Historical Archaeology of the Chesapeake

Historical Archaeology of the Chesapeake

EDITED BY

PAUL A. SHACKEL
AND BARBARA J. LITTLE

SMITHSONIAN INSTITUTION PRESS
WASHINGTON AND LONDON

Edited by Vicky Macintyre.
Production editing by Rebecca Browning.
Designed by Linda McKnight.

Library of Congress Cataloging-in-Publication Data

Historical archaeology of the Chesapeake/edited by Paul A. Shackel
and Barbara J. Little.
p. cm.
Includes bibliographical references.
ISBN 1-56098-257-8
1. Chesapeake Bay Region (Md. and Va.)—Antiquities.
2. Excavations (Archaeology)—Chesapeake Bay Region (Md. and Va.)
3. Archaeology and history—Chesapeake Bay Region (Md. and Va.)
4. Chesapeake Bay Region (Md. and Va.)—History. I. Shackel, Paul A.
II. Little, Barbara J.
F187.C5H56 1993
975.5′18—dc20 93-29078

British Library Cataloging-in-Publication Data is available.

Manufactured in the United States of America.

02 01 00 99 98 97 96 95 94
10 9 8 7 6 5 4 3 2 1

∞ The paper used in this publication meets the minimum requirements
of the American National Standard for Permanence of Paper for
Printed Library Materials Z39.48-1984.

On the cover are a 1680 map of Virginia and Maryland, courtesy
Maryland State Archives Special Collection MSASC 1427–47, and
the *Maryland Dove*, Historic St. Mary's City, under sail, courtesy
Historic St. Mary's City Commission.

With love and appreciation

we dedicate this book to our parents:

Paul and Gloria Shackel and Dorothy Oetjen Little

and to the memory of Willits Burkhardt Little

Contents

Acknowledgments

We wish to express our thanks to each of the authors who have contributed to this volume and to all those archaeologists who have advanced our understanding of the rich legacy of the historical Chesapeake. We also are grateful to those historians who have worked with Chesapeake materials and have built an impressive body of scholarly data and interpretations. Their influence is often apparent in the various works in this volume. Special thanks to our colleagues and our students who continue to make archaeology rewarding.

We thank the staff of the Smithsonian Institution Press, particularly Dan Goodwin for his enthusiastic support of this project, and Vicky Macintyre for her thoughtful and skillful editing. Anonymous reviewers provided helpful suggestions as the volume was taking shape. Stephen Potter supplied some important references.

With long-term gratitude, we thank our families, including Ian, who aspires to be an archaeologist, and especially our parents for their enthusiasm for what we do.

Contributor's Affiliations

KEITH L. BARR, Peoria Historical Society, 942 Northeast Glen Oak Avenue, Peoria, Illinois 61603

JOANNE BOWEN, Department of Archaeology, The Colonial Williamsburg Foundation, Williamsburg, Virginia 23187

MARLEY R. BROWN III, Department of Archaeology, The Colonial Williamsburg Foundation, Williamsburg, Virginia 23187

CHARLES D. CHEEK, John Milner Associates, Inc., 5250 Cherokee Avenue, #129, Alexandria, Virginia 22312

PAMELA J. CRESSEY, Alexandria Archaeology, Office of Historic Alexandria, 105 N. Union Street, City of Alexandria, Virginia 22314

MATTHEW C. EMERSON, Department of Anthropology, Princeton University, Princeton, New Jersey 08544

SUSAN E. WINTER, Chesapeake and Ohio Canal National Historical Park, P.O. Box 4, Sharpsburg, Maryland 21782

JULIA A. KING, Jefferson Patterson Park and Museum, 10515 Mackall Road, St. Leonard, Maryland 20685

ELIZABETH KRYDER-REID, National Gallery of Art, Smithsonian Institution, Washington, D.C. 20560

MARK P. LEONE, Department of Anthropology, Woods Hall, University of Maryland, College Park, Maryland 20742

BARBARA J. LITTLE, National Park Service, National Capital Region, 1100 Ohio Drive, S.W., Room 218, Washington, D.C. 20242

BARBARA H. MAGID, Alexandria Archaeology, Office of Historic Alexandria, 105 N. Union Street, City of Alexandria, Virginia 22314

ANN B. MARKELL, Department of Archaeology, University of Cape Town, Private Bag, Rondebosch, South Africa 7700

ANN SMART MARTIN, Advanced Studies Office, Winterthur Museum, Winterthur, Delaware 19735

HENRY M. MILLER, Historic St. Mary's City, St. Mary's City Commission, St. Mary's City, Maryland 20686

DENNIS J. POGUE, The Mount Vernon Ladies' Association of the Union, Mount Vernon, Virginia 22121

STEPHEN R. POTTER, National Park Service, National Capital Region, 1100 Ohio Drive, S.W., Room 218, Washington, D.C. 20242, and Research Associate, Department of Anthropology, Smithsonian Institution, Washington, D.C. 20560

Patricia Samford, Department of Archaeology, The Colonial Williamsburg Foundation, Williamsburg, Virginia 23187

Douglas W. Sanford, Department of Anthropology, University of Virginia, Charlottesville, Virginia, and Department of Historic Preservation, Mary Washington College, Fredericksburg, Virginia 22401-5358

Donna J. Seifert, John Milner Associates, Inc., 5250 Cherokee Avenue, #129, Alexandria, Va 22312

Paul A. Shackel, Division of Archaeology, Harpers Ferry National Historical Park, Harpers Ferry, West Virginia 25425

Gregory A. Waselkov, Department of Sociology and Anthropology, University of South Alabama, Mobile, Alabama, 36688

I
CHAPTER

Archaeological Perspectives
An Overview of the Chesapeake Region

PAUL A. SHACKEL AND BARBARA J. LITTLE

MANY HISTORICAL archaeologists are at work in the Chesapeake region. Although some of their ideas have been published in various journals, others are buried in the "grey literature" of cultural resource management reports that have limited distribution. The goal of this volume is to provide a representative collection of current substantive and theoretical contributions to historical archaeology in the Chesapeake Bay region. In keeping with the traditional divisions in the field, the work described here is confined to that done on land, for underwater archaeology in the bay deserves a volume in itself.

The analyses presented here are bound in time and space to the historic Chesapeake region, particularly its western shore in Maryland and Virginia. The bay area is well known for both its ecology and its history. The Chesapeake has a long geological history and complex ecology. The historic period is judged by European effect, from sixteenth-century contact with Native Americans to twentieth-century city life. In these introductory remarks, we define the region, sketch a background context, briefly discuss the historical archaeology already done in the region, and delineate the issues that have taken shape. These remarks provide a springboard for the work that follows in this book.

THE BAY

About 21,000 years ago, at the climax of the Wisconsin Glaciation, what is now the Chesapeake region was covered by a boreal coniferous forest. The ecological zones of today were displaced approximately 650 miles south. The temperature averaged five degrees cooler; days were about 25 percent more overcast; and approximately 25 more inches of snow fell every year. World water levels averaged 350 feet lower than today. The Chesapeake Bay did not exist as such, but the area in which it eventually developed contained the extension of the Susquehanna River, which flowed onto the exposed continental shelf. With the warming of the earth's temperatures, the Wisconsin glaciers receded, ecological zones slowly migrated northward, and the bay filled. By about 3,000 years ago, the marine transgression of the bay was complete. The area between the James River and the city of Baltimore now consists of an oak pine forest, which is a transition zone between the northern boreal coniferous forest and the southern temperate deciduous forest (Whitehead 1965; Brush 1986).

Habitation of the region dates to about 10,000 years ago, when Native Americans successfully exploited the resources of the Chesapeake. At that time the bay began to fill (Custer 1984). The Paleo-Indian artifacts caught by watermen in their oyster dredges attests to early human habitation along the shores of the ancient Susquehanna.

Today, the Chesapeake estuary is the largest and most varied estuary in the contiguous United States and is one of the most productive regions in the world. The bay is about 200 miles long and it ranges from 4 to 30 miles in width. Its 8,000 miles of related shoreline include tributary rivers, streams, and smaller embayments. Averaging less than 30 feet in depth, the bay contains about 18 trillion gallons of water. Salinity ranges from 0 parts per thousand (that is, completely fresh) near the source of the Susquehanna River, to about 35 parts per thousand near the mouth of the bay. Local estuaries like the Chesapeake form a critical link in the food chain of aquatic life. Approximately 70 percent of the fish in the Atlantic Ocean depend on the estuary system for at least part of their lives (Warner 1976: 4–12). About 2,700 species of plants and animals are able to adapt to the harsh, ever-changing ecosystem of the bay, where they find an abundance of food. Therefore populations are high (Capper, Power, and Shivers 1983:15–17). This bounty was present historically as well as prehistorically, as the documentary record indicates. John Smith's early exploration of the bay uncovered "diverse places [with an] abundance of fish lying so thicke with their heads above the water as for want of nets (our barge driving amongst them) we attempted to catch them with a frying pan" (Barbour 1986:228).

The bay itself, which lies within the Atlantic Coastal Plain, covers more than 2,200 square miles, but the drainage area, which includes at least 50 tributaries, covers approximately 64,000 square miles in five states. Parts of the Ridge and Valley physiographic province, the Allegheny Plateau, and the Piedmont Plateau, as well as the Coastal Plain, are in the bay's drainage basin. The coastal plain is relatively flat, with a maximum elevation of about 300 feet above sea level. The fall line that separates the coastal plain from the piedmont starts 15 to 90 miles west of the bay, where the elevation increases to approximately 1,100 feet above sea level. The fall line provides a source of water power, and many cities—including Fredericksburg, Richmond, Washington, D.C., and Baltimore—have been developed along it (EPA 1982). Figure 1.1 illustrates the geography of the bay and the locations of archaeological work described in this book.

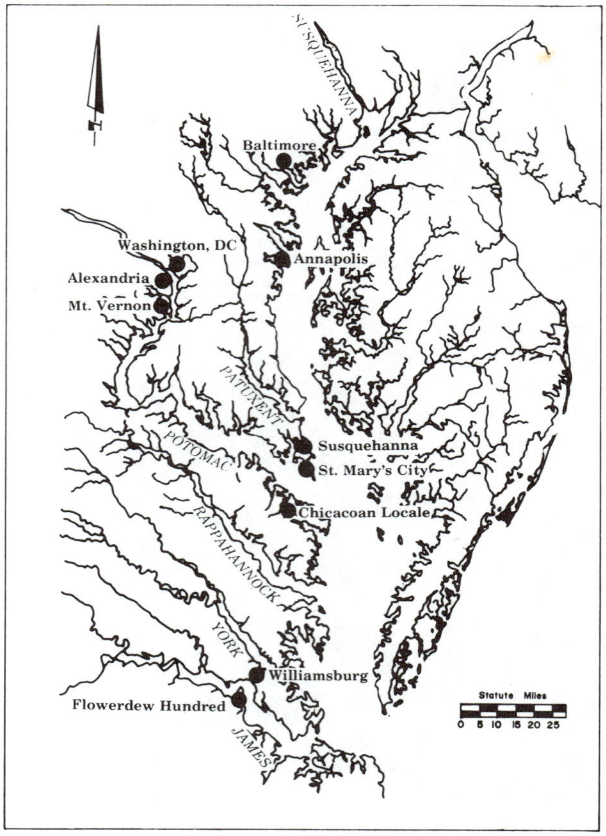

Figure 1.1. *Geography of Chesapeake Bay and locations of the archaeological work described in this volume.*

Exploration of the Chesapeake Bay Region

During the earliest intensive exploitation of the New World by Europeans from the late 1400s, the Chesapeake received rather limited attention as explorers and traders concentrated on areas to the north and the south. In the north, they visited Newfoundland, Nova Scotia, and Labrador. John Cabot for England and Caspar Corte-Real for Portugal, among others, led northern expeditions around the turn of the sixteenth century. Whaling in particular was attractive to Basque, Dutch, and other European entrepreneurs (Kaplan 1985). Fishing and the fur trade or other direct, intensive exploitation did not reach the Chesapeake during the 1500s (Wolf 1982). To the south were the Spanish, who controlled the Atlantic Ocean for most of the sixteenth century and conducted a profitable exploration and exploitation of South and Central America, as well as the circum-Caribbean region and the southeastern part of what is now the United States. The Spanish found early settlement in North America to be unprofitable, but when they were threatened by French Protestant intervention in the 1560s and by consistent pirating of their gold- and silver-laden fleets, they established a settlement at St. Augustine and by 1566 had several missions along the southeastern coast of North America (South 1988; Thomas 1988). Some ethnohistorical accounts suggest that a Spanish expedition may have traveled as far north as the Chesapeake in the 1520s (Lewis and Loomie 1953; Turner 1985). In the late 1500s the Spanish had limited contact with the Powhatan chiefdom in coastal Virginia. The Ajacan mission was established in 1570, purportedly on the York River. In founding that mission, the Spaniards brought with them a local Native American who had earlier been abducted to Spain. The mission was annihilated, and after a Spanish retaliation in 1572 there was little direct contact between natives and Europeans in the Chesapeake until the settlement of Jamestown (Turner 1985:208–209).

The English did not successfully inhabit the bay area until the early seventeenth century, although earlier settlements had been attempted. In 1585 Sir Walter Raleigh sponsored a settlement south of the Chesapeake at Roanoke. When Sir Francis Drake visited the colony in 1586 after attacking St. Augustine, he found miserable settlers in disastrous conditions. During that brief time the English military settlement had thoroughly alienated most of the native population in the region (Fausz 1985:234). Hope for friendly relations was gone; the English settlement was abandoned. In the following year John White, a member of the first settlement, convinced Raleigh and Queen Elizabeth to sponsor another expedition, this time to the Chesapeake. The English considered the area attractive, partly because it had many deep places to anchor, which would provide safe harbor for English privateers attempting to acquire supplies before or after raiding the Spanish fleets in the Caribbean. White proposed that, unlike Roanoke, which consisted mostly of soldiers, the new settlement should consist of families. He assumed that Native Americans would consider such settlers less of a threat. With 150 men, women, and children, the colonists set sail in the spring of 1587. White's ill-fated expedition fell short of its Chesapeake destination, however, and landed back at Roanoke, where it became the famous "lost colony." Some ethnohistoric accounts suggest that some members of the colony may have made it to the Chesapeake by 1587, probably near Norfolk County, Virginia, and that they were eventually assimilated by the Chessipians. During this time the Powhatan chiefdom was consolidating power in the region and conquered the Chessipians, who refused to acknowledge the Powhatan as their overlords (Quinn 1985). Others have suggested that the Roanoke colonists were assimilated by the Croatoans, an Algonquian group from the outer banks of North Carolina (Fausz 1985; Quinn 1985).

In 1603 the London Company explored the Chesapeake region intensively to gather data for another attempt at settlement. In 1607 the English founded Jamestown in the southern Chesapeake, in what is now Virginia. The Maryland region had no English settlements to speak of until 1631, when a fur trader began operating on Kent Island. In the 1620s George Calvert, the Lord Baltimore, sought to establish a permanent settlement for Catholics and was granted a patent to create a settlement in Newfoundland, but one long and miserable winter in 1628 was enough to change his mind. The crown refused to grant George Calvert's request for land in a more temperate climate, but soon after his death in 1632, his son Cecil Calvert received a charter to settle Maryland. In 1634 he founded St. Mary's City (Scarf 1879; Menard 1975; Quinn 1985).

One of the earlier reasons for settling the Chesapeake region was that it provided a port for raiding the Spanish, but in the seventeenth century the English were more interested in its economic potential (Wolf 1982; Fausz 1985). Thus between 1610 and 1620 settlers began capitalizing on the high price of tobacco in Europe. Within several decades tens of thousands of settlers had established plantations along the Chesapeake waterways, which facilitated the transport of tobacco and allowed them to readily obtain necessary supplies from the mother country. This tobacco economy created a dispersed settlement pattern, with the result that towns of substantial size were almost nonexistent in the seventeenth and eighteenth centuries. Even the early colonial capitals of St. Mary's City in Maryland and Jamestown in Virginia each had only a few hundred inhabitants. And the two centers established in the 1690s that later became provincial capitals—Annapolis, Maryland, and Williamsburg, Virginia—still had permanent populations of less than 2,000 at the end of the eighteenth century (McCusker and Menard 1986).

Early Archaeology in the Chesapeake Region

The Chesapeake's economy, ecology, and history make it an extraordinarily rich area for archaeological study. Indeed, the Chesapeake has been among the first regions in the United States to be studied by historical archaeologists. Historical archaeology is a relatively new discipline. James Deetz (1977:29) credits John Hall's 1856 excavation of Miles Standish's house in Duxbury, Massachusetts (Deetz 1977:29) as the first controlled historical archaeological excavation in the United States. Excavations in the Chesapeake began 41 years later. In 1897 the Association for the Preservation of Virginia Antiquities, which owned parts of James Island, uncovered the brick foundations of a church built in 1639 at Jamestown, the first permanent English settlement in the New World. A Jamestown ordinance of the time, passed after several devastating fires, required the use of bricks in construction, and thus many of the post-1620s components of the settlement are readily visible in the archaeological record. By 1901 and 1902 excavations had uncovered the 1617 church foundations, along with the churchyard and cemetery. In 1901 Col. Samuel A. Younge of the U.S. Corps of Engineers discovered brick foundations while constructing a sea wall. Two years later he revealed the foundation to be 240 feet long and 24–46 feet wide. The western and central parts of the structure had served as multifamily units, while the eastern end was used as the state house. This state house complex had been constructed about 1660–1665 but was burned during Bacon's Rebellion in 1676. After being rebuilt, the structure suffered another fire in 1698. The following year the capital was moved to Middle Plantation, later known as Williamsburg.

In 1934 the National Park Service initiated excavations at Jamestown with the main goal of architectural reconstruction. For several years it permitted only architects to excavate around foundations, while anthropologists were required to stop within 3 feet of architectural features. One of the more prominent architects associated with the early Jamestown project was H. Chandlee Forman. In 1936 the National Park Service reorganized the fieldwork and called upon J. C. Harrington to direct the archaeological investigation. He supervised the Jamestown excavations into the 1940s, during which time he concentrated on organizing and documenting what had already been excavated. John L. Cotter succeeded Harrington in the 1950s (Cotter and Hudson 1957; Cotter 1958).

Excavations at St. Mary's City, Maryland's first capital, were also pioneered by H. Chandlee Forman who worked there intermittently from 1936 to 1965. He uncovered the second state house (1666), parts of the Catholic chapel (ca. 1634–1638), and the site of St. John's (1637), the residence of Governor Charles Calvert (Forman 1986).

The archaeological resources of Virginia's second capital, Williamsburg, received considerable attention as well, through the assistance of the Rockefeller Foundation. Excavations there were also geared to architectural restoration. Beginning in the 1930s, many of the open lots were cross-trenched at 45-degree angles to the street to quickly identify foundations running at right angles to each other. During this endeavor, features between the trenches, such as wells or buildings constructed on piers, were sometimes missed (see, for example, Derry and Brown 1987). The work at Williamsburg came to a temporary stop during the peak of the Great Depression. Many of the resident architects and archaeologists who left the early Williamsburg reconnaissance project supplied the labor base for the 1934 Jamestown excavations (Noel Hume 1983:29).

Other early work in the region focused on plantations (see Singleton 1990:71), but it would be some time before scholars defined historical archaeology in an anthropologically productive way, and during this period of development there was considerable confusion over the proper role and potential contribution of historical archaeology (see, for example, Cleland and Fitting 1968). The large-scale excavations of the 1930s were concerned primarily with gathering details for architectural restoration, still a valid pursuit. Through the 1950s and 1960s, historical archaeology remained a subdiscipline of archaeology and ancillary to prehistory, and was often used as a testing ground for archaeological methods. In this role, it still failed to receive recognition as an independent discipline. Finally, during the 1960s, historical archaeologists questioned whether their activities were to be categorized as history or anthropology. This question has not yet been fully resolved. Historical archaeology is unquestionably an interdisciplinary entity, but like others of this nature, finds itself a poor stepchild of its parent disciplines. For an overview of the debate and the early development of the field, the reader is directed to the collection edited by Schuyler (1978a) and the overview by Deagan (1982).

Nonetheless, historical archaeology has strengthened its place within the field of anthropology since the 1970s by investigating a wide range of interesting questions and working from an abundant data base. The Society for Historical Archaeology established in 1967 has helped to provide a professional identity. In 1978 Schuyler argued that historical archaeology had the potential to become one of the most sophisticated and productive areas of archaeology (Schuyler 1978b). It still holds that promise. Many historical archaeologists have made important contributions to our understanding of the complexity of past cultures. Scholarly studies of the human experience have been concerned with many levels of that experience, from its local to its worldwide aspects. The theoretical orientations adopted by historical archaeologists vary as widely as the specific questions they ask. Functionalism, materialism, symbolic analysis, Levi-Straussian structuralism, and Marxian analysis have all shed light on our historic experience.

The work of historical archaeology—the examination, questioning, and presentation of conflicting elements from the past—is far from an "ivory tower" affair. Public access to our findings and interpretation have been part of our work from its beginnings. The interpretations that historical archaeology offers both reflect and influence what we think about our past and how we understand the contributions of various people of different ethnicity, race, class, and gender.

Jamestown and Williamsburg, in particular, provide examples of what historical archaeology can do in regard to public accessibility. At the outset, government and private interests, respectively, greatly influenced the interpretation of the historic past. At Jamestown the National Park Service presented the town not only as the first permanent English settlement in the New World, but also as the birthplace of modern democracy. The first representative legislative assembly in America convened at Jamestown from 1619 to 1699, when it was moved to Williamsburg (Hudson 1985:48). At Williamsburg, the Rockefeller Foundation celebrated the ideals of the planter elite as being timeless and inevitable American values (Wallace 1981:68–78; Patterson 1986:1–12). While each site celebrates Anglo-American history, other peoples whose histories were inextricably linked with the British were largely ignored or glossed over. Neither Native Americans nor African Americans figured in the initial vision of the Jamestown and Williamsburg restorations. However, in the 1980s the Colonial Williamsburg Foundation made substantial strides in incorporating the lives of those "others," who included black slaves, servants, and women (in general) in the restoration, archaeology, research designs, and public presentations. Moreover, the public has become increasingly aware, probably through greater exposure to critical histories, that the ideals of the planter elite were not "natural" in the sense of being inevitable, or timeless, but were embedded in their own contemporary social and political realities. At each of these sites, historical archaeology has challenged and changed research questions and messages about the past.

Some of the recent work in Chesapeake archaeology is briefly described here to provide an idea of the range of research being conducted, but it should be kept in mind that this is far from a comprehensive overview. Leading public and private institutions as well as private companies have worked in the region. Surveys and excavations have been small and large, and both short-term and long-term projects. Work has been sponsored by the federal government through the National Park Service, not only at Jamestown but also at parks in the National Capital Region and Mid-Atlantic Region. The area's state governments, through the Maryland Historic Trust and Virginia's Department of Historic Resources, both sponsor work and review that is done by private firms. Both St. Mary's City and Jefferson Patterson Park and Museum are run by the state of Maryland. Several counties in Maryland and Virginia employ archaeologists and carry out some excavation. Cities, too, have taken an active role, most notably, Alexandria and Baltimore, although Annapolis also offers some support. Private organizations have also been important sponsors. There would be much less to say about historical archaeology in the Chesapeake were it not for the likes of the Rockefeller Foundation (Colonial Williamsburg), the Association for the Preservation of Virginia Antiquities (Jamestown), the Thomas Jefferson Memorial Foundation (Monticello), the Mount Vernon Ladies' Association (Mount Vernon), Historic Gordonsville, Inc. (Spotswood's Plantation), the Flowerdew Hundred Foundation (Flowerdew Hundred Plantation), and the Historic Annapolis Foundation (Annapolis). Universities that have done considerable work in the area include the University of Maryland, the University of California at Berkeley, College of William and Mary, Virginia Commonwealth University, Mary Washington College, and Germana Community College.

Recent Archaeology in the Chesapeake Region

The following overview of recent work in the region follows the same thematic organization as the book: early European settlement, plantation and landscape studies, eighteenth-century life, and nineteenth-century life.

Early European Settlement

Early settlement encompasses diverse topics related both to the contact between native groups and Europeans and to the adaptations that settlers from the Old World had to make to the physical and social environments of the New. European settlers did not simply transplant culture, but had to create it anew. Decisions and challenges concerning subsistence ranged from where to locate settlements to the methods of raising crops (see chapter 2), to strategies for raising stock (see chapter 10). Trade, warfare, governance, and relations with the mother country were of constant concern in this frontier society. Archaeological work done on seventeenth-century sites is beginning to reveal forgotten facets of a complex and fascinating world. Only a handful of projects are mentioned here. Other important work done on early plantations includes that at Kingsmill (see, for example, Kelso 1984) and at Governor's Land (Outlaw 1989). Ivor Noel Hume (1963) provides an early account of work in Virginia. Michael Smolek et al. (1984) provide a bibliography of the extensive work that has been done in the Chesapeake region. Most of the sites in Virginia are discussed first in the following summary since settlement there preceded that in Maryland by a quarter of a century.

Martin's Hundred and Suffolk Fort. Noel Hume's work on Martin's Hundred is perhaps the most publicized and well-known excavation in Chesapeake historical archaeology. Martin's Hundred consisted of 20,000 acres along the James River settled in 1619. Its administrative center, known as Wolstenholme Towne, was a palisaded fort that was surrounded by several domestic buildings. In 1622 Native American attacks devastated the settlements along the James River; the population of Martin's Hundred, for example, fell from 140 to 62. The survivors may have fled to Jamestown. Shortly afterward about 20 people resettled Martin's Hundred, only to disband several years later. The burning of Wolstenholme Towne sealed a time capsule of early seventeenth-century plantation life (Noel Hume 1983). A possibly contemporary site is that of Suffolk Fort, on the Nansemond River in Suffolk. This trapezoidal fortification has bastions similar to those of Wolstenholme Towne. The fort contains the remains of five post-in-the-ground structures (Anonymous 1990).

Flowerdew Hundred and Early Manufacturing. The archaeological project at Flowerdew Hundred, Virginia—under the direction of James Deetz and sponsored in part by the University of California at Berkeley and the Flowerdew Hundred Foundation—has provided valuable information on early Chesapeake settlement. Sir George Yardley, Virginia's first governor, established Flowerdew Hundred in 1619 as one of many plantations along the James River. Archaeological surveys have located over 60 sites, half of which are related to European settlement. One of the project's goals is to study early relationships between European and African Americans (Deetz 1988; see also chapter 3).

Excavations have revealed a small, previously unknown iron smelting industry that operated in the last quarter of the seventeenth century (chapter 4). Early manufacturing industries have also been investigated by the National Park Service and by the College of William and Mary at the Poor Potter's site in Yorktown (see, for example, Barka 1973; Watkins and Noel Hume 1967). Work has also been done on a likely tannery and shoemaking operation on a plantation on the eastern shore of Virginia dating to the second half of the century. This work was conducted by the James River Institute for Archaeology under the auspices of the Virginia Division of Historic Landmarks.

Contact Sites and Jordan's Point. The Virginia Department of Historic Resources has been involved in several surveys and excavations of early contact and European settlements in the Chesapeake. An 800-acre survey along the south shore of the Rappahannock River at Camden National Historical Landmark in Caroline County revealed historic Native American and seventeenth-century Anglo- and African American sites. One important goal of this research has been to assess the impact of European culture on the aboriginal population. Land development along the James River has also necessitated excavations at Jordan's Point, Prince Georges County. An extensive Powhatan chiefdom settlement existed in the area that Samuel Jordan patented as a plantation in

1619. Nathaniel Bacon assumed leadership of his rebel forces and encamped at this location. Three early seventeenth-century Virginia Company sites were found here, along with a late seventeenth- to early eighteenth-century plantation. Jordan's Journey is one of the few excavated settlements of the Virginia Company period, which extended from 1607 to 1625 (Mouer 1990).

BERMUDA HUNDRED AND CURLES PLANTATION. Because of Richmond's urban sprawl, the Virginia Commonwealth University's Archaeological Research Center (VCUARC) was called on to perform an archaeological assessment around the city. This effort included a mapping project of Sir Thomas Dale's 1613 two-mile-long Bermuda Hundred palisade fortifications. Bermuda Hundred was designated a port town in 1691. Excavations revealed seventeenth- and eighteenth-century stores, taverns, and dwellings and evidence of free black merchants. The VCUARC is also exploring the archaeology at Curles Plantation. The site ranks among the earliest in the Chesapeake and is noted for being the residence of Nathaniel Bacon, Jr. Brief accounts describe the plantation as fortified with an earthwork and puncheon stockade. After Bacon's Rebellion in 1676, the ownership of Curles Plantation was contested in the courts into the late seventeenth century. William Randolf eventually purchased the land and became a leading supporter of the building of Williamsburg and the College of William and Mary. The plantation survived into the twentieth century (Mouer 1991).

ST. MARY'S CITY. Although Forman performed the earliest excavations of St. Mary's City, much of the recent archaeological work there is described by Henry Miller (1986). Excavations since 1981 have focused on the development of the town center. Several structures have been located, including the 1635 governor's residence and state house (see chapter 5), a lawyer's lodging, some private homes, and public inns. Archaeological evidence indicates that Maryland's first city did not develop haphazardly, as did many medieval towns, but was a planned settlement that incorporated concepts of baroque urban design (Miller 1988). Excavations also revealed the 1645 Pope's Fort, which played a role in the English Civil War and the Protestant's rebellion against Lord Baltimore.

The most recent excavations have concentrated on the 1630s Jesuit chapel, where three early sealed lead coffins were discovered buried to the right of the altar. The coffins have received a great deal of media attention since their discovery in 1990. It is likely that they contain the remains of members of the Calbert family. An interdisicplinary team, including archaeologists, forensic scientists, and National Aeronautics and Space Administration scientists interested in preindustrial air, have been working on Project Lead Coffins.

KING'S REACH AND HARMONY HALL. The Maryland Historical Trust and Jefferson Patterson Park and Museum sponsored an excavation of a ca. 1690– 1715 plantation site known as King's Reach (Pogue 1990). Excavations revealed post supports for a 30-by-30-foot dwelling and smaller 20-by-10-foot quarters. The quarters probably housed servants or slaves and were connected to the large house by a common fence. This configuration is common among late seventeenth-century plantations (Pogue 1988b:40–56; see also Keeler 1978; Deetz 1988). Other early historic sites include the National Park Service's excavations of Harmony Hall in Prince Georges County. The earliest component of the site consists of an earth-fast structure constructed at the turn of the eighteenth century (Sonderman et al. 1993).

JESUIT MISSIONS. Beginning in the 1630s the Jesuits established a string of missions along the Chesapeake Bay. In 1984 and 1985 the Maryland Historical Trust initiated an archaeological survey and excavations in lower St. Mary's County, Maryland, in advance of utility line construction at a Naval facility. Archaeologists located part of the Society for Jesus plantation that operated continuously from 1638 to 1942. Excavations concentrated around the Jesuit St. Inigoes mission priest's residence occupied ca. 1705–1755. An earlier site that was also found may be related to the seventeenth-century mission activities (King and Pogue 1985).

Plantation and Landscape Studies

Plantations were established as soon as Europeans arrived in the Chesapeake, and they continued to be vital parts of the economic and social landscape until the end of the Civil War. Through nearly three centuries plantations varied greatly, depending on the region in which they were found and on the economic status of their owners. Charles Orser (1988a, 1988b) discusses plantation archaeology, particularly issues concerning power and internal relations. Landscapes, too, vary a great deal and are of interest in any time period. Both elite and vernacular architecture are clearly essential parts of both plantations and landscapes. Landscape archaeology is a burgeoning field. *Earth Patterns*, edited by William Kelso and Rachel Most (1990), indicates the variety of work being done. Many of the projects cited in the preceding section also pertain to plantations. Miller's work in this volume (chapter 5) could easily fit into either section. Similarly, Julia King's study, included in this volume's section on nineteenth-century life (chapter 18), also considers landscape. The work on these topics continues to grow.

Monticello and Jefferson's Poplar Forest. Archaeology at Monticello, Thomas Jefferson's plantation, has been funded in part by the Thomas Jefferson Memorial Foundation, Inc., and has been directed by William Kelso. Excavations have focused on the kitchen yard, carpenter shop, and blacksmith shop. This work is concerned with the life-styles, working conditions, and accomplishments of white and black servants. As on other plantations (see, for example, McKee 1987), the analysis of food remains (Crader 1984) has provided insight into ethnic and economic variability. Attention has also been given to the distinct culture that developed among African Americans (chapter 8), and to Jefferson's landscape design and shaping of Monticello into an ornate farm. Poplar Forest, Jefferson's "other" plantation, is also under archaeological investigation, as is Shadwell, Jefferson's birthplace.

Mount Vernon. Archaeology at Mount Vernon in Fairfax County, Virginia, is sponsored by the Mount Vernon Ladies' Association. Excavations and survey work have focused on the area directly around the main house, including the blacksmith shop, as well as parts of the 500 acres of associated land (Pogue 1988a). Some of the work currently under way is aimed at interpreting landscape development in the context of Chesapeake regional events (chapter 7), as well as reinterpreting slave life. Excavation of the "House for Families" cellar has been a rich source of data on the latter topic.

Enchanted Castle. Excavations principally sponsored by Historic Gordonville, Inc., at Germana in Orange County, Virginia, have focused on the "Enchanted Castle," the plantation complex associated with Lt. Gov. Alexander Spotswood. Douglas Sanford has directed the excavations with the aid of field schools from Mary Washington College and Germana Community College. Analysis has concentrated on the establishment of this frontier plantation (in the second quarter of the eighteenth-century) and on its activities. Part of Sanford's (1990) work relates specifically to the gardens.

Clifts Plantation and Stratford Plantation. At Clifts Plantation, research has focused on the changing uses of and meanings in architecture from the late seventeenth to the early eighteenth centuries. The earlier-style "manner house" known as Clifts Plantation was razed, and Stratford Hall was built as the central architectural feature of the Lee family's 6,000-acre Stratford Plantation (Neiman 1978, 1980).

Pohoke and Portici. The National Park Service has surveyed and excavated some sections of Manassas National Battlefield. Recent work has been done on the Wheeler Tract, which was part of the Lower Bull Run Tract originally patented by Robert "King" Carter in 1724. Both the plantation Pohoke, built in 1728, and its nineteenth-century successor Portici were investigated. Portici, built in 1820 and burned in 1862, yielded important evidence of nineteenth-century colonoware made by African American slaves (Parker and Hernigle 1990). Portici also served as a hospital during the early part of the Civil War.

Annapolis. An analysis of the gardens and city plan of Annapolis (Leone et al. 1989) has shed considerable light on the landscape, particularly on the manipulation and design of space for ideological purposes. Most notable is Leone's (1984) analysis of the Paca garden and that of Mark Leone and Paul Shackel (1990) on the Carroll garden. Elizabeth Kryder-Reid (chapter 9) analyzes landscape as myth, focusing on the garden of Charles Carroll of Carrollton as an expression of cultural and social ideals.

Oxon Hill. Garrow and Associates, Inc., and John Milner Associates, Inc., conducted excavations at Oxon Hill Manor in Prince Georges County, Maryland. Archaeologists located a late seventeenth- to early eighteenth-century post-in-the-ground structure and a later manor house that was inhabited by some of the elite residents of the Chesapeake. A formal landscape surrounded the house. The project has been concerned with issues of status, culture change, function, and the use of space in an elite household (Garrow and Wheaton 1986).

LOCUST GROVE. The tobacco farm Locust Grove, later known as Oaks II, dates from 1800 until the Civil War. Because of constraints imposed by contract conditions, work there was limited to the material culture found at the main house and did not include outbuildings or quarters. Of particular interest is the unexpected gap between the relatively poor material possessions and the relatively great wealth and high status of the plantation owners, who worked their land with slave labor. Sorenson (1987) discusses these discrepancies and raises questions about the relationships between local folk cultures and national cultures.

BALTIMORE. The Baltimore Center for Urban Archaeology has conducted work at Mount Clare Mansion in the city of Baltimore. The project was co-sponsored by the city of Baltimore and the Colonial Dames of America in the State of Maryland. The plantation was the eighteenth-century residence of barrister Charles Carroll. Excavations of the orchard, bowling green, and other areas surrounding the buildings recovered data that made possible a more accurate landscape restoration (Comer and Stevens 1990).

Eighteenth-Century Life

The seventeenth century saw the character of European settlement in the Chesapeake change from frontier to settled community. At the end of the 1600s the capitals of both Maryland and Virginia were moved; as social and political centers, Williamsburg and Annapolis serve as symbols of eighteenth-century life in the Chesapeake. Plantations continued to be important, but cities became increasingly so. The eighteenth century also ushered in the Age of Reason, with its new rules of behavior (see, for example, Shackel 1993), and marked the beginning of the industrial revolution in the Anglo-American colonies. Manufacturing grew and spread to the interior as the frontier moved west. In this context Susan Winter (chapter 13) discusses ironworking in western Maryland. The changes of the eighteenth century included not only technological innovations but also a restructuring of class relations and gender relations. Barbara Little (chapter 12) uses the lives of two Chesapeake printers to suggest different gender expectations and to document female resistance to a masculine Age of Reason. Comparisons between regions and over time reveal the changes occurring in the colonies. Joanne Bowen (chapter 10) compares subsistence practices between the Chesapeake and New England over time. Ann Smart Martin (chapter 11) examines merchants and the availability of material goods in different regions of the Chesapeake.

Although the revolutionary war was the most important political event in the Chesapeake and the Anglo-American colonies as a whole, archaeological investigation on land in the region tends to focus instead on the cultural revolutions of the era. Yorktown, in particular provides an underwater archaeological perspective on the war for independence (see, for example, Sands 1980; Broadwater 1985).

The work referred to here pertains mainly to that done on the capital cities, although many other sites have also been explored. The port of Londontown, on Maryland's South River, for example, has received both terrestrial (Barse 1986) and underwater (Shomette 1978) attention. The plantations and landscapes of the preceding section could be included here as well.

WILLIAMSBURG. The Colonial Williamsburg Foundation's Office of Excavations and Conservation, under the direction of Marley Brown III, has continued to focus its excavations on the core of Virginia's second capital city. Williamsburg, founded in 1699, offers a unique opportunity to study many aspects of eighteenth-century colonial life. Some of this work is performed to recover archaeological resources prior to development. Excavation techniques continue to be a major concern of the program. Brown and Patricia Samford (chapter 15) provide an overview of archaeological research in this capital city.

Many kinds of sites have been investigated, including taverns and domestic structures. Work at Shields Tavern was initiated because of disturbances that occurred while the structure was being converted into an operational tavern. Because the tavern operated through most of the century, archaeologists were able to compare early and late eighteenth-century tavern use. Excavations at another tavern, Marot's Ordinary, uncovered several garden features. Further analysis will provide additional insight into both commercial and domestic occupation in the city.

Excavations at the Brush-Everard site, conducted in cooperation with the African American program at Colonial Williamsburg, have been concerned with locating outbuildings, since these structures often housed slaves. Excavations of the main structure produced domestic refuse from residents of differing occupations and status: Brush was a gunsmith, and Everard a mayor.

Backlot archaeology was the main concern of the Payton Randolph House excavations (see chapter 15). Data from the excavations established the dates of the structural foundations, walkways, fencelines, and other features and were useful for the eventual reconstruction of outbuildings.

ANNAPOLIS. Since 1981 Archaeology in Annapolis, a cooperative project between the University of Maryland and the Historic Annapolis Foundation, has excavated about 20 sites. The aim of the project is to study the eighteenth-century development of the town. Excavations have been done on domestic sites of groups of various economic levels and on commercial sites. Leone (chapter 14) provides an overview of the archaeology done in Annapolis in the 1980s.

Excavations at the Calvert House showed how the early eighteenth-century gentry responded to changing emphases of power (Yentsch 1990a). When originally built, the Calvert House probably faced the Annapolis harbor, but when the house was remodeled in the 1730s to house the governor, its orientation shifted and faced the State House. One of the more spectacular features uncovered was the hypocaust heating system for an orangery, which the governor may have used to grow exotic fruits (Yentsch 1990b).

The Jonas Green Printshop site, a domestic site and also the workplace of a printing family for nearly 100 years, has produced the largest excavated collection of handmade printer's type known in America. Studies of the site have shed light on the ordering of the printing craft and especially its products, including the *Maryland Gazette*. The newspaper is a reflection of the widespread influence of the rationalization demanded by the Age of Reason (Little 1988).

Excavations at the St. Mary's site have yielded a rich array of material, some of which survives from the earliest part of the eighteenth century and the later seventeenth, but it is buried under several feet of fill and is underneath the current water table. Three generations of the wealthy Carroll family lived on the property. Excavations have been most informative about the activities of the third, Charles Carroll of Carrollton, best known as the only Catholic signer of the Declaration of Independence. The discovery in the main house basement of a cache of materials used by Carroll's slaves provides the only known example of surviving Africanisms in the city.

The Archaeology in Annapolis project pioneered the critical presentation of archaeology to the public (Leone 1983; Leone and Potter 1987; Potter and Leone 1987; Leone et al. 1987). Conceived by Mark Leone and later coorganized with Parker Potter, the project emphasizes the presentation of critical theory to the public and explains how histories are created and are dependent upon the needs of specific interest groups. In part because of the success of this project, other archaeological projects are paying more attention to the importance of communicating the goals of archaeology to the public and the role of archaeology in helping communities understand the ways their histories have been created and re-created through time.

FREE BLACKS IN MARYLAND. The Maryland Historical Trust has sponsored excavations at the Benjamin Banneker site in Baltimore County. Banneker, a free black, was a scientist who assisted in the original survey of Washington D.C. He lived in Oella, Maryland, from 1737 to 1806. Excavations revealed a 17-by-17-foot stone foundation and a root cellar. This work provided insight into the architectural development of the site and the life of a free black scientist. Work has also been done on free blacks on the lower eastern shore of Maryland, particularly on some of the occupations dating to the end of the revolutionary war era (Davidson 1983).

Nineteenth-Century Life

Developments during the nineteenth century continued to add to the themes of earlier periods. The manufacturing that began in the colonies during the seventeenth and eighteenth centuries turned into full-blown industries during the nineteenth, and there was a corresponding rise in commerce. Industry changed the structure of wage labor, although slave labor continued for a time. King (chapter 18) provides an example of a southern Maryland plantation and the labor relations there. Urban-rural and core-periphery relations during this period shed light on economic conditions and social relations. Industry and agriculture contributed to regionalism and to the North-South differences that pitted the Chesapeake states against one another and divided the nation during the Civil War.

As in the preceding section, the central war of the century is not considered directly in these chapters. There are, of course, numerous sites of Civil War battles, encampments, hospitals, and others in the Chesapeake region. The archaeological work on battles and battlefields continues, and broader questions concerning the anthropology of war are currently being taken up (Stephen Potter, personal communication).

ALEXANDRIA. The Alexandria Urban Archaeology program, directed by Pamela Cressey, has excavated a variety of sites over the past decade, including domestic, commercial, church, and industrial sites. In preparation for building expansion, excavations were conducted in the churchyard of Christ Church. Prominent citizens who once attended the church include George Washington and Robert E. Lee. Over a dozen burials were found, some as close as 1 1/2 feet below the surface, and most with poorly preserved skeletal remains.

The Alexandria program has also examined the Quaker community's contributions to the development of nineteenth-century Alexandria. Excavations at the residence of a prominent Quaker merchant and businessman, Robert Miller, revealed a water filtration cistern in his backyard dating to ca. 1830. The fact that all 11 of his children lived to adulthood has been interpreted as testimony to his pioneering concern for health and hygiene. Miller later founded the Alexandria Water Company.

Another Quaker family operated the Stabler-Leadbeater Apothecary Shop continuously from 1796 to 1933. A well in the basement was supplied by both the water table and rainwater guided from the roof. Reconnaissance uncovered a wide range of medicinal products and other stock related to mercantile operations.

An early nineteenth-century sugar house and associated dwellings were excavated in Alexandria, and interpretations are offered by Keith Barr, Cressey, and Barbara Magid (chapter 17). The refinery operated with slave labor from 1804 to 1828 and imported raw materials from Havana, Cuba. Hundreds of earthenware shards that once served as cones and syrup jars in the refining process were uncovered and analyzed.

ANNAPOLIS. The Archaeology in Annapolis project has investigated several sites occupied by African Americans in the second half of the nineteenth century and the first half of the twentieth. The Burgess-Maynard house was occupied by a free black family after the 1840s and has yielded a rich assemblage of domestic artifacts and faunal remains.

BALTIMORE. In order to trace Baltimore Harbor's physical and economic development, the Maryland Historical Trust undertook the Fells Point Archaeology project centered along the waterfront in the downtown area. Fells Point grew as a national shipbuilding center in the late eighteenth and early nineteenth centuries. Later the area developed as a major coffee warehouse district. Several important sites that were located reflect a mix of residential and commercial areas around the waterfront.

At Fort McHenry National Monument and Historic Shrine in Baltimore, John Milner Associates, Inc., under the direction of Charles Cheek, investigated various drainage problems at the fort. The goal was to understand the original construction techniques and the various alterations made through the nineteenth century. This excavation represents the only investigation in the area of a site directly associated with the War of 1812.

WASHINGTON, D.C. Investigations at Federal Triangle in Washington, D.C., were done by John Milner Associates, Inc. Cheek and Donna Seifert (chapter 17) provide some insight into the dynamic nature of this urban neighborhood. Located two blocks from the White House, the area was transformed from a working class neighborhood to a red-light district during the course of the nineteenth century. The neighborhood later attracted European immigrants, native-born white and black laborers, and industry. As the area grew, it accommodated a mixture of domestic, commercial, and manufacturing activities.

Other recent work in the nation's capital includes excavation in the Howard Road Historic District by Louis Berger and Associates, Inc. in advance of construction for the D.C. Metro-Anacostia station. The area is associated with Barrys Farm Settlement established after the Civil War by the federal government. This new neighborhood served as a relocation settlement that aided in the transition of former slaves into a free society. Archaeological analysis has focused on the rate and extent of black assimilation into the white-dominated society and has yielded information on the persistence of foodways and self-sufficiency.

MANASSAS NATIONAL BATTLEFIELD. Over 500 acres were added to Manassas National Battlefield when the Stuart's Hill tract was purchased in 1988. Archaeological investigations by the National Park Service revealed a number of sites containing evidence not only from the first and second battles of Manassas fought there, but also from the many generations of people who lived and worked in the communities that were engulfed by the Civil War. The potential is particularly rich for understanding the lives of African Americans both before and after the war (Galke 1992).

HARPERS FERRY, WEST VIRGINIA. The National Park Service performed an archaeological survey of Maryland and Loudoun Heights. The survey of the heights that surround Harpers Ferry identified numerous eighteenth- and early nineteenth-century charcoal hearths, nineteenth-century domestic farms, and Civil War fortifications and encampments.

Harpers Ferry was established as an armory town in 1799, and after the Civil War the lower town area transformed into a residential and commercial district. Archaeological excavations since 1989 have concentrated on the domestic life of armory workers, boarders, and entrepreneurs. Investigations have shown the interrelationship between technology, culture, and landscape in the early nineteenth-century industrial town. Contextual analysis provides insight into the general material wealth and health conditions of subordinate and dominant groups in the town (Shackel and Winter, in press). Work currently focuses on the area's early industrial development in Virginius Island and examines the interrelationship between work and domestic life.

SUMMARY

The concerns of the authors in this volume are necessarily interrelated through the analytic techniques and concepts common to the discipline of historical archaeology. They are also connected by the historical commonalities of their subject matter, which are bound in time and space with the European economic system that began to develop with the Age of Discovery.

Interethnic relations and class conflicts are themes that play a major role in many of these chapters. The relationships among Native Americans, Europeans, and Africans clearly have bearing on the history of the Chesapeake. Thus it is important to examine class and social conflicts among economic groups, occupational groups, and regional groups as we strive to understand changing social and political situations (including the stratification within cities) between urban and rural areas, and between the Old World and the New.

The chapters in this volume could have been organized in a number of ways. They could have been arranged strictly by century, but half of the work focuses on the 1700s, while some of the chapters straddle centuries. If the urban studies were separated from plantation studies, we would find more archaeology in cities and towns, owing to our perception and methods of working in the present. As a result, we have settled on a combination of these topics.

As mentioned at the outset, much historical archaeology is described in the grey literature, hard-to-find or hard-to-afford books, unpublished Ph.D. dissertations and M.A. theses, and scholarly journals, some of which have rather limited distribution. These discussions are by and large inaccessible to members of other disciplines or to the general public. The purpose of this book is to take a much-needed step in collecting in one volume some of the work under way in Chesapeake historical archaeology.

Of course, one volume cannot cover the entire range of exciting work that is being done by historical archaeologists in the Chesapeake. For this reason the chapters collected here must be considered a sample. The essays presented here provide some answers and questions that merit further study, and, most important, should stimulate the reader to continue to reap the historical and archaeological bounty of the bay.

REFERENCES CITED

Anonymous

1990 Highlighting Virginia Historical Archaeology: 1930–1990. *Notes on Virginia* (Fall). Virginia Department of Historic Resources. pp. 24–28.

Barbour, Philip L.

1986 *The Complete Works of Captain John Smith (1580–1631)*, vol. 1. University of North Carolina Press, Chapel Hill.

Barka, Norman F.

1973 The Kiln and Ceramics of the "Poor Potter" of Yorktown: A Preliminary Report. In *Ceramics in America*, edited by I. M. G. Quimby, pp. 291–318. Winterthur Conference Report. University Press of Virginia, Charlottesville.

Barse, Mary Folsum

1986 A Preliminary Archaeological Reconnaissance Survey of Londontown Publik House and Gardens and Twelve-Acre Expansion, Anne Arundel County, Maryland. Manuscript Series from Maryland Historic Trust, No. 41.

Broadwater, John D.

1985 The York River Shipwreck Project: Results from the

1978 Survey. In *Realms of Gold*, edited by Wilburn A. Cockrell, pp. 33–44. Fathom Eight Special Publication No. 1, San Marino, Calif.

Brush, Grace S.
1986 Geology and Paleoecology of Chesapeake Bay: A Long-Term Monitoring Tool for Management. *Journal of the Washington Academy of Sciences* 76(3):146–60.

Capper, John, Garrett Power, and Frank R. Shivers, Jr.
1983 *Chesapeake Waters: Pollution, Public Health, and Public Opinion, 1607–1972*. Tidewater Publishers, Centerville, Maryland

Cleland, Charles E., and James E. Fitting
1968 The Crisis of Identity: Theory in Historic Sites Archaeology. *The Conference on Historic Site Archaeology Papers* 2, pt 2: 124–138.

Comer, Elizabeth Anderson, and Kristin Stevens
1990 Mount Clare: Introducing Baltimore to 18th Century Splendor. In *New Perspectives on Maryland Historical Archaeology*, edited by R. J. Dent and B. J. Little. Thematic issue of *Maryland Archaeology* 26:86–94.

Cotter, John L.
1958 *Archaeological Excavations at Jamestown, Virginia*. U.S. National Park Service Archaeological Research Series No. 4. Washington, D.C.

Cotter, John L., and Paul Hudson
1957 *New Discoveries at Jamestown*. Government Printing Office. Washington, D.C.

Crader, Diane
1984 The Zooarchaeology of the Storehouse and the Dry Well at Monticello. *American Antiquity* 49:3:542–558.

Custer, Jay
1984 *Delaware Prehistoric Archaeology: An Ecological Approach*. University of Delaware Press, Newark.

Davidson, Thomas E.
1983 Free Blacks on the Lower Eastern Shore of Maryland: Part 1—The Colonial Period 1662–1775. Maryland Historical Trust Manuscript Series No. 42.

Deagan, Kathleen
1982 Avenues of Inquiry in Historical Archaeology. In *Advances in Archaeological Method and Theory*, vol. 5, edited by Michael B. Schiffer, pp. 151–178. Academic Press, New York.

Deetz, James
1977 *In Small Things Forgotten: An Archeology of Early American Life*. Doubleday, New York.
1988 American Historical Archaeology: Methods and Results. *Science* 239:262–367.

Derry, Linda, and Marley R. Brown III
1987 Excavation at Colonial Williamsburg Thirty Years Ago: An Archaeological Analysis of Cross-Trenching behind the Peyton-Randolph Site. *American Archaeology* 6:1:10–19.

Environmental Protection Agency (EPA)
1982 *Chesapeake Bay: Introduction to an Ecosystem*. Reprinted 1989 by Chesapeake Bay Program, Washington, D.C.

Fausz, Frederick J.
1985 Patterns of Anglo-Indian Aggression and Accommodation along the Mid-Atlantic Coast, 1584–1634. In *Cultures in Contact: The Impact of European Contacts on Native American Cultural Institutions, A.D. 1000–1800*, edited by William W. Fitzhugh, pp. 225–68. Smithsonian Institution Press, Washington, D.C.

Fitzhugh, William W. (editor)
1985 *Cultures in Contact, The European Impact on Native Cultural Institutions in Eastern North America, A.D. 1000–1800*. Smithsonian Institution Press, Washington, D.C.

Forman, H. Chandlee
1986 Some Pioneering Excavations in Virginia and Maryland. *Maryland Archaeology* 22:2:1–19.

Galke, Laura J. (editor)
1992 *Cultural Resource Survey and Inventory of a War-Torn Landscape: The Stuart's Hill Tract, Manassas National Battlefield Park, Virginia*. Occasional Report no. 7. Regional Archeology Program, National Capital Region, National Park Service, Washington, D.C.

Garrow, Patrick H., and Thomas R. Wheaton, Jr.
1986 *Final Report: Oxon Hill Manor Archaelogical Site Mitigation Project, I-95/MD 210/I-295*. Prepared for the Maryland Department of Transportation.

Hudson, Paul
1985 Jamestown: Birthplace of Historical Archaeology in the United States. *Archaeological Society of Virginia* 40:1:46–57.

Kaplan, Susan
1985 European Goods and Socio-Economic Change in Early Labrador Inuit Society. In *Cultures in Contact, The European Impact on Native Cultural Institutions in Eastern North America, A.D. 1000–1800*, edited by William W. Fitzhugh, pp. 45–69. Smithsonian Institution Press, Washington, D.C.

Keeler, Robert W.
1978 *The Homelot on the Seventeenth Century Tidewater Frontier*. Ph.D. dissertation, University of Oregon, Eugene.

Kelso, William M.
1984 *Kingsmill Plantation, 1619–1800: Archaeology of Country Life in Colonial Virginia*. Academic Press, New York.

Kelso, William M., and Rachel Most (editors)
1990 *Earth Patterns: Essays in Landscape Archaeology*. University Press of Virginia, Charlottesville.

King, Julia A., and Dennis J. Pogue
1985 Archeological Investigations at the Antenna Field, St. Inigoes, Maryland. Report prepared for the Naval Electronics Systems Engineering Activity, St. Inigoes. Ms. on file at Maryland Historic Trust.

Lewis, Clifford M., and Albert J. Loomie (editors)
1953 *The Spanish Jesuit Mission in Virginia, 1570–1572*. University of North Carolina Press, Chapel Hill.

Leone, Mark P.
1983 Method as Message: Interpreting the Past with the Public. *Museum News* 62:34–41.

1984 Interpreting Ideology in Historical Archaeology: The William Paca Garden in Annapolis, Maryland. In *Ideology, Power and Prehistory*, edited by D. Miller and C. Tilley, pp. 25–35. Cambridge University Press, Cambridge.

Leone, Mark P., Julie H. Ernstein, Elizabeth Kryder-Reid, and Paul A. Shackel

1989 Power Gardens of Annapolis. *Archaeology* 42:2:34–37; 74–75.

Leone, Mark P., and Parker B. Potter

1987 Liberation Not Replication: "Archaeology in Annapolis" Analyzed. *Journal of the Washington Academy of Sciences* 76:2:97–105.

Leone, Mark P., and Paul A. Shackel

1987 Forks, Clocks and Power. In *Mirror and Metaphor: Material and Social Construction of Reality*, edited by Daniel Ingersoll, pp. 45– 61. University Press of America, Lanham, Md.

1990 Plane and Solid Geometry in Colonial Gardens in Annapolis, Maryland. In *Earth Patterns: Essays in Landscape Archaeology*, edited by W. Kelso and Rachel Most, pp. 153–168. University Press of Virginia, Charlottesville.

Little, Barbara J.

1988 Craft and Culture Change in Eighteenth-Century Chesapeake. In *The Recovery of Meaning: Historical Archaeology in the Eastern United States*, edited by Mark P. Leone and Parker B. Potter, Jr., pp. 263– 292. Smithsonian Institution Press, Washington, D.C.

McCusker, John J., and Russell R. Menard

1986 *The Economy of British America, 1607–1789*. University of North Carolina Press, Chapel Hill.

McKee, Larry

1987 Delineating Ethnicity from the Garbage of the Early Virginians: The Faunal Remains from the Kingsmill Plantation Slave Quarters. *American Archeology* 6:1:31–39.

Menard, Russell Robert

1975 *Economy and Society in Early Colonial Maryland*. Ph.D. dissertation on file at the Department of History, University of Iowa.

Miller, Henry M.

1986 *Discovering Maryland's First City: A Summary Report on the 1982–1984 Archaeological Excavations in St. Mary's City, Maryland*. St. Mary's City Archaeology Series No. 2. St. Mary's City, Md.

1988 Baroque Cities in the Wilderness: Archaeology and Urban Development in the Colonial Chesapeake. *Historical Archaeology* 22:2:57–73.

Mouer, L. Daniel

1990 New Revelations at Jordan's Point. *Notes on Virginia* (Fall). Virginia Department of Historic Resources, pp. 31–34.

1991 Digging a Rebel's Homestead. *Archaeology* 44(5):54–57.

Neiman, Fraser D.

1978 Domestic Architecture at the Clifts Plantation: The Social Context of Early Virginia Building. *Northern Neck of Virginia Historical Magazine* 28:3096–3128. Reprinted in *Common Places: Readings in American Vernacular Architecture*, edited by D. Upton and J. M. Vlach. University of Georgia Press, Athens.

1980 *The "Manner House" before Stratford: Discovering the Clifts Plantation*. Robert E. Lee Memorial Association, Stratford, Va.

Noel Hume, Ivor

1963 *Here Lies Virginia*. Alfred A. Knopf, New York.

1983 *Martin's Hundred*. Alfred A. Knopf, New York.

Orser, Charles E., Jr.

1988a *The Material Basis of the Postbellum Tenant Plantation; Historical Archaeology in the South Carolina Piedmont*. University of Georgia Press, Athens.

1988b The Archaeological Analysis of Plantation Society: Replacing Status and Cast with Economics and Power. *American Antiquity* 53:735–51.

Outlaw, Alain

1989 *Governor's Land*. University Press of Virginia, Charlottesville, Va.

Parker, Kathleen A., and Jacqueline L. Hernigle

1990 *Portici: Portrait of a Middling Plantation in Piedmont Virginia*. Occasional Report no. 5. Regional Archaeology Program, National Capital Region, National Park Service, Washington, D.C.

Patterson, Thomas C.

1986 The Last Sixty Years: Toward a Social History of Americanist Archaeology in the United States. *American Anthropologist* (88)1:7–26.

Pogue, Dennis

1988a *Archaeology at George Washington's Mount Vernon: 1931–1987*. File Report 1. Mount Vernon Ladies' Association, Mount Vernon, Va.

1988b Spatial Analysis of the King's Reach Plantation Homelot, Ca. 1690–1715. *Historical Archaeology* 22:2:40–56.

1990 King's Reach and 17th-Century Planation Life. Jefferson Patterson Park and Museum Studies in Archaeology No. 1. Maryland Historical and Cultural Publications, Annapolis, Md.

Potter, Parker B. Jr., and Mark P. Leone

1987 Archaeology in Public in Annapolis: Four Seasons, Six Sites, Seven Tours and 32,000 Visitors. *American Archeology* 6:1:51–61.

Quinn, David Beers

1985 *Set Fair for Roanoke: Voyages and Colonies, 1584–1606*. University of North Carolina Press, Chapel Hill.

Sands, John O.

1980 *Sea Power at Yorktown: The Archaeology of the Captive Fleet*. Ph.D. dissertation, George Washington University, Washington, D.C.

Sanford, Douglas

1990 The Gardens at Germana, Virginia. In *Earth Patterns: Essays in Landscape Archaeology*, edited by W. Kelso and Rachel Most, pp. 43– 58. University Press of Virginia, Charlottesville.

Scarf, Thomas J.

1879 *History of Maryland*, vol. 1. John B. Piet, Baltimore.

Schuyler, Robert

1978a Editor. *Historical Archaeology: A Guide to Substantive and Theoretical Contributions*. Baywood Publishing, Farmingville, N.Y.

1978b The Spoken Word, the Written Word, Observed Behavior and Preserved Behavior; the Contexts Available to the Archaeologist. Reprinted in *Historical Archaeology: A Guide to Substantive and Theoretical Contributions*, edited by R. L. Schuyler, pp. 269–77. Baywood Publishing, Farmingville, N.Y.

Shackel, Paul A.

1993 *Personal Discipline and Material Culture: An Archaeology of Annapolis, Maryland, 1695–1870*. University of Tennessee Press, Knoxville, Tenn.

Shackel, Paul A. and Susan E. Winter (editors)

In press An Archaeology of Harpers Ferry's Comercial and Residential District. *Historical Archaeology*.

Shomette, Donald G.

1978 Londontown: The Reconnaissance of a 17th-18th Century Tidewater Maryland Riverport Complex. In *Beneath the Waters of Time: Proceedings of the Ninth Conference on Underwater Archaeology*, edited by J. Barto Arnold III, pp. 167–174. Texas Antiquities Committee Publication No. 6. Austin.

Singleton, Theresa

1990 The Archeology of the Plantation South: A review of Approaches and Goals. In Historical Archaeology on Southern Plantations and Farms, edited by Charles E. Orser, Jr., *Historical Archaeology* 24(4):70–77.

Smolek, Michael A., Dennis Pogue, and Wayne Clark

1984 Historical Archaeology of the Seventeenth-Century Chesapeake: A Guide to Sources. Jefferson Patterson Park and Museum, Occasional Paper No. 1.

Sonderman, Robert C., Matthew R. Virta, Marilyn W. Nickels, and Stephen R. Potter

1993 *Archeology at Harmony Hall: Exploring the Late Seventeenth-Century Frontier of Maryland*. Occasional Report No. 9. Regional Archeology Program. National Park Service, National Capital Region.

Sorenson, James D.

1987 *Folk to National Culture in Nineteenth-Century Montgomery County: Archaeological and Ethnohistorical Evidence from a Maryland Plantation*. Ph.D. dissertation, American University, Washington, D.C.

South, Stanley

1988 "Santa Elena: Threshold of Conquest." In *The Recovery of Meaning: Historical Archaeology in the Eastern United States*, edited by Mark P. Leone and Parker B. Potter, Jr., pp. 27–72. Smithsonian Institution Press, Washington, D.C.

Thomas, David Hurst

1988 Saints and Soldiers at Santa Catalina: Hispanic Designs for Colonial America. In *The Recovery of Meaning: Historical Archaeology in the Eastern United States*, edited by Mark P. Leone and Parker B. Potter, Jr., pp. 27–72. Smithsonian Institution Press, Washington, D.C.

Turner, E. Randolph

1985 Socio-Political Organization within the Powhatan Chiefdom and the Effects of European Contact, A.D. 1607–1646. In *Cultures in Contact, The European Impact on Native Cultural Institutions in Eastern North America, A.D. 1000–1800*, edited by William W. Fitzhugh, pp. 193–224. Smithsonian Institution Press, Washington, D.C.

Wallace, Michael

1981 Visiting the Past: History Museums in the United States. *Radical History Review* 25:63–96.

Warner, William

1976 *Beautiful Swimmers: Watermen, Crabs and the Chesapeake Bay*. R. R. Donnelley and Sons Company, Harrisonburg, Va.

Watkins, C. Malcolm, and I. Noel Hume

1967 *The "Poor Potter" of Yorktown*. U.S. National Museum Bulletin No. 249. Smithsonian Institution Press, Washington, D.C.

Whitehead, P. R.

1965 Palynology and Pleistocene Phytogeography of Unglaciated Eastern North America. In *The Quaternary of the United States*, edited by H. E. Wright, Jr., and D. G. Frey. Princeton University Press, Princeton, N.J.

Wolf, Eric

1982 *Europe and the People without History*. University of California Press, Berkeley.

Yentsch, Anne E.

1990a An Interpretive Study of the Use of Land and Space on Lot 83, Annapolis, Maryland. In New Perspectives on Maryland Historical Archaeology, edited by R. J. Dent and B. J. Little. *Maryland Archaeology* 26(1,2):21–53.

1990b The Calvert Orangery in Annapolis, Maryland: A Horticultural Symbol of Power and Prestige in an Early Eighteenth-Century Community. In *Earth Patterns: Essays in Landscape Archaeology*, edited by W. Kelso and Rachel Most, pp. 169–187. University Press of Virginia, Charlottesville.

PART I

Early European Settlement

THE PRINCIPAL issues of concern in interpreting early settlement of the Chesapeake are cultural contact, the frontier, exploitation of people and resources, and self-sufficiency. European colonization in the Chesapeake, as in many other areas in the New World, was stimulated by the hope of finding new wealth (Wolf 1982). The French and English in the northern reaches of the Americas exploited the fur trade (Jennings 1975; Trigger 1976; Ray and Freeman 1978), the Spanish capitalized on the gold and silver resources in Central and South America (Quinn 1985; Thomas 1989), and the first English settlers came to the Chesapeake to make their fortunes in tobacco farming. The intruders also learned to exploit local resources—such as land and the fauna and flora—in their quest for wealth.

In the frontier situation, settlers exchanged ideas, material culture, and patterns of behavior with the indigenous peoples. Often early contact led to conflict and eventual removal or annihilation of those peoples (Feest 1973; Turner 1982; Ramenofsky 1987; Smith 1987). The various intercultural relations in the Chesapeake region have been studied by Randolph Turner (1985) and Frederick Fausz (1985). They describe hostility and warfare in early Virginia and relative peace and self-preservation in Maryland.

The chapters in this section discuss to varying degrees how Europeans gained and utilized the new-found and unfamiliar resources in the Chesapeake region as they exploited and changed the existing physical and social environment. Chapter 10 by Joanne Bowen in the next section is also of interest here because it discusses seventeenth-century subsistence in comparing strategies through time and across regions.

Conflict, cooperation, negotiation, and other forms of interaction among the groups that inhabited the bay area are central anthropological themes. Continual power struggles between Europeans, Native Americans, and Africans, and between wealth groups, religions, and European and colonial authorities characterize the period of early settlement, as well as later periods. Although aboriginal inhabitants are not the primary focus of this section, their influence on European settlement and adaptation is undeniable. It could be argued, of course, that the effects of the contact on Native American populations were more far-reaching: disease and warfare resulted in drastic depopulation (Dobyns 1966, 1983; Ramenofsky 1987); and trade in goods and land devastated native cultural structures (Fitzhugh 1985). However, as Stephen Potter and Gregory Waselkov point out (chapter 2), the English did not simply transplant their culture to the Chesapeake. Instead, largely because of the native inhabitants, settlers had to create a new culture and develop strategies to adapt to unfamiliar social and physical environments.

European settlers brought Africans to the Americas in the early seventeenth century but relied on white indentured servants as well as black slaves for labor. For several generations race relations were more flexible than later in the seventeenth century. Timothy Breen and Stephen Innis (1980) have provided a particularly interesting account of free blacks on the eastern shore of the Chesapeake. James Deetz (1988) has described master-slave and master-servant relations, architecture, the tobacco economy, the institutionalization of racially based slavery, and locally manufactured colonoware ceramics. These complex relationships provide the context for Matthew Emerson's (chapter 3) work on the production of tobacco pipes by African Americans.

Power struggles occurred within the Chesapeake and the wider colonial world during its transformation from frontier to settled land (Lewis 1977, 1984; Paynter 1982, 1985). The material culture strategies of those struggles in the second half of the seventeenth century, and again in the 1720s, prefigure in some ways the transformation in Virginia from 1740 to 1790 that Rhys Isaac (1982) has described. Architecture and manufacturing were particularly important in the later seventeenth century as Virginians sought some measure of independence from England (chapter 4). During the same period in Maryland's first capital, both architectural form and the town plan were blended with legislative effort to create a more stable class structure. Later in Maryland's second capital, particular consumer choices rather than home manufacturing add another dimension to the power struggle between wealth groups (chapter 6).

The Essays

Stephen Potter and Gregory Waselkov establish a context for examining the initial European settlement pattern and land-use practices in the Northern Neck of Virginia. Their essay in chapter 2 provides a solid methodological technique for a regional survey, including walk-over surveys, low-altitude aerial photography, and limited excavation. They also discuss settlement patterns and the material implications of early European contact in the New World.

Their archaeological survey revealed several small and intermediate-size Chicacoan occupations along and close to the Coan River in the Northern Neck. Smaller sites, probably briefly occupied by hunting and gathering groups, were located a further distance from the main settlements. Using a coefficient of spatial association, Potter and Waselkov notice a strong association between early English settlement and protohistoric and historic Chicacoan sites. Whereas ecological factors may have influenced Native American settlement, and cleared lands motivated the English to settle in these areas, historical events and individual actions also promoted colonization on Chicacoan sites. Legislation passed in 1652 called for the removal of various Indian groups from these highly sought-after lands. The practice of moving into native settlements was a common pattern in much early European colonization.

European settlers adapted many Native American techniques during initial occupation, such as tool forms, crops, and farming methods. Because draft animals were in short supply, Europeans used swidden agricultural practices and hoe cultivation. They constructed their homesteads on already depleted Chicacoan fields and cultivated the land on the nutrient-repleted homesites of the Indians.

Matthew Emerson (chapter 3) analyzes the form and decoration of 800 pipe bowls that were excavated from various tidewater sites. The craft of pipemaking developed on late seventeenth-century Chesapeake plantations and disappeared by the eighteenth century. The variety of pipe forms and decorations suggests that many individuals were involved in making these objects. Emerson notes that both Native Americans and Europeans practiced this local craft, but the design elements on the pipes also suggest an African influence. He supports this interpretation by tracing the styles of pipe manufacture and pipe art to West African origins. West African pipemaking was well established by the third quarter of the seventeenth century. Motifs and bowl forms found in West Africa, as well as in a contemporary slave burial in Barbados, are similar to some of those found in the Chesapeake. The appearance of the African decorative style coincides with the increased visibility of Africans in the Chesapeake. Emerson argues that by the late seventeenth century planters increasingly controlled access to imported commodities. Therefore, these Chesapeake pipes were probably produced by individuals who had neither power nor access to the market. These powerless people included landless people: newly freed indentured servants, indentured servants, and slaves. By the late seventeenth century, an increasing number of those without power were members of the black population, and therefore a large proportion of the Chesapeake pipes may be attributed to this peripheral group. The death of local pipemaking coincides with the reorganization of plantation life and the introduction of a more culturally diverse African population.

Ann Markell (chapter 4) explores some of the material symbols of seventeenth-century English colonists, such as architecture and manufacturing, and demonstrates how they were manipulated to facilitate social change. Markell notes the complex relationship between goods and meaning. A change in material culture indicates not only technological change but also changing perceptions of relationships and the creation and maintenance of group identity.

Virginians created an architectural form specifically attributed to this region. Although impermanent architecture was the norm for the seventeenth-century Chesapeake, some permanent architecture built by the later part of the century represented intentional, symbolic acts. The aspiring elite used brick chimneys, for example, to differentiate themselves from lower-class groups. In this context, Markell analyzes a middling planter's site from Flowerdew Hundred, dating from 1660 to 1690. Although this planter subscribed to the standard impermanent architectural form for the period, he did construct a brick chimney. The planter also exercised his desire for self- sufficiency and independence by experimenting with iron smelting. Other forms of small-scale industry also existed in the region, such as pipe manufacture, pottery manufacture, shoemaking, and shipbuilding.

Although manufacturing was encouraged by Virginia in 1682, it was not allowed by the English Commissaries of Customs. England thought this entrepreneurial activity posed a threat to its dominance over the colonies because self-sufficiency could foster independence. Many Virginians discreetly disregarded and resisted these laws. Similarly, individual settlers struggled for independence from the colony as a whole: as settlers increasingly used forms of permanent architecture, they broke their ties with local communities and craftsmen.

Henry Miller (chapter 5) analyzes the seventeenth-century landscape in Maryland's first capital city and provides an important example of how early Marylanders manipulated material attributes in the colony's center of power. In particular, Miller centers his argument on the Country House, the governor's domicile, which was later converted for public use in 1662. Miller recognizes the complex relationship between functional, social, and symbolic attributes in the landscape. He defines landscape attributes to include buildings, fences and other barriers such as ditches and hedges, and activity areas such as gardens, orchards, and chicken yards.

At first, the Country House was used solely as the governor's dwelling. Eventually a townhouse addition was constructed for government use. Three yardscapes were created over the seventeenth century. In the 1630s the built features followed the natural landscape. During the 1640s and 1650s, the spatial orientation of the built environment remained relatively unstructured. By the 1660s, the town had undergone a substantial organizational restructuring and formalization, as had the yardscape around the Country House. The yard's use became well defined. A recognizable rectangular lot developed, and the back areas became more spatially complex. The spatial distribution of functionally different artifacts indicates some spatial separation of activities. During the 1660s the Country House transformed from a rural plantation to the focal point of the center of power in Maryland's most urbanized seventeenth-century space.

In chapter 6 Paul Shackel explores the relationship between new material culture and social, political, and economic instability. He examines items that create separations in the community, give rise to strong group boundaries, and encourage the development of individuality. These items include architecture, town plans, and everyday material culture from Maryland's first capital city of St. Mary's City and second capital city of Annapolis.

As the number of freed white and black indentured servants increased and threatened the power of the gentry in the middle of the seventeenth century, white landholders marginalized peripheral groups by passing racist legislation. It is no mere coincidence that St. Mary's City, which developed as a center of political power rather than a center of commerce, was redesigned using particular baroque features. As monumental architecture emphasizing the power of the government and church became more widespread during the 1660s and 1670s, so too did the amount of racist legislation.

In Maryland more racist legislation was passed between 1710 and 1730 than in any other period. The social and economic effect of this legislation on the residents of Annapolis and the Chesapeake in general is examined through such factors as population increase, wealth redistribution, and inflation. During this time, the wealthy adopted a modern discipline, which included the use of a formal and segmented dining. The goods and behavior associated with this new discipline had appeared in England many decades before, but did not gain acceptance in Annapolis until this period of instability. Impermanent architecture was also replaced by more permanent building forms. This new material culture promoted individuality and discouraged interclass cooperation.

The period of early European and African settlement in the Chesapeake was a complex and dynamic time, the end of which may be marked conveniently as the end of the seventeenth century. By that time both Maryland and Virginia had moved their capital cities, the frontier had moved farther west, Europeans were indisputably dominant both militarily and culturally over Native Americans, and racially based slavery had been institutionalized. A native-born European American elite was in power.

References Cited

Breen, Timothy, and Stephen Innes
1980 *"Myne Owne Ground": Race and Freedom on Virginia's Eastern Shore, 1640–1676*. Oxford University Press, New York.

Deetz, James
1988 American Historical Archaeology: Methods and Results. *Science* 239: 362–367.

Dobyns, H.
1966 An Appraisal of Techniques for Estimating Aboriginal Population with a New Hemispherical Estimate. *Current Anthropology* 7: 395–416.
1983 *Their Number Become Thinned: Native American Population Dynamics in Eastern North America*. University of Tennessee Press, Knoxville.

Fausz, Frederick
1985 Patterns of Anglo-Indian Aggression and Accommodation along the Mid-Atlantic Coast, 1584–1634. In *Cultures in Contact: The Impact of European Contacts on Native American Cultural Institutions, A.D. 1000–1800*, edited by William W. Fitzhugh, pp. 225–271. Smithsonian Institution Press, Washington, D.C.

Feest, Christian
1973 Seventeenth-Century Virginia Algonquian Population Estimates. *Quarterly Bulletin of the Archaeological Society of Virginia* 37:45–64.

Fitzhugh, William W. (editor)
1985 *Cultures in Contact, The European Impact on Native Cultural Institutions in Eastern North America, A.D. 1000–1800*. Smithsonian Institution Press, Washington, D.C.

Green, S. W., and S. M. Perlman
1985 *The Archaeology of Frontiers and Boundaries*. Academic Press, Orlando, Fla.

Hemphill, John M.
1985 *Virginia and the English Commercial System 1689–1733*. Garland, New York.

Isaac, Rhys
1982 *The Transformation of Virginia, 1740–1790*. University of North Carolina Press, Chapel Hill.

Jennings, Francis
1975 *The Invasion of America: Indians, Colonialism, and the Cant of Conquest*. University of North Carolina Press, Chapel Hill.

Kulikoff, Allan
1986 *Tobacco and Slaves: The Development of Southern Culture in the Chesapeake, 1680–1800*. University of North Carolina Press, Chapel Hill.

Lewis, Kenneth
1977 Sampling the Archaeological Frontier: Regional Models and Component Analysis. In *Research Strategies in Historical Archaeology*, edited by Stanley South, pp. 151–201. Academic Press, New York.
1984 *The American Frontier: An Archaeological Study of Settlement Pattern and Process*. Academic Press, New York.

McCusker, John, and Russell Menard
1986 *The Economy of British America: 1607–1789*. University of North Carolina Press, Chapel Hill.

Paynter, Robert
1982 *Models of Spatial Inequality: Settlement Patterns in Historical Archaeology*. Academic Press, New York.
1985 Surplus Flow between Frontiers and Homelands. In *The Archaeology of Frontiers and Boundaries*, edited by S. W. Green and S. M. Perlman, pp. 163–211. Academic Press, Orlando.

Quinn, David Beers
1985 *Set Fair for Roanoke: Voyages and Colonies, 1584–1606*. University of North Carolina Press, Chapel Hill.

Ramenofsky, Anne
1987 *Vectors of Death: The Archaeology of European Contact*. University of New Mexico Press, Albuquerque.

Ray, Arthur, and Donald Freeman
1978 *"Give Us Good Measure": An Ecological Analysis of Relations between the Indians and the Hudson's Bay Company Before 1763*. University of Toronto Press, Toronto.

Smith, M. T.
1987 *Archaeology of Aboriginal Culture Change in the Interior Southeast: Depletion during the Early Historic Period*. University of Florida Press, Gainesville.

Thomas, David Hurst
1989 *Columbian Consequences I: Archaeological and Historical Perspectives on the Spanish Borderlands East*. Smithsonian Institution Press, Washington, D.C.

Trigger, Bruce
1976 *The Children of Aataentsic: A History of the Huron People to 1660*. McGill-Queen's University Press, Montreal.
Turner, E. Randolph
1982 A Reexamination of Powhatan Territorial Boundaries and Population, ca. A.D. 1607. *Quarterly Bulletin of the Archaeological Society of Virginia* 37:45–64.
1985 Socio-Political Organization within the Powhatan Chiefdom and the Effects on European Contact, A.D. 1607–1646. In *Cultures in Contact: The Impact of European Contacts on Native American Cultural Institutions, A.D. 1000–1800*, edited by William W. Fitzhugh, pp. 193–224. Smithsonian Institution Press, Washington, D.C.
Wolf, Eric
1982 *Europe and the People without History*. University of California Press, Berkeley.

Suggested Readings from the Contributors

Breen, Timothy, and Stephen Innes
1980 *"Myne Owne Ground": Race and Freedom on Virginia's Eastern Shore, 1640–1676*. Oxford University Press, New York.
Bruce, Philip Alexander
1895 *Economic History of Virginia in the Seventeenth Century: An Inquiry into the Material Conditions of the People*. Vols. 1 and 2. Peter Smith, New York.
Carson, Cary, Norman Barka, William Kelso, Gary Wheeler Stone, and Dell Upton
1981 Impermanent Architecture in the Southern American Colonies. *Winterthur Portfolio* 16:135–196.
Deetz, James
1988 American Historical Archaeology: Methods and Results. *Science* 239:362–367.
King, Julia
1988 A Comparative Midden Analysis of a Household and Inn in St. Mary's City, Maryland. *Historical Archaeology* 22(2):17–39.
Kulikoff, Allan
1986 *Tobacco and Slaves: The Development of Southern Culture in the Chesapeake, 1680–1800*. University of North Carolina Press, Chapel Hill.
Lewis, Kenneth
1977 An Archaeological Perspective on Social Change—The Virginia Frontier. In *The Frontier: Comparative Studies*, edited by D. H. Miller and J. O. Steffen, pp. 139–159. University of Oklahoma Press, Norman.
Main, Gloria
1982 *Tobacco Plantation: Life in Early Maryland 1650–1720*. Princeton University Press, Princeton, N.J.
Miller, Henry M.
1986 *Discovering Maryland's First City: A Summary Report of the 1981–1984 Archaeological Excavations in St. Mary's City, Maryland*. St. Mary's City Archaeological Series No. 2. St. Mary's City, Md.
Morgan, Edmund
1975 *American Slavery, American Freedom: The Ordeal of Colonial Virginia*. W. W. Norton, New York.
Neiman, Fraser D.
1980 *The "Manner House" before Stratford: Discovering the Clifts Plantation*. Robert E. Lee Memorial Association, Stratford, Va.
Pogue, Dennis J.
1990 *King's Reach and 17-Century Plantation Life*. Jefferson Patterson Park and Museum Studies in Archaeology No. 1. Maryland Historical and Cultural Publications, Annapolis, Md.
Potter, Stephen R.
1993 *Commoners, Tribute, and Chiefs; The Development of Algonquian Culture in the Potomac Valley*. University of Virginia Press, Charlottesville.
Upton, Dell
1986 *Holy Things and Profane: Anglican Parish Churches in Colonial Virginia*. Harvard University Press, Cambridge, Mass.
Walsh, Lorena S.
1988 Community Networks in the Early Chesapeake. In *Colonial Chesapeake Society*, edited by Lois Green Carr, Philip D. Morgan, and Jean B. Russo, pp. 200–224. University of North Carolina Press, Chapel Hill.
Waselkov, Gregory A., and R. Eli Paul
1981 Frontiers and Archaeology. *North American Archaeologist* 29:4:309–329.
Wood, Peter, Gregory A. Waselkov, and Thomas Hantley
1989 *Powhatan's Mantle: Indians in the Colonial Southeast*. University of Nebraska Press, Lincoln.

II
CHAPTER

"Whereby We Shall Enjoy Their Cultivated Places"

STEPHEN R. POTTER AND GREGORY A. WASELKOV

EARLY EUROPEAN invaders of Eastern North America, according to a widely accepted historical tenet, frequently settled on or near areas of earlier or extant Indian habitation. Yet few detailed studies present substantive archaeological or documentary evidence to support this contention. Toward that end, we examine the settlement pattern and land use practices of the first English colonists to settle Virginia's northern neck, a finger-like peninsula bounded by the Potomac and Rappahannock rivers and Chesapeake Bay (figure 2.1), and we compare them with those of local sixteenth- and seventeenth-century Virginia Algonquians. English adaptation to this new environment, which had been occupied for centuries by the Algonquians, led to a convergence in the settlement patterns of the two societies.

When English colonists began settling the Virginia shore of the Potomac River, around 1642, many of them already held specific ideas concerning what sort of settlement strategies, land-use practices, and farming methods were appropriate to the frontier. These included a complex amalgam of English and Native American customs forged over three decades of social interaction and cultural exchange elsewhere in the Chesapeake-tidewater region, particularly in the vicinity of Jamestown (Lewis 1975, 1977). Our interpretation of the development of this colonial English adaptive strategy is based upon the anthropological concept of a frontier as a zone of mixture and interaction between intrusive and indigenous societies (Waselkov and Paul 1981). Such an approach reveals that the pattern of successive settlement observed in Virginia's northern neck is not unique, but apparently represents a phenomenon common to frontier settings.

STUDY AREA AND METHODS

English settlement of the northern neck began in the locality known as Chicacoan, the anglicized name for an early seventeenth-century Indian district occupied by a small Algonquian chiefdom of about 120 to 130 people. The main territory of the Chicacoans—and location of the chief's or *werowance's* village shown on John Smith's 1612 map of Virginia as "Cekakawwon"—corresponds to the area of the Coan River and Hull Creek drainages in present-day Northumberland County, Virginia (Potter 1982a:1, 10, 87).

The Chicacoan area considered in this study covers approximately 65 square kilometers (25 square miles) and is bounded by the Potomac River in the north and in the south by a ridge in the interior uplands that marks the head of the Coan, Cod, Presley, and Hull drainages (see figure 2.1). The neck of land along the east bank of Hull Creek marks the eastern boundary, and the western boundary is the neck of land forming the west bank of the Coan River.

Surveys and excavations were conducted in the Chica-

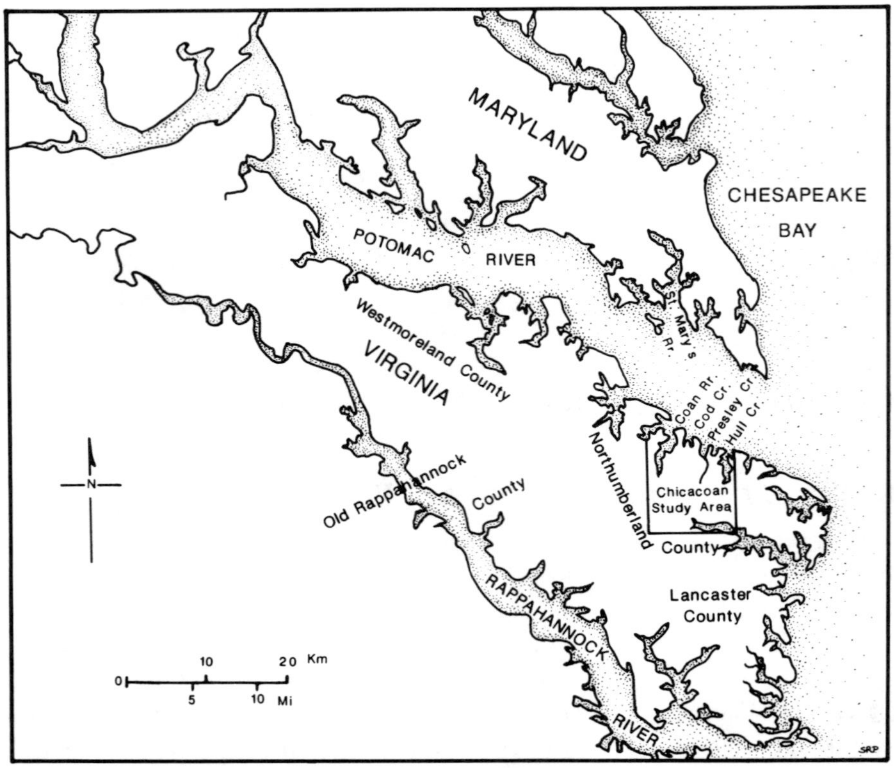

Figure 2.1. *Map of Virginia's northern neck and the Chicacoan study area.*

coan locality during 1976, 1978, and 1979 as part of the senior author's dissertation research. Fieldwork was devoted to collecting data on changes in the settlement system of the developing Chicacoan chiefdom over the period A.D. 200 to 1650. All archaeological sites discovered during the course of the investigations were documented, regardless of temporal or ethnic association, and the total came to 181 sites. Of that number, 15 had been occupied by the protohistoric-historic Chicacoans, as indicated by the presence of a Chicacoan component— an assemblage of contemporaneous artifacts—at each site, and 8 have seventeenth-century English components.

Approximately 60 percent of the total Chicacoan study area was surveyed on foot, by canoe, and by airplane. Figure 2.2 shows the areas examined and survey methods used. During the on-the-ground survey of cultivated fields, team members walked approximately 9.5 meters (30 feet) apart. Each person looked for artifacts, mollusc shells or animal bones, surface indications of features, or soil color or textural differences. Soil probes were used to determine the nature of the soil profile and to detect subsurface features or midden deposits. In wooded areas, team members relied heavily on random shovel test pits and soil probes but also examined eroded areas, tree falls, and banks.

A canoe was used to gain access to thickly wooded shorelines or to examine the shoreline for archaeological remains. Paddling close to the shore, the survey team looked for artifacts, mollusc shells, features, or soil discolorations. Whenever they saw any of these potential site indicators, they went ashore and thoroughly examined the area using the methods described above.

Low-altitude aerial survey provided a quick and relatively accurate means of covering large tracts of cultivated land. Experimentation at various times over three years proved that the optimum seasons for spotting archaeological sites from the air were late winter and early spring. Archaeological sites appeared as very green areas of small grain crops, such as wheat, or as gray-black soil marks (Potter 1982b). All tracts of land containing suspected archaeological sites observed from the air were completely surveyed on the ground.

Prior analysis of the historical sources suggested that the Chicacoans lived along the east bank of the Coan River in the early seventeenth century. It was also known that John Mottrom's Coan Hall, the first permanent English settlement on the Virginia side of the Potomac, was located in the same vicinity. Therefore, the land adjacent to the east bank of the Coan was purposely selected as an intensive sampling unit within the Chicacoan study area. This sampling unit consisted of all the land along the east bank of the Coan River drained by streams flowing into the Coan and Cod Creek, as well as parts of the west bank of the Coan near its mouth. About 22.3 square kilometers (8.6 square miles) were included in the sampling unit, or 33 percent of the total study area (figure 2.2). In addition, the sampling unit included a complete physiographic cross section of uplands, slopes, and necklands, with 45 percent of the unit consisting of uplands (the land above the 50-foot contour interval).

The team conducted an 85 percent on-the-ground survey of the sampling unit. The remaining 15 percent consisted of properties whose owners did not grant permission to trespass. Fortunately, of the 85 percent surveyed, the proportion of upland to neckland was the same as the proportion for the entire unit. Thus, given the state of land ownership at the time of the fieldwork, the sampling unit was surveyed as thoroughly as possible.

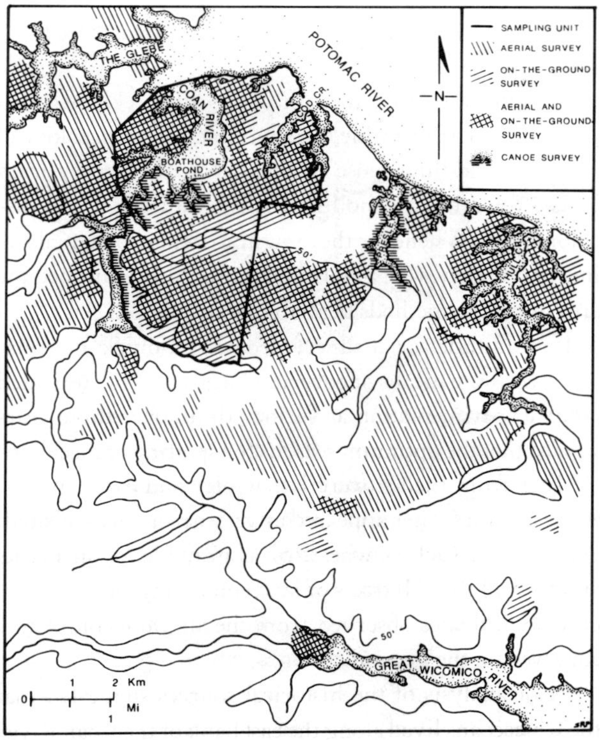

F I G U R E 2.2. *Map of the Chicacoan study area showing sampling unit, areas surveyed, and method used.*

Native American Settlement Pattern

Protohistoric and early historic Chicacoan components were identified by the presence of certain types of material culture known to occur with greater frequency or exclusively during the period circa A.D. 1500 to the 1650s. Items characteristic of this time include a predominately plain, thin-walled, fine shell-tempered pottery named Yeocomico ware (Egloff and Potter 1982:112–114); Potomac Creek Plain and Moyaone Plain pottery (Stephenson 1963:119–120, 124–125); hollow reed or cane punctate decoration on simple Rappahannock Incised and Townsend Corded pottery; small, elbow pottery pipes, usually with fine punctate designs; Levanna Small triangular points; ceramic vessels that imitated European vessel forms, but were made by Indians using traditional techniques; local copies of English pipes with roulette designs; seventeenth-century glass beads; iron objects such as cutlery; and European sheet copper cut into geometric shapes (MacCord 1965:98–104, 1969:9–38; Potter 1982a:137–139, 1989:161–172).

The distribution of the 15 protohistoric-historic Chicacoan components found during this study is shown in figure 2.3. Each component was classified by three empirically observable characteristics: midden composition, integrity, and size. Those in which more than 50 percent of the midden volume consisted of dark earth or mollusc shell were termed "midden sites" or "shell midden sites," respectively, depending on the predominant midden composition. Areas showing no evidence of dark earth or shell midden were called "decomposed" sites. These three categories were further subdivided into three, arbitrarily chosen, size classes: large, 1 hectare (2.47 acres) or larger; intermediate, between 1 hectare and 1,000 square meters (2.47 acres and 10,800 square feet); and small, 1,000 square meters (10,800 square feet) or less (Potter 1982a:143–145).

The only large site (44NB111) discovered during the survey is a dark earth midden covering 7.29 hectares (18 acres) adjacent to Boathouse Pond, on the east bank of the Coan River. Approximately 4.45 hectares (11 acres) of the site was occupied during protohistoric-historic times, making this the most extensive occupation of that period found thus far. Together with several other nearby components surrounding Boathouse Pond, this was probably the main protohistoric-historic Chicacoan village, where the district chief, or *werowance*,

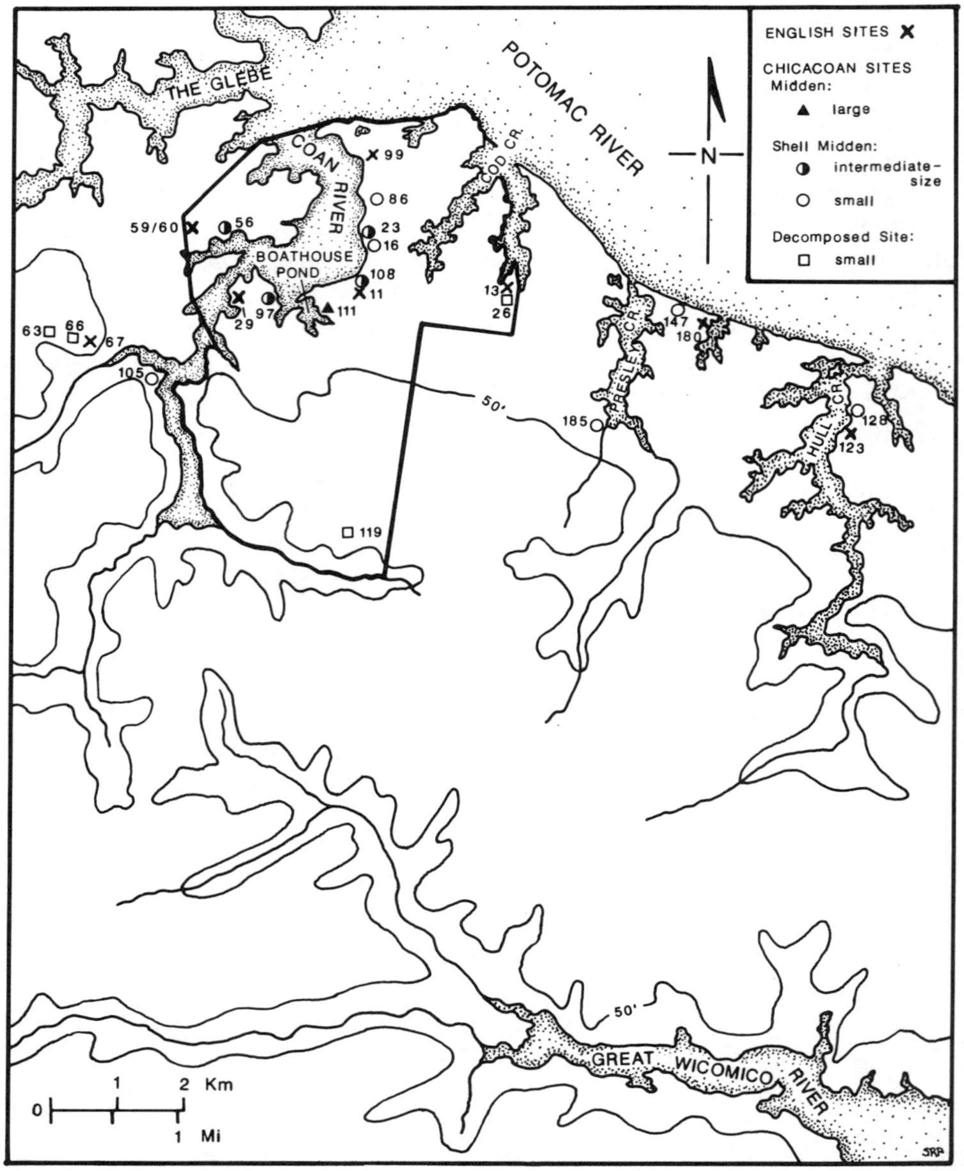

FIGURE 2.3. *Map of the distribution of protohistoric-historic Chicacoan components and seventeenth-century English components.*

lived, symbolized by the "King's howse" on John Smith's 1612 map of Virginia.

From the distribution of the protohistoric-historic components in the sampling unit, it appears that most of the Chicacoan occupation occurred in the necklands along the east bank of the Coan River. All but one of the protohistoric-historic intermediate-size and small components within 2 kilometers (1.24 miles) of the large Boathouse Pond site are in the neckland along the river's east bank. This confirms the predicted ethnohistoric pattern, wherein agricultural plots, outlying houses and hamlets, and favored spots for gathering shellfish were within a convenient walk or canoe ride of the main village (Potter 1982a:59–61, 87–90, 245–250).

All of the protohistoric-historic components beyond a 2-kilometer (1.24-mile) catchment radius of the Boathouse Pond site are either small shell middens or small decomposed sites. Small decomposed sites probably represent briefly occupied interior hunting-gathering sites, as evidenced by their assemblages, which typically consist of a triangular point, a scraper or biface, and a few flakes. Small shell middens, like the excavated component at Blue Fish Beach (44NB147), are indicative of estuarine gathering and camping sites used by small groups of people for relatively short durations (Potter 1982a: 204–244).

English Colonial Settlement Pattern

Sometime around 1642 John Mottrom established the first permanent English settlement on the Virginia shore of the Potomac River. Mottrom was a merchant-planter, formerly of Maryland, but more recently from York County, Virginia. He purchased from Machywap, *werowance* of the Chicacoan Indians, a tract of land along the eastern side of the Coan River. Not far from the high banks of the river's L-shaped bend, Mottrom built his seat, or plantation, named Coan Hall. As additional English settlers arrived shortly thereafter, the personal relationship between Mottrom and Machywap served as the foundation for early Indian–white diplomacy in Chicacoan (Anonymous 1908:53–54; Potter 1976:40).

Although John Mottrom represented the "inhabitants of Chicawone" as a burgess to the General Assembly of 1645, apparently Northumberland was not officially recognized as a county by the General Assembly until 1648 (Hening 1823:299, 352–353). Four years later the county commissioners were empowered to handle all affairs consistent with maintaining the peace with the Indians of their county. As a consequence of an act passed by the General Assembly in April 1652, the Indians of the Chicacoan and adjacent Wicocomoco chiefdoms were combined into a single political group and relocated to an area set aside for their use about 1655–1656 (Potter 1976:44–45). Thus, in less than seventeen years, the aboriginal people of Chicacoan were displaced, by and large in a peaceful manner, by the invading English.

The identification of the seventeenth-century Anglo-American components was based on historical and archaeological research, with the following items serving as diagnostic artifacts: locally made "terra cotta" pipes with roulette designs; English and Dutch pipes characteristic of the seventeenth century; a variety of seventeenth-century tin-glazed earthenwares; North Devon gravel-tempered pans with seventeenth-century rim forms; North Devon Sgraffito ware; Rhenish Brown stoneware; Surry-like ware; Morgan Jones pottery; and wine bottle seals bearing family names, such as "Presly" (Kelso and Chappell 1974:58–62; Henry 1979:19–32; Miller 1983:75–94).

The distribution of Anglo-American archeological sites having an origin in the seventeenth century is shown in figure 2.3. A total of eight were identified, and they all represent rural farmsteads or "plantations" consisting of a cluster of wooden post-in-the-ground structures. Recent archaeological salvage excavation and historical research at Newman's Nook (44NB180) confirm this interpretation (Hodges 1990; McCartney 1990).

Spatial Effects of Frontier Contact

To assess the overall level of spatial association between the distribution of protohistoric-historic aboriginal components and the seventeenth-century Anglo-American components, a coefficient of spatial association (C_s) was calculated (Sorenson 1974:172–176). The coefficient of spatial association is a pure number expressing the overall correspondence between two populations whose elements may be regarded as occupying points in space. The level of association is calculated on the basis of the distances between the elements or points of the two populations, first within each population and then one to another.

In order to apply this method of measuring the spatial association between point patterns, it must be assumed that the components assigned to each distributional pattern were contemporaneous, even though the protohistoric-historic Chicacoan components may have been occupied anytime between circa A.D. 1500 and the 1650s. The calculated crude C_s value equals 2.26 and the transformed C_s value equals 0.38. As indicated in table 2.1, the transformed value of 0.38 for the coefficient of spatial association indicates a *moderate association* between the overall correspondence or two-way relationship of Chicacoan to

Table 2.1. *Analysis of C_s Values*

Crude C_s Value	Transformed C_s Value	Degree of Association/Disassociation
1/3	<−0.5	High disassociation
1/3 to 2/3	−0.5 to −0.2	Moderate disassociation
2/3 to 1.5	−0.2 to +0.2	Indeterminate relationship
1.5 to 3.0	0.2 to 0.5	Moderate association
>3.0	>0.5	High association

Source: After Sorensen (1974:table 1).

FIGURE 2.4. *Aerial photograph showing the proximity of John Mottrom's Coan Hall (44NB11) to the Boathouse Pond village site (44NB111). Black arrows point to the sites that appear as soil marks in the cultivated fields in the center and upper right.*

English components, on the one hand, and of English to Chicacoan components, on the other.

More important to the thesis of this chapter, however, is the degree of association between the seventeenth-century English sites and the protohistoric-historic Chicacoan sites. This one-way relationship is defined by calculating a coefficient of partial association (C'_{sb}), which yields a transformed value of 0.68 (Sorensen 1974:174). A transformed value of 0.68 for the coefficient of partial association indicates a *high association* of seventeenth-century Anglo-American sites to protohistoric-historic aboriginal sites (table 2.1). Thus, English sites are more strongly associated with the Chicacoan sites than the two sets of sites are to each other.

Although there are several problems with this method, such as the assumption of contemporaneity, it does indicate that seventeenth-century English settlements are located very close to protohistoric-historic Chicacoan Indian sites. This is strikingly illustrated in an aerial view that shows the close juxtaposition of the two preeminent sites of the era, John Mottrom's Coan Hall (44NB11) in the foreground and the probable protohistoric-historic *werowance's* village site (44NB111) at Boathouse Pond, 350 meters (1,148 feet) away in the background (figure 2.4).

The second permanent English settlement in Chicacoan was the seat of William Presly (Keach 1926:92–93), which in the early eighteenth century was known as Northumberland House (44NB13). Presly's plantation is about 1.7 kilometers (1.05 miles) due east of Coan Hall and within a 2-kilometer (1.24-mile) catchment radius of the Boathouse Pond site (see figure 2.3). The location of this site is crucial to our understanding of seventeenth-century English settlement strategy and deserves detailed discussion.

In the estuarine coastal plain, one of the most important factors involved in selecting a site for a *werowance's* village was proximity to enough good-quality land suitable for slash-and-burn maize cultivation (Potter 1982a: 60, 245–49, 358). Villages were usually located in areas where soil associations contained significantly high percentages of silty loam, such as Matapeake, Mattapex, and Woodstown soils. Of the three soil associations within a 2-kilometer (1.24-mile) catchment radius of the Boathouse Pond site, the Mattapex-Bertie association is particularly suited for slash-and-burn subsistence cultivation. Given that only 10 percent of the soils in all of Northumberland County are included in the Mattapex-Bertie association, it is significant that 51 percent of the soils within a 2-kilometer (1.24-mile) catchment radius of the Boathouse Pond site are part of this soil association.

In order for the Chicacoans to stay in the locale along the Coan River, they required approximately 419 to 592 hectares (1,035 to 1,462 acres) of arable soil favorable to maize growth, with at least 36 to 41 hectares (89 to 101 acres) of maize under cultivation each year (Potter 1982a:

FIGURE 2.5. *Aerial photograph of site 44NB29, containing a seventeenth-century English component, visible as a dark concentration of winter wheat (see black arrow) in the narrow strip of field adjacent to a grass runway.*

76–78, 358– 360). At present, there are about 456 hectares (1,150 acres) of arable land within a 2-kilometer (1.24-mile) catchment radius of the Boathouse Pond site. If the protohistoric-historic component of this site does, indeed, represent part of the historic Chicacoan village, then there was enough arable land within the village's catchment area to support indefinitely a population of about 125. This figure corresponds well with the estimated population of about 120 to 130 for the Chicacoans circa 1608, which is based on John Smith's warrior counts (Potter 1982a:46–52).

Returning now to William Presly's settlement, it was located at the head of Cod Creek on the neckland adjacent to Mottrom's plantation, yet still within the agricultural catchment area of the Chicacoan village (Nugent 1934: 185). It is quite probable, therefore, that fields in varying stages of production or succession were located here. The same situation exists at site 44NB29, shown in an aerial view as a dark crop mark in the cultivated field (figure 2.5). The seventeenth-century English component at this site is approximately 360 meters (1,181 feet) from the protohistoric-historic Chicacoan occupation at site 44NB97, situated on the west side of Boathouse Pond at its entrance to the Coan River (see figure 2.3). Again, the probability is high that this was an area of Indian clear fields or fallow plots (often referred to in the colonial records as Indian old fields). The same association can be noted with respect to the later seventeenth-century English components at 44NB59/60 and 44NB99. With the exception of the first English settlement located near the site of the Chicacoan village, all other seventeenth-century English settlements in the vicinity of the Coan River occur near the periphery of the main village's catchment area, close to small or intermediate-size sites of protohistoric-historic Indian occupancy. It is no historical accident that an "ould Indian feild" is recorded in land patents dating from 1650 to 1664 on the west side of the Coan River (Nugent 1934:205, 319, 510).

A tendency on the part of the English colonists to establish their plantations near extant Indian sites and accompanying clear fields and old fields was not confined to the Chicacoan locality. A similar situation existed in adjacent Westmoreland County, where one of the earliest English farmsteads, Nominy Plantation, was described in 1659 as situated "near the side of an Indian field commonly known as the Pipemaker's field" (Westmoreland County 1653–1659:1:111–112) and next to an extensive Late Woodland–early historic village site (44WM13). Excavations at Nominy Plantation (44WM12) during 1978 revealed part of an earlier Indian structure beneath a seventeenth-century colonial structure (Virginia Department of Historic Resources, Archaeological Inventory Archives, Richmond).

A similar association occurs along Farnham Creek, on the north bank of the Rappahannock River, in Richmond County. In 1979 an archaeological survey of the Woodbury tract revealed two large midden sites, both containing small Late Woodland and possibly protohistoric-historic Indian components (the two sites appear as dark, gray-black stains on the adjacent headlands in figure 2.6). Ethnohistorical research indicates that the village of Oquomack, belonging to the Moratico chiefdom, was located in this vicinity (Barbour 1971:295).

In May 1650 Sir William Berkley granted 5,350 acres to Moore Fauntleroy on both sides "of a Creeke called Farnham." Land patents from 1660 and 1664 refer to an "Indian Field" near the head of Farnham Creek (Nugent 1934:408, 441, 501), and in 1667 mention is made of Pipemaker's Creek, which flows into Farnham Creek just above the Woodbury tract. This tract was referred to as the "Old Plantation" in a land transaction for old Rappahannock County dated April 29, 1667, which may indicate that this was the site of Moore Fauntleroy's original house (Ryland 1976:148).

Figure 2.6. *Aerial photograph of two large midden sites containing Late Woodland and possibly protohistoric-historic Indian components. Black arrows point to the sites that appear as dark, gray-black stains in the cultivated field adjacent to the creek.*

Discussion and Conclusions

When John Mottrom first sailed his sloop into the Coan River about 1642, a wave of English settlement followed in his wake. In quick succession, the slender peninsula of land between the Potomac and Rappahannock rivers was divided into four counties: Northumberland, circa 1645; Lancaster, 1651; Westmoreland, 1653; and old Rappahannock, 1656, most of which incorporated one or more Algonquian chiefdoms in their entirety (Hening 1823:352–353; Hiden 1957:11–12, 14–15). Some of the original English parishes in these counties, such as Chickacoan Parish in Northumberland County, were formed from what had been the core areas of the Algonquian chiefdoms. The hierarchical nature of Algonquian society, in which political power was controlled by a single individual—the *werowance*—and his or her immediate matrilineal relations, permitted enterprising colonists such as Mottrom to usurp the heartland of entire chiefdoms by purchase or agreement with a *werowance*. Europeans who colonized areas of North America occupied by more egalitarian societies seldom acquired legal title so easily to lands that could only be given with the consent of all tribal members.

Indian and English settlement patterns also converged at the level of the individual settlement. The earliest English settlers to this region of Virginia's northern neck dispersed themselves in a pattern modeled after the coastal Algonquian prototype. This dispersal indicates that the short-fallow, plow agriculture typical of the English midlands was impractical here, given the small labor supply and shortage of draft animals (Carrier 1957:31; Lewis 1975:76). The method eventually chosen by the colonists was swidden planting of Native American crops tended by hoe cultivation (Craven 1965:34–36).

The English decided to adopt a dispersed settlement pattern partly because it was necessary for the intensive cultivation of a particular native American plant—tobacco. After Sir Walter Raleigh helped popularize tobacco smoking in England, the demand for the product created a profitable market, once restrictions were lifted on tobacco growing in Virginia. Landowners, servants, and slaves who soon began to grow the crop found that the intensive cultivation and care required for each plant limited the manageable crop to about three acres per year per individual. They also discovered that the Algonquian method of planting among the stumps, fallen logs, and ashes of a swidden plot reduced soil erosion and runoff and thereby maintained soil fertility. When the soil did become exhausted of nutrients, English farmers learned from their Indian counterparts to shift cultivation to a new plot, letting the old fields recover their fertility under second growth, in the aboriginal manner, rather than in pasture, as in England (Craven 1965:30–36; Earle 1975:217; Waselkov and Paul 1981:317; Carr 1987:2, 5–8).

This method of maintaining field fertility may have some relevance to the previously documented tendency of the earliest English colonists in the northern neck to settle adjacent to the former sites of Late Woodland–historic Indian villages with accompanying old fields. In 1619 the English noted "many grounds here cleared by the Indians to our handes, which being much worn out, will beare no more of their corne " (Carrier 1957:27; Morgan 1975: 53). The archaeological evidence presented here suggests that by the 1640s and 1650s the colonists had recognized the temporarily low fertility of the most recent old fields and were selecting those sites as the most vegetation-free locations for their houses, while reserving the nearby nutrient-enriched Indian village sites for field locations. Similarly, early historic-period farmers in the Midwest located their croplands within areas of prehistoric Indian sites (Woods 1987:281).

The usurpation of indigenous settlement patterns by colonizing peoples has been noted in many other frontier situations. Jamestown, St. Mary's City, Plymouth, and most of the other early colonial towns on the eastern seaboard were planted on or near recently abandoned Indian town sites (Hall 1925:73– 76; Walsh 1988:204; Washburn 1978:95–96; Cronon 1983:90). Although mainly of anecdotal value, it is interesting to note that the earliest Saxon settlements in England were on lands already cleared and cultivated by the native Britons. Celtic place names are clustered in the same areas as early Saxon place names, so evidently "the first English settlers were taking over clearances made by their Celtic precursors" (Alcock 1971:193–194). In the vicinity of the earliest French colonial settlement on the Gulf coast of the United States, the first French plantations were placed either adjacent to or directly on the sites of recently abandoned Indian villages. The location finally selected in 1711 for the town of Mobile, capital of French Louisiana, had been previously occupied by a village of Chato Indians (Lankford 1983:58–61). Numerous other examples could be cited.

This convergence of settlement strategies is by and large a reflection of the "colonization gradient" produced when agricultural peoples from western European states settled territories "inhabited by peoples at a lower level of socio-cultural integration" (Casagrande et al. 1964:311; Miller 1984:15). As colonists moved from their homeland to a region of active contact with native societies, those colonial settlements farther from the mother country tended to become socially and culturally simpler, and increasingly dissimilar from the parent state, whereas those nearer the homeland tended to be more stable and complex. Distance, in this case, was as much a matter of the nature and extent of the transportation system connecting the colony and the mother country as it was the actual spatial separation between them (Miller 1984:13–17). Where distances were great or when links to the homeland were poorly developed, the earliest phases of colonization were more likely to be marked by adoption of native land-use practices and subsistence strategies until transportation networks between the colony and the homeland improved or the frontier environment was altered to accommodate land-use practices and farming methods typical of the homeland. Colonists who simultaneously encountered new challenges of an unfamiliar environment while meeting individuals from different societies with novel approaches to settlement and subsistence often displayed greater flexibility and willingness to experiment than their countrymen farther from the exigencies of the frontier.

Certainly the English colonists in Virginia quickly recognized the benefits of preferentially appropriating cleared lands in a heavily forested country. And they were also aware of the differences between the soils of the necklands and those of the uplands (Smolek 1984). The latter eventually were found to be quite suitable for large-scale tobacco agriculture and were extensively farmed beginning late in the seventeenth century as the population, tobacco production, and chattel slavery increased (Craven 1965:35–36; Kulikoff 1986:45–78; Lukezic 1990). But they were virtually ignored at first, because only the broad necklands of the first and second terraces provided an appropriate combination of factors for the intensive hoe cultivation of tobacco by a small English colonial population—they were close to waterways, clear springs, and good-quality soils suitable for swidden agriculture—some of the same factors that determined the location of Algonquian Indian villages (Potter 1982a:59–60, 249–250; Smolek 1984; Walsh 1988:206). It would be a mistake, however, to conclude that the English were only interested in cleared land because it would save them the labor of felling trees, or that Indian fields were the only lands suitable for agriculture. The early English settlers adapted to the seventeenth-century Chesapeake frontier by combining Anglo and Algonquian settlement patterns because they had nearly identical agricultural needs.

The English colonists seized Virginia from its native inhabitants by preempting their adaptive strategy and selectively adopting many of their cultigens, tool forms, and farming methods. After several decades of struggle, the English learned their lessons well, perhaps heeding the exhortations of Edward Waterhouse who, in the aftermath of the Algonquian attack of 1622, penned the following passage:

> We, who hitherto have had possession of no more than their waste, . . . may now by right of Warre, and law of Nations, invade the Country, and destroy them who sought to destroy us: whereby we shall enjoy their cultivated places. . . . Now their cleared grounds in all their villages (which are situate in the fruitfullest places of the land) shall be inhabited by us. (Kingsbury 1933:556–557)

Acknowledgments

The authors would like to thank Martha W. McCartney, Helen C. Rountree, Dennis J. Pogue, Michael A. Smolek, Henry M. Miller, and Francis P. McManamon for their comments on earlier versions of this chapter. Martha McCartney, Dennis Pogue, Michael Smolek, Henry Miller, and Charles T. Hodges also graciously provided us with copies of unpublished and published papers. In addition, our thanks go to Albert Clark of Heathsville, Virginia, for his time, the use of his plane, and his skill as a pilot. Without his unselfish assistance and that of his wife, Geraldine, the aerial survey would not have been as successful. Stephen Potter completed the research for this chapter through the auspices of a Horace M. Albright grant received from the National Park Foundation and administered by the National Park Service.

References Cited

Alcock, Leslie
1971 *Arthur's Britain.* Penguin Press, London.

Anonymous
1908 Mottrom-Wright-Spencer-Ariss-Buckner. *William and Mary Quarterly* 17(1):53–57.

Barbour, Philip L.
1971 The Earliest Reconnaissance of Chesapeake Bay Area: Captain John Smith's Map and Indian Vocabulary. *The Virginia Magazine of History and Biography* 79(3):280–302.

Carr, Lois Green
1987 *Adaptation and Settlement in the Colonial Chesapeake.* St. Mary's City Research Series No. 6. St. Mary's City, Md.

Carrier, Lyman
1957 *Agriculture in Virginia, 1607–1699.* Jamestown 350th Anniversary Historical Booklet No. 14. University Press of Virginia, Charlottesville.

Casagrande, Joseph B., Stephen Thompson, and Philip Young
1964 Colonization as a Research Frontier. In *Process and Pattern in Culture, Essays in Honor of Julian Steward*, edited by Robert A. Manners, pp. 281–325. Aldine, New York.

Craven, Avery O.
1965 *Soil Exhaustion as a Factor in the Agricultural History of Virginia and Maryland, 1606–1860.* Reprinted. Peter Smith, Gloucester, Mass. Originally published 1925, University of Illinois, Urbana.

Cronon, William
1983 *Changes in the Land.* Hill and Wang, New York.

Earle, Carville V.
1975 *The Evolution of a Tidewater Settlement System: All Hallow's Parish, Maryland, 1650–1783.* Research Paper No. 170. Department of Geography, University of Chicago.

Egloff, Keith T., and Stephen R. Potter
1982 Indian Ceramics from Coastal Plain Virginia. *Archeology of Eastern North America* 10:95–117.

Hall, Clayton C.
1925 *Narratives of Early Maryland, 1633–1684.* Charles Scribner's Sons, New York.

Hening, William W. (editor)
1823 *The Statutes at Large; Being a Collection of all the Laws of Virginia, From the First Session of the Legislature in the Year 1619*, vol. 1. R. and W. and G. Bartow, New York.

Henry, Susan L.
1979 Terra-Cotta Tobacco Pipes in 17th Century Maryland and Virginia: A Preliminary Study. *Historical Archaeology* 13:14–37.

Hiden, Martha W.
1957 *How Justice Grew—Virginia Counties: An Abstract of Their Formation.* Jamestown 350th Anniversary Historical Booklet No. 19. University Press of Virginia, Charlottesville.

Hodges, Charles T.
1990 Excavations at 44NB180 and 44NB174: An Early English Colonial Plantation and Prehistoric Shell Midden in Northumberland County, Virginia. Draft report submitted to the Virginia Department of Historic Resources, Richmond.

Keach, O. A.
1926 The Preslys of Northumberland. *The Virginia Magazine of History and Biography* 34(1):92–92.

Kelso, William M., and Edward A. Chappell
1974 Excavation of a Seventeenth Century Pottery Kiln at Glebe Harbor, Westmoreland County, Virginia. *Historical Archaeology* 8:53–63.

Kingsbury, Susan M. (editor)
1933 *The Records of the Virginia Company of London*, vol. 3. U.S. Government Printing Office, Washington, D.C.

Kulikoff, Allan
1986 *Tobacco and Slaves: The Development of Southern Cultures in the Chesapeake, 1680–1800.* University of North Carolina Press, Chapel Hill.

Lankford, George E.

1983 A Documentary Study of Native American Life in the Lower Tombigbee Valley. In *Cultural Resources Reconnaissance Study of the Black Warrior–Tombigbee System Corridor, Alabama*, edited by Eugene M. Wilson, vol. 2, *Ethnohistory*. University of South Alabama, Mobile.

Lewis, Kenneth E.

1975 *The Jamestown Frontier: An Archaeological Study of Colonization*. Ph.D. dissertation, Department of Anthropology, University of Oklahoma. University Microfilms, Ann Arbor.

1977 An Archaeological Perspective on Social Change—The Virginia Frontier. In *The Frontier: Comparative Studies*, edited by D. H. Miller and J. O. Steffen, pp. 139–159. University of Oklahoma Press, Norman.

Lukezic, Craig

1990 Soils and Settlement Location in 18th Century Colonial Tidewater Virginia. *Historical Archaeology* 24(1):1–17.

MacCord, Howard A.

1965 The DeShazo Site, King George County, Virginia. *Archeological Society of Virginia Quarterly Bulletin* 19(4): 98–104.

1969 Camden: A Postcontact Indian Site in Caroline County. *Archeological Society of Virginia Quarterly Bulletin* 24(1): 1–55.

McCartney, Martha W.

1990 44NB180 and Its Historical Continuum. Draft report submitted to the Virginia Department of Historic Resources, Richmond.

Miller, Henry M.

1983 *A Search for the "City of Saint Maries": Report on the 1981 Excavations in St. Mary's City, Maryland*. St. Maries Citty Archaeology Series No. 1 (rev. ed.). St. Mary's City Commission.

1984 *Colonization and Subsistence Change on the 17th Century Frontier*. Unpublished Ph.D. dissertation, Department of Anthropology, Michigan State University, East Lansing.

Morgan, Edmund S.

1975 *American Slavery—American Freedom: the Ordeal of Colonial Virginia*. Norton, New York.

Nugent, Nell Marion

1934 *Cavaliers and Pioneers: Abstracts of Virginia Land Patents and Grants 1623–1800*, vol 1. Dietz Press, Richmond.

Potter, Stephen R.

1976 *An Ethnohistorical Examination of Indian Groups in Northumberland County, Virginia: 1608–1719*. Unpublished Master's thesis, Department of Anthropology, University of North Carolina, Chapel Hill.

1982a *An Analysis of Chicacoan Settlement Patterns*. Unpublished Ph.D. dissertation, Department of Anthropology, University of North Carolina, Chapel Hill.

1982b Low Budget and Low Altitudes: Aerial Photography and Archeological Survey in Tidewater Virginia. Paper presented at the 47th Annual Meeting of the Society for American Archaeology, Minneapolis.

1989 Early English Effects on Virginia Algonquian Exchange and Tribute in the Tidewater Potomac. In *Powhatan's Mantle: Indians in the Colonial Southeast*, edited by Peter H. Wood, Gregory A. Waselkov, and M. Thomas Hatley, pp. 151–172. University of Nebraska Press, Lincoln.

Ryland, Elizabeth L. (editor)

1976 *Richmond County, Virginia: A Review Commemorating the Bicentennial*. Warsaw, Va.

Smolek, Michael A.

1984 "Soyle Light, Well-Watered and on the River": Settlement Patterning of Maryland's Frontier Plantations. Paper presented at the 3d Hall of Records Conference on Maryland History, St. Mary's City, Maryland.

Sorensen, A. D.

1974 A Method for Measuring the Spatial Association between Point Patterns. *Professional Geographer* 26(2):172–176.

Stephenson, Robert L., A. L. L. Ferguson, and H. G. Ferguson

1963 *The Accokeek Creek Site: A Middle Atlantic Seaboard Culture Sequence*. Anthropological Papers No. 20. Museum of Anthropology, University of Michigan, Ann Arbor.

Walsh, Lorena S.

1988 Community Networks in the Early Chesapeake. In *Colonial Chesapeake Society*, edited by Lois Green Carr, Philip D. Morgan, and Jean B. Russo, pp. 200–224. University of North Carolina Press, Chapel Hill.

Waselkov, Gregory A., and R. Eli Paul

1981 Frontiers and Archaeology. *North American Archaeologist* 2(4):309– 329.

Washburn, Wilcomb

1978 Seventeenth-Century Indian Wars. In *Northeast*, edited by Bruce G. Trigger, pp. 89-100. Handbook of North American Indians, vol. 15, William C. Sturtevant, general editor. Smithsonian Institution, Washington, D.C.

Westmoreland County

1653–1659 Court Record Book I. Westmoreland County Courthouse, Montross, Va.

Woods, William T.

1987 Maize Agriculture and the Late Prehistoric: A Characterization of Settlement Location Strategies. In *Emergent Horticultural Economies of the Eastern Woodlands*, edited by William F. Keegan, pp. 275–294. Occasional Paper No. 7, Center for Archaeological Investigations, Southern Illinois University, Carbondale.

III
CHAPTER

Decorated Clay Tobacco Pipes from the Chesapeake
An African Connection

MATTHEW C. EMERSON

OVER THE PAST few decades, historical archaeologists have added a great deal to the recent history of North America. They have uncovered many details about our recent past while digging up sites and studying the vast range of the American experience, from seventeenth-century colonial Virginia to twentieth-century Marin County, California. In many cases, the information from physical remains is not available in the documentary record. In addition to uncovering the minutiae of past life, archaeologists have also discovered evidence for some widespread cultural and cognitive changes through the study of settlement plans, building traditions, refuse discard, human remains, and objects in well-documented contexts. The best studies of the past draw on the data sets of both archaeology and history to construct a narrative that neither data set could provide alone (Deetz 1987:22).

One assemblage of artifacts and a documented context for the Chesapeake Bay region have made it possible to construct such a narrative about the activities and interactions of a specific group of people who are underrepresented in the surviving written record—*African Americans*. Locally made clay tobacco pipes of the seventeenth century are the earliest surviving evidence of African craftsmanship in the Chesapeake and are testimony to the interaction of blacks and whites on the plantations of the early colonial period.

THE ARCHAEOLOGY OF CHESAPEAKE PIPES: A SAMPLE

Although individual tobacco pipes made from North American clays have been recovered from archaeological sites from Massachusetts to South Carolina, the greatest concentration of locally made tobacco pipes is found in late seventeenth-century plantation deposits in the Chesapeake Bay region. Unlike the white clay pipes that colonists imported from England and Holland during the seventeenth-century, these tobacco pipes were made from local tidewater clays and appear in a range of colors from orange to brown. Although previous researchers have referred to these tobacco pipes as "Virginia-made pipes," "Colono-pipes," "terra cotta pipes," or "aboriginal pipes" (Henry 1979), they are described here as *Chesapeake pipes* because they are made from Chesapeake clays and because all locally made pipes are not exclusively made by one group of people. While scant documentary references and archaeological evidence suggest that European colonists and Chesapeake Indians were involved in pipemaking, many Chesapeake pipes appear to have been made and decorated by seventeenth-century Africans.

I first encountered Chesapeake pipes during the excavation of a typical seventeenth-century Chesapeake dwelling at Flowerdew Hundred farm near Hopewell, Virginia. Hundreds of locally made pipe stems and many different types of pipe bowls were discovered (Emerson 1987). These smoking pipes are either hand- or mold-made, and many are decorated with a variety of abstract designs and representational motifs. Since the documentary record makes few references to seventeenth-century pipemaking in Virginia or Maryland, I decided to investigate more closely these and other tobacco pipes recovered from sites throughout the Chesapeake region.

Locally made pipes from 25 site areas in the Chesapeake Bay region were examined (figure 3.1). Collections of pipes are stored at federal, state, and private institutions throughout Virginia and Maryland. In Virginia, hundreds of broken pipebowls, pipestems, and pipe fragments are stored at Flowerdew Hundred Farm, Colonial Williamsburg, the Colonial Historical National Park at Jamestown, and the Virginia Historic Landmarks Commission. In Maryland, a large pipe collection is stored at the St. Mary's City Archaeological Commission laboratory. Because I was particularly interested in pipebowl forms and their decorations, I examined a qualitative sample of 200 distinctly different decorated pipebowls and fragments from a total of approximately 800 bowls and fragments selected from these collections. This total also reflects the number of specimens that were made available to me by particular host institutions at the time of my study. Many Chesapeake pipes are still waiting to be cleaned and catalogued in some of the collections at these institutions. In addition, I examined excavation records and site reports and spoke with other archaeologists about the archaeological context and dating of Chesapeake pipes (Emerson 1988). My sample of decorated and undecorated locally made pipe bowls, fragments, and stems was examined with the following questions in mind. Where were Chesapeake tobacco pipes made and by whom? How and why were they decorated? What is the significance of tobacco pipemaking in the seventeenth-century Chesapeake? Locally made tobacco pipes are examined here not only as a region-wide assemblage of artifacts that were made, used, and discarded during the second half of the seventeenth-century, but also as a phenomenon that reflects the culture of seventeenth-century tidewater society.

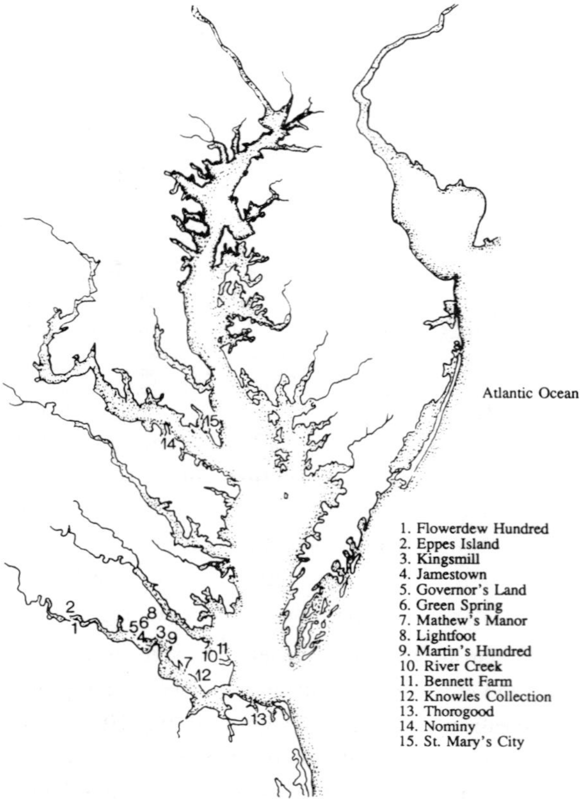

FIGURE 3.1. *Selected seventeenth-century sites in the Chesapeake-tidewater region.*

LOOKING FOR EVIDENCE OF CHESAPEAKE PIPEMAKING

Archaeologists have had difficulty finding physical evidence for pipemaking at seventeenth-century sites. Although seventeenth-century pottery kiln sites have been uncovered (Cotter 1958:66; Hudson 1975; Noel Hume 1975:170-174; Kelso and Chappell 1974), there is no conclusive evidence for pipe manufacture at these pottery-making locations. Perhaps the occasional nature of pipemaking, coupled with the use of in-house fireplaces or firing pits well outside the homelot, may explain this lack of physical evidence for Chesapeake pipemaking.

Pipemaking required little skill, given the few tools needed, the molds available, and the abundance of local clays. Pipemaking consisted of digging and preparing the clay, molding, decorating, and firing. The individual steps may have taken place in as many as three locations: a source site, a manufacturing and decorating site, and a firing site. Some evidence for pipemaking has been discovered in the form of small lumps of fired clay called "wasters" (Cotter 1958:145–147; Emerson 1987; Mitchell 1983:31; Outlaw, personal communication 1985).

Unfortunately, only a small number of wasters have yet been found, making it difficult to arrive at any firm conclusions about pipemaking at particular sites. It has also been difficult to identify the source locations for Chesapeake pipe clay. Even if clay samples from multiple locations at each site were collected and analyzed, it is highly unlikely that one original source area for pipe clays would be found. Pipe clay was probably collected from lowlands or exposed riverbanks near settlement areas.

Furthermore, archaeologists have recovered few pipemaking tools from Chesapeake settlement sites. To date, no pipemaking molds have been recovered. There is little hope of finding metal pipemolds owing to the frequent recasting of metals on plantations, while molds made of perishable materials would be unlikely to survive. Natural materials, such as bone and clam shell, as well as fragments of metal or ceramic, may have been used to decorate pipes. One possible decorating tool has been recovered from an archaeological site (MacCord 1969:41, fig. 17), but small natural tools may not have survived. Even if they did, they would be difficult to recognize.

Because of this lack of direct information in both the physical and the written record, our insight into Chesapeake pipemaking has been quite limited. The pipes themselves, however, are a rich source of information—not only on plantation activities, but also on the cultural milieu in which they were made. Chesapeake pipe forms and decorative art reveal that local pipes were made by many individuals expressing themselves through a generalized decorative tradition.

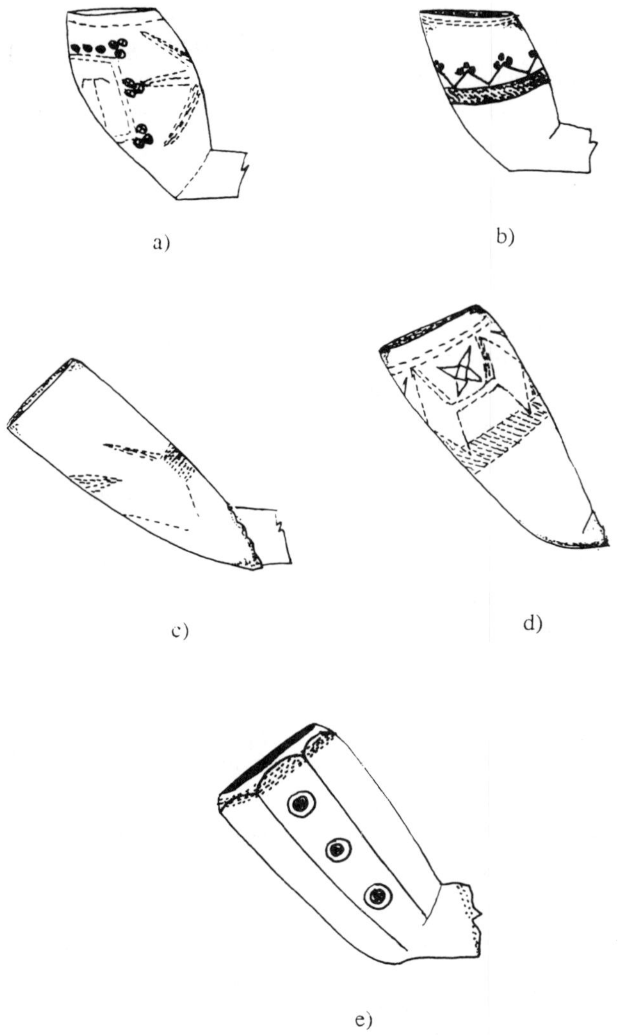

FIGURE 3.2. *Examples of seventeenth-century Chesapeake pipes: a. Elbow pipe with star and panel decoration, Virginia. b. Elbowpipe with zigzag band and complementary triple rosette clusters, Virginia. c. Obtuse-angled pipe with stylized quadruped motif on front and back surfaces, Maryland. d. Obtuse-angled pipe with encircling band of repeating* Kwardata *motifs, Virginia. e. Faceted pipe with stamped decoration, Virginia.*

PIPEMAKERS AND PIPEMAKING TRADITIONS: EXAMINING PIPE FORMS

The shape of Chesapeake tobacco pipe bowls varies greatly. About 200 bowl forms were used during the brief half-century that local pipes appear in the Chesapeake (Emerson 1988). They range from obtuse-angled and elbow pipes to faceted pipes (figure 3.2). Prior to firing, some pipemakers modified their pipe forms by polishing, bending or cutting facets into the clay. The diversity of both decorated and undecorated hand- or mold-made pipe bowls found in plantation deposits suggests that many individuals were involved in occasional pipemaking.

The range of pipe forms in archaeological collections may be a reflection of the number of European pipemakers arriving in the Chesapeake. Emigrating English pipemakers are mentioned briefly in the documentary record, and it is certain that some of them made pipes on Chesapeake plantations. Although the majority of Chesapeake pipes from plantation deposits are close imitations of European mold-made pipes, not all Chesapeake pipemakers were European. European written records indirectly mention that Chesapeake Indians continued to make and use traditional clay tobacco pipes through the end of the seventeenth-century (Durand and Chinard 1934:153). Their distinct pipes stem from a precontact Woodland tradition and are occasionally found in plantation deposits. A closer examination of a few Chesapeake pipe forms, however, reveals more than does the written record about the identity of Chesapeake pipemakers. Along with specific pipe forms, the style and subject matter of Chesapeake pipe art does not suggest its origins lay in the precontact Woodland period. This formal and decorative evidence points to a group of people whose participation in pipemaking is unknown from documentary records. These people were Africans.

Seventeenth-Century Africans and Tobacco

Africans were introduced to Virginia in small numbers as early as 1619 and to Maryland in 1634 (Craven 1971; Vaughan 1972; Franklin 1980). Unfortunately, American historians have limited documentary evidence on the origins of the Chesapeake's seventeenth-century Africans (Minchinton et al. 1984:ix–x). Scholars have suggested that many of the slaves brought to the Chesapeake in the seventeenth century were not directly imported from Africa (Curtin 1969; Kulikoff 1986), but arrived via the Caribbean and other colonies, where they were first taken. Although a few seventeenth-century slaves were taken from the Congo and Madagascar (Curtin 1969: 125), the majority of the Chesapeake's slaves originated in the coastal and inland states of West Africa (Curtin 1969: 122, table 35). Therefore, one might expect to find antecedents for some New World cultural traditions, ideas, behaviors, and artifacts in present-day Senegal, Ghana, Togo, and Nigeria and in the hinterland areas of Mali and Burkina Faso (figure 3.3). Furthermore, the history of tobacco use and pipemaking in these areas of West Africa is relevant to a study of Chesapeake pipes.

Written records indicate that Europeans introduced the use of tobacco to West Africa early in the sixteenth century. Although Europeans reported the use of smoking pipes in isolated coastal areas as early as the first decade of the seventeenth century (Jobson 1623 in Arents 1938:13; Copes Tobacco Plant Office 1895:11:52–54), the history of local pipemaking in West Africa is largely unknown from written records.

West African Pipemaking and Chesapeake Pipe Forms

Archaeology has begun to provide some insight into local pipemaking in several areas of West Africa. Clay smoking pipes have been recovered from the seventeenth-century site of Great Accra in Ghana. These pipes and others from Gold Coast sites suggest that a local West African pipemaking industry was well-established by the third quarter of the seventeenth century (Ozanne 1962). West African pipemakers chose to incorporate European bowl styles into a reed-and-bowl pipe for greater durability and ease of cleaning (Ozanne 1964:38). These late seventeenth-century pipes were made in a variety of forms and reflect the development of local styles, which may also have been influenced by an influx of metal trade pipes from Northern Africa (Shinnie and Ozanne 1962:97;

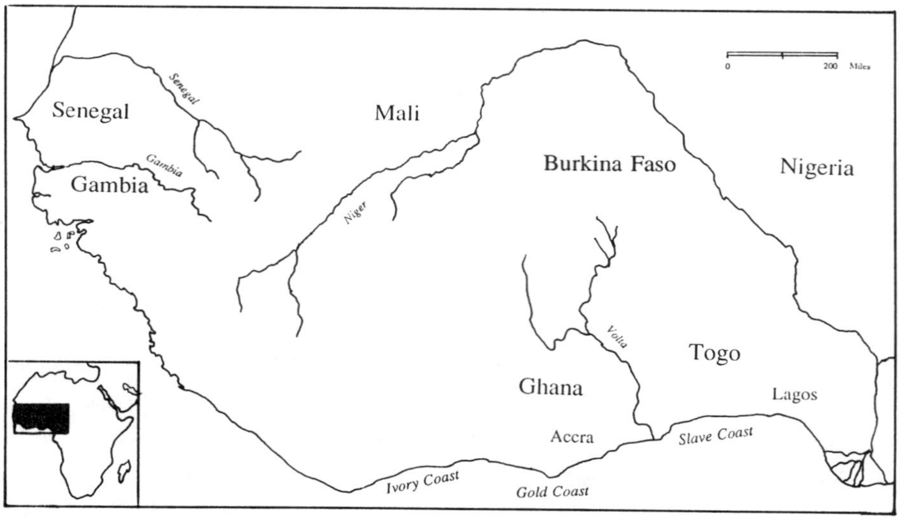

FIGURE 3.3. *The West African homelands of seventeenth-century Chesapeake slaves.*

Ozanne 1964:23). Their surface decorations are relevant to the study of Chesapeake pipes and are discussed later. An example of a reed-and-bowl pipe from Ghana is illustrated in figure 3.4a. Archaeologists working in the Caribbean on the island of Barbados have recovered a West African–style smoking pipe from an eighteenth-century slave grave (Handler 1978:132). It is a reed-and-bowl pipe that is identical to pipes found in Ghana, and archaeologists have concluded that its form, if not the pipe itself, is African. Although local pipemaking in Ghana was contemporary to pipemaking in the Chesapeake, these reed-and-bowl tobacco pipes are different from Chesapeake pipe bowl forms. Those from another area of West Africa, however, suggest a connection between the Chesapeake and West Africa.

Some Chesapeake tobacco pipes have faceted sides or flutes cut into the sides of the pipe bowl (figure 3.2e). Faceted forms have no clear antecedent in European or Indian pipemaking traditions. Decorated and undecorated faceted tobacco pipes have been recovered from almost all of the major settlement areas in the Chesapeake. The Barbadian pipe mentioned above also shares this fluting characteristic. Archaeologists working in Mali and other areas of the Middle Niger River Valley have recovered seventeenth-century faceted forms that are nearly identical to those found at Chesapeake sites (figures 3.2e, 3.4e,f). Continuing research indicates that other Chesapeake pipe forms may have West African antecedents as well (Emerson 1993). Similarities in form across the Atlantic are only a small part of the evidence for an African connection to Chesapeake pipes.

Locally made pipes appear in plantation deposits at approximately the same time that Africans appear in visible numbers throughout the Chesapeake-tidewater region. These concurrent factors may explain not only the variety of pipe forms in plantation deposits, but the sudden and prolific appearance of decorative art on many Chesapeake pipes. An analysis of Chesapeake pipe art, strongly suggests African inspirations in Chesapeake pipemaking.

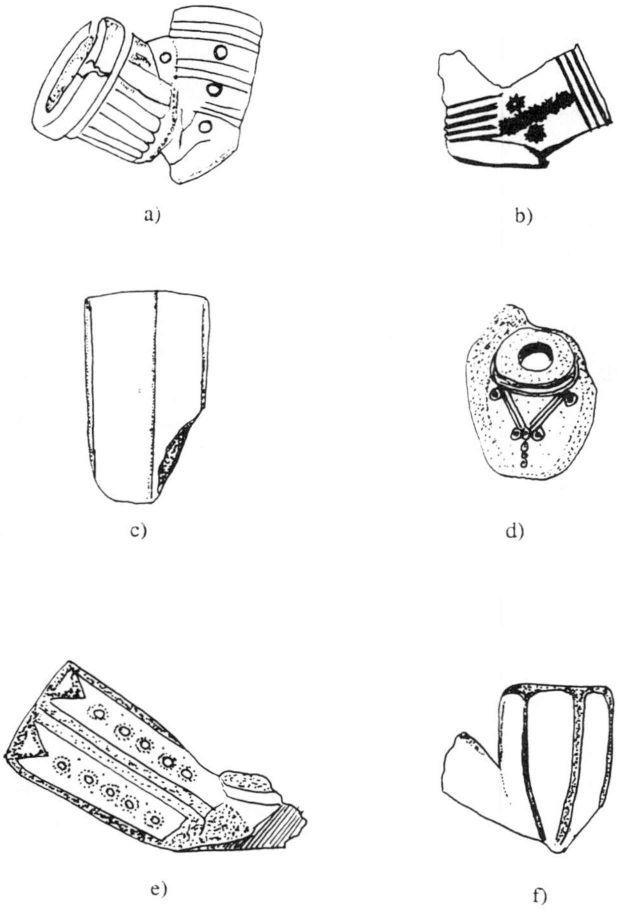

FIGURE 3.4. *African-made clay tobacco pipes: a. Fluted slave pipe decorated with punches, Barbados (after Handler and Lange 1978:130, fig. 23). b. Seventeenth-century pipe decorated with stamps and white fill, Ghana (after Ozanne 1962:56, fig. 2). c. Seventeenth-century faceted pipe, Gambia (after Hill, personal communication 1989). d. Seventeenth-century pipe decorated with denticulate lines and stamps, Gambia (after Hill, personal communication 1989). e. Seventeenth-century faceted pipe with stamped decorations, Mali (after Daget and Ligers 1962:33, fig. 5.2). f. Seventeenth-century faceted pipe, Mali (after Daget and Ligers 1962:19, fig. 2.3).*

CHESAPEAKE PIPE ART: INSPIRATIONS AND ANTECEDENTS

The Quadruped Motif Problem

It is tempting to look back into a past plural society such as colonial Virginia and try to identify people and their residences by artifacts, particularly decorated ones. However, tracing the origins of and inspirations for a particular Chesapeake pipe design or decorative motif is a difficult task. For example, one decorative motif drawn on some Chesapeake pipes is very similar to a motif found on a Native American cloak collected by an English colonist in 1608 (figure 3.5a; Wood et al. 1989:307, fig. 8). Quadruped motifs decorate Powhatan's cloak and some locally made pipes in Virginia and Maryland. The visual

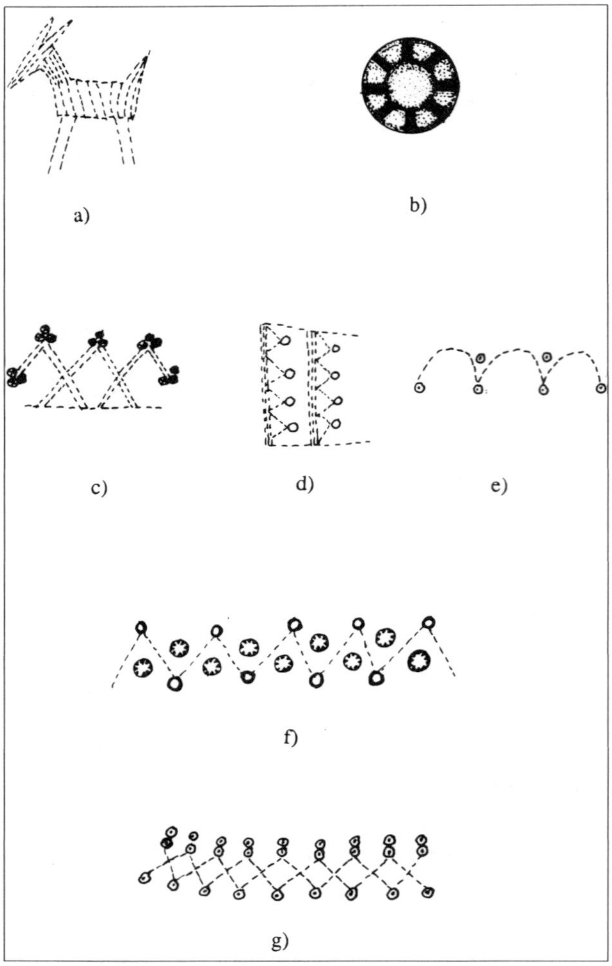

FIGURE 3.5. *Examples of designs and motifs in pipe and pottery art. a. Pointille-line quadruped motif from a Chesapeake pipe. b. A decorative stamp element from a Chesapeake pipe (10 X). c–e. Pointille-line decorations with complementary decorative stamps from Chesapeake pipes. f–g. Pointille-line decorations with complementary decorative stamps from a West African tobacco pipe (after Daget and Ligers 1962: plate C:5) and from a West African pot (after Stobel 1984: 233). Both pipe and pot were found in seventeenth-century deposits in Mali.*

similarities between pipes and cloak might lead one to conclude that all artifacts decorated with quadrupeds were made and used by Indians. It has been suggested that Virginia white-tailed deer were one of the original inspirations for this motif, and thus, some Chesapeake pipes have been colloquially described as "deer pipes." This visual conclusion and interpretation have their problems. Although most Chesapeake pipes were made and decorated a half-century after this unique cloak was created, stylized quadruped motifs are almost pancultural. Quadruped motifs on Chesapeake pipes are drawn in many ways and suggest many hands, and perhaps different original inspirations for the motif. Quadruped motifs are found on some seventeenth-century English glassware (Edwards and Ramsey 1956:84, plate 46c) and on European ceramics (Arneberg 1951:plates 86, 87). West African artifacts are also decorated with depictions of quadrupeds, some of which are similar to those found on Chesapeake pipes (Griaule and Germaine 1934:205). Consequently, it is possible that not only Indians, but also Europeans and Africans, identified with this quadruped motif and drew it on their tobacco pipes. The fact that quadruped motifs are found on a wide variety of tobacco pipe forms may illustrate the degree to which the motif was used by Europeans and non-Europeans in the Chesapeake. Moreover, many Chesapeake pipes may be syncretic decorative types and may reflect the influence and antecedent inspiration of more than one culture group.

In view of the difficulties of tracing a single motif, one must take a conservative approach in tracing the origins of and inspirations for Chesapeake pipe art. Consider, first, the techniques of decoration, use of materials, and organization of decorative characters.

Decorating Techniques, Media, and Style

Most Chesapeake pipe art consists of denticulated lines, patterns, and motifs incised into the clay before firing. This technique is generally called pointille (see figure 3.2 a–d). Pointille-decorated Chesapeake pipes exhibit consistent and clean patterns of denticulate lines applied in a continuous motion. Other pipes are decorated with a cord-wrapping technique. Cord-impressed decorations commonly appear on Algonquian pottery, and the pipes decorated in this manner were likely made by Chesapeake Indians. Another form of decoration found on some Chesapeake pipes is incised dentate stamping. This technique is characterized by single, irregularly impressed stamps of dentate lines. Although incised dentate stamping is known from Lenape tobacco pipes in the Delaware River Valley (Leslie 1970), it is both technically and artistically different from most of the pointille-line pipes found in seventeenth-century plantation deposits. As mentioned earlier, archaeological finds indicate that some Chesapeake Indians made tobacco pipes from local clays. The few traditional forms with cord-wrapped or incised dentate decorations recovered from English plantation deposits confirm that Indians occasionally visited the English settlements known from documentary sources.

An extensive survey of seventeenth-century European artifacts contemporary with Chesapeake pipes shows little indication of intensive and consistent use of pointille-line decorations. Although pointille-line decoration is not uncommon in the English decorative tradition and can be found embellishing English country pottery from the thirteenth century on (McCarthy and Brooks 1988), the most widespread and intensive use of pointille-line decoration in the seventeenth century is found in West African decorative arts. Moreover, the current decorative arts traditions of some West African societies demonstrate that this technique has not died out (Wolff, personal communication 1987). However, pointille-line decorated pipes are not conclusive evidence of Africans decorating pipes in Virginia and Maryland. Chesapeake pipe art encompasses other decorative techniques and elements in a generalized style.

Punched or stamped decorative characters are also common on Chesapeake pipes (figures 3.2 a,b; 3.5b–e). The variety of stamped characters suggests that many different tools and perhaps many different pipemakers made them. Decorative stamping is a common element in examples of seventeenth-century Algonquian pottery, European pottery and furniture, and West African pottery, metalwork, and tobacco pipes. The characters stamped on Chesapeake pipes, however, are quite different from the punctates seen on Algonquian pottery and the maker's marks impressed on European pipes and other goods. Impressed stamps on Chesapeake pipes are similar to the characters that decorate some West African artifacts.

The majority of Chesapeake pipes also have white material rubbed into these lines and stamped decorations. The use of white fill is not an exclusive decorative technique of any particular culture in the New or Old World. Iroquoian Indians used decorative shell inlays in some of their wooden objects, and medieval Europeans used ceramic inlays in tiles for an intaglio effect (Rutsch 1973:86). The most widespread use of white fill inlays appears in West African decorative arts traditions. White clays, chalk, bone, ash, and a variety of other white substances were, and still are, used to highlight decorated calabashes, pottery, tobacco pipes, wooden artifacts, and human bodies in West and Central Africa. In some West African societies, white decorative materials are often associated with a range of medical, social, and spiritual ideals (Cole and Aniakor 1984:62, 216). The concept of whiteness is a common denominator of some West African cosmologies and is strongly conserved across time and space as a decorative expression.

Although individual denticulate lines, patterns or figures, stamped characters, and decorative fill are found independently in the decorative arts traditions of many cultures, in combination they define the unique decorative style of Chesapeake pipe art. This style is closely paralleled in some West African craft traditions, particularly in pipes and pottery from Mali.

Seventeenth-century tobacco pipes found in Mali resemble some Chesapeake pipes not only in form, but also in decoration (figure 3.4e). Decorations on clay pipes (figure 3.4e; Daget and Ligers 1962:plate C:5) and pottery (figure 3.5g) from Mali are similar to Chesapeake pipes in the technical application of decoration, the organization of pointille-line and stamping elements, and the use of white fill. This generalized style was not unique to one small area of West Africa, however. Archaeologists have recovered similarly decorated pipes from seventeenth-century sites in the Gambia region (figure 3.4d; Hill, personal communication 1989). Reed-and-bowl pipes from Ghana also exhibit decorative stamping and the use of white fill (figure 3.4b; Shinnie and Ozanne 1962:96, Ozanne 1964:20). Furthermore, early European travelers to West Africa commented on this decorative style (Bowditch in Cole and Ross 1977:57).

Chesapeake pipe art may have been inspired by other West African decorative art traditions. Although Senegal, Ghana, and Mali were the source of some Chesapeake slaves, several of the largest seventeenth-century slave ports were situated on the coast of Nigeria. Slaves from a variety of inland cultural groups were captured and exported from coastal Nigerian ports to the Caribbean and Chesapeake. Therefore, Nigeria is also an important geographic region to search for antecedents of Chesapeake pipe art.

West African Antecedents for Chesapeake Pipe Art

Chesapeake pipe art may be described by the particular organization of decorative elements put on a pipe. Although different designs appear on different pipes, all of the pipes could be described with a series of rules that define how decorative elements are put together to form designs. In studying Chesapeake pipe art, one considers not only the physical techniques of decoration but also stylistic pattern in the hopes that a decorative aesthetic can be identified. Following this, technical affinities and aesthetic principles can be described and compared, to confirm the transmission or translation of a decorative tradition across time and space. Chesapeake pipe art exhibits an interesting patterned use of stamped characters. Stamped characters appear singularly or in clusters of three or four in bands, positioned at the ends of lines, at line intersections, and often surrounding bands or motifs (figures 3.2a,b; 3.5c–e). As a rule, stamped characters complement line designs and motifs. The pattern of lines and stamps found on Chesapeake pipes is also found on Malian pottery (Stobel 1984:232–235). Stamps are used to complement zigzag lines on seventeenth-century decorated pipes from the Chesapeake and the Gambia region (figure 3.4d). Stamped characters were also used by Chesapeake pipemakers to surround bands and patterns of lines. Nupe pottery from Central Nigeria and a few Chesapeake pipes share bands of zigzag lines with surrounding punched circlets (Biedermann 1981:66, fig. 6). Bands of repeating stamped characters that appear on Chesapeake pipes and on Malian pottery (Stobel 1984:232–235, figs. 102–3, 108), are also found on West African musical instruments (Parrinder 1982:64), modern textiles (Seiber 1972:223), and body art (Cole and Aniakor 1984:46, fig. 67). Single stamped characters or clusters of characters also complement designs and motifs on Chesapeake pipes (figure 3.5c–e). This aspect of decoration is also seen in the pottery, metalworking, and jewelry-making traditions of southeastern Nigeria (Eyo 1979:66, 49; Biedermann 1981:69, figs. 12, 13). Seventeenth-century Akan gold weights from Ghana also illustrate a similar use of stamped characters and lines (Garrard 1973). The articulation of stamped characters complementing line designs is a consistent attribute of Chesapeake pipes and a range of West African material culture.

The patterned use of decorative denticulate lines and stamps filled with additional white inlays is widely seen in Chesapeake pipes. Although not all locally made pipes in the Chesapeake are decorated, many of the decorated Chesapeake pipes recovered from plantation deposits share this decorative style. An extensive examination of seventeenth-century European and Chesapeake Indian artifacts has failed to reveal a similar stylistic story. In contrast, West African artifacts demonstrate a patterned use of lines, stamps, and inlay that is almost identical to the decorative art of Chesapeake pipes. A grammar consisting of rules for the articulation of this style would easily "fit" examples of West African artifacts and many Chesapeake pipes. This generalized decorative style was widespread in West Africa and predates the mass shipment of Africans to the Chesapeake. The appearance of this African decorative style on seventeenth-century tobacco pipes clearly coincides with the increased visibility of Africans in the Chesapeake colonies. The strength of African inspirations in Chesapeake pipe art is further demonstrated by the appearance of exact African motifs on Chesapeake pipes.

African Symbolism on Chesapeake Pipes

A few pipes firmly demonstrate the African connection. Despite the oppressive social context of plantation slavery, some West African symbols were remembered by plantation slaves and depicted on some Chesapeake pipes. A few examples are presented here.[1]

Cattle Symbol

A Chesapeake pipe recovered from excavations at Green Spring Plantation, the home of Governor William Berkeley, is decorated with a distinctive motif that is shaped like an apple core with concave lines containing a vertical section of lines at the top and bottom (figure 3.6a). It is identical to a common symbol for cattle in Central Africa (Jefferson 1973). Livestock represented an important high-return, low-labor investment for free blacks in the Chesapeake, and herding was one of many plantation tasks reserved for slaves (Breen and Innes 1980:81–83). Documentary and archaeological evidence indicates that Governor Berkeley had a number of servants, slaves, and livestock at Green Spring Plantation in the middle seventeenth century (Caywood 1957:70). A black pipemaker at Green Spring Plantation may have decorated a pipe with this African motif.

A Lozenge Motif with Surrounding Circlets

One Chesapeake pipe is decorated with a distinctive line-and-stamped motif, described as two lozenges surrounded by punched circlets (figure 3.6b). This motif is also a highly visible decorative element on an Ashanti black earthenware pot (Trowel 1960: plate 72). Over large West African culture areas such as the Akan lands of

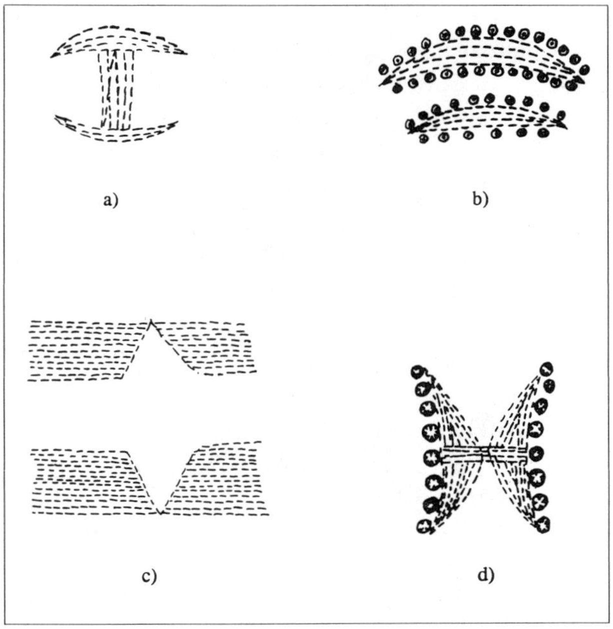

FIGURE 3.6. *African Motifs found on Chesapeake Pipes: a. Cattle symbol. b. Lozenge motif. c.* Kwardata *motif. d. Double-bell motif.*

Ghana, pottery making was a skill daughters inherited from their mothers (Antwi 1976:22). Black females were present in seventeenth-century Virginia and Maryland and may have directed their individual artistic skills to pipemaking. Although no published source documents the significance or meaning of this motif, it is undoubtedly West African and was probably inscribed on a Chesapeake pipe by a slave.

The Kwardata Motif

An exact replication of a West African decorative motif and design on a Chesapeake pipe is the *Kwardata* motif. This distinctive diamond-shaped motif in a band appears on a variety of Chesapeake pipes (figures 3.2d, 3.6c) and on Nigerian pottery. The *Kwardata* motif, when placed on a ritual beer vessel, represents "the transition from youth to adulthood" in contemporary Ga'anda society (Berns and Hudson 1986:135). Chesapeake pipes decorated with this motif, or design, were found at several sites in Virginia and Maryland, including St. Mary's City, Jamestown, Governor's Land, and Martin's Hundred.

The Double-Bell Motif

Chesapeake pipes from Nominy, Jamestown, Governor's Land, and the River Creek sites in Virginia are decorated with a motif that is clearly derived from the decorative arts traditions of Nigeria and areas in neighboring Cameroon. This motif is depicted in a variety of ways on Chesapeake pipes and on some West African artifacts. A Cameroonian clay tobacco pipe exhibits this motif (figure 3.6d; Gebauer 1979:251). The design indicates that the owner of the pipe is a member of the ruling class and a regulatory sect within Cameroonian society (Gebauer 1979:251—252).

The double-bell or double-gong shape is also found in recent Tiv scarification (Bohannon 1956:118, figs. a, g), Igbo metalwork (Basden in Cole and Aniakor 1984: 39), and in the Nsibidi symbols of Ejagham peoples in southwestern Nigeria (Thompson 1983:227–268, 244). Ejagham peoples developed a language that consisted of both commonly used and secret gestures, words, and ideograms. The graphic symbols of this language were often reminders of status, but many also represented emotions, places, people, and things. Thompson (1983) has demonstrated that this lexicon of ideograms was reborn among Africans in some New World contexts such as the Caribbean.

INTERPRETING CHESAPEAKE PIPE ART AND PIPEMAKING

The decorative style, designs, and motifs of Chesapeake tobacco pipe art are clear evidence that Africans made pipes in seventeenth-century Virginia and Maryland. Unfortunately, there are no witnesses, testimony, or documents from this place or period to indicate why Africans and others decorated their tobacco pipes.

One suggestion is that pipe decorating was a means of describing personal identity and status. Near the end of the seventeenth century, English indentured servants and Africans shared living conditions and tasks on the plantation. Their individual status and personal identity were probably linked with their age, sex, and tasks on the plantation. It is interesting to note that English initials, the *Kwardata* motif, and the cattle symbol reflect the identity of a person, a stage in one's life, and possibly an occupation, respectively. In addition, bonded blacks may have identified themselves with the foodstuffs, clothes, pipes, and other goods that they produced. Their worldview and status were local and personal. Thus, personal items such as tobacco pipes exhibit both representational and idiosyncratic decorative art. Some of the motifs (for example, quadrupeds, boats, cattle, and tobacco plants) clearly reflect the physical environment and perhaps the social realities of life on a Chesapeake plantation (that is, through marks of personal identity [initials], symbols of occupational identity [herdsman, boatman], and adulthood [*Kwardata* motifs]). As the number of blacks increased in the seventeenth-century Chesapeake, their social opportunities, status, and identity changed. Chesapeake pipe decoration may reflect such changes.

The Social Context of Plantation Pipemaking

European-style mold-made Chesapeake pipes decorated with African techniques may provide clues to the interaction of whites and black on seventeenth-century tidewater plantations. To find further evidence of such interaction, one needs to look at the social contexts of plantation pipemaking.

By midcentury, the majority of English people emigrating to the Chesapeake were bound by some form of contract or indenture (Galenson 1981). The key to success in tidewater society lay in acquiring land and labor to cultivate tobacco. As the number of emigrating servants increased in the third quarter of the seventeenth century, however, their opportunities to secure land, labor, and status decreased because established planters had acquired more land through servant headrights. Consequently, arable land near river routes of transportation became increasingly scarce, and many servants who had completed their contracts had difficulty becoming established. As a result, the documentary record reveals little about these landless freedmen and servants.

Although pipemaking was a common occupation in seventeenth-century England, it is unknown how many pipemakers came to the Chesapeake in the seventeenth century. To date, only one English pipemaker who practiced his trade in the Chesapeake has been identified from the extant documentary record. John Bennett, a late seventeenth-century pipemaker in Charles City County, was ordered to appear in court on charges of clay pipe collecting on Sunday (Weisiger 1980:179). Unfortunately, nothing is mentioned about where Bennett lived, his status, or the extent of and motivations for his pipemaking activities. Thus, the documentary record offers little direct insight into the lives of seventeenth-century European colonist-pipemakers or their helpers.

The absence of documentary or archaeological evidence for major pipe manufacturing sites in the Chesapeake strongly suggests that tobacco pipemaking was not as important as other trades, such as carpentry, brick and tile manufacture, and pottery. Moreover, archaeological evidence reveals that imported pipes were continuously deposited during all periods of the seventeenth century. Thus, there is no evidence that Chesapeake pipemaking was a stable seventeenth-century livelihood or that it was needed to offset a colony-wide shortage of tobacco pipes. Further study of the documentary record, however, gives some interesting insight into the occupations of freemen and servants, and into the identities of Chesapeake pipemakers.

It is unlikely that major planters made Chesapeake tobacco pipes. By midcentury, prominent planters had their own ships to carry goods from England and thus could keep themselves supplied with European products, including tobacco pipes. The opportunities for smaller planters to purchase imported goods may have been limited by these same planters, who often controlled local accounts and crop sales (Pagan 1982:490). Therefore, some smaller planters may have allowed their servants or slaves to make certain goods, including pipes, for themselves. Decorated Chesapeake pipes were probably not produced by poorer planters only in difficult economic times, as suggested by Henry (1979), but rather by a widespread group of people who were landless, bonded, and without any access to even the most inexpensive imported commodities.

Among the landless colonists in seventeenth-century tidewater society were the freemen, who traveled from plantation to plantation to earn day wages at various trades. Although these freemen used tobacco pipes, it is unlikely that they were involved in plantation-based pipemaking. Since the demand for tobacco pipes on plantations was probably greatest among people who had little or no capital, freemen would have had little economic incentive to fill this demand. In fact, freemen skilled in other trades were enthusiastically courted by major planters because their skills were in such demand (Bruce 1935:410). Furthermore, there is no archaeological evidence of a particular pipemaker's form or decorative style at contiguous sites that would indicate the plantation pipemaking activities of a traveling journeyman.

Indentured servants were one of the fastest-growing groups in the seventeenth-century tidewater. The immigration of servants to Virginia reached a peak in the late 1660s (Galenson 1981:221, table 1.1), and by 1671, according to Governor William Berkeley's estimate, the servant population accounted for approximately 6,000 of the 15,000 residents in the colony (Hening 1823:2:515). Indentured servants and slaves probably had the least access to imported goods, and their need for locally produced goods such as clothes, shoes, and tobacco pipes grew dramatically as their numbers increased in the second half of the seventeenth century. Servants made shoes, candles, cider, beer, and a variety of other daily goods for themselves and their masters, who in turn sold these commodities to other planters (Fleet 1942:13:99). Documentary evidence suggests that some locally made products, such as shoes, were made by servants explicitly for servants (Beverley in Wright 1947:295). Because of their demand for but limited access to imported pipes, indentured servants were motivated to participate in occasional pipemaking. As discussed above, it is doubtful if there was any demand for servant-made pipes among planters, who likely procured imported pipes for themselves. Although servant pipes may have been used occasionally for casual exchange (Breen and Innes 1980:66), it is unlikely that servants were allowed to make pipes for personal sale. Servant time and goods were probably strictly budgeted, and planters were discouraged by law from illegally "trucking" with servants (Fleet 1942:13:91; Weisiger 1980:143). Although county court records indicate some barter of services, home-made goods, and food between plantations, there is no direct or indirect evidence to suggest that pipes were made in number or were valuable as an exchange commodity. Therefore, the manufacture of local pipes by white servants on English plantations to fill personal needs is a plausible Chesapeake pipemaking context. It is also likely that this pipemaking was infrequent and short-lived. Former servants probably had little time or desire to make pipes after their contract was completed, because with their new freedom came the ability to earn cash and gain access to market channels that were not available to them as bonded servants. Making and using Chesapeake pipes was probably an exclusive practice of bonded statusless individuals who identified more with their local world than with the distant one whose goods seldom reached their hands. Toward the end of the seventeenth-century, the majority of these individuals were black.

Africans, Plantation Crafts, and Pipemaking

The arrival of numbers of African slaves in the Chesapeake-tidewater region corresponds closely with the appearance of many decorated Chesapeake pipes in plantation deposits. Although no documentary evidence identifies black pipemakers in tidewater Virginia and Maryland, the possibility that slaves on English plantations made pipes can be discussed and evaluated in light of the documentary evidence concerning other slave activities.

During the second half of the seventeenth century, Chesapeake tobacco plantations began competing for incoming slaves because their supply of indentured servants was dwindling (Breen 1973; Menard 1977; Galenson 1981). Historians estimate that by the mid-seventeenth century, blacks constituted approximately 3–5 percent of the colonial population. During the next three decades, the number of slaves in the Chesapeake grew dramatically, reaching 2,000 in 1670 and more than 6,000 by the turn of the century (Berkeley in Hening 1823:2:515; Donnan 1969:4:6). Living on small farms and numbering fewer than 10 per farm, blacks in the mid-seventeenth century were easily incorporated into their masters' houses and daily plantation tasks (Kulikoff 1986:319). This lifestyle was a more intimate relationship than that between whites and plantation-based Indians. The lives of seventeenth-century blacks varied widely, depending on the status of their masters, the proximity of other plantations with blacks, and the everyday interactions of blacks and whites. Although all seventeenth-century Africans entered the Chesapeake as slaves, some were freed, some testified in County courts, and some even owned small amounts of property, livestock, and labor (Brewer 1955; Breen and Innes 1980). Therefore, it is difficult to generalize about the lives of plantation blacks in the second half of the seventeenth century.

Planters employed blacks in a variety of small manufactures centered on the plantation. The description of one mid-seventeenth-century James River planter and his plantation offers some insight into the industries and use of blacks on a Virginia plantation:

> He hath a fine house, and all things answerable to it; he sowes yeerly store of Hempe and Flax, and causes it to be spun; he keeps Weavers, and hath a Tan-house, causes Leather to be dressed, hath eight Shoemakers employed in their trade, hath forty Negroe servants,

brings them up to Trades in his house. (Anonymous 1649:14)

Although this reference mentions the training of blacks in small manufactures, there is no specific documentary evidence to indicate that slaves made pipes on Chesapeake plantations. Pipemaking was most likely omitted from this and other written records because it was not a skilled or market-oriented local industry. As discussed earlier, Chesapeake pipe art clearly demonstrates that slaves were involved in plantation pipemaking. The manufacturing context of local pipemaking may have varied from plantation to plantation, as some slaves were probably given European-style molds to make pipes or were permitted to use them temporarily, while others may have worked alongside white servant pipemakers, decorating only those pipes they used for themselves. Seventeenth-century plantation pipemaking clearly involved whites and blacks working cooperatively or in close proximity. Local tidewater clays, European molds, and West African decorating techniques and motifs were combined to produce pipes by people whose access to imported goods was very limited or nonexistent. Some decorated Chesapeake pipes may be the first physical evidence of Africans in the Chesapeake. Furthermore, the appearance of hearts, initials, stars, ships and other European-inspired motifs drawn and complemented in the generalized decorative style described above may be the only surviving evidence of the sharing and syncretism of European and African cultures that occurred on seventeenth-century Chesapeake plantations. This scenario does not exclude Native American participation in pipemaking in the Chesapeake. In fact, the continual discovery of traditional Indian tobacco pipe forms at aboriginal sites through the seventeenth-century and the recovery of a few of these unique pipes from plantation deposits suggest that, although Indians visited and worked on some English plantations, they were not part of this local and occasional crafting context on the plantation.

The pipemakers and pipemaking contexts proposed in this essay reflect a balanced consideration of documentary and artifactual evidence. While both documentary and archaeological evidence indicate the participation of some Indians and English people in Chesapeake pipemaking, some of the pipes recovered from plantation deposits strongly demonstrate the decorative traditions and craftsmanship of seventeenth-century African slaves—a people about whom we know very little.

The Death of Chesapeake Pipemaking

The death of local pipemaking in the Chesapeake can be attributed to a variety of factors, including changes in the relations between blacks and whites and the physical reorganization of plantation life in the late seventeenth century. At the end of the seventeenth century, the social distance between English planters and their servants reflected the development of a tidewater class structure that limited the opportunities for landless men to acquire land and compete in a depressed international tobacco market. The number of servants emigrating to the Chesapeake dropped, and many resident white servants left for better opportunities in other Atlantic colonies. Concurrently, the number of imported blacks increased sharply, and their slave-for-life status was routinized by English colonial law and attitude. With the completion of a slave code in Virginia at the beginning of the eighteenth century, slavery was fully institutionalized. This eighteenth-century legal institutionalization of bonded black labor, however, had its beginnings earlier in the seventeenth century, as colonial authorities had begun limiting the rights and opportunities of blacks in the 1670s. As increased numbers of Africans were brought to the Chesapeake, their identity as property became more defined. Furthermore, changes toward both white and black bonded labor were expressed earlier in the physical world of the plantation.

In some cases, the social distancing of bonded labor from planters resulted in a gradual physical reorganization of plantations and a change in housing size and structure (Upton 1979). The move of indentured servants and slaves out of the planter's house to quarters in the yard was a physical and emotional statement about the changing roles and opportunities of bonded people in the Chesapeake colonies. This physical and social separation, coupled with the increase in black slaves and decrease in white servants marked the end of any occasional pipemaking, and decorated Chesapeake pipes disappear from eighteenth-century plantation deposits. Although there was a feeble attempt to raise the status of white servants above enslaved blacks, servants continued to emigrate out of the Chesapeake. The remaining slaves were legally and socially reduced from people to property.

As planters became increasingly alarmed about the interplantation social networks that their slaves maintained over long distances, they limited slave travel, banned slave funerals, and attempted to suppress any vestiges of African tribal identities. Planters attempted to provide a new identity for their slaves and themselves by distancing themselves physically, emotionally, and materially from this new species of property. Plantation slaves no longer had access to individual time and crafts, but they did continue to make a few items for everyday communal use, such as colonoware, a type of undecorated, low-fired earthenware pottery (Ferguson 1980; Deetz 1988). This colonoware may also be evidence of the gender-related division of labor among the plantation slave population on bigger operations. As the number of Africans swelled on these estates, the plantation labor force and the diversity of Africans with different cultural backgrounds also increased. Along with decorated pipes, descriptive, symbolic, and highly personalized decorative art may have disappeared as well, not because of a lack of skill, but perhaps because of the lack of desire to affect or offend others who, although black, were culturally different.

It was not until the tremendous increase in imported slaves later in the eighteenth century that African-inspired creole traditions are highly visible in the surviving material culture of the American South. Although the lives of eighteenth-century plantation blacks were rigidly directed by a racially xenophobic planter society, by this time slaves had already developed a new way of life that was separate from that of their masters and was uniquely Afro-American.

Notes

1. A more detailed discussion of Chesapeake pipe art and African motifs is found in Emerson (1988).

References Cited

Anonymous

1649 A Perfect Description of Virginia . . . , London. Reprinted in *Tracts and Other Papers Relating to the Origin Settlement, and Progress of the Colonies in North America, From the Discovery of the Country to the Year 1776*, vol. 2, edited by Peter Force. Washington, D.C., 1836–1846.

Antwi, Ibraham Kwabena (editor)

1976 *The Historical and Cultural Significance of Ashanti Artifacts: An Annotated Bibliography*, University of Ghana Legon.

Arents, George Jr.

1938 *Books and Manuscripts Relating to Tobacco from the Collection of George Arents Jr.* Library of Congress, Washington, D.C.

Arneberg, Halfdan

1951 *Norwegian Peasant Art: Men's Handicrafts*. Fabritius and Sonner, Oslo.

Berns, Marla C., and Barbara Rubin Hudson

1986 *The Essential Gourd Art and History in Northeastern Nigeria*. Museum of Cultural History, University of California, Los Angeles.

Biedermann, Galerii

1981 *Nupe Kakanda Basa-Nge*. Fred Jahn, Munich.

Bohannon, Paul

1956 Beauty and Scarification amongst the Tiv. *Man* 129:117–121.

Breen, Timothy H.

1973 A Changing Labor Force and Race Relations in Virginia 1660–1710. *Journal of Social History* 8:3–25.

Breen, Timothy H., and Stephen Innes

1980 *Myne Owne Ground, Race and Freedom on Virginia's Eastern Shore, 1640–1676*. Oxford University Press, New York.

Brewer, James H.

1955 Negro Property Holders in Seventeenth-Century Virginia. *William and Mary Quarterly*, 3d ser., 12:575–580.

Bruce, Philip Alexander

1935 *Economic History of Virginia in the Seventeenth Century.* Vols. 1 and 2. Macmillan, New York.

Caywood, Louis R.

1957 Green Spring Plantation. *The Virginia Magazine of History and Biography*, 65:67–84, January.

Cole, Herbert M., and Doran H. Ross

1977 *The Arts of Ghana*. Museum of Cultural History, University of Los Angeles, Calif.

Cole, Herbert M., and Chike C. Aniakor,

1984 *Igbo Arts: Community and Cosmos*. Museum of Culture History, University of California, Los Angeles.

Copes Tobacco Plant Office

1895 *The Pipes of Asia and Africa*. Smoke Room Booklets No. 11. Liverpool.

Cotter, John L.

1958 *Archaeological Excavations at Jamestown*. Virginia Archaeological Research Series No. 4. National Park Service, Washington, D.C.

Craven, Wesley Frank

1971 Twenty Negroes to Jamestown in 1619? *Virginia Quarterly Review* 47:416–420.

Curtin, Philip D.

1969 *The Atlantic Slave Trade–A Census*. University of Wisconsin Press, Madison, Wis.

Daget J., and Z. Ligers

1962 Une Ancienne Industrie Malienne:les Pipes en Terre.

Bulletin de L'Institut Français d'Afrique Noire. 24:1–2, 12–53.

Deetz, James,
1988 American Historical Archaeology: Methods and Results. *Science* 239:362–367.

Donnan, Elizabeth
1969 *Documents Illustrative of the History of Slave Trade to America*. Vols. 1–4. Octagon Books, New York.

Durand, Dauphine de, and Gilbert Chinard (translators)
1934 *A Huguenot Exile in Virginia, or Voyages of a Frenchman Exiled for His Religion*. Press of the Pioneers, New York.

Edwards, R., and L. G. G. Ramsey (editors)
1956 *The Tudor Period 1500–1603*. Connoisseur Period Guides, London.

Emerson, Matthew
1987 Excavations at the Barker-Lucy Site at Flowerdew Hundred: A Preliminary Report. Unpublished ms. Flowerdew Hundred Foundation, Hopewell, Va.
1988 *Decorated Clay Tobacco Pipes from the Chesapeake*. Ph.D. diss. University Microfilms, Ann Arbor.
1993 *African Inspirations in a New World Art and Artifact*. University of Georgia Press, Athens, Ga. (in press).

Eyo, Ekpo
1979 *Nigeria and the Evolution of Money*. Central Bank of Nigeria and Federal Department of Antiquities, Lagos.

Ferguson, Leland
1980 Looking for the "Afro" in Colono-Indian Pottery. In *Archaeological Perspectives on Ethnicity in America*, edited by Robert Schuyler pp. 14–20. Baywood, Farmingville, N.Y.

Fleet, Beverley
1942 *Virginia Colonial Abstracts Charles City County Court Orders 1664–1665, Fragments 1650–1696*. Vol. 13. Beverley Fleet, Richmond.

Franklin, John H.
1980 *From Slavery to Freedom: The History of the Negro Americans*. 3d ed. Alfred Knopf, New York.

Galenson, David W.
1981 *White Servitude in Colonial America: An Economic Analysis*. Cambridge University Press, New York.

Garrard, Timothy F.
1973 Studies in Akan Goldweights (IV): The Dating of Akan Goldweights. *Transactions of the Historical Society of Ghana* 14:2:149–168.

Gebauer, Paul
1979 *Art of Cameroon*. Portland Art Museum Association. Portland, Oreg.

Griaule, Marcel, and Germaine Dieterlen
1935 Calabasses Dahomeennes. *Journal del la Societie des Africanistes*. 5:203–207.

Handler, Jerome S., and Frederick W. Lange
1978 *Plantation Slavery in Barbados, An Archaeological and Historical Investigation*. Harvard University Press, Cambridge, Mass.

Hening, W. W. (editor)
1823 *Statutes at Large: Being a Collection of All the Laws of Virginia from the First Session of the Legislature in the Year 1619*. 13 vols. Richmond 1809–1823.

Henry, Susan L.
1979 Terra-Cotta Tobacco Pipes in 17th Century Maryland and Virginia: A Preliminary Study. *Historical Archaeology* 13:14–37.

Hudson, Paul J.
1975 Pottery-Making in Virginia in the Seventeenth Century. *Quarterly Bulletin, Archaeological Society of Virginia* 30:1:41–52.

Jefferson, Louise E.
1973 *The Decorative Art of Africa*. Viking Press, N.Y.

Kelso, William, and Edward A. Chappell
1974 Excavations of a Seventeenth Century Pottery Kiln at Glebe Harbor, Westmoreland County, Virginia. *Historical Archaeology* 8:53–63.

Kulikoff, Allan
1986 *Tobacco and Slaves, The Development of Southern Cultures in the Chesapeake, 1680–1800*. University of North Carolina Press, Chapel Hill.

Leslie, Vernon
1970 The Pointille Pipe in the Upper Delaware Valley: Contribution to Tocks Island Reservoir Area Archaeology. *The Chesopiean* 8:3:57–66.

MacCord, Howard A.
1969 Hungar's Neck Trash Pit, Northampton County, Virginia. *Quarterly Bulletin, Archaeological Society of Virginia* 27:1:59–64.

McCarthy, Michael R., and Catherine M. Brooks
1988 *Medieval Pottery in Britain* A.D. 900–1600. Leicester University Press, U.K.

Menard, Russell R.
1977 From Servants to Slaves; The Transformation of the Chesapeake Labor System. *Southern Studies* 26:355–390.

Minchinton, Walter, Celia King, and Peter Waite
1984 *Virginia Slave-Trade Statistics 1698–1775*. Virginia State Library, Richmond.

Mitchell, Vivienne
1983 The History of Nominy Plantation with Emphasis on the Clay Tobacco Pipes. In *Historic Clay Tobacco Pipe Studies*, edited by Byron Sudbury, vol. 2, pp. 1–38. British Archaeological Reports, International Series 60:151-341.

Noel Hume, Ivor
1975 *Historical Archaeology*, W. W. Norton, New York.

Ozanne, Paul
1962 Notes on the Early Historic Archaeology of Accra. *Transactions of the Historical Society of Ghana* 6:51–70.
1964 Tobacco Pipes of Accra and Shai Institute of African Studies: Legon, Ghana. University of Ghana.

Pagan, John R.
1982 Dutch Maritime and Commercial Activity in Mid-

Seventeenth-Century Virginia. *Virginia Magazine of History and Biography* 90:4:485–501.

Parrinder, Geoffrey
1982 *African Mythology*, Peter Bedrick Books, New York.

Rutsch, Edward S.
1973 *Smoking Technology of the Aborigines of the Iroquois Area of New York State*. Associated University Presses, Cranbury, N.J.

Seiber, Roy
1972 *African Textiles and Decorative Arts*. Museum of Modern Art, New York.

Shinnie, P. L., and Paul Ozanne
1962 Excavations at Yendi Dabari. *Transactions of the Historical Society of Ghana*. 6:87–118.

Stobel, Arnulf
1984 *Afrikanische Keramic*. Hirmer Verlag, Munich.

Thompson, Robert Farris, and Joseph Cornet
1983 *Flash of the Spirit*. Random House, New York.

Trowel, Margaret
1960 *African Design*. Praeger, New York.

Upton, Dell
1979 *Early Vernacular Architecture in Southeastern Virginia*. Unpublished Ph.D. dissertation, Department of American Civilization, Brown University, Providence, R.I.

Vaughan, Alden T.
1972 Blacks in Virginia: A Note on the First Decade. *William and Mary Quarterly* 29:3:469–478.

Weisiger, Benjamin B. (compiler)
1980 *Charles City County, Virginia Court Orders 1687–1695*. Benjamin B. Weisiger, Richmond.

Wood, Peter H., Gregory A. Waselkov, and M. Thomas Hatley (editors)
1989 *Powhatan's Mantle: Indians in the Colonial Southeast*. University of Nebraska Press, Lincoln.

Wright, Louis B. (editor), with Robert Beverley
1947 *The History and Present State of Virginia*. Chapel Hill, N.C.

IV
CHAPTER

Solid Statements
Architecture, Manufacturing, and Social Change in Seventeenth-Century Virginia

ANN B. MARKELL

THIS CHAPTER is about the use of material symbols by the English colonists in seventeenth-century Virginia. Virginia had first been colonized in 1607; the last half of the seventeenth century was a pivotal period for the colony, in which it shifted from frontier society to settled community and established the social foundations necessary for the birth of a nation independent from England. Social and cultural upheaval was visible in the material world of the colonists, both as a reflection of change and as a symbol used in the creation of that change. Architecture and manufacturing are just two types of material culture that were used symbolically to facilitate social change in the late seventeenth century and are ideally suited to this study because of their clear archaeological visibility.

Flowerdew Hundred plantation (figure 4.1) lies on the south shore of the James River, halfway between Williamsburg and Richmond. First settled by the English in 1618, when Sir George Yeardley began a "particular plantation" of 1,000 acres, it had been split into smaller landholdings in the late seventeenth and eighteenth centuries and then in the nineteenth century was reassembled into a tract whose boundaries now closely parallel the original ones. The site being examined here, 44PG92 (figure 4.2), dates to the period between 1660 and 1690. No documentary records survive to indicate the name of the planter who built his home here, but we can conclude from the material recovered—shattered wine goblets, fragments of leaded glass windows, gold-plated upholstery tacks—that this was a person whose status lay somewhere between the wealthy elite and the landless freemen and tenants of late seventeenth-century Virginia. He was a middling planter, whose aspirations to membership in the elite class of Virginia became evident in the ruins he left behind. Among these were the remains of a dwelling, its architectural form still discernible after 330 years, and the debris from his small attempts at manufacturing.

The material world with which people like this early Virginian surround themselves performs a myriad of functions, some quite obvious and mundane and others more obscure in nature. For the archaeologist, who must rely on the tangible remains of past societies for information, the obvious can be only the beginning of the search for the content and substance of past cultures. Because the material world of a society is created in response to specific needs, conditions, and perceptions (Hodder 1986:3), it is unique to that time and that people. It is part of a text that can inform us not only about the physical world, but also about the social and psychological world. Change in material culture implies social change, which

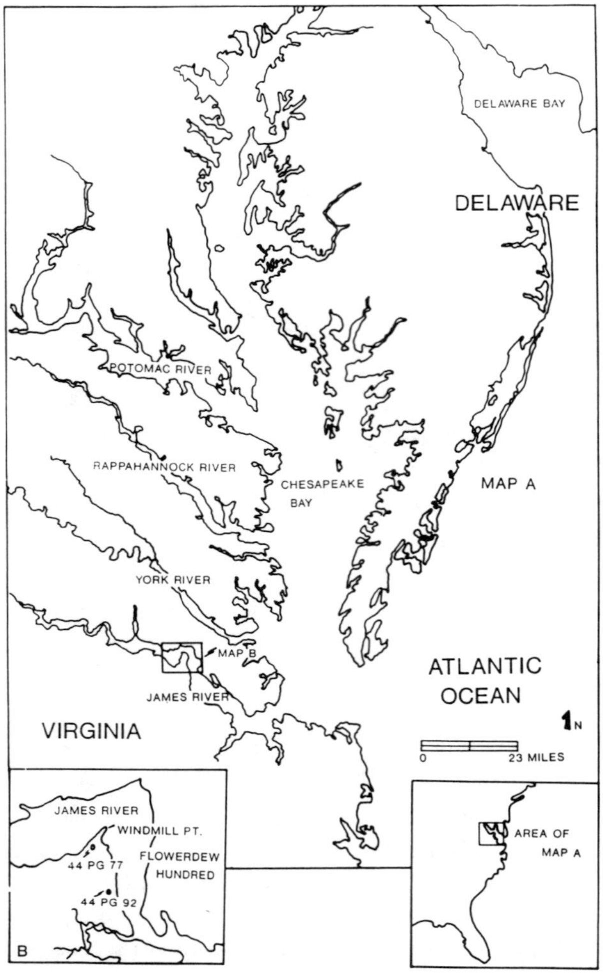

FIGURE 4.1. *Chesapeake Bay region showing the location of Flowerdew Hundred and Site 44PG92.*

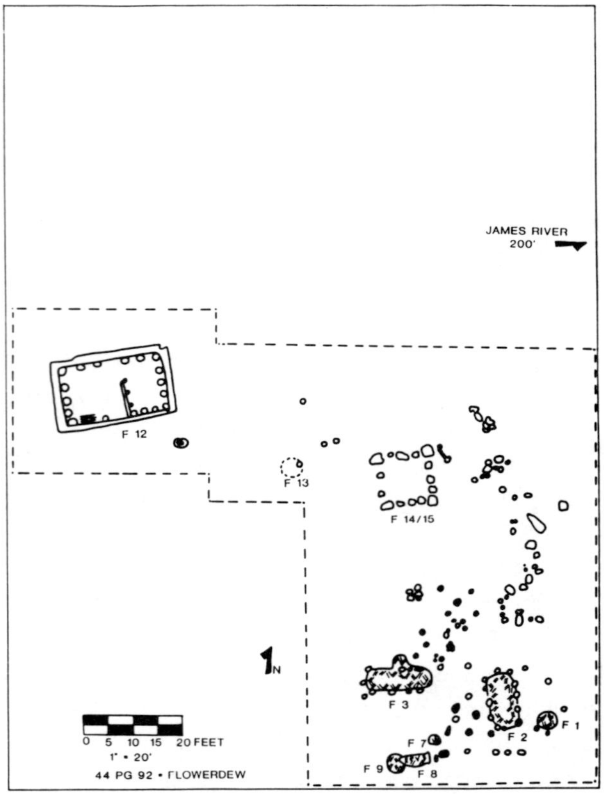

FIGURE 4.2. *Site plan of 44PG92.*

includes change in relationships within a specific society and between that society and the larger world. Here, material culture plays a reflective role, conveying information about change that has already transpired.

Material culture is also actively employed to create and affirm change in a society (Miller and Tilley 1984; Hodder 1986). Exposing this often ephemeral and highly contextual function of material culture is difficult, but if it can be teased out of the data, we are able to gain another perspective of the past that brings us that much closer to an understanding of human relationships in the past and in the present. Ian Hodder (1986) emphasizes the relationship of material culture to changes in human organization and takes into account not only the reflective nature of material culture, but also the active nature, by recognizing the formative role of the artifact in social and cultural dynamics. The artifact is not only a text to be read after the fact, it is an integral part of the life of the maker or user. "To understand the meaning of artifacts in the broadest sense, we need to focus on the imaginative act by which people fuse their surroundings into a meaningful whole" (Upton 1989:4). The material world is a means to that end. The use of artifacts to create order out of potential chaos, to mediate differences, and to bridge the transitions in life is universal. We can perhaps read the material record after the fact to document the change, but we also need to look for the process.

The relationship of material culture to the formation and maintenance of group identity is complex. Among its many functions, material culture serves as a form of communication. In most definitions of collective group identity, one of the most powerful components of the identity system is its material symbols, which are used not only to communicate group membership, but also to maintain the boundaries between groups (Weber 1961; Spicer 1971).

Upton (1989) points out, using the same approach as

Sperber (1974), that the difference between sign and symbol is seldom noted by the researcher. Material culture can be symbolic without any item acting as sign. In fact, this is what gives material culture its power as symbol; a sign communicates a specific message, which is rigidly encoded, whereas a symbol by its very nature is subject to interpretation. A sign also implies conscious intent, whereas the meaning of symbol often seems inadvertent, having its basis in the changing ideology of the people. This changeable symbolic nature of material culture is a necessary element in its ability to enhance social and cultural development.

A symbol, then, can be used at times to affirm relationships and to solidify boundaries, and at other times to create rifts in those relationships (Hodder 1986). Material symbols are intelligible only within the context in which they are created or used. In order to interpret this symbolic communication, there must be an understanding of the "ideas, beliefs and meanings which interpose themselves between people and things" (Hodder 1986:3). Social structure and ideological conflict that spur the definition and redefinition of group boundaries must be placed in historical context before material statements can be interpreted. The planter who left behind the remnants of his created world at Flowerdew Hundred was a part of the larger seventeenth-century colonial society. Placing the various material elements found at this site into the larger historical context joins this small planter's voice to those around him—and enables us to hear it in a way not possible before.

Architecture

Seventeenth-century Virginia architecture has been described as impermanent, calculated to last only 20 or 30 years in a world that saw no gain in substantial housing (Carson et al. 1981). For much of the century, the wealthy as well as the poor lived in the same types of dwellings, scorned by their peers in England as "the worst in the world" (Bruce 1895:1:148; cf. Butler 1623 in Proceedings of the Virginia Company). The features that gave the housing this "impermanent" status were the use of posts set directly into the ground to frame the house, and the general lack of brick or other masonry construction. Although there were a number of variations in the form of the impermanent, post-built house, by the last quarter of the seventeenth century a form emically termed the "ordinary Virginia" house had evolved (Carson et al. 1981: 159). This was in direct opposition to the "English framed house" referred to in written records (British Colonial Office 1677) and probably bearing more relationship to architecture found acceptable in England.

At 44PG92, an unusual structure was excavated, one that fit the preceding description only in part. Dating to the period between 1650 and 1667, it was built with post-in-the-ground construction, typical of most seventeenth-century Virginia architecture, but it had a number of features that lead to questions about the conclusion of impermanent intent.[1] In 1638, Samuel Symonds of Ipswich, Massachusetts, gave building instructions for a house, stating:

> I would have it sellered all over, and soe the frame of the howse accordingly from the bottom. . . . Let the frame begin from the bottom of the seller, & soe in the ordinary way upright, *for I can hereafter (to save the timber within grounde) run up a thin brickwork without*. . . . It were not amisse to leave a dore-way or two within the seller, that soe hereafter one may make comings in from without. (Carson et al. 1981:146; emphasis added)

In these instructions Symonds has described much of what was found in the cellared structure of 44PG92 (figure 4.3). The cellar posts are on 4-foot centers and of sufficient size and depth (figure 4.4) to support a structural weight above. The cellar was wood lined, with much of the wall planking still surviving, fully partitioned, with a surviving wooden partition wall, and had a clay floor. Wooden stairs entered from the outside of the structure into the larger of the two rooms.[2]

The unusual evidence from this structure, however, points not to the expected impermanent features of the structure—the wooden posts, the wood-lined walls, and the clay floor—but to those that contradict this norm. First, the structure had a brick chimney; large amounts of brick rubble, some with clear evidence of burning, were found on the floor of the cellar on the western end. Tile fragments, similar in size to floor tiles, with clear burning on one face were also found here. Second, the builder's trench that surrounds the cellar was fully 2 1/2 feet wide on three sides of the cellar and narrowed to 1 foot on the fourth side (figure 4.3).

Excavation revealed that the trench had been intentionally stepped, to produce a foot-wide shelf at a depth of 1 foot (figure 4.5). There is no evidence that this trench

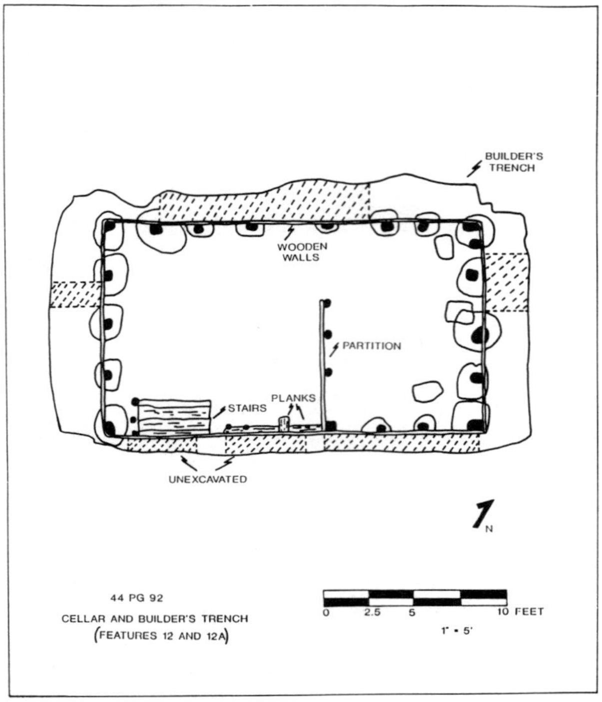

FIGURE 4.3. *Plan of cellar AT 44PG92.*

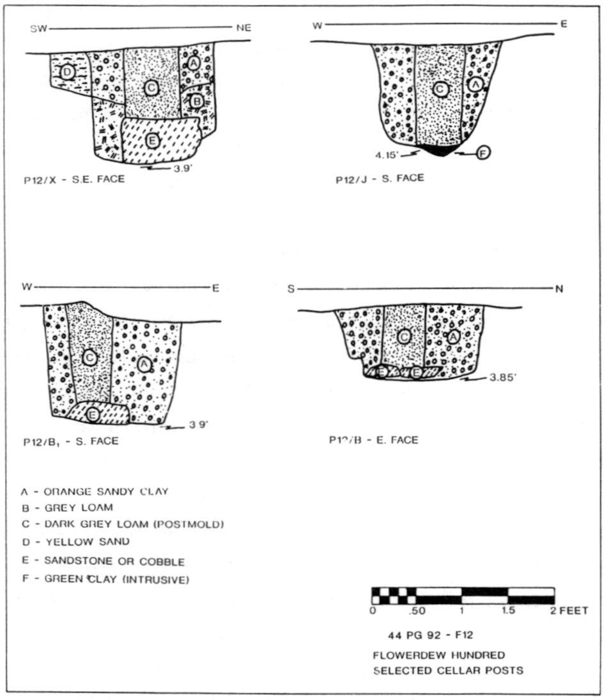

FIGURE 4.4. *Sections of selected profiles from feature 12 (cellar) at 44PG92.*

was necessary for the building of the cellar itself, since the posts are set to the interior of this trench, and the wood planking of the walls of the cellar, while placed behind the posts, was nailed to the posts from the interior. A second possible explanation for the trench is that the cellar was built in a larger hole originally dug for another purpose, or that the size of the structure was altered after the original hole was dug, and the excess was later filled. The carefully notched corners of the builder's trench appear too intentional for this explanation. The third possibility is that the trench was intentionally dug to allow for the addition of masonry facing, as was suggested in Symond's building instructions (Upton, personal communication 1989). If this was the case, the masonry work was never carried out, and the trench was later filled. Apparently the trench stood open for at least a short while. Crossmends in some of the ceramics from the site indicate that the upper part of the trench was open while the cellar was in use; the ceramics and other debris had gathered on the stepped shelf of the trench, rather than being incorporated into the fill (Markell 1990a).

It appears the builder of this structure hoped to improve upon it in the future; that he seems to have failed in this attempt, for economic or other reasons, does not alter the fact that he had intended to construct a more permanent dwelling than was common at the time in Virginia. If this were the only case of intended permanence in an otherwise impermanent architectural landscape, it could perhaps be considered idiosyncratic. Numerous documentary records, and the recent excavation of other sites from the last half of the seventeenth century that exhibit a trend toward permanence long before the general rebuilding of Virginia in the eighteenth century, argue against this. Inventories of the rebels executed in 1677, in the aftermath of Bacon's Rebellion, list an unexpected number of "English framed" and brick houses. These inventories, taken in close sequence by peers of the deceased, are careful to distinguish between "ordinary Virginia housing" (British Colonial Office CO5/1371:240) and "framed" dwellings (British Colonial Office CO5/1371:237), which indicates that the distinction was one clearly recognized in the seventeenth century. Of these 23 inventories, 5 mention the presence of framed housing, or of brick housing, all with brick chimneys rather than the common wood and daub stacks. Other inventories indicate either "very good" or "new" dwellings (British Colonial Office CO5/1371:243). The majority of these executed rebels were members or potential members of Virginia's elite.

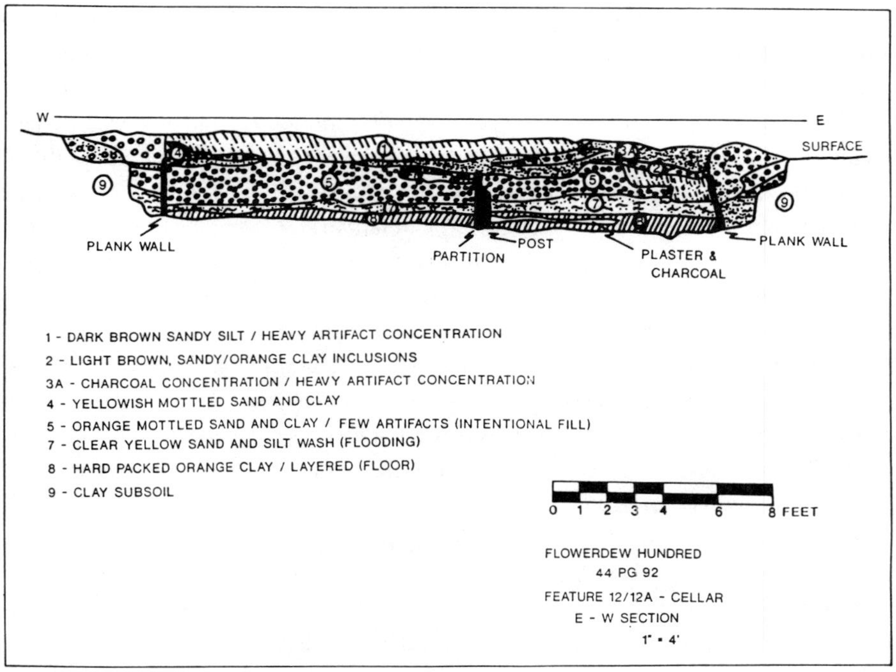

FIGURE 4.5. *Section of feature 12 (cellar) at 44PG92.*

Another document sheds light on the seventeenth-century perception of the proper form for a dwelling. This letter, written by William Fitzhugh in 1686 to Nicholas Hayward in England, offered advice on setting up a plantation in the colony. If the plantation were intended for tenants on a year-to-year lease, Fitzhugh advised, then the building of a "Virginia house" would be appropriate. If there were a longer lease, he suggested that the tenants build for themselves, because of the expense. If Hayward intended to build for himself, however, or for a child or near relative, he should attempt a "very good house, not only for their comfortable, but *creditable* accommodations" (Davis 1963:202; emphasis added). Continuing his instructions, Fitzhugh recommended that Hayward find and bring to Virginia "a Carpenter and Bricklayer Servants, and send them in here to serve 4 or five years, in which time they might reasonably build a substantial good house" (Davis 1963:202). Fitzhugh here implied that at the end of the seventeenth century, a "creditable" house in Virginia required the use of brick.

Archaeological evidence also indicates a trend toward increased permanence in the houses of the elite, or those who aspired to the elite. Documentary evidence related to Jamestown reveals that the form and materials of some dwellings were mandated by statute. They were to have brick foundations and tile or slate roofs, and even the thickness of the brick walls was specified (Hening 1823:2:171–176). Archaeological excavations at the site of Jamestown have revealed brick foundations and roof tile that suggest some conformity with the statutes (Harrington 1950:19). At Greenspring, the home of Governor William Berkeley, excavations in the 1950s revealed a structure with brick and sandstone foundations, two brick-lined cellars, and brick fireplaces, probably dating to the period between 1641 and 1677 (Caywood 1955:8–10). At Arlington plantation in Northampton County on the eastern shore of Virginia, excavation of the Custis house has revealed a double-pile house with a full brick foundation and brick chimneys, dating to the 1670s (Bedell and Luccketti 1988).

The increased use of brick to make structures more permanent is evident from a site at Kingsmill plantation, Littletown Manor, where Thomas Pettus added brick chimneys and a brick and tile cellar in the last quarter of the seventeenth century (Kelso 1984:79). At St. Mary's City in Maryland, the St. John house underwent renovations in 1678 that included rebuilding the chimney with brick and repairing and paving the cellar with brick (Carson et al. 1981:185–186). And at 44PG77, another site from the last half of the seventeenth century at Flowerdew Hundred, researchers have excavated a cellar with a fully tiled floor (Emerson 1988).

The move toward the use of more permanent building techniques seems sporadic but determined. This was not a great rebuilding, but a gradual addition of new materials and techniques. As was seen at 44PG92, the intent often did not match the reality, and the economic circumstances of the time, difficult at best, often did not cooperate. On one level, these architectural changes suggest that the attitude toward Virginia had changed— it was now seen as a settled colony and home and no longer as a way station in a tobacco boom economy. Permanent housing could have implied a commitment to take up residence in the colony, but there seems to be an additional statement being made. The fact that the great majority of these houses were those of the politically dominant elite seems to hold more than economic significance.

An artifact such as architecture is an integral part of the life of its maker or user. Architecture as a symbolic statement can only be understood when interpreted as one part of the cultural text. If the architectural symbol is examined through another class of material culture, the manufacturing process, we may be able to gain more insight into the social world of the Virginia elite in the seventeenth century.

MANUFACTURING

Although the act of producing an object cannot be classified strictly as material culture, it is responsible for the existence of that culture. Choices made during production—about type, form, and function—are directly related to the needs of the person producing the item. The propriety of these choices must be anticipated by the manufacturer if the object is intended for someone else. The success of that anticipation has much to do with the success of the product in a market situation.

In the case of colonial Virginia, this situation seems to have had an effect on the establishment of manufacturing efforts in the colony. The shift in manufacturing locus for some items could indicate not only an economic strategy, but a need for more congruity between artifact form and culture. The manufacture of material goods then becomes a statement of social and cultural independence, as intelligible as is the statement made by the artifacts themselves.

The outer yard of the cellared structure at 44PG92 had three features that suggest another inconformity with the currently extant histories of Virginia in the seventeenth century. According to historical sources, iron smelting did not take place in late seventeenth-century Virginia (Swank 1892; Bruce 1895; Mulholland 1981). The shallow pits found at 44PG92 (figures 4.6 and 4.7), which date to 1670–1690 (Markell 1990a), contained evidence suggestive of iron manufacturing. This evidence centers on the form and content of these small trashpits. The main components of features 1, 2, and 3 were charcoal, brick, baked clay, iron ore, oyster shell, coral, and iron (Markell 1990a). When these components of the fill were examined in the light of the direct or bloomery method of iron smelting, there appeared to be some fit. The charcoal, iron ore, and possibly the limestone and coral, play a direct role in the smelting process.

A bloomery furnace employs a mechanically simple technique for smelting iron on a small scale. These furnaces have been used in North America, Africa, Asia, and Europe, and they vary in form from small hearths excavated into the ground to large shaft furnaces (Killick and Gordon 1988:120). When a small amount of iron-

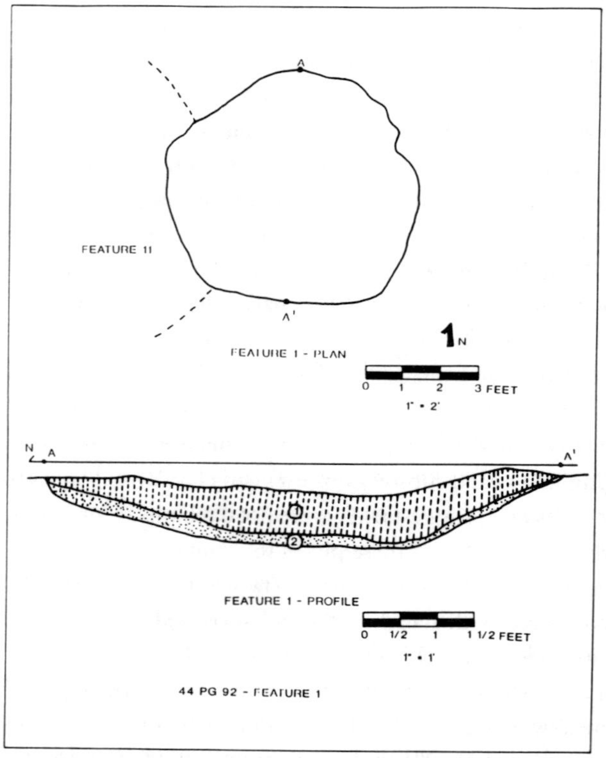

FIGURE 4.6. *Plan and section of feature 1 at 44PG92.*

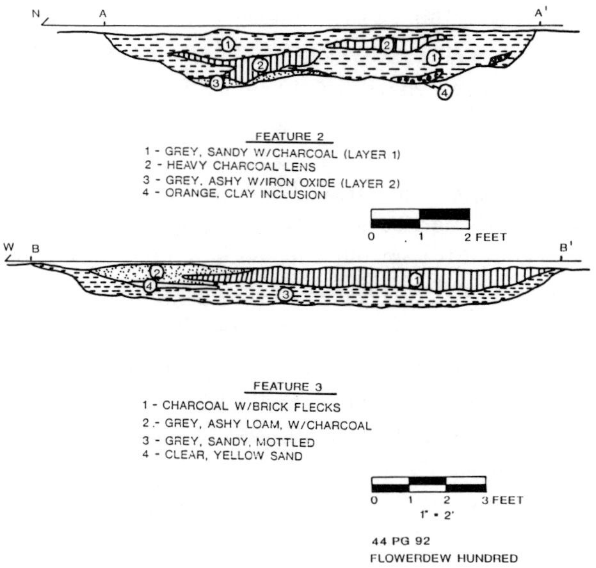

FIGURE 4.7. *Sections of features 2 and 3 at 44PG92.*

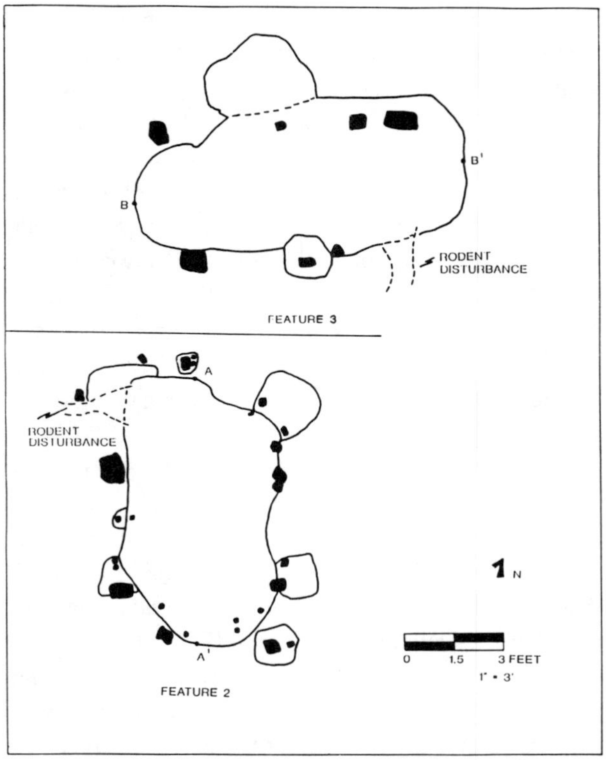

FIGURE 4.8. *Plans of features 2 and 3 at 44PG92.*

bearing ore is heated with charcoal, a spongy mass of slag and iron forms in the furnace bottom. This mass, or bloom, is then removed and hammered and reheated repeatedly to force out the remaining impurities. The smith then shapes it into an iron bar (Schubert 1957:150; Harvey 1986). Although this method calls for a good deal of skill, it requires a small outlay of labor and capital, in comparison with a larger, more complex blast furnace operation (Langston 1657). It is ideally suited to small supplies of ore, such as the outcrops of bog ore in the Chesapeake area of Virginia and Maryland (Heite 1983). Through the use of the bloomery method, a single plantation could obtain a supply of iron at a relatively small cost.

The form of the pits also ties them to the smelting process. Although they are consistent in size and shape with daub pits, which are common in this area because the local clay was used as architectural daub, the fact that they were dug into a sand subsoil, while a good clay subsoil lay only 50 feet away, suggests they were not daub pits. One clue to the primary use of these pits is the ring of postholes surrounding both features 2 and 3 (figure 4.8), which can be compared with stakeholes found surrounding pits at the site of St. Neots, Huntingdonshire, in England (Teebutt 1966:158). This thirteenth-century iron smelting and metalworking site revealed shallow bowl or pit furnaces surrounded by stakeholes, apparently used to support a domed clay roof over the furnaces. Burned daub was found in those pits, along with other debris from the destruction of the furnaces (Teebutt 1966:159). The Flowerdew pits also contained burned brick and clay, possibly the remains of roof or lining. While the bowl furnaces at St. Neots correspond in form with the features at 44PG92, the latter lack the intense fire reddening found in the St. Neot's furnaces and therefore may not have been used primarily as smelting furnaces, but as part of an earlier stage of the smelting process.

A description of ore roasting pits, used to heat the iron ore in the first stages of the smelting process, was offered by Agricola in 1556. "By digging out the earth they make the areas much larger and square; walls should be built along the sides and back to hold the heat of the fire more effectively, and the front should be left open." This is consistent with the configuration of posts around the features at 44PG92. Agricola spoke also of using wood 12 feet long, the approximate longitudinal dimension of both features 2 and 3. It is possible that the posts that ringed the features supported the enclosure of a roasting pit. The fact that feature 3 showed evidence of heat-reddened walls is also consistent with this conclusion. If these features were used in the roasting of the ore, rather than in the actual smelting process, it would explain the lack of any large quantities of slag on the excavated portion of the site.

The industrial activity that took place at 44PG92 was clearly done on a small scale. It was also carried out for a short period of time, possibly as a single experiment. As in the case of the cellar house, the intent seems to have outshone the reality. Again, if this were the only case of apparent iron smelting in this period in Virginia, it could be described as an anomaly. There is, however, another excavated example of a bloomery in late seventeenth-century Virginia, and still another apparently dating to the second quarter of the century.

Excavations at the Drummond site at Governor's Land near Williamsburg revealed an area of shallow trashpits dating to the last half of the seventeenth century that contained evidence of smelting and of smithing. William Drummond was a politically important, wealthy member of the Virginia elite, who fell out of favor with Governor Berkeley and became a supporter of and participant in Bacon's Rebellion of 1676. He was executed for treason in 1677 (Outlaw 1977). Materials found in these pits were similar to those found at 44PG92—charcoal, iron ore, iron scrap, slag, and cinder (Harvey 1986:7). Analysis completed on debris from this site has shown conclusively that the waste is from an iron-smelting process (Harvey, personal communication 1989). There is not, unfortunately, any clear evidence of the form of the smelting furnace itself. Drummond's inventory, taken after his execution in 1677, makes no mention of smelting, but lists 15,000 6- and 8-penny nails (British Colonial Office 1677), a large quantity in comparison with numbers in other inventories. Although this is certainly not conclusive evidence of smithing, the assumption could be made that these nails were made from iron smelted on the premises.

At Jamestown, excavations in 1955 uncovered a complex of three features, one of which seems to have been used primarily for the smelting of iron. Approximately 10 feet in diameter, it contained quantities of iron ore, charcoal, limestone, and burned oyster shell. This area may also have been used as a smithing forge, as is suggested by the presence of large quantities of nails, armor fragments, sword parts, and kettle fragments (Cotter 1958). Although these features appear to date to the second quarter of the seventeenth century, there were not enough clearly datable artifacts to rule out a slightly later time period (Cotter 1958), which would align this site temporally with 44PG92 and with Governor's Land. The materials associated with this suspected furnace are almost identical to those from the trashpits at 44PG92, and they appear in similar ratios. Whatever the industrial activity that took place at Jamestown, it is reasonable to conclude that a similar activity was conducted at Flowerdew Hundred a few years later.

There may be no documentary evidence for smelting, but there is ample indication of smithing in the last part of the century. Smithing, while certainly carried out for the normal maintenance of tools and implements in the colony, also contributed to the creation of material culture. Although it is difficult to assign manufacturing sources to iron implements, documentary evidence suggests the manufacture of distinct forms of tools in Virginia, such as the "Virginia hoe" mentioned in inventories (Bruce 1895:1:463; Egloff 1980). Nathaniel Bacon, instigator of the rebellion of 1676 and owner of a new brick house, also owned a smith shop with bellows and tools and had among his servants a smith named Peter. William Hunt, also a participant in the rebellion, owned a smithy with tools, forges, bellows, and large supplies of new and old iron (British Colonial Records 1677). Virginia statutes also reveal a concern with the establishment of the smith's trade (Hening 1823:1:488, 2:124).

Iron production was not the only manufacturing activity to increase in the latter part of the seventeenth century. Of the five excavated sites that have shown evidence of ceramic production in Virginia, three date to the last half of the century. Greenspring, the home of Governor Berkeley, had a kiln dating to between 1660 and 1680 that produced coarsewares made from the local red clays (Caywood 1955:12). A kiln at Glebe Harbor, run by a potter named Morgan Jones during the 1670s, produced a variety of utilitarian wares (Kelso and Chappell 1974). And at the Challis site, near Jamestown, lead-glazed utilitarian wares were produced from about 1680 until the 1730s (Noel Hume 1963).

To date, these are the only excavated seventeenth-century ceramic production sites, but the existence of others can be presumed from the large quantities of unidentified, but locally made, ceramics commonly found on sites throughout the region. At 44PG92, approximately 10 percent of the vessels found were presumably locally made and thus had a tie with regional distribution networks. Other sites, such as Kingsmill, have an even higher proportion of local ceramics (Kelso, personal communication 1989).

Evidence of clay pipe production in the last half of the seventeenth century is also strong. Excavations on sites from this time period have yielded large numbers of decorated and undecorated pipes that were locally made. Comparative work on many of these, carried out by Emerson (1988), suggests a possible regional distribution of decorative pipe designs (Emerson 1988:101). There is no evidence of centralized manufacture; rather, pipemaking seems to have been carried out as a small, plantation-based industry. There is sparse documentary evidence; one mention is made of punishment accorded for the digging of pipe clay on a Sunday (Weisiger 1980:179), and there is a reference to "pipmoulds" in the inventory of Edmund Choosman, executed for his part in Bacon's Rebellion (British Colonial Office 1677:239).

Although no pipe kilns have been located archaeologically, many sites from the last half of the century have yielded pipe wasters and the trimmings from their manufacture. Among these is the middling planter's site at Flowerdew, 44PG92, where not only trimmings and wasters were found, but also quantities of bulk, unfired, high-quality clay, suitable for the production of pipes. This appeared to have been in blocks, stored in the cellar at the site (Markell 1990a). Wasters have also been found at Governor's Land (Outlaw 1977:133), at Jamestown (Cotter 1958:145), at Nominy Plantation (Mitchell 1983:31), and at 44PG77, also at Flowerdew Hundred (Emerson 1988:34). All of these materials date to the last half of the seventeenth century.

Documentary records confirm the growth of other miscellaneous manufacturing efforts toward the end of the century. Clothing and cloth manufacture was promoted by Virginia's government (Hening 1823:2:238, 266, 287), and the success of these efforts is alluded to in Fitzhugh's statement in 1681 that "there's little of any wool left in our parts not wrought up either in stockings etc., therefore no hopes of the purchase of any here" (Davis 1963:103). Furthermore, under Virginia statute, each county was required to have a tanhouse (Hening 1823:2:123), and private ones were erected on many plantations (Bruce 1895:2:476–477). Shoemakers were often sought as servants; Edmund Scarborough had nine shoemakers in his employ in 1662 (Northampton County Records 1657–1664:153). Shipbuilding also increased in the last quarter of the century. By the end of the century small sloops suitable for trade with New England and the Caribbean were being built, as well as ships of 300 tons (Evans 1957:25–27).

Manufacturing efforts had never been completely absent from the Virginia Colony in the seventeenth century, but they clearly enjoyed a tremendous increase toward the end of the century. England's general view of manufacturing in this colony was not benign. Although England was not opposed to first-stage manufactures in Virginia, because this would provide it with a supply of raw materials, it saw the free manufacture of goods that were earlier supplied by the mother country as a threat to its economy (Bruce 1895:2:394). Virginia's statute of 1682, passed to promote manufacture in the colony, was disallowed by the English Commissioners of Customs, who stated clearly: "The plantations are inhabited by his Majesty's subjects for the maintaining a greater correspondence and . . . firmer dependence upon it. These laws break the correspondence between the plantation's dependence on his Majesty's kingdom" (McDonald n.d.:6:-267). The economic situation in the Virginia colony was such that it became necessary to provide an impetus for local manufacturing efforts. The Navigation Acts of the 1660s, the Dutch wars, and the depressed tobacco prices had all taken their toll, with the result that Virginia's very survival now depended on expanding local industry. Britain, however, remained impassive, and Virginians, rather than challenging Britain's decisions outright, went ahead with their efforts discreetly, regardless of the law. The true extent of manufacturing seems to have been hidden from England. Governor Berkeley, in his communications with England, denied not only the existence of good sources of iron, which had been documented earlier (Hening 1823:2:514), but also the fact that sizable ships had been built in the colony (Hening 1823:2:515). There were even veiled threats, long after manufacturing was established in the colony, to begin manufacturing if trade laws and levies were not eased. Governor Edmund Andros, for example, addressing the Privy Council in 1692, stated that if the people were not supplied with appropriate goods at usual cost, they might be forced to begin manufactures. He further stated that if this happened, the people would have to leave the planting of the usual amount of tobacco, further lessening the King's revenues (Palmer n.d.:1: 38–39). These denials of the existence of certain industries, or misrepresentations of the extent of those industries, indicate a conflict between England and its colony that went beyond a purely economic struggle. The act of manufacturing had become a statement of independence from England.

The Social World

By the last half of the seventeenth century, many of those who had arrived in the early years of the colony and had survived its rigors had already ascended to positions of wealth and power. These were the men who sat on the council and in the House of Burgesses. These were the men who wielded the political power in the colony, and these were the men who used whatever means they could to add to their wealth and maintain their power. The best and most accessible land was theirs, and in the seventeenth century this meant river frontage convenient to merchant ships. Small planters, removed from such ports, were forced to consign their crops to the larger planters, who thus became merchants as well (Morgan 1975:224). Not only did the wealthy elite have control of the political power, they also had control of the economic power in the colony. By the 1660s, a distinct social structure had been defined in Virginia. At the top were the elite—the wealthy and politically powerful planters—and below them were the smaller or "middling" planters who had succeeded in establishing households. Below the planters were the ever-increasing numbers of landless freemen, who had served their indentures and been released from servitude into an uncertain economic future. Indentured servants formed the next rung down the social ladder, and at the bottom were the few slaves (approximately 1,000 at this time). The Native Americans seemed to be completely outside of the structure (Morgan 1975:224).

The constant flow of servants into the country, so necessary to the planters' continued success, had spawned a large body of young, single, impoverished, and landless freemen; many were recent immigrants from England, with little stake in their new country. Servants, too, were strangers to Virginia and to those who had lived most or all of their lives in the colony. Those at the lower ends of the social and economic scales were sorely pressed economically, while those at the upper ends of the scales were concerned with the maintenance of power in the face of so much discontent. "During the last thirty or forty years of the seventeenth century, while tobacco was enriching the king and so many others, most of the men who worked in the fields were losers and they did not much like it" (Morgan 1975:216).

The elite of Virginia not only had to maintain their positions within the colony, they were also faced with proving their acceptability in English society. The upper classes in England regarded Virginia and Virginians with disdain. The image of Virginia was that of a rough uncultured frontier, peopled with social inferiors: "Believing the colony to be the habitat of convicts, whores, poorhouse veterans, and bankrupt citizens, people at home considered it especially fitting that such base creatures chose to cultivate a base crop like tobacco" (Shammas 1979:275). Virginia's elite may have had wealth and public office, but they were still, in the eyes of England, Virginians. This opinion of Virginians seems also to have been held by some recent immigrants, as evidenced by statements made by Nathaniel Bacon, himself newly arrived, in his "Manifesto," in which he defended rebellion against the "juggling Parasites whose tottering Fortunes have bin repaired and supported at the Publique chardg" (Billings 1975:278).

The social stress that led to change at the end of the seventeenth century in Virginia was exacerbated by the world economic situation. Virginia held a small place in that global economy, but felt its effects strongly. The difficulties created by extracolonial affairs would have perhaps been more bearable had they not come in tandem with natural disasters, such as the "great gust," or hurricane, of 1667, which was preceded by a hail storm that ruined many of the crops, and by a rainstorm that supposedly lasted a biblical 40 days and 40 nights (Sainsbury n.d.:129, Ludlum 1963:15).

This was the volatile social and economic world of the late seventeenth century in Virginia—factionalism among the elite, huge gulfs dividing the wealthy and the poor with rebellion a very real possibility at any time, impotency in the face of English policy decisions, and the ever-present knowledge that those in England regarded the colonists as slightly distasteful, regardless of wealth or power. The material world created by the colonists not only reflected the social change brought by conflict, but served as a symbolic reinforcement of the new order.

The Symbolic World

Virginia's elite—those who had built the brick houses and who had initiated manufactures—needed to establish clear boundaries between themselves and the landless freemen and servants, and between themselves and England in order to maintain their status and power in Virginia. One method of communicating collective identity and creating and maintaining boundaries is through the use of material symbols (Spicer 1971; Blu 1980). Architecture and manufacturing were two of those symbols, statements in an ideological text that declared economic and social dominance over the less privileged and a measure of independence from England.

The architectural statement came in the form of more permanent and, to some, "creditable" (Davis 1963:202) housing. Certainly economics provided the means to effect this formal change, but much of the impetus was found in the conflict between Virginia's elite and both England and the Virginia underclasses in the late seventeenth century. This is precisely the same time period for which Dell Upton has demonstrated a shift toward the segregation of living quarters in Virginia architecture, signaling and fostering a growing social differentiation between master and servant (Upton 1982). The use of more permanent building methods and materials spoke to this same conflict, as well as to the conflict between the English and the elite. It communicated membership in a distinct group. The owner, through his house, asserted his economic status and his awareness of the civility required of the elite. It set him apart as one of a select group distinct from the Virginia "rabble."

The landless freemen, servants, tenants, and small planters were to see in such architecture a statement of wealth, permanence, and power in a community that equated land ownership with the ability to produce income and in which those without land were denied political power by statute and economic power through circumstance (Hening 1823:2:280; Morgan 1975:221). It was the maintenance of this order and of this division that was aided by the construction of permanent brick or English framed houses.

Another, more subtle statement was made by the shift to more permanent construction methods. Robert St. George (1983) has outlined the process, which he termed "maintenance relations." Maintenance, he said, implies "an exchange relation whose purpose is not the acquisition of property, but rather its constant reclamation" (St. George 1983:3). High-maintenance housing, such as post-constructed dwellings, required a relationship between the owner and those who would keep it in good repair. This was a social as well as an economic relationship, requiring interaction with and a social obligation to the workmen contracted to repair and maintain the house. A move toward more permanent, less maintenance-intensive materials in housing created a break in this relationship. This change, according to St. George, "often occurs at the same time that house forms change . . . from experiential and socially open to conceptually complete and closed. Both changes are symptomatic of intensive social reorganization" (1983:13). This coincidence of the change to more permanent building techniques with the change to a more closed house plan, characterized by features such as interior chimneys and symmetrical facades, was described by Upton (1982). Not only did the brick fabric of the house reinforce the differences between the elite and the rest of Virginia, but it effectively diminished the social exchange relationship between the groups and created a more solid wall between them.

If architecture helped create social boundaries between Virginians, the development of manufacturing made a statement of independence from England. Although there is some indication that the form of the artifacts produced by colonial manufacturing efforts differed from their English counterparts, there is not yet enough evidence to build a strong case for formal change as a material statement. In the production process, however, the colonists were able to assert some independence from England and its economic and legal hold on the colony.

Colonial manufacturing was clearly a consistent area of conflict between England and Virginia. Moreover, Virginia continued to promote manufactures despite the disapproval of England, and despite English legislation opposing it. The denial and veiled threats that surrounded Virginia's discussions of colonial manufacturing imply that manufacturing was being used not only to supply the immediate needs of the colonists and to boost the economic holdings of the elite, but also as a social strategy to manipulate the English. It was used to maintain a social boundary between England and Virginia, and to confirm the Virginia identity as politically and economically distinct from England. The desire for a degree of autonomy from England was tempered by a need for both social approval and acceptance (evidenced by the concern for creditable housing) and a lingering economic reliance; this required that some manufacturing efforts—specifically those that competed with England's craftsmen—be covert.

Again, the concept of maintenance relations is applicable, but in slightly altered form. The ability to manufacture goods was a statement of independence and of permanence very much akin to the replacement of a high-maintenance thatched roof with tin, and was an indication of the colony's ability to function without the dominance of the mother country. Virginia did not replace the roof, however. The manipulation that took place through manufacturing was merely a threat to replace the roof. Manufacturing became the statement of intent, rather than the act of independence. As Upton (1986:23) has stated:

> The study of intention becomes the ultimate one in vernacular architecture studies, because it is the study of people acting. It shows us people in charge of their own lives, people engaged with their surroundings in a critical way, people making their own histories in the face of authorities trying to make it for them.

With this notion of the importance of intent in mind, consider now the struggling planter at 44PG92, because through him can be seen the intimate reality of these large-scale conflicts. He was a middling planter, caught between the wealthy elite, on the one hand, who had achieved power and sought to maintain it, and the tenants and freemen, on the other, who, in his perception, threatened to overrun him. Standing on uncertain economic and social ground, he used material statement to try to consolidate his position through more permanent architecture and the instigation of manufactures. Whether or not he was successful in his attempts has little bearing on the intent of the statements he made. He had declared his identity and, for a brief time, defined his place in the world.

ACKNOWLEDGMENTS

The generous support of the Flowerdew Hundred Foundation and of David Harrison III is gratefully acknowledged. Thanks are also due to Dr. J. F. Deetz for his direction and support, to the Lowie Museum of Anthropology, Margot Winer, Taft Kiser, Charles Hodges, and numerous colleagues who offered help and advice. This project would not have been possible without the contribution of time and effort by the many students and volunteers whose work was invaluable to the project.

NOTES

1. The dating of the cellar is based on excavated material. On the clay floor of the cellar we found a wine bottle with a seal, identified as coming from the Mitre Inn in London and bearing William Proctor's initials. This bottle was dated at ca. 1655 by Ivor Noel Hume (1988 personal communication). The floor was sealed by sediment associated with the flooding of the cellar, which was rapid enough to preserve the wood lining and the wooden partition wall of the cellar. This flooding episode was severe enough to deposit sand and clay to a depth of a foot or more and is believed to have occurred at the time of the 1667 hurricane. The structure above appears to have been severely damaged and later dismantled. The deposits subsequent to the flooding all date to 1670–1685. See Markell (1990a, 1990b).

2. The only archaeological comparison has been to a site at Thetford in East Anglia, dating to the eleventh century. One of the structures at this Saxon site (building J) was underlain by a cellar measuring approximately 15 x 20 feet, which contained postholes of a similar configuration to those at 44PG92. The posts of building J were supports for the structure above, the floor of which was supported by struts that extended at a 45-degree angle from the posts below. This cellar did not have a builder's trench, and there was no evidence mentioned of the structure of the walls or lining of the cellar. Although grubenhausen were present at this site, there was a distinction made between these and this structure (Davison 1967:192).

3. The lime in the fill was in the form of fossilized coral, oyster shell, and limestone. Lime is used as a flux in the indirect or blast furnace method of smelting, but it is not necessary for the bloomery method, although it is sometimes used. It was in the debris from the supposed bloomery found at Jamestown, Virginia (Cotter and Hudson 1957), as well as the blast furnaces at Saugus, Massachusetts (Hartley 1957), and at Falling Creek in Virginia (MacCord 1964).

REFERENCES CITED

Agricola, Georgius
1556 *De Re Metallica*. Translated and annotated by Henry Clark Hoover and Lou Henry Hoover, 1950. Dover Publications, New York.

Bedell, John C., and Nicholas M. Luccketti
1988 *An Archaeological Assessment of Arlington, Northampton County, Virginia*. James River Institute for Archaeology, Inc., Jamestown, Va.

Billings, Warren M. (editor)
1975 *The Old Dominion in the Seventeenth Century: A Documentary History of Virginia, 1606–1689*. The Institute of Early American History and Culture. University of North Carolina Press, Chapel Hill.

Blu, Karen
1980 *The Lumbee Problem: the Making of an American Indian People*. Cambridge University Press, Cambridge.
British, Colonial Office
1677 *Inventories of the Men Tried and Executed for Treason during the Rebellion*. C.O. 5/1371, part 2. British Public Record Office, London.
Bruce, Philip Alexander
1895 *Economic History of Virginia in the Seventeenth Century: An Inquiry into the Material Condition of the People*. Vols. 1 and 2. Peter Smith, New York.
Carson, Cary, Norman Barka, William Kelso, Gary Wheeler Stone, and Dell Upton
1981 Impermanent Architecture in the Southern American Colonies. *Winterthur Portfolio* 16:135–196.
Caywood, Louis R.
1955 *Excavations at Greenspring Plantation*. Colonial National Historical Park, Yorktown.
Cotter, John L.
1958 *Archaeological Investigations at Jamestown*. Archaeological Research Series No. 4. National Park Service, Washington.
Cotter, John L., and J. Paul Hudson
1957 *New Discoveries at Jamestown, Site of the First Successful English Settlement in America*. U.S. Government Printing Office, Washington, D.C.
Davis, Richard Beale (editor)
1963 *William Fitzhugh and His Chesapeake World, 1676–1701: The Fitzhugh Letters and Documents*. University of North Carolina Press, Chapel Hill.
Davison, Brian K.
1967 The Late Saxon Town of Thetford: An Interim Report on the 1964–6 Excavations. *Medieval Archaeology* 11:189–207.
Egloff, Keith
1980 *Colonial Plantation Hoes of Tidewater Virginia*. Research Report Series No. 1. Virginia Research Center for Archaeology, Williamsburg, Va.
Emerson, Matthew Charles
1988 *Decorated Clay Tobacco Pipes from the Chesapeake*. Ph.D. Dissertation, University of California, Berkeley.
Evans, Cerinda W.
1957 *Some Notes on Shipbuilding and Shipping in Colonial Virginia*. The Mariner's Museum, Newport News, Va.
Harrington, J. C.
1950 Seventeenth Century Brickmaking and Tilemaking at Jamestown, Virginia. *Virginia Magazine of History and Biography* 58(1):16–39.
Hartley, E. N.
1957 *Ironworks on the Saugus*. University of Oklahoma Press, Norman.
Harvey, David
1986 A Progress Report on the Reconstruction of the American Bloomery Process. Paper prepared for the Colonial Williamsburg Foundation, Williamsburg, Va.
Heite, Edward F.
1983 The Pioneer Phase of the Chesapeake Iron Industry: Naturalization of a Technology. *Quarterly Bulletin of the Archaeological Society of Virginia* 38(3):133–181.
Hening, William Waller
1823 *Virginia Statutes at Large*. Vols. 1–3. Facsimile edition, 1969. University Press of Virginia, Charlottesville.
Hodder, Ian
1986 *Reading the Past: Current Approaches to Interpretation in Archaeology*. Cambridge University Press, Cambridge.
Kelso, William
1984 *Kingsmill Plantation 1619–1800*. Academic Press, New York.
Kelso, William M., and Edward A. Chappell
1974 Excavation of a Seventeenth Century Pottery Kiln at Glebe Harbor, Westmoreland County, Virginia. *Historical Archaeology* 30(1):53–62.
Killick, D. J., and R. B. Gordon
1988 The Mechanism of Iron Production in the Bloomery Furnace. In *Proceedings of the 26th International Archaeometry Symposium*. Toronto, May 1988.
Langston, Anthony
1657 Anthony Langston on Towns, and Corporations; and on the Manufacture of Iron. Reprinted in *William and Mary Quarterly*, 2d ser., 1921.
Ludlum, David M.
1963 *Early American Hurricanes, 1492–1870*. American Meteorological Society, Boston.
MacCord, Howard A., Sr.
1964 Exploratory Excavations at the First Ironworks in America (44 CF 7). *Quarterly Bulletin of the Archaeological Society of Virginia*, 19(2):2–13.
Markell, Ann B.
1990a 44 PG 92—Flowerdew Hundred: Site Report. Manuscript on file at Flowerdew Hundred Foundation.
1990b *Manufacturing Identity: Material Culture and Social Change in 17th Century Virginia*. Ph.D dissertation, University of California, Berkeley.
McDonald
n.d. *Transcripts*. Vols. 5–7. Virginia State Library, Richmond.
Miller, Daniel, and Christopher Tilley
1984 Ideology, Power and Prehistory: An Introduction. In *Ideology, Power and Prehistory*, edited by Daniel Miller and Christopher Tilley, pp. 1–12. Cambridge University Press, Cambridge.
Mitchell, Vivienne
1983 The History of Nominy Plantation with Emphasis on

the Clay Tobacco Pipes. In *Historic Clay Tobacco Pipe Studies*, edited by Byron Sudbury, pp. 1–38.

Morgan, Edmund

1975 *American Slavery, American Freedom: The Ordeal of Colonial Virginia*. W. W. Norton, New York.

Mulholland, James A.

1981 *A History of Metals in Colonial America*. University of Alabama Press, University.

Noel Hume, Ivor

1963 A Late Seventeenth-Century Pottery Kiln Near Jamestown. *Antiques* 83(5):550–552.

Outlaw, Alain

1977 *An Interim Report: Governor's Land Archaeological District Excavations: The 1976 Season*. Virginia Research Center for Archaeology, Richmond.

Palmer, Charles

n.d. *Calendar of Virginia State Papers*. Vol. 1. Virginia State Library, Richmond.

Sainsbury, Noel E.

n.d. *Abstracts of Records in British Public Record Office Relating to Virginia in the 17th Century*. Calendar of State Papers, Colonial (1574–1660), (1661–1668). Original at Virginia State Library, Richmond.

Schubert, H. R.

1957 *History of the British Iron and Steel Industry*. Routledge and Kegan Paul, London.

Shammas, Carole

1979 English-Born and Creole Elites in Turn-of-the-Century Virginia. In *The Chesapeake in the 17th Century*, edited by Thad W. Tate and David L. Ammerman, pp. 274–296. University of North Carolina Press, Chapel Hill.

Sperber, Dan

1974 *Rethinking Symbolism*. Cambridge University Press, Cambridge.

Spicer, Edward

1971 Persistent Cultural Systems. *Science* 174(4011):795–800.

St. George, Robert Blair

1983 Maintenance Relations and the Erotics of Property in Historical Thought. Paper presented at the American Historical Association meetings, 1983.

Swank, James M.

1892 *History of the Manufacture of Iron in All Ages, and Particularly in the United States from Colonial Times to 1891*. . . . Burt Franklin, New York.

Teebutt, C. F.

1966 13th Century Buildings and Metal Workings at St. Neots, Huntingdonshire. *Journal of the Society for Medieval Archaeology* 10:158–160.

Upton, Dell

1982 The Origins of Chesapeake Architecture. In *Three Centuries of Maryland Architecture: A Selection of Presentations Made at the 11th Annual Conference of the Maryland Historical Trust*. Maryland Historical Trust, Annapolis, Md.

1986 Introduction. In *Common Places: Readings in American Vernacular Architecture*, edited by Dell Upton and John Vlach, pp. xiii–xxiv. University of Georgia Press, Athens.

1988 New Views of the Virginia Landscape. *Virginia Magazine of History and Biography* 96(4):403–470.

1989 Form and User: Style, Mode, Fashion and the Artifact. Unpublished manuscript in possession of the author.

Weber, Max

1961 The Ethnic Group. In *Theories of Society*, edited by Talcott Parsons and Edward Shils, et al., pp. 305–9. The Free Press, New York.

Weisiger, Benjamin B.

1980 *Charles City County, Virginia Court Orders 1687–1695*. Benjamin B. Weisiger, Richmond.

V
CHAPTER

The Country's House Site
An Archaeological Study of a Seventeenth-Century Domestic Landscape

HENRY M. MILLER

ONE OF THE MOST dramatic and dynamic periods of America's past is the seventeenth century. This was the era in which a new and distinctive British colonial culture took root on the east coast of North America. One of the key areas in this development was the Chesapeake, but, surprisingly, not a great deal is known about the colonial society in this region. In the early 1970s, historians and archaeologists began a concerted effort to understand this largely forgotten time and place through a sustained program of research. Historians traced the demographic, economic and social events that shaped the new society. Archaeologists excavated a variety of sites and learned much about the lives of the early settlers.

One of the subjects largely overlooked in this effort, however, is the nature of the vanished landscapes that once surrounded the colonist's homes. This subject is important to consider because a community's network of buildings, fences, yards, pens, and gardens plays a central role in transforming a natural setting into a human landscape. This built environment is culturally determined, and it provides a rich source of information about a society. A vanished landscape can not only tell us something about the physical setting of past life, but "it unconsciously reveals so much about the ideas of the men and women who devised it" (Jackson 1980:115). The built environment can also be seen as a cultural means of ordering human behavior in that it designates specific locations for specific activities (Rapoport 1980, 1982). The cultural setting often contains certain codes or signals that serve to cue humans about the appropriate behavior in that location. Thus, any landscape contains a mix of functional, social, and symbolic attributes. This chapter explores the cultural landscape associated with one of the first prominent buildings erected in colonial Maryland.

THE COUNTRY'S HOUSE

The site investigated here is the Country's House (18-ST 1-13), located in St. Mary's City, Maryland. It is one of the most significant archaeological sites in the state, having served as the residence of the colony's first governor and Maryland's first state house. The Country's House was also the nucleus around which Maryland's earliest city and also its seventeenth-century capital developed.

Construction of this building began shortly after Maryland's founding in 1634, and it was occupied by the colony's first governor, Leonard Calvert. He acquired the surrounding 100 acres of land and rapidly developed it as a working tobacco plantation (Stone 1982: 21). Little is known about the size or appearance of the house during this early period, although it was described as a "large fram'd house" in Calvert's probate inventory, written shortly after his death in 1647. Afterward, Governor William Stone occupied the building, using it as his St. Mary's City residence until his death in 1659 (Carr 1971).

In 1662 the provincial government purchased the building for use as the first official statehouse of Maryland. Because the colony had acquired the building for public use, it was named the "Country's House." The General Assembly and courts met for only short periods each year, however, and to avoid maintenance costs, the legislature leased the structure to innkeepers, who were responsible for its upkeep. Thus, by the early 1660s, the function of the site underwent an important change, from a private plantation to a public inn and government meeting place.

For the last third of the seventeenth century, the Country's House was the largest public inn or "ordinary" in Maryland, and a series of innkeepers leased the property. Among them were William Smith (1665–1668), Daniel Jennifer (1668–ca. 1670), Richard Moy (ca. 1672–1675) and John and Elizabeth Baker (1678–1693). Throughout this period, the Country's House was a popular establishment, and it attracted a large portion of the hotel business in St. Mary's City. Following the construction of a new brick state house in 1676, most governmental functions were transferred from the Country's House, although committees still occasionally met there.

The final historical reference to this building is a 1694/95 petition for a 21-year lease of the property for use as an ordinary. At that time, the structure was in poor condition: "one side of the said house and the whole covering is now quite decayed and unless speedily repaired will fall to the Ground" (Md. Archives 19:120). The petitioner promised to repair the structure if given the lease, but archaeological evidence suggests that the renovations were not made. Since the government moved from St. Mary's City to Annapolis in 1695, no innkeeper was likely to expect sufficient business to justify making expensive repairs. As a result, the Country's House collapsed or was demolished in the early eighteenth century. The surrounding lands were soon converted to tobacco and wheat fields, and they remained in agricultural use until 1841. In that year, Dr. John Brome built a large mansion that still survives on the site (but is to be moved in June 1993).

Interest in finding the Country's House dates to the 1930s, when an architectural historian, H. Chandlee Forman, located the foundation (1938). Archaeologists with Historic St. Mary's City relocated the site in 1981 with the support of a National Endowment for the Humanities grant, and three seasons of exploration followed (Miller 1983, 1986). The Country's House is an especially suitable site for investigating the early colonial landscape. It was inhabited for virtually the entire period of seventeenth-century settlement in Maryland (ca. 1635–1700), and the basic architectural form of the main house remained essentially unchanged for nearly six decades. This long occupation, the architectural stability, and the intensive archaeological excavations provide an unusual opportunity to study the changing vernacular landscape in the early Chesapeake. Among the questions this chapter raises about that landscape are the following: How did the colonists shape the new land into a domestic setting? What factors were responsible for the organization, form, and use of space during the period? And did the landscape at this site change over time, and if so, how and why?

ELEMENTS OF THE VERNACULAR LANDSCAPE

The seventeenth-century Chesapeake setting has completely vanished beneath generations of eighteenth-, nineteenth-, and twentieth-century landscapes. Some historical documents provide a few clues, but detailed information about this subject can only come from archaeological study. The limited historical evidence and few archaeological studies that have been completed on the early colonial landscape (Keeler 1978; Neiman 1980; Pogue 1988; King 1990) suggest that there was little effort at formal design during the period, apart from that evident in a formal garden found at Bacon's Castle in Virginia, which may date to the late 1680s (Luccketti 1990). Instead, a vernacular landscape dominated the region. That is to say, the landscape surrounding most colonial homes was a work environment shaped by the needs of a functioning household, but it was also deeply influenced by tradition, the social setting, and the cultural perspectives of the residents.

Study of a vanished cultural setting must include all of the prominent elements that made up that landscape. Houses and other structures were the first and probably main element because they were the center of most human activity, and thus domestic landscapes formed around them. Second in importance were the various fences and other barriers (ditches, hedges) that acted to physically structure open spaces and organize them into functional areas. Third were activity areas. These special-purpose spaces ranged from gardens, orchards, and chicken yards to work areas and garbage dumps. Fortunately, many activities leave behind evidence (artifacts, features, soil chemicals, and the like) that suggests how certain spaces both within and outside structures were used. Note, however, that many types of human behavior do not leave behind clear physical evidence and are therefore invisible for the purposes of archaeological study. Only documentary information and the use of analogy can occasionally be used to infer that some of these "invisible" activities occurred at a site. Fourth, doors, gates, pathways and roads make up the access routes that linked all the above elements together. Pathways and roads are often difficult to find archaeologically but can be inferred by studying doorway and gate locations, the distribution of refuse and soil chemicals, and even aerial photographs (Keeler 1977). Since the principal building at a site was usually the focal point of the domestic landscape, the Country's House itself will be considered first.

Architecture of the Country's House

The Country's House was one of the largest and most complex buildings in seventeenth-century Maryland. Excavations have revealed the remains of a brick and stone foundation 40 feet wide and 67.5 feet long. The surviving brickwork indicates that the interior was divided into two rows, or banks, of rooms separated by a central passage. These foundations imply that it was a double gable (pile) structure, that is, one covered with two parallel A-frame roofs (Stone 1982:378). Several generations of H-shaped brick chimney bases are also present, signifying room divisions. Archaeologists detected two large cellars from different periods under the western end of the structure.

Given the complexity of this site and limited funding for analysis, the evolution of this structure is not yet fully understood. However, by meshing the available archaeological data with the documentary evidence, it is possible to decipher the principal stages of its architectural development. Stone (1982) has already made an important contribution to this endeavor in his thorough study of the historical data pertaining to this building and its architectural changes.

Archaeological evidence indicates that the original building was smaller than previously thought. An early cellar with fired clay walls found under the southwest end of the building and some early artifacts found under the northern part imply that the south half was the original section. It was apparently a hall-and-parlor house measuring 18 by 50 feet, with a central H-shaped fireplace (figure 5.1A). A similar architectural plan was used at the nearby St. John's house site, built in 1638 (Stone 1974, 1982). Doorways in the structure are inferred from various architectural clues and artifact distributions. Remnants of sandstone and the lack of structural postholes probably indicate that the original building was constructed on a foundation of dry laid stones.

Even if it began as a modest farmhouse, this structure was enlarged at an early date. The early artifacts consistently cluster around the brickwork that replaced the earlier stone foundation. This implies that the house was expanded to its full 40-by-67-foot size during the first decades of settlement (figure 5.1B). Support for this assumption comes from the discovery of a 1645 fort, known as Pope's Fort, that encircled Calvert's home. The ditches of this fortification are roughly the same distance from the north and south walls of the house. In addition, a large, well-defined bastion on the east end of the fort was clearly built with reference to the house (Miller 1986:51). This is strong archaeological evidence that the Country's House reached its maximum size before 1645. Note that the assembly passed an act in 1639 ordering that a "Townhouse" be built for government use (Md. Archives 1:75–76). There is no further reference to this "Townhouse", but the assembly did begin meeting at Calvert's home in 1642. Stone (1982: 381) suggests that the colonists enlarged the governor's house in accordance with this act. If correct, the Country's House reached its full size by 1641. Historical records provide few clues as to the construction or layout of the building during the early years. Calvert's probate inventory merely refers to a large framed house, probably with walls and roofs of riven clapboard.

The earliest detailed information regarding the number, names, and functions of the rooms in the building comes from the inventory of William Smith, taken in early 1668 (Test. Proc. 3:127–159). It is a room-by-room listing and mentions a "Lodging Chamber" that contained a "Parlor" and a "Bed chamber," a "Hall," a

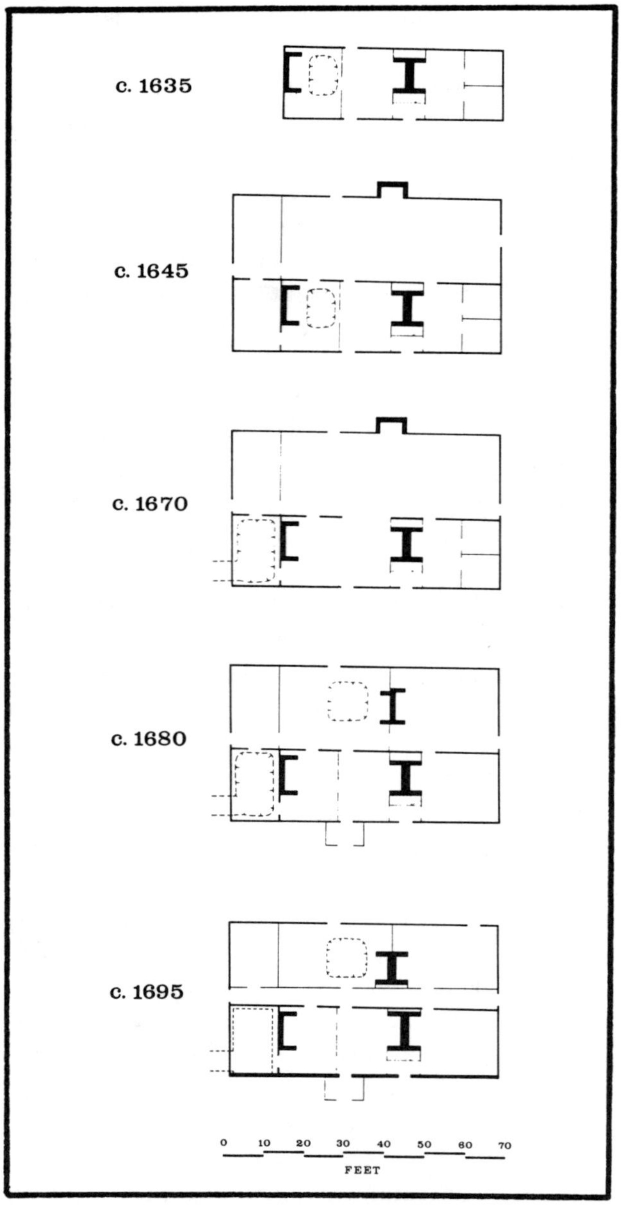

FIGURE 5.1. *The architectural evolution of the Country's House.*

"Kitchen" and adjoining store room and wine and meat cellars, and rooms over the lodging chamber and hall. Also mentioned is "the Great Roome called St. Marys," which had one fireplace. The architectural plan revealed by archaeology suggests that this "Great Roome" occupied most of the rear or northern half of the building (figure 5.1C). Its size was indeed great, measuring 22 feet by 45–50 feet. In other words, this single room was twice as large as the homes of most colonists. Such a large space was probably necessary to accommodate the assembly and courts that regularly met there. According to the inventory, there was a smaller chamber, located directly adjacent to the St. Mary's room, which served as a "cellar" or storage room. The other rooms mentioned in the inventory were apparently located in the southern half of the building, with the parlor and bedchamber on the east end and the hall in the center. The presence of cellars under the west end of the house suggests that the kitchen and pantry were located there.

Nearly 20 years later, in 1687, appraisers took a second room-by-room inventory of the building when innkeeper John Baker died. Baker and his wife are known to have spent thousands of pounds of tobacco bricking up the walls and chimneys of the Country's House. This work along with other renovations, probably conducted around 1680, left an excellent archaeological record of the building's outline and internal divisions in the surviving brickwork. A long passageway ran down the central axis of the building (figure 5.1D) and was connected to external doors at each end. Baker apparently created this passageway by partitioning off a section of the old St. Mary's room. He also added a substantial double chimney, thus splitting the St. Mary's room in half. Excavators found fragments of tin-glazed tiles in this area, indicating that these new fireplaces were also attractively decorated. Uncovered at the southwest corner of the building was an external bulkhead entrance leading to a brick-lined cellar. It and a new porch on the front of the building were probably added before 1680. Artifacts from the 1680s and 1690s suggest that a new doorway was cut into the back side of the building near its northeast corner during the final years of site occupation. Figure 5.2 presents a conjectural drawing of the Country's House as it may have appeared when the Bakers ran it as an inn.

Archaeology has thus revealed the basic nature of this important structure, which evolved from a modest English-style farmhouse into the largest building in early Maryland. It served as the home of the governors and was a frequent meeting place for the assembly. After becoming the first state house in 1662, it served both as a government structure and a public inn. When a brick state house was constructed in 1676, the Country's House was converted to a full-time public inn, and continued to serve as such for the rest of the seventeenth century. Despite

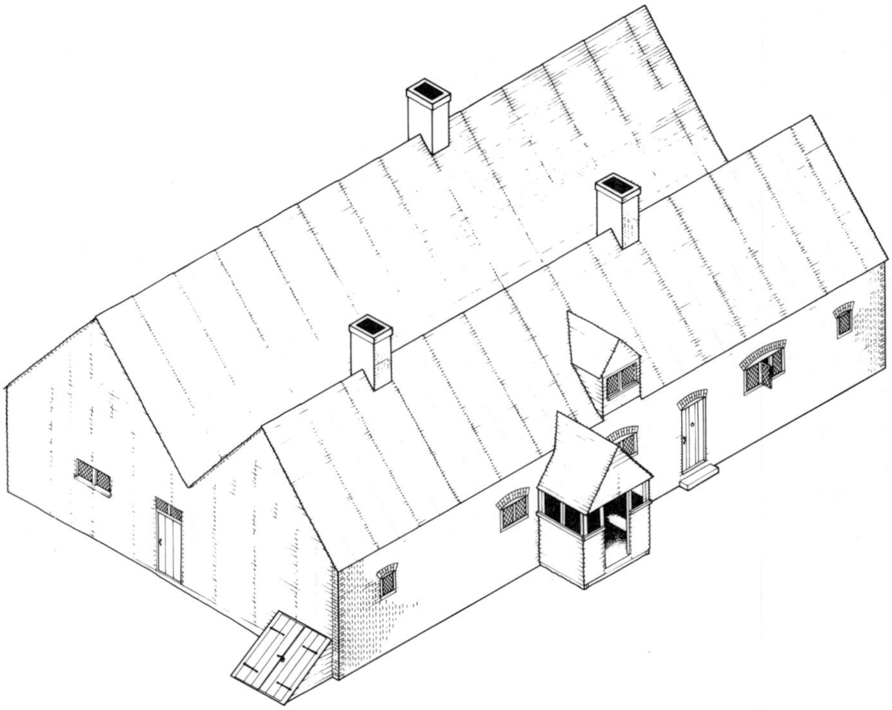

FIGURE 5.2. *Conjectural drawing of the Country's House, 1685.*

these pronounced shifts in site function, the basic layout of the structure was not significantly altered after its enlargement in the 1640s.

The Landscape of the Country's House

Numerous outbuildings were associated with the Country's House during its existence, including stables, tobacco houses, various work buildings, and possibly servants' quarters. All of these were apparently constructed of wood and their archaeological visibility is low. However, in a broad sampling of the yard areas around the main house, excavators detected traces of a number of these structures. These buildings were identified on the basis of structural features and artifacts. Structural postholes are an obvious indication, but scatters of nails, ceramics, or tobacco pipes far from the main house also signify some type of activity. When found together, these were used to infer the locations of outbuildings.

In addition, evidence of fences was sought to determine, as already mentioned, how the colonists organized space and laid out their yards into functional areas, and to identify former property boundaries. In a place like St. Mary's City, fence remains often are the key evidence for linking the historical and archaeological records together. Perhaps the most commonly encountered evidence of fencing on seventeenth-century Chesapeake sites are trenches. There are traces of three types of ditch or trench-set fencing. Some were stout palisades that consisted of whole or quartered logs placed upright in a deep, narrow trench. Some consisted of palings made with thin, riven boards or pales placed vertically in a more shallow trench and nailed to a horizontal timber. Usually, these were reinforced with vertical posts placed at intervals of 10 feet or more. The third type, the wattle fence, consisted of small stakes placed at close intervals in a shallow trench. Branches, vines, and other materials were then woven between the stakes to mesh them together into a rugged fence. Because these trenches were shallow, any surviving evidence for wattle fences can be easily destroyed by later agricultural activities.

Another type of fencing that archaeologists can identify, but that is not constructed in a trench, is the post-and-rail fence. The widely spaced postholes of these fences are more difficult to detect, although they can be found by studying various posthole alignments. Yet another type of colonial fencing is the stake-and-rider, or worm fence, which was made of rails horizontally stacked in a zigzag pattern. These fences were extremely common in the Chesapeake region but because they were built on the ground surface, little evidence of them survives where subsequent plowing or other soil disturbance has occurred.

Excavations around the Country's House yielded evidence of paling, palisade, and post-and-rail fences. The relative date of the fences was ascertained from a variety of information, including the physical nature of the remains, their artifact contents, the stratigraphic relationship of fencelines to other features, and their association with the architectural remains. The process of yardscape development is dynamic and usually continuous. Consequently, it is virtually impossible to trace precisely every step in this process at a site by using archaeological data. Nevertheless, the many changes in the yards at this site appear to fall into five general phases (figure 5.3).

1630s–1640s Yards

Evidence for fencing during the first years of settlement is sparse and the excavators found few traces of the earliest outbuildings, probably because of the construction of Pope's Fort in 1645. This military activity had a tremendous impact on the yards surrounding the house and certainly destroyed most of the early fences and nearby structures. In addition, the first settlers may have used shallow wattle fences, which leave only slight traces in the soil.

The earliest known fence extends from the northeast corner of the house. It runs at a diagonal to the house orientation (figure 5.3A) and can be dated to before 1645 because it was cut by the palisade line of Pope's Fort but was erected after the enlargement of the Country's House to its full size around 1641. Another fence placed at an angle to the house foundation was found to the west of it. Also, a possible stock pen complex of early date found to the south of the Calvert home was built at a 45-degree angle to the cardinal directions. All the later fences found at the site run north-south or east-west, as do the walls of the Country's House. Why were these early fences oriented differently? One possible clue is that the early fence alignments match the topography of the site. The river bank and a ravine in this area are roughly oriented northwest-southeast, which suggests that the earliest colonial landscape conformed to the natural setting.

1650s Yards

Excavations produced more evidence regarding the yards during the late 1640s and 1650s. Military activities forced the next occupant of the house, Governor Stone, to start over in creating a yardscape around the structure. At least two outbuildings were constructed during this period (figure 5.3B). One was located about 85 feet north of the Country's House, while the other was 40 feet to the

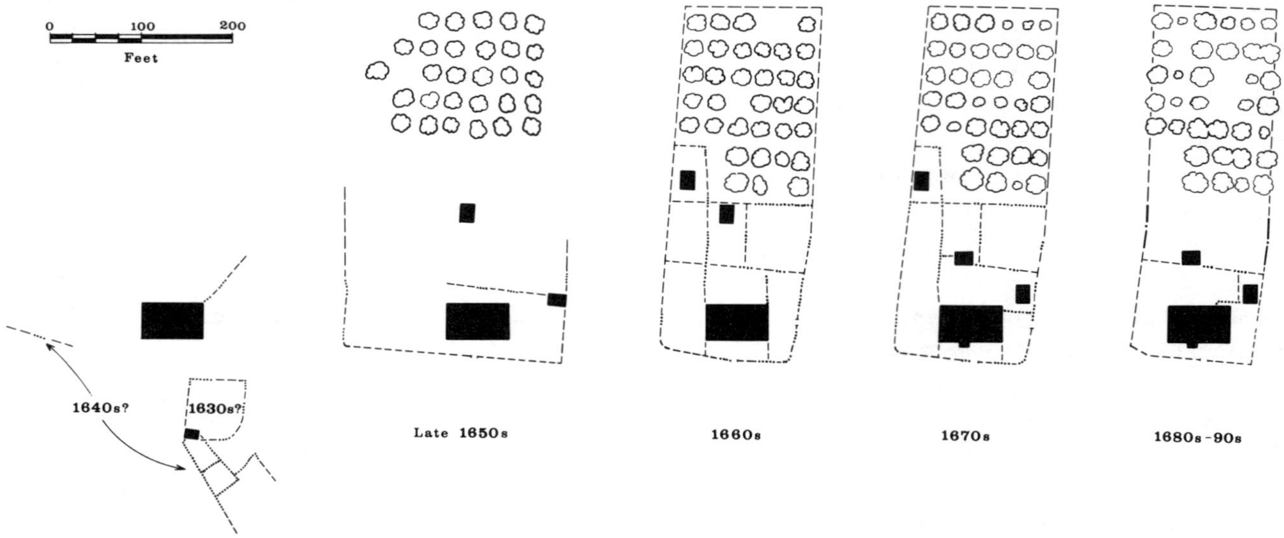

FIGURE 5.3. *Phases in the development of the Country's House yards.*

east. Two fences were also identified from this phase. The first is represented by a ditch running north-south that is located 110 feet to the west of the Country's House. The second was a north-south ditch uncovered some 60 feet to the east of the Country's House. These fences probably define the east and west boundaries of the Country's House yard during the 1650s. Available evidence suggests the homelot was at least 250 feet wide during this period, when the Country's House was the only major structure in the vicinity. No evidence was found regarding the location of the northern boundary during this phase, but the southern boundary is probably defined by one of several generations of paling fences uncovered just south of the house. The yards were apparently quite extensive during this time, with little restraint exercised on the use of space.

1660s Yards

In the 1660s significant development began in St. Mary's City: a street system was established and construction started on other lots in the center of town. The first formal efforts to limit the size of the Country's House lot were made at this time. Because the house had changed from a governor's residence and working plantation to a leased ordinary, the land associated with this structure had to be clearly defined. Thus, it is not surprising that the oldest document defining the yard boundaries of the Country's House dates from 1666, when William Smith received a lease for the property. A memorandum written on this document describes paling fences surrounding the "ordinary" and notes the presence of an adjacent "highway" (Prov. Ct. Proc. 10, f. 351–352). One fence extended from the house westward to the highway, later known as Aldermanbury Street, then turned north and ran till it reached another paling fence near an "office." The property line then ran eastward until it met another fence coming from the north side of the ordinary. Since the approximate location of the office is known, the information in this lease can be used to deduce that the lot was rectangular in shape and 350 to 400 feet long. Its width is uncertain, but the southwest corner was no more than 60 or 70 feet west of the ordinary, since there was enough space between the fence and the ravine edge for a "Highway."

Another part of the lease describes additional yardscape elements. It states that the lease is for "the Mansion or dwelling house of the said William Smith with the orchard Garden and all outhouses in the said Orchard and Garden" (Prov. Ct. Proc. 10, f. 351–352). This statement suggests that most of the outbuildings stood in the orchard and garden, and were not immediately adjacent to the house.

Archaeological evidence for fences is much stronger in this phase (figure 5.3C). Excavators discovered several generations of paling ditches approximately 20 feet to the south and 30 feet to the east of the structure. Another paling fence section was detected about 50 feet to the west of the Country's House. Excavation of a portion of this trench yielded fragments of ceramics made by Morgan Jones, a local potter who came to Maryland in 1661. These fences continued for at least 100 feet north of the house, and it seems clear that they mark the east, south, and west boundaries of the property. They enclosed an area approximately 150 feet wide and several hundred feet long.

There are indications of two small outbuildings within this space, both located to the north of the Country's House. The one nearest the house was probably constructed in the 1650s and continued in use during the 1660s. Some domestic artifacts are associated with it, including Morgan Jones pottery. The second building was to the northwest, but few artifacts other than wrought nails were found around it. This structure may have served as a stable; traces of fence ditches indicate that it was within an enclosure. Fencing data show that the Country's House lot was divided into small yards, perhaps for special functions. One major yard division, located approximately 40 feet north of the main building, existed for a considerable time period, as indicated by several generations of fences. These fences form the southern boundary of a zone measuring 70 by 150 feet with three subdivisions. There are few features or artifacts within this space, except in the central section, where a small building stood. Available data suggest that this zone was the garden noted in William Smith's 1666 lease. The northern boundary of this garden area lies near the center of the Country's House lot. Excavations further to the north recovered few artifacts and found no evidence that the northern half of the property was subdivided by fences, except around the possible stable noted earlier. Archaeologists did uncover a large number of amorphous features in this area that appear to be tree root molds. This finding suggests that the orchard, also noted in the 1666 lease, covered much of the northern half of the lot.

Fences also extended north and south from the corners of the main house, thereby dividing the space around this building into four yards. On the south or front side, these apparently created a forecourt at the main entrance to the structure. Thus, the above information indicates that the spaces surrounding the Country's House became more restricted, subdivided, and perhaps more functionally specific in the 1660s.

1670s Yards

During the 1670s the layout of the Country's House lot remained similar to that of the previous decade (figure 5.3D). Several generations of paling fences in the same general locations certainly imply that the basic yard arrangement persisted for a considerable time. Some changes are evident, however, including the construction of new outbuildings. A new structure was erected in the central section of the garden area, about 50 feet from the main house. Another building was apparently built near the northeast corner of the main house. A new paling fence extended from the same corner and ran to the east.

1680s–1690s Yards

John Baker and his wife Elizabeth dominated the final decades of occupation at the Country's House. They leased the property between 1678 and 1694 and made a number of alterations to the structure and its surrounding yards. Of particular relevance here is John Baker's 1678 lease for the property (Pat. Lib.20, f. 381). This document provides the only precise historical description of the size of the lot. A new survey was made at this time and, unlike the 1666 document, which exclusively used cultural landmarks to demarcate boundaries, the 1678 surveyor defined the property lines with compass bearings and measured distances while also noting relevant cultural features. This survey defines a 1.25-acre tract measuring 138 feet by 396 feet (figure 5.3E). No paling fences are noted in the document. A likely reason is that most of the trench-set fences were being replaced by post-and-rail fencing at this time. Many postholes were detected, and a number of these cut through earlier paling ditches. It is significant that the distance between several lines of postholes found on the eastern and western sides of the house is about 140 feet, which is very close to the 138-foot width specified in the lease. At the nearby St. John's site (Keeler 1978), and at Smith's Townland (Miller 1986), trench-set fences were also being replaced by post-and-rail fencing during this same period. This shift in fencing types was apparently a general trend throughout the region during the late seventeenth and early eighteenth centuries.

The tripartite division of the garden area seems to have ended during the 1680s because someone dug several large borrow pits near the center of it, cutting through the paling ditches that had previously defined the garden. Artifacts in these pits date to the 1680–1690 period. The pits contained large quantities of architectural debris, probably deriving from the Baker's remodeling of the Country's House.

Both outbuildings near the main house continued in use, but there is no evidence that the stock pen and stable survived. Another stable must have existed on the property because innkeepers were required by law to have them, but it has not yet been found. Some change is apparent in the spatial arrangement around the small outbuilding at the northeast corner of the Country's House. Specifically, a post-and-rail fence was constructed to separate it from the rear work yard. At the same time, a paling fence was built along the back or north side of the Country's House. This fence was associated with the cutting of a new door into the rear wall of the main house and created a 20-foot-long corridor along the backside of the house. It probably kept customers out of the backyard and directed them toward the adjacent street.

The above information indicates that the Country's House lot became slightly narrower during the last decades of the seventeenth century, and the palings previously used at the site gave way to post-and-rail fences. Although there is some suggestion that the yards became less subdivided during this period, this change is more likely related to the greater use of post-and-rail fences, which are difficult to detect without excavating broad areas.

To summarize, the landscape of the site underwent diverse changes over the seventeenth-century. Initial archaeological study has identified at least five phases in yard development, but a number of other changes no doubt occurred, although they have not yet been recognized owing to limitations in the data. Despite these numerous alterations, three distinct yardscapes are evident at the Country's House over this period. The earliest one occurred during the first decade of settlement, when the yard arrangements apparently followed the natural landscape. A second yardscape was created in the late 1640s or early 1650s, when the fences became oriented with the standing architecture. The spatial structure during this period was apparently loose and quite extensive, with large yards used for various plantation activities. The final landscape, beginning in the 1660s, was a well-defined, rectangular lot that was more spatially complex. Over time, this rectangular lot became smaller, probably because the structure changed from a private plantation to a leased property in the center of an expanding community.

Building Functions and Artifact Distributions

Documentary evidence and architectural data can be combined to create a tentative model of how the various parts of the Country's House were used. First, the presence of several generations of cellars suggests that the kitchen was on the west end of the house. A hall apparently occupied the central front section, and the east front section served as a parlor. The east room on the rear was initially the meeting place for the assembly, but was later subdivided into rooms for patrons of the inn. The west rear of the house contained several small rooms initially used for lodging or socializing but later incorporated into the kitchen. Thus, each section of the main house apparently served discrete purposes (figure 5.4) for which there should be archaeological evidence. No relevant documentary evidence survives for the outbuildings and yards, but the associated artifacts can reveal their roles in the Country's House landscape.

The pronounced functional differences in the main house should be discernible in the artifact concentrations. The assumption is that different activities employing different objects will, if they occurred in different places, leave diagnostic archaeological evidence. This is, of course, a simplified assumption and it is obvious that many factors can influence the relationship between an activity and its surviving archaeological residue. This subject has received much scholarly attention (cf. Yellen 1977; Gould 1980; Gould and Schiffer 1981; Kent 1984, 1987), which demonstrates that the direct relationships archaeologists would like to find are not always present. Nevertheless, many recurring activities eventually do leave distinctive physical traces that are identifiable through archaeological analysis.

In the Chesapeake, one clue to the relationship between an activity and its artifact residue can be found in disposal behavior, which in early colonial sites consisted mainly of throwing garbage directly out the door into surface midden deposits. Although some materials were deposited in pits, cellars, or other features, the majority of the artifacts used at colonial sites appear to have ended up in surface

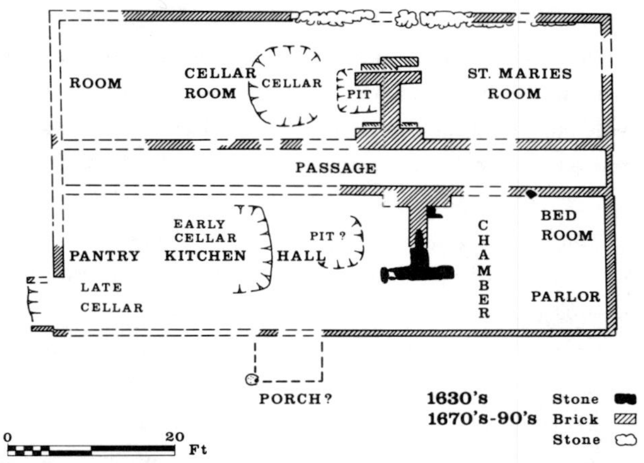

FIGURE 5.4. *Plan of the Country's House with likely room functions identified.*

deposits (King and Miller 1987). These middens or dumps were usually locations of intentional disposal, meaning that the artifacts were often removed from the locations where they were originally used and carried or swept out the door. Thus, the resulting artifact deposits do not necessarily correspond with the actual place of use.

Nevertheless, the middens can still tell us about activity locations because the settlers did not go further than absolutely necessary to dispose of their garbage. There is usually a close relationship between the middens and the associated structure and often with specific doorways in a building, as is evidenced by the data from a number of seventeenth-century sites (Keeler 1978; Neiman 1980; Miller 1986; Pogue 1988; King 1990). Likewise, outbuildings often have their own middens nearby, even when they are located quite near a main structure. Although artifacts from several activities are still likely to have been blended, these deposits can show significant variations in content if functions were spatially separated within or between buildings.

Information about artifact distributions from colonial Chesapeake sites, outside of urban areas are usually obtained from plowed soils. Although plowing tends to mix artifacts from various strata and can also move objects horizontally, research indicates that the basic distribution patterns remain, if somewhat blurred (Roper 1976; Trubowitz 1978; Lewarch and O'Brien 1981). Thus, it is possible to examine spatial patterning and functional variation with plowzone data.

The plowzone artifact data from the Country's House

were obtained from the excavation of 285 5-by-5-foot units. Artifact distribution analysis was conducted with the aid of the SYMAP computer graphics program, which creates a contour map of artifact densities over a site (see Miller 1986 for a discussion of how SYMAP was used in the Country's House analysis). Although not without flaws, this method provides a systematic and standardized means of comparing the spatial distributions of various artifacts.

To begin, four functionally distinct artifact groups (table glass, white clay tobacco pipes, tin-glazed earthenwares, and coarse utility wares) were mapped. Most of the table glass fragments are from elegant wine glasses that were used primarily for consuming alcohol in social and dining settings. Tobacco pipes indicate a common daily activity for most colonial Marylanders and the fragments of the pipes suggest where leisure time was spent. Tin-Glazed earthenware is considered a fine ceramic, and most of the shards are from plates, dishes, drinking pots, and cups. In general, this group represents dining and beverage consumption activities. The utility ware category is made up of North Devon Gravel Tempered Ware and Black Glazed Earthenware (Buckley-Like) shards. The primary vessel forms are milk pans and butter pots, and both wares typically served dairying, food storage, and cooking functions. They do not appear in dining or drinking forms in the Chesapeake. As figure 5.5A shows, the table glass at the site is strongly associated with the main house. The dark shading on these maps represents greater densities of artifacts. One concentration occurs at the southeast corner of the Country's House, corresponding with a door to the possible parlor. A second large cluster is found along the north or rear wall where there was an exterior door from the St. Mary's Room, and a less dense cluster occurs along the east end of the house, also near a doorway. A smaller cluster is found off the southwest corner of the house, presumably near the kitchen. Social activities that involved the use of elegant wine glasses were obviously restricted to the main house, and the table glass distribution strongly implies that it was used mostly in the parlor and adjacent St. Mary's Room. Although not illustrated, the distribution map of glass bottle fragments shows an almost identical pattern, implying that these two artifact groups were used together.

In contrast, tobacco pipe fragments are far more broadly distributed (figure 5.5B). This composite view of all pipes shows that most were used at the main house. The possible kitchen dump on the west end has the largest concentration, but substantial deposits also occur east and southeast of the structure. This broad and nearly continuous distribution of pipes all around the east end of the structure is notable and suggests this was where the inhabitants did much pipe smoking.

Pottery fragments display a quite different distribution. Tin-glazed earthenwares occur mostly to the south of the Country's House in three major deposits (figure 5.5C). These include the presumed kitchen dump, a refuse cluster associated with the possible parlor, and a dump to the southeast of the house. A small deposit is found at the east-end door, but few tin-glazed shards occur over the rest of the site. Significantly, the distribution of another type of fine ceramic—Rhenish Blue and Gray Stoneware (not illustrated)—is very similar with shards occurring in these same dump areas. Rhenish Blue and Gray Stonewares occur primarily in drinking vessel forms at this site. In sharp contrast are the utility wares (figure 5.5D). Although they are well represented in the west-side dump and do occur in the southeast-corner dump, the largest cluster is north of the main house near the outbuildings. Food processing or storage must have occurred in these structures, but a lack of tobacco pipes and other materials implies that they were not used as dwellings. Most likely, these served as work buildings, used for processing milk and produce from the garden and orchard.

These maps reveal pronounced differences in the distribution of functional groups, which strongly suggest that activities were spatially segregated at the site. Higher-quality artifacts associated with food consumption and drinking occur adjacent to the rooms thought to have been used by the innkeeper and his customers or in a possible kitchen dump. Utility wares were generally restricted to the western dump and outbuildings. Tobacco smoking occurred primarily at the main house and per-

FIGURE 5.5. (OPPOSITE). *Distribution of artifacts around the Country's House. Cross-hatching indicates locations of the densest artifact clusters: A. Tobacco pipe fragments. B. Table glass fragments. C. Tin-glazed earthenwares. D. Coarse utility wares. + Indicates 50-foot grid point.*

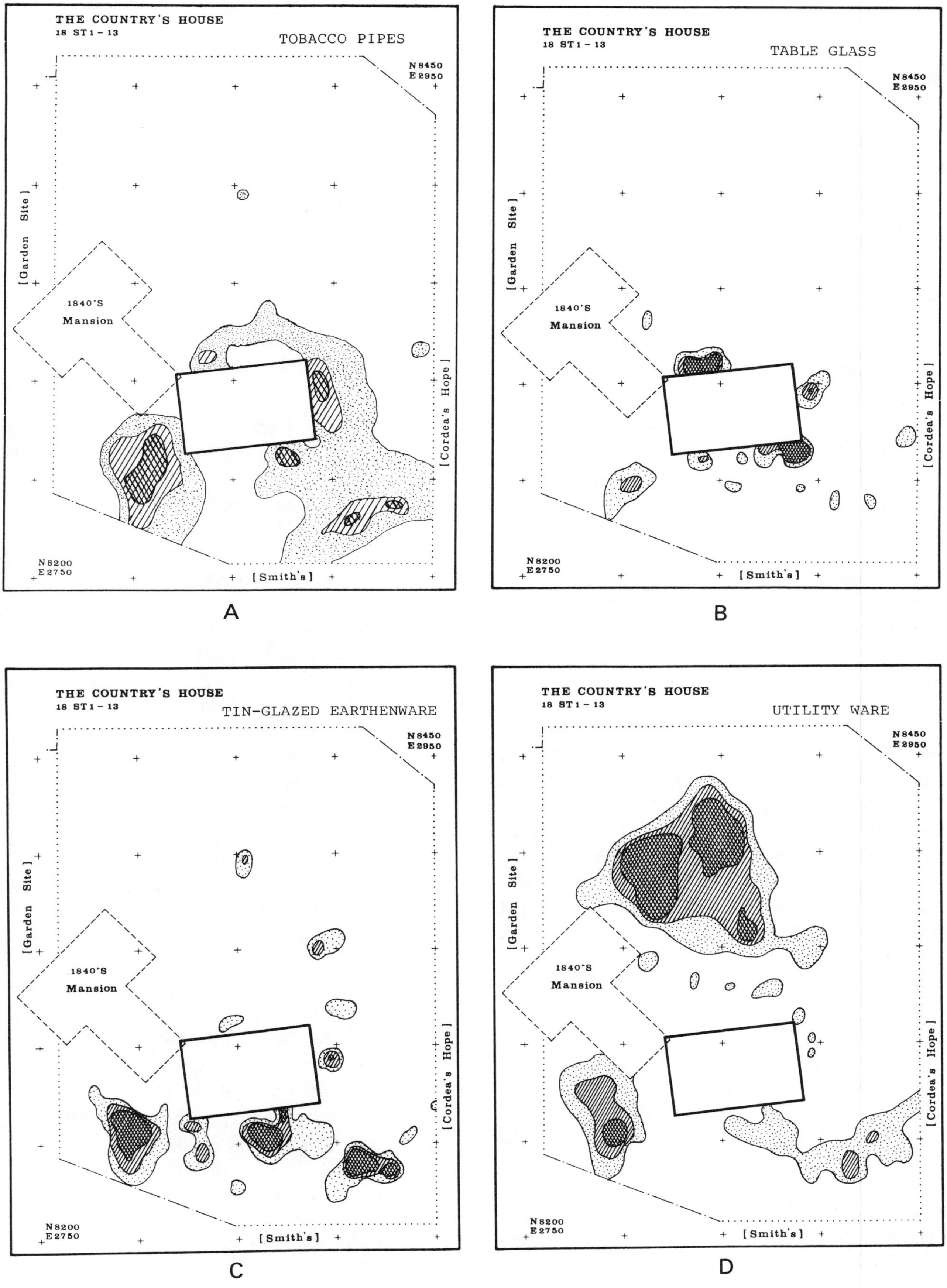
THE COUNTRY'S HOUSE
18 ST1-13
TOBACCO PIPES
N8450
E2950
[Garden Site]
1840'S
Mansion
[Cordea's Hope]
N8200
E2750
[Smith's]
A
THE COUNTRY'S HOUSE
18 ST1-13
TABLE GLASS
N8450
E2950
[Garden Site]
1840'S
Mansion
[Cordea's Hope]
N8200
E2750
[Smith's]
B
THE COUNTRY'S HOUSE
18 ST1-13
TIN-GLAZED EARTHENWARE
N8450
E2950
[Garden Site]
1840'S
Mansion
[Cordea's Hope]
N8200
E2750
[Smith's]
C
THE COUNTRY'S HOUSE
18 ST1-13
UTILITY WARE
N8450
E2950
[Garden Site]
1840'S
Mansion
[Cordea's Hope]
N8200
E2750
[Smith's]
D

haps in the east yard. Although more sophisticated analysis of these distributions using data on vessel form and the statistical evaluation of artifact associations will certainly expand and enhance these initial findings, even these relatively simple maps shed new insight on where the colonists conducted various activities.

Further information on how the various parts of the site were used was obtained from the composition of the artifacts in the various middens, as indicated by the distribution maps. The highest density of total artifacts at the site (38.5 per square foot) and the greatest concentrations of ceramics, pipes, bottle glass, and nails occur in the dump west of the Country's House. Bones were especially abundant in this area, and the mean density was 25.2 bone fragments per square foot. In contrast, the dumps at the east end of the house, where the soil is of similar depth, had bone densities of only 4.4 and 7.9 bones per square foot. This huge concentration of artifacts, especially bone, supports the architectural hypothesis that the west end of the house served as the kitchen. However, the east-end middens, had the highest densities of table glass fragments and bottle glass. The dumps associated with the outbuildings have much lower artifact densities, especially of bone and tobacco pipes, than the dumps near the main house.

To summarize, functionally different artifacts do display notable differences in their distributions at this site, which indicates that there was some spatial separation of activities. Evidence from the west end of the Country's House supports the hypothesis that this part of the structure was used for food processing and was probably the kitchen. The middens at the east end of the structure have far less bone but larger percentages of bottle glass, table glass, and fine ceramics, which suggests more social and dining activities. These findings support the inferences about the uses of the Country's House derived from the historical and architectural data.

Temporal Change in Spatial Patterns

As architectural and yard fencing data have shown,the physical structure of the Country's House site changed considerably during the seventeenth-century. Given these changes and the relatively long site occupation, similar changes can be expected in the way spaces were used, and the artifact distributions should provide this information. To test this assumption, I prepared computer-generated maps of ceramics and tobacco pipes that date to three phases of the Country's House occupation, as follows:

1. ca. 1635 to about 1660: Surry-like ware, Dutch coarse earthenware, Merida micacious ware, early tin-glazed earthenwares, and 3.2- to 3.8-millimeter tobacco pipes.
2. ca. 1660 to about 1680: Morgan Jones pottery and 2.8-millimeter pipes.
3. ca. 1680 to c.1700: Staffordshire-like slipware, manganese mottled ware, English brown stoneware, and 1.8- to 2.4-millimeter pipe stems.

The artifact distributions were merged with data about the fences and outbuildings to gain an overall perspective of the site during these phases. These materials were retrieved mainly from soils mixed by plowing. As a result, many artifacts such as nails, bottle glass, and bones, cannot be temporally distinguished. However, by selecting artifacts available for relatively short periods (within the context of a site), it is possible to obtain some temporal control. Previous research indicates that the artifact groups used here reached a peak of availability during these periods at St. Mary's City.

Figure 5.6A shows that during the early decades of occupation, the site inhabitants deposited ceramics mostly on the south or front side of the house and in a midden on the west side. Colonists also threw shards out the rear door of the structure, as indicated by the clusters on the north side. The only other ceramic concentrations of note are associated with the two early outbuildings. Tobacco pipes (figure 5.7A) occur in the same general areas, but they are much more frequent in a dump on the west end of the house. An important distinction between these maps is that a large cluster of pipes occurs along the east end of the house, where only small amounts of ceramics are found. This difference may suggest that smoking rather than dining occurred most frequently in and directly outside the St. Mary's room, a finding in keeping with the presumed function of that space as a meeting room.

During the second phase, when the Country's House served as both state house and ordinary, the disposal patterns changed (figures 5.6B and 5.7B). Occupants continued to throw garbage on the west-end midden and at the southeast corner of the yard in a dump that extended into the road. On the east side of the house, the residents discarded quantities of broken ceramics and tobacco

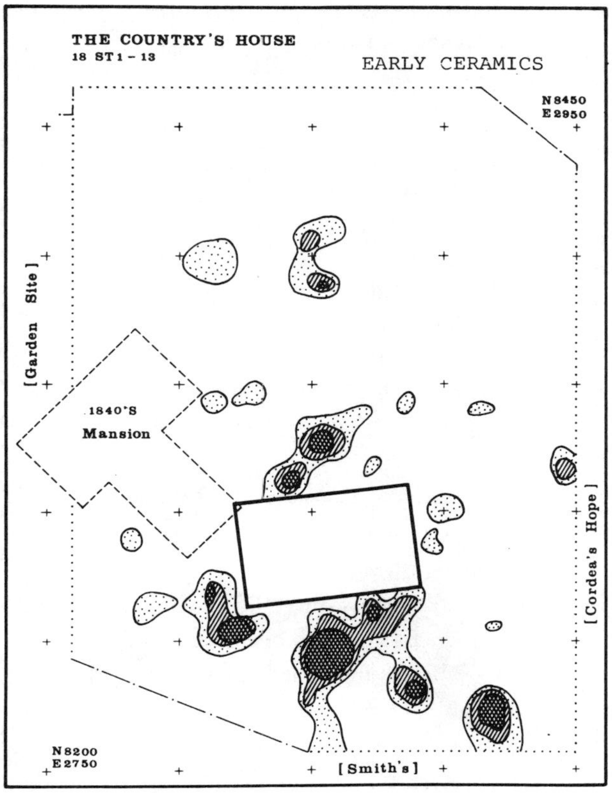

A

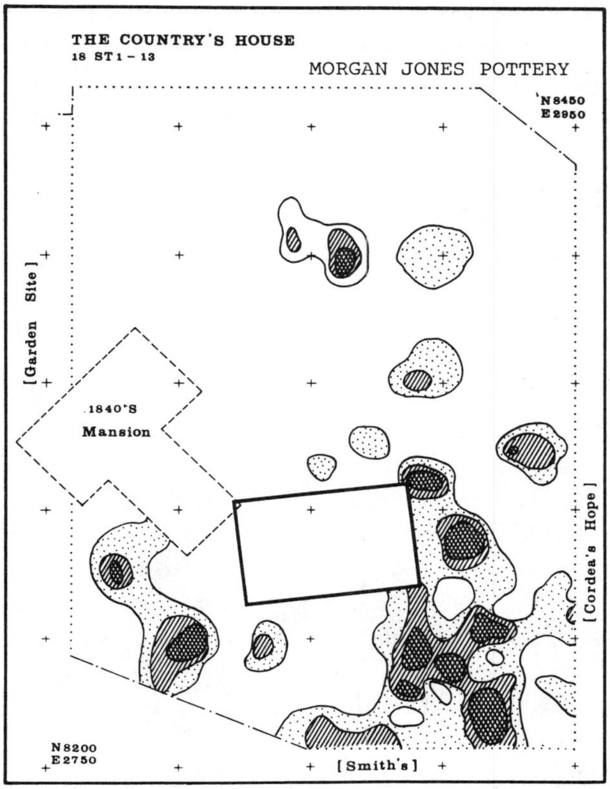

B

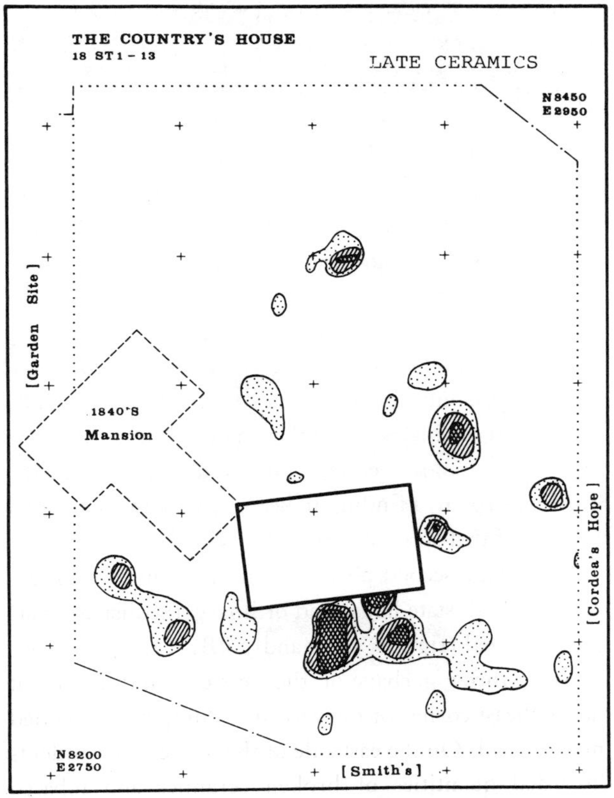

C

FIGURE 5.6. *Ceramic distributions through time: A. Early seventeenth-century ceramic fragments. B. Morgan Jones pottery (1661–ca. 1680). C. Late seventeenth-century ceramics. + Indicates 50-foot grid point.*

pipes. The most distinctive feature of this phase is the virtual absence of materials in the front yard and the reduced quantity of ceramics in the rear yard. Artifacts tend to be distributed in a pattern falling more toward the east and west of the house than was the case in phase 1, especially for ceramics. Such a pattern strongly suggests that the residents maintained certain areas as clean spaces during this period, especially the front yard. The small cluster of Morgan Jones pottery on the southwest side occurs at the juncture of two fence lines and may represent the accumulation of materials in an unswept corner. Although not as clean as the front, the backyard was also kept relatively free of refuse during this period. Greater control was now being exercised over trash disposal, but why? This prac-

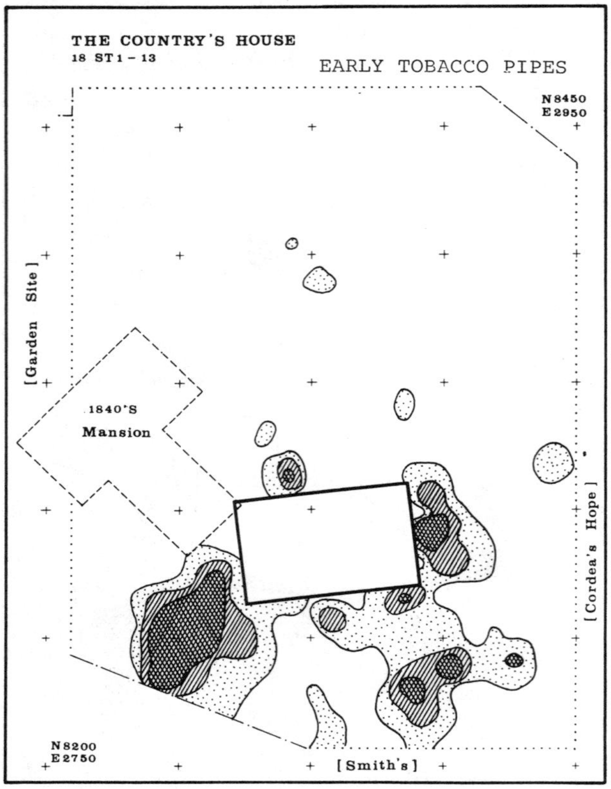

A

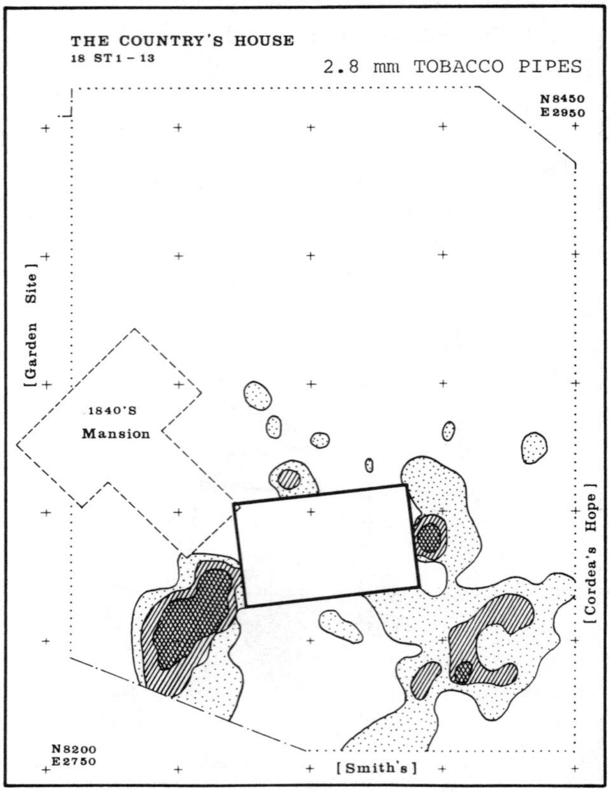

B

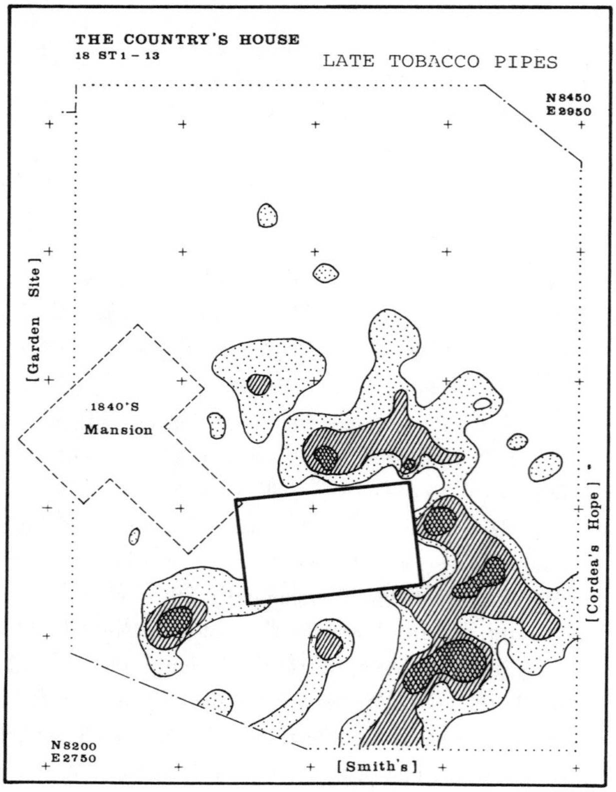

C

FIGURE 5.7. *Tobacco pipe distributions through time: A. Early tobacco pipes. B. 2.8-millimeter tobacco pipes. C. Late seventeenth-century tobacco pipes. + Indicates 50-foot grid point.*

tice cannot simply be attributed to one particular innkeeper because at least five individuals ran the Country's House inn during the availability period of Morgan Jones pottery and 2.8-millimeter pipes. Perhaps the explanation lies in the governmental function of the structure during this period, when a more formal space uncluttered by trash was thought appropriate.

This explanation is given some support by the distributions in phase 3, during which time the Country's House was used almost exclusively as an inn. The late ceramic and pipe maps (figures 5.6C, 5.7C) suggest a quick reversion to earlier practices, with the front and rear yards again used as disposal areas. This shift back to the earlier pattern would suggest that a different set of standards guided space usage during the middle phase of occupation. When a building served only as a residence or an inn, disposal of waste was apparently a matter of little concern. When it served as a state house, however, a less cluttered and perhaps more formal yardscape was maintained in certain areas, even though the building also continued to be used as an inn. When the political function of the site was removed in the late 1670s with the construction of a new brick state house, patrons rapidly returned to more typical disposal behavior. What is curious is that the ceramic and pipe patterns are so different during this last period. Most of the shards occur in the front yard while the major concentrations of pipes appear in the rear of the house and all along the east side of the lot. The pipe distribution is so broad and intense in those areas that it may indicate these yards were more intensively used by smokers, perhaps while relaxing outdoors during the hot Chesapeake summers. Archaeological evidence does suggest that a large tree stood in the yard off the southeast corner of the house. In addition, analysis of the likely height of the Country's House and solar angles indicates that parts of the east and north yards would have been shaded by the house itself at various times of the day.

Discussion

Study of the Country's House site has revealed a rich and complex story of pronounced change and striking continuity. The physical structure of the site did change as the Maryland frontier developed into a settled, colonial society. Many significant shifts took place in the site structure over the 65 years of occupation, and more intensive study would undoubtedly define additional changes. Indeed, the many alterations in fencing and outbuilding locations offer a picture of almost constant change. This finding is not surprising because early Maryland society experienced high death rates, nearly constant immigration, and abundant economic opportunity coupled with great social fluidity (Walsh and Menard 1974; Menard 1975; Carr and Menard 1979). All these factors combined to produce a society that did not achieve social and demographic stability until the end of the seventeenth century (Menard 1975; Jordan 1979). Hence, in one sense the frequent changes in the landscape at this site can be viewed as a reflection of the overall demographic and social instability of the colony.

Perhaps the most pronounced change seen at the site is in the form of the Country's House lot. The early landscape was apparently oriented to the natural setting, with topographic features being most important. Such conformity between the cultural and natural landscapes may reflect an attitude of adapting to the environment during the early years of colonial settlement rather than attempting to impose order on it. Certainly the first years of frontier settlement represent a crucial period in the process of colonization, during which settlers must learn about and cope with a new cultural and environmental setting (Thompson 1973). The initial orientation toward the natural setting quickly gave way to a mid-seventeenth-century landscape that was arranged with reference to cultural features, namely, the predominant architecture. This change suggests that as the colonial society became more firmly established, cultural factors took on a primary role in shaping the domestic landscape.

In the 1660s this landscape was again altered. A rectangular lot with precise boundaries was laid out. Such a lot form, with the house at one end and the outbuildings, work yards, gardens, orchards and stock pens behind it, follows a traditional British landscape arrangement that was commonly used from medieval times in villages and towns throughout England (Sharp 1946; Conzen 1960; Burke 1971). Its appearance at St. Mary's probably represents the transfer of a traditional landscape model to the Chesapeake region. However, no other known property in St. Mary's City had this shape. One reason may be that the Country's House was the first lot formally defined in the city, and that the colonists initially employed a familiar plan. By the 1670s, however, they developed a 1-acre lot, measuring 198 by 220 feet, which was used regularly throughout the rest of the seventeenth century. Why this nearly square lot was chosen as a standard at St. Mary's City instead of the traditional rectangular form is unknown. Perhaps the more square-shaped lot was easier to survey or somehow better served the domestic needs of the city residents. The cultural factors involved in determining lot shape have received little attention but could prove an interesting avenue for future research.

The changes in the Country's House landscape also indicate a notable shift in the cultural setting. Specifically, the lot took on a more concise form, was gradually reduced in size, and became increasingly subdivided over time. All these changes were probably responses to the greater urbanization of the St. Mary's City landscape. In less than 15 years, this site had gone from being a rural plantation to serving as the center point of the most urbanized space in seventeenth-century Maryland. Urban development was slow to begin anywhere in the Chesapeake region and at St. Mary's, there was only slight growth before 1660. Development was rapid after that date, however, and by the mid-1670s, a formal town plan utilizing Italian baroque ideas of urban design was in place, and a variety of structures, including several imposing brick buildings were standing or under construction (Miller 1988). Although the number of people who lived in St. Mary's City is unknown, a population of several hundred permanent residents is likely. The above findings imply that even a relatively small population concentration was sufficient to initiate the process of urbanization. It also suggests that the evidence of former landscapes can be employed to measure the early phases of this process. Recent work at the Shields Tavern site in Williamsburg, Virginia, has found a similar response in the development of that eighteenth-century community. At the Shields site, there was notable architectural stability, but "what was changed, and what is of utmost concern when evaluating the effect of urbanization, was the physical and cultural landscape that the occupants used to surround themselves" (Brown et al. 1990:173–175). Williamsburg was not a major urban center, but it was larger than St. Mary's City with a population that reached perhaps 2,000. Neither place was urbanized in the sense of colonial Philadelphia, New York, Boston, or later nineteenth- and twentieth-century cities. Nevertheless, it appears that urbanization and the shift to an urban cultural setting can begin with a relatively small population. Because domestic landscapes can be sensitive indicators of this process, studies of urban development can benefit from cultural landscape data along with information on architecture and demographics.

The preceding discussion has focused on numerous changes, but certain continuities can also be seen in the Country's House landscape through time. The architecture of the main house and the principal activity areas apparently remained relatively fixed throughout the occupation. The greatest concentrations of early and late seventeenth-century artifacts, for example, appear in the same locations, and thus attest to certain continuities in the use of space at this site. Although continuity might seem unlikely in view of the unstable nature of the society and rapidly changing cultural setting, it can be explained by the fact that major structures serve as anchor points in a landscape. They represent substantial economic investments and hence endure longer than relatively inexpensive outbuildings or cheap fences. Although any structure can be modified, when various sections of a building (a kitchen, bedroom, or formal reception space) were constructed with particular purposes in mind, these spaces by and large continued to be used in these ways. Hence, it is not surprising that certain aspects of the built environment will display stability even in a rapidly changing cultural setting.

One example of strong continuity can be seen in the basic patterns of artifact dispersal, which were similar from the early and the late periods. Although the Country's House was a private residence during the first period and a public inn during the last, the disposal behavior was remarkably similar. The stability of the Country's House architecture explains some of this, but it should also be noted that the disposal behavior of the colonists did not apparently change. In general, colonial trash disposal can be characterized as "out the nearest door," regardless of site function. Such a practice persisted into the eighteenth century on British colonial sites, where it is labeled the "Brunswick pattern" of refuse disposal (South 1977:47–48). The evidence from the Country's House clearly shows that this method of disposal was commonly used on British colonial sites from the earliest decades of settlement in the New World. Although such behavior may be considered inappropriate by late twentieth-century American standards, it was an appropriate response in a society with different notions of sanitation and with relatively few durable materials requiring disposal, especially when compared with the huge quantities of trash generated by modern industrial societies. Also, the wheeled vehicles that residents would have needed to transport refuse any distance from a site were very rare in Maryland during the 1600s (Earle 1975:145; Lois Green Carr, personal communication 1991).

Excavators did find two dumps a short distance from the Country's House. One is located off the west end of the house and contains materials from every period. This space probably served as a work area and general dump for kitchen waste. Computer maps suggest that this dump often extended into the adjacent road during the second half of the seventeenth century. Another dump, located at the southeast corner of the yard, also stretched into the roadway. A similar pattern of trash disposal has been identified at the nearby van Sweringen site, where an extensive midden developed in Aldermanbury Street during the late seventeenth century (King and Miller 1987:42). Data from Smith's Ordinary, located just south of the Country's House, also show that the occupants of this structure discarded their trash in the road (Miller 1986). This pattern occurs at several sites and thus indicates that public spaces such as roads were also considered appropriate locations in which to deposit garbage during the seventeenth century.

It is perhaps surprising to modern sensibilities that even the home of governors during the 1600s had yards strewn with garbage and dumps flanking every doorway. In part, this might be a reflection of the rough frontier conditions of early Maryland, but it is probably due even more to the practices of seventeenth-century British society. England had just emerged from the medieval period, and traditional perspectives, attitudes, and values were still strongly held. As James Deetz (1977:39–40) has written, the early colonial peoples had a worldview that was communal, less formal, and more resigned to nature. More sophisticated manners, formal behavior, and efforts to control nature were attributes of the new cultural outlook that came to dominate eighteenth-century British society. Called the "Georgian worldview," this emphasis on symmetry and order was to influence many aspects of life in the new century. In the 1600s, however, the old ways still dominated and neat, tidy yards were not yet a cultural requirement for those with social position and wealth. The disposal patterns decidedly reflect this more organic, informal outlook. Why then did the disposal pattern during the 1660s and 1670s at the Country's House feature a clean front yard?

This relatively clean space only appeared during the time when the building served as a state house. The reason for this shift in behavior is puzzling, but it must somehow relate to the change in site use. Amos Rapoport, a student of the built environment, has shown that buildings and landscapes have obvious, primary functions but also serve less obvious purposes. Specifically, he finds that "buildings and settings (landscapes) are ways of ordering behavior by placing it into discrete and distinguishable places and settings, each with known and expected rules, behaviors and the like. Built environments thus communicate meanings to help serve social and cultural purposes" (Rapoport 1980:300). In addition to serving various physical and economic purposes, the built environment can be seen as a symbolic system that is coded to elicit proper behavioral responses (Rapoport 1982; Sanders 1990). During the 1660s and 1670s, the Country's House took on a different meaning because it was the seat of the provincial government as well as a public inn. In this new role it symbolized political power and held great social significance for the colony. Indeed, social responsibility was associated with serving in the assembly or participating in a court, which therefore required a different behavior. Serious business was at hand and it required careful thought and more deliberate, formal action. Even a brief review of the *Archives of Maryland* reveals the formal nature of the assembly and court proceedings that were held at the Country's House. Could it be that this maintenance of the landscape served as a sensory cue, a coded message about expected behavior? At least four innkeepers apparently followed this practice, so it cannot be dismissed as an idiosyncrasy. When used as a state house, the site likely took on a new meaning, which entailed different expectations and rules of behavior. Although the physical structure of the landscape remained much the same during this period, it may be the subtle changes in the ways spaces were used and maintained that signaled the more serious and formal purpose that the Country's House took on during that time.

Conclusion

The Country's House site has provided much new information on colonial architecture and landscape. The traces of fence ditches and artifact scatters often seem of little importance until they are viewed as essential elements of vanished landscapes. Fence data show how the colonists physically organized the landscape, and artifact distributions provide vital evidence about how these spaces were used. Archaeological data demonstrate clear functional divisions of space at this site into work areas, more formal spaces, and special-purpose zones. Undoubtedly, more detailed analysis of the ceramics and other artifact groups will permit a more thorough interpretation of this site.

The information presented here offers dramatic testimony of the insights that lie hidden in the soils over archaeological sites. Past landscapes are rich but largely untapped sources of knowledge that are generally accessible only through archaeological study. Unlike the principal architecture at a site, the many minor actors in vernacular landscapes—outbuildings, fences, work areas, gardens and dumps—were almost constantly changing. Because of this malleability, the domestic setting may be a far more sensitive indicator of culture change and continuity than architecture. Landscape patterns and artifact distribution can provide information on cultural stability and adaptation, the beginnings of urbanization, and a people's perspective on the world. This analysis of the Country's House demonstrates a few of the possibilities.

Acknowledgments

The excavations at the Country's House site were conducted by Historic St. Mary's City with support from a National Endowment for the Humanities research grant (RO-1244-81) and funding provided by the citizens of Maryland. Field excavations were skillfully directed by Garry Wheeler Stone, Fraser D. Neiman, and the late Alexander H. Morrison II. Laboratory analysis of the artifacts was conducted by Julia King, Charles Fithian, and James O'Connor, who also prepared most of the graphics. Lois Green Carr assembled the relevant historical documentation about the Country's House and aided in its interpretation. Finally, Edward Chaney and other reviewers offered many valuable comments on the manuscript. I am most grateful for the many contributions of each of these talented persons.

References Cited

Brown, Gregory J. et. al.
1990 *Archaeological Investigations of the Shields Tavern Site, Williamsburg, Virginia*. Department of Archaeological Research, Colonial Williamsburg Foundation. Williamsburg, Va.

Burke, Gerald
1971 *Towns in the Making*. Edward Arnold, London.

Carr, Lois Green
1971 The Governor's Field: A Compilation of Documents Pertaining to this Tract in St. Mary's City. Manuscript on File, Historic St. Mary's City, Md.

Carr, Lois Green, and Russell R. Menard
1979 Immigration and Opportunity: The Freedman in Early Colonial Maryland. In *The Chesapeake in the Seventeenth Century*, edited by Thad W. Tate and David Ammerman, pp. 206–242. University of North Carolina Press, Chapel Hill.

Conzen, M. R. G.
1960 *Alnwick, Northumberland: A Study in Town-Plan Analysis*. Institute of British Geographers Publication No. 27. London.

Deetz, James
1977 *In Small Things Forgotten: The Archaeology of Early American Life*. Anchor Press, Garden City, N.J.

Earle, Carville V.
1975 *The Evolution of a Tidewater Settlement System: All Hallows' Parish, Maryland, 1650–1783*. Research Paper No. 170. Department Geography, University of Chicago.

Forman, Henry Chandlee
1938 *Jamestown and St. Mary's: Buried Cities of Romance*. Johns Hopkins Press, Baltimore, Md.

Gould, Richard
1980 *Living Archaeology*. Cambridge University Press, Cambridge.

Gould, Richard, and Michael Schiffer (editors)
1981 *Modern Material Culture: The Archaeology of Us*. Academic Press, New York.

Jackson, John Brinckerhoff
1980 *The Necessity of Ruins and Other Topics*. University of Massachusetts Press, Amherst.

Jordan, David W.
1979 Political Stability and the Emergence of a Native Elite in Maryland. In *The Chesapeake in the Seventeenth Century*, edited by Thad Tate and David Ammerman, pp. 243–273. University of North Carolina Press, Chapel Hill.

Keeler, Robert Winston
1977 An Earthy View of Life on a Seventeenth-Century Farm. Paper delivered at the Society for Historical Archaeology Annual Meeting, Ottawa, Canada. Copy on file, Historic St. Mary's City, Md.
1978 *The Homelot on the Seventeenth Century Chesapeake Tidewater Frontier*. Ph.D. dissertation, Department of Anthropology, University of Oregon. University Microfilms, Ann Arbor.

Kent, Susan
1984 *Analyzing Activity Areas: An Ethnoarchaeological Study*

of the Use of Space. University of New Mexico Press, Albuquerque.
1987 *Method and Theory For Activity Area Research: An Ethnoarchaeological Approach*. Columbia University Press, New York.

King, Julia A.
1988 A Comparative Midden Analysis of a Household and Inn in St. Mary's City, Maryland. *Historical Archaeology* 22(2):17–39.
1990 *An Intrasite Spatial Analysis of the van Sweringen Site, St. Mary's City, Maryland*. Ph.D. Dissertation, University of Pennsylvania. University Microfilms, Ann Arbor.

King, Julia A., and Henry M. Miller
1987 The View from the Midden: An Analysis of Midden Distribution and Composition at the van Sweringen Site, St. Mary's City, Md. *Historical Archaeology* 21(2):37–59.

Lewarch, Dennis E., and Michael J. O'Brien
1981 Effect of Short Term Tillage on Aggregate Provenience Surface Pattern. In *Plowzone Archaeology: Contributions to Theory and Technique*, edited by Dennis E. Lewarch and Michael J. O'Brien, pp. 7– 50. Vanderbilt University Publications in Anthropology No. 27. Nashville, Tenn.

Luccketti, Nicholas
1990 Archaeological Excavations at Bacon's Castle, Surry County, Virginia. In *Earth Patterns: Essays in Landscape Archaeology*, edited by William M. Kelso and Rachel Most, pp. 23–42. University Press of Virginia, Charlottesville.

Maryland Archives
The Archives of Maryland. Maryland Historical Society. Baltimore, Md. Published since 1883.

Menard, Russell R.
1975 *Economy and Society in Early Colonial Maryland*. Ph.D. Dissertation. University of Iowa. University Microfilms. Ann Arbor.

Miller, Henry M.
1983 *A Search for the "Citty of Saint Maries": Report on the 1981 Excavations in St. Mary's City, Maryland*. St. Mary's City Archaeology Series No. 1. St. Mary's City, Md.
1986 *Discovering Maryland's First City: A Summary Report on the 1981–1984 Archaeological Excavations in St. Mary's City, Maryland*. St. Mary's City Archaeology Series No. 2. St. Mary's City, Md.
1988 Baroque Cities in the Wilderness: Archaeology and Urban Development in the Colonial Chesapeake. *Historical Archaeology* 22(2): 57–73.

Neiman, Fraser D.
1980 *The "Manner House" before Stratford: Discovering the Clifts Plantation*. Robert E. Lee Memorial Association. Stratford, Va.

Pogue, Dennis
1988 Spatial Analysis of the King's Reach Plantation Homelot, Ca. 1690–1715. *Historical Archaeology* 22(2):40–56.

Rapoport, Amos
1980 Vernacular Architecture and the Cultural Determinants of Form. In *Buildings and Society*, edited by A. D. King, pp. 283–305. Routledge and Kegan Paul, London.
1982 *The Meaning of the Built Environment: A Nonverbal Communication Approach*. Sage Publications, Beverly Hills, Calif.

Roper, D.C.
1976 Lateral Displacement of Artifacts Due to Plowing. *American Antiquity* 41:372–374.

Sanders, Donald
1990 Behavioral Conventions and Archaeology: Methods for the Analysis of Ancient Architecture. In *Domestic Architecture and the Use of Space*, edited by Susan Kent, pp. 43–72. Cambridge University Press.

Cambridge. Sharp, Thomas
1946 *The Anatomy of the Village*. Penguin Books, Harmondsworth, Middlesex, Great Britain.

South, Stanley
1977 *Method and Theory in Historical Archaeology*. Academic Press, New York.

Stone, Garry Wheeler
1974 St. John's: Archaeological Questions and Answers. *Maryland Historical Magazine* 69(2):146–168.
1982 *Society, Housing and Architecture in Early Maryland: John Lewger's St. John's*. Ph.D. Dissertation, Department of American Civilization, University of Pennsylvania, Philadelphia. University Microfilms, Ann Arbor.

Thompson, Stephen J.
1973 *Pioneer Colonization: A Cross-Cultural View*. Addison-Wesley Module in Anthropology No. 33. Reading, Mass.

Trubowitz, Neal L.
1978 The Persistence of Settlement Pattern in a Cultivated Field. *Occasional Publications In Northeastern Anthropology* 5:41–66. Department of Anthropology. Franklin Pierce College, Rindge, N.H.

Walsh, Lorena S., and Russell Menard
1974 Death in the Chesapeake: Two Life Tables for Men in Early Colonial Maryland. *Maryland Historical Magazine* 69(2):211–227.

Yellen, John
1977 *Archaeological Approaches to the Present*. Academic Press, New York.

VI
CHAPTER

Town Plans and Everyday Material Culture
An Archaeology of Social Relations in Colonial Maryland's Capital Cities

PAUL A. SHACKEL

DURING THE seventeenth century, Chesapeake society was transformed from "crude egalitarianism" (McCusker and Menard 1986) into a society that emphasized the modern values of class structure and individuality. Many of the changes in the landscape and material culture of seventeenth- and eighteenth-century Chesapeake are a product of these broad sociocultural changes. For instance, James Deetz (1988) hypothesizes that colonoware made by African Americans can be linked to the changing relationship between white masters and black slaves. Mark Leone (1987) also suggests that the instability of the social order in Annapolis during the 1760s led the aristocracy to create formal gardens.

In this analysis I use the town plans of the two Maryland capitals, their architecture, and everyday material goods to demonstrate the relationships between changes in social, political, and economic conditions and the introduction of a new material culture. These new material forms helped to separate the community into various social groups, created strong group boundaries, and promoted individuality.

There is more than a coincidental relationship between the rise of the naturalizing ideology of racism and the development during the 1660s and 1670s of explicit uses of monumental architecture in Maryland's first capital, St. Mary's City. The redesign of the town incorporated baroque elements and emphasized the dominant powers of the church and state. The redesign of St. Mary's city in the 1660s and the 1670s occurred in conjunction with the increasing concern of the wealthy about a growing lower class and the legalization of racism against African Americans. Racism created a new underclass and reduced the threat from an uneasy land-poor group.

During a subsequent era of sociocultural instability in the Chesapeake and in Maryland's second capital city, Annapolis, tensions apparently developed between wealth groups. The elite responded by introducing a new set of material goods and a new set of rules for formal dining. This new etiquette emphasized individuality. Also during the 1720s, changes in architecture from impermanent to permanent structures reveal the breakdown of community maintenance relationships.

Changes in material culture can be more than an index of wealth or a product of diffusion. They can also be a reaction to sociocultural change and an expression of relationships in society. The meanings and uses of material goods change with the increased ambiguity of social hierarchy and can be used to symbolically reinforce the hierarchy. An analysis of the meanings and uses of goods therefore provides a fruitful analysis of cultural change in the Chesapeake.

MEANINGS AND USES OF GOODS

The meanings of goods can be controlled by groups defined by such factors as wealth, class, occupation, or gender to support a dominant ideology. This control can be exercised in two ways: (1) by making artificial phenomena and their meanings appear to be "natural" or part of the natural order, or (2) by placing the meaning in the past, making it appear that there is a historical precedent and, therefore, that the meaning is inevitable. The group in control will establish the meanings that are to be used to dominate others (Hodder 1986:150). Ideologically based asymmetrical relationships in society occur as power relationships in many everyday interactions.

Historical archaeologists of colonial America should find interesting Daniel Miller's (1987:135–137) and Neil McKendrick's (1982) interpretation of the changing material culture in England during the Enlightenment. This period marked a change in the symbolic use of goods by interest groups to reinforce their position in the social hierarchy.

> In a society in which the social distance between classes is *too great to bridge*, as, say, between a landed aristocracy and a landless peasantry, or in which the distance is *unbridgeable*, as in a caste society, then new patterns of increased expenditure on consumer goods are extremely difficult if not impossible to induce. (McKendrick 1982:20)

In a period of unquestioned social stratification, material goods often indicate the established hierarchy and are sometimes reinforced by sumptuary laws. In such circumstances, restrictions tend to be imposed on mercantile practices, and the meanings of goods and their place in the hierarchy are relatively uncomplex and firmly controlled.

With the disintegration of power of the old regime in Renaissance Europe, the amount and type of goods used in society were radically transformed. Goods that had relatively static symbolic meanings during times of unquestioned hierarchy, were now more active in creating new meanings and reinforcing social asymmetry, since the old order was increasingly being questioned and threatened. With the increased production of goods, those lower in the order began emulating the higher groups. The demand for goods increased as the social hierarchy became more ambiguous (Miller 1987:136). Feeling threatened by emulation, the upper levels of the hierarchy attempted to reestablish differences. The elite found it necessary to produce new goods, new behaviors, and new social actions to keep their social distance (Shackel 1987, 1993).

RACISM IN THE CHESAPEAKE

Racism and the material culture and behavior that reinforced it were not codified in the Chesapeake in the first half of the seventeenth century. The demands and rewards of the tobacco economy before 1660 unleashed a fierce individualism that worked against the social cohesion necessary to forge highly structured hierarchies. As the number of freed white and black indentured servants increased, they competed with the wealthy for land. This competition threatened the emerging social order. Consequently, the gentry championed the legislation and introduced new material culture patterns that would establish a hierarchy and marginalize peripheral groups such as African Americans through codification. An example of this can be seen in the development of racism in parts of the colonial Chesapeake.

A study of Northampton County, Virginia, shows that before the Reformation took place in England all blacks who came to Virginia's eastern shore entered as slaves. African Americans had to develop strategies to escape their bondage: sometimes they were freed by their masters; the other option was self-purchase, but in this case they had to rely on the cooperation of the master. Planters usually used self-purchase as a way to motivate slaves to attain higher productivity. Freedom served as a powerful goal and often increased the planter's profits with greater output. Obviously some planters lived up to their promise, as 29 percent of the African Americans in Northampton County were free in 1668 (Breene and Innes 1980:10–17; see also Deal 1988:275–305). Interaction between nongentry whites, such as small planters and indentured servants, and African Americans occurred on a daily basis. In fact, up until Bacon's Rebellion "the two races exchanged land, traded livestock, worked for each other, sued one another, and socialized together" (Breene and Innes 1980:104). Some white servants lived with and worked for African American planters (Breene and Innes 1980:105).

Timothy Breene and Stephen Innes trace the accounts of Anthony and Mary Johnson, free African Americans who lived in Northampton County, Virginia. By 1651 Johnson owned a modest estate of 250 acres, bred cattle and hogs, and grew tobacco. A 1653 court record indicates that Johnson owned a black slave. Johnson's oldest son accumulated an estate of 450 acres. The Johnsons moved to Somerset County, Maryland, where Anthony died. In the 1670s his children were able to increase their estates. A third generation of free landowning Johnsons existed until 1706, when the last survivor died without an heir. In the communities that the Johnsons inhabited, racial boundaries appeared nonrestrictive in court cases and land deed transactions (Breene and Innes 1980:10–17).

Some historians believe that planters preferred white skilled servants to the unskilled, unwesternized, alien blacks (Kulikoff 1986). Breene and Innes (1980:49) claim "the planters were, in one important respect, quite without prejudice: they were willing to employ any kind of labor, and under any institutional arrangements, as long as the labor force was politically defenseless enough for the work to be done cheaply and under discipline." It was under these circumstances that indentured servants and free whites and blacks operated in their Chesapeake communities.

To encourage the immigration of white servants, the Chesapeake gentry created legislation that improved the conditions of the servants. Specifically, at the end of their servitude they were to become freemen and landowners (Maryland Archives 1640:1:52, 97). Legislators set limits to the terms of servants without indentures (Handlin and Handlin 1950:241). The aim of shortening the term of indenture was to encourage laborers to emigrate in the hope of becoming freemen and establishing their own plantation. Early legislation applied stiff penalties to blacks and whites equally for running away, drunkenness, and carrying arms. Until the 1660s the statutes applied to blacks were similar to those for white servants. These regulations grew less stringent for white servants but little changed for the African Americans (Handlin and Handlin 1950:244; Morgan 1975). Within a decade the plantation system introduced a growing number of freedmen into a society in which much of the agricultural land was occupied by large plantation owners. Limited opportunities for advancement existed.

The gentry felt that the freedmen were a threat to their livelihood. Their fears increased as the proportion of African Americans in the labor force increased. In Virginia the African American population totaled less than 2,500 in 1660s, but by the 1700s slave traders were importing several thousand black slaves per year. The increased alien black population threatened a hierarchy dominated by white planters (Breene and Innes 1980:108). The gentry's answer was legalized racism. The substitution of slaves for servants in the 1660s gradually eased the threat of insurrection and functioned as a way of keeping labor docile (Kulikoff 1978). As Edmund Morgan (1975:328) notes, "If freemen with disappointed hopes should make common cause with slaves of desperate hopes, the results might be worse than anything Bacon had done."

Differential treatment between blacks and whites created a division of interest through racial contempt. For instance, white servants who ran away with slaves had their sentences doubled—for their time lost and that of the slave (Handlin and Handlin 1950:244). The division between whites and blacks in the consciousness of the freedmen appeared to be working by the 1660s. As Winthrop Jordan (1978:278) points out, "White men were loudly protesting against being made 'slaves' in terms which strongly suggest that they considered slavery not as wrong but as inappropriate to themselves." Even African American servants were unable to protect themselves against this racist legislation. "White men were more clearly free because Negroes had become so clearly slave" (Jordan 1978:278). Freedmen's social unrest over the lack of economic mobility had threatened the upper class. In response to this unrest, the colonial upper class created a new, lower class and promoted racial prejudice where it had previously not existed, thus dividing the power of the poor and creating a new labor base.

Reasserting the Dominant Culture: The Redesign of Maryland's First Capital

In the early seventeenth-century Chesapeake settlement, all social groups owned the same type of goods, although the wealthy owned more. All social groups lived in the same type of home. The region included a mix of recently freed indentured servants, a small proportion of which comprised African Americans, as well as young Anglo men and women in search of economic opportunity (McCusker and Menard 1986:141). White plantation owners worked alongside white and black indentured servants.

St. Mary's City, Maryland's first capital, was settled in

1634. Historians are united in claiming that the development of the town was slow, especially in its first several decades of existence (Carr 1974; Menard 1975). The town conformed to John McCusker and Russell Menard's (1986) model of "crude egalitarianism." Probate inventory analyses of St. Mary's county indicate that members of all wealth groups accumulated few luxury items (Carr and Walsh 1977:34). The town center consisted of little more than the home and plantation of Leonard Calvert, governor of the colony.

However, Henry Miller (1986:123–125, 1988: 62ff.) has demonstrated through archaeology that by the late 1660s and early 1670s the design of the center of the town had changed considerably. Miller (1986:125) notes that the Maryland assembly's concern for redeveloping the town plan may have occurred as early as 1662. At the same time, the ruling class created and legislatively codified a difference between whites and blacks. Five years later Lord Baltimore granted a charter to create the City of St. Mary's. The new design of the town—which is the earliest documented baroque plan in the New World—probably took shape during the 1660s. As Morris (1979:124–25) points out, immense centralized autocratic powers initiate baroque urban design. This new design emphasized stratification and class structure, particularly in religious and governmental institutions. During the 1680s and 1690s St. Mary's town plan was "fleshed out" by the building of monumental architecture (Miller 1986, 1988).

As the town developed, so too did racist legislation. In 1662 Virginia declared that "'if any Christian shall commit Fornication with a Negro man or woman, he or she soe offending' should pay double the usual fine" (Jordan 1978:277). The following year the Maryland legislature declared "Negroes were to serve 'Durante Vita'", that is, their entire lives (Jordan 1978:279; Handlin and Handlin 1950:241). By 1669 the beating of slaves was formalized by legislation (Morgan 1975:312). Within several years of the 1676 Bacon's Rebellion—an insurrection of small planters, indentured servants, and black slaves—Virginia passed "An Act preventing Negroe Insurrection" and stated that negroes and slaves could not own guns (Breene and Innes 1980:27). In 1681 a Maryland act described mixed marriages as a "disgrace not only of the English butt also of many other Christian Nations" (Jordan 1978:277). After 1691 marriages between slaves and freemen were made illegal. Consequently, by the end of the seventeenth century, legislation was couched in the terms of race, that is, black and white. The fact that by the first decade of the 1700s "white servants were as much the exception in the tobacco fields as slaves had been earlier" (Morgan 1975:308) reflects the effectiveness of this codification.

Three points in particular should be made about the creation of St. Mary's new baroque town plan. First, three important buildings—Smith's Ordinary, the Lawyer's Lodging, and Cordea's Hope—were all built in close proximity to the Country's House (Miller 1986, 1988; see also chapter 5). The County's House functioned both as inn and as the state house, and these buildings surrounded a "commons" area. Second, avenues replaced disordered paths. Third, these avenues connected prominent institutions: the state house and the Chapel, with the center of town. The Jesuits built the Chapel in the late 1660s, while the state house was completed in 1676. Each was constructed of brick, stood about 1/2 mile from each other and 1,400 feet from the town center, and each was surrounded by a substantial amount of open space. "A line drawn from the Chapel through [the town center] to the state house forms an angle of 140 degrees" (Miller 1986:126).

Miller suggests that because of the economic situation in the Chesapeake, where it was more economically advantageous to establish tobacco plantations than towns, these cities served primarily as administrative centers, that is, as centers of power, rather than centers of commerce. "The Baroque cities of the seventeenth-century Chesapeake can be seen as a skillful response to the need for expression of ideology and authority in an agrarian society lacking a centralized economy" (Miller 1988:70). It is also clear that the need for authority had increased, not only because the region lacked a centralized economy or because baroque town planning had been introduced in England at this time, but also because social, political, and economic conditions were rapidly changing in the Chesapeake.

The development and completion of the plan (that is, the placement of monumental architecture) was implemented during the legalization of explicitly racial inequalities. The plan may have been conceived by the aristocracy as an expression of their power in the local society in the face of their increasing concern over a growing lower group that had little economic mobility. A new lower class was formed to divide and disarm a portion of the subordinates, and the entrenched aristocracy propped its position through explicit uses of material goods, such as town planning and architecture that emphasized governmental and religious institutions.

Culture and Material Change in Maryland's Second Capital City

In 1689 William and Mary ascended the throne of England. Protestants in Maryland took this opportunity to gain control of the colonial government, and in 1694 the capital was moved from the Catholic stronghold of St. Mary's to a Protestant concentration known as Anne Arundel Town, renamed Annapolis in 1695 (Riley 1887:54–58). In 1698 the town consisted of 40 dwellings and about 250 inhabitants (Papenfuse 1975:9). Described in 1708 as a place "where scarce a house will keep out rain" (Cook 1900:29–30), Annapolis did not initially grow as an economic center because it lacked a dependent hinterland (Walsh 1983a:1).

Francis Nicholson is credited with the design of the Annapolis baroque town plan in 1695, which was imposed on an earlier, gridlike plan. The Anglican church and the state house were placed on the highest points of the town, encompassed by circles that had streets radiating from them (Reps 1972; Ramirez 1975). The two monumental structures could be seen from any location in the city, and many of the streets framed a vista that led the eye to these two institutions of power. This visual attention reinforced the church's and state's authority (Leone et al. 1989; see also Miller 1988).

The 1710s and 1720s witnessed another dramatic surge in racist legislation in Maryland. Sometimes this prohibiting legislation was masked as a naturalizing ideology. For instance, interracial marriage or copulation was prohibited because it was "unnatural or inordinate." In 1728 an act was passed "for the punishment of negro women, having bastard children by white men; and for as much as such copulation are as unnatural and inordinate as between white women and negroe men" (Kilty 1799:IV B No. 5:203). Quotas were also placed on segments of the white population. Numerous laws were enacted to "prevent the importing [of] too great a number of Irish papists into the province" (Kilty 1799:XXXVI, LL No.4:197).

The 1710s and 1720s had more racist legislation passed than any other decade before or after. This legislation was a product of an increasing number of family dynasties elected to the Maryland assemblies in the early eighteenth century who developed political monopolies to protect their place in the hierarchy. By the 1720s, 60 percent of those elected had Maryland-born fathers. After this date the number increased to 84 percent (Kulikoff 1986). Racist legislation was one tool that created a clear position in the hierarchy for an increasing number of slaves and indentured servants so that they would not threaten the power of established hierarchy.

This legislation must be viewed in the light of the social and economic crises that befell Annapolis and Chesapeake residents around the 1720s. For instance, Edward Papenfuse (1975:14–15) and Lorena Walsh (1983b:6) estimate that between 1720 and 1730 the city's population increased between 65 and 70 percent. This was twice the rate of any other ten-year period during the colonial era. During the 1710s and 1720s there was also a drastic redistribution of wealth. Original research by Jean Russo (1983:3), expanded upon by Paul Shackel (1987, 1993) and by Leone and Shackel (1987, 1990), indicates a restructuring of wealth holdings in Annapolis from 1710 to 1732 (table 6.1). (All wealth has been deflated to the 1700 pound in order to make these comparisons.) The poorest wealth group (those whose estates were valued at £0 to £49) in seventeenth-century Annapolis made up 75 percent of the population while possessing only 28 percent of the city's total wealth held at death. By the 1720s their wealth had decreased disproportionately faster than the decrease in membership in this segment of the population. Between 1723 and 1732, 30 percent of the population making up the lower wealth group owned about 2 percent of the total wealth in that city. Therefore, the average wealth per estate in this group decreased with time.

However, the scenario is just the opposite for the wealthy. In the first decade of the eighteenth century the wealthiest group in Annapolis (those with estates valued at £1,000 or more) accounted for 8 percent of the population and had accrued 21 percent of the wealth held at death. By the 1710s this share in wealth had increased to 56 percent, and increases in wealth held by the elite did not slow down until after the 1730s. By 1725 four Annapolitans owned more than half of the town's land, and the landless were subjugated to a leasehold system (Baker 1986). Between 1722 and 1735 the Chesapeake became engulfed in the most devastating and persistent tobacco depression in the colonial era (Hemphill 1985:54). The cost of imported labor and manufactured goods began to rise during the 1720s and thus indicated the possibility of inflation (Carr and Walsh 1977:15). As tobacco values

TABLE 6.1. *Percentage of Wealth Held by Wealth Groups in Annapolis, Maryland*

	Group I		Group II		Group III		Group IV		Total Wealth and Population from Those Inventoried	
Year	%W	%P	%W	%P	%W	%P	%W	%P	Wealth (£s)	Population
1689–99	28	75	0	0	72	25	0	0	321	4
1700–09	8	46	14	23	51	23	21	8	2,175	13
1710–22	5	38	18	42	21	13	56	8	8,444	40
1723–32	2	30	7	30	13	21	78	18	41,769	33
1733–44	3	37	8	27	12	16	77	20	19,804	51
1745–54	3	48	4	13	7	13	86	26	15,292	31
1755–67	2	26	7	34	7	15	84	25	32.673	53
1768–77	2	30	8	43	5	13	85	20	17,697	30

NOTE: Group I = estates valued at £0–50; Group II = estates valued at £51–225; Group III = estates valued at £226–1,000; Group IV = estates valued at more than £1,000; %W = percentage of wealth; and %P = percentage of population.

SOURCE: Russo (1983); Leone and Shackel (1987, 1990).

declined, the Virginia legislation imposed a tobacco inspection act, which required that tobacco be brought to public warehouses for inspection. Middling planters, fearing that their tobacco would be overlooked in favor of the crops of wealthier planters, began rioting and burning tobacco warehouses from Northern Virginia to Southern Maryland (Kulikoff 1986:107–11).

During times of economic stress, within a competitive system or when the existing social order is being threatened by a new and growing population, the meanings goods establish can create overt distinctions between groups and standardize behavior in order to reinforce or reestablish the hierarchy (Hodder 1979, 1982; Douglas and Isherwood 1979; Miller 1987). Not only did a colonial Chesapeake naturalizing ideology enforce itself through legal means and confirm the established order, but the material culture and the behavior associated with it actively created these boundaries.

As remarked earlier, material culture refers to items that do more than merely reflect human behavior; they are also products having symbolic meaning that actively shapes and creates society through the actions that individuals or groups take in response to those symbols. Indeed, material objects may be the most fundamental and unnoticed aspect of socialization. They not only play an important role in social reproduction, but they can also act as a bridge between the mental and physical world and between the conscious and unconscious (Bourdieu 1977; Miller 1987).

PROBATE ANALYSIS OF FORMAL DINING

As the crises mentioned above affected the Chesapeake region, rules and meanings may have been uncertain and an attempt made to reinforce the traditional order. These new social relations were based on a modern discipline (see Foucault 1979), a behavior that was regular, predictable, and replicable and that manifested itself in a new code of manners and material culture. The wealthy could reaffirm their place in the hierarchy by dismembering the communal values of medieval society and using a new form of social discipline and material culture to create social differences between them and the lower classes. The new modern discipline can be demonstrated in part by the new etiquette and material culture used in the process of eating, such as sets of plates, knives, and forks—which are formal and segmenting items. The assumption is that these sets of items reflect a new formal behavior departing from the medieval communal tradition. Items in groups were intended to relate to each other functionally and to serve socially as the material expression of formalized social structures. No longer were people sharing the same dishes; one plate was used by one person. Relatively few of these formal and segmenting items existed in the earliest estate inventories in Annapolis, but by the 1720s there was a sharp increase in the consumption of these goods by the elite, which reflects the use of a new modern behavior (table 6.2). The fact that etiquette books existed in the probate inventories among the wealthiest Annapolitans in the 1720s indicates that not only did they use these new items of etiquette, but they also paid particular attention to the new rules of social behavior. This new behavior was effectively used to segment the wealthy from the lower poorer groups. Interestingly, this new behavior was prominent among the English elite in the seventeenth century and was nonexistent in colonial Annapolis—one of only a few urban centers in the Chesapeake—up until the 1710s. The new behavior did not emerge gradually, but was instead rapidly introduced into Chesapeake society (Shackel 1991, 1993).

Some Chesapeake historians have argued that the decrease in explicitly segmenting goods in the 1730s and 1740s was a result of the influx of a new rural population into the city. These people did not know the rules of the new etiquette. Since the new immigrants did not know the rules of high society, they would not have the goods to continue the material stratification of the community (Carr, personal communication 1987). I would like to propose an alternative interpretation. I have argued elsewhere (Little and Shackel 1989) that once social hierarchy is reestablished there may be little point in maintaining chattels that explicitly segment groups. If the reestablished order were considered to be unbridgeable, there would be little need to reinforce the hierarchy with material goods, thus the material culture that reinforced the new etiquette would decrease.

Archaeological Analysis of the Transition from Impermanent to Permanent Architecture

During the social, political, and economic fluctuations in the Chesapeake and Annapolis during the late seventeenth and early eighteenth centuries, there was a change not only in the types of chattels owned by people, but also in the kind of architecture used, which moved to more permanent structures after 100 years of earthfast construction. These structures used wood posts as foundations,

Table 6.2. *Some Formal Dining Items Found in Annapolis, Maryland, Probate Inventories*

Wealth in Pounds	1688–1790			1710–1732			1733–1754			1755–1777		
	C	N	%	C	N	%	C	N	%	C	N	%
Set of Plates												
000–49	9	1	11	24	3	13	33	2	06	33	1	03
50–225	3	0	00	27	3	11	18	2	11	30	5	17
226–490	4	1	25	12	2	17	11	1	09	9	2	22
491+	1	0	00	9	2	22	15	3	20	17	7	41
Sets of Forks												
000–49	9	0	00	24	0	00	33	1	03	33	3	09
50–225	3	0	00	27	5	19	18	6	33	30	3	10
226–490	4	0	00	12	3	25	11	6	55	9	7	78
491+	1	0	00	9	4	44	15	2	13	17	12	71
Sets of Knives												
000–49	9	0	00	24	0	00	33	0	00	33	3	11
50–225	3	1	33	27	5	19	18	5	28	30	4	30
226–490	4	0	00	12	3	25	11	6	55	9	7	78
491+	1	0	00	9	5	56	15	4	27	17	13	76

Note: C = total number of cases; N = presence of item; and % = percentage of cases.

and the buildings only lasted an average of 10 years but did not require high expenditures for maintenance (Carson et al. 1981). I use the ideas of Henry Glassie (1987) and Robert Blair St. George (1983) to argue that the decision to prolong the use of earthfast structures was based on the need to maintain social relations between different wealth groups. When earlier relationships disintegrated, a new order of behavior and material culture were created to reestablish a hierarchy in society. From archaeological investigations in Annapolis, Maryland, it appears that the dissolution of social relations in the 1720s was accompanied by a shift to a more permanent architecture, and that this move severed some historically maintained relationships. The change toward permanent architecture in Virginia and Maryland began in the 1660s (see chapter 4; Miller 1986, 1988).

Maintenance relationships are established when action is taken to keep objects or buildings in working order by supplying the necessary funds or needed provisions to replace decayed or damaged parts. Social relations are also created and maintained. Maintenance-related tasks "insured a fundamental continuity in economic, as well as social, relations in communities. . . . [This allowed owners to] seek periodic contractual obligations with a local worker capable of mending the product" (St. George 1983:2). From this perspective, it might be argued that members of all wealth groups built earthfast buildings for more than a century as a way of structuring social relations by maintenance relationships. The change to a more permanent, maintenance-free architecture is better understood when considered as an ideologically influenced decision to clearly distinguish between wealth groups. Intentions of mobility or permanency based on economic success and type of crop, as suggested by Carson et al. (1981) are also recognized as factors in the development of permanent architecture, but these factors alone do not fully explain why these maintenance relations were abandoned.

The limited documentation of social interaction in rural seventeenth-century Chesapeake suggests that these maintenance relationships had a complex character in both the urban and rural context. Although most settlers chose not to live close to each other, informal neighborhoods did appear. "Some cooperation—whether warmly supported or grudgingly extended—was essential to survival" (Walsh 1988:206). Rural social exchange was limited because the intensive care tobacco required left little time for interaction. Also, tobacco goods were exchanged mainly between the planter and a foreign merchant. Walsh (1988:206) argues that as long as most of the Chesapeake residents were immigrants, neighborhood relationships remained weak. But by 1700 nearly half of the region's residents were native-born (Kulikoff 1986:273–274), and the amount of social interaction, especially in new and growing urban areas, increased.

Maintenance relationships may develop in three distinct forms. First, explicit formal relationships are created where a laborer is hired to perform a task, whether in an urban or industrial setting. Second, maintenance relationships may take the form of a balanced or general reciprocity wherein neighbors or relatives are called upon to assist in a task. These are implicit and expected relations and are typical of rural, agrarian communities. Third, work might be performed in-house, either by the owner or servants and slaves. The latter two cases may have predominated during the early Chesapeake settlement. But as the native population increased and urban areas began to develop at the turn of the eighteenth century, settlers began to differentiate between social and economic exchange. The first type of maintenance relationship became increasingly important, as was the case in early eighteenth-century Annapolis, discussed below.

St. George (1983:2) argues that the "maintenance of material forms implies, perhaps is identical with, the maintenance of social forms." An economy based on maintenance-related tasks would ensure a continuation of economic and social relations as well as impose contractual obligations on local workers (St. George 1983:2). Maintenance relationships create a form of reciprocity and may symbolically create a form of communality. Note, too, that vernacular technologies involve local materials and local labor (Glassie 1987:121). The actors are diverse and interlock their talents. When people start opting for more permanent architecture, they are withdrawing from the "local economic system/exchange relations." With the withdrawal from the local system, there occurs a radical change that may disrupt the existing social order (Glassie 1987:237). The change in house forms and material culture forms are associated with a reorganization of social relations in the community. No longer do people rely on the community to organize their social relations. Instead, they take these responsibilities upon themselves. This withdrawal from the local economic system is one manifestation of the new Renaissance ideal of individuality.

The Sands House in Annapolis is a case in point. During the spring of 1988, the Historic Annapolis Foundation was notified that this house was to be remodeled and that the ground might be disturbed. Since this structure dates to the turn of the eighteenth century, archaeologists considered it important to determine when and how it was made "more permanent" through renovations that created a maintenance-free foundation. The Sands House (18AP47) was originally an impermanent structure built on blocks and was underpinned with fieldstone during some of the earlier eighteenth-century renovations, with at least one post mold filled with stone. Excavations have found diagnostic artifacts under the fieldstone as well as in the post-mold fill with a terminus post quem of 1700 and a mean date of manufacture of 1738. Therefore, the underpinning of the structure may have occurred some time around the end of the first quarter of the eighteenth century, the same time that many of the interior renovations took place.

The concept of maintenance relationships helps explain why people used earthfast structures during the seventeenth century. Repairs to the earthfast posts had to be performed on an occasional basis (usually at 10-year intervals) in order to increase the longevity of the structure. It is probably true that the residents of the Sands House were also involved in a maintenance relationship up until the 1720s. Archaeology has demonstrated that about the 1720s the Sands House was made more permanent for it was underpinned by a stone foundation.

This change from an impermanent to a more permanent architecture was an indication of increased individuality and a shift in community relationships. The change from an earthfast construction technique that lasted on the average of about 10 years without upkeep to a more permanent and more maintenance-free architecture was in part an ideological decision. During this era of dramatically changing social relations, the elite in the city not only acquired different types of chattels, but they also began expressing their new social position through architecture. During the 1720s the most affluent citizens of Annapolis began to build with stone foundations, brick exterior walls, and brick chimneys (Yentsch and McKee 1987:46). It appears that interclass cooperation diminished among the upper class as the meaning of their goods, services, and wealth changed. The earliest brick dwelling known to have been built in Annapolis was erected by 1721 by Charles Carroll. Soon after, other wealthy merchants followed Carroll's lead. Unlike the use of formal and segmenting dining items, which decreased in the 1730s and 1740s, the use of more permanent architecture increased from the 1720s and may have temporarily replaced other forms of material culture that distinguished the wealth groups.

Discussion

The interdisciplinary approach to material culture studies brings both an historical and archaeological perspective to bear on important questions and thus offers a powerful tool for interpreting the past. In this study, historical data indicated a change in the material culture goods found in probate inventories. The archaeological analysis contributed data on town planning and changing vernacular architecture. When these data are combined and placed in a social context, the dynamic meaning of the goods becomes clearer, as does the change in their meanings during times of social, political, or economic instability. Changing town plans, increased permanent architecture, and an increase in formal dining—all demonstrate the meanings of changing material goods in the seventeenth- and eighteenth-century Chesapeake.

Material culture is more than an expression of wealth. It is also a mechanism that may create, structure, and reshape social relations. Changes in sociocultural systems and in power relations are often reinforced by new symbols in the form of everyday material goods. With a strong and unquestionable hierarchy, symbolic change seldom occurs and material goods maintain a character that reflects that hierarchical relationship in the community. When the social hierarchy is threatened, new goods are introduced in an attempt to reestablish social asymmetry.

When the Chesapeake hierarchy was threatened by an increasing number of white and black freedmen, the elite divided the lower socioeconomic group by introducing racist legislation. Legalized racism in the 1660s gradually eased the threat of insurrection and was a way of keeping labor under control. The aristocracy essentially created a new, lower class and promoted racial prejudice where it had previously not existed. Racism divided the power of the poor and created a new labor base. Harsh penalties made it undesirable for whites to associate with blacks. New expressions of material culture were introduced to explicitly segment groups. It is more than a coincidence that New World baroque town planning developed during the 1660s, during the radical shift between white and black relationships. Undoubtedly this is not the only variable related to the town planning, as Miller (1988) explains, but it played a vital role.

This new baroque plan in St Mary's City emphasized the power of the two leading institutions in the community, church and state. When the capital was moved to Annapolis in 1694, the royal governor reestablished a major presence of authority and retained the symbolic citing of these central buildings. Both the state house and the church were placed on the highest points in town, surrounded by circles with streets radiating from them.

The 1720s was marked by social, political, and economic fluctuations. The population increased sharply, inflation and a depression took hold, and wealth restructuring prevailed in the city of Annapolis. Racist legislation became embedded in a naturalizing ideology and community relations began to disintegrate. Legislation stated that it was unnatural for whites and blacks to marry, socialize, and have sexual intercourse. Discriminatory legislation against Irish papists grew and legitimized the subordination of additional groups. Racist, ethnic, and religious legislation defined new roles in society during this period of sociocultural instability.

Early Chesapeake settlers probably did not differentiate between social and economic exchange until at least the turn of the eighteenth century. When these exchange systems became distinct, the relationships maintaining the social structure transformed dramatically. The perception of the new social structure that promoted a visible hierarchy was supported by a new material culture. These changes brought shifts in consumption patterns and the styles of architecture used by the elite. The upper wealth group began to dismember the medieval tradition. No longer were they satisfied with sitting on benches, eating communal meals with knives, and sharing goblets. Rather, they began to adhere to a new set of rules, or etiquette, and to sit on individual chairs, eat off their own plates, and use their own utensils. This movement toward individuality among the elite began in Maryland around the 1720s.

The shift away from community relations during the 1720s can also be documented archaeologically. Medieval-style architecture, which reflected traditional maintenance relationships, dissolved. Earthfast structures gave way to more permanent and ostentatious facades. In the case of the Sands House in Annapolis, the residents removed themselves from the community work network by replacing the impermanent wood posts with a stone foundation. Periodic maintenance was no longer needed and neither was the regular assistance of craftsmen in the community.

The development of distinct class boundaries and the concept of the modern individual was not historically inevitable but rather was a product of the changing social values and the reaction of the elite to an increasingly powerful lower group. The wealthy in the Chesapeake reacted toward sociocultural instability by using material symbols that reinforced the established order. The new material goods associated with the new behavior emphasized individuality and defined class boundaries and thereby changed the landscape and material culture of the seventeenth- and eighteenth-century Chesapeake.

ACKNOWLEDGMENTS

I am grateful to Mark Leone for inviting me to participate in the Archaeology in Annapolis project. Some of the data presented here were collected while I was employed by the Historic Annapolis Foundation. I am especially grateful to Mrs. Margaret Dowsett, proprietor of the Sands House, for allowing archaeologists from the foundation to excavate in the house while it was under renovation. Henry Miller insightfully suggested that I explicitly distinguish between various types of maintenance relationships. His analysis on the St. Mary's City town plan has facilitated this comparison between Maryland's capital cities. I appreciate Barbara Little's suggestions during the formulation of the ideas of this essay and her comments on various drafts. Paul Mullins also made valuable suggestions on an earlier draft.

REFERENCES CITED

Baker, Nancy

1986 Annapolis, Maryland 1695–1730. *Maryland Historical Magazine* 81(3):191–209.

Breene, T. H., and Stephen Innes

1980 *"Myne Owne Ground": Race and Freedom on Virginia's Eastern Shore, 1640–1676*. Oxford University Press, New York.

Bourdieu, Pierre

1977 *Outline of a Theory of Practice*. Cambridge University Press, Cambridge.

Carr, Lois Green

1974 The Metropolis of Maryland: A Comment on Town Development along the Tobacco Coast. *Maryland Historical Magazine* 69(2):124–145.

Carr, Lois Green, and Lorena Walsh

1977 Inventories and the Analysis of Wealth and Consumption Patterns in St. Mary's County, Maryland,

1658–1777. The Newberry Papers in Family and Community History, paper 77-46. Newberry Library, Chicago.

Carson, Cary, Norman F. Barka, William Kelso, Gary Wheeler Stone, and Dell Upton

1981 Impermanent Architecture in Southern American Colonies. *Winterthur Portfolio* 16(2/3):135–196.

Cook, Ebinezer

1900 [1708] The Sot-Weed Factor, or A Voyage to Maryland. In *Early Maryland Poetry*, edited by Bernard C. Steiner, pp. 29–30. Fund Publication No. 36, Maryland Historical Society, Baltimore.

Deal, Douglas

1988 A Constricted World: Free Blacks on Virginia's Eastern Shore, 1680–1750. In *Colonial Chesapeake Society*, edited by Lois Green Carr, Philip D. Morgan, and Jean B. Russo, pp. 275–305. University of North Carolina Press, Chapel Hill.

Deetz, James

1988 American Historical Archaeology: Method and Results. *Science* (239): 362–367.

Douglas, Mary, and Baron Isherwood

1979 *The World of Goods*. Basic Books, New York.

Foucault, Michel

1979 *Discipline and Punish*. Vintage Books, New York.

Glassie, Henry

1987 Vernacular Architecture and Society. In *Mirror and Metaphor: Material and Social Construction of Reality*, edited by Daniel Ingersol and Gordon Bronitsky, pp. 229–246. University Press of America, Lanham, Md.

Handlin, Oscar, and Mary Handlin

1950 Origins of the Southern Labor System. *William and Mary Quarterly* 7:199–222.

Hemphill, John M. II

1985 *Virginia and the English Commercial System 1689–1733*. Garland, New York.

Hodder, Ian

1979 Economic and Social Stress and Material Culture Patterning. *American Antiquity*. 44(3):446–454.

1982 *Symbols in Action: Ethnoarchaeological Studies of Material Culture*. Cambridge University Press, Cambridge.

1986 *Reading the Past: Current Approaches to Interpretation in Archaeology*. Cambridge University Press, New York.

Jordan, Winthrop

1978 Unthinking Decision: Enslavement of Negroes in America to 1700. In *Interpreting Colonial America*, edited by Kirby Martin, pp. 140–161. Harper and Row, New York.

Kilty, William

1799 *The Laws of Maryland*. Vol 1. Frederick Green, Printer, Annapolis, Md.

Kulikoff, Allan

1978 The Origins of Afro-American Society in Tidewater Maryland and Virginia, 1700–1790. *William and Mary Quarterly* 35:226–259.

1986 *Tobacco and Slaves: The Development of Southern Culture in the Chesapeake, 1680–1800*. University of North Carolina Press, Chapel Hill.

Leone, Mark P.

1987 Rule by Ostentation: The Relationship between Space and Sight in 18th-Century Landscape Architecture in the Chesapeake Region of Maryland. In *Method and Theory for Activity Area Research*, edited by Susan Kent, pp. 604–633. Columbia University Press, New York.

1988 The Georgian Order as the Order of Merchant Capitalism in Annapolis, Maryland. In *The Recovery of Meaning: Historical Archaeology in the Eastern United States*, edited by Mark P. Leone and Parker B. Potter, Jr., pp 235–262. Smithsonian Institution Press, Washington, D.C.

Leone, Mark P., and Paul A. Shackel

1987 Forks, Clocks and Power. In *Mirror and Metaphor: Material and Social Constructions of Reality*, edited by Daniel W. Ingersoll, Jr., and Gordon Bronitsky, pp. 45–62. University Press of America, Lanham, Md.

1990 The Georgian Order in Annapolis, Maryland. In New Perspectives on Maryland Archaeology, edited by Richard J. Dent and Barbara J. Little. *Maryland Archaeologist* 26(1&2):69–84.

Leone, Mark P., Julie Ernstein, Elizabeth Kryder-Reid, and Paul A. Shackel

1989 Power Gardens in Annapolis. *Archaeology*. 42(2): 34–39, 74–75.

Little, Barbara J., and Paul A. Shackel

1989 Scales of Historical Anthropology: An Archaeology of Colonial Anglo-America. *Antiquity* (62)240:495–509.

McCusker, John J., and Russell R. Menard

1986 *The Economy of British America: 1607–1789*. University of North Carolina Press, Chapel Hill.

McKendrick, Neil

1982 Commercialization and the Economy. In *The Birth of a Consumer Society: The Commercialization of Eighteenth-Century England*, edited by Neil McKendrick, John Brewer, and J. H. Plumb, pp. 9–194. Indiana University Press, Bloomington.

Menard, Russell Robert

1975 *Economy and Society in Early Colonial Maryland*. Ph.D. dissertation on file at the Department of History, University of Iowa.

Miller, Daniel

1987 *Material Culture and Mass Consumption*. Basil Blackwell, New York.

Miller, Henry

1986 *Discovering Maryland's First City: A Summary Report on the 1981–1984 Archaeological Excavations in St. Mary's City, Maryland*. St. Mary's City Archaeology Series No. 2. Alexander H. Morrison Fund Publication, St. Mary's City.

1988 Baroque Cities in the Wilderness: Archaeology and Urban Development in the Colonial Chesapeake. *Historical Archaeology* 22(2):57–73.

Morgan, Edmund S.
1975 *American Slavery American Freedom: The Ordeal of Colonial Virginia*. W. W. Norton, New York.
Morris, A. E. J.
1979 *History of Urban Form: Before the Industrial Revolution*. John Wiley and Sons, New York.
Papenfuse, Edward C.
1975 *In Pursuit of Profit: The Annapolis Merchant in the Era of the American Revolution, 1763–1805*. Johns Hopkins University Press, Baltimore, Md.
Ramirez, Constance Werner
1975 *Urban History for Preservation Planning: The Annapolis Experience*. University Microfilms, Ann Arbor, Mich.
Reps, John W.
1972 *Tidewater Towns: City Planning in Colonial Virginia and Maryland*. Colonial Williamsburg Foundation, Williamsburg, Va.
Riley, Elihu
1887 *The Ancient City: A History of Annapolis, in Maryland 1649–1887*. Record Printing Office, Annapolis, Md.
Russo, Jean
1983 Economy of Anne Arundel County. In Annapolis and Anne Arundel County, Maryland, A Study of Urban Development in a Tobacco Economy, 1649–1776, edited by Lorena S. Walsh. N.E.H. Grant No. RS 20199-81-1955. On File at Historic Annapolis, Inc., Annapolis, Md.
St. George, Blair
1983 Maintenance Relationships and the Erotics of Property in Historical Thought. Paper presented at the American Historical Association Meetings, Philadelphia.
Shackel, Paul A.
1987 *A Historical Archaeology of Personal Discipline*. Ph.D. dissertation, State University of New York at Buffalo. University Microfilms, Ann Arbor.
1991 Consumerism and the Structuring of Social Relations: An Historical Archaeological Perspective. In *Digging into Popular Culture: Theories and Methodologies in Archeology, Anthropology and Other Fields*, edited by Ray Browne and Pat Browne, pp. 31–41. Bowling Green State University Popular Press, Bowling Green, Ohio.
1993 *Personal Discipline and Material Culture: An Archaeology of Annapolis, Maryland, 1695–1870*. University of Tennessee Press, Knoxville, Tenn.
Walsh, Lorena S.
1983a Annapolis as a Center of Production. In Annapolis and Anne Arundel County, Maryland, A Study of Urban Development in a Tobacco Economy, 1649–1776, edited by Lorena S. Walsh. N.E.H. Grant No. RS 20199-81-1955. On File at Historic Annapolis, Inc., Annapolis, Md.
1983b Anne Arundel County Population. In Annapolis and Anne Arundel County, Maryland, A Study of Urban Development in a Tobacco Economy, 1649–1776, edited by Lorena S. Walsh. N.E.H. Grant No. RS 20199-81-1955. On File at Historic Annapolis, Inc., Annapolis, Md.
1988 Community Networks in Early Chesapeake. In *Colonial Chesapeake Society*, edited by Lois Green Carr, Philip D. Morgan, and Jean B. Russo, pp. 200–41. University of North Carolina Press, Chapel Hill.
Yentsch, Anne, and Larry McKee
1987 Footprints of Buildings in Eighteenth-Century Annapolis. *American Archaeology* 6(1):40–51.

II
PART

Plantation and Landscape Studies

PLANTATION AND landscape studies are closely related, particularly in the chapters in this section. The landscape environment played an important role in the creation of planters' self-perceptions and in developing an external image for others to observe (see chapters 7 and 9). Most of the chapters in this section elaborate on the landscapes of some of the most prominent forefathers in American history, those who challenged the English Crown for "life, liberty and the pursuit of happiness": George Washington (chapter 7), Thomas Jefferson (chapter 8), and Charles Carroll (chapter 9). The ideal of liberty for which these men and many others fought stands, in some ways, as a contradiction to their actual practices. These planters and gentlemen developed and shaped the environment around them in urban and rural areas with the exclusive aid of bonded labor. Even as plantation economies were redirected from tobacco to mixed grain and therefore no longer needed as sizable a labor force, planters transferred slaves to other activities rather than free them (see chapters 7 and 8).

Plantation studies in historical archaeology began in the early 1970s with Robert Ascher and Charles Fairbank's landmark study of a slave cabin in Georgia, which was found to contain various unexpected material goods (Ascher and Fairbanks 1971; Fairbanks 1974). Through the analysis of colonoware, Leland Ferguson (1978, 1992) opened whole new areas of research into the material expression of slave culture. Matthew Emerson (chapter 3) has further contributed to this research through the identification of African-made pipes in the Chesapeake. Many in-depth studies of particular plantations have been carried out, including those by Jerome Handler and Frederick Lange (1978) in Barbados, John Otto (1984) and Theresa Singleton (1980) in Georgia, William Kelso in Virginia (1984), and Charles Orser (1988) in the South Carolina Piedmont. In particular, Otto's methodology of comparing material differences between owners, overseers, and slaves has been quite influential. The technique of pattern recognition inspired by Stanley South (1977) has also been used extensively in plantation studies (for example, Singleton 1985; see also Orser 1989). Recently, archaeologists such as Orser (1988), Singleton (1988), and Sanford (chapter 8) have begun to address many of the social, political, and economic implications of plantation economy, its place in a profit-making system, the creation and integrity of an African American culture, and implications for an archaeology of racism today (Babson 1990; Epperson 1990).

In a recent overview, Charles Orser (1990) sets out three viewpoints taken in the archaeology of plantation slavery. The supraordinate view focuses on the planter elite, the subordinate on the slaves, and the dialectical on master–slave relations. In this section Pogue takes the supraordinate viewpoint in discussing George Washington's intentions at Mount Vernon. Sanford provides a primarily subordinate perspective in discussing changing slave life at Monticello, but also sets up a model for a dialectical analysis.

Landscapes, as Henry Miller explained in chapter 5, are important expressions in Western culture and play a role in the symbolic, social, economic, and functional definition of activities. Landscape studies have become an increasingly important focus of attention in historical archaeology. Since the early 1980s archaeologists have realized that landscape is very much an artifact. The landscape features serve as more than ornaments attached to the great houses of the Chesapeake; they are also expressions of baroque and Renaissance ideals, expressions of emulation, assertions of power over the natural environment, and sometimes vehicles used to display control and reinforce hierarchy. In chapter 9 Elizabeth Kryder-Reid examines the power of landscape as myth. Studies of landscape in American historical archaeology have included analyses of town plans (Miller 1988; Leone et al. 1989), houselots (Beaudry 1984; Harrington 1989), factories and boardinghouses (Beaudry 1989; Mrozowski and Beaudry 1990), ranches (Praetzellis and Praetzellis 1989), and gardens (Leone 1984; Leone and Shackel 1990). One of the first and most influential landscape studies in the region was Mark Leone's (1984) study of the Paca garden in Annapolis, Maryland. More recently, Kelso and Most (1990) compiled a review of landscape studies using a variety of approaches and data.

The Essays

In chapter 7 Dennis Pogue interprets changes in the design of Mount Vernon plantation. George Washington acted as his own architect and designer and emulated many of the architectural and landscape trends in the Chesapeake. Pogue divides Washington's occupation of Mount Vernon into three phases, tracing the development through historical documents, maps, and archaeology. During the first phase, between 1758 and 1766, Washington aspired to many of the goals and ambitions of Chesapeake planters. He developed and expanded the tobacco-producing plantation, acquired more land, and increased the number of slaves he owned. One of Washington's objectives for his plantation was to regularize many of the diverse features of his landscape—by developing a geometric plan for his landscape, presenting an orderly facade for his house, and creating a formal garden. During the second phase, between 1766 and 1774, Washington switched from tobacco production to grain, developed home-produced goods, and enlarged his fisheries. During the third phase, between 1774 and 1799, he altered the Mount Vernon landscape once again. Strictly geometrical landscape designs were replaced with carefully planned undulating greens, serpentine wilderness, and elliptical walls. Washington's continuous redevelopment of Mount Vernon displays his active intention to display ostentatiously his power and authority among Chesapeake planters.

Douglas Sanford focuses his discussion in chapter 8 on the development of African American culture on Thomas Jefferson's Monticello plantation. Sanford provides an interdisciplinary approach and addresses issues that reach beyond slave status to the nature of slave society. He develops a contextual and processual framework at the local and regional levels by using primary and secondary documentary sources. Because African American sites are variable, generalities about slave culture need to be examined in the context of specific situations and compared with larger regional contexts. Hence, Sanford notes, plantation archaeologists need to counter the growing trend toward studies confined to single sites.

Sanford examines seven domestic slave sites on Monticello and compares the data between two time periods: 1770–1800 and 1800–1825. In the later era he notices the development of an identifiable African American culture and finds that individual household differences indicate self-sufficiency and probably variations in status. Signs of slave autonomy include materials related to gardening, raising poultry, hunting and trapping, and gathering fruit. Money found in these cabins also indicates that the slaves earned monetary rewards for special chores or for selling garden surplus to the Jefferson household. Other material goods such as ceramics indicate that status differences existed between the African American households. Important to this analysis is the use of middle-range theory to search for ambiguities and contradictions between the archaeological and historical records.

In chapter 9 Elizabeth Kryder-Reid examines the eighteenth-century garden of Charles Carroll of Carrollton in Annapolis, Maryland, and explores the changing meanings of the landscape, comparing Carroll's use to that of the Redemptorists, a Catholic order whose members inhabited the property from the mid-nineteenth century. Kryder-Reid notes that the gardens can be seen as myths that resolve contradictions by calling upon precedent, or some glorious past, to naturalize the present, as well as to legitimize future claims of inequity. Landscapes are experienced, have public and private meanings, and construct and negotiate social identity.

Under Carroll's ownership this land was used not only to ostentatiously display power and wealth, especially since as a Roman Catholic he was unable to hold political office, but also to serve other purposes through its mythical qualities. The garden portrayed the owner as a master of nature and also erased any hints of its production process, such as slave labor. This latter myth served to mask the contradiction in Carroll's political ideology of sovereignty. The later inhabitants of the property, the Redemptorists, operated as a self-sufficient closed community. Soon after acquiring the land they began to conceal or destroy the ostentation of the Carroll property. The ornamental garden became functional, and the Redemptorists performed their labor themselves, rather than employing slaves or paid craftsmen. The privacy that they sought was an expression and construction of their own identity, and this was reflected in their changes in and around the Carroll property.

Archaeologists have always been concerned with environment and its effects on human lives. The study of landscape, including whole plantations, gardens, and any physical setting that people create for themselves or people under their control, extends this interest in environment. The material interaction between physical environments and the people that inhabit, build, and alter them provides an inescapable dynamism to the past.

References Cited

Ascher, Robert, and Charles H. Fairbanks

1971 Excavations of a Slave Cabin: Georgia, U.S.A. *Historical Archaeology* 5:3–17.

Babson, David W.

1990 The Archaeology of Racism and Ethnicity on Southern Plantations. Historical Archaeology on Southern Plantations and Farms, edited by Charles E. Orser, Jr. *Historical Archaeology* 24(4): 20–28.

Beaudry, Mary C.

1984 Archaeology and the Historical Household. *Man in the Northeast* 28:27–38.

1989 The Lowell Boott Mills Complex and Its Housing: Material Expressions of Corporate Ideology. *Historical Archaeology* 23(1):19– 33.

Emerson, Matthew

1988 *Decorated Clay Tobacco Pipes from the Chesapeake.* Ph.D. dissertation, Department of Anthropology, University of California, Berkeley.

Epperson, Terrance W.

1990 Race and Discipline of the Plantation. Historical Archaeology on Southern Plantations and Farms, edited by Charles E. Orser, Jr. *Historical Archaeology* 24(4):29–36.

Fairbanks, Charles

1974 The Kingsley Slave Cabins in Duval County, Florida, 1968. *Conference on Historic Site Archaeology Papers* 7:62–93.

Ferguson, Leland

1978 Looking for "Afro" in Colono-Indian Pottery. *Conference on Historic Site Archaeology papers* 12:68–86.

1992 *Uncommon Ground: Archaeology and Colonial African-America.* Smithsonian Institution Press, Washington, D.C.

Handler, Jerome S., and Frederick W. Lange

1978 *Plantation Slavery in Barbados: An Archaeological and Historical Perspective.* Harvard University Press, Cambridge.

Harrington, Faith

1989 The Emergent Elite in Early 18th Century Portsmouth Society: The Archaeology of the Joseph Sherburne Houselot. *Historical Archaeology* 23(1):2–18.

Kelso, William

1984 *Kingsmill Plantations, 1619–1800: Archaeology of Country Life in Colonial Virginia.* Academic Press, Orlando.

Kelso, William, and Rachel Most (editors)

1990 *Earth Patterns: Essays in Landscape Archaeology.* University Press of Virginia, Charlottesville.

Leone, Mark P.

1984 Interpreting Ideology in Historical Archaeology: Using the Rules of Perspective in the William Paca Garden in Annapolis, Maryland. In *Ideology, Power, and Prehistory*, edited by Daniel Miller and Christopher Tilley, pp. 25–35. Cambridge University Press, Cambridge.

Leone, Mark P., and Paul A. Shackel

1990 Plane and Solid Geometry in Colonial Gardens in Annapolis, Maryland. In *Earth Patterns: Essays in Landscape Archaeology*, edited by William M. Kelso and Rachel Most, pp. 153–168. University Press of Virginia, Charlottesville.

Leone, Mark P., Julie Ernstein, Elizabeth Kryder-Reid, and Paul A. Shackel

1989 Power Gardens in Annapolis. *Archaeology* 42(2):34–39, 74–75.

Miller, Henry

1988 Baroque Cities in the Wilderness: Archaeology and Urban Development in the Colonial Chesapeake. *Historical Archaeology* 22(2):57–73.

Mrozowski, Stephen, and Mary C. Beaudry
1990 Archaeology and the Landscape of Corporate Ideology. In *Earth Patterns: Essays in Landscape Archaeology*, edited by William M. Kelso and Rachel Most, pp. 189–210. University Press of Virginia, Charlottesville.
Orser, Charles
1988 *The Material Basis of the Postbellum Tenant Plantation: Historical Archaeology in the Eastern United States*. University of Georgia Press, Athens.
1989 On Plantations and Patterns. *Historical Archaeology* 23(2):28–40.
1990 Archaeological Approaches to New World Plantation Slavery. In *Archaeological Method and Theory*, vol. 2, edited by Michael B. Schiffer, pp. 111–154. University of Arizona Press, Tucson.
Otto, John Solomon
1984 *Cannons Point Plantation, 1794–1860: Living Conditions and Status Patterns in the Old South*. Academic Press, Orlando.
Praetzellis, Adrian, and Mary Praetzellis
1989 "Utility and Beauty Should Be One": The Landscape of Jack London's Ranch of Good Intentions. *Historical Archaeology* 23(1):33–44.
Singleton, Theresa
1988 An Archaeological Framework for Slavery and Emancipation, 1740– 1880. In *The Recovery of Meaning: Historical Archaeology in the Eastern United States*, edited by Mark P. Leone and Parker B. Potter Jr., pp. 345–370. Smithsonian Institution Press, Washington, D.C.
1980 *The Archaeology of Afro-American Slavery in Coastal Georgia: A Regional Perception of Slave Household and Community Patterns*. Ph.D. dissertation, University of Florida. University Microfilms, Ann Arbor.
1985 (editor) *The Archaeology of Slavery and Plantation Life*. Academic Press, Orlando.
South, Stanley
1977 *Method and Theory in Historical Archaeology*. Academic Press, New York.

Suggested Readings from the Contributors

Berlin, Ira, and Richard Hoffman
1983 *Slavery and Freedom in the Age of the American Revolution*. University of Virginia Press, Charlottesville.
Betts, Edwin M.
1976 *Thomas Jefferson's Farm Book*. University of Virginia Press, Charlottesville. Originally Published in 1953.
Breen, Timothy H.
1985 *Tobacco Culture: The Mentality of the Great Tidewater Planters on the Eve of Revolution*. Princeton University Press, Princeton, N.J.
Crader, Diana C.
1990 Slave Diet at Monticello. *American Antiquity* 55(4):690–717.
Flexner, James T.
1974 *Washington, the Indispensable Man*. Little Brown, Boston.
Genovese, Eugene D.
1972 *Roll Jordon Roll: The World Slaves Made*. Random House, New York.
Kelso, William M.
1984 *Kingsmill Plantations, 1619–1800: Archaeology of Country Life in Colonial Virginia*. Academic Press, New York.
Kelso, William, and Rachel Most (editors)
1990 *Earth Patterns: Essays in Landscape Archaeology*. University Press of Virginia, Charlottesville.
Leone, Mark P.
1984 Interpreting Ideology in Historical Archaeology Using Rules of Perspective in the William Paca Garden in Annapolis, Maryland. In *Ideology, Power, and Prehistory*, edited by Daniel Miller and Christopher Tilley, pp. 25–35. Cambridge University Press, Cambridge.
Orser, Charles E., Jr. (editor)
1990 *Historical Archaeology on Southern Plantations and Farms*. A thematic issue for *Historical Archaeology* 24(4).
Morgan, Philip, and Michael L. Nicholls
1989 Slaves in Piedmont Virginia, 1720–1790. *William and Mary Quarterly* 46(2):211–251.
Singleton, Theresa (editor)
1985 *The Archaeology of Slavery and Plantation Life*. Academic Press, New York.
Sobel, Mechal
1987 *The World they Made Together: Black and White Values in Eighteenth-Century Virginia*. Princeton University Press, Princeton, N.J.
Wall, Charles C.
1980 *George Washington: Citizen-Soldier*. University Press of Virginia, Charlottesville.

VII
CHAPTER

Mount Vernon
Transformation of an Eighteenth-Century Plantation System

DENNIS J. POGUE

OVER THE 45-YEAR period that George Washington was the proprietor of Mount Vernon, he transformed the modest holding established by his father, Augustine, into a sprawling, 7,600-acre plantation with four outlying "farms" in addition to his home at the "Mansion House Farm." The house was enlarged and the homelot reorganized into a late-Georgian "mansion" with a variety of supporting outbuildings and a pleasure ground with extensive gardens and ambitiously planned ornamental landscape features. The economic foundation of the plantation also was altered, turning from dependence on tobacco as a cash crop to diversified grain production, together with a variety of crafts and other commercial enterprises.

The story of George Washington's transformation of his home is informative on a number of levels. Fundamentally, the entire process reflects the personal expression of the tastes and desires of one man and how they changed over time. But as a member of Virginia's planter elite, his desires clearly reflect, and their implementation was made possible by, his position of social and economic prominence. Washington acted as his own architect and designer, depending on a variety of published sources and the advice of his peers to guide his attempts to emulate the current fashionable trends in architectural and landscape design. As such, Mount Vernon serves as a case study, providing insight into the mentalité of the highest level of the Virginia gentry during a half-century of remarkable changes in American culture and society.

As with all large Southern plantations in the eighteenth century, Mount Vernon was a complex multifunctioning entity, dependent on the labor of hundreds of slaves as the engine to drive it. The recent emphasis in "plantation archaeology" generally has taken the form of intensive study of the African American component of the plantation community in an attempt to balance an earlier focus on the lives and homes of the great planters. It now seems more appropriate, however, to study plantations as whole, complex systems that incorporate agricultural, economic, social, and cultural subsystems.

SYSTEMS THEORY

The anthropologically oriented archaeological investigation of plantations has developed over the past 20 years as a significant subfield within historical archaeology, complete with an impressive listing of site reports and a growing number of contributed volumes, monographs, and journal articles of both substantive and theoretical orientation. From a traditional emphasis on the material culture of the great planter families, by the mid-1970s the focus had broadened significantly to include other components of plantations, in particular the study of the lifeways of African American slaves (Fairbanks 1984; Orser 1984).

The recognition that plantations are complex socioeconomic entities has led researchers to seek methods that are better suited to their study. In regard to the analysis of slave lifeways, for instance, Orser (1987 and 1988) cautions that the broader context of plantation relationships must be carefully examined before synthetic analyses should proceed. In addition, the likelihood of variability between plantations according to the period of occupation, location, size, and the economic standing of the planter dictates that each plantation must be intensively and holistically analyzed before comparative studies will be feasible.

At Mount Vernon a systemic perspective is being used to provide an analytical framework for the archaeological research program, which seems to offer a useful means of interpreting the 45-year history of George Washington's proprietorship. Such a paradigm recognizes the complex nature of plantations and, therefore, ensures a more holistic approach to plantation research than has been the norm to date. Its advantage in this context is that by definition it calls for the broadest possible consideration of the factors affecting plantations, a perspective that seems sorely needed at this time.

From this perspective, plantations are viewed as systems, composed of "intercommunicating" attributes, or subsystems, which together represent a sophisticated adaptation to their social and natural environment. Such systems are envisioned as dynamic, or always undergoing minute change, but at the same time, continuous, implying a certain degree of behavioral regularity and predictability. In such a system, the component attributes or entities are viewed as intercommunicating, in that changes in the values or states of some of these components can be shown to alter the value or state of their neighbors. Any such change is customarily termed a transformation (Binford 1962; Watson et al. 1973; Clarke 1978). George Washington's decisions to radically redesign the landscape and realign the economic foundation of Mount Vernon seem instructively viewed as such systemic transformations.

Plog (1975) suggests that archaeologists may use systems theory effectively in a number of ways—as a unified body of concepts, a set of modeling techniques, a source of testable propositions, and a model of explanation. In reference to the study of Mount Vernon, and colonial plantations in general, systems theory serves as a means of conceptualizing processes and ordering diachronic trends that otherwise might seem unrelated.

Criticisms of the use of systems theory in a cultural context include the difficulty of strictly defining systems and in formulating testable principles that apply to any system. As a result, systemic analyses have proven exceedingly difficult to test. Because of this lack of falsifiability, systems "theory" has been criticized as being atheoretical and has even been characterized as nonexplanatory historical description (Salmon 1978). Although systems theory thus appears to have inherent explanatory limitations, even critics such as Salmon (1978) grant that a general outlook that might be described as taking a "systemic approach" to archaeological data will enhance understanding. One of the advantages of this approach is its broadly contextual nature, which is the characteristic that seems most beneficial in this instance.

The Plantation System

The Chesapeake plantation system may be viewed as the adaptation of English colonization to the Chesapeake environment. Even though the initial goals of the English colonizers were to establish extractive industries such as gold mining, within a few years environmental constraints combined with the needs of British mercantilism to foster the development of the region as an agriculturally based colony, which provided commodities to the mother country in return for manufactured goods. The region continued to play this economic role—source of raw materials and market for British goods—throughout the colonial period (Middleton 1953; Morgan 1975; Isaac 1982; Kulikoff 1986).

World systems theorists such as Wallerstein (1974) have effectively linked North American plantations with their interactive global model as the consequence of the planters' role in the colonial English economic system. In this context, the Chesapeake planter class operated on the periphery, economically dependent on the English core. Other materialist scholars such as Wolf (1982) and Roseberry (1989) support the interpretation of the dependent nature of plantations, but reason that as a group planters had greater autonomy than the classic core–periphery model implies. Economic dependence on overseas trade and the vagaries of that type of market, however, guaranteed that American planters producing a cash export crop would continue to be placed in a dependent, reactive position.

Tobacco served as the region's first major export crop, a plant that required unusually intensive care in its cultivation and preparation for the market. Chesapeake soils were well suited to growing tobacco, although they were quickly exhausted by the crop's nutrient demands. Fortunately, virgin land was abundant, and fertility could be replenished through field rotation. The myriad rivers and smaller streams feeding into the Chesapeake Bay served as the necessary conduit through which the crop began its trans-Atlantic journey. The final component of the system, the labor to cultivate, process, and ship the crop, initially was provided by English indentured servants and, by the end of the seventeenth century, through the institution of chattel slavery (Middleton 1953; Morgan 1975).

By the mid-eighteenth century, the fluid social structure of the previous century had been replaced with a rigid hierarchy comprised of a planter elite at the top and African American slaves at the bottom (Kulikoff 1986: 262–263). The cultivation of grain as a cash crop increased during this period, and in some regions it completely replaced tobacco (Carson et al. 1981:171–176). Tobacco remained the focus of the great planters and the economic bulwark of the system as a whole, however, even though recurring depressions in the market ensured a measure of continuing instability. The 1750s were a decade of generally high prices, which resulted in prosperity for the planter class (Kulikoff 1986:119).

The large plantations, therefore, were complex operations that often included hundreds of laborers and thousands of acres of land, with the planter's seat and one or more outlying farms, or quarters. The home farm usually was the site of a number of specialized crafts, while the outlying quarters were the primary agricultural units. In fundamental terms, the plantation represented an economic system with the planter at the top of a rigidly stratified hierarchy. The plantation subsystem, in turn, was intimately connected with the larger English colonial market network. In this period, tobacco was the product that the system was designed to exploit (Orser 1988).

Embracing the System, 1758–1766

After his return from the French and Indian War in 1758, George Washington sought to earn a place among Virginia's planter elite via the time-honored method of expanding his inherited holdings in slaves and in land and by devoting those resources to the cultivation of tobacco as a cash crop. His marriage the following year to the wealthy widow, Martha Dandridge Custis, provided him with the additional resources necessary to carry out that program. The plantation that George Washington acquired in 1754 was much different in almost all respects from the one he left behind at his death 45 years later. In addition to being only a fraction of the size it would later achieve, the planter's house and homelot reflected a more humble outlook and station in society (Flexner 1974; Wall 1980).

Between 1757 and 1761 Washington more than doubled the size of Mount Vernon, from approximately 2,300 to almost 4,800 acres. Although this program of acquisition placed him deeply in debt, he continued to purchase small adjoining parcels when they became available, and by 1764 the plantation totaled approximately 5,500 acres. At this point he halted expansion and did not acquire additional land until he found a way to reduce his indebtedness (figure 7.1) (Rhodehamel 1983).

At the same time George Washington was rapidly expanding his landholdings, he was also acquiring large numbers of slaves. Between 1752 and 1773 he purchased at least 50 slaves, to add to the 36 slaves he had inherited and the more than 50 slaves added as a result of his marriage to Martha Custis (Clark 1988). The earliest surviving enumeration of the occupations of the slaves at Mount Vernon dates to 1786, when the total number was 216 (Jackson and Twohig 1978:277–282). Therefore, it is not known how many of the slaves were engaged in tobacco production in the early period, but the percentage probably was quite high since tobacco was the main agricultural pursuit at Mount Vernon until 1766.

Washington's unqualified adoption of the system is evidenced by his entrance into the transatlantic consignment trade. The consignment of their tobacco crop to individual merchants in England was the preferred arrangement among Virginia's planter elite. The planter was responsible for all charges incurred in shipping his crop to England. In return, the merchant personally supervised the sale of the crop and offered other services prized by the larger planters. Chief among these was the extension of credit, allowing planters to draw bills of exchange against present and anticipated tobacco sales. Washington sent his first modest shipment of tobacco to England in 1755, with increasingly larger cargoes over the next decade (Ragsdale 1989:133–136).

As George Washington was enlarging his plantation and entering the tobacco trade, he also was expanding and rearranging his new home and the surrounding land-

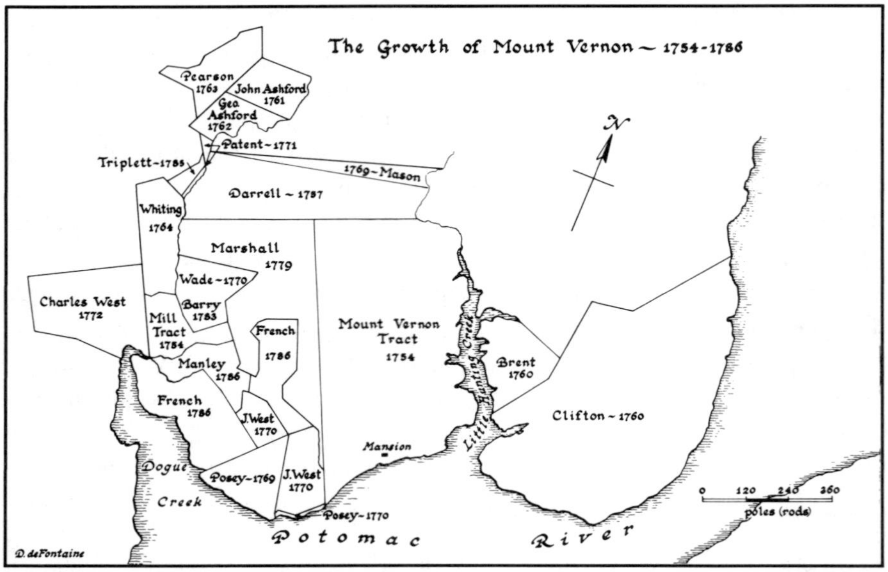

FIGURE 7.1. *The growth of Mount Vernon, 1754–1786. (Courtesy of the Papers of George Washington)*

scape. The result was an ambitious reordering of the dwelling and domestic seat he had inherited. The new configuration was more unified and visually regular, with the existing outbuildings and two new structures connected with the enlarged main house, and with those structures flanked by two rectangular walled gardens, all of which were oriented toward a driveway and circle (figure 7.2).

Although the early history of Mount Vernon is shrouded in uncertainty, it seems likely that George Washington's father, Augustine, built the first house on the site by 1735. The property was then known as Little Hunting Creek Plantation and consisted of one-half of a larger tract first patented in 1674 by John Washington, great-grandfather of George, in partnership with Nicholas Spencer. George Washington appears to have lived at Mount Vernon for several years as a boy during his father's ownership. With Augustine Washington's death in 1743, young George periodically returned to Mount Vernon to live with his elder half-brother, Lawrence, who had been ceded the plantation in 1740. With the death of Lawrence Washington in 1752, George first rented Mount Vernon from Lawrence's widow, Ann, and finally acquired clear title to the plantation in 1761 (Wall 1945, 1980).

An inventory of Lawrence Washington's estate was made in March 1753, which provides important evidence pertaining to the layout of the residence and the configuration of the homelot in this early period. The house plan apparently consisted of a central passage, with four flanking ground floor rooms and a second floor with a landing and three or four bedrooms (Inventory 1753). It is clear from later documentary evidence that this structure was incorporated within the existing Mansion House, which George Washington created by adding to the earlier building during two phases of construction (figure 7.3; Wall 1945). The hall and parlor listed in the 1753 inventory are likely to correspond with the two largest rooms in the apparent old section of the existing house, flanking the passage, on the west side. This arrangement—with the hall serving as the more formal, public room and the parlor as the dining room, and with the back rooms and second floor rooms serving mainly as bedchambers—conforms well to the pattern for living spaces that has been identified in mid-eighteenth-century Virginia houses (Upton 1982).

The document also lists four outbuildings: a kitchen, dairy, washhouse, and storehouse (Inventory 1753). At least three additional outbuildings are known to have been in existence at this time: a blacksmith shop, barn, and slave quarter (Pogue 1988). The locations of the four outbuildings listed in the inventory, along with numerous other structural remains, were discovered via archaeological excavations conducted by Morley J. Williams in the 1930s. Williams was a trained landscape architect who undertook research at Mount Vernon beginning in

1931 as part of a larger study of Southern colonial plantations and gardens. His initial work was performed as a member of the faculty of Harvard University; he then served as Mount Vernon's director of research and restoration from 1936 to 1939 (Williams 1938; Pogue 1988).

George Washington built two additional structures that may have been privies and linked them and the four earlier outbuildings to the house by means of "running Walls for Pallisades" (Jackson and Twohig 1976:258, 268). The four original outbuildings were placed in pairs on line and at angles to the house, so that the walls would have connected them to the west facade of the dwelling at the north and south corners. He also completed the enclosure of two matching rectangular gardens that flanked the driveway. The drive terminated at a circle on the west front of the house, with it and the four outbuildings oriented toward the circle (figure 7.2) (Williams 1938; Pogue 1988).

Interestingly, the new homelot layout bears a striking resemblance to that of Belvoir, the home of Washington's great friends, the Fairfax family. Belvoir is located less than four miles down-river from Mount Vernon and was built between 1736 and 1741. George Washington visited it on countless occasions, both in his youth and as an

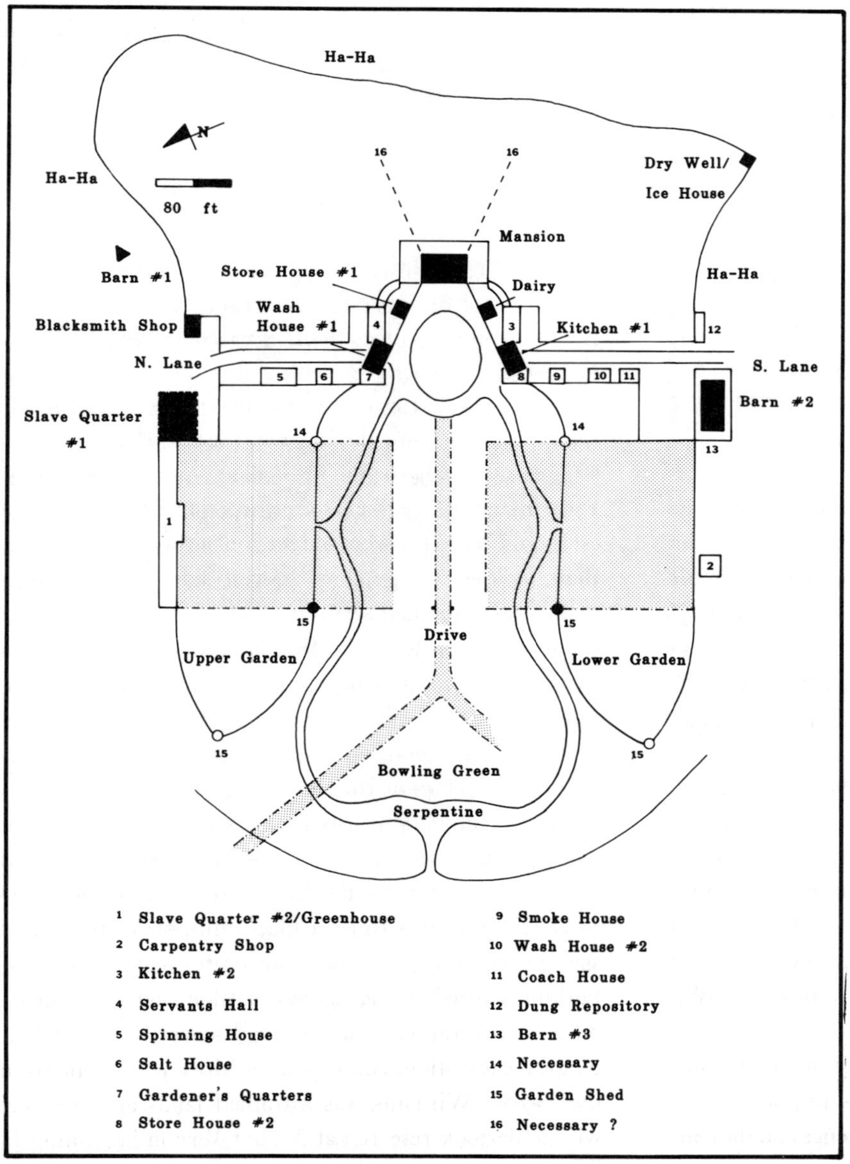

FIGURE 7.2. *Early layout of Mount Vernon, contrasted with later plan: earlier structures darkened and labeled, earlier gardens and drive stippled; later structures and features open and listed 1–15. Two areas marked 16 indicate the site of one known foundation (to the south) that may relate to a privy erected as part of the early plan and that continued in use until 1796, with the second location marked (to the north) being the possible site of another privy, which, according to documentary evidence, may have been built at the same time. The blacksmith shop and the dry well/ice house (stippled) spanned both periods; the Ha-Ha walls date to the later plan.*

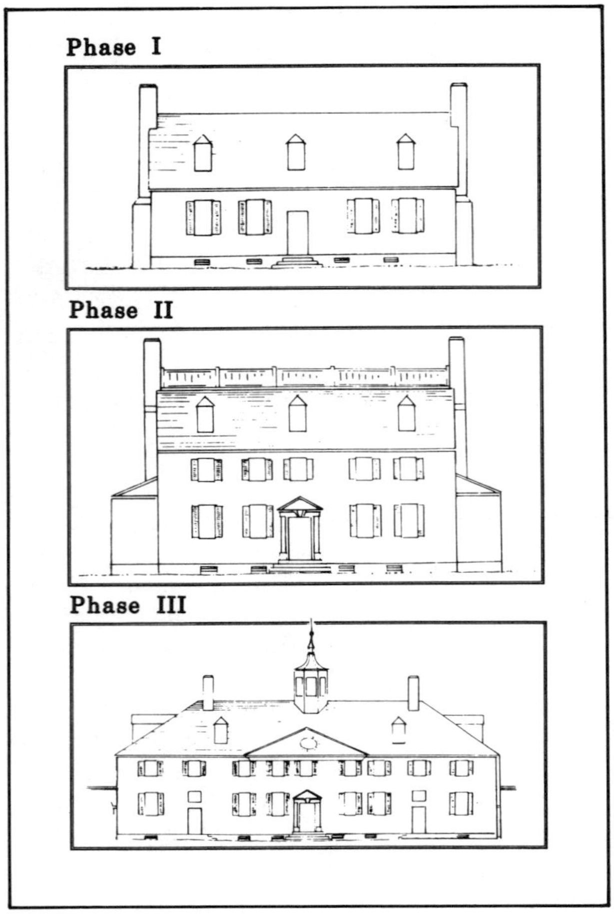

FIGURE 7.3. *Hypothesized evolution of Mansion, west front.*

adult, before it and several outbuildings were destroyed by fire in 1783. The layout of Belvoir has been established through a number of archaeological investigations conducted there, the most extensive of which occurred in the 1970s (Shott 1978). That plan includes three major brick outbuildings, flanking the house at angles on the west, or landward, side, with two on the north and the third on the south. The two nearer structures were connected to the main house by brick walls, which extended beyond the house to the east and finally terminated at the corners of two smaller brick foundations that may have been privies (Shott 1978).

Taken as a whole, Washington's modifications appear to have been a well-conceived plan to regularize the diverse elements of Mount Vernon's earlier layout. Its geometric plan fit with current fashion (Kornwulf 1984) and succeeded in presenting an ordered facade to anyone approaching from either the land or water sides. The rectangular gardens bounded the drive, with the house directly ahead and flanked by the four symmetrical outbuildings with their connecting walls. The two privies may well have been similarly linked to the house on the east front. The other outbuildings were out of sight some distance away.

Washington's expansion of his plantation and of its labor force was the manifestation of his intention to emulate the leading men of his colony and engage in the region's traditional agricultural pursuit—production of tobacco for export to England as a cash crop. Eager to secure his position as a planter of the first rank, he acquired the land and labor that were essential for the production of large, quality crops of tobacco. The expansion of his home and regularization of the layout of the buildings, gardens, and grounds reflected his ambitions and signified his claim to gentry status.

TOBACCO TO GRAIN, 1766–1774

In 1766 George Washington broke from the staple-crop system based on tobacco production that he had wholeheartedly embraced less than a decade before. In its place, he turned to mixed grain cultivation, combined with redoubled efforts at self-sufficiency and a greater commitment to other commercial enterprises. Chief among the nonagricultural activities aimed at turning a profit were his Potomac River fisheries and the production of cloth. The reconstruction of a grist mill in 1770 was an attempt to increase profits from the production of his own grain and to generate income through serving the needs of his neighboring farmers. Such a major restructuring of the plantation's economy implies a transformation in the systemic definition.

The proximate cause of Washington's conscious decision to embark upon such an altered course seems to have been growing dissatisfaction with the vagaries of the tobacco consignment system. An important factor in his decision undoubtedly was the narrowing margin of profit from tobacco resulting from a sharp downturn in the market during the 1760s. The steady decline in the price paid for his crop forced Washington deeply into debt to his London consignment house, totaling more than £1,800 by 1764 (Ragsdale 1989:146–148). By way of comparison, the revenue from the sale of all Mount Vernon tobacco in the year 1762 totaled only £463 (Ledger A:154).

The decline in tobacco prices beginning in the early 1760s was primarily the result of a glut of the leaf on the international market. Overproduction was the natural consequence of the inflated prices paid in the 1750s, which also encouraged significant numbers of smaller planters to concentrate on tobacco cultivation. In addition, the structure of the tobacco trade was undergoing a transformation. Most of the small planters marketed their product directly with the growing number of resident factors representing Glasgow firms, which paid high prices but operated on a strictly "cash-and-carry" basis. In other words, they did not offer the many benefits, most notably the extension of credit, provided by the consignment merchants that were so prized by the large planters. Finally, a widespread economic downturn in Britain began in 1761, further depressing the market and tightening credit (Ernst 1988:197–200). All these factors combined to undermine the consignment system favored by George Washington and his peers.

George Washington appears to have realized the implications of these events at an earlier date than most of his fellow large planters (Breen 1985:175–182) and he turned to a variety of crops and other products to supplant tobacco. In the early 1760s he began to increase the quantity of wheat grown at Mount Vernon, and by 1766 he had abandoned all tobacco cultivation on his Potomac River holdings. In September of 1765 Washington inquired as to the feasibility of shipping hemp and flax in addition to flour for sale in the British market. At that time he also acquired the tools and equipment needed to produce cloth and diverted the labor of several of his slaves to that activity full-time. By 1768 his weavers were producing more than 1,200 yards of homespun each year, most of which was used on the plantation (Ragsdale 1989:157–158), but custom work was carried out for neighboring planters (Macomber 1954:21). Washington's Potomac River fishery also was expanded during this period, with portions of the catch reserved for slave rations and for the use of his household, and the remainder marketed both locally and abroad (Wharton 1952).

The withdrawal from the tobacco market, however, also meant discontinuation of the credit from the consignment merchants on which George Washington had come to depend. Therefore, either he had to purchase English products with cash, always in short supply, or reduce dependency on the imported goods (Ragsdale 1989:158). The marketing of cloth, fish, and flour provided varying levels of income, but, of equal significance, it also reduced expenditures. Other plantation crafts, such as blacksmithing, carpentry, shoemaking, and coopering also were instrumental in approximating the self-sufficiency for which Washington strove.

With the transfer from labor-intensive tobacco cultivation to more diversified grain production, the number of field hands required was reduced significantly. Although by the 1770s Washington is on record as favoring the abolition of slavery, he was unwilling to divest himself of the surplus. Instead, he diverted some of the excess labor to the various crafts. In the census of the Mount Vernon slaves that was made in 1786, 14 of the 41 adult slaves at the Mansion House Farm are listed as seamstresses, spinners, knitters, carpenters, and smiths, the remainder as house servants, drivers, laundresses, gardeners, and laborers (Jackson and Twohig 1978:277–278).

Refinement, 1774–1799

Isaac (1982), among others, has portrayed the decades immediately preceding the American Revolution as a period of dramatic change in Virginia. At midcentury Virginia society was dominated by the landed gentry, whose power and self-image were closely intertwined with the established Church of England. A series of popular religious evangelical movements beginning in the 1740s led to the eventual disestablishment of the church and intensified a growing crisis in social authority, however. The decline in the tobacco market, a demographic shift brought about by the changing economy and westward expansion, and the patriot movement culminating in the Revolution and break with England all combined with the religious upheaval to cause a major redefinition of the roles of the various components of Virginia society. To varying degrees, all of these developments served to erode the authority of Virginia's planter elite (Isaac 1982).

In light of this erosion of the traditional powers of the gentry, Isaac (1982:265) suggests that "the patriot ideology" may have gained "in appeal among the Virginia gentry partly because it served as a defensive response to the open rejection of deference that was increasingly manifested in the spread of evangelicalism." In other words, although in certain respects the conflict with England exacerbated the local conflict between the gentry and the rest of society, it also provided an opportunity for the elite to reestablish their authority by adopting a role of leadership in the patriotic movement.

A number of scholars—including Isaac (1982), Deetz (1977), and Greene (1988)—contend that in the years just before the Revolution American culture had come to resemble that of Britain more than ever before. Evidence for the increasing similarity has been seen in changes in architectural design, foodways, burial practices, and a variety of other components of material culture (Deetz 1977, 1988).

Leone (1988) applies the paradigm of the crisis in gentry authority, combined with the trend toward re-Anglicization, to his study of eighteenth-century Annapolis. He suggests that patterns in architectural and landscape design and in material culture support both hypotheses. For instance, the Annapolis gentry responded to the crisis by building a series of formal gardens "to convince people that a rational social order based on nature was possible and that those with such access to its laws were its natural leaders" (Leone 1988:250).

Given the twin trends of the growing cultural similarity with England and the crisis in leadership experienced by the gentry, it is interesting that George Washington initiated the second round of alterations to his home beginning in 1774. There certainly is no indication that George Washington's patriotism was the result of any conscious realization that it had the potential to stem the erosion of the authority of his class. When this second phase of modification is viewed in the context of the broader social and cultural change, however, it may signify an attempt to reify both Washington's personal authority and that of the gentry elite. That Washington's new architectural and landscape designs were consciously imitative of English fashion, as he received and interpreted them, also suggests that American culture was achieving a closer approximation of the English, at least at the highest level of society.

Once again Washington enlarged his house, as well as demolished and replaced numerous outbuildings and reorganized the gardens and grounds. Much of this program was carried out by his plantation manager, Lund Washington, during Washington's eight-year wartime absence from Mount Vernon (Wall 1980). With his return in 1783, George Washington personally supervised the completion of this phase of construction, which culminated in an ambitiously arranged ornamental landscape design. The result was a nearly complete transformation of the domestic seat, which incorporated current fashionable trends in naturalistic design within the constraints of the existing layout (figure 7.4).

Not only was the house substantially enlarged—wings were added to both gables and it was raised to three stories—but numerous architectural details were also added that were designed to produce a symmetrical and fashionable facade (figure 7.3). These include a columned, two-story piazza running the length of the east front, a pediment on the west, a central cupola, a "Palladian" window placed in the newly added and ornately decorated large dining room, and colonnades linking the house with two new, symmetrically placed dependencies. The architectural conceits were generally successful in masking the flaws inherent in almost doubling in size what had been a modest, 1 1/2-story farmhouse (Macomber 1969).

The layout of the outbuildings and of the gardens and grounds also were changed, replacing the constricted geometric plan with a more open, naturalistic scheme (figure 7.1). Most of the outbuildings, many of which were in existence when George Washington acquired the plantation in 1754, were demolished and replaced. The driveway was removed, the geometric garden enclosures were reconfigured into a narrower, elliptical shape, and a bowling green bounded by a serpentine walk and naturally planted "wildernesses" were laid out between the gardens. This virtually complete makeover is documented by a plan of Mount Vernon drawn by Samuel Vaughan during a visit to the plantation in 1787 (figure 7.4). The accuracy of this remarkable document was attested to by Washington himself, and has been verified archaeologically on numerous occasions (Pogue 1988).

The construction of a substantial brick greenhouse in 1784 greatly increased Washington's capacities for growing and experimenting with exotic plants, as well as for ornamental gardening in general (Wall 1980). Those activities, and especially the investment in specialized gardening structures like greenhouses, also have been postulated as a particularly conspicuous claim to high status. If the manipulation of the natural world by establishing and maintaining intricate and fashionable gardens served to announce the exalted position of the gardener, the possession of a greenhouse made an even stronger claim (Yentsch 1990).

George Washington designed his greenhouse with the help of Tench Tilghman, his former military aid, who in turn enlisted the assistance of Mrs. Charles Carroll of Baltimore. Mrs. Carroll was extremely knowledgeable on the subject, and was able to offer advice on a wide range of topics (Macomber 1953). Over the years Wash-

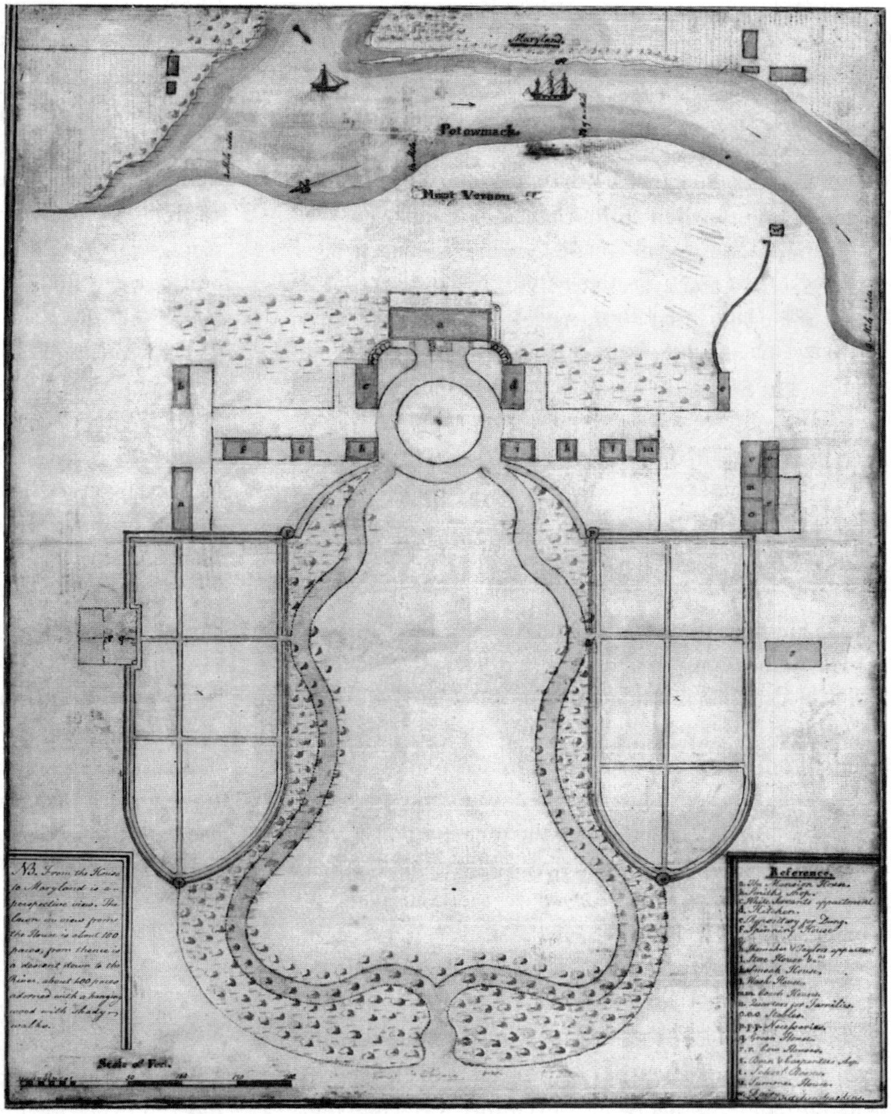

FIGURE 7.4. *Vaughan plan, 1787.*

ington appears to have received advice from other associates and from his employees when it came to designing the myriad alterations to his house and grounds.

In addition, while relatively poorly educated and little traveled abroad, Washington was well-read, and his library contained numerous gardeners' dictionaries and other treatises on landscape design. Notable among them was Batty Langley's *New Principles of Gardening* (1728), which was a strong advocate of the picturesque. In addition, the design of several of the new architectural details he ordered—particularly the Palladian window, chimney pieces, and doorways—have been linked with various builders' pattern books (Reiff 1986:277). The use of these sources, combined with the advice provided by friends, acquaintances, and workmen, seems to have been quite a common practice for gentry builders (Macomber 1969).

The contrast between the geometric and rigidly symmetrical layout of the earlier grounds and homelot and Washington's new plan is a remarkable record of the changes in fashion in landscape design that occurred during this period. The combination of the undulating shape of the bowling green, bounded by the serpentine and wildernesses, which are in turn flanked by the elliptical walled gardens, clearly owes much to the new picturesque fashion in landscape design gaining popularity at the time. Numerous Ha-Has, or walls that served simultaneously as physical barriers but not as visual impediments, also were erected in the 1780s and are consistent with the naturalistic orientation (Kornwulf 1984).

The third transformation of Mount Vernon, between 1774 and the late 1780s, seems to have occurred in response to fundamental changes in Virginia society. Washington's earlier switch from tobacco to diversified grain production was a transformation on the technomic level. But this second and more extensive reorganization of the layout of his home may be interpreted as a transformation of the socio- and ideotechnic domains, for the changes made at that time seem to imply a more fundamental concern with reinforcing his social position by adopting the current fashions in design.

Decline: 1799–1858

The fashionable facade thus created would perform its intended role as symbol of the social position of its owner and of the success of the plantation it epitomized for less than three decades. With George Washington's death in 1799, his beloved Mount Vernon passed into the custody of his wife, Martha, until her death in 1802 activated the subdivision of the plantation that was stipulated in his will. Over the next 50 years the property associated with the Mansion House continued to shrink in size, and the farming operation suffered a long and gradual decline. For decades George Washington had struggled with infertile soils, an overabundance of labor, evolving agricultural practices, and changing market demands in attempting to maintain Mount Vernon as an economically viable system. Washington's heirs were significantly less successful than he, and the last Washington owner, John Augustine, finally despaired of the financial drain and in 1858 sold the 200-acre remnant of Mount Vernon to the Mount Vernon Ladies' Association (Wall 1980).

One of the continuing problems inherent in the Mount Vernon system after 1766 was the surplus slave population, which, through natural increase, had reached a total of 316 in 1799 (Fitzpatrick 1937:256–268). Washington many times expressed his opposition to slavery as an institution, as well as his intention to free his slaves. In addition, he realized the strain placed on his resources caused by the growing slave population. However, he was unwilling "To sell the overplus . . . because I am principled against this kind of traffic in the human species. To hire them out is almost as bad because they could not be disposed of in families to any advantage, and to disperse the families I have an aversion. What then is to be done? Something must or I shall be ruined" (Fitzpatrick 37:338–339).

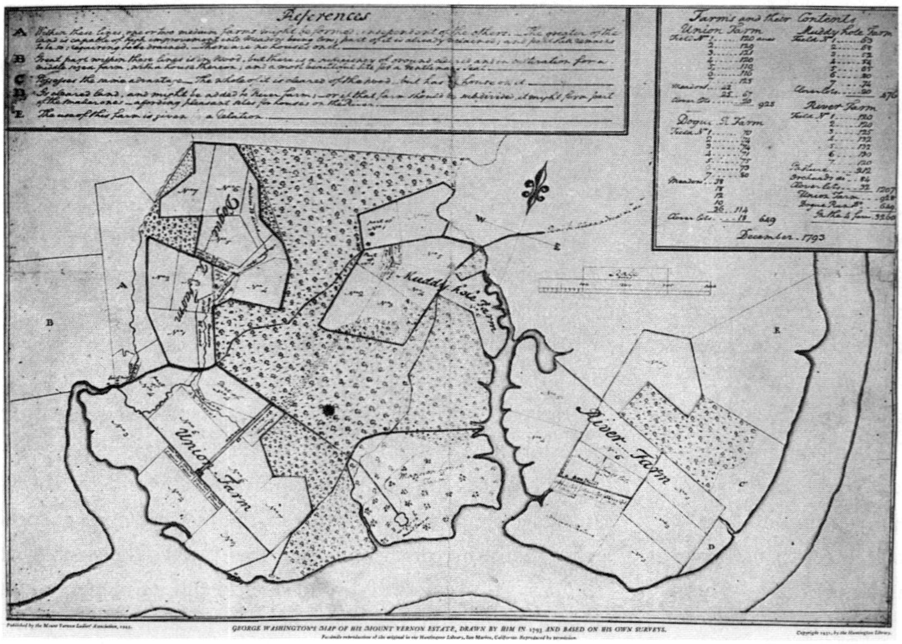

Figure 7.5. *Plan of Mount Vernon's five farms (1793), used in advertising property for rent. (Courtesy of the Huntington Library)*

Washington hoped that his problem could be resolved by renting his outlying farms, with tenants hiring his slaves as paid laborers (Fitzpatrick 34:433–438). He had no takers for his proposition, however, and a resolution finally occurred with the freeing of the slaves, as stipulated in his will (figure 7.5).

Neiman (1977) has postulated a model of the changes experienced by the plantation system of the large tidewater planters during the period from the Revolution to the mid-nineteenth century. According to this model, Washington and his peers were all faced with the same fundamental economic challenge—how to survive the decline in the tobacco market as they knew it. Neiman's study is based on a combination of archaeological and documentary data drawn from primarily two substantial tidewater plantations, Kingsmill in James City County, owned by the Burwells (Kelso 1984), and the Lee family's Westmoreland County seat, known as Stratford. Isaac's (1990) study of Landon Carter's attempts to systematize his Sabine Hall plantation during the period from 1756 to 1778 suggests a similar transformation in response to the changing economic climate. This model seems to possess considerable utility for explaining the long-term decline of Mount Vernon in terms of systems theory.

At midcentury, Kingsmill, Stratford, and Sabine Hall also typified the large tobacco plantations operated by Virginia's landed elite. They were tied to the tobacco trade, and the large slave populations its cultivation entailed, but also included a variety of crafts aimed at promoting self-sufficiency. Like Mount Vernon, they were large, multifunctioning systems that justified their owners' positions in the colony's leading class.

Like George Washington, the Lees, the Burwells, and Landon Carter all recognized that the tobacco market was in a long-term downward spiral that threatened their economic survival, and they, too, made the decision to abandon tobacco and emphasize grain production. As a result of the less labor-intensive nature of grain cultivation, the proprietors of the three estates found themselves with an ever-expanding surplus of field hands. The overabundance of labor necessitated additional adjustments to the system, with two likely alternatives. The first was to sell off slaves until a man-to-land ratio that made grain production profitable was reached. The second form of readjustment was that selected by George Washington—not to reduce his work force, and instead to transfer that labor to other activities that would generate income or at least help increase self-sufficiency.

At Stratford, the Lees seem to have adopted a similar strategy, and with the same limited success. By the end of the century, Stratford had shrunk from 6,500 acres with approximately 90 field hands to less than half that size and only 23 slaves. At Kingsmill, the labor force was similarly reduced and land had to be sold off. By the second quarter of the nineteenth century, however, both properties had rebounded, although in significantly altered forms. Instead of the complex plantation systems of the eighteenth century, both holdings were reduced to being farmed in numerous small parcels by tenants. Such a system did not lead to the diversification of activities or to the close-knit plantation communities that had characterized the earlier period (Neiman 1977).

Therefore, this model postulates an equilibrium state achieved only after the plantation labor supply was drastically altered to take into account the replacement of tobacco with grain as the main agricultural product. Through a combination of hard work, attention to detail, and the creative use of the extensive resources available to him, George Washington was able to keep Mount Vernon an economically viable operation, even though his growing slave population placed tremendous strains on the system. Diversification was an important tool in this effort, which brought significant long-term success to his fishery and mill in particular.

In systemic terms, Mount Vernon was transformed, but did not achieve equilibrium, however. Thus an eventual readjustment occurred after the passing of George and Martha Washington. When Mount Vernon was divided among several heirs in 1802, it effectively marked the plantation's demise. In terms of Neiman's (1977) model, this would mark the beginning of the final period of readjustment that ultimately would lead to equilibrium and a viable, if radically altered, system.

With Augustine Washington's sale in 1858 of the 200-acre parcel containing the remnant of the Mansion House Farm to the Mount Vernon Ladies Association, the property's "final" transformation had begun—from the Washington family's domestic seat and the hub of the extended plantation system, to the country's first "historic" landmark. The history of that transformation also might profitably be portrayed as a series of stages in development and in shifting philosophies that would be an instructive chapter in the study of the historic preservation movement in America. For in many ways the history of the past 130 years of Mount Vernon and its management by the association, the oldest historic preservation organization in the country, is at least as interesting as the Washington family period of ownership. That long and entertaining story will need to be told elsewhere, however.

"Systems Archaeology"

The three phases of transformation identified here seem to correlate fairly well with the archaeological record and make it possible to formulate research designs aimed at investigating their impact on various plantation components. To date, the best material evidence for the transformations consists of changes in the layout and embellishment of the landscape and in structural modifications, which seem strongly correlated with the first and third phases. In the long run, the economic realignment seems to have the greatest interpretive potential, however, as it affected virtually all components of plantation life.

The transfer from tobacco to grain production and to increased self-sufficiency probably would have most directly affected the slave community. For example, with the reordering of the entire system of labor, many more positions for craftspeople were created, with a corresponding reduction in the proportion of field hands. Given that the dichotomy between skilled and nonskilled laborers was a primary means of status identification on plantations (Blassingame 1979; Kulikoff 1986; Sobel 1987), this change could have a significant impact on patterns in the archaeological record.

The decision to improve self-sufficiency might have had a similarly significant impact on slave diet, with a likely increase in the proportion of foods that were available from the plantation itself. Analysis of faunal remains excavated from the "House for Families" slave quarter, the main quarter at the Mansion House Farm from ca. 1760 to 1793 (Wall 1980), has revealed an extremely diverse diet, with at least 46 species identified. Fish and wild species that could have been collected from the plantation and from the nearby Potomac River make up a high percentage of the total, with fish comprising 80 percent of the total assemblage (Pogue 1990; Atkins 1991). While the presence of wild taxa in slave-associated faunal assemblages now appears to be a common pattern at plantations (Singleton 1988), the proportion of wild to domestic fauna at Mount Vernon may be higher than usual.

Inasmuch as George Washington operated a fishery for many years and is on record as using fish as rations for his slaves (Atkins 1991), their presence in the assemblage is not surprising. But the quest for self-sufficiency suggests the likelihood that fish and wild species became more important as rations over the course of the century. As additional slave domestic sites are investigated, and if they span a sufficiently broad time period, it will be possible to test this hypothesis.

Conclusion

Under this study's systemic paradigm focusing on a half-century of change at Mount Vernon during George and Martha Washington's lifetimes, the trajectory of the plantation's alterations reflects broad cultural and social transformations. The specific changes carried out by Washington may be understood as one man's responses to these outside stimuli, which, as demonstrated earlier, were similar to the responses of others of his class. The adoption of systems theory in this context does not imply that Washington's decisions were predetermined by the events at hand, however. Washington selected from among a number of possible options available to him in each instance, although his choices were limited by commanding social, economic, and political constraints.

Given his inherited position in Virginia society, as the younger son of a member of the midlevel gentry, George Washington's career opportunities were limited, but he was not without options. It was only after his disillusionment with the military as a result of his participation in the abortive Forbes campaign that he turned to the planter's life-style. Even then, it was only his inheritance from his elder brother's estate, combined with his marriage to the wealthy widow of Daniel Parke Custis, that provided him with the resources needed to enter the ranks of the large planters (Flexner 1974). Once on this track, Washington easily settled into the affairs of his class, but realized before most of his peers that changing circumstances made it necessary to transform the economic foundation of his plantation.

In retrospect, although Washington's move to diversify his activities was successful in the short run, the decision to retain all of his slaves made it unlikely that the new system could achieve long-term equilibrium. Sooner or later the plantation would no longer be able to support itself, a fact that late in his life Washington himself seems to have recognized. The plantation's long-term decline was well under way when its 200-acre core was purchased by the Mount Vernon Ladies' Association in 1858.

Similarly, the third transformation of Mount Vernon, the rearrangement and redesign of the domestic seat carried out between 1774 and 1787, may be viewed ultimately as unsuccessful. If the subconscious goal of those changes was to reify the authority of Washington's gentry class during a period of social upheaval, posterity must judge it a failure as well. Within a generation of its implementation, the traditional role of authority in Virginia society enjoyed by the large tidewater planters was being usurped by the new merchant middle class and by a subtle shifting of power, along with population, to the west.

References Cited

Inventory of the Estate of Lawrence Washington
1753 Collection of Mount Vernon Ladies' Association. Mount Vernon, Va.

Atkins, Stephen C.
1991 A Closer Look: Reconstructing Slave Diet from the House for Families Cellar. A paper presented at the Society for Historical Archaeology Annual Conference, Richmond, Va.

Binford, Lewis
1962 Archaeology as Anthropology. *American Antiquity* 28:217–225.

Blassingame, John W.
1979 *The Slave Community: Plantation Life in the Antebellum South*. Oxford University Press, New York.

Breen, T. H.
1985 *Tobacco Culture: the Mentality of the Great Tidewater Planters on the Eve of Revolution*. Princeton University Press, Princeton, N.J.

Carson, Cary, Norman F. Barka, William M. Kelso, Garry W. Stone, and Dell Upton
1981 Impermanent Architecture in the Southern American Colonies. *Winterthur Portfolio* 16(2/3):135–196.

Clark, Ellen M.
1988 George Washington and Slavery at Mount Vernon. Ms. on file, Mount Vernon Ladies' Association, Mount Vernon, Va.

Clarke, David L.
1978 *Analytical Archaeology*. Columbia University Press, New York.

Deetz, James F.
1988 Material Culture and Worldview in Colonial Anglo-America. In *The Recovery of Meaning: Historical Archaeology in the Eastern United States*, edited by M. Leone and P. Potter, pp. 219–233. Smithsonian Institution Press, Washington, D.C.
1977 *In Small Things Forgotten*. Doubleday, New York.

Ernst, Joseph A.
1988 The Political Economy of the Chesapeake Colonies, 1760–1775: A Study in Comparative History. In *The Economy of Early America: The Revolutionary Period, 1763–1790*, edited by R. Hoffman, J. J. McCusker, R. R. Menard, and P. J. Albert, pp. 196–243. University Press of Virginia, Charlottesville.

Fairbanks, Charles H.
1984 The Plantation Archaeology of the Southeastern Coast. *Historical Archaeology* 18(1):1–18.

Fitzpatrick, John C. (editor)
1931–1944 *The Writings of George Washington from the Original Manuscript Sources: 1745–1799*. Vols. 1–39. U.S. Government Printing Office, Washington, D.C.

Flexner, James T.
1974 *Washington, The Indispensable Man*. Little Brown, Boston.

Greene, Jack P.
1988 *Pursuits of Happiness: The Social Development of Early Modern British Colonies and the Formation of American Culture*. University of North Carolina Press, Chapel Hill.

Isaac, Rhys
1982 *The Transformation of Virginia: 1740–1790*. University of North Carolina Press, Chapel Hill.
1990 The Enlightenment and the Problem of Systematizing the Plantation: Colonel Landon Carter's Sabine Hall, 1756–1778. Paper presented at the conference, "Recreating the World of the Virginia Plantation, 1750–1826," Charlottesville, Virginia.

Jackson, Donald, and Dorothy Twohig (editors)
1976–1979 *The Diaries of George Washington*. Vols. 1–6. University Press of Virginia, Charlottesville.

Kelso, William M.
1984 *Kingsmill Plantations, 1619–1800: Archaeology of Country Life in Colonial Virginia*. Academic Press, New York.

Kornwulf, James D.
1984 The Picturesque in the American Garden and Landscape before 1800. In *British and American Gardens in the Eighteenth Century*, edited by R. P. Macubbin and P. Martin, pp. 93–106. Colonial Williamsburg Foundation, Williamsburg, Va.

Kulikoff, Allan
1986 *Tobacco and Slaves: the Development of Southern Cultures in the Chesapeake, 1680–1800*. University of North Carolina Press, Chapel Hill.

Langley, Batty
1728 *New Principles of Gardening*. London.

Ledger A: Accounts of George Washington Mount Vernon Ladies' Association, Mount Vernon, Virginia.

Leone, Mark P.
1988 The Georgian Order as the Order of Merchant Capitalism in Annapolis, Maryland. In *The Recovery of Meaning: Historical Archaeology in the Eastern United States*, edited by M. Leone and P. Potter, pp. 235–261. Smithsonian Institution Press, Washington, D.C.

Macomber, Walter M.
1969 Mount Vernon's "Architect." *Historical Society of Fairfax County, Virginia* 10:1–10.

1953 The Rebuilding of the Greenhouse-Quarters. *Mount Vernon Ladies' Association, Annual Report* 1952:19–26.

1954 The Spinning House Restoration. *Mount Vernon Ladies' Association, Annual Report* 1953:19–27.

Middleton, Arthur P.

1953 (1984) *Tobacco Coast: A Maritime History of Chesapeake Bay in the Colonial Era*. Johns Hopkins University Press, Baltimore, Md.

Morgan, Edmund S.

1975 *American Slavery, American Freedom*. W. W. Norton, New York.

Neiman, Fraser D.

1977 Responses of the Chesapeake Plantation System to Culture Changes in the late Eighteenth Century: The Evidence from Kingsmill and Stratford. Paper presented at the Society for Historical Archaeology Annual Conference, Ottawa, Ontario.

Orser, Charles E., Jr.

1984 The Past Ten Years of Plantation Archaeology in the Southeastern United States. *Southeastern Archaeology* 3(1): 1–12.

1987 Plantation Status and Consumer Choice: A Materialist Framework for Historical Archaeology. In *Consumer Choice in Historical Archaeology*, edited by S. Spencer-Wood, pp. 121–137. Plenum Press, New York.

1988 Toward a Theory of Power for Historical Archaeology: Plantations and Space. In The *Recovery of Meaning: Historical Archaeology in the Eastern United States*, edited by M. Leone and P. Potter, pp. 313–343. Smithsonian Institution Press, Washington, D.C.

Plog, Fred T.

1975 Systems Theory in Archeological Research. *Annual Review of Anthropology* 4:207–224.

Pogue, Dennis J.

1988 *Archaeology at George Washington's Mount Vernon: 1931–1987*. Mount Vernon Ladies' Association Archaeology Department, File Report No. 1. Mount Vernon, Va.

1990 Slave Life at Mount Vernon. *Archaeology* 43(6)26.

Ragsdale, Bruce A.

1989 George Washington, the British Tobacco Trade, and Economic Opportunity in Prerevolutionary Virginia. *Virginia Magazine of History and Biography* 97(2) 133–162.

Reiff, Daniel D.

1986 *Small Georgian Houses in England and Virginia: Origins and Development through the 1750s*. Associated University Presses, London.

Rhodehamel, John

1983 The Growth of Mount Vernon. *Mount Vernon Ladies Association, Annual Report* 1982:18–24.

Roseberry, William

1989 *Anthropologies and Histories: Essays in Culture, History, and Political Economy.* Rutgers University Press, New Brunswick, N.J.

Salmon, Merrilee H.

1978 What Can Systems Theory Do for Archaeology? *American Antiquity* 43(2): 174–183.

Shott, George C.

1978 U.S. Army Engineer Museum Archaeological Investigations of Belvoir Historic Site, Fort Belvoir, Virginia. U.S. Army Engineer Center and Fort Belvoir, Fort Belvoir, Virginia.

Singleton, Theresa A.

1988 An Archaeological Framework for Slavery and Emancipation, 1740–1880. In *The Recovery of Meaning: Historical Archaeology in the Eastern United States*, edited by M. Leone and P. Potter, pp. 345–370. Smithsonian Institution Press, Washington, D.C.

Sobel, Mechal

1987 *The World They Made Together: Black and White Values in Eighteenth-Century Virginia*. Princeton University Press, Princeton, N.J.

Upton, Dell

1982 Vernacular Domestic Architecture in Eighteenth-Century Virginia. *Winterthur Portfolio* 17(2/3):95–119.

Vaughan, Samuel

1787 Plan of Mount Vernon. Mount Vernon Ladies' Association, Mount Vernon, Va.

Wall, Charles C.

1945 Notes on the Early History of Mount Vernon. *William and Mary Quarterly*, 3d ser., 2:173–190.

1980 *George Washington: Citizen-Soldier*. University Press of Virginia, Charlottesville.

Wallerstein, Immanuel

1974 *The Modern World-System*. Academic Press, New York.

Watson, Patty Jo, Steven A. Leblanc, and Charles L. Redman

1973 *Explanation in Archaeology: An Explicitly Scientific Approach*. Columbia University Press, New York.

Wharton, James

1952 Washington's Fisheries at Mount Vernon. *Commonwealth* (August):11–13, 44.

Will of George Washington

1799 Mount Vernon Ladies' Association, Mount Vernon, Va.

Williams, Morley J.

1938 Washington's Changes at Mount Vernon Plantation. *Landscape Architecture* 28(2):63–73.

Wolf, Eric R.

1982 *Europe and the People without History*. University of California Press, Berkeley.

Yentsch, Anne

1990 The Calvert Orangery in Annapolis, Maryland: a Horticultural Symbol of Power and Prestige in an Early Eighteenth-Century Community. In *Earth Patterns: Essays in Landscape Archaeology*, edited by W. Kelso and R. Most, pp. 169–187. University Press of Virginia, Charlottesville.

VIII

CHAPTER

The Archaeology of Plantation Slavery in Piedmont Virginia
Context and Process

DOUGLAS W. SANFORD

RECENT ARCHAEOLOGICAL studies of American slavery and plantations point to the need for an overarching methodological and analytical framework, one that can encompass diverse sites and research issues. Such a framework has become necessary because plantation archaeology has begun shifting away from its former descriptive objectives and the material demarcation of the status and ethnic identity of slaves (Hantman and Sanford 1986; Singleton 1985). A rethinking of analytical categories has propelled this movement as well. Although the new direction has no particular name or single theoretical paradigm, it appears increasingly centered on contextual and processual information supplied by documentary records and secondary historical studies (Orser 1988a, 1988b; Singleton 1988: 345–370; Sanford 1991). Theresa Singleton's call for greater contextual focus within archaeological studies of slave and African American life and culture marks a critical step in this direction, especially with regard to identifying historical phases of distinctive material culture and living conditions. By concentrating on periods of perceived change in plantation economies and cultures, archaeologists can contribute to the understanding of the diversity and evolution of American plantation slavery.

The growing archaeological interest in context and process parallels the movement by historians of slavery away from grand synoptic and thematic studies toward a concern with chronology and economic geography. The roles of particular plantation crops and slaves' occupations now receive greater emphasis, as do periods deemed crucial to the development of American slavery and African American culture as a whole. Plantation archaeology has likewise acknowledged the need "to reveal the vast texture and experience of plantation life and slavery" (Silberman 1989:68) and paradigmatic shifts within the field over the past 10 years mirror this movement from universal themes to issues of regional and temporal diversity.

Initial archaeological studies searched for artifact patterns distinctive of a slave status or African American identity and for African "survivals" (Ascher and Fairbanks 1971; Otto 1975; Deetz 1977; Singleton 1985). Later work explicitly recognized the need for regional analysis and archaeological inferences concerning distinctive modes of social and cultural interaction (Wheaton et al. 1983; Fairbanks 1984; Orser 1988b; Singleton 1988). According to Charles Orser (1989:28, 37), for example, plantations cannot be studied as "distinct, complex, historical, spatial entities that embodied change" without developing "artifact classes to address social relations" within particular plantation contexts.

The type of analytical framework I propose stresses the contextual definition of plantation systems and of archaeological correlates for the behaviors of various residents therein. To define the plantation context one must delineate the spatial demographies of planters, slaves, and land use; outline the practices of slave management and the distribution of slave work and domestic activities; and determine the material culture and landscape that conditioned the nature of slave and planter life at a given place and time. Process—here meaning change or evolution—implies that although plantation slavery in general employed similar institutional means for balancing land, labor, staple crop growth, and capital, local and regional occurrences developed within unique contexts and in dissimilar sequences. Hence, defining process means establishing when and how slavery changed as a labor system, as an ideology, and as a way of life. Researchers can use these contextual and processual definitions in combination to formulate a model of plantation slavery, which they can then evaluate and refine with the aid of archaeological data and further historical study. This type of investigation moves historical research beyond the straightforward rendition of historical background and should head plantation archaeology in the direction advocated in 1984 by the late Charles Fairbanks (1984:7), namely, toward "summaries about the cultural process and trajectories of slave life."

This essay applies the contextual and processual framework to Thomas Jefferson's piedmont Virginia plantation, Monticello (ca. 1770–1825). This Albemarle County plantation represents a "settled" agrarian and early national society dependent on mixed agriculture and slave labor. Social and economic alterations within this evolving Southern plantation system effected, but also reflected changes within the associated African American slave community. These changes can be found in documentary sources and in archaeologically recovered material culture.

Documentary and archaeological data from several domestic slave sites provide the basis for the analysis. The extensive collection of primary documents related to Jefferson's plantation operations makes it possible to define the local context for slave life and plantation management. Records such as Jefferson's *Farm Book*, his multifaceted memorandum books, and numerous letters to and from his family, friends, and overseers provide one basis for the diachronic modeling of the labor system/routines, social structures, and living conditions of Monticello's slaves.

The Monticello archaeological data base has developed from a long-term research effort at Monticello focused on plantation landscapes and on African American slave life (Crader 1984; Kelso 1984, 1986; Sanford 1985). The particular data for this case study originate from the completed excavations of seven slave quarter sites from the "main street" area of the Monticello plantation known as Mulberry Row (figure 8.1). Artifactual and architectural information from these sites provides a complementary and comparative basis for evaluating the material and social conditions of slave domestic life over time and space.

Beyond defining undocumented aspects of slaves' everyday lives, archaeological evidence supplies a contrasting source for investigating slave-based means of subsistence, resistance to oppression, and notions of identity. It also sheds light on slave housing, provisioning, and access to resources. Archaeology can uniquely contribute to these issues and thereby provide insight into the definitive attributes of slave life and African American culture (Berlin 1980; Herman 1984; Vlach 1987; McGuire and Paynter 1991).

Methodological Framework

Plantations, long recognized as pervasive economic and social institutions, figured prominently in the international expansion of European capitalism and in particular represented a key historical factor in the evolution of Britain's southern colonies in America, later the southern region of the United States. At certain times and places slavery coincided with these plantation systems, which thereby evolved into physically distinctive, cultural institutions. Their study remains crucial to an understanding of regional settlement patterns and the accompanying socioeconomic structures and multiethnic cultures.

Historically, the institutions of slavery and plantations encompassed great spatial and temporal diversity. Methodologically, then, archaeological interpretations of plantation slavery should take place within a contextual and processual framework designed to address such differences. The first step is to define the local and regional contextual factors from primary documents, secondary historical studies, and anthropological treatments of slavery. The constraining and defining variables include plantation demography, labor structure, and slave management, as well as types of economic, political, and social change, or process, that influenced plantation slavery during the specified time frame. It is essential to define the contextual and processual framework at both the local and regional levels in order to arrive at a more compre-

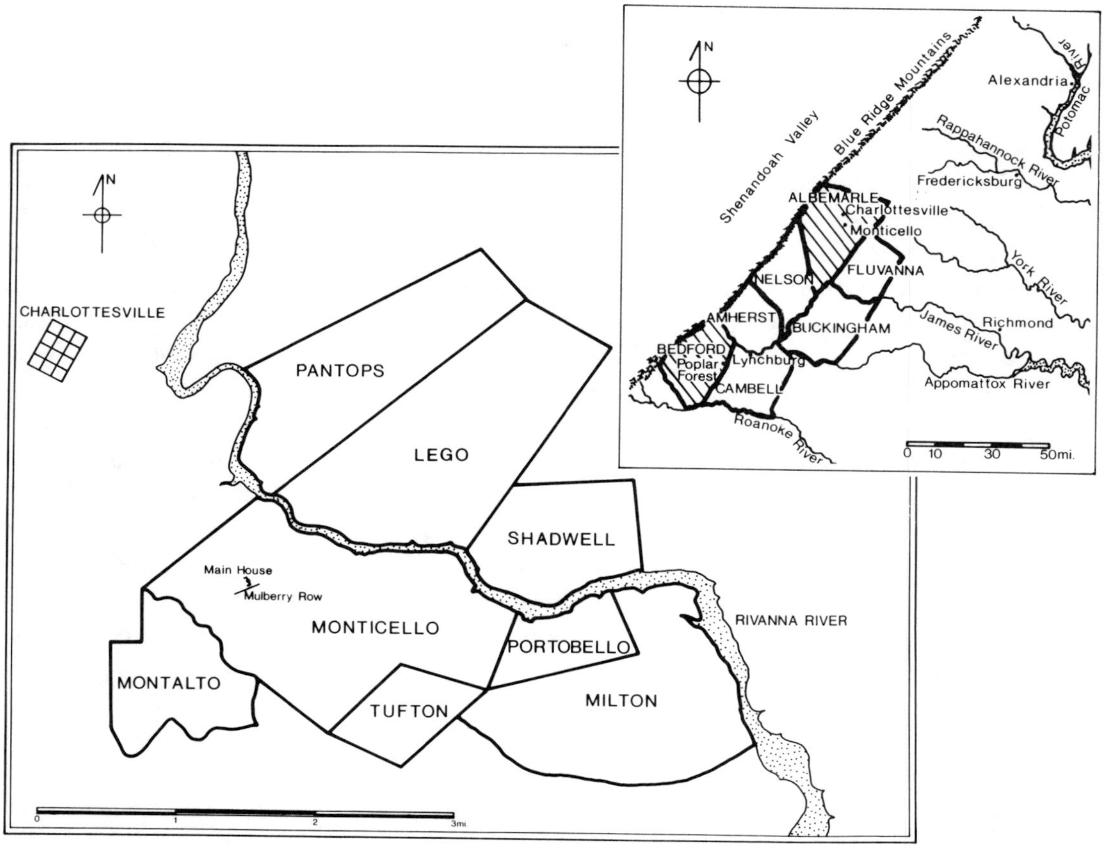

FIGURE 8.1. *The Monticello plantation, showing areas of archaeological excavation.*

hensive picture of a slave plantation system than is usually available.

The second methodological step is to derive local implications concerning the changed conditions and behaviors of intraplantation groups from this contextual model of evolving plantation slavery. These implications are then applied to the available documentary and archaeological records, to ascertain whether the model is applicable to the case study at hand. Conversely, the broader model is used to assess the representativeness of the case study.

One advantage of this method is that it integrates the plantation site, often the archaeologist's point of reference, into a larger frame of analysis, that of regional history and historical anthropology. Plantation sites, as case study examples of plantation slavery, provide the needed counterpoints to the regionally scaled, social demography approach taken by most historians (Kulikoff 1986; Lee 1986; Carr et al. 1988; Morgan 1988). A regional historical model first points to the greater degree to which historians have addressed this topic. It also underscores archaeologists' need to interact with historians and to analyze the same primary documents for the initial definition of plantation and slavery contexts.

Another advantage is that the model reinforces the interdisciplinary nature of historical archaeology, wherein archaeologists can use their own and anthropological insights to broaden our understanding of a bicultural institution. The evolution of plantation slavery involved both European American and African American influences. Until recently, the slave-based internal dynamics have received less attention than those of planter origin. Archaeology—wherein artifacts are thought to shed light on slave life, slave social meanings, and culture change—can address these dynamics.

The framework also denotes a methodology of comparison similar to middle-range theory, as recently discussed by Leone and Potter (1988:11–14). In their view, the differences ("contradictions") that emerge from a comparison of a context's documentary record, functioning approximately as an ethnographic analogy, and its archaeological record provide critical information or sources of meaning. These differences signify more than quirks of survival, but rather are clues to past cultural systems. In this case, though, archaeological and documentary records are compared in two stages in order to recover meaning. First, archaeological data concerning plantation slavery are examined alongside primary documents to identify and interpret their differences. Both sources are assumed to have certain limitations. For example, the surviving documentary record of slave life and culture is admittedly incomplete and biased. Slaveowners' documents recorded what European Americans thought important and thus embodied, at least in part, their ideology of slave management and treatment and their ideals of proper slave behavior and relations. Conversely, archaeological data represent evidence of both the masters' political economy of slavery and the slaves' daily lives and cultures.

At the second stage of analysis the results of this mutual evaluation at the case study level are compared to the model of evolving slavery. This additional comparison further refines our understanding of both the general development of slavery and its particular practice. This analytical method, by providing data to support new interpretative frameworks, attempts to move archaeology's role in slave plantation studies beyond the mere description of undocumented past peoples.

Monticello as a Representative Plantation

A word of caution is in order concerning the use of Monticello as a representative case study of plantation slavery in the piedmont of Virginia. Certainly, Thomas Jefferson was an unusual individual in Virginia and in American history. Furthermore, Jefferson and other "great planters" of his status (who constituted 3 to 5 percent of the Albemarle County adult population) were statistically unrepresentative of piedmont planters in general, the majority of whom owned far fewer slaves and much less land (Ayres 1968:17, 24). The county household average in 1785, for instance, was 7.9 slaves, in contrast to the 129 slaves owned by Jefferson. His 5,000 acres ranked high even among the county's top 4 percent of households, which averaged about 2,200 acres (Dabney 1951:124–125; Moore 1976:84).

But great planters like Jefferson do offer interpretive value. On the one hand, they provide a wealth of documentary information—not only about planters' personal and political lives, but also about the range of operations, social statuses, and behaviors typical of large plantations. Many demographic and individualized details concerning slaves survive. On the other hand, elite plantations, although they usually accounted for less than 10 percent of all plantations within localities, did represent a repeated pattern of land and slaveholding. Within most tidewater and piedmont counties, members of the gentry controlled a disproportionate amount of acreage, and over time, often a near majority of slaves. Thus many slaves had some experience, if not long-term experience, with large plantation settings. In that sense, Monticello is representative of a typical Virginia and Chesapeake pattern. The documentary and archaeological data bases of such plantation sites provide a key source for analyzing the material and social conditions of slave domestic life.

Another reason for interpreting the context of one particular plantation in piedmont Virginia is that historical and archaeological studies have by and large neglected this region and time frame. Historians, acknowledging this problem, have called for more studies of the "context of local plantations and neighborhoods" (Schlotterbeck 1989:2). Most archaeological studies of plantation slavery have dealt with monocrop plantations of the antebellum period (1815 to 1860) that were located in the coastal areas of the lower South (Wheaton et al. 1983; Fairbanks 1984; Otto 1984; Singleton 1985). While although a neglected context, piedmont Virginia is, as the historians point out, a region where slavery eventually became adapted to a more diversified form of agriculture, which contributed to the institution's geographical expansion and its "long-term" viability. Historians also consider this Upper South context crucial to a better understanding of the formative growth of American slavery and African American culture (Berlin 1980; Kulikoff 1986).

The Piedmont Regional Context and Historical Model

Virginia's piedmont is the physiographic province located west of the fall line and east of the Blue Ridge Mountains. This was the region in which the tobacco- and slave-based plantation system of the eighteenth century expanded outward from the tidewater region. At first the tidewater's frontier roughly corresponded to the piedmont, which retained this hinterland position until the middle of the century. Between 1750 and 1800 Virginia's population and agricultural production came to be centered in the piedmont, and during this transition the slave plantation system took firmer hold. In the second and third quarters of the eighteenth century, more permanent slave plantations supplanted pioneering quarters and gradually came to dominate landholdings and to contain more slaves per unit.

The contextual and processual model for piedmont plantation slavery during the late eighteenth and early nineteenth centuries postulates that changing economic and political conditions in the local, regional, and international contexts in which the system operated created new circumstances for slaves. As plantation agricultural economies diversified and stressed self-sufficiency, slave and plantation life took a new form, one detectable in the archaeological record. These new circumstances were also the result of transformed ideals of slave management and changed demographic conditions.

In the 1770-to-1825 time frame, the Southern gentry became more paternalistic, reform-minded, and racist (Genovese 1972; Breeden 1980), and this ideological shift had a great effect on slave management, as did the geographical expansion of and increase in slaveownership. The institution had managed to thrive despite economic and ideological challenges to its structural stability. On the economic level, for example, it was threatened by the winding down of the international slave trade, which came to an end between 1783 and 1808, and by the demise of slavery in the northern colonies and states. Furthermore, tobacco markets had become unstable, for wheat had replaced tobacco as the major commercial crop of the American states. This was a blow to slavery in Virginia, which had hitherto depended on worldwide slave and staple marketing systems (Berlin 1983:xv–xxvii; Kulikoff 1986:118–161).

Most piedmont planters responded to the new conditions by diversifying their operations. That is to say, they replaced the monocrop orientation with a mixture of commercial and subsistence crops and placed increased emphasis on livestock, vegetables, and grasses. As a risk-reduction strategy for dealing with fluctuating markets for agricultural staples and externally imposed credit restrictions, diversification insulated planters from economic uncertainty. Planters seeking self-sufficiency found it advantageous to have slaves support themselves rather than have to subtract subsistence costs from plantation profits. This response to altered market "forces" and regional demographics profoundly affected the slave system. Diversification meant employing slaves in an expanding variety of crop and craft activities. Activities that promoted the plantation's self-sufficiency also promoted slaves' relative self-sufficiency and theoretically, at least, altered their material circumstances and opportunities for power within the system (McColley 1964; McCusker and Menard 1985:117–143, 351–377).

Specifically, the shift from tobacco to wheat drew plantations closer to agricultural technologies, mills, transportation systems, and local and regional markets. What was important for slaves, the emphasis on wheat, a crop of seasonal labor intensity, meant they had more time to engage in a variety of tasks and to support themselves. That is, it gave them relatively more autonomy within slavery's ultimate limits. Diversification also raised the levels of plantation industries and crafts, and encouraged the hiring-out of slaves to other planters and business entrepreneurs. In adapting to these various changes, slaves not only made diversification possible for planters, but they also widened their own opportunities for travel and for gaining access to new skills and resources.

Two strong forces emerged at this time to challenge the planter-held ideals of slavery: the egalitarian ideologies of the American Revolution and the evangelical revivalism of the Second Great Awakening. The democratic beliefs underlying these systems undermined the gentry's hegemony and cast doubt on the moral legitimacy of their slave regimes. Traditional systems of hierarchy and deference experienced serious disruptions. These ideological struggles and the inclusion of African Americans in the newly formed Baptist and Methodist churches made slavery a morally and politically charged public issue. Southerners such as Jefferson had to defend slavery in more direct fashion, while continuing to incorporate it into the fabric of their social order and cultural identity (Isaac 1982). In one sense piedmont planters "successfully" met the above contextual changes within southern plantation slavery. In other words, they adapted plantation slavery to these altered circumstances, with the result that the institution remained structurally important to the region and its cultures.

The transformational period of Southern plantation economies coincided with the development from within of a more complex and stable slave social structure. By 1775 piedmont plantation society had experienced a phenomenal population growth, with slaves accounting for approximately 120,000 people as compared to the 40,000 in 1750 (Morgan 1988:433). At the time of the American Revolution the "center of Virginia's slave system shifted from tidewater to piedmont" (Morgan and Nicholls 1989:217). Between 1750 and 1800, increased African American demographic dominance and stability permitted more permanent slave communities to become established, often with large plantations at their center. As the slave population increased and sex ratios became more balanced, familial and social stability among slaves also increased. Furthermore, as the percentage of slaves on large plantations grew, the density of residential slaves and kin networks became higher. Overall, these conditions, while obviously not ideal from the perspective of slaves, reflected a more viable basis for African American communities and cultures (Berlin and Hoffman 1983; Kulikoff 1986:96–99, 142–143; Carr and Walsh 1988; Morgan 1988).

Deriving the Model and Its Implications for Monticello

Given the diversity of factors surrounding the contextual model, the following analysis tests only a part of the overall model and its implications for piedmont plantation slavery. The method consists of extracting from the general model more particular implications or hypotheses amenable to documentary and archaeological evaluation. It proceeds from the assumption that social, economic, and cultural changes can be observed at the individual plantation level. Predicted changes within Monticello's slave community over time center on alterations in social and material conditions brought about by diversification. Those changes can be archaeologically measured, for example, as a modest increase in slaves' ability to provide their own subsistence. While this directional movement reflected an altered economic status, it obviously did not remove the fundamental conditions of enslavement and domination.

The task of defining specific contextual factors for Monticello begins with the analysis of primary and secondary historical documents. This procedure simultaneously builds and evaluates the general model. Relevant variables include the demography of slavery, patterns of land and slave ownership, practices of slave management and treatment, and the manner in which local slavery fit into regional and international economic and political systems. By examining the ideology of slavery at this level we are able to delineate the changing political economy of the institution and determine Thomas Jefferson's role in this process.

Jefferson's documents allow a close study of slave demography, kin networks, and slave behavior in relation to planter methods of control. Furthermore, they provide some insight into slave-based notions of cultural identity and values. Jefferson's extensive writings record not only his philosophical reflections on slavery and so-called black-white differences, but also the daily behavior of slaves that accommodated, resisted, and creolized this institution (Gutman 1976; Sobel 1987).

By comparing slave household assemblages synchronically and diachronically, and then juxtaposing archaeological inferences with documentary evidence, the analytical method for examining Monticello slavery as a whole remains inherently comparative. The methodological objective consists first of testing the overarching hypothesis of a change in slaves' socioeconomic conditions. Theoretically, for slaves a diversifying plantation system meant improved provisioning, more training in diverse skills, and increased self-sufficiency, which presumably entailed more consumerism, subsistence activities, and local mobility. Hypothetically, the artifact analyses should diachronically demonstrate more diversified activities and greater diversity of goods and market access among the slave sites.

A two-stage model provides the means for testing this general hypothesis and its ancillary predictions (figure 8.2). The seven domestic sites are divided into two time periods or stages, ca. 1770–1800 and ca. 1800–1825, with a change in slaves' relative socioeconomic conditions expected between stage one and stage two. Figure 8.3 lists specific artifactual correlates derived from past archaeological studies of slave and nonslave economic status and from logical deductions made from the study of plantation records and histories that pertain to slave subsistence

Figure 8.2. *Two-Stage Model of Changing Conditions for Mulberry Row Slave Households.*

Stage 1 Sites, ca. 1770–1800	Stage 2 Sites, ca. 1800–1825
Building "l", ca. 1770–1809	Building "r", ca. 1790–1810
Building "m", ca. 1770–1809	Building "s", ca. 1790–1830
Building "o", ca. 1770–1800	Building "t", ca. 1790–1830
"Negro Quarter", ca. 1778–1790	

1770 - - - - - - - > - - - - - - - > - - - - - - - 1825

Stage 1 to Stage 2 Hypotheses

Prediction of relative increase in:

1. Slave households' socioeconomic status.
2. Assemblage diversity.
3. Provisions (housing, diet, clothing).
4. "Self-sufficiency" of slave households, that is, access to resources, variety of activities and craft skills. Also, evidence for augmented local mobility and domestic economy.
5. Consumerism, that is, market access and individual purchasing.

FIGURE 8.3. *Potential Archaeological Correlates for Testing the Model's Hypotheses*

SOCIOECONOMIC STATUS

a. Ceramic evidence:
   1. Decreased relative percentages of bowls, hollowwares, banded wares, undecorated wares (Otto 1984).
   2. Increased relative percentages of flatwares, storage vessels, porcelain, teawares, transfer-printed wares, matched vessel sets (Otto 1984; Spencer-Wood 1987).
   3. Increased quantity of quality ware types, decorative attributes with higher price indices (Miller 1980).
   4. Increased quantity of ware types and vessel forms.
   5. Increased diversity of ware types and vessel forms.

b. Faunal evidence:
   1. Improved meat quality, better meat cuts, greater selection of body elements.
   2. Increased relative quantity of faunal elements.
   3. Increased relative diversity of species and meat cuts.

ASSEMBLAGE DIVERSITY*

Increased number of:

a. Artifact categories (richness).
b. Artifacts within categories (evenness).
c. Artifact forms within a given category.

PROVISIONING

a. Improved housing:
   1. Larger spaces and more substantial architecture.
   2. Increased quantity of interior furnishings.
   3. Decreased adaptive re-use of existing structures.

b. Improved meat diet:
   1. Increased quantity of meat cuts, choicer elements.
   2. Increased diversity of meat cuts.
   c. Increased evidence for clothing, food-related objects.

SELF-SUFFICIENCY

Increased evidence for:

a. Local ceramics.
b. Trades and craft skills.
c. Local hunting and gathering.
d. Material goods for foods storage and preparation.

CONSUMERISM

a. Increased relative percentage of current ceramic wares.
b. Reduced dominance of planter-provided wares that exhibit time lag effects (via relative percentages of pre- and post-Mean Ceramic Date wares).
c. Increased purchases of local ceramics and individual market items indicative of market access.
d. Increased quantity and variety of personal possessions.

*Diversity measurements obtained by way of the Shannon-Weaver information statistic, where the evenness value (the order of abundance values for individual items among artifact categories) is expressed as J. The formula for deriving J is as follows:

$$J = \frac{H}{H_{max}} \qquad H = \frac{n \log n - (\Sigma fi \log fi)}{n}$$

$$H_{max} = \log k$$

where f = frequency of category i, k = number of categories, and n = sample size.

J values can range from 0 to 1.0 with higher values indicating greater diversity.

(Ascher and Fairbanks 1971; Otto 1975, 1984; Deetz 1977; Miller 1980; Singleton 1985; Spencer-Wood 1987; Adams and Boling 1989). The analysis draws on various artifact categories and attributes that offer comparative and potentially converging lines of evidence with respect to predicted changes in slave material conditions.

The comparison of site assemblages both within and between stages must first identify differences that are due to site formation and transformation processes or to variable length of occupation or household size. Then, when examined against documentary sources, the correlations between assemblages can test whether the observed degree of similarity occurred because of Jefferson's systematic provisioning methods or occurred because of the growing self-provisioning and access to resources in slave households. This kind of assemblage variability supports the proposition that slave status and subsistence were creolized entities, in that slaves' own means for self-identification and for material existence both conflicted and contrived with Jefferson's system for doing the same.

DOCUMENTARY ANALYSIS OF THE MONTICELLO CONTEXT OF SLAVERY

The primary historical record of slavery at Monticello supports the model of piedmont plantation slavery obtained from secondary sources. Monticello, on one level, was a plantation community of up to 100 people (slaves, Jefferson family members, and hired workers) within 1,000 acres, which included fields, the main house and numerous outbuildings, functional and ornamental gardens, and small-scale industries. On a larger scale, Monticello stood as the main unit in a plantation system consisting of four other Jefferson-owned quarters. Together with associated fields, mills, and roads, these plantation operations encompassed more than 100 slaves and some 5,000 acres that straddled the Rivanna River in the central part of Albemarle County (see figure 8.1). Organizationally, Jefferson's Albemarle plantation system operated in tandem with his Bedford County holdings, the latter composed of three quarters totaling some 4,000 acres. Depending on seasonal needs and shifting management strategies, the numbers of slaves at the plantations' various quarters oscillated, but in Albemarle County the majority of slaves worked and resided at Monticello, and those in Bedford County at Poplar Forest (Jefferson in Betts 1976:32, 127).

Wheat and tobacco represented the main commercial crops on Jefferson's Bedford and Albemarle County plantations. Beyond these staples, Jefferson's slaves planted, tended, and harvested Indian corn for human and animal subsistence (Betts 1976:201, 255). The emphasis on commercial crops at each plantation underscores the piedmont's agricultural context. Wheat, the dominant staple at Monticello, reflected the general trend away from tobacco among Chesapeake region plantations. While Jefferson also grew wheat at Bedford, tobacco remained the principal staple there, no doubt because of the western piedmont's fresher and cheaper soils. Tobacco remained a viable cash crop longer (beyond the 1770s) in the piedmont than in tidewater, with piedmont counties dominating tobacco production at the turn of the century.

Jefferson's record keeping amply demonstrates the range of plantings and kinds of animals on diversifying plantations. Crops grown for subsistence or local markets included oats, rye, peas, clover, barley, potatoes, hemp, and millet. These plantings and various grasses for pasture and hay aided the plantation's scheme of crop rotation for preserving land fertility. Raising small fowl, sheep, and particularly pigs and cattle added another significant dimension. In sum, a substantial degree of the plantation activities, capital, land, and slave labor went "for the support of the farm" (Betts 1976:227), that is, self-sufficiency.

The tendency of bonded African Americans to become the demographic majority in piedmont counties occurred quickly in Albemarle County. In 1755, 30 to 39 percent of Albemarle's population was African American, and by 1782 the proportion reached 40 to 49 percent (Dunn 1983:55–57). Later census figures show the same trend: the county's slave population was 44.3 percent in 1790, 50.5 percent in 1810, and 53.8 percent in 1820 (U.S. Bureau of the Census 1790, 1810, 1820). More and more of these slaves came to dwell on larger plantations, the owners of which acquired more slaves and land over time. Between 1757 and 1770 the wealthiest 10 percent of the European American male population owned 42 percent of all slaves in Albemarle County (Ayres 1968:28), and by 1785 41 percent of all piedmont slaves resided on agricultural units with more than 21 slaves (Kulikoff 1986:338). On large plantations like Monticello, African American slaves obviously represented the plantation community's overwhelming majority group.

During his adult years Jefferson owned between 150 and 375 slaves in several counties, the total varying with changing birth and death rates, sales, inheritance, and management practices. In 1773–1774 Jefferson held 383 slaves: 49.3 percent were under the age of 15, and the remaining 50.7 percent were considered adults. The latter figure was divided fairly evenly into 24.3 percent male and 26.4 percent female (Norton et al. 1983:183). In 1774, 127 of these slaves lived and worked in Bedford County, whereas in 1805 only 73 slaves resided there (Jefferson in Betts:7, 60). In Albemarle County Jefferson divided his slaves among four plantation units. In 1794, for example, the Monticello plantation had 64 slaves, Tufton 15, Shadwell 11, and Lego 15 (Jefferson in Betts 1976:30). In 1810, Jefferson recorded 85 slaves at Monticello, 28 at Tufton, and 8 at Lego for a total of 121, which, together with 86 in Bedford County, came to a population of 207 (Jefferson in Betts 1976:128–129). Jefferson subdivided the 85 at Monticello by category, identifying 40 as house servants, 22 as tradesmen, and 23 as being associated with the farm.

Some slaves at Monticello resided in quarters located away from plantation's main house complex, closer to the farming operations situated farther down the mountainside and toward the river. These slaves probably experienced less daily contact with European Americans in their work and domestic affairs than did the majority of slaves at Monticello who resided either at the main house or along Mulberry Row. This main street area contained numerous outbuildings (totaling 19 in 1796) for housing slaves, animals, and various craft activities essential to the plantation's operation. Mulberry Row slaves were predominantly house servants or tradesmen, that is, domestic slaves with diverse skills, or skilled artisans and trained crafts people (Betts 1976).

Table 8.1 lists the range of tasks assigned to slaves and indicates the skills inherent to those tasks and learned trades. Thus, slaves first performed the agricultural chores required by a fully diversified plantation. Second, they engaged in trades related to the construction of mills, other buildings, and farm machinery; worked with wood to produce tools, buildings, furniture, and transportation vehicles; and worked with metal in both plantation and commercial operations.

Research to date indicates the slaves at Monticello represented a tightly knit kin network that exhibited several of the traits of more stable slave plantation societies. For instance, most slaves at Monticello lived in family groupings of parents and children or kin-related households; marriages tended to continue over several years; and child-naming practices evidence these kin groups and the importance of slaves' families. In 1810 the 42 slave artisans and house servants at Monticello belonged to eight extended families, four of which were linked by marriage (Norton et al. 1983:181–182).

Through their family ties, slaves also passed on acquired skills. More than half of the aforementioned tradesmen and servants belonged to three families wherein children obtained the skills and occupational status of their parents (Norton et al. 1983). Archaeological evidence of such crafts and trades occurred within the slave domestic sites along Mulberry Row. Besides the artifacts associated with such domestic skills as sewing and bone button manufacture, the excavations revealed a common pattern of the tools, materials, and products of ironworking, particularly nailmaking—presumably a cottagelike industry carried out by slaves that possibly netted monetary payments or other rewards (Sanford 1985; Kelso 1986).

TABLE 8.1. *Documentary Evidence for Slaves' Occupational Activities and Terms*

Activities	Terms
Agriculture (general farming, planting, weeding, harvesting, plowing, land clearing)	Laborer or ground laborer; Field or farmhand
Livestock (raising, tending, butchering)	Hireling
Gardening and landscaping (utilitarian and ornamental)	
Fencing	
Roadwork	
Boating	
Carting	Wagoner/Carter
Housework (cleaning, personal service, horse/vehicle attendance)	Servant
Kitchen work (cooking, storage, preparation, serving)	Cook
House maintenance (painting, carpentry)	
Cloth manufacture (spinning, carding, loomwork, weaving)	Factory (worker)
Shoe manufacture	
Carpentry/joining (house construction, furniture, carriages, venetian blinds, doors, obtaining and preparing lumber)	Tradesman (joiner, nailer, smith)
Coopering (barrels, casks)	
Blacksmithing (iron, brass, tinware)	
Nail manufacture	
Stone masonry and quarrying	
Brickwork	
Charcoal production	
Canal construction	
Mill construction and operation	

ARCHAEOLOGICAL ANALYSIS OF THE MONTICELLO SLAVERY CONTEXT

Archaeological evidence offers mixed results with respect to the model's implications, especially concerning the hypothesized change in socioeconomic status (see figure 8.4). In part because of the chronological overlap among the archaeological assemblages from the two stages,the distinctions in economic status or subsistence capability are rather unclear. For example, all slave sites exhibited craft-related artifacts, but none more significantly than any other. In addition, the lack of consistent results between stages perhaps indicates the Monticello planta-

FIGURE 8.4. *Results of Analyses Testing the Model's Hypotheses*

STRONG SUPPORT FOR HYPOTHESES

1. Status/Self-Sufficiency: Relative percentage of storage/preparation vessels: Sites l,o (4.6%, 7.0%) vs. Sites s,t (13.6%, 14.4%).
2. Status: Relative percentages of bowls: Site o (16.2%) vs. Sites s,t (4.0%, 5.4%).
3. Status: Relative percentages of teaware vessels: Site o (21.7%) vs. Site s (33.7%).
4. Diversity/Self-sufficiency: Richness/diversity of coarsewares: Site o (14 types) vs. Sites s,t (24 types each).
5. Status/Diversity/Provisioning: Faunal diversity (evenness) for body part representation of three domestic species: Site l (combined J = 2.16) vs. Site s (combined J = 2.43).
6. Status: Miller Ceramic Price Index Value: Site o (1.64) vs. Site s (2.17).
7. Status: Miller Index for Cups & Saucers: Site o (1.66) vs. Site s (2.50).
8. Status: Miller Index for Plates: Site o (1.26) vs. Sites s,t (1.97, 2.10).

MODERATE SUPPORT FOR HYPOTHESES

1. Status: Relative percentages of post-Mean Ceramic Date wares: Sites l,o (46%, 48%) vs. Site s (58%).
2. Status: Relative percentages of flat and hollowwares: Flat wares: Sites l,o (37.4%, 31.9%) vs. Sites s,t (41.0%, 44.7%). Hollowwares: Sites l,o 62.5%, 68.1%) vs. Sites s,t (59.0%,55.3%).
3. Status: Relative percentages of teaware vessels: Site o (21.7%) vs. Site t (28.7%).
4. Diversity/Provisioning: Faunal diversity (evenness) for number of elements for three domestic species: Sites l,o (J = 0.70, 0.62) vs. Sites s,t (J = 0.88 each).
5. Diversity/Provisioning: Faunal diversity (evenness) for sheep body part representation: Site l (J = 0.53) vs. Sites s,t (J = 0.73, 0.80).
6. Status: Miller Ceramic Price Index Value: Site o (1.64) vs. Site t (1.76).
7. Status: Relative percentages of higher-priced decorative wares from Miller Index: Site o (30%) vs. Sites s,t (48.3%, 55.1%).

CONFLICTING EVIDENCE

1. Consumerism: Mean Ceramic Dates, implying more current wares at earlier sites than expected: Sites l,m vs. Sites s,t.
2. Status: Relative percentages of post-Mean Ceramic Date wares: Sites l,m (46%, 59%) vs. Site t (46%).
3. Diversity: Ceramic diversity (evenness) for number of shards per ten, main ceramic types: Site o (J = 0.64) vs. Sites s,t (J = 0.41, 0.47).
4. Diversity: Ceramic diversity (evenness) for number of shards per three dominant ceramic types: Site o (J = 0.93) vs. Sites s,t (J = 0.76, 0.86).
5. Status/Diversity: Faunal diversity (evenness) for cow body part representation: Sites l,o (J = 0.81, 0.70) vs. Site t (J = 0.59).

EVIDENCE FOR SIMILARITY OF ASSEMBLAGES

1. Status: Same relative percentages of pre- and post-Mean Ceramic Date wares: Sites l,m and Sites t,s.
2. Diversity: Same J values for general "domestic" diversity (ceramic, glass, metal, architectural, personal artifact categories). Sites l,o and Sites s,t.
3. Diversity: Same J values for ceramic diversity (evenness), for number of shards and vessels per main types, for number of shards per dominant types, for number of forms per dominant types, and for number of vessels per tableware forms. Site o and Sites s,t.
4. Diversity/Provisioning: Same J values for faunal diversity (evenness) for number of elements for all species, for number of individuals per main domestic species, and for body part representation of pig. Sites l,o and Sites s,t.

tion became diversified at an early date. Diversification typically occurred sooner and faster on large plantations, namely those with more capital and labor (Carr and Walsh 1988). Hence, this transformation obviated the expected archaeological transition predicted for slave quarter sites associated with an evolution in plantation economy and management.

Nonetheless, archaeological items associated with daily subsistence afford one way of examining slave self-sufficiency through time. The possession of a wide range of ceramic wares and forms, together with metal vessels and utensils, indicates that slaves could materially support activities for storing, preparing, and serving food (see table 8.2). A comparison of the proportions of food storage and preparation vessels at two early sites (buildings "l" and "o") and at two later sites (buildings "s" and "t") suggests that this ability increased over time among Mulberry Row slave quarters. At the earlier sites, 4.6 percent and 6.6 percent of all vessels were related to storage and preparation, whereas at the later sites, the figures were 13.6

percent and 14.4 percent. Similarly, the first-stage assemblage at building "o" displayed 14 different coarse wares (earthenware and stoneware) associated with food activities, while the second-stage assemblage at quarter "s" contained 24 varieties of ware.

Further indications of elevated economic ability and augmented material conditions among the slaves come from other ceramic attributes denotative of general socioeconomic status (see figure 8.3). The relative percentages of flatware and hollowware derived for the abovementioned four sites (with higher proportions of the latter associated with lower status) imply increased economic status diachronically. The assemblages at buildings "l" and "o" exhibited 62.5 percent and 68 percent hollowware respectively, while those at buildings "s" and "t" displayed slightly decreased hollowware figures of 59 percent and 55.3 percent. In similar fashion, decreased percentages of bowls also connote an increase in economic status (Otto 1975). At slave quarter "o" bowls made up 16.2 percent of tableware vessels, while at second-stage buildings "s" and "t" the figures came to 5.4 percent and 4.0 percent, respectively. Higher percentages of lower-priced, undecorated ceramics are said to indicate lower economic status (Miller 1980). At building "o" the lower-range ceramic wares made up 58.9 percent of the mass-marketed English ceramics, while at buildings "s" and "t" the same wares accounted for 19.7 percent and 20.2 percent, respectively.

Conditional support for the model's hypotheses concerning slave self-sufficiency and autonomy comes from combined archaeological and documentary data. Because no consistent differences were found between stages in this analysis, the assemblages from the sites under investigation are collapsed into one body of synchronic evidence. For example, the finding that slaves had the time and resources to carry out craft activities reinforces the proposed conditions of enhanced self-sufficiency and autonomy, as does the evidence of their gardening and poultry-raising activities. Gun-related hardware and shot, together with nondomestic faunal remains, point to slaves' hunting practices and the time and mobility (or need) to carry out those activities. Similarly, archaeological remains of fruit, nuts, and small game suggest the gathering and trapping of additional food sources (see tables 8.2, 8.3, and 8.4).

Another indication of slaves' autonomy and access to resources comes from the archaeological and documentary evidence for their having had and having received money. Small coins were found at most slave-quarter sites, although some of these possibly functioned as items of personal adornment or as symbols of religious belief. Jefferson's memorandum books and letters state that slaves received money for specific chores or personal favors, as a work incentive, and as traditional gratuities. Slaves generated additional funds by selling the produce of their garden and their livestock to the Jefferson family. What

TABLE 8.2. *Slaves' Food-Related Items and Objects*

Documented	Archaeological
Food Items	
Hog meat (bacon, salt pork, offal)	Pig
Beef	Cow
Mutton (sheep)	Sheep
Fish	Fish
Poultry (slaves' livestock)[a]	Birds (wild and domestic)
Milk	Horse/mule
Flour	Deer
Cornmeal	Turtle
Bread	Opossum
Molasses	Squirrel
Salt	Rabbit
Field peas	Woodchuck
Beans ("snaps")[a]	Muskrat
Squash ("cymlins")[a]	Clam shells
Melon ("potato pumpkin")	Oyster shells
Jamaica rum	Egg shells
Whiskey	Beans
	Pumpkins
	Peaches
	Watermelon
	Chestnut
	Walnut
Food-Related Objects	
Pot (cast iron)	Cast iron vessels
Sifter (iron or tinware)	Colander (metal)
	Basin (metal)
	Tinware vessels
	Utensils (spoons, knives, forks)
	Pot hook
	Glass wares (bottles, pitcher, stemware, tumblers)
	Ceramic wares (approximately 28 different ware types and 25 vessel forms)

[a]From slaves' documented gardens, livestock.

TABLE 8.3. *Slaves' Nonwork Activities*

Documented	Archaeological
Gardening	Some seed evidence
Raising small livestock	Faunal evidence
Social drinking	Various liquid containers
Raising pets (dogs)	
Wrestling and other games	Gaming/play (marbles, toys)
Folk songs and tales	Music (Jew's harps, harmonica)
"Pilfering" (theft)	Tobacco smoking
	Boneworking crafts (buttons, pin case, handles, brushes, combs)
	Metalworking crafts (Nailmaking, iron and brass object repair and manufacture)
	Trapping and Hunting (lead shot, gun flints, gun parts)

TABLE 8.4. *Slaves' Personal Possessions*

Documented	Archaeological
Money	Money (metal coins)
	Coins as objects of adornment or religious belief
Tools (hoe, axe, wedge)	Tools and utensils (pen and case knives, drill, punch, hammer, chisel, file, sickle, blades)
	Bone brushes, combs
	Beads
	Brass objects (rings, rivets, screws, springs, staple)

slaves spent their money on remains an unanswered question at present; research to date suggests that slaves particularly valued food and clothing, which was needed to augment their allotments from the plantation (Genovese 1972:524–566). It is also conceivable that slaves purchased other material goods to supplement their domestic economies, as Adams and Boling (1989) argue with respect to certain ceramics seen on plantations in Georgia, and such behavior may have affected the nature of the artifact assemblages seen at Monticello (see below). The presence of coins on all these sites, together with repeated evidence for metalworking crafts and for slaves' ability to hunt, trap, and gather wild food form the basis for describing a subsistence mode. In addition, the similarities between the assemblages suggest a status of sorts shared by slaves, namely a condition of resource access defined by themselves.

AN ALTERNATIVE COMPARISON: MIDDLE-RANGE THEORY

Middle-range research offers another means of evaluating the model's implications for this context. The range of primary documents dealing with Jefferson and Monticello make possible a detailed rendering of his ideology of slavery, his slave management practices, and the contradictions contained therein. Methodologically, these written records define a "descriptive grid" (Leone and Potter 1989:13) of Jeffersonian slavery, a network of period terms, beliefs, and behaviors. By testing the grid with archaeological information we are able to determine which documentary strands of the network contrast with excavated data, and thus identify questions requiring further study.

Jefferson, like other "scientific" farmers of the era, believed in the rational management of agriculture and slaves. He considered slaves to be predictable and interchangeable units of labor and believed he could calculate both the slave division of labor and provisions of food, bedding, and clothing based on the basis of slaves' age, sex, and skills, and by seasonal agricultural requirements (Jefferson in Betts 1976). Jefferson followed standard practices, employing a mixture of incentives (food, clothing, money) and punishments (occupational demotion, whipping, family separation, sale) to obtain desired behaviors and production performances. As a slaveowner he felt it was his duty to adequately feed, clothe, and house his slaves, "protecting them from all ill usage" and requiring "reasonable labor only" (Jefferson in Betts 1976:5).

A familial model of slave life accompanied rational management. Nuclear slave families would literally reproduce the system while housed in individual structures "fit up . . . in an entirely comfortable and decent manner" (Jefferson in Betts 1976:28). But reality conflicted with the ideals of familial slavery and rational management geared to maximizing production. Where whole families had to be supported, this disrupted calculations of workers' rates and efficiencies. Jefferson's own management practices disrupted slave families, with the result that household forms departed from the nuclear family ideal.

A similar conflict issued forth during the summer wheat harvest of 1795. After experiencing difficulties with his slaves' sense of work discipline and efficiency, Jefferson wrote down his ideal organization of slaves for this short but intense task. Altogether 66 slaves—including men, women, and children—would work in nine groups. If all went according to plan, "in this way the whole machine would move in exact equilibrio, no part of the force would be lessened without retarding the whole, nor increased without a waste of force" (Jefferson in Betts 1976:46). This episode, beyond reflecting a slave management ideology based on notions of machinelike efficiency with humans as integral parts, delineates Jefferson's conflict with keeping slaves with diverse backgrounds properly motivated, constantly at work, and in balance with their presumed occupational statuses.

Documentary sources at Monticello reveal a more complex range than the stereotypical, and perhaps mythical, three-part hierarchy of house servants, artisans, and field hands. Although Jefferson often imposed that scheme, he also used up to eight different terms in defining work-related slave statuses. A documentary-based compilation of slave tasks suggests that even a wider range of skills and activities existed (table 8.1). More important, these sources reveal that work-oriented status categories were not rigid, but shifted with age, skill level, kinship ties, and the demands of a changing plantation regimen. Furthermore, the archaeological interpretations from Mulberry Row denote differences in economic status between slave households grouped together within the house servant and tradesmen categories. The actual determination of slave status obviously involved a creolized process, one in which both slaves and masters participated. Contrasting with masters' status notions are documentary and archaeological indications of slave-based hierarchies based on alternative systems of social identity and authority.

As tables 8.2 and 8.5 demonstrate, archaeological remains of slave household furnishings, architectural materials, and food-related objects are in marked contrast with documentary references to similar goods provisioned by Jefferson. Some of the discrepancies may simply be explained by the failure of Jefferson to record certain items. But this answer poses another question: why didn't Jefferson record many items, especially those seen in large quantity at all sites? Presumably many of the nonrecorded items were supplied by him, such as building materials, furniture, and glass and ceramic wares. Were these goods too inexpensive or unimportant to be noted? Or was their method of distribution too informal and therefore not conducive to a written system of listed provisional units? Although these questions are difficult to resolve without further study, one possible answer lies in the discrepancy produced by slaves' own means of subsistence.

For example, Jefferson regularly recorded slaves' allotments of domesticated meat. These accounts suggest a meat diet dominated by salt pork and bacon issued in standard cuts. Alternatively, archaeological evidence for slaves' meat diet points to the wholesale use of pig and cattle carcasses, and near equal proportions of pork and beef (Crader 1984). In related fashion, information on the furnishing and treatment of the interior spaces of

TABLE 8.5. *Slave Housing*

Documented	Archaeological
Furnishings	
Beds	Root/storage cellars
	Furniture hardware
	Spikes, hooks
	Glass lamp globe
	Andiron
	Barrel (storage?)
Architectural Elements	
Wood (logs, shingles, chimneys)	Wood (logs, lathing, cellar linings and lids)
"Cramming" (chinking)	Chinking, daub (mud)
Earth (flooring)	Earth, mixed with stones
Nails	Nails
	Stone (foundations, cellar linings, hearths)
	Brick (paving, cellar lining, hearths)
	Whitewash (?)
	Window glass
	Door hardware (pintle, hinge, lock, latch, key)
	Outbuilding
	Possible shed addition

slave quarters comes almost entirely from archaeological sources (table 8.5). The repeated use of underground storage cellars and the addition of furniture, fixtures, and domestic goods point to slave-based notions of defining cultural space and social status. Finally, slave ceramic assemblages hold to a common pattern featuring both currently popular and out-of-date wares. This pattern suggests that slaves supplemented their provided ceramics (presumably Jefferson family hand-me-downs or wares specifically purchased for slaves) with purchases of fashionable pottery. Together with the above evidence concerning hunting, gathering, and gardening, these data reveal that slaves maintained their own system of provisioning beyond Jefferson's system of rational management, one that undoubtedly combined self-production, theft, purchase, and trade.

CONCLUSIONS

The foregoing evaluation of the contextual and processual model for plantation slavery in piedmont Virginia did not provide clear support for all of the model's implications. Nonetheless, the analyses that supported several aspects of the model suggest it has analytical value and together with the negative results indicate the avenues by which it might be refined. The future application of archaeological data from additional plantation sites from the same regional and chronological context will best determine the worth of the general model, especially if assemblages from small and middle-sized slave plantations are included.

On the whole, the implementation of an analytical framework based on contextual modeling has its advantages. First, it necessitates an interdisciplinary approach to research sources and demands constant comparisons between archaeological data, documentary materials, and the interpretive models proffered by archaeologists, historians, and anthropologists. Second, it pushes analyses of archaeological data beyond purely substantive issues and toward sociocultural issues such as the nature of slave society and African American culture in a given place and time. Third, the method, by way of its close attention to local and regional variables of plantation slavery, addresses the acknowledged variability of slave sites.

Through its emphasis on making comparisons and identifying contradictions, the methodology also enhances the archaeologist's ability to consider the bicultural aspects of artifacts from slave plantations. For example, the ceramic assemblages from the Monticello slave sites exhibited common attributes with respect to ware types, decorative treatments, and vessel forms. But they also demonstrated diversity within and between the proposed stages of plantation development because the assemblages embody not only Jefferson's management standards but also the slaves' methods of provisioning and self-definition. This artifactual contrast underscores both the bicultural nature of slave site assemblages and the contradiction inherent to slavery.

Jefferson's provisioning system enacted his ideology of paternalistic slave management as much as it attempted to rationally distribute goods. As other scholars have noted, the standardization of slave treatment promoted by reform-minded planters likely embodied an additional attempt to control slaves and impose European American cultural norms (Singleton 1988:354–355). Contradicting this control and domination were slaves' means of resistance and their creation of opportunities for enhanced autonomy. Slaves' own systems of status determination and cultural identification and their material displays of self-sufficiency further enacted strategies of empowerment. In sum, the attempted control of slaves via increased paternalism was contradicted in turn by the resultant alteration of slaves' skills and their material and social conditions. This conflict implicitly recognized planters' actual dependence on slaves.

This sense of contradiction ran throughout slavery's ideology and practice. Jefferson's stance on slavery has been called a "web of contradictions" (McLaughlin 1988:96), because it denounced slavery's principles, on one hand, while defending its practice on the other (McColley 1964:116). Given slavery's contradictory nature, this conflict is not unexpected. As an institution attempting to be humane, familial, and moral, and yet rationally economic, slavery encased both an ideology of paternalism and reason and a reality of hierarchy, patriarchy, and exploitation. From an archeological standpoint, the contradictory aspects of plantation slavery in piedmont Virginia offer the opportunity to better understand this institution and its "other" culture, that of African American slaves.

REFERENCES CITED

Adams, William H., and Sarah Jane Boling
1989 Status and Ceramics for Planters and Slaves on Three Georgia Coastal Plantations. *Historical Archaeology* 23(1):69–96.

Ascher, Robert, and Charles H. Fairbanks
1971 Excavations of a Slave Cabin: Georgia, U.S.A. *Historical Archaeology* 5:3–17.

Ayres, S. Edward
1968 Albemarle County, Virginia, 1744–1770: An Economic, Political, and Social Analysis. M.A. thesis, History, University of Virginia, Charlottesville.

Berlin, Ira
1980 Time, Space, and the Evolution of Afro-American Society on British Mainland North America. *American Historical Review* 85(1):44–78.
1983 Introduction. In *Slavery and Freedom in the Age of the American Revolution*, edited by Ira Berlin and Richard Hoffman, pp. xv–xxvii. University of Virginia Press, Charlottesville.

Berlin, Ira, and Ronald Hoffman (editors)
1983 *Slavery and Freedom in the Age of the American Revolution*. University of Virginia Press, Charlottesville.

Betts, Edwin M. (editor)
1976 *Thomas Jefferson's Farm Book*. University of Virginia Press, Charlottesville. Orig. 1953.

Breeden, James O. (editor)
1980 *Advice among Masters: The Ideal in Slave Management in the Old South*. Greenwood Press, Westport, Conn.

Carr, Lois Green, and Lorena S. Walsh
1988 Economic Diversification and Labor Organization in the Chesapeake, 1650–1820. In *Work and Labor in Early America*, edited by Stephen Innes, pp. 144–188. University of North Carolina Press, Chapel Hill.

Carr, Lois Green, Philip D. Morgan, and Jean B. Russo (editors)
1988 *Colonial Chesapeake Society*. University of North Carolina Press, Chapel Hill.

Crader, Diana C.
1984 The Zooarchaeology of the Storehouse and the Dry Well at Monticello. *American Antiquity* 49(3):542–557.

Dabney, William M.
1951 *Jefferson's Albemarle: History of Albemarle County, Virginia, 1727–1819*. Ph.D. dissertation, History, University of Virginia.

Deetz, James
1977 *In Small Things Forgotten*. Doubleday, New York.

Dunn, Richard S.
1983 Black Society in the Chesapeake, 1776–1810. In *Slavery and Freedom in the Age of the American Revolution*, edited by Ira Berlin and Ronald Hoffman, pp. 49–62. University of Virginia Press, Charlottesville.

Fairbanks, Charles H.
1984 The Plantation Archaeology of the Southeastern Coast. *Historical Archaeology* 18(1):1–14.

Genovese, Eugene D.
1972 *Roll, Jordan, Roll: The World Slaves Made*. Random House, New York.

Gutman, Herbert G.
1976 *The Black Family in Slavery and Freedom, 1750–1825*. Pantheon Books, New York.

Hantman, Jeffrey L., and Douglas W. Sanford
1986 Review of *Cannon's Point Plantation 1794–1860: Living Conditions and Status Patterns in the Old South*, by John S. Otto. In *Journal of American Folklore* 99(391):92–94.

Herman, Bernard L.
1984 Slave Quarters in Virginia: The Persona Behind Historic Artifacts. In *The Scope of Historical Archaeology*, edited by David Orr and Daniel Crozier, pp. 253–283. Laboratory of Anthropology, Temple University, Philadelphia.

Isaac, Rhys
1982 *The Transformation of Virginia, 1740–1790*. University of North Carolina Press, Chapel Hill.

Kelso, William M.
1984 *Kingsmill Plantations, 1619–1800: Archaeology of Country Life in Colonial Virginia*. Academic Press, New York.
1986 The Archaeology of Slave Life at Thomas Jefferson's Monticello: 'A Wolf by the Ears.'" *Journal of New World Archaeology* 6(4):5–20.

Kulikoff, Allan
1986 *Tobacco and Slaves: The Development of Southern Cultures in the Chesapeake, 1680–1800*. University of North Carolina Press, Chapel Hill.

Lee, Jean B.
1986 The Problem of Slave Community in the Eighteenth-Century Chesapeake. *William and Mary Quarterly* 43(3):333–361.

Leone, Mark P., and Parker B. Potter, Jr. (editors)
1988 *The Recovery of Meaning: Historical Archaeology in the Eastern United States*. Smithsonian Institution Press, Washington, D.C.

McColley, Robert
1964 *Slavery and Jeffersonian Virginia*. University of Illinois Press, Urbana.

McCusker, John, and Russell R. Menard
1985 *The Economy of British America, 1607–1789*. University of North Carolina Press, Chapel Hill.

McGuire, Randall H., and Robert Paynter (editors)
1991 *The Archaeology of Inequality*. Basil Blackwell, Oxford, England.

McLaughlin, Jack
1988 *Jefferson and Monticello: The Biography of a Builder*. Henry Holt and Company, New York.

Miller, George
1980 Classification and Economic Scaling of 19th Century Ceramics. *Historical Archaeology* 14(1):1–41.

Moore, John H.
1976 *Albemarle, Jefferson's County, 1727–1976*. University of Virginia Press, Charlottesville.

Morgan, Philip D.
1988 Slave Life in Piedmont Virginia, 1720–1800. In *Colonial Chesapeake Society*, edited by Carr, Morgan, and Russo. pp. 433–484. University of North Carolina Press, Chapel Hill.
Morgan, Philip D., and Michael L. Nicholls
1989 Slaves in Piedmont Virginia, 1720–1790. *William and Mary Quarterly* 46(2):211–251.
Norton, Mary B., Herbert Gutman, and Ira Berlin
1983 The Afro-American Family in the Age of Revolution. In *Slavery and Freedom in the Age of the American Revolution*, edited by Ira Berlin and Ronald Hoffman, pp. 175–192. University of Virginia Press, Charlottesville.
Orser, Charles E., Jr.
1988a Toward a Theory of Power for Historical Archaeology: Plantations and Space. In *The Recovery of Meaning: Historical Archaeology in the Eastern United States*, edited by Mark P. Leone and Parker B. Potter, Jr., pp. 313–343. Smithsonian Institution Press, Washington. D.C.
1988b The Archeological Analysis of Plantation Society: Replacing Status and Caste with Economics and Power. *American Antiquity* 53(4):735–751.
1989 On Plantations and Patterns. *Historical Archaeology* 23(2):28–40.
Otto, John S.
1975 *Status Differences and the Archaeological Record: A Comparison of Planter, Overseer, and Slave Sites from Cannon's Point Plantation (1794–1861), St. Simon's Island, Georgia*. Ph.D. dissertation, University of Florida.
1984 *Cannon's Point Plantation, 1794–1869: Living Conditions and Status Patterns in the Old South*. Academic Press, Orlando.
Sanford, Douglas W.
1985 A Report on the Archaeological Excavations of Servants' Houses 'r', 's', and 't', and the Related Landscape. In Monticello Black History/Craft Life Archaeological Project, 1985-1985, Progress Report, by William M. Kelso et al. Submitted to the National Endowment for the Humanities.
1991 Middle Range Theory and Plantation Archaeology: An Analysis of Domestic Slavery at Monticello, Albemarle County, Virginia, ca. 1770–1830. *Quarterly Bulletin of the Archeological Society of Virginia* 46(1):20–30.
Schlotterbeck, John T.
1989 Slavery and Slave Life in an Upper South Mixed Agriculture Region, 1800 to 1880. Paper presented at "Cultivation and Culture: Labor and the Shaping of Slave Life in the Americas," University of Maryland, College Park, April, 1989.
Silberman, Neil A.
1989 Letter from Mississippi: The Black Experience in America. *Archaeology* 42(5):62, 68–71, 82.
Singleton, Theresa A.
1988 An Archaeological Framework for Slavery and Emancipation, 1740–1880. In *The Recovery of Meaning: Historical Archaeology in the Eastern United States*, edited by Mark P. Leone and Parker B. Potter, Jr., pp. 345–370. Smithsonian Institution Press, Washington, D.C.
Singleton, Theresa A. (editor)
1985 *The Archeology of Slavery and Plantation Life*. Academic Press, New York.
Sobel, Mechal
1987 *The World They Made Together: Black and White Values in Eighteenth-Century Virginia*. Princeton University Press, Princeton, N.J.
Spencer-Wood, Suzanne M. (editor)
1987 *Consumer Choice in Historical Archaeology*. Plenum Press, New York.
U.S. Bureau of the Census
1801 *Second Census of the United States, 1800*, pp. 1–2H. Washington, D.C.
1811 *Aggregate Amount of Persons within the United States in the Year 1810*, pp. 54-56.
1821 *Census for 1820*, pp. 23–24. Gales and Seaton, Washington, D.C.
1832 *Fifth Census: Enumeration of the Inhabitants of the United States*. Duff Green, Washington, D.C.
1908 *First Census of the United States, 1790*, pp. 9–10. Government Printing Office, Washington, D.C.
Vlach, John M.
1987 Afro-American Domestic Artifacts in Eighteenth-Century Virginia. *Material Culture* 19(1):3–23.
Wheaton, Thomas R., Patrick Garrow, and Amy Friedlander
1983 *Yaughn and Curriboo Plantations: Studies in Afro-American Archaeology*. Soil Systems, Marietta, Georgia.

IX
CHAPTER

"As Is the Gardener, So Is the Garden"
The Archaeology of Landscape as Myth

ELIZABETH KRYDER-REID

THE CHESAPEAKE and Virginia tidewater areas contain the largest concentration of gardens surviving from the second half of the eighteenth century in America. The most famous of these gardens—such as Monticello, Mount Vernon, Gunston Hall, and the Paca garden—have been restored and are open to the public. The vast majority, however, remain in private hands and in varying degrees of preservation. The St. Mary's site (18AP45) has been in the hands of private owners for more than 300 years and has been disturbed remarkably little, despite its urban setting in the Historic District of Annapolis (figure 9.1). These conditions make the St. Mary's site an ideal test case in which to reconstruct past landscapes and to interpret the changing perceptions and meanings of the built environment.

The European American history of the site is examined in this study as a series of superimposed landscapes. Two of these landscapes, a 1770s terraced garden and a late nineteenth- and early twentieth-century religious community's grounds, are interpreted as a means by which the owners articulated an ideology and displayed their place in the world. The late eighteenth-century landscape garden was the product of Charles Carroll of Carrollton, a member of the colonial economic elite, albeit disfranchised because of his Catholicism, and his garden is interesting as a self-representation of a politically aspiring member of the dominant class in a capitalist, hierarchical society. Similarly, the nineteenth-century landscape examined here is viewed as a medium for constructing and negotiating social identity, but in this case the self-representation of the Redemptorists, an all-male Catholic congregation of priests and brothers in a community professing poverty, chastity, obedience, and perseverance in the Congregation until death (Anonymous 1928:34). In contrast to Carroll's bid to join the politically empowered, the Redemptorist landscape offers a perspective on the formation of a self-conscious and self-proclaimed marginal group.

The Chesapeake region's heritage of formal gardens preserved from the eighteenth century and the historical archaeology of these landscapes have much to contribute to an understanding of colonial self-representation. In the eighteenth century, geometrically planned, terraced gardens were powerful statements of wealth and the right to own it. Gardens were displays of financial resources, but more importantly they were displays of knowledge; a garden implied familiarity with literature, classics, and art, as well as the "natural sciences" of geometry, botany, husbandry, hydraulics, surveying, and architecture. Gardens, as controlled domains of nature, were therefore

FIGURE 9.1. *A view of the St. Mary's site looking north, taken from the Spa Creek bridge.*

powerful media for men, and occasionally women, of the colonial elite to communicate and negotiate their social identity.[1]

The eighteenth-century saying "As is the Gardener, so is the Garden" invokes this notion of self-presentation, but the relation between the encoded meanings of the garden and the diverse colonial audience who observed and toured these groomed spaces is less simple than the maxim suggests.[2] Gardens were places where social constructions were expressed and empowered, but these messages were also resisted and denied. The readings of visiting planter gentry were clearly different from those of the slaves who weeded and tilled (Upton 1988). Despite this diversity of audiences and received meanings, the gardens were powerful symbols that in many ways operated like myths in the construction of social identity. Like myths of the past that are told to explain the present, colonial gardens drew on precedents to naturalize the present and to project claims on the future. Elite gardens evoked their owners' associations with the past through neoclassical architecture, mythological or heroic figures, and other symbols of an Arcadian ideal. Like myths also, the gardens legitimated their owners by embedding the present in seemingly natural or eternally inevitable powers. The control of time, the manipulation of perspective, and the propagation of the natural world resonated in sundials, optical illusions, hot beds, and topiary. Furthermore, just as myths evolve, so too through time the changing needs, beliefs, and interests of the occupants are expressed and reinforced in the transformation of the landscape.

In historical archaeology much has been written about the ways in which material culture—whether scientific instruments, tea sets, musical compositions, architecture, or gravestones—actively shaped and continues to shape our world and how we perceive it. A premise of these writings has been that artifacts are not simply expressive entities, the results or products of human behavior and thought. Instead, they are productive; they shape our motions, perceptions, and categories. This recursive relationship between human creatures and their physical world is part of the ongoing construction of meaning, or, what we know as reality. Landscapes are particularly powerful symbolic artifacts because they are three-dimensional spaces, which, unlike portable artifacts, are volumes literally entered into and experienced. Space is not simply viewed, held, or worn; it is enacted by being within and moving through it. A landscape, through the structure of its space, directs what one sees and how one moves. For instance, the organization of a garden may control movement through it by means of a series of ramps that promote continuous motion or by stairs that enable visitors to stop at discrete viewing platforms. The placement of trees and the proportions of falls and terraces create vistas both for viewers within the garden and for spectators from without. Garden books, such as Langley's popular *New Principles of Gardening* (figure 9.2), provided the geometry and planting instructions "necessary to be well understood by every good Gardener that's employed in making and laying out Gardens" (1728:viii). By manipulating laws of perspective, these directions in-

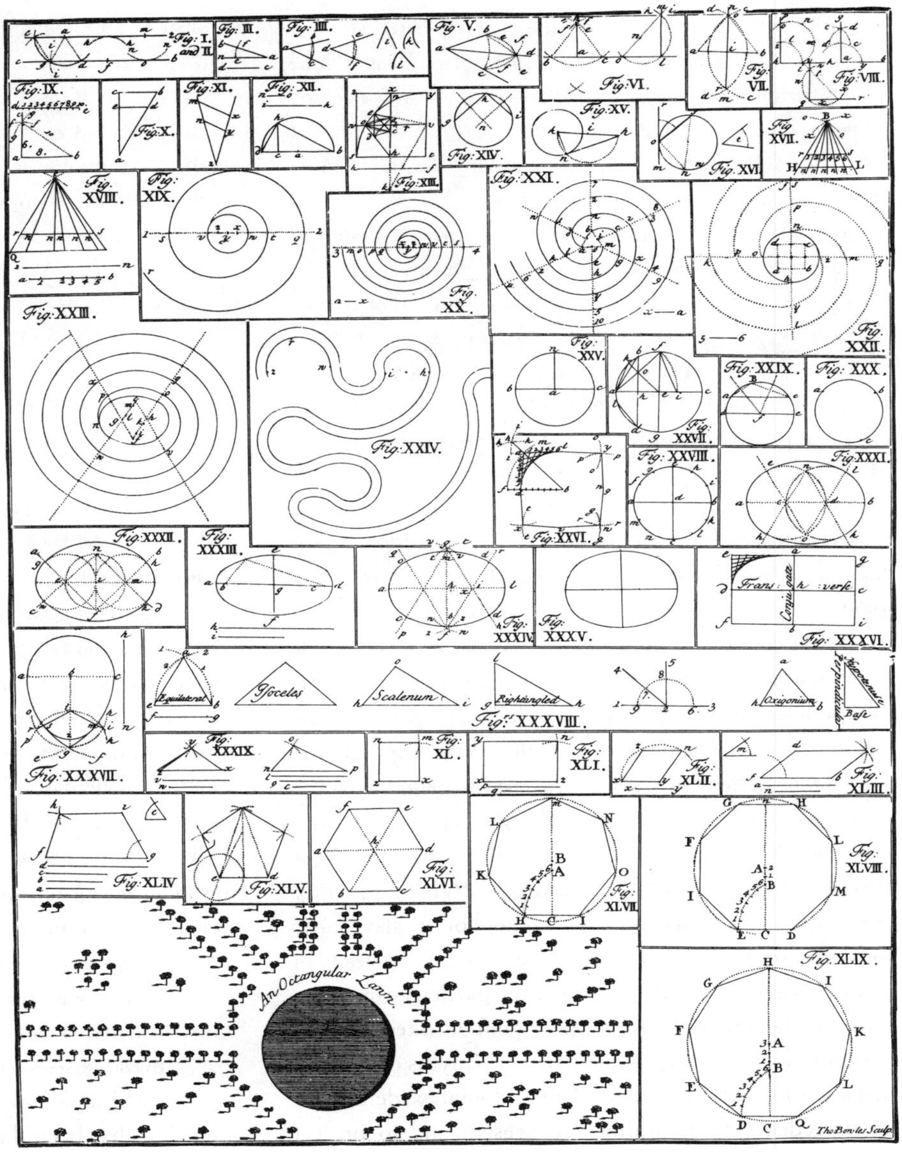

FIGURE 9.2. *Plate 1 from Batty Langley's* New Principles of Gardening *providing instructions for creating geometrical forms in a garden. (Photograph courtesy of Dumbarton Oaks, trustees for Harvard University)*

dicated how to make a small space appear larger or a distant object closer. For the visitor versed in such literature, the experience of being in and moving through the garden was a sensory and intellectual interaction with the space.

THE EIGHTEENTH-CENTURY CHESAPEAKE LANDSCAPE

Although the St. Mary's site encompasses approximately 9 acres, 2 of which make up the Carroll garden, the landscape is most meaningful when seen as part of its larger historical and geographic context. The natural harbor and surrounding waterways of the Chesapeake made Annapolis an obvious center of trade and shipping, and the area's first settlers in the 1650s selected protected sites on peninsulas and often chose the clearings of Indian "old fields" for farmsteads (Wright 1977:183). It was not until 1694, however, when the colony's capital was moved from strongly Catholic St. Mary's City to Protestant-dominated Annapolis, that the settlement flourished. The economic basis of mercantile centers in the Chesapeake such as Annapolis was the developing agrarian capitalism based mainly on the tobacco production of independent plantations (Middleton 1984). Owing to the Chesapeake's temperate climate, the abundance of arable land, and the intertwined water routes that allowed dispersed shipping points throughout the Chesapeake Bay and its estuaries, land-intensive tobacco plantations flourished in the tidewater area (Stilgoe 1982:60, Middleton 1984:94). Rent rolls of the seventeenth century divided the area that is now Anne Arundel County into hundreds, and land grants within those areas generally consisted of 100 to 400 acres (Wright 1977:183). These plantations, although small compared to the plantations of other southern states, were self-sufficient units; what could not be produced or manufactured on the farm was acquired through an English agent or local merchant for credit earned with tobacco crops, which became the de facto currency of the colonies (Compton 1977:61). The tidewater's intricate network of navigable rivers and creeks (48 in Virginia and Maryland alone) supported the dispersed settlements required to produce the land-intensive crop because it eased transportation problems, as well as frustrating attempts to regulate exportation (Middleton 1984:353, Compton 1977:60).

Chartered in 1708, Annapolis grew rapidly during the eighteenth century, supported by the business of craftsmen, merchants, and government activities. By the 1760s it emerged as the social and commercial center of the Chesapeake. In 1769 Thomas Eddis, a visitor to the town, wrote

> It is . . . the seat of Government; the public offices are here established; and as many of the principal families have chosen this place for their residence, there are few towns of the same size in any part of the British dominions that can boast a more polished society. . . . In the vicinity of Annapolis there are many pleasant villas, whose proprietors are eminent for their hospitality. (As quoted in Trostel 1981:33)

For approximately 30 years, from 1760 to 1790, the cultural and social florescence that accompanied this prosperity—the social clubs, theater, musical performances, balls, fashions, distinguished visitors—gave Annapolis a prominence in the colonies it has never regained (Lemay 1972; Davis 1978). During this time the elite of Anne Arundel County, like others in the Chesapeake colonies, were engaged in consolidating their wealth and buttressing their authority vis á vis English rule, Evangelical religious movements, and the underclasses (Isaac 1982). The most successful entrepreneurs of this period were those plantation gentry who expanded their agrarian-based wealth with speculative ventures in land, money lending, shipping, and industrial investment. These entrepreneurs were the same gentlemen who in the latter half of the eighteenth century invested such time, energy, and capital into grooming their estates, country and urban, into idyllic green spaces.

The gardens crafted by the colonial elite cannot be fully understood without a sense of how the spaces were organized, as well as what they looked like. Most important was the intimate relation of house and garden, which were linked not only by proximity, but by their geometrical proportions, vistas, and entrances. Sight lines, boundaries, access points, and planting arrangements were more than mere aesthetic elements; they dictated how the garden was viewed and experienced. Garden doorways to the house were as much a part of the garden as a gate, mediating between the inside and outside worlds (Lockwood 1934:119). The terraces were graced with parterres or beds planted in elaborate geometrical designs that provided both intricate paths to navigate and platforms from which to view distant vistas of focal points within the garden. Plantings included flowering shrubs, bulbs, roses, vegetables, fruit trees, and border plants such as privet and boxwood. Fragrant plants were particularly popular, as were tulips; by 1760 more than 50 varieties of tulips were advertised for sale in Boston (Taylor 1952:88). Shade trees were often planted around the perimeter of a garden or to frame a vista. Water works such as fountains and jet d'eaux were almost unknown in the colonies, in contrast to their English counterparts, although still-water features such as the ponds and the canals at the Paca garden and the governor's palace in Williamsburg appear to have been more common.[3] Grass surrounded the beds on the terraces that were connected by turfed ramps rather than stairs, as was more common in England (Lockwood 1934:129; Sarudy 1989:126). These ramps offered continuous processional routes from level to level, rather than the punctuated, potential stopping places of the stairs. Often the approach to the house was lined with trees creating dramatic alleys and vistas both to and from the house, as well as strictly controlling the passage of approach.

Garden architecture was also a significant part of Chesapeake terraced gardens. Outbuildings such as summerhouses, pavilions, temples, dovecotes, icehouses, springhouses, and bathhouses of brick and wood served as focal points for vistas, and provided specialized functions. Small garden houses such as those at Mount Vernon and Montpelier were relatively common, while more sophisticated designs such as Jefferson's temple, Paca's domed summerhouse, and the Wye Island orangerie graced more elaborate gardens. The design and ornamentation of these garden outbuildings were generally neoclassical in character although rustic, naturalistic, and exotic designs such as the hermitage, grotto, or Chinese pagoda fashionable in England in the late eighteenth century were known through garden literature and occasionally constructed in America.[4]

In addition to the falling gardens, the Chesapeake abounded with flat-quadrangle or "four bed gardens" such as the Colonel Nicholas Rogers garden in Baltimore. One of the 13 that historian Barbara Sarudy records in the city during the eighteenth century, the Rogers garden was typical of the symmetrical, ordered combination of "utility and decoration" (Sarudy 1989:129). Oddly, the flat gardens do not appear to be a disproportionately urban phenomenon, as one might expect given the space constrictions and lack of relief in many urban lots. The Paca garden in the center of Annapolis is comprised of five terraces on a lot 198 feet by 396 feet (Paca-Steele and Wright 1986), while an 1801 map of Baltimore shows numerous flat four-bed gardens in the "environs" of the city (Sarudy 1989).

The question posed here is why these entrepreneurs of the latter half of the eighteenth century invested such time, energy, and capital into grooming their estates, country and urban, into idyllic green spaces. The most obvious answer is that they did so to create displays of wealth or status symbols, and this thesis has been argued at length. Williams (1985) points convincingly to the "great" country houses of eighteenth-century England as symbols:

> Look at the sites, the facades, the defining avenues and walls, the great iron gates and the guardian buildings. These were chosen for more than the effect from the inside out. . . . They were chosen for the other effect, from the outside looking in: a visible stamping of power, of displayed wealth and command: a social disproportion which was meant to impress and overawe. (Williams 1985:106)

In the Chesapeake, similar wealth displays were presented in the form of large, brick Georgian-style houses perched on prominences along the James, the Potomac, and the Chesapeake Bay, as well as in urban centers such as Annapolis and Alexandria. From the mid-eighteenth century until the revolutionary war, gardens relying on the same principles of geometry and proportions as the buildings were constructed adjacent to these homes. The timing of this period of construction and popularity of landscape gardens in the Chesapeake has been examined by Leone (1987) using Braudel's (1979) idea that ostentatious displays are employed when the right to govern is challenged. The display is particularly prominent when that right is based not on money, but on other forms of authority such as lineage, religious affiliation, or appointment. Leone uses Braudel's hypothesis to argue that the construction of formal gardens in the years preceding the revolutionary war can be seen as an attempt to reinforce elite claims on leadership.

The Chesapeake's rural seats and townhouses clearly boasted substantial economic investment, but their architectural statements go beyond mere ostentation. Through their demonstration of classicizing architectural principles of proportion, symmetry, and ornamentation, the homes bespoke the authority of one who had a classical education. They told of one who understood the interrelated orders of mathematics, optics, music, astronomy, and architecture. This unity of the arts, philosophy, and politics in the eighteenth century makes clearer the ideological import of changes in landscape design that might otherwise be seen simply as "fashion." According to the precepts of the New Science of the seventeenth century, nature was linked with music, astronomy, mathematics, and physics as part of a natural philosophy that considered the world to be in a fixed state of order and harmony. Laws of motion, proportion, and harmonics were attempts to understand and codify the natural state of the world.

> [I]t was not the ambiguity of 'Nature' which people felt most strongly; it was the clarity of the authority, and the universal acceptability of Nature and Nature's laws. The Laws of Nature are the laws of reason; they are always and everywhere the same, and like the axioms of mathematics they have only to be presented in order to be acknowledged as just and right by all men. (Willey 1940:2)

But the buildings and gardens of the eighteenth-century must be seen as far more than wealth displays or even statements of mastery of the laws of nature; they were inherently political statements because of an integral link between power and nature in the Lockean theory of society, a theory that was accepted as a basic principle of Enlightenment rationalism in the colonies. Historian Bernard Bailyn explains that in colonial American political theory, power was explicitly the control of some people over others. The basis of a government's power was seen to be the voluntary surrender of the rights of individuals to the society's leaders. This compact meant that power "inhered naturally in the government" and liberty "inhered naturally in the people" (Bailyn 1967:59). An interpretation of the political implications of colonial gardens is not in itself a novel approach. Leone (1984) has examined the William Paca garden (ca. 1765) and proposed that, through the rationalization of space (by manipulating geometry and laws of optics) and through precedent (the display of knowledge of the past), Paca was attempting to naturalize the existing social hierarchy and his position in it. By embedding that which was not natural (his wealth and social position) in that which appeared natural (the garden and the principles it represented), Paca was creating not just an attractive landscape, but an ideology.

I suggest, however, that it is not simply the rationalization of space or even the use of precedent that is the ideological import in these Annapolis landscapes. I believe these gardens were created as idealized pastoral landscapes—mythical settings presenting their owners as master not only of nature, but of a nature in which all hints of production are erased and only a landscape to be consumed remains. As in the more naturalized pastoral landscapes of England (Williams 1985:125), the geometrical gardens of Annapolis presented an objectified, idealized vision of nature that mystified the profit-making exploitation on which the estate was based. That the setting appeared natural served all the more to legitimize the exploitation that made its very existence possible.

THE CARROLL GARDEN

For four seasons from 1987 to 1990, Archaeology in Annapolis has been researching and excavating the landscape of the St. Mary's site (18AP45) in Annapolis, Maryland, with a particular focus on the formal terraced garden created in the 1770s by Charles Carroll of Carrollton and changes to the space by the Redemptorists since 1853.[5] The excavations proceeded under a combination of strategies aimed at obtaining information on both the layout and stratigraphy of the garden. Broad areas were opened in intensive-use areas such as the foundations of the early eighteenth-century wing, which had been the site of the garden entrance and principal viewing platform from the house until it was demolished in the mid-nineteenth century.[6] The construction sequence and topography of the garden were investigated by dividing the garden into units and taking cores at 20-foot intervals along perpendicular transects throughout the garden.[7] The coring demonstrated how workers cut into the natural hillside and filled it out to create the terraces. Excavation units dated the stratigraph established by the coring and also recovered several architectural and planting features. Of particular interest was the discovery that the entire lowest terrace (5) was created by building the seawall and filling the area behind it, thereby raising the original shoreline 6 feet and extending it approximately 50 feet into the creek.

The St. Mary's site is remarkable for several reasons. First, after 200 years of continuous occupation, the garden topography remains relatively intact. Second, its construction and the Carroll family activities at the time are recorded in the voluminous Carroll papers. Third, it was built in the years leading up to and during the revolutionary war by the wealthiest man in Annapolis who, because of his Catholicism, was disfranchised politically and discriminated against socially. These three factors lead to two conclusions about the 1770s garden: that it is retrievable at least in part through archaeological data and detailed textual information, and that it was the creation of a man with a self-acknowledged paradoxical social identity. His wealth and education positioned him for a leading role in colonial politics, yet his religion threatened to deny him that access. Carroll was aware of this contradiction and wrote of it to a friend in London.

> [D]esigning & selfish men invented religious tests to exclude from posts of profit and trust their weaker or more conscientious fellow subjects; thus to secure to themselves all the emoluments of government. . . . If my countrymen judge me incapable of serving them in a public station for believing ye moon to be made of green cheese . . . I will serve them notwithstanding, nay, I have done it. (Charles Carroll of Carrollton [CCC] to William Graves, August 15, 1774, Maryland Historical Society [MdHi] Ms. 203, No. 2, p. 30 [591])

Three biographical points set up the interpretive context for Carroll's garden built from 1770 until 1778.[8] The first is that the Carroll family was as firmly established economically as any in the colonies. Carrollton's grandfather emigrated from Ireland in 1688 to take the post of attorney general of Maryland. Despite the revolt of Maryland Protestants in 1689 and his subsequent imprisonment, Carroll the Settler, as he came to be called, retained close ties to the Calverts (proprietors of Maryland) and established an impressive financial basis. By the time of his death in 1720, his wealth included six manors, 47,777 acres (the largest holdings in the colony), and an estate of £40,000 sterling (Hanley 1982:4–5; Hoffman 1988:219, 225). The Settler's son, Charles Carroll of Annapolis, diversified the family estate with investments in the Baltimore Iron Works in 1731, and in rental properties, shipping interests, agriculture, bonds, mortgages, and money lending. By the time Carroll of Carrollton was born in his father's recently constructed house in Annapolis (figure 9.3), he was heir to the largest fortune in the colony.

The second point is that Charles Carroll of Carrollton, like his father, was educated by Jesuits in Europe, where he received training in the classics, the Enlightenment philosophy (particularly in the works of Voltaire and the physiocrats), law, art, poetry, music, painting, surveying, mathematics—in short, all the skills needed to take his place as the gentleman manager of the Carroll estate. He traveled extensively in France and England, visiting Versailles, touring the Loire Valley, living in Paris and London. As his book orders and correspondence indicate,

Figure 9.3. The Carroll house as seen from the lowest terrace looking north.

Carroll continued to keep up with the currents of intellectual and political thought abroad and at home after he returned to Maryland. Not only could his life-style be described as that of a landed English aristocrat (Papenfuse 1975), but his intellectual world was, like that of Jefferson, a product of the European Enlightenment.

The third point is that Charles Carroll of Carrollton has been hailed as a signer of the Declaration of Independence, indeed the "Last Living Signer," and, as an exemplar of revolutionary America, he "typified all that was best in the new civilization that was beginning to illuminate this Western World" (Address of the Hon. T. Scott Offutt at the celebration of the 200th anniversary of Carroll's birth, as quoted in Scarff 1937:8).[9] Until the outcome of the revolutionary war was clear, however, Carroll's position within the developing authority structure of the colonies was less than certain, in his own mind at least. Although Carroll was politically active in the years leading up to war with Britain, his correspondence at the time indicates that his own perception of that role was tenuous. Throughout his education, Carroll realized the cost of his religious convictions. While still in Europe he confided to his father, "Rural amusements such as farming & other country occupations unified to Philosophy (its best allies) form that plan of life wh appears of all others ye most eligible: the Laws of my country exclude me from acting in any public capacity" (CCC to Charles Carroll of Annapolis [CCA], July 15, 1761, MdHi Ms. 206, No. 68). While a member of a delegation to Canada, Carroll wrote, "These public honors set very heavy on me, I think I am fitter for a private station, at least such a one is more suited to my feelings & inclination" (CCC to CCA, March 29, 1776, MdHi Ms. 206, No. 330), And writing from Montreal to his father he added, "If the Congress has any opinion of my abilities, they were certainly mistaken" (CCC to CCA May 5, 1776, MdHi Ms. 206, No. 341). Even his appointment to the Continental Congress appeared to be incidental, according to Carroll's account:

> Contrary to my expectation I am appointed a Deputy to Congress, and much against my inclination I find myself obliged to set off for Pha. in a week at farthest—Mr. Johns cant go his wife is near her time—Mrs. Chase is too ill to permit Chas to go—Mr Tilghman is prevented by something or other so I am reduced to the necessity of being there very soon as we now have no Representation. (CCC to CCA, July 5, 1776, MdHi Ms. 206, No. 354)

These three points portray a garden built by a man secure in his wealth, well-versed in Enlightenment political philosophy, and unsure of his position in the emerging colonial power structure.

The garden that Carroll built looked, for the most part, like its contemporaries in the Chesapeake, which also means that it looked much like the gardens in England in the first quarter of the eighteenth century (Leone et al. 1989). It was arranged on a geometrical grid (Leone and Shackel 1990), but as a triangle, rather than the more common rectangle of other urban gardens such as Paca's (Paca-Steele 1986) and Ridout's (Hopkins 1986). The triangular shape may have been dictated in part by the lot's existing borders of the creek, house, and street; but the shape may also have been a reference to Catholic symbolism such as the Trinity, as in the case of the well-known Triangular Lodge built at Rushton Hall by Sir Thomas Tresham (Pevsner 1961:399).

Topographic mapping, historic photographs, coring, and four seasons of excavation and coring have revealed the stratigraphy of garden construction and demonstrated that the garden was originally composed of six terraces and five falls descending from the shortest terrace to the creek below in ever-lengthening widths (figure 9.4). Two "pavilions" marked the east and west end of the stone seawall that runs along the creek (Peale n.d.; Plat map 1853). Parterres, some of which were planted with cabbages and other vegetables (Peale n.d.), graced the terraces and earthen ramps ran perpendicular to the terraces. Like the Paca garden, which invokes the Palladian proportions of the house (Paca-Steele 1986:305), Carroll's design was based on the basic 90-foot measurement of his house, and like the Paca garden, it manipulated lines of sight to enhance the vistas of the landscape (Leone and Shackel 1990).

Carroll's geometrically regular garden may be seen as an expression of the Enlightenment concept of nature discussed above: an ordered, rational space created through the principles of plane and solid geometry. It was a science Carroll understood in theory as well as practice:

> I have begun trigonometry: and one more month of close application I hope will make me a master of surveying. I have taken great pains with Geometry, my pains have been rewarded by the pleasure resulting from . . . Geometrical demonstrations and from the thorough conviction of their truth: would there were the same certainty, the same fixed principles in the Law.

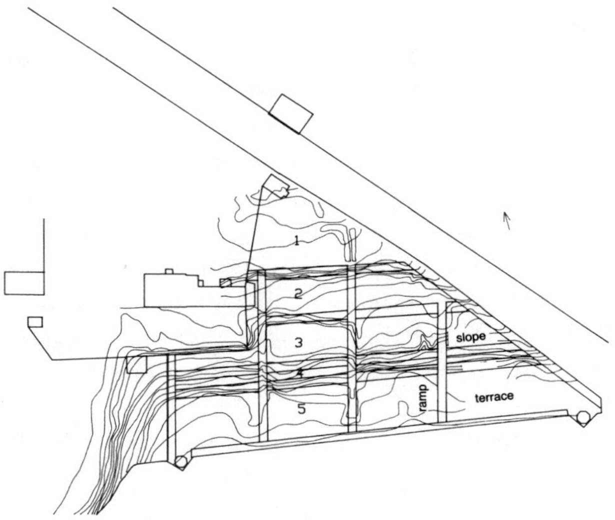

FIGURE 9.4. *A topographic map of the St. Mary's site in 1986, with an overlay reconstructed plan of the Carroll garden and footprint of the house and outbuildings, ca. 1782.*

> (CCC to CCA July 2, 1763, MdHi Ms. 206, No. 97 [296])

In its geometry and ordered view of nature, the garden is no more remarkable than any in the Chesapeake. As Leone (1984) argued for the Paca garden, Carroll's garden identified him as a member of the elite able to manipulate the laws of nature and one whose position of power was derived from seemingly natural sources (Leone 1984).

The question posed in this analysis, however, is how the garden conveyed a connection between nature and power, and, in doing so, resolved the contradictions of Carroll's identity. At the time Carroll was constructing his garden, he was in the process of turning the agrarian-based wealth of his grandfather and the early industrial ventures of his father into one of the largest fortunes in America by investing increasingly in iron production (and later in railroad and canal construction) and expanding his moneylending and tenancy activities. In both his plantation-based agrarian capitalism and his industrial investments, Carroll's profit was based on the labor of others, worker or slave. Williams has noted a similar agrarian root of capitalism in England:

> [O]ur first really ruthless capitalist class, taking up things and men in much the same spirit and imposing an at once profitable and pauperizing order on them, were those eighteenth-century agrarians who got themselves called an aristocracy, and who laid the real foundations, in spirit and practice . . . for the industrial capitalists who were to follow them. (Williams 1980:79)

During this time of financial expansion, Carroll was also achieving his first recognition in political circles as the author of the First Citizen letters in his published debate with Daniel Dulaney over the right of the proprietary government to set fees. Carroll won public support for his stand that only the legislature, as the elected representative of the people, had the right to control finances. He portrayed the Proprietary initiative and Dulaney's defense of it as a threat to the basis of the Constitution, the same threat of unlimited parliamentary sovereignty that was to be challenged by the Revolution (Onuf 1974:12).

There lies an inherent contradiction, then, between Carroll's political ideology of the sovereignty of the people and his capitalist profit based on their exploitation. The conflict is resolved in part by the contemporary notion that property owning is a natural right (Locke 1727, 1759), a right Carroll passionately defended in his First Citizen debate:[10] "'Whatever another may rightfully take from me without my consent, I have certainly no property in'—if you render property thus insecure, you destroy the very life, the soul of liberty" (Carroll quoting Molyneux 1770:129 in Onuf 1974:144). In the terms of this logic, Carroll could own slaves and continue to defend the American people as sovereign because of the concept that liberty and power were separate. Carroll was able to speak as the "First Citizen" expounding the rights of the individual while also writing "I am informed that negroes sell cheap in Virginia: as they are much wanted at ye works [Baltimore Iron Works] would it not be proper to direct Clt. Brooke to attend ye sales" (CCC to the Baltimore Company partners, August 29, 1767) because sovereign liberty surrendered to the government made the government's power natural. By extension—and it is this extension that is mystified in the garden—the laborer, slave, or tenant farmer surrendered the control over his or her means of production to the foreman, owner, or landlord, in whom the right to own property was then also natural.

The contradiction of identity, resolved in Carroll's political ideology, is also mystified and legitimated in his landscape. The view of nature presented in Carroll's garden was not simply an ordered, rational, and segmented one (Leone and Shackel 1987); it was a self-generating idyllic pastoral nature, a "simple vision of natural plenty" (Williams 1985:24). The basis of Carroll's wealth and status, as mythically portrayed in the garden, was that of an agrarian squire for whom nature turned herself effortlessly into produce and profit. This display of a self-generating nature required two elements: an understanding of nature as separate from humans, objectified and autonomous, and of nature as an effortless source of abundance. The first characteristic was described by Carroll during his tour of southern France:

> Nothing contributes more to the beauty and ornament of this so delightful country than the River Loire. Charmed with the beauties of this place he peacefully glides along the meadows in so many and various meanders, that he often seems to return upon himself and quit this enchanting abode with reluctance. (CCC to Elizabeth Brooke, July 14, 1758, MdHi Ms. 206, No. 32 [132])

The second view of nature implicated in resolving the contradiction of Carroll's identity is not hard to associate with a garden that was an abundant, idyllic, green oasis in the midst of Annapolis's mud and smells. Carroll's slopes were turfed in verdant English clover. The parterres thrived with cabbages and other vegetables, and low-growing privet planted in quincunxes added an intricate patterning to the flat terraces. Catalpa trees near the wall offered shade during the oppressive Chesapeake summers. Furthermore, this was a private oasis designed to be enjoyed by a privileged few, but admired by many. Walled in on the street side, the garden was an inaccessible private haven; but on the creek side—the open side—it was a public display.

Even more significantly, this green, abundant landscape was stripped of any evidence of the labor that built and maintained it. Impressions of a self-generating nature were reinforced by the seemingly ornamental landscape. The labor to produce and maintain the garden was made invisible: all evidence of the stone masons and their workshed was torn down, the slaves and their wheel barrows were housed elsewhere, and the "functional" outbuildings were placed out of sight to the west of the house. Excavations, documentary records, and maps suggest that the only structures in the garden were ornamental and deliberately anachronistic—"one is a Summer House and probably the other is a temple" (Peale n.d.). The garden, in this respect, was self-referential. For the viewer at the base of the garden, lines of sight were directed to the house. From the top of the garden, perspectives were to the extended landscape of the creek and beyond. The formal entrances to the house—the porticos on the north and the porch on the east—were accentuated while the access to the kitchen on the ground floor was screened from view from most parts of the garden by the terrace wall to the south of the house. The combination of visual effects obscured the more utilitarian buildings and workspaces. The slaves, the sweat, and the labor that produced the garden were as invisible as the industry and usury that funded it.

I suggest that Carroll, in removing all traces of labor, attempted, consciously or unconsciously, to erase evidence of the means of production—the exploitation of slaves, workers, and the land itself—by fashioning a self-evident, self-abundant source of bounty, an unencumbered place of consumption. In this landscape myth, the owner is the beneficent giver of this bounty; he is never called to account for its source, but simply praised for his good fortune and, by those he chose to share it with, his generosity. Carroll's wealth, based in profitable rental properties, money lending, and early industrial ventures, is made to appear in his landscape to be founded on the agrarian ideal of a bounteous nature. The contradictions between who he was and who he wanted to be seen as (industrialist versus agrarian, owner of slaves versus defender of liberty) were resolved in part in his garden, which became, as Nisbet suggests, a "means of effecting instantaneous fusion of two separated realms of experience into one illuminating, iconic, encapsulating image" (1969:4). The myth, written in nature, with its inherent roots in a concept of an ordered, reasoned, and harmonious nature, was legitimated by the constancy of those laws of nature: the present made legitimate by the past and projected into the future. The myth of Carroll's identity, as communicated in the garden, was reified by the process of being repeatedly viewed and walked through.

The Redemptorist Landscape

> Gone were the Carrolls. Silent were their halls
> Beside the Severn: yea the strife was o'er,
> New pilgrims walked by Maryland's green shore
> And preached the Love which human souls enthralls.
> Then rose Religion's sacred temple walls,

Here in their cells these pilgrims node and bore
Abroad, the honey of both love and lore.
(Anonymous 1928:32)

In 1852, 20 years after Charles Carroll of Carrollton's death, his four granddaughters transferred the Annapolis property to the Congregation of the Most Holy Redeemer (*Congregationis Sanctissimi Redemptoris* [C.Ss.R]), a Roman Catholic congregation of priests and brothers known commonly as the Redemptorists. The congregation has retained ownership of the site ever since, and their occupation is recorded in a remarkable set of documents: 12 volumes of *Chronicles*, which record in daily entries the spiritual and practical activities of the congregation's life. The Redemptorists' primary ministry has been the care of Catholics in the city ("*ipsi curam Catholicorum huius civitas eiusque vicinitas susciperant*," *Chronicles*, introduction), although it has expanded to include a Novitiate (a school to train young men for the priesthood), St. Mary's primary and secondary school, and various missionary activities.

The Redemptorist Congregation was founded in 1732 in Germany and a hundred years later the first American province was established in northern Ohio and Michigan. After seven years the priests settled in Pittsburgh and in 1844 founded the Baltimore Province, of which St. Mary's is a part (Borgmann 1904:13). The *Chronicles* record few details of daily life at the Annapolis house, but conditions were austere and the routine highly regimented. Under the direction of the first rector, Father Rumpler, a strict schedule of meditation, manual labor, and spiritual exercise was performed in silence, except for "an hour of fraternal conversation" during recreation times (Borgmann 1904:25).

The group that took over the Carroll House in 1853 defined itself as distinct from the previous owner—poor where he was wealthy, productive where he was ornamental, and private where he was public. Where Carroll had diplomatically bridged many of the barriers between Protestant and Catholic during his life, the Redemptorists consciously distanced themselves from the strongly Protestant and obviously secular town. These contrasts were manifest in many ways, but particularly in the transformation of the house and surrounding property. Some of the renovations were necessary because of the dilapidated condition of the estate after almost 30 years of renters and because of the logistical needs of the new owners. But the changes were also active forces in the construction of the Redemptorists' communal identity, an identity based on their vows of poverty, chastity, and obedience, and of perseverance in the congregation until death (Anonymous 1928:34).[11]

The most obvious evidence of the differentiation of the Redemptorists from their past was the masking of the Carroll House itself. A landmark visible enough to be one of the four structures listed in the key of a 1781 map was made invisible to the town within 20 years after the Redemptorists' arrival. In 1857 stones were shipped for the construction of a new church, St. Mary's, to be built to the northeast of the Carroll House along Duke of Gloucester Street. With the addition of the massive rectory to the north of the house finished in 1862, the Carroll house was obscured from public view, except from the creek. And even along the waterfront, barns were raised in front of the house and trees were planted along the terraces, profoundly altering the vistas from the garden and essentially screening the house from view.

Another aspect of this change was the transformation from formal terraced garden to working farm. What had been primarily ornamental became utilitarian. In April of 1853 the chronicler recorded:

Domus in quantum fieri potuit reparta est, Hortus in ordinem restitutus Religiosis convenientem. Fratres Servientes sicut et Novitii multi erant in laboribus rusticis obeundis, quum multae manus necessariae essent ad ordinem illum restituendum. Viae et Semitae in horto erant sternendae, herbae inutiles eradicandae quae utilia essent plantata, inter alia, arbores pomiferae, vites, etc. (*Chronicles*, April 1853)	The house was repaired to the fullest extent possible. The garden was restored in a manner appropriate to the Religious. There were many Brothers and Novices who performed manual labor since many hands were necessary so that it might be restored to order. Roads and narrow paths in the garden had to be spread out, and useless plants had to be eradicated in order that useful ones might be planted, among others, fruit bearing trees, vines, etc.

Indeed, the opening sentence of their *Chronicles* records the transfer of the Fathers to "*Caroli Carroll domum hunc cum agris adjacentibus*" (this Charles Carroll house together with the adjacent fields). The congregation viewed the ornamental, formal garden of the Carrolls as convenient, arable land. An 1864 photo depicts the radical transformation of the landscape (figure 9.5). The grounds housed domestic animals (cows, horses, ducks, chickens), as well as fields for crops. A vineyard, a substantial underground vault, and a wine press were added in the late 1860s to

FIGURE 9.5. *The earliest known photograph of the Carroll site from 1864 showing the Redemptorists boating on Spa Creek with the house, rectory, and numerous outbuildings in the background. (Photograph courtesy of the St. Mary's Archives)*

produce wine for domestic use (Kryder-Reid 1987). In addition to the above-ground barns known from photographs and maps, an underground outbuilding, probably a springhouse constructed in the latter part of the nineteenth century, was revealed in the excavations on the lowest terrace. Excavations also uncovered the foundations of a Redemptorist greenhouse. The sum of these changes in the Redemptorists' first 20 years on the property was that, with the exception of the terracing, all signs of Carroll's ornamental, ordered garden had been removed, and a productive, working farm had taken its place.

Part of the power of the landscape transformation was that it was done by the occupants themselves, rather than hired craftsmen or designers. A note added to the 1862 *Chronicles* recounts that

> In May the students and novices began to inhabit the new house. The labors of Frs Rosenbaum & Bone & Werner & Strict are ever worthy of remembrance. Plastering (at least pitching mortar into crevices), lathing, painting, etc. were ordinary occupations. Studying was out of the question. The new house has been solemnly blessed by Rev. P. Provincial before anyone was permitted to inhabit it. (Note on file, Redemptorist Archives, Brooklyn, N.Y.)

Furthermore, these labors were part of the devotional routine of the priests and brothers. The chronicler writes:

Vix notare necesse est paupertatum in omnibus regnasse nihilominus omnes quam maxima animi pace ac tranquillitate perfunctantur, quum in hac domo omnia . . . Regulis magis conformiter peragere valerens (*Chronicles*, introduction)	It is scarcely necessary to note that poverty reigned in everything . . . Nonetheless everyone enjoyed the greatest possible peace and tranquillity of spirit/mind because [insofar as] they were able to do so, [they] performed everything in this house in conformity with the rules

The cooperative action of rebuilding the landscape was in itself part of the construction of the community. Manual labor was part of the service of the lay brothers and the training of the novices. The Chronicles contain numerous references to painting, mending, cleaning, and, most frequently, to agricultural activities such as grape picking, or gardening. In 1868 the congregation's history records that

> To promote the health of the young men, Father Anwander had part of the garden divided into plots, one of

> which was assigned to each student for cultivation of flowers or other plants he might fancy. It afforded unspeakable delight to the good Rector to see the success of some in raising flowers; or that of others, more given to utility in their views, in the cultivation of beans, peas, or corn. (Borgmann 1904:55)

In contrast to Carroll's pastoral setting, the Redemptorists' was one of utility and production. Whereas the source of Carroll's wealth was mystified by his garden, the Redemptorists' landscape was a consecration of their poverty.

Another aspect of the landscape that articulated the Redemptorist community identity was its differentiation from the town. Although relations between the congregation and the town improved rapidly, the first few years were marked by tension and even open hostility. The difficulties may be attributed in large part to the "Know-nothings," members of a secret society who eventually organized into the "American party" and achieved success in local elections with anti-Catholic and xenophobic platforms. Several incidents—such as a letter accusing the Redemptorists of holding hostages, burying bodies in the garden, and placing statues over the victims' graves (Borgmann 1904:23)—exemplify not only a hostility to the congregation but also the extent to which their landscape was read as an expression of their identity by the town.

The walls around the property served as both physical and symbolic barriers to those within and without. For the students, they defined the boundaries of the community—boundaries that could be resisted. The 1886 chronicler reports a student's departure: "Novice Fr. Spengler jumped the fence early this Sunday morning" (*Chronicles*, August 12, 1886). The walls also kept the outside world at bay. In 1884 there was a small fire in the house: "The news caused some excitement. A large number of people assembled in front of the church but few gained access to the grounds." (*Chronicles*, December 8, 1907). The significance of these two examples of piecing the borders suggests that the walls reinforced the boundaries of self and other between the Redemptorists and the world beyond.

Beginning in the last two decades of the nineteenth century, there was a change in the use of the landscape and a change in the references in the *Chronicles* to both the town and the property's past. A number of catalysts may have been responsible for this change. The founding of St. Mary's School in 1867 entailed increasing interaction with the Annapolitans. The Redemptorist Congregation and the St. Mary's Parish were growing and becoming financially more secure. The Redemptorists assumed charge of Catholics enrolled in the Naval Academy, and Know-nothingism had been eclipsed by the Civil War. Whatever the cause or causes, the Redemptorists' diversification of activities, their less insular outlook, and their acceptance of their place in the town was reflected in changes in and uses of the landscape.

The property was made available to many more activities: public bazaars in the school, concerts in the church, recreation days at the garden or nearby farm for visiting religious groups. To the boating and swimming facilities already in place, the rector added a motorized launch for rides up and down the creek. Riding in it became a favorite pastime. A farm outside of town that provided a source of vegetables and grapes was also a popular day-trip destination for picnics. Improvements in the landscape around the house reflect the outward focus of the Redemptorists.

> To render the entrance from Gloucester Street more respectable as well as more solid and suitable for the transportation of all sorts of goods, the same concrete and vitrified pavement was wisely procured by Father Rector. It forms an united whole and presents a good appearance conjointly with the main street with which it connects. (*Chronicles*, October 26, 1901)

In 1911, as part of the beautification project, the *Chronicles* report that "One of our working is putting holes in the wall along Gloucester St. between the Church and the school for the purpose of covering this wall with greens" (March 22, 1911). The result was that the wall that had once been a barrier was made to appear a decorative hedge.

Part of this identification with the town seems to also include an acceptance of the history of the property. The *Chronicles*, which in 1884 were recorded in English rather than in Latin or German, increasingly refer to the house as the "old house" and the "Carroll Mansion." The *Chronicles* recount visitors requesting tours of the illustrious patriot's former home:

> About 5 PM, four prominent members of the Legislature . . . came to the Rectory and asked to be shown about the grounds. Rev. F. Bonia accommodated them. After showing them the Old House and the grounds, he brought them to the church and explained to them,

> for they were all Protestants, the meaning of the Stations, Confessionals, etc. (*Chronicles*, March 13, 1901)

The opening of the property to a variety of activities made the grounds not only physically more accessible, but also increasingly segmented with the use of specific areas for specialized purposes. The southwest waterfront was graded and continued to serve as a small farmyard, while the lots to the west of the house and church were taken up with school buildings. The space to the south of the church was cultivated as a garden and a "Mortuary Chapel" was built for Redemptorist burials. Most significantly—and this aspect of the landscape change goes beyond the scope of this essay—the area of the former Carroll garden was gradually cleared of the more utilitarian structures and transformed into an ornamental space that came to be viewed as an extension of the church itself.

The process by which the landscape was transformed was a gradual one of reification. The perceptions and physical changes mutually reinforced each other. During the first decade of the twentieth century, a planting program, paths, an arbor, and statuary, restored the garden to a recreational and ornamental space, although in a more Victorian style. In 1910 the chronicler writes:

> Even the gardens have put on a new appearance. Instead of the old straight formal walks, there is now a continuous stretch of lawn, through which winds a pretty serpentine gravel path beginning at the step of the Father's Common Room and ending at the old [house]? road which leads down to the water. (*Chronicles*, March 15, 1910)

Although access was still restricted to the Redemptorists and their guests, the garden was opened for various parish occasions such as the annual bazaar and Sunday school picnics. The garden became a showpiece to honored guests. During the visit of the Most Rev. General, the chronicler writes:

> At this hour he . . . repaired to the garden. Three beautiful trees were lying there ready to be planted by our august guests. Father General chose a beautiful, well-branched tulip tree, as a living reminder to perpetuate the memory of the Visit. Father Hedel planted a silver maple and Father Foure an elm. (*Chronicles*, October 10, 1910)

A detailed analysis of the remaining history of the changes in the twentieth-century landscape goes beyond the scope of this essay (Kryder-Reid 1991). Throughout the twentieth century the physical boundaries of the garden shifted, but the remaining garden area, now much closer to the original 1770s configuration, remains the private reserve of the Redemptorists. A school recreation field has replaced the mortuary chapel, most of the area to the west of the Carroll house has been paved to provide a needed parking space, and the last of the cowyard has been sodded over. Fences, "no trespassing" signs, and guard dogs continue to preserve the sanctuary. It is therefore a remarkable fact that, at the Redemptorists' invitation, a group of approximately 20 archaeologists have spent the past four summers digging up this space and asking questions about its occupants of 200 years ago. The meaning of the landscape is obviously being transformed again, but the process of the myth making remains the same.

Conclusion

The 2-acre property on the point of land projecting into the Chesapeake Bay has been a privately owned space for almost three hundred years. It is a powerful artifact, both for its contemporary observers and for those trying to understand the past, because of the relation of owner and landscape. As the property of its owners, it was and is recognizably the site of their productions of self. Historian Stephen Orgle notes that frames became significant when paintings became "commodities, objects to be bought and collected. . . . A framed painting is possessed, limited, defined; and what it depicts becomes an epitome, life in miniature and under control" (Orgle 1975:21). So, too, gardens surrounding the estates of their owners become worlds in miniature, and these privately produced visions depict not only how they wish to be seen, but how they see themselves. These gardens are not just external displays, they are the constitution of self as well—the relation of self and others, the relation of self and God. This constructed space, shaped and reshaped through the years, offers a glimpse into the meaning of and is created by the landscape.

Documents, photographs, and archaeology provide a picture of the physical changes of the St. Mary's landscape, while the Carrolls' writings and the Redemptorists' *Chronicles* offer clues to how those changes were perceived and endowed with meaning. Carroll legitimated his wealth, asserted his social position, and claimed his political rights by associating himself through the medium of his garden with the myth of "natural" rights and power. Since 1952 the site has changed from the historic landscape and shrine of a patriot to a closed community's self-sufficient farm to a sacred extension of the church itself. Through these changes and the symbolic process that brought them about, the landscape became an expression of and active force in Carroll's bid for social and political authority and in the redemptorists' changing identity in relation to the past, the public, and the secular.

The current chapter of the landscape known in the state Historic Trust Office as 18AP45 continues to be written. The myth is being constructed by the Redemptorists, tourists, some dedicated parishioners, state officials, and a handful of archaeologists. In the course of a 10-year restoration of the Carroll House and a 4-year excavation of the garden, the landscape is being made into a new myth: the "house and grounds of Charles Carroll of Carrollton," a fascinating remnant from the past, and symbol of Maryland's revolutionary heritage. It is also a Catholic landscape, "a property dedicated to the purposes of religion" and preserved by the fortuitous stewardship of the Redemptorists. It is also the subject of a research design—"The archaeology and political meaning of Charles Carroll of Carrollton," which has cost thousands of dollars, trained four classes of field school students, been presented to thousands of tourists, and generated several publications to date.

The shaping of the landscape—what to do on it, what to do with it, and what to call it—continues to be an issue debated by those with different perceptions of the landscape. In short, the perception of the landscape and the molding of the landscape to that image continue to be an active process of a political process. The question of what the garden should look like is still undetermined, but the result will be not just a decision of "historical authenticity." It will be one of power—literally a question of who is in control—and of self-presentation. The construction of the myth of the landscape will continue to serve the same functions it has for 300 years: to resolve contradictions, maintain social relations, and display one's place in the world.

Acknowledgments

I am indebted to Robert Worden for his generous offers of information, his cooperation and enthusiastic participation during field seasons, and his support of this research at every turn. The 1987–1990 field crews made this work possible and a whole lot of fun. No one could ask for better colleagues than the Archaeology in Annapolis team, and I particularly thank Barbara Little and Paul Shackel for all they have taught me. Thanks also go to the Redemptorists for access to the property, and particularly to Father Rush for his assistance in the Redemptorist Archives in Brooklyn. Borys Gudziak and Jeffrey Featherstone lent their expertise in Latin translation. Patricia Rubertone and Therese O'Malley have offered valuable encouragement and guidance. Barbara Sarudy has been very helpful in providing references and information about eighteenth-century gardens. Finally, I offer my gratitude to Dr. Mark Leone for his intellectual guidance in the understanding of landscapes and the organization of archaeological thought. Significant funding for the St. Mary's site excavations and their interpretation to the public was provided by the Maryland Humanities Council. The author's research has been generously supported by a Dumbarton Oaks Junior Fellowship.

Notes

1. Women's participation in gardening activities is less well known than men's mainly because of their relative invisibility in the documentary record. However, sources such as Eliza Lucas Pinckney's letterbook (1972), written from 1739 to 1762, present a picture of an active and creative participation in plantation management, garden design, and plant exchange.

2. "As is the Gardener, so is the garden." Collected by Thomas Fuller in 1732. In *Gnomologia: Adagies and Proverbs, Wise Sentences and Witty Sayings, Ancient and Modern, Foreign and British* London, no. 701. (As quoted in Hunt and Willis 1975:2)

3. The earliest example of a fountain in a garden in the English colonies that I am aware of is the jet d'eau at Charles Willson Peale's garden at Belfield outside Philadelphia, begun in 1810 and painted by Peale in 1816 (O'Malley 1986:156). Although instructions in hydraulics were available through garden treatises during the eighteenth century, still-water features such as fish ponds and basins were much more common.

4. Examples in America of the sort of architecture associated with the more "picturesque" landscape gardens in England during the late eighteenth century are the hermitages at Gray's Tavern in Philadelphia and at the Hasket Derby farm in Massachusetts and the grotto described by Josiah Quincy in John Dickerson's Philadelphia garden.

5. Archaeology in Annapolis is jointly sponsored by Historic Annapolis Foundation and the University of Maryland at College Park.

6. Excavators of the house interior conducted in 1991 are reported in Logan et al. (1992).

7. Coring was done using a split-spoon assembly that recovered cores 3/4 of an inch in diameter in 2-foot sections up to a depth of 8 feet. The cores were driven into the ground using a hand-dropped 35-pound weight. Cores were recorded by soil texture, color, and artifact content.

8. The Carroll family history has been recorded in numerous biographies (Rowland 1898; Smith 1942; Hoffman 1975; Mason 1975; Papenfuse 1975; Hanley 1982, 1983), and only the details pertinent to this study are highlighted here.

9. A comparison of representations of Charles Carroll of Carrollton in the Archaeology in Annapolis public program and in the 200th and 250th anniversaries of Carroll's birth is discussed in Leone and Kryder-Reid (1992).

10. Both texts are listed in Carroll's library.

11. The active role of the Redemptorist built environment in the training of priests is discussed in more detail in Kryder-Reid (in press).

References Cited

Note: The Carroll papers are housed at the Maryland Historical Society in Baltimore with microfilm copies there and at the Annapolis Hall of Records in Annapolis. The correspondence is currently being prepared for publication under the editorship of Dr. Ronald Hoffman.

Anonymous
1928 *St. Mary's Church Diamond Jubilee, 1853–1928.* Annapolis: Privately published.

Bailyn, Bernard
1967 *The Ideological Origins of the American Revolution.* Cambridge, Mass., Belknap Press.

Borgmann, Henry
1904 *History of the Redemptorists at Annapolis, Md., from 1853 to 1903.* College Press, Ilchester, Md.

Braudel, Fernand
1979 *The Wheels of Commerce: Civilization and Capitalism, 15th–18th Century*, vol. 2. Harper and Row, New York.

Chronicles, Redemptorist
1853–1983 13 volumes of bound manuscripts. In the Redemptorist Archives, Brooklyn, N.Y.

Compton, William R.
1977 The Tobacco Industry. In *Anne Arundel County, Maryland, a Bicentennial History, 1649–1977*, edited by James C. Bradford, pp. 59–67. Anne Arundel County and Annapolis Bicentennial Committee, Annapolis.

Davis, Richard Beale
1978 *Intellectual Life in the Colonial South, 1585–1763.* University of Tennessee Press, Knoxville.

Hanley, Thomas O'Brien
1982 *Charles Carroll of Carrollton: The Making of a Revolutionary Gentleman.* Loyola University Press, Chicago.
1983 *Revolutionary Statesman: Charles Carroll and the War.* Loyola University Press, Chicago.

Hoffman, Ronald
1975 Charles Carroll of Carrollton: Conservative Revolutionary, 1776–1781. In *'Anywhere So Long as There Be Freedom': Charles Carroll of Carrollton, His Family and His Maryland*, an exhibition and catalogue organized by Ann C. Van Devanter. Baltimore Museum of Art, Baltimore, Md.
1988 "Marylando-Hibernus": Charles Carroll the Settler, 1660–1720. *William and Mary Quarterly* 3d series, 45(2):207–236.

Hopkins, Joseph W. III
1986 A map of the Ridout Garden, Annapolis, Maryland. Manuscript on File at Historic Annapolis Foundation. Annapolis, Maryland.

Hunt, John Dixon, and Peter Willis (editors)
1975 *The Genius of the Place: The English Landscape Garden 1620–1820.* Paul Elek, London.

Isaac, Rhys
1982 *The Transformation of Virginia, 1740–1790.* University of North Carolina Press, Chapel Hill.

Kryder-Reid, Elizabeth
1987 Investigations of a 19th-century Wine Vault: Changing Social Landscapes. Manuscript on file, Historic Annapolis Foundation, Annapolis, Md.
1991 *Landscape as Myth: The Contextual Archaeology of an Annapolis Landscape.* Ph.D. dissertation, Department of Anthropology, Brown University. University Microfilms, Ann Arbor.
1992 The Construction of Sanctity: Landscape and Ritual in a Religious Community. In *Case Studies in Landscape Archaeology*, edited by Rebecca Yamin and Karen Besherer Metheny. CRC Press, Boca Raton, in press.

Langley, Batty
1728 *New Principles of Gardening: Or, Laying Out and Planting Parterres, Groves, Wildernesses, Labyrinths, Avenues, Parks, &c.* . . . A. Bettesworth and J. Batley, London.

Lemay, J. A. Leo
1972 *Men of Letters in Colonial Maryland.* University of Tennessee Press, Knoxville.

Leone, Mark P.
1984 Interpreting Ideology in Historic Annapolis Using Rules of Perspective in the William Paca Garden in Annapolis, Maryland. In *Ideology, Power, and Prehistory*, edited by Daniel Miller and Christopher Tilley, pp. 25–35. Cambridge University Press, Cambridge.
1987 Rule by Ostentation: The Relationship between Space and Sight in Eighteenth-Century Landscape Architecture in the Chesapeake Region of Maryland. In *Method and Theory for Activity Area Research: An Ethnoarchaeological Approach*, edited by Susan Kent, pp. 604–633. Columbia University Press, New York.

Leone, Mark P., and Elizabeth Kryder-Reid
1992 Critical Perspectives on Work Concerning Charles Carroll of Carrollton. In *Representations in Archaeology*,

edited by Jean-Claude Gardin and Christopher S. Peebles. Indiana University Press, Bloomington.

Leone, Mark, Elizabeth Kryder-Reid, Paul Shackel, and Julie Ernstein
1989 Power Gardens of Annapolis. *Archaeology* 42(2):34–39, 74–75.

Leone, Mark P., and Paul S. Shackel
1987 Forks, Clocks and Power. In *Mirror and Metaphor: Material and Social Constructions of Reality*, edited by Daniel W. Ingersoll, Jr., and Gordon Bronitsky, pp. 46–61. University Press of America, Lanham, Md.
1990 Plane and Solid Geometry in Colonial Garden in Annapolis, Maryland. In *Earth Patterns: Essays in Landscape Archaeology*, edited by William Kelso, pp. 153–167. University Press of Virginia, Charlottesville.

Locke, John
1727 *The Works of John Locke*. 3 vols. Printed for A. Bettesworth, London.
1759 *Essay Concerning Human Understanding*. 3 vols. Printed for R. Urie, Glasgow.

Lockwood, Alice G. B.
1934 *Gardens of Colony and State: Gardens and Gardeners of the American Colonies and of the Republic before 1840*. Vol. 2. Compiled and edited for the Garden Club of America by Alice G. B. Lockwood. Charles Scribner's Sons, New York.

Logan, George C., Thomas W. Bodor, Lynn D. Jones, and Marian C. Creveling
1992 *1991 Archaeological Excavations at the Charles Carroll House in Annapolis Maryland*. A report prepared for Charles Carroll House of Annapolis Inc. On file, Historic Annapolis Foundation, Annapolis, Md.

Mason, Sally
1975 Charles Carroll of Carrollton and His family, 1688–1832. In *'Anywhere So Long as There Be Freedom': Charles Carroll of Carrollton, His Family and His Maryland*, an exhibition and catalogue organized by Ann C. Vany Devanter. Baltimore Museum of Art, Baltimore, Md.

Middleton, Arthur Pierce
1984 *Tobacco Coast: A Maritime History of the Chesapeake Bay in the Colonial Era*. Johns Hopkins University Press, Baltimore, Md. (Original edition, Mariners' Museum, Newport News, 1953.)

Molyneux, William
1770 *The Case of Ireland Being Bound by Acts of Parliament in England Stated*. Printed for J. Almon, London.

Nisbet, Robert A.
1969 *Social Change and History: Aspects of the Western Theory of Development*. Oxford University Press, London.

O'Malley, Therese
1986 Landscape Gardening in the Early National Period. In *Views and Visions: American Landscape before 1830*, edited by Edward J. Nygren, pp. 133–159. Corcoran Gallery of Art, Washington, D.C.

Onuf, Peter S.
1974 Introduction. In *Maryland and the Empire, 1773: The Antilon-First Citizen Letters*, edited by Peter S. Onuf, pp. 3–39. Johns Hopkins University Press, Baltimore, Md.

Orgle, Stephen
1975 *The Illusion of Power: Political Theater in the English Renaissance*. University of California Press, Berkeley.

Paca-Steele, Barbara, with St. Clair Wright
1986 The Mathematics of an Eighteenth-Century Wilderness Garden. *Journal of Garden History* 6(4):299–320.

Papenfuse, Edward C.
1975 Charles Carroll of Carrollton: English Aristocrat in Any American Setting. In *'Anywhere So Long as There Be Freedom:' Charles Carroll of Carrollton, His Family and His Maryland*, an exhibition and catalogue organized by Ann C. Van Devanter. Baltimore Museum of Art, Baltimore, Md.

Peale, Charles Wilson
n.d. The Diary of Charles Wilson Peale, Manuscript on file at the American Philosophical Society, Philadelphia, Pa. Description of Carroll Garden appears in vol. 20., pp. 52–54, June 11, 1804.

Pevsner, Nikolaus
1961 *Northamptonshire*. The Buildings of England. Penguin Books, Middlesex.

Pinckney, Eliza Lucas
1972 *The Letterbook of Eliza Lucas Pinckney, 1739–1762*, edited by Elise Pinckney. University of North Carolina Press, Chapel Hill.

Plat map
1853 Chancery Court. Document on file, Maryland Hall of Records.

Rowland, Kate
1898 *The Life and Times of Charles Carroll of Carrollton, 1737–1832, with His Correspondence and Public Papers*. 2 vols. G.P. Putnam's Sons, New York.

Sarudy, Barbara Wells
1989 Eighteenth Century Gardens of the Chesapeake. *Journal of Garden History* 9(3):104–159.

Scarff, John H. (editor)
1937 *The Bicentenary Celebration of the Birth of Charles Carroll of Carrollton*. Lord Baltimore Press, Baltimore, Md.

Smith, Ellan Hart
1942 *Charles Carroll of Carrollton*. Harvard University Press, Cambridge, Mass.

Stilgoe, John R.
1982 *Common Landscape of America, 1580 to 1845*. Yale University Press, New Haven, Conn.

Taylor, Raymond
1952 *Plants of Colonial Days: A Guide to One Hundred and Sixty Flowers, Shrubs, and Trees in the Gardens of Colonial Williamsburg*. Colonial Williamsburg Foundation, Williamsburg, Va.

Trostel, Michael F.
1981 *Mount Clare: Being an Account of the Seat Built by Charles Carroll, Barrister, upon His Lands at Patapsco.* National Society of the Colonial Dames of America in the State of Maryland, Baltimore, Md.

Upton, Dell
1988 White and Black Landscapes in Eighteenth-Century Virginia. In *Material Culture in America, 1600–1860,* edited by Robert Blair St. George, pp. 357–69. Northeastern University Press, Boston.

Willey, Basil
1940 *The Eighteenth Century Background: Studies on the Idea of Nature in the Thought of the Period.* Columbia University Press, New York.

Williams, Raymond
1980 *Problems in Materialism and Culture.* Verso, London.
1985 *The Country and the City.* Hogarth Press, London.

Wright, St. Clair
1977 The Preservation of Annapolis. In *Anne Arundel County, Maryland, A Bicentennial History, 1649–1977,* edited by James C. Bradford, pp. 183–188. Anne Arundel County and Annapolis Bicentennial Committee, Annapolis, Md.

III
PART

Eighteenth-Century Life

RESEARCH INTO the eighteenth century must deal with a host of issues: subsistence and economic strategies; settlement patterns; the group relations of class, race, ethnicity, and gender; and cultural and political tensions between the mother country and the colonies. The eighteenth century witnessed transformations in every aspect of life, as the dominant culture came under the influence of the rationalization of the Enlightenment. James Deetz (1977, 1983, 1988) has described the Georgian mind set as it developed in the New World: communality was replaced by individuality, segmentation, symmetry, and standardization. Mark Leone (for example, 1988) relates the changes observed in this "Georgianization" to the developing culture of capitalism. Rhys Isaac's (1982) work on eighteenth-century Virginia provides a context of power relations in which to interpret material culture, as upper wealth groups found it necessary to distance themselves socially but at the same time ally themselves politically with the lower classes.

Continuing analysis of eighteenth-century sites is enhancing and complicating our vision of eighteenth-century life. The imposition of and resistance to dominant culture and the creation and maintenance of subcultures are themes that run throughout American culture from early settlement to the present. Work in Annapolis, Maryland (chapter 14), makes it clear that this pattern cannot be defined and accepted simply as "modernization," with its implication of progress and inevitability. Work in Williamsburg (chapter 15) is challenging views held about class behaviors: material goods from several sites do not follow predictions. Other research (chapter 12) suggests gender differences in the acceptance or rejection of the developing culture of capitalism. Work on plantation sites included in the previous chapters provide insight into slave life and resistance as well. Ann Smart Martin's work (chapter 11) also challenges traditional archaeological notions of when certain materials became available and affordable. Her data will force a serious reconsideration of some of our ideas about consumption patterns and even the dating of sites.

Much urban archaeology in the United States has focused on the eighteenth century, although historical archaeology has certainly devoted attention to urban places of earlier times—such as St. Augustine, Florida, founded in 1565 (Deagan 1983), and Port Royal, Jamaica, a thriving port and a center of economic activity until it was destroyed by an earthquake and sealed underwater in 1692 (Hamilton and Woodward 1984). In the Chesapeake, the capitals of St. Mary's City (Miller 1986) and Jamestown (Cotter and Hudson 1957) provide early city contexts. However, urban areas of the eighteenth century have received greater attention, in part because that is when cities became increasingly important within the colonial political, economic, social, and cultural structures. Some recent work in the northeastern United States has focused on the eighteenth-century components of New York (Rothschild 1990), Charlestown, Massachusetts (Pendery 1986), and Middletown, Connecticut (Dyson 1982), among others. Frederick Gorman (1982) has also discussed some broad implications of urban manufacturing.

Both Roy Dickens (1982) and Edward Staski (1987) have edited collections of work on urban contexts. The only Chesapeake city included in those volumes is Alexandria, Virginia (Cressey and Stephens 1982; Cressey et al. 1982), which is represented in the next section of this volume. Researchers in Alexandria (Cressey et al. 1982) have considered the important theme of core–periphery relations, which can be analyzed on global, national, regional, and local scales. The regional scale is important for Susan Winter's consideration (chapter 13) of iron production in western Maryland; manufacturing there was connected to the Chesapeake as the economic system expanded and affected this interior frontier land. Changing core–periphery relations on a local level are part of Joanne Bowen's comparisons (chapter 10) of animal-use strategies. Bowen raises basic questions about subsistence strategies, the role of the marketplace, and the relationships between rural producers and urban consumers. Urban and rural participation in the market also comes into play in Martin's (chapter 11) analysis of ceramic availability.

The Essays

Joanne Bowen develops a method for analyzing faunal remains in a broad context of interregional comparisons. Her work responds to Crabtree's (1990) recent call for an archaeological and anthropological, rather than strictly zoological approach to the study of animal remains. Bowen analyzes herding systems and compares the New England and Chesapeake regions through the seventeenth and eighteenth centuries and demonstrates how these two English settlements developed different herding strategies. The herding systems for each region are compared on the basis of ethnographic and archaeological/biological factors. The factors that contribute to the development of a herding system include primary use of livestock, sex and age composition of the herd, physical environment, and agricultural and field management system.

Bowen challenges the common notion that the English transplanted their culture to the New World (see also chapter 2); in fact, groups committed themselves to different survival strategies in different areas. Earlier sites in New England, where colonists focused on dairying, reveal that cows were not slaughtered until the age of three to four and in some cases five to six. By the mid-eighteenth century, urban demand pressured rural areas for the production of meat, and the kill-off age dropped to about two. In the earlier periods, kill-off in the Chesapeake was about three years and older, a phenomenon that, if taken out of context, could mislead archaeologists into believing that cattle may have been primarily used for dairying. Instead, in the labor-intensive tobacco industry, cattle usually ran freely in woodland "reserves," received little shelter, and had poor grazing lands. Chesapeake planters actually did very little dairying, as their cattle tended to have poor milk production.

Ann Smart Martin (chapter 11) examines the meanings and uses of goods in the context of the colonial Chesapeake. She applies an emulation model to ceramic purchases and the adoption of these goods by all strata of society. Her data base includes over 125,000 objects from Maryland and Virginia store account books. Before 1760 three-quarters of the plates found in stores were made of pewter. In the 1770s delft surged in popularity. After 1770 there is a dramatic increase in the consumption of creamware. Even though creamware was being imported into the colonies in the 1760s by some of the wealthiest families, Martin concludes that creamware did not appear in the nonelite households until the 1770s, and most likely not until after the American Revolution.

Even though a creamware revolution was under way, pewter still remained popular, and urban and rural differences existed. Stores in the rural areas in the 1770s provided mainly pewter, whereas in the urban areas creamware became increasingly popular. Throughout the Chesapeake, stores provided a greater proportion of porcelain teawares than plates. An aspiring merchant might have creamware plates while also owning porcelain teas. Many variables need to be examined during the consumer revolution, including personal needs, practicality, and the cultural and local meanings of these goods.

Barbara Little (chapter 12) examines the life and material culture of a colonial printer, Anne Catharine Green, in the context of feminist historical archaeology. Little notes that a feminist archaeology is not about finding goods known to be attributed to women's activities, but rather explores the historical constructions of gender bias and gender ideology. She finds that muted groups, including women, can express themselves through various media. The possibility for a feminist historical archaeology relies on an understanding of the material culture expressions of muted groups within dominant ideology. In the seventeenth and eighteenth centuries masculine and feminine attributes began to be seen as natural and therefore unnegotiable. This changing ideology, which may be related to increasingly centralized power, is associated with the transformation and subordination of women's roles. The scientific revolution reinforced the polarization of gender.

Anne Catharine Green became the official colonial printer after the death of her husband, Jonas Green. She continued the standardized layout of the *Maryland Gazette*, but made some changes in design. She also expanded the newspaper content during the pre-revolutionary era. Both Jonas and Anne Catharine's probate inventories, taken in 1767 and 1775, respectively, contained nearly the same goods, but the items were arranged differently. Jonas kept an eight-day clock in his printshop and probably subscribed to the discipline of time for himself and his employees. In contrast, Anne Catharine appears to have been concerned with the reintegration rather than the separation of domestic and work life. She kept some of her printing equipment and the eight-day clock in the house instead of in the shop. It is suggested that task-orientation rather than time-orientation guided Anne Catharine's work process.

Susan Winter (chapter 13) explains the development, context, and the local and international implications of the ironworks industry in Maryland. The Carroll family invested in ironmaking in the early eighteenth century and by the middle of the century the family owned the largest ironmaking enterprise in the Chesapeake region. After 1750 it was almost impossible to compete against the giant ironmaking firms (such as that owned by the Carrolls) that controlled the iron exports to England. New ironmaking firms that developed after the mid-eighteenth century exploited untapped inland markets.

The ironmaking industry grew during the 1760s, and the Antietam Valley of Maryland experienced tremendous growth during the 1770s. Winter traces the development and growth of the Antietam and Mt. Aetna Furnace. These enterprises, owned by Samuel and Daniel Hughes, became large centers of production that serviced not only much of the local population, which was primarily of German descent, but also the Continental Army. By using indentured and slave labor the Hugheses successfully saturated the local market and became the wealthiest property owners in Washington County, Maryland.

Mark Leone (chapter 14) provides an overview of many of the archaeological finds in the historic district of Annapolis and ties them together with the theme of ideology, one of the primary research topics of the Archaeology in Annapolis project. The earliest sites discovered in Annapolis, dating to the late seventeenth century, are located near the state house and on the waterfront. These locations demonstrate the early multiple uses of the town by the government and for commerce. In the early 1700s, during its infancy as the colonial capital, the town underwent dramatic social and economic changes. Archaeological and historical data demonstrate the collapse of the community network system and the eventual internalization of a modern discipline. This new discipline became part of domestic and work life. Leone explains that Jonas Green the colonial printer (see chapter 12) increasingly standardized the layout of the colonial newspaper. Businesses, including Green's printing establishment, were gradually removed from houselots and were established in other areas of the town.

Formal gardens in eighteenth-century Annapolis helped to strengthen inequalities in society. Between 1765 and 1790 the elite of Annapolis constructed many of the terraced gardens there. The elite utilized landscape perspectives to manipulate visions and thereby to claim that they had a natural right to rule (see chapter 9). After the American Revolution, Annapolis was no longer a social and political center in the New World. The town instead survived as a small regional port.

Marley Brown and Patricia Samford (chapter 15) use the themes established by the Colonial Williamsburg Foundation in the 1980s for their archaeological research design, one objective of which is to examine history from the bottom up. Research on African Americans, for example, has become increasingly important. The use of new technologies to allow for more precise measurements of artifacts and topography in the town has played a major role in defining landscape, houselots, and the town as a whole.

Recent archaeology has begun to challenge some assumptions about eighteenth-century urban life. For instance, the estate of John Brush contains unexpected data. Probate inventory analysis of this gunsmith's belongings ranked him in the middle wealth group of York county.

Material goods and pollen samples recovered from Brush's estate indicate that his household owned materials and acquired foods and spices that were not typical for his standing. He had instead a consumption pattern more typical of the wealthiest residents in the county.

The archaeology of Block 29 around the Palace Green and Market Square, the town's most important political and social center, is described through historical, architectural, and archaeological data. In the early eighteenth century the area's use is mixed commercial and residential. By the middle of the century the square lost most of its commerce, owing to the general decline of the city. In 1780, when Thomas Jefferson moved the capital to Richmond, the Palace Green lost its status as a focal point. Several of the houselots were rearranged or moved to face the Market Square. The frontage along Palace Street was relegated to outbuildings.

Archaeology of the eighteenth century includes research on all aspects of life as society and culture were being transformed through the developing culture of capitalism that we call modernization. Continuing work on sites from this period reveal the complexity that we should expect from culture change. Further interesting questions are being asked of this period and its connections to earlier and later time periods. The next section, on the nineteenth-century Chesapeake, continues the themes of urbanism, industrialization, and the changing context of rural life.

References Cited

Crabtree, Pam J.
1990 Zooarchaeology and Complex Societies: Some Uses of Faunal Analysis for the Study of Trade, Social Status, and Ethnicity. In *Archaeological Method and Theory*, vol. 2, edited by Michael Schiffer, pp. 155–205. University of Arizona Press, Tucson.

Cressey, Pamela J., and John F. Stephens
1982 The City-Site Approach to Urban Archaeology. In *Archaeology of Urban America: The Search for Pattern and Process*, edited by Roy S. Dickens, Jr., pp. 41–61. Academic Press, New York.

Cressey, Pamela J., John F. Stephens, Steven J. Shephard, and Barbara H. Magid
1982 The Core–Periphery Relationship and the Archaeological Record in Alexandria, Virginia. In *Archaeology of Urban America: The Search for Pattern and Process*, edited by Roy S. Dickens, Jr., pp. 143–174. Academic Press, New York.

Cotter, John L., and Paul Hudson
1957 *New Discoveries at Jamestown*. U.S. Government Printing Office, Washington, D.C.

Deagan, Kathleen
1983 *Spanish St. Augustine: The Archaeology of a Colonial Creole Community*. Academic Press, New York.

Deetz, James
1977 *In Small Things Forgotten: The Archaeology of Early American Life*. Doubleday, Garden City, N.Y.

Dickens, Roy (editor)
1982 *Archaeology of Urban America: The Search for Pattern and Process*. Academic Press, New York.

Dyson, Stephen L.
1982 Material Culture, Social Structure, and Changing Cultural Values: The Ceramics of Eighteenth- and Nineteenth-Century Middletown, Connecticut. In *Archaeology of Urban America: The Search for Pattern and Process*, edited by R. Dickens, pp. 361–380. Academic Press, New York.

Gorman, Frederick
1982 Archaeological Implications of a Manufacturing Industry in Eighteenth-Century American Cities. In *Archaeology of Urban America: The Search for Pattern and Process*, edited by R. Dickens, pp. 63–104. Academic Press, New York.

Hamilton, D. L., and Robyn Woodward
1984 A Sunken 17th-Century City: Port Royal Jamaica. *Archaeology* 37:1:38–45.

Isaac, Rhys
1982 *The Transformation of Virginia 1740–1790*. University of North Carolina Press, Chapel Hill.

Leone, Mark P.
1988 The Georgian Order as the Order of Merchant Capitalism in Annapolis, Maryland. In *The Recovery of Meaning: Historical Archaeology in the Eastern United States*, edited by Mark P. Leone and Parker B. Potter, Jr., pp. 235–261. Smithsonian Institution Press, Washington, D.C.

Miller, Henry
1986 *Discovering Maryland's First City: A Summary Report on the 1981–1984 Archaeological Investigations in St. Mary's City, Maryland*. St. Mary's City Archaeology Series, No. 2., St. Mary's City, Md.

Pendery, Steven R.
1986 Artisans and Merchants in Colonial Charlestown, Massachusetts. *Archaeology 39(3): 64–77*.

Rothschild, Nan A.
1990 *New York City Neighborhoods, the 18th Century*. Academic Press, New York.

Staski, Edward
1987 *Living in Cities: Current Research in Urban Archaeology*. Special Publication Series No. 5 for the Society for Historical Archaeology.

Suggested Readings from the Contributors

Bushman, Richard L.
1984 American High-Style and Vernacular Culture. In *Colonial British America: Essays in the New History of the early Modern Era*, edited by Jack P. Greene and J. R. Pole, pp. 345–383. Johns Hopkins University Press, Baltimore.

Carr, Lois Green, and Lorena S. Walsh
1988 The Standard of Living in the Colonial Chesapeake, in Forum: Toward a History of the Standard of Living in British North America. *William and Mary Quarterly* 3d ser., 45:116–170.

Carson, Barbara
1990 *Ambitious Appetites: Dining, Behavior, and Patterns of Consumption in Federal Washington*. American Institute of Architects Press, Washington, D.C.

Deetz, James
1977 *In Small Things Forgotten*. Doubleday, New York.

Glassie, Henry
1975 *Folk Housing in Middle Virginia*. University of Tennessee Press, Knoxville.

Greene, Jack P.
1988 *Pursuits of Happiness; The Social Development of Early Modern British Colonies and the Formation of American Culture*. University of North Carolina Press, Chapel Hill.

Isaac, Rhys
1982 *The Transformation of Virginia, 1740–1790*. University of North Carolina Press, Chapel Hill.

Leone, Mark P., and Parker B. Potter, Jr. (editors)
1988 *The Recovery of Meaning: Historical Archaeology in the Eastern United States*. Smithsonian Institution Press, Washington, D.C.

Leone, Mark P., and Paul A. Shackel
1987 Forks, Clocks and Power. In *Mirror and Metaphor: Material and Social Construction of Reality*, edited by Daniel Ingersoll and Gordon Bronitsky, pp. 45– 62. University Press of America, Lanham, Md.

McKendrick, Neil, John Brewer, and J. H. Plumb
1982 *The Birth of A Consumer Society: The Commercialization of the Eighteenth Century*. Indiana University Press, Bloomington.

Martin, Anne Smart
1989 The Role of Pewter as Missing Artifact: Consumer Attitudes toward Tablewares in Late Eighteenth-Century Virginia. *Historical Archaeology* 23(2)1–27.

Mercer, Henry C.
1961 *The Bible in Iron*. The Bucks County Historical Society, Doylestown, Pa.

Miller, George L., Ann Smart Martin, and Nancy S. Dickenson
1992 Changing Consumption Patterns, English Ceramics and American Markets from 1770 to 1840. In *Everyday Life in the Early Republic, 1780–1828*, edited by Kate Hutchens. W. W. Norton, New York, in press.

Mitchell, Robert D.
1977 *Commercialism and Frontier: Perspectives on the Early Shenandoah Valley*. University Press of Virginia, Charlottesville.

Morgen, Sandra (editor)
1989 *Gender and Anthropology, Critical Reviews for Research and Teaching*. American Anthropological Association, Washington, D.C.

Paskioff, Paul F.
1983 *Industrial Evolution: Organization, Structure, and the Growth of the Pennsylvania Iron Industry, 1750–1860*. Johns Hopkins University Press, Baltimore, Md.

Reps, John
1972 *Tidewater Towns; City Planning in Colonial Virginia and Maryland*. University Press of Virginia, Charlottesville.

Shackel, Paul A.
1993 *Personal Discipline and Material Culture; An Archaeology of Annapolis, Maryland, 1695–1870*. University of Tennessee Press, Knoxville.

Upton, Dell, and John Michael Vlach
1986 *Common Places, Readings in American Vernacular Architecture*. University of Georgia Press, Athens.

X
CHAPTER

A Comparative Analysis of the New England and Chesapeake Herding Systems

JOANNE BOWEN

THE MOST COMMON goal of faunal analysis is to reconstruct broad subsistence patterns and the way in which a historic site's occupants adapted to their environment. In practice, however, faunal studies focus primarily on household consumption patterns. To assess a household's diet, faunal analysts generally determine the meat diet and preference for certain cuts of meat and explain these consumption patterns in relation to environmental constraints, cultural values, or the household's social and economic status.

This focus on the household level of analysis has narrowed our views of what environmental, economic, social, and cultural variables actually influence dietary patterns. We need to break from this pattern and begin looking at the much broader context of the herding system and how it shapes the selection of foods. This analysis focuses on the subsistence system and its production and distribution of food, with a view to better understanding the diet of historic peoples.

The colonial New England and Chesapeake herding systems are compared to show how two English settlements adapted to their respective environments and developed herding systems with different priorities, which ultimately affected their diet. Documentary sources are used to reconstruct the outlines of the two herding systems. Kill-off patterns, age data that have been derived from cattle long bones, will be analyzed for evidence on cattle husbandry and the extent to which the New England and Chesapeake colonists relied on their cattle for beef and dairy products.

Every data base has its own biases, and faunal remains are no exception (Gifford 1981; Maltby 1982). As animals mature, the epiphyses, or joints, fuse to their long bone at a certain age and in a prescribed sequence. By noting the proportion of fused and unfused specimens for each bone element, we can determine the relative age at which these animals were slaughtered and can reconstruct the relative proportions of age groups represented in any given faunal assemblage. The ages of these groups, however, are those that have been established with modern cattle. Because the exact age at which these bones fuse varies somewhat—depending on environmental differences, breed, and care given the animal—they should be taken as relative age groups (Silver 1969; Chaplin 1971; Payne 1973; Wilson et al. 1982; Maltby 1982; 1985; Barker and Gamble 1985). Since cattle tend to be slaughtered only after they have either served out their usefulness or reached their optimum weight, we can read backward from these age profiles to infer certain facts about whether these individuals were raised primarily for their meat and milk, or for draft purposes. But they have been subjected to many natural processes that modify bone in ways we are only beginning to understand and as a result kill-off patterns can underrepresent young individuals.

Moreover, as Cribb, Redding, and others have pointed out, kill-off patterns only represent what has been slaughtered. They do not inform us about the living herd or herds the archaeological bone came from, and they do not provide enough detail to explain variability encountered in the kill-off patterns. Redding and Cribb have proposed a way of better understanding herding systems and determining the extent to which livestock were raised for their meat, milk, and other purposes (Dahl and Hjort 1976; Redding 1981; Cribb 1985). The dynamics of a living herd can be reconstructed with the aid of ethnographic and biological data. Several factors need to be considered in analyzing a herding system: (1) the primary uses of the livestock, (2) sex and age composition of the herd, (3) the physical environment, and (4) the agricultural and field management systems of the group under study (Redding 1981:2). Archaeological kill-off patterns, when measured against the demographic structure of the living herd, can be analyzed much more precisely.

Documentary sources are a relatively untapped resource, but secondary sources provide sufficient information on the essential characteristics of these herding systems. When archaeological data on cattle from southern New England and the Chesapeake, the coastal region of Maryland and Virginia, are compared with documentary evidence, two very different systems of herd management and cattle use emerge. In both regions beef was an extremely important food resource; but climatic differences between the cold North and warmer tidewater, as well as their distinctive systems of agriculture, meant a difference in the degree to which dairying was emphasized. Together, these two independent data bases can reveal important characteristics of cattle husbandry and the different uses for cattle.

The herding systems and the effect they had on the relative importance of beef and milk are described below for both regions. New directions for research are suggested—directions that can help us better understand the complex interaction between the environment, households, their principles of herd and field management, and desired uses of livestock.

New England farmers had well-developed field systems and excellent pastures. They raised cattle for meat, milk, and draft purposes—each of which remained equally important. In the Chesapeake a very different system evolved, one that altered the important position dairying had held in the Old World. Coastal Virginia and Maryland colonists developed a slash-and-burn form of agriculture, a system that relied on manual labor to clear fields for the cash crop, tobacco. Chesapeake planters had little time or inclination to invest in subsistence activities, and they let their cattle fend for themselves in the woodlands. Milking was done, but never on the same scale as in New England. The effect of this type of herding, combined with the fact that the Chesapeake climate was too warm for good cheese making, meant that dairying remained relatively unimportant throughout the colonial period.

The New England Herding System

From the early years of settlement, New Englanders had ample pastures for grazing cattle (see figure 10.1). During the summer, the young stock were sent to remote virgin or partly cleared tracts, while milch cows and working oxen were kept on nearby pastures to be milked daily or used for various tasks (Bidwell and Falconer 1925:21; Russell 1977). When fall arrived and temperatures dropped, grass stopped growing and pastures could no longer support the herds. So after the crops had been harvested, cattle were turned into fields to graze on the stubble. There, those to be culled from the herd could be fattened quickly for slaughter, and those to be kept could prepare themselves for the long winters (Bidwell and Falconer 1925:22–25; Russell 1977).

Cattle were important to New England farmers for their meat, dairy products, and ability to perform a variety of tasks. This was subsistence-oriented agriculture and cattle were raised with all uses in mind: butter and cheese were made in quantities; castrated bull calves were allowed to mature and become oxen; and all were slaughtered for their meat. What is clear from the documentary sources is that from the early seventeenth century cattle and the production of butter and cheese were important in New England. Much of the land was thin, rocky, difficult to plow, and therefore ill-suited to tillage. But it made excellent pastures for cattle, and most households kept at least one cow (Bidwell and Falconer 1925; Bailyn 1955; McManis 1975). Moreover, the northern climate, with its cool summers, was perfect for dairying, and virtually every farm wife and her daughters milked, churned butter, and made cheeses for immediate use, as well as for the

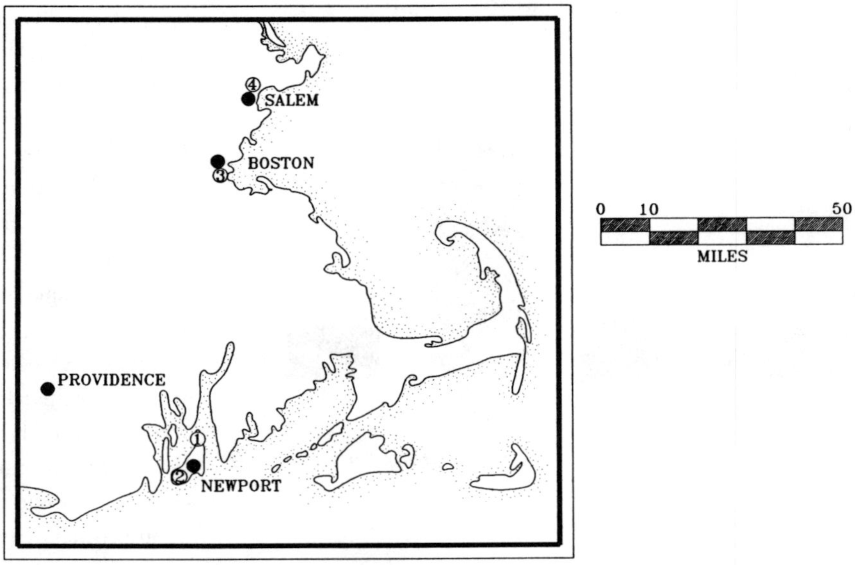

1. Mott Farm, Portsmouth, Rhode Island (Bowen 1975)
2. Carr House, Newport, Rhode Island (Young 1987)
3. African Meeting House, Boston, Massachusetts (Bowen 1986)
4. Narbonne House, Salem, Massachusetts (Bowen 1982)

FIGURE 10.1. *New England.*

winter (Bidwell and Falconer 1925; Deetz 1972:26, 1977:53; Russell 1977).

A subsistence study of Suffield, Connecticut, during the late eighteenth century and an analysis of Suffield farm account book entries has shown that virtually every household in Suffield consumed quantities of cheese and butter, which they could have used on bread much as we would use cheese (Bowen 1990; Sandra Oliver, personal communication 1989). Those households that had more cows, particularly those owning five or more, could produce all the cheese, butter, and milk their households consumed, plus a surplus that could be sold on the export market or loaned or sold to neighbors and kin who could not produce sufficient amounts on their own (Bowen 1990).

Beef, too, was highly desired. Faunal assemblages show that New Englanders had a strong preference for beef (Bowen 1975, 1982, 1986). The Suffield subsistence study also reveals a preference for beef over other types of meat; the wealthier households consumed more of it than the poorer households, and they tended to give it to their kin and wealthier friends (Bowen 1990). Finally, nineteenth-century references show farmers slaughtered three-year-old dairy cows, young animals that probably had given birth to only one calf (Andrew Baker, personal communication 1987). If milk had been more important than beef, farmers probably would have kept their cows longer. Beef was an important part of their diet.

The cattle kill-off patterns derived from the Mott Farm, an early eighteenth-century site in Portsmouth, Rhode Island, illustrates this subsistence strategy (Bowen 1975). Figure 10.2 shows a preponderance of cattle slaughtered in their prime, at approximately three to four years of age. Had the Motts valued milk more highly, they would have kept their cows longer, and the data would show a higher percentage of older animals. In the youngest age group, there are a few calves, probably bull calves not needed as oxen. There are also a few young individuals killed sometime before they reached 18 months of age. And there were a few oxen and more productive milch cows aged four years and older.

The Mott Farm data illustrate the essential characteristics of New England's subsistence-oriented agriculture and herding system, but we lack sufficient comparative

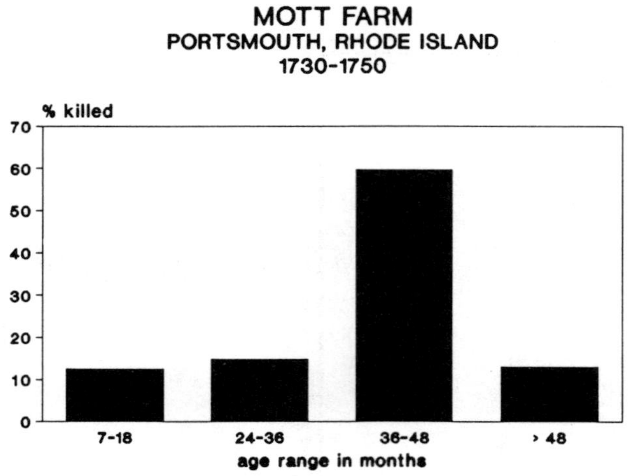

FIGURE 10.2. *New England rural kill-off pattern.*

data from other contemporary sites to assess the variability over time, among individual farmsteads, and between regions in New England. More analyses of documents are required—analyses of probate inventories, tax lists, agricultural sources, and account books—to determine the demographics of their live herd population, field and grazing systems, and herd management strategies on individual farms. This information will make it possible to build a model of live herd management practices and household strategies that can be used to measure our estimates of cattle mortality. A comparison of these two populations will provide the best inferences about the New England herding system and relative importance of meat and dairy products.

By as early as the late eighteenth century, agriculture in some regions of New England had developed from a subsistence-based activity to a commercially oriented one (Bidwell and Falconer 1925; Gates 1960; Danhof 1969; Russell 1977; Bowen 1990). Along the coast and in some inland areas urban populations had grown. Many farmers continued to function in the traditional manner, but in response to increased demand, more began specializing in the production of beef and milk, which they sold at nearby markets. Some scholars have assumed farmers simply fit this commercial endeavor in with their multipurpose cattle husbandry. It is said that farmers without sufficient grain and fodder to fatten their older cattle sold them to those with better lands. These farmers quickly fattened the aged cattle and sent them on to market (Bidwell and Falconer 1925:227; Russell 1977:357–359; Danhof 1969:167; Lewis 1984; Garrison 1985:173–193).

But by the early nineteenth century large numbers of urban households had become dependent on rural produce, and their demand for food exerted pressure on traditional subsistence-based agricultural methods to produce additional surpluses (Friedman 1973; Smith and Bridges 1982). To meet these demands, farmers shifted from subsistence-based agriculture to commercialized agriculture and focused on raising livestock specifically for sale.

Unlike subsistence farmers, whose basic intent is to provide for their family's needs, these farmers focused on producing a cash crop. Subsistence farming became secondary, and the emphasis was on carefully managing livestock to produce the greatest profit. Since this was best accomplished by concentrating on a single livestock product, and since fattening older livestock for the beef market was neither as efficient nor as profitable as raising young cattle specifically for this purpose, farmers specialized in what their farm could best support (Colman 1841:86–90; Bidwell and Falconer 1925:226–227, 388–393, 421–422, 433; Danhof 1969:173; Bundy et al. 1982; Blakely and Bade 1985).

Colman, in his descriptions of the state of New England cattle husbandry in the early nineteenth century, vividly recalls for us an entire region in which the traditional husbandry was becoming commercial and highly specialized (Colman 1837, 1839). Where lands were best suited to dairying, farmers focused on that aspect of cattle husbandry; where lands could not support the demands of a dairy herd, farmers raised beef cattle; and in areas of rapidly expanding urban markets, farmers practiced a diversified form of commercial farming that supplied urban residents with vegetables and fresh milk (Colman 1841). In Franklin County in 1841 dairying did not enter much into the river farmers' economy. Instead, they kept only enough cows to supply their own families with milk and butter, and devoted their commercial enterprise to raising young stock or fattening beef cattle (Colman 1841:41).

Colman's descriptions of fattening cattle indicate that not all farmers practiced the same husbandry. Depending on the type and quality of land they owned, some farmers preferred to fatten older oxen aged four to six, others preferred cattle aged three to five, and a third group preferred young stock one to three years old. "It is obvious," Colman (1841:63) states, "that different kinds of stock may be properly preferred by different farmers, according to the peculiar situation and circumstances." On more than one occasion Colman indicates these young steers were fattened for market because they needed less feed than the older cattle. The experienced farmer was shrewd and picked the small-boned and thrifty one- and two-year-old animals for stall-feeding (Colman 1841:54–55, 63–64). Yearlings could be purchased cheaply in the fall, fed hay throughout the winter, then in the spring simply put out to pasture. By June or July they were ready for market at approximately double their purchase value. How many farmers actually followed this scheme is not known; undoubtedly the quality and type of land had much to do with what choices were made.

The faunal record can be used to monitor the activities of large-scale marketing systems (Maltby 1979, 1985; Bourdillon 1980; Zeder 1988). Kill-off patterns from several urban sites illustrate the presence of this specialized form of cattle husbandry system in New England as early as 1790 (figure 10.3). Eighty percent or more of the cattle were less than two years old in assemblages from the Carr House in Newport, Rhode Island, occupied by an upper-class household; the Narbonne Site in Salem, Massachusetts (circa 1790 and 1805), occupied by the upper middle-class household of Mary Gardner; and an African American site in Boston (1830s), occupied by several lower-middle and lower-class African Americans (Moran et al. 1982; Bowen 1986; Bower 1986; Young 1987).

Modern animal science claims that the most profitable

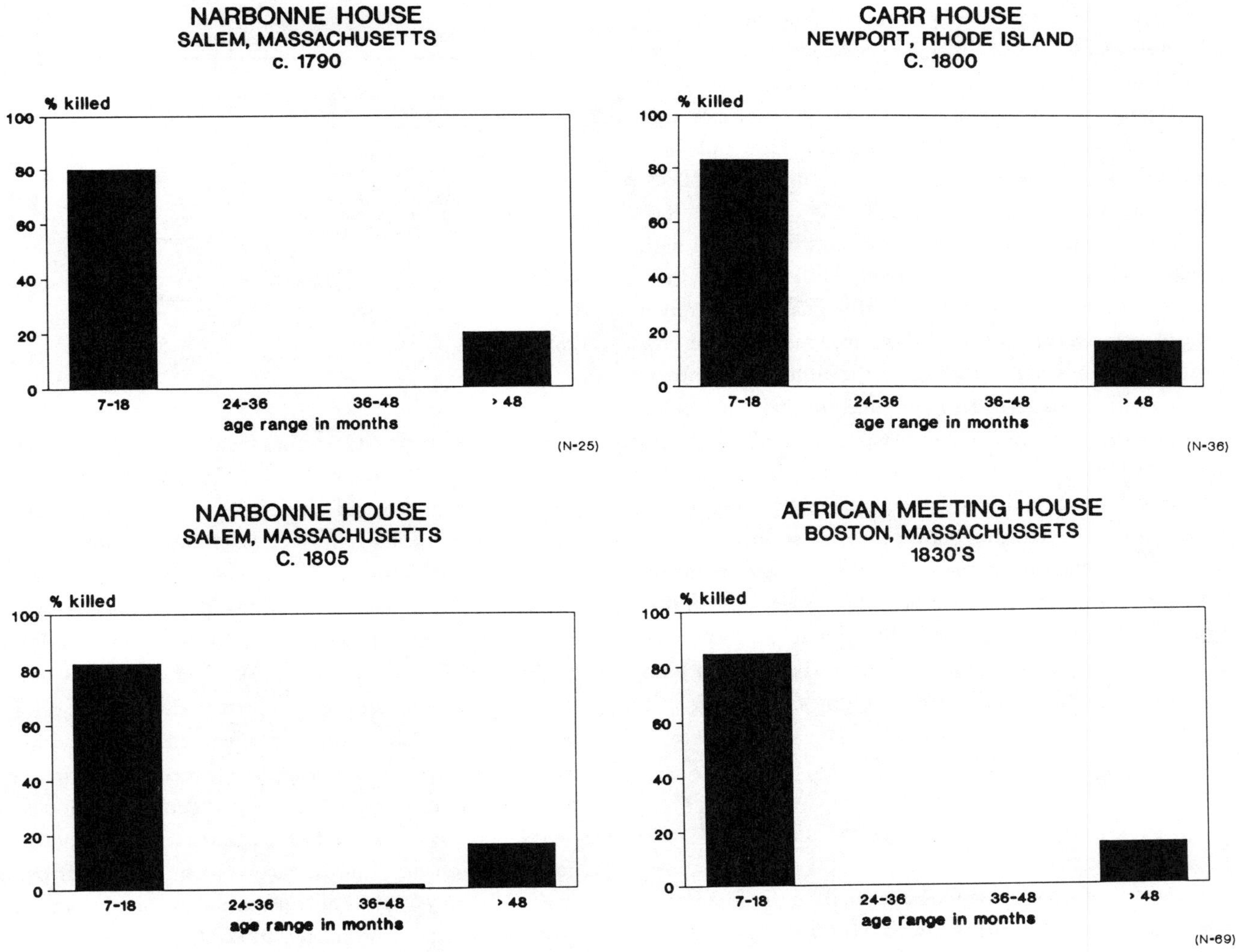

FIGURE 10.3. *New England urban cattle kill-off patterns.*

age to slaughter beef cattle is just when they have gained most of their adult weight; each pound gained after this stage in their development requires more grain. In modern husbandry this tends to be between 18 and 24 months of age (Bundy et al. 1982; Blakely and Bade 1985). Some of these individuals are represented in these kill-off patterns, along with a large number of calves, probably bull calves, that were produced on dairy farms and quickly fattened before being sent to market. The second largest group of cattle that found their way to urban markets were the older cattle—a group that probably included dairy cows whose milk production had dropped off, as well as oxen past their prime.

These data show a highly commercialized herding system from the *urban* perspective. These changes cannot be adequately explained, however, without further documentary analysis of the dynamics of the urban market system. We need to learn more about when western cattle began to be sold in the eastern markets. How and when did New England farmers begin to specialize in raising beef and dairy cattle? Just what were the dynamics of the herding system and the raising of market-bound cattle on farms in towns of colonial New England? How and when did this activity affect their own consumption of beef, veal, and dairy products?

We also need to compare the urban kill-off data with that from rural sites. No data from rural sites have been produced for this time period, unfortunately, and much more research must be done if we are to understand how this system evolved by the end of the eighteenth century. Cattle kill-off patterns from eighteenth- and nineteenth-century rural sites can help us determine whether farmers who had begun to raise these commercial crops also stopped producing their own food and instead began purchasing it with their profits. Or did they simply continue to produce their own food in the traditional manner, merely adding the commercial enterprise onto a multipurpose form of cattle husbandry? These are important questions— questions that the combined analysis of both urban and rural kill-off patterns might some day be able to answer.

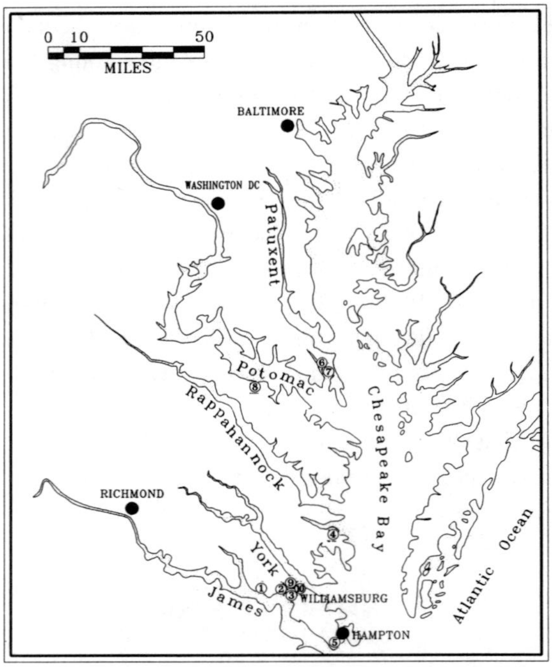

(After Miller 1984)

1. Drummond Plantation (Miller 1984)
2. Pettus Plantation (Miller 1984)
3. Utopia (Miller 1984)
4. Bennett Farm (Miller 1984)
5. Hampton HT55 (Brown 1989)
6. St. John's (Miller 1984)
7. Pope's Fort (Miller 1984)
8. Clifts Plantation (Bowen 1976)
9. Peyton Randolph (Bowen ND)
10. John Draper (Brown 1989)

Figure 10.4. *The Chesapeake.*

The Chesapeake System

A number of sites in the Chesapeake have disclosed pronounced cattle kill-off patterns (figure 10.4; Miller 1984; Bowen 1979). Miller's impressive data base allows us to examine mortality profiles from different time periods and different areas within the Chesapeake, as well as assess the variability and consistencies present in the data. Taphonomic problems must be taken into account in this exercise. In all cases the faunal assemblages came from closed, relatively protected contexts such as wells, cellars, and trashpits. Sample sizes were also checked for statistical bias (Miller 1984:200–226). This study uses only those large assemblages with adequate numbers of cattle bone for which age could be determined. Thus, neither natural modifications nor sample size seems to be a major problem. Status was another variable considered, but no correlation was found. In fact, a planter and tenant household living on the same land show identical kill-off patterns (Miller 1979). The variability in these mortality profiles appears to be related to the Chesapeake subsistence system.

In contrast to the agricultural systems of England and New England, which were based on intensive animal husbandry and crop production, Chesapeake agriculture consisted of a slash-and-burn field system in which hoes and manual labor were used to clear fields and plant around stumps. The entire system revolved around the production of the labor-intensive, but highly lucrative cash crop, tobacco.

In this scheme, an extensive herding system provided an easy source of meat for the tobacco-focused society. Settlers abandoned most British husbandry methods, allowing their cattle to run free and exercising little control over their movements (Gray 1941; Laing 1954; Main 1982:62–68; Miller 1984; Walsh n.d.). Throughout the seventeenth century planters kept expansive woodland areas as "reserves" for when land already under cultivation became exhausted. These reserve areas were perfect for their cattle to graze in; and when exhausted fields had been allowed to grow over, they provided even more area for livestock. Durand, a seventeenth-century French traveler, remarked that farmers generally kept the proportions of their lands at about half in woodland, a fourth as pastures, and the other quarter under cultivation (Laing 1954:105–106). This was a perfect environment for keeping large herds of cattle. They could fatten themselves, withstand losses, and still multiply on their own. In short, the Chesapeake was a perfect environment for raising beef cattle.

It was not, however, the perfect environment for dairying. First, tidewater summers were (and are) too warm for making hard cheeses (Main 1982). And from the perspective of the herding system, little or no shelter, care, or fodder was given the cows, so they produced relatively little milk. Second, even though small farmers kept between 10 and 40 cattle, and planters 100 to 500 or more, they milked only as many as were needed to supply their households. Calves were penned close by so the cows would come in for milking, but in contrast to New England, there was apparently no organized, consistent system of dairying here. Moreover, it seems that in the South only the rich had the equipment or facilities to make butter and cheese for use later in the year (Laing 1954:51; Main 1982:199–200, 221). So striking was the difference between the involvement in cheese making in New England and Virginia that a New Englander remarked in 1863 that the southern half of the United States did not have the lush pastures cows needed to produce quantities of milk, and they were kept too far from home to be regularly milked. Consequently, "they make no cheese, never made much, and never will" (Goodale 1863:383).

This herding system and the relative importance of meat and dairy products are not that obvious from the kill-off patterns, however. In fact, when judged solely on the basis of cattle behavior, kill-off patterns erroneously suggest cattle were raised primarily for their milk. In all cases, cattle three years and older predominated among the slaughtered animals, a pattern very similar to New England's.

The documentary sources, however, emphatically state that dairying played a minimal role in the subsistence strategy of the colonial Chesapeake. It seems, then, that kill-off patterns alone are not sufficient for interpreting herding systems. They must be measured, as Cribb (1985) and Redding (1981) have advised, against a model of the live herd and system of field and herd management, in order to accurately interpret the kill-off patterns. My analysis of the range of the variability found in the kill-off patterns for the very early years of settlement, unfortunately, was inconclusive (see figure 10.5). Only two sites—HT55 located in Hampton, Virginia, and Pope's Fort, located on the St. Mary's River in Maryland—have produced reliable kill-off patterns. Although they show what appears to have been a preference for the middle-aged group over the older cattle, there is too much variability and no good documentary evidence to account for this variability. One possible explanation is that farmers were experimenting with various adaptive strategies during the early years of settlement. Cattle were in short supply, and newcomers who wished to establish their own herds placed a constant demand on established herds. Owners responded by slaughtering their young males and barren cows for meat and selling their more productive cows (Miller 1984:315). More archaeological work needs to be done to produce additional kill-off patterns; further documentary analysis might provide critical information on this very early attempt by the colonists to adapt the herding system they had known in their homeland to a new frontier.

Although the analysis of these kill-off patterns remains inconclusive for the early seventeenth century, there are enough kill-off patterns for the later periods to discern a regional pattern despite some variability and one unique kill-off pattern. The largest single age group represented in the kill-off patterns from the second half of the seventeenth century were four years and older (see figure 10.6; Miller 1984).

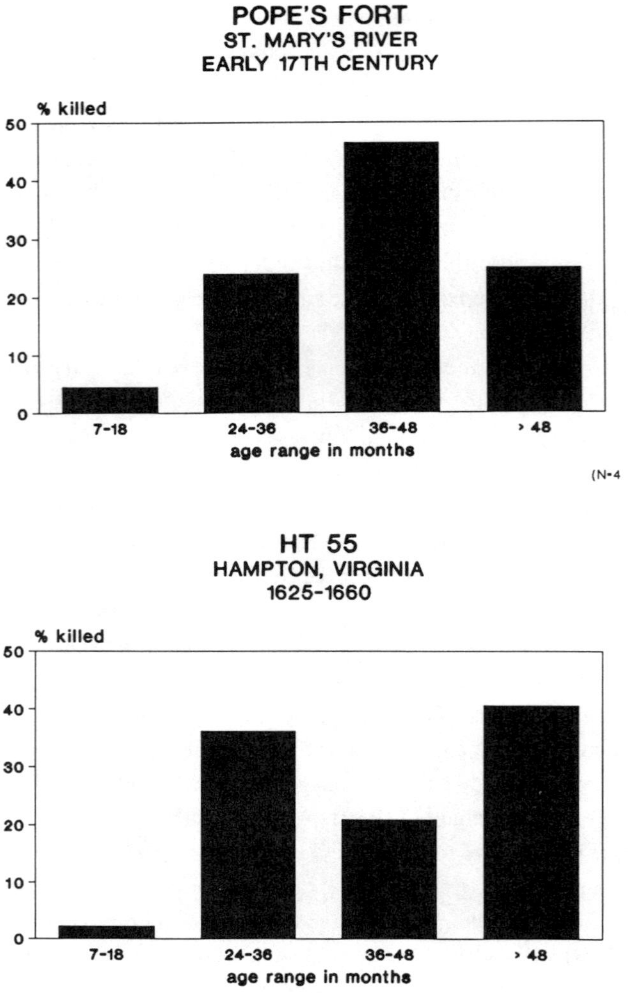

FIGURE 10.5. *Early seventeenth-century Chesapeake cattle kill-off patterns. (Miller 1984)*

Beaudry's work with Chesapeake probate inventories indicates a distinct shift in cattle husbandry occurred during the last quarter of the seventeenth century (Beaudry 1980:113–136). Descriptions of cattle in this period no longer merely identify color and refer to age in general terms, such as "old" or "very old," but provide much more specific details. By the turn of the century probate inventories list the ages of most mature female cattle from 4 to 12 years old (Beaudry 1980:122). Beaudry attributes this shift to the development of a more supervised system of penning, regulating slaughter age, and breeding (Beaudry 1980:135).

By the early eighteenth century another change in husbandry is evidenced by the appearance of a substantial number of cattle aged three to four years (see figure 10.7). Despite this shift, however, a basic continuity in the kill-off patterns is apparent. First, at no time were the youngest cattle, 0–18 months of age, the target group. Second, despite the periodic presence of the middle-aged group, the oldest animals were almost always the dominant group. The presence of the middle-aged group in the early eighteenth century indicates that some changes, however subtle, occurred within the system. To explain this shift in herd management, we need to look closely at shifts in agriculture and regional economics.

There are two possible reasons for the increase in the middle-aged group. Maybe the overriding cause is that during this time the Chesapeake was experiencing a period of economic stress. Tobacco prices in Europe had slumped, and the soil had begun to wear out (Walsh n.d.:3:1–20). Planters responded by diversifying, that is, by growing wheat and other grains and keeping flocks of sheep on a much larger scale than before. The combination of the reduced tobacco crops and increased tillage for grains meant a more intensive form of agriculture. More oxen plowed more fields. Cattle dung, which had not been used for tobacco fields because it imparted a bad flavor to the weed, was increasingly used as fertilizer (Miller 1984; Walsh n.d.). And with more sheep, a better pasture system had to have evolved. Sheep are less able to survive in a woodland environment than cattle, hogs, and goats. They need protection from wolves and other predators, open spaces so their coats are not torn, and pastures to graze in. Cattle, too, must have benefited from these improvements.

The second reason for the increase in younger cattle slaughtered might be that frontier settlements had by this time thousands of cattle roaming over woodlands and reportedly luxuriant grazing lands. Some have claimed many were brought east when they were three and four years old and were sold in the markets (Gray 1941; Laing 1954).

Whether either of these changes influenced the shift toward slaughtering younger cattle remains debatable. Some only marginally resembled the patterns described earlier. One must conclude, then, that there was considerable household variation in herd management. To understand the overall similarities, as well as how individual households worked within their region's agricultural system, it will be necessary to reconstruct environmental relationships, the demographic structures of live herds, herding strategies, and system of field and woodland

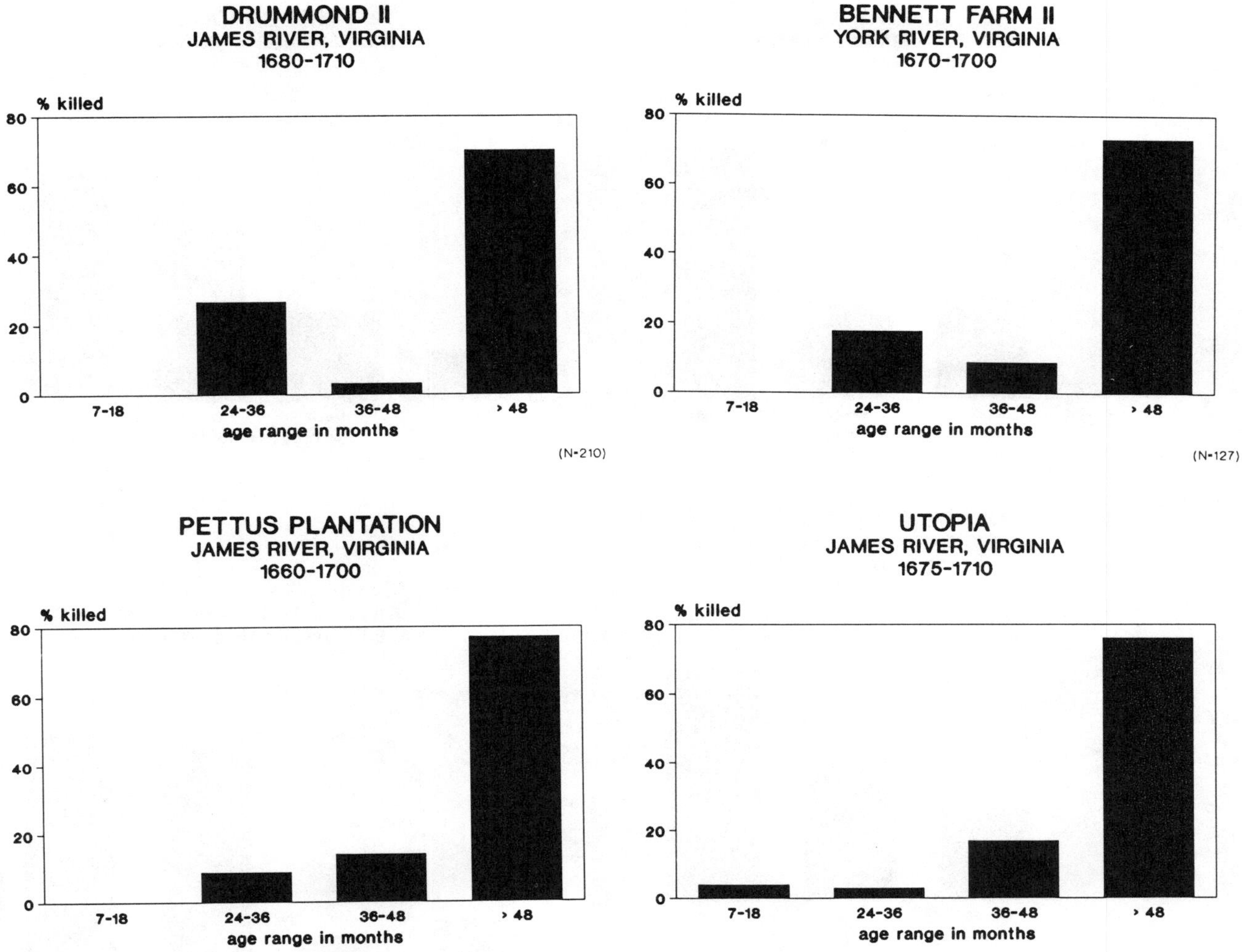

FIGURE 10.6. *Late seventeenth-century Chesapeake cattle kill-off patterns. (Miller 1984)*

management. Ultimately, this approach will enhance our understanding of Chesapeake herding strategies and the effect they had on diet. For rural households, we can determine who kept more cows so they could produce more milk and who kept more steers so they could produce more beef.

It should also be possible to reconstruct the Chesapeake market system. The combined analysis of urban and rural kill-off patterns, herd management strategies, and a better delineation of the importance of western cattle in the Chesapeake will help us determine the extent to which cattle from local plantations or western herds supplied the eastern markets. Most excavations of archæological sites, unfortunately, have not produced sufficient numbers of bones for us to reconstruct the kill-off patterns, so at present there are very few data to work from (see figure 10.8). There is one kill-off pattern from early eighteenth-century Williamsburg, however, and it is essentially the same as contemporary rural kill-off patterns. Does this mean that market vendors, butchers, and urban residents got their meat from local plantations, either their own, their friends' or their relatives'?

There is only one reliable kill-off pattern from late eighteenth-century Williamsburg (Brown 1989). It shows about equal amounts of the three-to-four year old group and the four years and older group—the exact ages at which cattle were sold from western Virginia, according to Gray (1941) and Laing (1954). Does this mean that during the eighteenth century Williamsburg came to rely more and more on cattle brought in from the west?

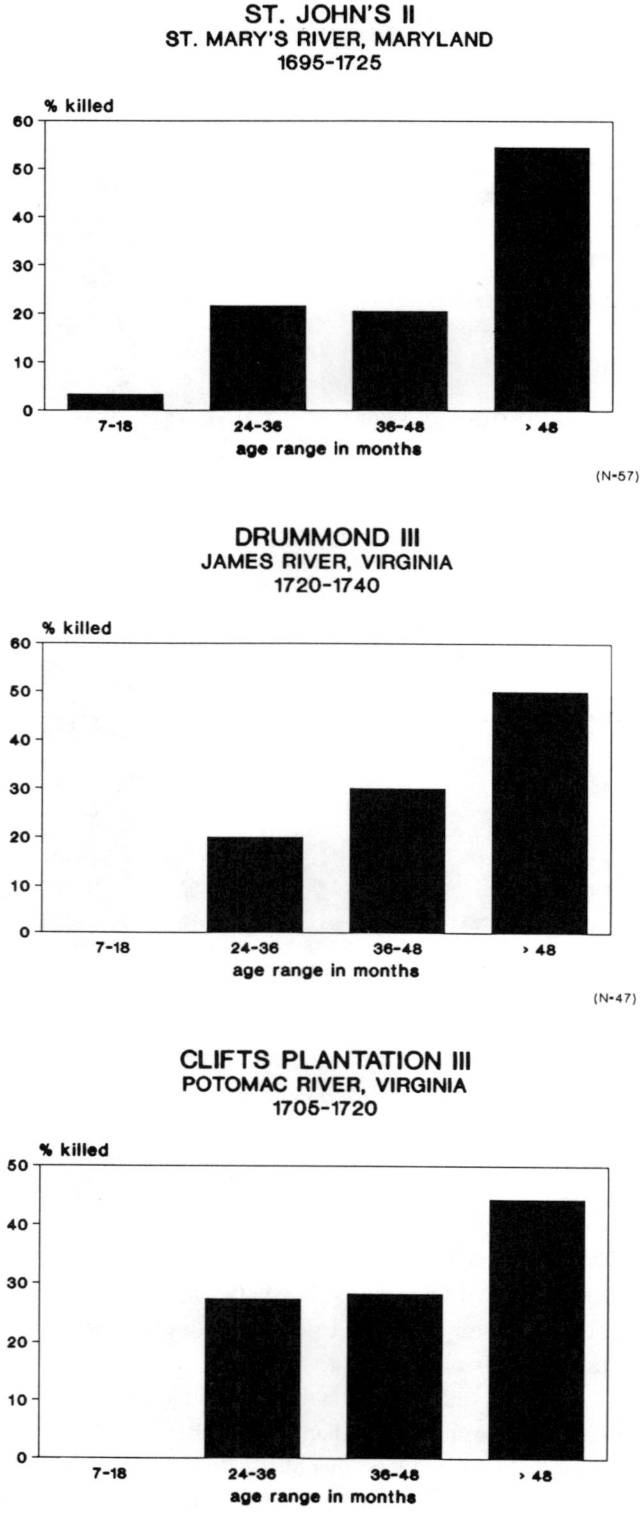

FIGURE 10.7. *Early eighteenth-century Chesapeake cattle kill-off patterns. (Bowen 1979; Miller 1984)*

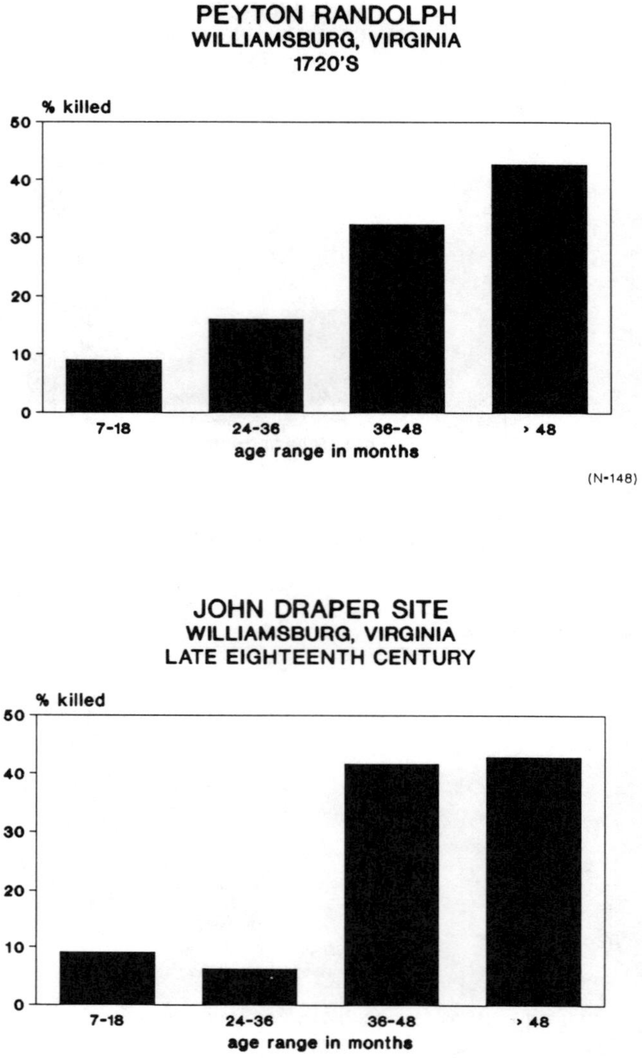

FIGURE 10.8. *Chesapeake urban kill-off patterns. (Bowen 1979; Brown 1989)*

Answers to these questions remain elusive, since there are no kill-off patterns from any rural site in any part of Virginia for the second half of the eighteenth century.

Conclusion

One of the points not yet adequately addressed is whether the New England and Chesapeake kill-off patterns really show how the subsistence system and its environmental constraints shaped diet. Specifically, do they show how climate, agricultural methods, and field and herd management systems interact to shape the relative importance of meat and dairy products in the colonial diet?

From surface observations, one could only say "no"—because the Virginian pattern of keeping cattle for three years and more before slaughtering them has been shown to be misleading. From these data one could also claim that the kill-off pattern proves milk to have been an important part of the diet in Virginia. We know, however, that this was not the case, and the conclusion I have come to is that if left to stand alone, kill-off patterns do not necessarily reveal the relative importance of milk and meat in the diet.

But if these assessments are combined with reliable studies of the biological characteristics of cattle, reconstructions of households, the demographic structure of herds, and field and herd management strategies, we can begin to produce a working model of how a farmer managed his livestock. Such studies should be able to determine: (1) how much and what types of land a farmer had; (2) his individual priorities in the potential uses of the animal; and (3) given his herd management strategy, how policies ranging from virtual neglect to the extreme care and feeding of livestock affected their growth and maturation.

If our interpretations of herding systems are ever going to approach reality, we must realize kill-off patterns are the product of their agricultural and herding systems and, therefore, always must be analyzed from this perspective, in conjunction with documentary information. The resulting estimates can be useful in pinpointing shifts in the herding system both on a household level and on a broader regional level.

The comparison of the New England and Chesapeake subsistence systems has helped in assessing the relative importance of meat and dairy products in the diet of each region. Dairy products played an important part in the Englishman's diet, and it is tempting to assume they were just as important in the New World. But, as we have seen from this comparative analysis of the New England and Chesapeake herding systems, this preference cannot be simply transferred to any new English colony. Englishmen settled in a variety of environments, brought with them different goals, and developed a subsistence system for each region that directly influenced how they kept their animals, what they kept them for, and ultimately what they ate.

Acknowledgments

I want to thank those who have given me permission to use their faunal data. I am indebted to Henry Miller, who has been so generous with his data over the years. This comparative analysis would not have been possible without his substantial data base and impressive synthesis of dietary patterns in the Chesapeake. Gregory Brown and Timothy Young both kindly allowed me to use their data as well. I also want to thank James Deetz, Marley Brown, Geoffrey Moran, Beth Bower, and Frazier Neiman, each of whom has given me the opportunity to analyze faunal remains excavated from sites in New England and the Chesapeake. Kim Wagner reproduced Henry Miller's map and produced the New England map. Marley Brown and Lorena Walsh both provided helpful criticisms. Finally, I want to thank Andrew Baker and Sandra Oliver, who were generous with their knowledge of New England agriculture and diet. I am, of course, responsible for the results.

References Cited

Bailyn, Bernard
1955 *The New England Merchants in the Seventeenth Century.* New York, Harper Torchbooks.

Barker, Graeme, and Clive Gamble
1985 Beyond Domestication: A Strategy for Investigating the Process and Consequence of Social Complexity, In *Beyond Domestication in Prehistoric Europe*, edited by Graeme Barker and Clive Gamble, pp. 1–31. New York, Academic Press.

Beaudry, Mary C.
1980 *"Or What Else You Please to Call It": Folk Semantic Domains in Early Virginia Probate Inventories.* Unpublished Ph.D. dissertation, Brown University.

Bidwell, Percy, and John Falconer
1925 *History of Agriculture in the Northern United States 1620–1850.* New York, Peter Smith.

Blakely, James, and David H. Bade
1985 *The Science of Animal Husbandry.* 4th ed. Reston Publishing, Reston, Va.

Bowen, Joanne
1975 Probate Inventories: An Evaluation from the Perspective of Zooarchaeology and Agricultural History at the Mott Farm. *Historical Archaeology* 9:11–25.
1979 Analysis of Faunal Remains from Clifts Plantation. Report submitted to the Robert E. Lee Memorial Association, Inc.

1982 Faunal Analysis of Two Trash Pits. In *Archaeological Investigations at the Narbonne House*, edited by Geoffrey P. Moran, Edward Zimmer, and Anne Yentsch. Cultural Resources Management Study No. 6. Salem Maritime National Historic Site, Massachusetts. National Park Service.

1986 Analysis of the African Meeting House Faunal Remains. In *The African Meeting House, Boston, Massachusetts: Summary Report of Archaeological Excavations 1975–1986*, edited by Beth Anne Bower. Museum of Afro-American History, Boston.

1990 *A Study of Seasonality and Subsistence: Eighteenth-Century Suffield, Connecticut*. Unpublished Ph.D. dissertation, Brown University, Providence, Rhode Island.

Bower, Beth Anne

1986 The African Meeting House, Boston, Massachusetts: Summary Report of Archaeological Excavations 1975–1986. Manuscript report submitted to the National Park Service by the Museum of Afro-American History, Boston, Massachusetts.

Bourdillon, Jennifer

1980 Town Life and Animal Husbandry in the Southampton Area, as Suggested by the Excavated Bones. *Proc. Hants. Field Club Archaeol. Soc.* 36:1818–191.

Brown, Gregory

1989 *The Faunal Remains from the John Draper Well: An Investigation in Historic-Period Zooarchaeology*. M.A. thesis, San Francisco State University.

Bundy, Clarence E., Ronald V. Diggins, and Virgil W. Christensen

1982 *Livestock and Poultry Production*. 5th ed. Prentice-Hall, Englewood Cliffs, N.J.

Chaplin, Raymond

1971 *The Study of Animal Bones from Archaeological Sites*. London, Seminar Press.

Colman, Henry

1837 Letter to the Farmers of Massachusetts on the Subject of an Agricultural Survey of the State by the Authority of the Legislature. Weeks, Jordan & Co., Boston.

1839 *Second Report of the Agriculture of Massachusetts, County of Berkshire*. Dutton & Wentworth, Boston.

1841 *Fourth Report of the Agriculture of Massachusetts, Counties of Franklin & Middlesex*. Dutton & Wentworth, Boston.

Cribb, Roger

1985 The Analysis of Ancient Herding Systems: An Application of Computer Simulation in Faunal Studies. In *Beyond Domestication in Prehistoric Europe*, edited by Graeme Barker and Clive Gamble, pp. 75–106. New York, Academic Press.

Dahl, Gudrun, and Anders Hjort

1976 *Having Herds: Pastoral Herd Growth and Household Economy*. Stockholm Studies in Social Anthropology No. 2. Department of Social Anthropology, University of Stockholm.

Danhof, Clarence

1969 *Change in Agriculture: The Northern United States, 1820–1870*. Harvard University Press, Cambridge, Mass.

Deetz, James J. F.

1972 Ceramics from Plymouth, 1635–1835: The Archaeological Evidence. In *Ceramics in America*, edited by Ian M. G. Quimby, pp. 15–40. University Press of Virginia, Charlottesville.

1977 *In Small Things Forgotten: The Archeology of Early American Life*. Anchor Books, New York.

Friedman, Karen J.

1973 Victualling Colonial Boston. *Agricultural History* 42:190–205.

Garrison, John Ritchie

1985 *Surviving Strategies: In Commercialization of Life in Rural Massachusetts, 1790–1860*. Unpublished Ph.D. dissertation, University of Pennsylvania.

Gates, Paul

1960 *The Farmer's Age: Agriculture, 1815–1860*. Harper Torchbooks, New York.

Gifford, Diane P.

1981 Taphonomy and Paleoecology: A Critical Review of Archaeology's Sister Disciplines. In *Advances in Archaeological Method and Theory*, edited by Michael Schiffer, vol, 4, pp. 365–438. Academic Press, New York.

Goodale, S. L.

1863 The Manufacture of Cheese as a Staple Article of Export. In *Report of the Commissioner of Agriculture for the Year 1862*. U.S. Government Printing Office, Washington, D.C.

Gray, Lewis Cecil

1941 *History of Agriculture in the Southern United States to 1860*. Vols. 1 and 2. Peter Smith, New York.

Laing, Wesley Newton

1954 *Cattle in Early Virginia*. Unpublished Ph.D. Dissertation, University of Virginia.

Lewis, James Hoffman

1984 *Farmers, Craftsmen and Merchants: Changing Economic Organization in Massachusetts, 1730 to 1775*. Unpublished Ph.D. Dissertation, Northwestern University.

Main, Gloria L.

1982 *Tobacco Plantation: Life in Early Maryland 1650–1720*. Princeton University Press, Princeton, N.J.

Maltby, J. M.

1979 *Faunal Studies on Urban Sites: The Animal Bones from Exeter 1971–1975*. Department of Prehistory and Archaeology, Exeter Archaeological Reports 2. Sheffield University, England.

1982 The Variability of Faunal Samples and their Effects on Ageing Data, In *Ageing and Sexing Animal Bones from Archaeological Sites*, edited by Bob Wilson, Caroline

Grigson, and Sebastian Payne, pp. 81–90. British Archaeological Reports, British Series No. 109. Oxford, England.

1985 Patterns in Faunal Assemblage Variability. In *Beyond Domestication in Prehistoric Europe*, edited by Graeme Barker and Clive Gamble, pp. 33–74. Academic Press, New York.

McManis, Douglas R.

1975 *Colonial New England: A Historical Geography*. Oxford University Press, New York.

Miller, Henry M.

1979 Pettus and Utopia: A Comparison of the Faunal Remains from Two Late Seventeenth Century Virginia Households. *Conference on Historic Site Archaeology Papers* 13:158–180.

1984 *Colonization and Subsistence Change on the 17th Century Chesapeake Frontier*. Unpublished Ph.D. dissertation, Michigan State University, Lansing.

Moran, Geoffrey P., Edward Zimmer, and Ann Yentsch (editors)

1982 *Archaeological Investigations at the Narbonne House*. Salem Maritime National Historic Site, Massachusetts. Cultural Resources Management Study No. 6. National Park Service.

Payne, Sebastian

1973 Kill-Off Patterns in Sheep and Goats: The Mandibles from Asvan Kale. *Anatolian Studies* 23:281–303.

Redding, Richard

1981 *Decision Making in Subsistence herding of Sheep and Goats in the Middle East*. Unpublished Ph.D. Dissertation, University of Michigan, Ann Arbor.

Russell, Howard S.

1977 *A Long Deep Furrow: Three Generations of Farming in new England*. University Press of New England, Hanover, N.Y.

Silver, I. A.

1969 The Aging of Domestic Animals. In *Science in Archaeology*, edited by Don Brothwell and Eric Higgs, pp. 283–302. Praeger, New York.

Smith, David, and Anne E. Bridges

1982 The Brighton Market: Feeding Nineteenth-Century Boston. *Agricultural History* 56(1):3–21.

Walsh, Lorena

n.d. Plantation Economy. Manuscript on file at Colonial Williamsburg Foundation Research Department. Williamsburg, Va.

Wilson, Bob, Caroline Grigson, and Sebastian Payne

1982 *Ageing and Sexing Animal Bones from Archaeological Sites*. British Archaeological Reports. British Series No. 109. Oxford, England.

Young, Timothy

1987 Analysis of Faunal Remains from Queen Anne's Square, Newport, Rhode Island. *Northeast Historical Archaeology* 16:67–82.

Zeder, Malinda

1988 Urban Process through the Study of Specialized Subsistence Economy in the Near East. *Journal of Anthropological Archaeology* 7:1–55.

XI
CHAPTER

"Fashionable Sugar Dishes, Latest Fashion Ware"
The Creamware Revolution in the Eighteenth-Century Chesapeake

ANN SMART MARTIN

"WRETCHED, MISERABLE and unhappy Mug! I pity thy luckless Lot." So begins Benjamin Franklin's "A Meditation on a Quart Mug," published in the *Pennsylvania Gazette* in 1733. One of the few eighteenth-century sources to breathe life into such humble household objects, Franklin's satire woefully relates the miserable status of the earthenware mug in tavern duty and its coarse treatment by louts, drunkards, and servants, each of whom would as soon hurl it at an adversary as drink from it. But it was the unavoidable end of the mug that received Franklin's greatest sympathy, for "thou must at last untimely fall, be broken to Pieces, and cast away." The bottom might survive to hold a candle or shoe blacking or salve, but "all thy other Members will be for ever buried in some miry Hole." If "less carefully disposed of," those shards might be used by children "to furnish out their baby houses," or, if cast on a dung pile, be carted to the meadow field where "unlucky Boys," might throw them at dogs or birds. Finally, the poor pottery members meet their peace, for "by length of time and numerous Casualties, they shall be press'd into their Mother Earth, and be converted to their original Principles" (Lemay 1987:216–218).

Franklin underestimated the strength of his earthenware mug to withstand the ravages of time and rest unchanged in those "miry holes." So, too, when he mourned that the mug would "never more . . . be recollected and form'd into a Quart mug," he could not have predicted that some 250 years later, a host of scholars might spend their lives piecing together and puzzling over such a humble artifact.

Few colonial Americans had the literary abilities to comment on such simple household objects. But even if more were as prolific as Benjamin Franklin, such testimony no doubt would have been rare. Few of us today would likely write a paean to the things from which we eat and drink. Thus, the physical evidence of that mug must be used in creative ways to understand life in the past.

For the ubiquitous ceramic shard is one of the most common markers of human presence from prehistoric to modern times, and archaeologists rely heavily on ceramic evidence to excavate and analyze their sites. Even if the subject of inquiry is house construction or garden layout, one shard can explode a hypothesis about site formation, and another lead the archaeologist with confidence through complex features.

At the same time, an assemblage of ceramics can provide great insight into the lives of colonial households in the past. A huge volume of information has been amassed in the past several decades from the ceramics used in colonial households of varying economic rank, sex, race, and ethnic affiliation, and found from the farthest frontier to the heart of burgeoning urban areas. Because these many pots, cups, and mugs are the tangible markers of human behavior, they have been fruitfully used to assess the whole constellation of activities related to foodways, such as eating, drinking, food preparation, and storage. Because ceramic items could soar from the prosaic to the luxurious—with accompanying price differentials—these artifacts speak of the investments people made and their potential as material symbols of wealth and power. Because all of these values and behaviors are cultural variables, ethnic and racial variations on Anglo-American patterns have also been formulated.

The vast majority of these studies would have been impossible without the tools of the archaeological trade, not just the trowels and shovels, but the methods of dating and identification that have been copiously culled from the records of ceramic production. Teamed with such documentary information, ceramic artifacts are the cornerstone of historical archaeology.

Yet, much of what we know about ceramics comes from the records of their manufacture, particularly the Staffordshire pottery industry in England, which provides dates of varying degrees of precision to the beginning and end of manufacture. Although not formally stated, four propositions seem to underpin such temporal assignments: (1) that colonial Americans had equal access to the products of the factories of England through some form of distribution system; (2) that such access was obtained in a timely manner; (3) that colonial households desired these products, and were somehow active players of that rapidly changing dialectic between producer and consumer of the incipient industrial revolution; and (4) that colonial Americans somehow gained information about products manufactured both in England and at home and made decisions based on a number of factors, including availability, utility, aesthetics, price, and myriad social intangibles.

Each of these ideas are, of course, broadly correct. While historians still argue about the degree of self-sufficiency or commercial participation of colonial households, the fact remains that English ceramics carpet the sites of colonial America. As the colonial economy matured and the exploding population created a larger body of consumers, a complex distribution system developed, trading many agricultural commodities for just those household goods like Mr. Franklin's mug. But it *is* reasonable to question whether the access of colonial consumers was equal to that of the home market of England, and if the acquisition of English goods was accomplished in a timely manner. The proposition may also be tested that the colonists shared with their English cousins a number of values about English manufactured goods that our temporal assignments imply. This inquiry thus challenges the ideal that England and its North American colonies were bound into a virtually seamless Anglo-American cultural empire in the mid-eighteenth century and shared a kaleidoscope of values in a time of rapid social, economic, intellectual, and behavioral change (Breen 1986:467–499).

Several of these propositions can be examined by studying the kinds of ceramics available to colonial consumers in the predominant local distribution system of the colonial Chesapeake—the local store. By determining when particular wares were introduced, popular and obsolete, more precise dating tools can be formulated. But, more important, the choices colonial men and women made, out of a wide range of wares in production for eating and drinking, are valuable clues to the meanings that such items conveyed to both user and observer. Such preferences can particularly help gauge the power of the fashion-driven culture of metropolitan London to woo and win colonial consumers, and track the prevalence of elite high-style social behaviors through varying social ranks.

Funding by the National Endowment for the Humanities and the Colonial Williamsburg Foundation in 1986 and 1987 has enabled me to address these questions through an analysis of consumer demand at more than 40 Virginia and Maryland retail stores from about 1750 to 1810. With this data, it is possible to delineate a common core of table- and teawares available at local stores in the Chesapeake and to test archaeological notions about temporal assignments of new ware types. Moreover, such information makes it possible to examine any local or regional variability on that baseline of consumer choice; an index perhaps of the penetration of fashion and elite behaviors into the differing social contexts of urban areas, established eastern rural areas, or the newer western countryside.

A Time of Change

Almost a year to the day before Franklin wrote of that humble earthenware mug, a letter to the editor appeared on the pages of the *Pennsylvania Gazette*. It was a sad tale told by one Anthony Afterwit, a man who worked hard and "with care and industry" might have lived "tolerably easy, and in Credit" with his neighbors. But his wife "had a strong inclination to be a Gentlewoman" and thus began the march of new household furniture into their home. His "Wife being entertain'd with Tea by the Good Women she visited," they could "do no less than the like when they visited us," and a new "Tea-Table with all its Appurtenances of China and Silver" was the next necessity. So on came a maid, a clock, a horse, and all the trappings, and though poor Anthony "could see all Along, that this Way of Living was utterly inconsistent with my circumstances," he "had not Resolution enough to help it" (Lemay 1987:185–187).

Once again, the author was the keenly observant Benjamin Franklin. Like many of his literate peers, Franklin was protesting remarkable changes in the attitude toward—and use of—material objects in his lifetime. Many factors had combined to bring a number of material objects into the lives of more and more common people, and a host of scholars still struggle to untie the gordian knot of supply and demand (Gilboy 1967; McKendrick, et al. 1982; Crafts 1985). It is clear, however, that a number of circumstances—greater prosperity; improvements in manufacturing, distribution, and retailing; and lowering prices—somehow combined with a new willingness to spend to bring a range of new items of comfort and convenience into the lives of the Anglo-American middling ranks of the eighteenth century (Weatherill 1988; Carr and Walsh 1991).

Thus many items that were once luxuries, the exclusive purview of the elite or ruling class, tumbled from royal or noble households to more common ones in the course of the late seventeenth and eighteenth centuries. But the very power of luxury items, their ability to stand as potent symbols of power and wealth, hinges on their rarity, expense, and a fascination of those below (Braudel 1985:1:184). When such objects are no longer able to serve as exclusionary "fences" against the middling ranks by their rarity and expense, the intense interest of the watching crowd and whatever latent wish to live like one's betters are released (Douglas and Isherwood 1979:71–94). One common result may be social emulation: Mrs. Afterwit's wish to live like a gentlewoman.

What is one result of such imitation? The elite raced off for new social symbols; the middling ranks galloped after them; even the poorer sorts jogged along, at least to the degree that their economic abilities enabled them. As each group desperately sought to guard its borders from improper intruders, the wheel of fashion change spun faster and faster. The idea of fashion was not new to the eighteenth century. What *was* new was the hectic pace of change and the scope of population that ran the race. This is the heart of what the historian Neil McKendrick has dubbed "the consumer revolution" (McKendrick, et al. 1985).

But the elite were far from powerless in the chase. As more and more of the population obtained access to the material objects of social prestige, the wealthy were able to change the rules. Not only must one now own a proper set of accoutrements for smart living, but know a complex set of rules on how to use them. For it was in this same era that notions of gentility began to spread, as more of the English gentry invested time and money in proper education, manners, and leisure. Many Chesapeake elites, anxious to be considered up to date, modeled their behavior and their life-styles on their peers in England. Genteel and sociable behavior became the hallmark of the well-bred or wealthy, including accomplished dancing, games of skill, tea drinking, and elaborate dining (Bushman 1984). By thus linking their status to the superiority of the English aristocracy, eighteenth-century Virginia elites sought to establish a cultural leadership to consolidate their considerable political and economic power (Greene 1976:18; Isaac 1982; Kornblith and Murrin 1985:23–24).

With the increasing social importance of these behaviors came a necessity for newly appropriate props. The newest luxuries of the mid-eighteenth century were thus often symbols of those refined behaviors and appearances. But it was not just the objects that mattered; one had to know how to use them in socially dictated ways to convince the observer that one was an appropriate participant.

The wealthy Alexander Hamilton traveled with a loud, boorish fellow named William Morrison. When Morrison was not treated at a tavern in the manner he felt appropriate to his standing, he was incensed. He had good linen and silver buckles in his baggage, his wife at home drank tea twice a day; why should he not be treated as a gentlemen? Hamilton knew the answer, as did the tavernkeeper and all who watched. Morrison was a "roughspun, forward, clownish blade . . . at the same desirous to pass for a gentleman" (Bridenbaugh 1948:13–14). He represented the quintessential social riser that Franklin derided as a "mulatto gentleman," one who had the trappings of wealth but not the "natural and easy manner of those who have been genteely educated" (Lemay 1987:219).

But to return to Franklin's proverbial Mr. and Mrs. Afterwit. Having a "strong inclination to be a Gentlewoman," Mrs. Afterwit dragged the couple into a cycle of conspicuous consumption that poor Anthony had not "resolution to stop." But note how the process was hastened by the new sociable behaviors, like entertaining neighboring women at tea (Lemay 1987:186).

The drinking of tea summarizes well the process of the marked changes in both objects and behaviors of the eighteenth century. A classic case of a luxury item, tea was an appropriate gift for seventeenth-century royalty. But the increasing trade of the East India Company, as well as sharp drops in taxes throughout the century, gradually cut price. In the earlier eighteenth century, the rarity and expense of tea and sugar, the costly equipment to serve it, and the leisure considered necessary for entertainment all served to limit tea drinking to the very upper class. Indeed, the Virginian Devereux Jarrett was precise about the social station of those who drank tea before the middle of the eighteenth century. Remembering his childhood in a poor family, he recalled that "we made no use of tea or coffee . . . nor did I know a single family" that did. He "supposed" that the "richer sort might make use of these and other luxuries, but to such people I had no access." Those he called "Gentle Folks" moved in a different world (1952:361).

Yet by the last quarter of the eighteenth century, so many more were able to enjoy the small luxury of tea that travelers reported the custom to be "near universal" and even extended its custom to Indians and slaves (Blanchard 1873:78; Repplier 1932:99–100; Krzyzanowski 1961:26). But even though an indentured servant in Virginia could sit down to tea with a tailor's wife and daughters in 1773, their social superiors were still able to distinguish themselves by choosing expensive and elaborate silver and china tea services (Harrower 1963:5). The elite also erected barriers by creating complex rituals that the more common sort had to learn before they could participate (Roth 1961:72). Without proper warning, uneasy new initiates could not know, for instance, that if a woman were to use too much sugar or cream, "people will certainly take you for the daughter of a dairy maid" (Repplier 1932:87).

In a similar way, notions of proper dining were transformed in the eighteenth century. Labor-intensive and exotic foods were luxuries in themselves, requiring specially prepared sauces, trimmings, confections, and other elaborations alongside the main cut of meat (Douglas 1982:93). Contemporary cookbooks reinforced this new complexity by dictating several courses, with diagrams to demonstrate how to display abundance in a highly symmetrical balance of matching ceramic plates and serving dishes (for example, see Smyth 1742). This elaboration of food serving forms such as sauce boats, tart pans, and sweetmeat dishes further separated the well-to-do by their expense. Finally, this choice of complex and intricate meal structures and standards of hospitality at great expense take on an important role in social competition by focusing one's resources on impressing the few—the few that mattered for social promotion or marriage. The less wealthy may have been practicing the time-honored system of community inclusion, spreading consumption widely through community links as a strategy ensuring reciprocity in tough times (Douglas 1984:33–36).

The use of food by the wealthy in the eighteenth-century Chesapeake was a complex cultural phenomenon that balanced occasional community-wide largesse (the rich planter throwing the barbecue for the county) with elaborate foods for a select few. Food carried important social meanings in its own right. But when served on mahogany tables in newly specialized dining spaces with proper seating, serving, and even subjects of conversation, these socially charged food customs gained a new potency.

Thus, just as the uninitiated stumbled at proper tea-table behavior, so those uninformed in the ritual of dining marked their inappropriate presence. For example, Barbara Carson has recently demonstrated the transformation in table manners produced by the introduction of the three-tined fork in the later eighteenth century. Putting food in one's mouth with a knife was once the standard practice at American tables. At least by the early nineteenth century, however, such an action was a certain avenue to social rejection in urban places like the new federal capital (Carson 1990:59–73).

We might therefore think of tea drinking and dining for the rich as an elaborate kind of theater with roles that must be properly learned, and expensive props that must be correctly handled. A modern analogy might be just knowing which fork to use in a fine restaurant or how to sample wine with the steward staring, situations that still leave many uncomfortable without knowing the proper rules in using these objects.

The cultural dominance of the elite was consolidated by new genteel and sociable behaviors, complex unwritten rules, and specialized artifacts of dining and tea drinking.

But their efforts were buttressed in one final way: by the quality, expense, and fashionability of the objects they chose. Throughout the eighteenth century, the high-end luxury of the market was Chinese or European porcelain. European porcelains remained prohibitively expensive, in some cases matching the cost of silver equivalents. But Chinese producers responded to greater European demand by creating a wider range of quality in their wares. Thus, the bottom end, the cheaper wares with less painstaking decoration, continued to drop in the eighteenth century. Just as lower grades of tea began to flood the market, more and more were able to purchase the cheaper forms of Oriental porcelains to drink it from (for example, see Curtis 1987).

Yet porcelains remained so anxiously sought after by the elite that one historian claims that "no mania for material objects has ever been so widespread, so general to the rich of all nations," as was the china rush of the eighteenth century (McKendrick, et al. 1982:101). Given this madness for china, efforts to compete with porcelains by producing a fine, light-bodied ware to which could be applied precise and controlled decoration would become the driving force of innovation in the Staffordshire potteries. Josiah Wedgwood and other potters solved the dilemma with the perfection of creamware, a light and sturdy refined-body ware with a clear lead glaze that could be decorated with many techniques, most newly discovered themselves. It was Wedgwood's brilliant marketing, however, that gave the new ceramic the patronage of royalty and the new name "Queen's ware." First royalty were impressed, then nobility flattered, then the wishes of the common people to be like their betters were finally realized—each separated by the appropriate quality, decoration, forms, and hence price.

But the story of Wedgwood's Queen's ware has a slightly different twist on the classic tale of luxury items, such as porcelain. Like porcelain, creamware gained its status as a luxury from a royal endorsement, and the rich and fashionable flocked to buy it. Like porcelain, it was available in fabulously decorated and costly styles or relatively plain and inexpensive ones. But it took generations for porcelains to move from being the costly traditional symbol of wealth and power to a common tea and tableware. Wedgwood, however, managed to compress the whole cycle of luxury consumption in less than a decade, without losing the interest of any group. And unlike porcelains—which remained a traditional symbol of prestige for centuries—a particular variety of Queen's ware was not "in" for very long. Although the common plain form continued in use for another 50 years, Wedgwood was forced to continually bring out new forms and designs to keep the interest of the "smart set" in the buying public.

It was that pace of change that is so striking. In a 1789 novel, the protagonist contemplates his Staffordshire tea set, noting "this was quite an old set purchased two years ago." He had "seen some beautiful new specimens when last in town" and felt that "the manufacture was much improved" (Hillier 1968:9). The fact that a two-year-old tea set was considered quite old and worthy of replacement, and that new wares could seem so improved, is shocking testimony to the speed and power of changing fashion that was a hallmark of the late eighteenth century and the so-called consumer revolution. At its heart was a thorough transformation from the value of a luxury item in terms of its age—symbolizing old family wealth—to its value based on newness or fashion (McCracken 1988:31–43).

So just as the burgeoning nouveau riche merchant class was no longer disenfranchised from symbols of wealth in Europe, Chesapeake grandees spent lavishly to align themselves to London trend-setters and to divorce themselves from locals below. By the middle of the eighteenth century, letters and diaries of the wealthy are filled with reports of dances and dinners and teas. So, too, wealthy colonists seemed anxious to be in the latest mode; a contemporary reported in 1769 that "a new fashion is adopted earlier by the polished and affluent American" than by their peers in England (Eddis 1969:57).

However, few of those below the elite left these kinds of documents that could tell us about their own life-styles. The question must then be: how far down the social scale did those elite behaviors descend? The degree to which these more middling people participated in that fashionable English dining and tea drinking should be seen in the demand for the necessary supporting objects. And if the non-elite wanted such items, they should be found in the most common distribution network of the Chesapeake—the local store.

The Distribution of Consumer Goods

If the urban merchant or wealthy planter usually ordered goods directly from England, the middling man—a smaller planter or artisan—most likely shopped at the local retail store. Eighty percent of all Chesapeake tobacco by the 1770s passed through the hands of local merchants in a procedure standardized by tobacco inspection acts (Price 1974:168). These storekeepers allowed their customers to trade a wide variety of other local cash-producing crops or services, preferably paying in credit with store goods. Most of their customers were those who could not afford the risk and cost of marketing their own crops abroad.

Satisfying such middling consumers was important to the local merchants, for as the number of year-round stores exploded after 1750, keenly competing for customers and their crops, the items for sale became even more important for attracting and keeping business. The merchant John Hook pleaded with his suppliers to send him all the goods he requested, noting in despair in 1773 that "for me to make money without Goods is as absurd as to suppose a Taylor to make a Coat without cloth by the needle." He pointed out that even in the backcountry, the "sucess of the Trade depends first on the orders for the different cargoes being completed with dispatch, exactness and judgement in the choice of the goods . . . respecting the quality, collours, patterns and fashions" (Hook 1773).

While basic utilitarian wares formed the bulk of the inventories of these stores, as competition between stores increased, the stocking of nonessentials and even small luxuries became of utmost necessity. John Wilkins was so anxious to have the edge on his competitors that he wanted *whatever* was most in style to please his customers: he ordered "most fashionable sugar dishes, latest fashion ware" (Wilkins ca. 1773). The presence of creamware and teawares in these stores will thus attest to the conscious quest of less affluent colonists to behave as the more wealthy did: to live in the vogue of the cosmopolitan center of the British empire.

THE CREAMWARE REVOLUTION

A data base has been assembled of more than 125,000 foodways-related objects in Maryland and Virginia stores, ranging from fine decanters to common griddles. Among this wide variety of utensils and vessels, one of the most common items stocked was the basic component of all tablewares—plates. These serving forms are thus an excellent item to analyze for basic changes in ceramic popularity. Combining the invoices of plates ordered by all the stores in the study produces a clear picture of changing consumer demand (table 11.1). Before 1760, three-quarters of the plates stocked were not ceramic at all, but pewter. In the next decade, delftware surged in popularity, forming about 40 percent of all plates ordered, about equal to the number of pewter ones. Stone, earthen, porcelain, and agate wares were also available, albeit in smaller quantities.

But note the change after 1770 (figure 11.1)! The introduction of creamware formed an important watershed in the use of ceramics in the colonial era; consumers flocked to purchase the new cream-colored wares in a variety of dining and tea forms, leaving older styles languishing on store shelves. A few white salt-glazed plates were ordered by merchants early in the 1770s, but delft plates were simply no longer in demand.

Creamware quickly appealed to the public's taste and their pocketbooks. For, unlike later decorated Staffordshire wares, this ceramic was *introduced* at a cheap price in

TABLE 11.1. *Popularity of Ceramic Types: Percentage of All Plates in Store Sample, 1750–1799*

Type	1750–59 (n = 1,248)	1760–69 (n = 5,071)	1770–79 (n = 3,902)	1780–89 (n = 1,932)	1790–99 (n = 1,674)
Delftware	2.08	40.5			
Agate	1.4				
Porcelain	10.2	0.7	4.1		
White stone	13.1	6.8			
Cream/pearlware	73.3		43.0	96.2	91.0
Pewter	1.2	43.0	40.0	3.7	9.0
Unknonwn ceramic		6.1			

SOURCE: See the appendix to this chapter.

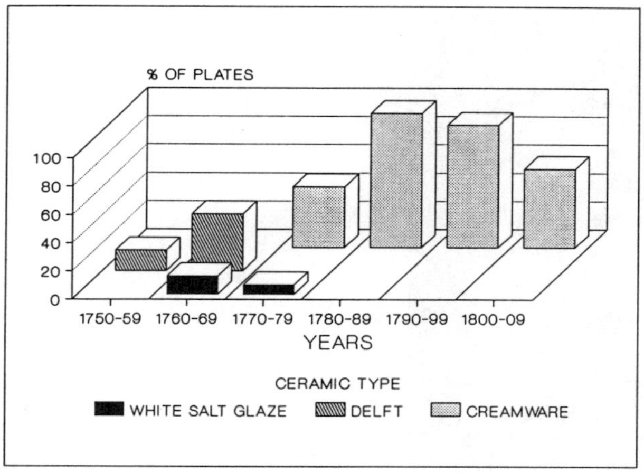

FIGURE 11.1. *The creamware revolution: rise of creamware and decline of delft and white salt-glazed plates, 1750–1809.*

relation to other options (Miller 1980). Plain creamware plates cost about the same as delft or white salt-glazed stoneware and at least a third of the price of pewter or porcelain. With its technical improvement, novelty, price, and the marketing push of Josiah Wedgwood, creamware could easily outpace its rivals (figures 11.2 and 11.3).

It is clear that creamware was phenomenally popular among the middling ranks of Virginia and Maryland consumers. But of greater importance was the scope and timing of that popularity. Remembering that part of the power of fashionable items was being the first to have them, to be the most in fashion on the block, so to say, how quickly did information about new products flow across the Atlantic?

Josiah Wedgwood claimed to have perfected creamware by 1762, drawing upon several decades of experimentation by other potters. He gained the patronage of the Queen—and the new name Queen's ware—at least by 1767 (Noël Hume 1973:227). In only a year, he is doing a brisk business at a London warehouse, is advertising his royal or noble patronage in the morning newspapers of England, and giving notice via soft news of how "in" his wares are. One such puff appeared in 1768 in the *Virginia Gazette* in Williamsburg in a letter from Burslem, Staffordshire, reporting the new popular interest in the potting industry. It noted that men went to see a new canal, an engineering marvel linking the Trent and Mersey rivers, but "Ladies go to Warburton's to buy the Queen's sets of cream coloured ware." Remember, though, that even the Virginia newspaper notice was quoting a letter from Burslem nine months old, from September 5, 1767.

FIGURE 11.2. *Eighteenth-century nonceramic tablewares: wood and pewter. (Photograph courtesy of the Colonial Williamsburg Foundation)*

FIGURE 11.3. *Creamware's ceramic rivals: creamware, delft, white salt-glazed stoneware, and blue underglaze painted porcelain. (Photograph courtesy of the Colonial Williamsburg Foundation)*

But nearly two years passed between the time that English women were reported in the Chesapeake press to be flocking to admire the fashionable Queen's ware and the acquisition of the ware by even the wealthiest colonists of North America. For example, George Washington had ordered a set of porcelain tablewares in 1762, and another in 1763. Yet, even all that porcelain was not enough; in July of 1769 he asked for an assortment of over 250 pieces of Queen's ware "ye. most fash[ionabl]e kind." The wide variety of specific functional shapes that Washington requested suggests that he was either ordering from a retailer's lists, a pattern book, or a service seen elsewhere, perhaps in Philadelphia or Williamsburg (Detweiler 1982:54).

Washington liked his new creamware so much that he reordered even a greater quantity only six months later. The future political leader of our country seems to have been quite a fashion leader as well. Not only can one of the earliest documented colonial orders for creamware be found in his correspondence, but tentative archaeological evidence suggests that he was already enjoying creamware prior to his 1769 order. Postholes of a smith's shop on Washington's property at Mount Vernon, most likely built or renovated in 1768, contain three tiny shards of creamware (Pogue 1989).

Documentary references to creamware in the colonies fall thick and fast after the prescient Mr. Washington's orders. For instance, a wealthy Yorktown woman ordered

"Some necessaries for House Keeping," including two sets of Queen's ware, from her London agent a month after Washington did, joking that at her age she probably should have consulted the undertaker before ordering (Mason 1937:103). The timing of these orders does not seem to be an accident. In that same year, creamware is first advertised in a newspaper in Quebec, Canada, and a store inventory in Providence, Rhode Island (Collard 1967:105–106, Teller 1968:574). Similarly, the advertising of creamware or Queen's ware does not begin until the fall of 1769 in the *Virginia Gazette*. And finally, a New York City agent for a wealthy upstate New Yorker wrote him in September 1769 that "the Table Crockery I now send are quite new fashioned, several principal Families have lately got them over from England, they are very much admired, but come Very High. . . . I hope you will approve of my sending them rather than the common White Ones . . . for I do not See why you Should not be in the fashion as well as anybody Else" (Howard 1984:62–63). Such urban places with their wealth of merchants in constant correspondence with England were "hot houses" of information, and it is there that creamware most likely first became known and used (Brown 1989:110–130).

These dates fit neatly with the earliest documentation for either the names "cream colored" or "Queen's ware" in Virginia discovered by Ivor Noël Hume. But problems do arise when trying to judge the early presence of creamware in the colonies. Noël Hume, for instance, points to a letter in 1764 from Thomas Bentley to Josiah Wedgwood, passing on a "small Order which we have just rec[eive]d from Boston . . . from a very Careful man who has sent us Cash to pay for them." Although most of these items would be categorized by archaeologists as Whieldon wares—pineapple tea pots and the like—cream-colored mugs were included (1973:223). Kathleen Deagan (1975:24) also reports early creamware in a Florida Indian archaeological context clearly sealed by a 1763 floor in St. Augustine and even speculates that such shards could have been deposited as early as 1750, perhaps part of those early experiments with cream-bodied wares associated with Whieldon. It does seem that a few crates of creamware were shipped to the colonies as early as 1763 from John Sadler of Liverpool, who provided transfer-printing on the ceramics of Josiah Wedgwood. When Wedgwood complained about the quality of some of his work, Sadler assured him that "we hope to have the opportunity of transporting those that are not so good, you'll have little to complain of" (Price 1948:38). Other wares may have arrived earlier under different names such as Yellow Liverpool ware (Noël Hume 1973:228–230).

But even if one gives credit to a few possible shipments for cash at an earlier date from English manufacturers to major urban centers, there is little indication that any such trade was more than sporadic, perhaps even used to dump inferior products. From all evidence in hand to date, it was not until *after* Wedgwood's marketing campaign transformed mere cream-colored ware into Queen's Ware that colonists pricked up their ears and took notice. The technical transition from clouded Whieldon wares to cream-colored ones by the perfection of the clear lead glaze *in itself* did not seem to have been of great concern.

For it was not just the elite planter or urban merchant who ordered creamware in the colonies in the late 1760s, but a host of small shopkeepers in the Chesapeake. A lone tidewater Virginia merchant, Edward Dixon, seemed to have his finger firmly on the pulse of London fashion, for he precociously ordered enameled creamware teacups and saucers in 1768, in what is perhaps the first irrefutable reference to creamware in the colonies. But not until 1770 did the rush of orders begin by Virginia and Maryland merchants. Thus, a time lag of about eight years existed between production and initial availability to the majority of the population. But creamware's popularity in stores did not peak until the first half of the *1780s*, a full two decades after its initial production or perfection. It was not until after the Revolution that creamware became the predominant tableware, but its victory over competing wares was by then impressive. This is confirmed in the probate record of the three Maryland counties of Anne Arundel, Kent, and Baltimore; creamware reached its maximum use there between 1780 and 1800 (Allen 1988:75).

Archaeological evidence from around the colonies firmly buttresses such claims to both creamware's introduction and popularity. No creamware is found among the thousands of shards excavated with rather precise temporal control at Fort Michilimackinac prior to 1771. There, too, can be seen the replacement of white salt-glazed stoneware by creamware, falling from just over 20 percent of all ceramics in the 1760s to less than 10 percent by 1774–1781. (Heldman and Grange 1981; Heldman 1983).

Excavation at Miles Brewton's house in Charleston

similarly demonstrates how quickly creamware spread throughout the English empire in the early 1770s. The wealthy merchant constructed a large house between 1765 and 1769, and probably added a neoclassical garden some time shortly after the house was complete, and before his family was lost at sea in 1775. A feature with many ceramics broken in situ—perhaps even serving as drainage—contains a number of creamware vessels (Zierden, personal communication 1990).

George Washington's excellent records indicate that the elite rushed to purchase creamware, in spite of already owning ample tablewares of porcelain. But the wealth of archaeological evidence from Thomas Jefferson's home can verify both the date of elite purchase and long-term and widespread use throughout society. For instance, a dry well there dates rather precisely to sometime between 1770 and 1771, and broken within it are 35 fine creamware tablewares, as well as Chinese porcelains in a number of decorative styles. The spread of creamware down through society can also be hinted at by the numerous creamware vessels found in slave quarters at Monticello, dating between the 1770s and 1790s. But the resilience of creamware meant that even as more of society obtained it, the wealthy did not necessarily abandon its usage. A small deposit at Monticello in a garden retaining wall seems to be the receptacle for what may be none other than a dropped dinner tray in 1806, perhaps for Jefferson himself. Along with a number of Chinese porcelain vessels are several well-worn feather-edged creamware platters and a plate (Gruber and Whitley, personal communication 1989). It is tantalizing— although unprovable—to think that a man that owned four cases of French porcelain still enjoyed his old feather-edged creamware (Jefferson 1790).

What are the archaeological implications for such findings? Archaeologists most often assign a date of 1762 as a terminus post quem for creamware, the date after which that ware could have been deposited. Technically, of course, that is correct if no creamware was produced prior to 1762, an assumption increasingly questioned by ceramic historian Terence Sockett's ongoing research (Sockett, personal communication 1992). Yet creamware found on the sites of those households below the elite—the families who shopped at local retail stores—were almost certainly purchased after 1770, and most likely after the Revolution. Even the wealthiest and most fashion-conscious Virginians do not *seem* to have been choosing creamware until after Wedgwood's royal marketing of the late 1760s, and it was not until 1771 that a well-to-do rural Virginia planter could report that it was much in use among his peers (Downman 1771).

In contrast, delftware and white salt-glazed plates, although continuing in production after 1770, were probably purchased before that period. But looking back to the middle of the century, the popularity of pewter was so pronounced that few Virginia consumers may have chosen ceramic wares at all! While clearly these store documents do not contain evidence of all local potters, the fact remains that the use of pewter continues long after the supposed market control of the Staffordshire potters (Martin 1989).

In any case, the introduction of creamware into the colonial market is an important watershed. It is a "revolution" in the sense that up to this time there was an immense variability of imported tablewares for sale in the colonies, even if each kind was not available in each different store. These wares included pewter, porcelain, white salt-glazed stoneware, Whieldon-Wedgwood or green-glaze, slipware, or tin-glazed earthenware, to name the most common. Of those choices, the last three were considerably lower in price than either pewter or porcelain. After 1770, however, the refined body earthenwares of creamware and later pearlware seem to sweep other low-cost ceramics before them. Pewter remains popular until the turn of the century, and porcelain continues as a luxury to modern times, but creamware seems to be what many, especially middling, colonists wanted on their dining tables on the eve of the American Revolution.

Yet, if technical improvements did not initially make the difference, creamware remained a popular standard so long after any novelty wore off that its technical superiority should not be overlooked. For instance, creamware's surface could stand up to long-term wear and tear that delftware could not. The only delftware forms that creamware did not seem to replace were bowls, continuing in popularity until the end of the century. Most likely used for punch drinking, these vessels were not subjected to the rigors of the increasingly standard knives and forks of polite eating. Nor can particular preferences for the simple designs of creamware be discounted in colonial choices. For instance, Chesapeake residents often chose the word "neat" to qualify their requests for fashionable items, suggesting a desire for the plain rather than the highly ornamental. But even this seeming aesthetic preference may have had a pragmatic basis. The Marylander Charles Carroll of Carrolton specifically requested a Queen's ware service "of the newest pattern, but no ways decorated to harbour Dirt," although he added that the fruit dishes and bowls, and small pickle dishes "may admit of an Ornament without that Inconvenience" (Carroll 1775). Unlike white salt-glazed stoneware, most new creamwares did not have highly molded surfaces, which perhaps indeed decreased labor to keep it clean.

But it remained the colonists' own knowledge about the prevailing English taste that led both the elite and local merchants to begin their orders. Wedgwood and other potters did not race to woo the colonial market; little mention is found in Wedgwood's letters of the free 1.8 million potential consumers in the North American colonies at the eve of the Revolution. The fact that creamware first became a popular purchase a full eight years after Wedgewood's claim of perfection, and a good three years after "fashionable marketing," is all the more remarkable when that temporal lag is compared to the situation in the early nineteenth century. Five months after Lafayette landed in New York in 1824, transfer-printed plates recording that scene were on their way to those old colonies across the Atlantic, now the Staffordshire potteries' major consumers (Miller et al. 1993:n.p.)

Rural/Urban Variability

However sweeping this creamware revolution, there *was* variability in different rural and urban places (table 11.2). Looking again at the types of plates ordered for all the stores between 1770 and 1779, it is clear that pewter and creamware were the most popular, with white salt-glazed stoneware and porcelain requested in small quantities. Yet a closer look at stores in several Virginia communities demonstrates some important differences (figure 11.4).

William Allason was a merchant in Falmouth from about 1760 to 1774. On the fall line on the north side of the Rappahannock River near Fredericksburg, his store drew a large number of customers from the Shenandoah Valley backcountry. What kinds of plates were stocked in Allason's store in the fourteen years from 1760? The majority—about two-thirds—were pewter. Of the ceramic plates, Allason ordered mostly delftware in the 1760s, along with a small number of earthenware and porcelain plates, until he introduced creamware in 1770, which left all ceramic rivals gathering dust on his shelves. In the next decade, Allason ordered only pewter and creamware plates, but pewter continued to be the workhorse of his tablewares.

Table 11.2. *Popularity of Most Common Plates in Chesapeake Stores, 1770–1779 (percent)*

Type	All Merchants (n = 3,902)	William Allason (n = 864)	Hooe, Stone and Company (n = 286)
Creamware	43	33	37[a]
White salt-glazed	7	0	21
Porcelain	4	0	25
Pewter	40	67	17
Unknown ceramic	6	0	0

[a]Half of this number were gilded.

Source: See the appendix to this chapter.

Compare that to the orders of a large commission house and store in booming Alexandria, Virginia, with satellite stores on either side of the Potomac. The first plates that Hooe, Stone, and Company received in 1771 were "white stone barley corn plates," an order repeated two years later. During this time they were also supplied with four dozen pewter plates, and by 1774 half of them had been sold, as well as 80 percent of the white salt-glazed plates. However, although old-fashioned white salt-glazed or pewter plates were sold, creamware ones were far more popular. The first creamware was highly decorated and quite expensive. The price of these four dozen "gold-bordered" Queen's ware table and dessert plates was two to three times ordinary creamware and greater than blue-and-white porcelain. Although these luxuries sold slowly, Hooe, Stone, and Company ordered more than 500 plain creamware plates and six dozen porcelain ones in the next eleven years.

But the differences in the range of goods available at the Alexandria store cannot be suggested merely by looking at only plates. The firm also stocked two "compleat dining setts Queens Ware," each containing a full 240 pieces at a cost of £66. Yet, such hugely expensive matched sets included only part of the props for the serving of abundant and elaborate foods. Additional expense was necessary for appropriate glassware, cutlery, silver, bread baskets, "straw matts for dishes," and a host of other items, all available in Hooe, Stone, and Company's store. Added to

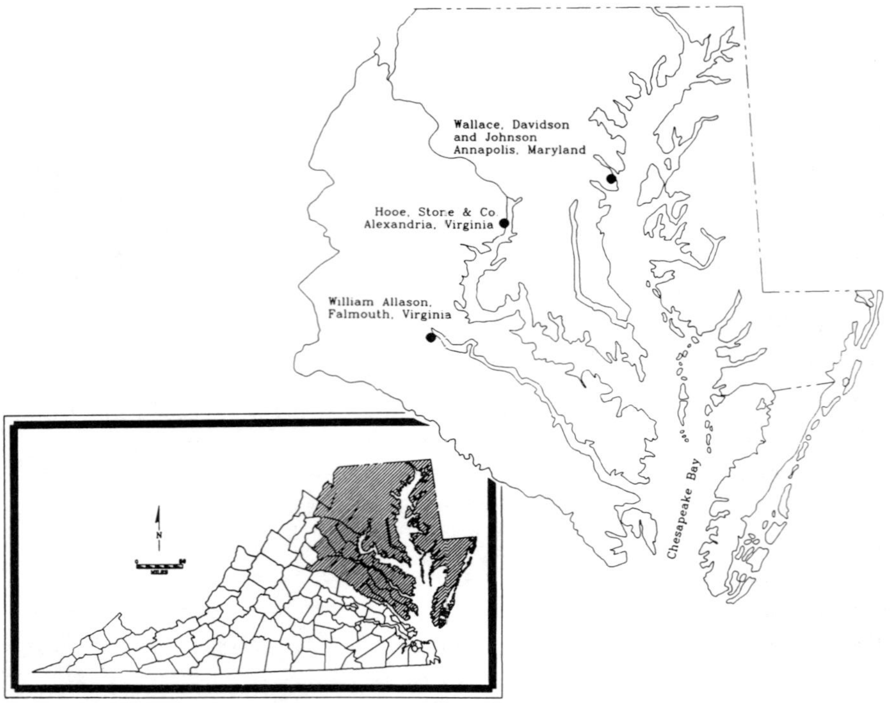

FIGURE 11.4. *Location of selected sample merchants, c. 1760–1784.*

their stock were also lemons, sweetmeats, spices, the finest oils and wines, and cookbooks. The combined effect is a picture of a truly urban difference in life-style.

Many of Allason's customers were drawn from the more recently settled piedmont and backcountry. Those that came to his store in the 1770s to purchase salt or osnaburg would undoubtedly see the gleaming creamware plates, so delicate and refined and new, and certainly cheaper than the old standard pewter. Did they buy those vessels, carefully tucking them in straw for the journey homeward across jolting country roads? While some were wooed and won by the fashions of the Staffordshire ceramic industry, others could not or would not be swayed.

In contrast, town dwellers were both able and anxious to purchase fashionable creamware, as well as porcelains, cut glass decanters, and large matched dining sets. Here the urban life-style—great dinners, teas, and card parties—placed a greater emphasis on entertaining and social display. One critic lampooned urban society as a city made out of bandboxes where "fashion intermeddled with everything and *descended to all ranks*" (*Norfolk Gazette and Publick Ledger*, 1814). These urban—perhaps even urbane—customers wanted and received far greater choices at their local stores.

Although creamware plates were immensely popular in both rural and urban places, their more expensive alternatives were distinctly different. The ever-practical pewter held its sway among the more wealthy middling ranks in the countryside, while their urban peers may have stepped up to porcelain, relegating their old pewter to the kitchen. Wise businessmen stock what sells. Allason could not rid himself of six porcelain plates and never reordered. But Hooe, Stone, and Company stocked and sold gold-bordered creamware and a variety of porcelains.

But a very different picture emerges in the sale of teawares. Although only urban stores successfully added porcelain plates to their store inventory, porcelain teawares were far more common throughout the Chesapeake. Overall, about half of all teacups and saucers stocked between 1770 and 1779 were creamware, and another one-fourth of teawares were porcelain (table 11.3). Yet, in the same decade only 4 percent of plates were of the same luxury material. Even in more rural areas, such as Allason's store, five grades of porcelain teacups were offered, costing two to four times the least expensive tin-glazed equivalents. This trend is only exacerbated in urban places: Wallace, Davidson, and Johnson in Annapolis, for instance, ordered 21 different kinds of tea and coffee cups in their first shipments in 1771 and 1772. In 1774, the most expensive colored and enameled porce-

TABLE 11.3. *Popularity of Types of Table- and Teawares in Chesapeake Stores, 1770–1779 (percent)*

Type	Cups and Saucers[a] (n = 2,727)	Plates (n = 3,902)
Creamware	48	43
White salt-glazed	13	7
Porcelain	25	4
Unknown	14	6
Pewter	0	40

[a]Not including sets

SOURCE: See the appendix to this chapter.

lain teacup cost 25 times the cheapest one. Teawares were offered at a wide range of prices; a few quite inexpensive cups and saucers, a large number at varying costs in the middling range, and a few that might cost a week's wages of a common laborer or the equivalent of Hume's eight-volume *History of England*.

Thus, many consumers could afford to participate in tea drinking from special apparatus, but enough gradations of price remained that varying social groups could maintain prestige. Indeed, when the full range of objects at the formal tea table were added—tea pots, sugars, silver spoons, and the like— the cost mounted quickly. But the true high cost was for a matching tea service, often ordered by the elite, but in general store stock at both Alexandria and Annapolis. It seems other households most likely mixed teawares, choosing creamware or porcelain cups and saucers and perhaps a creamware, black basalt, or white salt-glazed stoneware teapot.

Why were porcelain teawares so common in both urban and rural Chesapeake stores and porcelain tablewares for sale mainly in urban places? One explanation of course leads us back to urban living. Rural families of the middling and lower ranks did choose to participate in the "small piece of luxury" of tea drinking with porcelain teawares. However, they did not seem to join in the prestigious display of high-style dining, or at least place a premium on the investment in the highest price tablewares. This choice was due perhaps to the lack of time necessary for preparation, or continued rural patterns of simple inclusive yeoman hospitality. Similarly, tea drinking was most likely not the high-style entertainment of tea parties, but took place at the more informal gatherings of family or neighbors, or, for the poorest, was even a form of subsistence diet, a hastily gulped hot drink with bread (Mintz 1985).

Another part of the answer lies in the simple economics of consumer choice. To "step up" into the "luxury" of the least expensive blue and white porcelain for tea drinking was a much smaller investment than to do so for the least expensive china tablewares (figure 11.5). Put another way, the small luxury of tea from porcelain tablewares was a smaller strain on the middle class budget wherever one lived.

To an upwardly mobile man of middling ranks, careful choices were made on how to invest in symbols of social rank. An excellent case in point is Robert Nicholson. At the age of 26 with a wife and two children, he purchased a lot on what was then the outskirts of Williamsburg. Most in the neighborhood were craftsmen and young men starting their careers, like himself in the tailoring business. He constructed a rather unpretentious two-story house between 1751 and 1753, measuring approximately 24 × 26 feet, and took in boarders to supplement his income. Nicholson added two bays to his house in about 1766, creating a more up-to-date double-pile central passage structure and nearly doubling its size to its appearance today. By 1773, he was able to move his business from near his home to the city core, buying a shop on the Duke of Gloucester Street and expanding his business to include a general store and a post office. In only a few years, he stopped taking in boarders. On the basis of limited ar-

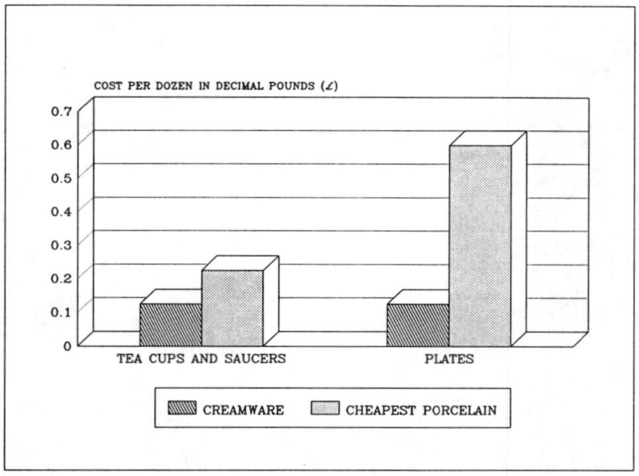

FIGURE 11.5. *The price of stepping up: relative costs of creamware and porcelain, Virginia 1772.*

chaeological investigation, it can be suggested that with Robert Nicholson's rising fortune, he replaced his old white salt-glazed stoneware and delftware ceramics with new, more fashionable table and teawares. Nicholson chose creamware tablewares and porcelain teawares (Samford 1985). Archaeological investigation of another Williamsburg craftsman, John Draper, indicates that the farrier and blacksmith similarly selected creamware plates and Chinese porcelain teawares in the late 1770s (Brown et al. 1990) (figure 11.6).

Distinctions in the quality and cost of cups and saucers aside, a salient point must be that vessels for the drinking of tea were, for a large majority of Chesapeake residents, increasingly de rigueur as a part of the standard household assemblage. Between 20 and 30 percent of even the poorest inventoried rural households in numerous counties in the Chesapeake invested in some kind of teawares by the 1760s and 1770s (Stone 1976; Gregory 1987; Carr and Walsh 1993). By 1800, Baltimore County residents of the poorest rank were spending slightly more on teawares than tablewares, a pattern reversed from the 1760s. When one moves to the middling ranks—a broad spectrum, indeed—the number of both rural and urban households in the Chesapeake containing teaware increased to well over half, and in the rank of the elite, more than 80 percent had some part of the assemblage relating to tea drinking (Gregory 1987:95; Carr and Walsh 1991). While this type of analysis does not give details of the number and kinds of teawares chosen, it does help explain, once again, just what the store data tell us. Since more of the population drank tea, spending on a particular *quality* of teawares became more significant.

SUMMARY

How can this analysis inform our study of the ceramics we recover archaeologically? First, by looking at the introduction, popularity, and obsolescence of wares in retail stores we can gain better dating tools. Of course, creamware could have been deposited on Virginia or Maryland sites in only the time it took for a ship to sail from England and a person to drop it on the ground. Yet, the likelihood remains that most in the middling ranks purchased creamware after 1770, perhaps after the Revolution. Probate and store evidence combine to demonstrate that creamware peaked in popularity sometime between 1780 and 1800. Similarly, delft and white salt-glazed plates

FIGURE 11.6. *Common choice of the aspiring middling ranks: creamware tablewares and blue underglaze painted porcelain teacups. (Photograph courtesy of the Colonial Williamsburg Foundation)*

were most likely purchased before 1770; this, of course, changes their median date range.

Second, it is too simplistic to state that a certain ware—in any vessel—suggests a certain social status. Consumers based their choices on a number of variables: what their neighbors or superiors used, what one ware cost in relation to another, what they thought was attractive or practical, or what was considered "suitable" for a certain function by a certain social rank. Consider that one so lofty as the Assistant Keeper of the Wardrobe to Queen Charlotte wrote as late as 1783 that "our Tea and Coffee set were of common India china, our dinner service, of earthenware, to which, *for our rank*, was nothing superior, Chelsea porcelain and fine India china being only for the wealthy. Pewter and Delft ware could also be had but were inferior" (Elliot 1986:11–12). So, too, Virginia and Maryland consumers of the middling rank chose creamware tablewares and porcelain teawares. Yet delftware bowls continued in standard service even as dinnerwares of the same type may have been considered inferior or old-fashioned. Thus, varying vessel forms in different wares have different tales to tell. Porcelain plates on archaeological sites are not simply the same as porcelain teawares.

Finally, with the greater emphasis on social display in urban areas, expensive, high-style wares were not uncommon even among the artisan ranks. Not only was sociability more important, but the audience to impress was larger and less likely to be intimately aware of one's family history or current economic position. Thus, porcelain teacups on rural sites speak far more loudly of higher household social rank, or at least pretension, than those on urban ones. Such urban and rural distinctions found in the eighteenth century, even among the small but increasingly cosmopolitan urban centers of the Chesapeake, would become even more marked in the early nineteenth century (Smart 1986).

A story ties together many of the themes presented here. In 1772, Anne Hulton, a wealthy Brookline, Massachusetts, woman, wrote to the wife of a merchant in Liverpool requesting a crate of creamware for her sister. The items in the previous crate sent were already "demolished," but the family had liked their new creamware so well that they wanted replacements. Anne Hulton's instructions for the purchase of her ceramics are telling. She carefully stipulated that "if there's any new fashion or invention of Mr. Wedgwood for this kind of ware, that is approvd, Shod prefer it to the yellow over again." She also stressed that they were for "common and daily use" and should be "usefull and neat, rather than Ornamental . . . and by no means gilt cream colored," suggesting instead a "plain or figured edge [which] we esteem genteeler." She did not want more than one tureen as the family already owned several made of porcelain, nor sauce boat with spoons because they tended to break. Rather than buy these wares in town, her family wrote to England assuming that there was some new "variety in the fashion from Liverpool" that had not yet reached colonial shops (Gorely 1944:109–111).

What can Anne Hulton's letters tell us? Obviously, a whole broken crate of creamware by 1772 is strong evidence of high rates of breakage, and helps explain why so many ceramics are found archaeologically in relation to a single household. But her requests also speak loudly about notions of fashion change, function, and social meaning. In Hulton's mind, everyday wares should be simple, and even though she wrote to Liverpool to get the latest fashion, she inserted her notions of what *she* and her social peers considered genteel. This was the paradox: she wrote to England for her ceramics, expecting rapid fashion turnover and knowing such change would be felt first in England, not in her local shop. Yet she was not a slave to that fashion. She knew what was considered proper for a certain function, and what kind of decoration was considered refined. Nor was she concerned that all her tablewares matched. She had several perfectly good porcelain tureens at home, and hoped she could break a manufacturer's set for her own needs. She also knew from experience that certain forms were less practical and suffered a higher rate of breakage. Personal needs, practicality, and local social meaning all mediated her wish to have the latest mode.

Only the elite—and few of them—have left so detailed a testimony to their purchases for ceramics. So we must turn to multiple types of indirect evidence to piece together the complex social drama of the demand for creamware and teawares by the less wealthy. We know that just as social mobility was becoming blocked in some places in the eighteenth century by pressures on land and resources, the desire to behave like those at the top as a means of social progress was exacerbated. Yet, we must not be satisfied with a monocausal explanation for changing consumer behaviors, but seek the range of economic, social, cultural, and personal factors that led one person to purchase, another to abstain. It was not more "primitive" conditions of the more recently settled parts of the Chesapeake that caused the customers at Allason's store to only slowly accept certain artifacts deemed desirable by the dominant Anglo-American culture. Fashionable emulation and genteel behaviors became more important as they began to serve a necessary function, and even then may have been modified to suit the needs of a new group. Artifacts of the newest style for dining and tea drinking found on archaeology sites thus suggest more than just the ability or desire to spend money to acquire a particular object. They are signals that site occupants chose to be active players in the cultural game of eighteenth-century Anglo-America.

ACKNOWLEDGMENTS

Research of this kind always incurs large debts. Primary thanks must go to the National Endowment for the Humanities for funding research in merchants' records under the grant "English Ceramics in America, 1760–1860: Prices, Availability, and Marketing" RO #-21158-86. Marley R. Brown of the Department of Archaeological Research, Colonial Williamsburg Foundation, supported my continued research and analysis. A continual joy of working at Colonial Williamsburg was the encouragement of a host of associates; this chapter benefited from the specific input and information of George Miller and Patricia Samford and the comments of Greg Brown and William Pittman, all in the Department of Archaeological Research. From the Department of Collections, Robert Hunter and John Davis graciously helped arrange the photographs taken by Hans Lorenz. Kim Wagner of the Department of Archaeological Research prepared the map. Earlier comments from Paul Shackel and Barbara Little were quite useful, as more recently were long discussions with English ceramic historian Terence Lockett about the earliest production of creamware.

Archaeological colleagues from around the country also provided a wealth of information. Special thanks must go to Dennis Pogue of the Mt. Vernon Ladies' Association; Anna Gruber, Cindy Whitley, and William Kelso of the Thomas Jefferson Memorial Foundation; Donald Heldman of Fort Michilimackinac; and Martha Zierden of the Charleston Museum. Each of these people heeded my pleas for information on tightly dated creamware in their archaeological excavations. It is only through this kind of cooperation that this story could be told.

REFERENCES CITED

Allen, Gloria Seaman
1988 Ceramics in Maryland, *American Ceramic Circle* IV:53–104.

Blanchard, Claude
1873 *The Journal of Claude Blanchard, 1780–1783*. J. Munsell, Albany.

Braudel, Fernand
1985 *The Structures of Everyday Life*, vol. 1, *Civilization and Capitalism: 15th–18th Century*. Harper and Row, New York.

Breen, T. H.
1986 An Empire of Goods: The Anglicization of Colonial America, 1690–1776. *Journal of British Studies* 25 (October 1986):467–499.

Bridenbaugh, Carl
1948 *Gentleman's Progress: The Itenerarium of Alexander Hamilton in 1744*. University of North Carolina Press, Chapel Hill.

Brown, Gregory J., Thomas F. Higgins III, David Muraca, S. Kathleen Pepper, and Roni H. Polk
1990 *Archaeological Investigations of the Shields Tavern Site, Williamsburg Virginia*. Department of Archaeological Research, Colonial Williamsburg Foundation, Williamsburg, Va.

Brown, Richard D.
1989 *Knowledge Is Power: The Diffusion of Information in Early America, 1700–1865*. Oxford University Press, New York.

Bushman, Richard L.
1984 American High-Style and Vernacular Cultures. In *Colonial British America: Essays in the New History of the Early Modern Era*, edited by Jack P. Greene and J. R. Pole, pp. 345–383. Johns Hopkins University Press, Baltimore.

Carr, Lois Green, and Lorena S. Walsh
1991 Changing Lifestyles and Consumer Behavior in the Colonial Chesapeake. In *Of Consuming Interest: The Style of Life in the Eighteenth Century*, edited by Ronald Hoffman and Cary Carson, in press.

Carroll, Charles
1775 Invoice for goods ordered through Wallace, Davidson, and Johnson, January 25. Wallace, Davidson, and Johnson Order Book. Maryland Hall of Records. Microfilm Collections, Foundation Library, Colonial Williamsburg Foundation. Willliamsburg, Va.

Carson, Barbara
1990 *Ambitious Appetites: Dining, Behavior, and Patterns of Consumption in Federal Washington*. American Institute of Architects, Washington, D.C.

Collard, Elizabeth
1967 *Nineteenth Century Pottery and Porcelain in Canada*. McGill University Press, Montreal.

Crafts, N. B. R.
1985 *British Economic Growth during the Industrial Revolution*. Clarendon Press, Oxford.
Curtis, Julia
1987 Chinese Export Porcelain in Eighteenth-Century Tidewater Virginia. In *Studies in Eighteenth-Century Culture*, edited by John Yolton and Leslie Ellen Brown, 17:119–144. Colleagues Press, East Lansing, Mi.
Deagan, Kathleen
1975 Architecture, Archeology, and History in Spanish St. Augustine: New Data from Sealed Contexts. *Conference on Historic Sites Archaeology Papers*, 9:13–29.
Detweiler, Susan Gray
1982 *George Washington's Chinaware*. Harry Abrams, New York.
Douglas, Mary
1982 Food as a System of Communication. In *The Active Voice*, pp. 82–124. Routledge and Kegan Paul, London.
1984 Standard Social Uses of Food: Introduction. In *Food in the Social Order: Studies of Food and Festivities in Three American Communities*, edited by Mary Douglas, pp. 1–39. Russell Sage Foundation, New York.
Douglas, Mary, and Baron Isherwood
1979 *The World of Goods: Toward an Anthropology of Consumption*. W. W. Norton, New York.
Downman, Raleigh
1771 Letter to Clay and Midgeley, July 2, 1771. Joseph Ball Letterbook, Library of Congress. Microfilm Collections, Foundation Library, Colonial Williamsburg Foundation. Williamsburg, Va.
Eddis, William
1969 *Letters from America*, edited by Aubrey C. Land. Belknap Press of Harvard University, Cambridge, Mass.
Elliot, G. W.
1986 The Technical Characteristics of Creamware and Pearl-Glazed Earthenware. In *Creamware and Pearlware*, edited by T. A. Lockett and P. Halfpenny. Fifth Exhibition from the Northern Ceramic Society, Stoke-on-Trent Museum and Art Gallery.
Gilboy, Elizabeth Waterman
1967 Demand as a Factor in the Industrial Revolution. In *The Causes of the Industrial Revolution*, edited by R. M. Hartwell, pp. 121–38. Metheun and Company, London.
Goreley, Jean
1944 *Old Wedgwood*. Wellesley Press, Wellesley, Mass.
Greene, Jack P.
1976 Society, Ideology and Politics: An Analysis of the Political Culture of Mid-Eighteenth-Century Virginia. In *Society, Freedom and Conscience: The Coming of the Revolution in Virginia, Massachusetts, and New York*, edited by Richard M. Jellison, pp. 14–76. W. W. Norton, New York.
Gregory, Stacia M.
1987 *The Elements of Consumption: Tea and Tablewares in Baltimore County, Maryland before and after the Revolution*. Unpublished M.A. thesis in Early American Culture, University of Delaware.
Harrower, John
1963 *The Journal of John Harrower: An Indentured Servant in the Colony of Virginia*, edited by Edward Miles Riley. Colonial Williamsburg, Williamsburg, Va.
Heldman, Donald P.
1983 *Archaeological Investigations at French Farm Lake, 1981–1982: A British Colonial Farm Site*. Archaeological Completion Report Series No. 6, Mackinac Island State Park Commission, Mackinac Island, Mich.
Heldman, Donald P., and Roger T. Grange, Jr.
1981 *Excavations at Fort Michilimackinac: 1978–1979: The Rue de la Babillarde*. Archaeological Completion Report Series No. 3, Mackinac Island State Park Commission, Mackinac Island, Mich.
Hillier, Bevis
1968 Two Centuries of China Selling. *English Ceramic Circle* 7(2):2–20.
Hook, John
1773 Letter to Walter Chambre, December 28, 1773. Letter Book 1763–1784, 1796, 1797, n.d. Virginia State Library, Richmond.
Howard, David Sanctuary
1984 *New York and the China Trade*. New York Historical Society, New York.
Isaac, Rhys
1982 *The Transformation of Virginia, 1740–1790*. University of North Carolina Press, Chapel Hill.
Jarrett, Devereux
1952 The Autobiography of the Reverend Devereux Jarrett, 1732–1763. William and Mary Quarterly, 3d ser., 9:346–393.
Jefferson, Thomas
1790 Memorandum of the Objects Made and Furnished by Me Greven Master Boxmaker for Mr. de Jefferson minister of the United States of North America. July 17. Typescript on file, Thomas Jefferson Memorial Foundation, Charlottesville, Va.
Kornblith, Gary J., and John Murrin
1985 Class and the Language of Class in Colonial and Revolutionary America. Unpublished paper presented at the Anglo-American Social History Conference, Williamsburg, Va., September 5–7.
Krzyzanowskii, Ludwik (editor)
1961 *Julian Ursyn Niemcewicz' American Diary*. Polish Academy of Arts and Sciences in America, New York.
Lemay, J. A. Leo
1987 *Benjamin Franklin: Writings*. Library of America, New York.
McCracken, Grant
1988 *Culture and Consumption: New Approaches to the*

Symbolic Character of Consumer Goods and Activities. Indiana University Press, Bloomington.

McKendrick, Neil, John Brewer, and J. H. Plumb
1982 *The Birth of Consumer Society: The Commercialization of the Eighteenth Century*. Indiana University Press, Bloomington.

Martin, Ann Smart
1989 The Role of Pewter as Missing Artifact: Consumer Attitudes toward Tablewares in Late Eighteenth-Century Virginia. *Historical Archaeology* 23(2):1–27.

Mason, Frances Norton
1937 *John Norton and Sons, Merchants of London and Virginia*. Repr. ed. David and Charles, Newton Abbott.

Miller, George L.
1980 Classification and Economic Scaling of Nineteenth Century Ceramics. *Historical Archaeology* 14(1):1–40.

Miller, George L., Ann Smart Martin, and Nancy S. Dickinson
1993 Changing Consumption Patterns, English Ceramics and the American Market from 1770 to 1840. In *Everyday Life in the Early Republic, 1780– 1828*, edited by Kate Hutchens. W. W. Norton, New York, in press.

Mintz, Sidney
1985 *Sweetness and Power: The Place of Sugar in Modern History*. Viking Penguin, New York.

Noël Hume, Ivor
1973 Creamware to Pearlware: A Williamsburg Perspective. In *Ceramics in America*, edited by Ian M. G. Quimby, pp. 217–54. Charlottesville, University Press of Virginia.

Norfolk Gazette and Publick Ledger
1814 January 26. Norfolk, Va. William Davis, publisher.

Pogue, Dennis
1989 Archaeology at George Washington's Mount Vernon: The Blacksmith Shop. *Fairfax Chronicles* 12(4):1–4.
1989 Letter, August 11.

Price, Jacob L.
1974 Economic Function and the Growth of American Port Towns in the Eighteenth Century. In *Perspectives in American History*, edited by Donald Fleming and Bernard Bailyn, vol. 8, pp. 123–186. Charles Warren Center for Studies in American History, Cambridge.

Price, Stanley
1948 *John Sadler: A Liverpool Pottery Printer*. West Kirby.

Repplier, Agnes
1932 *To Think of Tea!* Houghton, Mifflin, Boston.

Roth, Rodris
1961 *Tea Drinking in Eighteenth-Century America: Its Etiquette and Equipage*. Bulletin No. 225, Paper 14. Contributions to the Museum of History and Technology, Smithsonian Institution.

Samford, Patricia
1985 *The Nicholson House: Report on the 1982 Archaeological Investigations*. Office of Archaeological Excavation, Colonial Williamsburg Foundation, Williamsburg, Va.

Smart, Ann Morgan
1986 *The Urban/Rural Dichotomy of Status Consumption: Tidewater, Virginia 1815*. Unpublished M.A. Thesis, Program in American Studies, College of William and Mary, Williamsburg, Va.

Smyth, E.
1742 *Compleat Housewife*. William Parks, Williamsburg, Va.

Stone, Gary Wheeler
1976 Artifacts Are Not Enough. *Conference on Historic Sites Archaeology Papers* 11:43–63.

Teller, Barbara Goreley
1968 Ceramics in Providence, 1750–1800: An Inventory Survey, *Antiques* 94(4):570–577.

Weatherill, Lorna
1988 *Consumer Behavior and Material Culture in Britain, 1660–1760*. Routledge, New York.

Wilkins, John
ca. 1773 Letter to John Norton and Sons, London. John Norton and Sons Papers, Special Collections, Colonial Williamsburg Foundation Library, Williamsburg, Va.

APPENDIX: DATA AND METHODOLOGY

This study is based on invoices for goods ordered by more than two dozen Virginia and Maryland merchants in the second half of the eighteenth century. These records detail the shipments of goods from England to a partner or employed shopkeeper in the colonies, recording quantities, prices, and various levels of detail concerning type and decoration. Some 273 invoices and store inventories between 1740 and 1811 were recorded on a computer data base, representing nearly 125,000 vessels and utensils of ceramic, pewter, glass, tin, brass, wood, and iron.

Qualifications and cautions are always in order in a quantitative study like this. Judgment was occasionally necessary in sorting out various categories, although there seemed to be little doubt over the identification of creamware. Moreover, these prices represent a base cost—discounts and drawbacks were taken by the merchant, retail markup varied in time and place, and the actual purchasing power of the consumer was integrally tied to exchange rates and commodity prices. The invoices themselves are the result of an intensive search at a number of archives through extant eighteenth-century merchants' accounts, and undoubtedly reflect the curation rates of the documentary record. Because nearly 90 percent of these vessels were ordered between 1760 and 1790, I have confined my analysis to this better-represented period.

Although there was variety in these stores—as this chapter demonstrates—the orders of more than two dozen merchants show far more similarities than distinctions. Larger stores contained more variety, and were perhaps more likely to have a particular item at a given time. But these documents reflect what was available to and desired by thousands of eighteenth-century consumers. Two dozen merchants would be poor businessmen, indeed, to miss the pulse of the buying public.

These documents can be found in the following collections:

Microfilm Holdings, Foundation Library, Colonial Williamsburg Foundation, Williamsburg, Virginia

William Allason Papers, Virginia State Library.
Edward Dixon Papers. Library of Congress.
John Hook Papers, Special Collections, Duke University.
John Glassford and Company Papers, Library of Congress.
Frederick Hall Account Books. Southern Historical Collection, University of North Carolina at Chapel Hill.
Hooe, Stone, and Company Papers. Invoice Book. New York Public Library.
Neil Jamieson Account Books, Library of Congress.
James Lawson–John Semple Accounts, Scottish Record Office, Currie-Dal Misc. Bundle 20.
Logan, Dunmore and Company Inventory, Original: P.R.O./A.O. 13/30 Loyalist Claims 1782–1790, Reel 252.
John Norton and Sons Papers, London, 1769–1780.
Wallace, Davidson and Johnson Order Book, Annapolis. Maryland Hall of Records.
Dr. Thomas Walker Papers, Rives Papers, Library of Congress.
Willison, Stewart and Company Invoice. U.S. Circuit Court, Eastern District of Virginia Records, Record Books # 1 A–# 2 B, 1790–November 1794.

Swem Library, Manuscripts Department, College of William and Mary, Williamsburg, Virginia

Henry Bedinger Invoice Book, 1785–1796.
Briggs and Blow Letter Book, Blow Family Papers.

Virginia State Library, Richmond, Virginia

William Allason Papers, Loose papers.
Dramgoole Family Papers.

XII
CHAPTER

"She Was . . . an Example to Her Sex"
Possibilities for a Feminist Historical Archaeology

BARBARA J. LITTLE

IN THIS CHAPTER I use the life of Anne Catharine (Hoof) Green as a starting point from which to examine the possibilities for a feminist historical archaeology. If we as anthropologists and historians accept that gender is a structuring principle in all societies (see, for example, Moore 1988:vii; Morgen 1989a) then the possibility of incorporating gender into archaeological interpretation is not only interesting, but also essential for any historical archaeology that purports to be about people. My purpose is also that of archaeologists beginning to engender *pre*history: to produce a *visibility* of gender rather than attempt to identify gender per se in the archaeological record (see, for example, Conkey 1991; Hastorf 1991; Tringham 1991).

Anne Catharine Hoof traveled to Philadelphia from Holland with her parents sometime during her early childhood in the first quarter of the eighteenth century (Thomas 1970:531). Other facts of her life until her marriage to Jonas Green are obscure. It is likely that her parents provided her with a basic education; she was literate in adulthood. Benjamin Franklin remarks favorably on the education provided Dutch girls when he comments in his autobiography on widow Elizabeth Timothy's able management of the printing business left her by her husband (Labaree et al. 1964:166). Such a comment is not proof of a Dutch girl's education in the colonies, but perhaps indicates the value Anne Catharine's parents may have attached to it.

Anne Catharine Hoof and Jonas Green were married in Christ Church in Philadelphia in April of 1738, moved to Annapolis in May, and had their first child in October.[1] During the next 22 years Anne Catharine bore 14 children, only 5 of whom survived to adulthood. Until her husband's death in 1767, Anne Catharine managed a household that consisted of children, servants, apprentices, employees, and occasionally slaves. She provided the household support necessary for her husband's social and political successes, and she almost certainly worked in the print shop as well.

Anne Catharine took over the printing business and continued to manage the household when Jonas died. The General Assembly of Maryland awarded her the same terms of payment that her husband had enjoyed and appointed her to the official position of printer to the province. Until her death in 1775, Anne Catharine printed under her own name as well as with her son William and later her son Frederick. She bought the lot where she lived and printed, and she bought another lot in town as well, which she later sold to her son-in-law.

In an obituary for his mother on March 30, 1775, Frederick Green wrote in the *Maryland Gazette*:

Last Thursday Morning departed this Life, Mrs. ANNE CATHARINE GREEN, relict of the late Mr. Jonas Green, Printer to the Province; and on Friday Evening her Remains were decently interr'd in Saint Anne's Churchyard: She was of a mild and benevolent Disposition, and for conjugal Affection, and parental Tenderness, an Example to her Sex.

The statement that Anne Catharine Green was an "Example to her Sex" can be seen to be true in a variety of ways. She was an example of proper womanly behaviors and values to Frederick Green, not necessarily because he was her son, but because he was a man we can understand as signifying the contemporary conventional wisdom regarding women. Anne Catharine Green was also an example of the roles and limited options available to women in the eighteenth-century Chesapeake. She was a member of a gender whose power was muted in a society where women had little autonomy. She took on many roles: daughter, wife, mother, mother-in-law, businesswoman, mistress, landowner, printer, patriot, and "relict," or widow—all of them in part defined and structured by gender. Finally, Anne Catharine Green serves as an example now, not to her sex but of her sex and its visibility in a feminist historical archaeology.

FEMINISM IN ANTHROPOLOGICAL ARCHAEOLOGY

An anthropology of gender must be distinguished from a feminist anthropology. The latter, which grew out of the "anthropology of women" of the 1970s, has as its object gender relations rather than simply "women" and understands gender as a principle of human social life (Moore 1988:186). The same sort of distinction can be made between an archaeology of gender, which implies an approach of looking for women's artifacts, and a feminist archaeology, which aims at changing interpretive frameworks (see Conkey 1991; Conkey and Gero 1988). Feminism is a politics aimed at changing gender-based power relations (see, for example, Weedon 1987:1). A feminist archaeology contributes to this end by reexamining historical constructions and by assessing material conditions of gender relations.

As Conkey and Spector (1984) originally pointed out, archaeology as a subdiscipline of anthropology has been quite slow in acknowledging gender as an important structure in social organization and in the archaeological record. Compared to gender studies within anthropology as a whole (see Morgen 1989b for an overview), there are few archaeological publications at the time of this writing. Nevertheless, there has been an explosion recently in the number of conferences, sessions at professional meetings, and publications specifically concerned with archaeology and gender. Spector and Whelan (1989) could cite only 11 in their annotated bibliography but correctly anticipated more. Gero and Conkey's recent (1991) collection on gender in prehistory adds considerable work and will stimulate much more. Especially within historical archaeology, where researchers have just begun to ask the questions of the rich data available, gender relations and their visibility in material culture will become the focus of further analysis.[2]

Structuralist oppositions—including Nature::Culture, Communal::Individual, and Public::Private—have become well-known and appreciated by historical archaeologists since they were introduced to the field's literature and logic by James Deetz (1977, 1983). Structuralism, as Leone and Potter (1988) have pointed out, is one of the three principal approaches that historical archaeologists use to make sense of their data. Recognition and serious consideration of the often unspoken Female::Male opposition is long overdue. Sexual dichotomy is central to the Levi-Straussian style of structuralism that has become mainstream in historical archaeology, but its implications have been all but ignored. Gender ideology is also of central concern in the poststructuralist thinking now affecting archaeology and, of course, in feminist anthropology; the issue will remain important.

The logic for assuming that data relevant to gender will be present and discernible in the archaeological record is based on the cultural construction and variability of gender. Spector and Whelan (1989:70) write:

> In fact, gender constructions may actually be "built" with the aid of material objects that mark the gender of individuals using, wearing, or otherwise displaying them. . . . The objects or spaces themselves are used to actively construct and perhaps modify notions of gender because they carry social meaning in addition to their utility as tools, clothing or ornaments.

Conkey (1991:71) writes:

> Thus, a feminist archaeology (cf. Conkey and Gero 1988) that takes gender as a primary structuring prin-

ciple and as a process of relations *and* that takes material culture as active and constitutive of social life, including gender relations and forces, is thus methodologically empowered to look at how material culture is part of the processes of gender relations: how and in what ways do people make and use material culture in establishing, producing, changing, and challenging gender relations?

Material culture may be necessary for defining gender in a living society precisely because the basis for much of gender ideology is not natural but cultural.

Archaeologists may be able to pinpoint the objects that determine gender attribution and identity. We may also learn to identify usual, and unusual, gender roles and the materials associated with them. We cannot stop there, however. It would be a mistake to identify, for example, particular items or domains of material culture with women and then use such material to define women's presence and women's roles. Such logic creates the danger that domestic items may be called "female" artifacts and then be used tautologically to identify women's activities.

Perhaps one way to avoid the uncomfortable and indefensible position of relating archaeology and gender to "discover" what we already "know" about gender roles is to place gender ideology at the center of analysis, as has been suggested by many feminist writers. Other aspects of gender cannot be understood except in conjunction with culturally constructed gender ideology, those rules and rationalizations for appropriate gender behavior and interrelationships (Spector and Whelan 1989). A feminist archaeology aims at interpreting the mutual effects of gender ideology and material culture. Gender ideology and gender roles are closely intertwined. Both the symbolic valuations of gender ideology and sociological gender roles must be taken into account to create any holistic view of gender relationships and their material realities. The dynamic nature of gender relationships becomes apparent in any historical exploration, and an archaeological viewpoint assumes that the meanings and uses of related material culture will also be dynamic.

Teaching Women How to Be Women

Eighteenth-century gender ideology polarized the sexes and used sexual difference as a basis for evaluating appropriate roles and attitudes, differentiating rationality and educability, and judging relative worth. The domestic/public dichotomy was in place. Natural law and supernatural decree were used to support the social relations of gender and their strict division. In 1712 Joseph Addison wrote in the English periodical the *Spectator*: "I think it absolutely necessary to keep up the Partition between the two Sexes and to take Notice of the smallest Encroachments which the one makes upon the other" (quoted in Anderson and Zinsser 1988:114).

Works aimed at "improving the fair sex" became increasingly available and popular from the last quarter of the seventeenth century through the eighteenth century. In her classic study of southern colonial women, Julia Cherry Spruill provides some insight into the behaviors and attitudes expected of Anglo-American women. Handbooks on domestic economy were popular through the seventeenth and eighteenth centuries (Spruill 1972:204), and Spruill refers to a selection of 19 such books published between 1596 and 1759. These books included not only recipes and directions for running a household but also "the inward and outward vertues which ought to be in a compleate women" (Spruill 1972:209; Best 1986).

Spruill's lists are not exhaustive but are representative of the advice manuals aimed at eighteenth-century women (see Browne 1987 for other writings). Many of these books had long influence and were read well into the nineteenth century (Browne 1987:114). Such books were advertised in colonial newspapers, including the *Maryland Gazette*. Certainly Anne Catharine Green knew of them. Whether or not she owned any is unknown; her probate inventory lists "a parcel of books" without specific titles.

One of the most enduring of these popular books, Richard Allestree's *The Ladies Calling* written in 1673, was much paraphrased and incorporated into other works. Spruill summarizes its basic message, which will serve as an example of the kinds of behavior and attitude expected of a lady. The underlying principle is that masculine and feminine virtues were divinely ordained, therefore natural and not open to negotiation. What is "comely for the one Sex, . . . often is not (at least in the same degree) for the other" (quoted in Spruill 1972:214). Modesty, meekness, compassion, affability, and piety are the feminine virtues. "Modesty as opposed to wantonness was presented as 'the most indispensable requisite of a woman; a thing so essential and so natural to the sex, that even the least declination from it, is proportionate receding from Womanhood'" (Spruill 1972:214). A wife's primary duty of obedience to her husband, according to these manuals, is required both because of marriage vows and because of Eve's disobedience (1972:215). The ideological appeal to both the natural and the supernatural is clear. By establishing "common sense" through appeal to such authority, both history and the possibility of change are denied: women are frozen into their duties (see Weedon 1987:1ff.).

The stages of a woman's life—that is, maid, wife, and widow—described in various "ladies' books" make it clear that marriage was to be the most important event in that life (Browne 1987:30ff.). In eighteenth-century literature women are discussed in relation to men and are defined by those relationships. Many of the eighteenth-century arguments made on behalf of women's education constitute an "instrumental feminism"; that is to say, the result of bettering women's education would be to improve men's lives (Browne 1987:5). In 1710 Sir Richard Steele proposed a "Female Library" to provide women with "reflections and sentiments proper for the companions of reasonable men" (Spruill 1972:213). The argument was also made that better-educated women would be able to better educate their children, thus benefiting society as a whole. Although women's equality before God was argued with the aphorism "there is no sex in souls," any difference between men and women were interpreted, at least by men, as signs of women's inferiority (Browne 1987:4).

The rules, restrictions, and expectations placed on women were both specific and general. Such rules and the proliferation of rule books and guides for behavior reflect a social structure in constant need of re-creation. One of Henry Glassie's insights about architecture serves as an illustration of an analogous process. He writes: "The existence of plans is an indication of cultural weakening. The amount of detail in a plan is an exact measure of the degree of cultural disharmony" (Glassie 1987:234). The creation of guidebooks to teach women how to be women indicates that the expectations held for women were not deeply embedded enough to be unquestioned; rather, they were often questioned, if not effectively challenged. Shackel (1993) argues similarly in reference to the proliferation of etiquette books in general from the sixteenth through the eighteenth centuries: as social relationships altered, specific rules for behavior changed and the need for etiquette books to enumerate the rules increased.

There has been a great deal of debate in anthropology over the universality of women's subordination (for an overview, see Morgen 1989a). Although apologists for male superiority often have appealed to natural law and to supernatural decree in insisting that women were inferior to men, the gender hierarchy in place in the eighteenth-century Anglo-American world was not universal in time and place. Gender ideologies develop and change along with other cultural constructs, influenced by and influencing political structures, religious authority, scientific epistemology, economic systems, and social organization.

Joan Kelly-Gadol (1987) argues that the new etiquette and the changing gender ideology were related to changing political power and other ideologies. In the early modern period, monarchies were centralizing power and resisting feudal attempts at maintaining power. The new etiquette, exemplified in books like Castiglione's *The Courtier* (1528), created a way of life and a code for behavior that gave a sense of self-determination to the nobility who had lost economic and political control. The theme of both Castiglione and the new etiquette as a whole was that detachment allowed men to maintain a sense of self, which was threatened by the loss of independent power. The courtier renounced the power of self-determination, being pleased and humble in the presence of his lord. To make up for such loss of power, the political order of servant and lord was transferred to gender ideology. In seventeenth-century guidebooks, often written for women, the role of obedient servant is made explicit for a wife who must submit to the will of her husband (Kelly-Gadol 1987:194ff.).

Evelyn Fox Keller (1985:63) suggests that the scientific revolution responded to and supported the polarization of gender that was required by developing industrial capitalism. As both scientist and feminist, Keller analyzes natural science and its emergence. She focuses on the dynamic that supports a conjunction of science and masculinity and a disjunction between science and femininity. Tracing the associations of male with objectivity, reason, and mind and of female with subjectivity, feeling, and nature is valuable in understanding some relationships between gender ideology and the development of Western science, which functions as a dominant mode of expression in Western culture and authority.

The Enlightenment in eighteenth-century Western thought established the male individual as both the source and purpose of knowledge (Fox-Genovese 1987). The precepts of the scientific revolution of the seventeenth century were brought to bear on society and the rights of man. According to Anderson and Zinsser, "Enlightenment thinkers questioned all the traditional limits on men—and indeed challenged the validity of tradition itself. They championed the rights of commoners, the rights of citizens, the rights of slaves, Jews, Indians, and children, but not those of women" (1988:113). Although the European salons, the sites of much discussion and philosophical debate that crystallized Enlightenment thinking, were frequently sponsored by women, male participants in the salons often explicitly denied women any proper role outside of the domestic life (Anderson and Zinsser 1988:117).

The eighteenth century witnessed a great many changes in Western culture and society: the political upheavals of the American and French revolutions, technological changes of the industrial revolution, and cultural developments in worldview, ideology, and social relationships. Historical archaeologists refer to these changes as the developing Georgian worldview, which Deetz (1977) tied to material culture evidence. This shift in male worldview from valuing community to valuing the individual can be identified in most domains of material culture, including archaeologically discernible artifacts such as architecture and equipment for serving meals. The shift is seen as incorporating increasing segmentation, separation, and standardization. Deetz (1977, 1988) suggests that the communal::individual, public::private (implicitly involving female::male) shift in worldview was tied to the eighteenth-century "Age of Reason," embedded in the Renaissance. Leone (for example, 1988) suggests an emerging culture of capitalism was responsible for the observed changes: the "Georgian" individual was created as a wage laborer through the segmentation of time, of work from domestic life, of space, and of social position through adherence to particular rules of behavior. The separation of people from each other and the segmentation of their work supports part of the social relationship necessary for capitalism to develop and thrive. Gender ideology is an essential element in the development of capitalism, which demanded a rigid distinction between domestic labor and labor in the workplace (Moore 1988: 53). Eighteenth-century gender ideology relied on religious authority, scientific authority, and natural law. Both custom and the legal code enforced the ideology (see, for example, Salmon 1986).

Anne Catharine Green

There is not a great deal of historical documentation that explicitly concerns the lives of middle-class and working-class women in the Chesapeake. Anne Catharine Green, however, is visible in the colonial newspaper, first in the advertisements and then as its printer. She appears intermittently in official documents. A few glimpses of her life are visible in her husband's activities. The probate inventory of her estate survives. The material culture most clearly associated with her consists of the imprints she produced and the things listed at probate. Although the archaeological assemblage reflects an entire household made up of individuals of different gender, age, and legal status, certain aspects of the record can be directly attributed to Anne Catharine Green.[3]

Anne Catharine Green and Jonas Green both sold merchandise at their home. Perhaps Anne Catharine was acting as *feme sole*—that is, independent from her husband—in her selling, but there is no supporting documentation. Advertisements for coffee, raisins, and chocolate that mention Anne Catharine Green specifically as the seller appear in the *Gazette* in 1746 and 1749. Ads for long London pipes, "European goods," medicine, nails, and molasses mention Jonas Green or the house of Jonas Green (implying that his wife could act as agent) in 1746, 1751, 1763, and 1765. Whether the sale of goods was as sporadic as the timing of the ads is unclear.

Anne Catharine Green is most visible in her role as printer because the *Maryland Gazette* and other imprints survive. Her role as a producer of such documentary artifacts is more visible than her role as a consumer of other craft or factory products. Jonas Green had started the weekly newspaper in 1745 and it was continued by his heirs with little interruption until 1839. I have argued elsewhere (Little 1987, 1988) that characteristics of the *Gazette* layout and grammatical content indicate the increasing order and segmentation an archaeologist expects of eighteenth-century material culture. During the relatively short span of time that Anne Catharine published the newspaper (April 1767–March 1775), the general trend toward standardization continued. However, her hand is apparent in the design of the front page and in the newspaper content. She revived a form of decorative embellishment surrounding the first letter of an issue. The embellishment, which first appears in November 1767, is for a time varied in nearly every issue and occasionally disappears. The design of the embellishment itself becomes standardized early in 1769.

Aubrey Land observes that after Anne Catharine and her sons took over the press, it "thereafter seemed even more identified with the country interest" (Land 1981: 260). She reprinted all the installments of the John Dickinson's "Letters of a Pennsylvania Farmer" and printed Boston letters and the Boston "Journal of Occurrences."

Opposition to the Townshend Acts was clear. Demeter summarizes his view of Anne Catharine's press: "Mrs. Green [transferred] the Gazette into a chronicle of intercolonial events and a propaganda organ for the patriot cause. In doing so, of course, the widow served as midwife to an aroused American political consciousness" (Demeter 1979:97).

Aside from the *Maryland Gazette*, Anne Catharine, either alone or with one of her sons, printed a yearly almanac, annual editions of the Laws of Maryland and the Votes and Proceedings of the Assembly, the Acts of Assembly, and the Bylaws of Annapolis. She also printed political pamphlets and broadsides and miscellaneous items both for the provincial government and for individuals. The printer's colophon of the *Gazette* advertised further work:

> At same Place may be had, ready Printed, most kinds of BLANKS, viz, COMMON and BAIL BONDS; TESTAMENTARY LETTERS of several sorts, with their proper BONDS annexed; BILLS of EXCHANGE; SHIPPING-BILLS, &c, &c. All Manner of PRINTING-WORK performed in the neatest and most expeditious Manner, on applying as above.

There are also documentary clues to some of the social roles played by Anne Catharine Green. As wife to Jonas Green her duties consisted of more than the "conjugal affection" referred to in her obituary. She was also mistress of their household, providing the social support necessary for Jonas's social endeavors. A look at the minutes of the Tuesday Club provide hints about women's roles in Annapolis society.

The Tuesday Club was a gentlemen's social club in Annapolis that was started by 1745 and continued to meet until 1756. Dr. Alexander Hamilton founded the club to provide a place for social interaction in the sort of (all-male) institution familiar to him in his native Scotland (Breslaw 1988:xiii). There were a dozen regular members and at least 150 visitors during the life of the club. A wide range of occupations and social standings were represented. Breslaw (1988:xxiii–xxvi) points out that the Tuesday Club used humor to cross class boundaries and to create social mobility and acceptance. One purpose of the club was to satirize social conventions, always done in a humorous and therefore supposedly inoffensive, but still effective, manner (Breslaw 1988:7).

Jonas Green applied for membership and was invited to join in February 1748. He was an active participant, known by the appellation P.P.P.P.P., which stood for Poet, Printer, Punster, Purveyor, and Punchmaker General. Meetings were held at members' houses on a rotating basis. The host was to entertain the club, providing "vittles."

It is reasonable to surmise that Anne Catharine Green provided the food for the meetings that were held in her house: the minutes of the club hint that wives did so. Initially, bachelors were permitted to host the meetings, but during the fifth meeting of the club the members agreed to Law VI: "That Such as are Batchellor members of this Society May be permitted to have a cheese, Instead of dressed vittles" (Breslaw 1988:7). By July the group resolved that "cheese is not any more to be deemed a dish of vittles," and its use was forbidden (1988:10). There was even a proposal that no more "batchellors" be admitted to the club (1988:13). Wives themselves or wives directing servants were apparently the providers of the food essential for the weekly meetings.

No women were recorded as members or visitors in the Tuesday Club minutes. However, some women witnessed at least part of club meetings. The men's toast "to the ladies" immediately after supper was established as a law of the club. Although there is no indication whether the toast is made to ladies present, absent, or about to depart, a humorous petition to the club's president from a group of single women in the city makes it clear that they have at least heard the toast. Some of the Tuesday Club cartoons also make apparent the often public nature of the meetings, suggesting that while the club's members were men, the club's activities were neither isolated nor secret from household members, other onlookers, or passers-by.

Records of the Tuesday Club provide more insight into class relations and the renegotiation of hierarchy than into women's roles, but they do provide some insight into the gender ideology behind a men's social club. Relationships among entertaining, the new etiquette, Enlightenment values, and social and political negotiation may hold some indications of the centrality of gender relationships. Proper courtesy and manners and correct behavior were needed in any social situation. After a 1795 trip, the writer Mary Wollstonecraft observed: "The women seem to take the lead in polishing the manners everywhere, that being the only way to better their condition" (quoted in Anderson and Zissner 1988:110). Although Wollstonecraft was referring to European women, colonial women probably also tried to adapt changing rules of behavior to their advantage.

The new etiquette required that particular forms of material culture be used in particular ways. Shackel (1993) has discussed at length such requisite material culture and its archaeological evidence. Little and Shackel (1989) use archaeological and probate data from the Green family house to compare etiquette items among Annapolis wealth groups. There is evidence that Jonas and Anne Catharine Green owned only a few of the dining items of the new etiquette; compared to their son Frederick, they owned very few (Little 1987:137). It is possible that Anne Catharine Green was using the new etiquette to her advantage in social situations at home, but the archaeological evidence for this is vague at best. She and her husband seem to rely on "old-fashioned" displays of expensive items, particularly porcelain, to convey their desired status, rather than on the use of the new etiquette.

Probate inventories are one source of data that specifically associate material culture with gender. The inventories of Jonas Green in 1767 and of Anne Catharine Green in 1775 suggest one possible relationship between gender and material culture. As one might expect, the items in each probate are largely the same. Acquired while Jonas was head of household and within a legal system wherein husbands were expected to be responsible for purchases (Salmon 1986:41ff.), most of the items listed have little to say directly about Anne Catharine's choices. Anne Catharine has some items Jonas does not, but fewer items overall. The point in comparing inventories, then, is not to identify particular items with the gender of the head of household. Instead, I want to raise a question about the organization of the items within the house and shop. I suggest that while Jonas was alive material was organized in a way we would recognize as more "orderly" in the Georgian sense. Anne Catharine rearranged material to reflect a different set of values, one in which domestic labor and craft labor were not entirely separated. My reading of the probate inventories is admittedly impressionistic and is intended to encourage further such comparisons.

When Jonas Green died in 1767 he left an estate of personal property reported in probate to be worth £376.10.6 (Anne Arundel County, 1767). If adjusted to 1700 money in a standard devised by Carr and Walsh (1980), the worth of the estate is £255.43. This adjustment puts Jonas Green in the second highest of four wealth groups in the city (see Russo 1983). The possessions and their organization indicate something of the degree to which the new eighteenth-century ideas of rationality and order were being followed. Knowing that an assessor would proceed room by room and building by building, whether or not those rooms and buildings were specified, allows us to gain an impression of the order of the rooms. Judging from the types of material listed, the inventory begins in the library/study, moves to the pantry, the office, bedrooms and kitchen, then moves to outbuildings, stable, lumbershed, and storage, before ending up in the print shop itself. (see the appendix).

Several items are particularly interesting. One is an "electrical wheel and some apparatus" and another is an eight-day clock in the printing office. Both are artifacts of eighteenth-century modernization. The electrical wheel, along with glass tubes and burning glasses, implies an interest in science, in rationalizing nature. The scientific revolution was appreciated in the colonies, encouraged notably by Benjamin Franklin (Jonas Green's former employer) and by the traveling lecturers who spread the word of Franklin's inventions and experiments (see Hare 1963). The clock in the workshop is expected by the modern mind, but time discipline was not always part of the workplace. The creation of commodified time and the replacement of task-oriented time are part of the system that makes wage labor and capitalism work. In a classic article E. P. Thompson (1967) explains how commodified time came to control workers and their output when the factory system started.

Anne Catharine Green's estate had a value of £304.1.10, adjusted to a 1700 value of £196.64 (Anne Arundel County 1775). This value places her estate in the second lowest wealth group. Comparing her inventory with that of her husband suggests that Anne Catharine was less concerned with separating domestic life from business life. While Jonas Green apparently kept all printing and bookbinding material in the shop and kept a separate office for himself, Anne Catharine rearranged the printing material, keeping paper and tools in the house rather than in the shop. The eight-day clock was moved out of the print shop. A bookstand, printing paper, and some imprints were listed among kitchenwares and ceramics. The bookbinders press was moved out of the shop and into the house. The order and function of the rooms in the inventory are more difficult to summarize since the items one expects in each is "disordered," but the order seems to be sitting/dining, bedroom, pantry, kitchen, printing office, bedroom, print shop (appendix). I suggest that a domestic task orientation rather than a wage-labor time orientation guided Anne Catharine's workplaces.

The sequence of building of the Greens' house and shop also indicates a changing configuration of space and suggests that while Anne Catharine was head of the household she rearranged more than objects. While Jonas was alive, the house and shop were remodeled several times (Little 1987:178–186). By his death in 1767 there stood a house with a two-story kitchen possibly connected by a ground floor passageway and a separate print shop. Jonas Green himself stated that the shop was completely unconnected to the house. He wrote so in the newspaper (*Maryland Gazette*, December 12, 1756), trying to allay fears of contagion during a small pox epidemic after one of his children died of the disease.

During her tenure as head of household from 1767 to 1775, Anne Catharine built a rather wide hyphen with its own fireplace to connect the southern el of the house with the shop. Creamware, present in the builders' trench for the hyphen, was almost certainly not available to Jonas (see chapter 11), although it was to Anne Catharine. The probate listings of ceramics are too general to document ownership of such items. However, the probates otherwise support Anne Catharine's building. Jonas Green's probate lists "2000 feet of very indiff plank . . . 7500 cypress singles . . . and 500 clapboards," whereas Anne Catharine Green's lists only "a small parcel of planks . . . a parcel of lumber." Whether Jonas himself was planning to reconnect house and shop or to build something else on the property is open to question. Frederick Green almost certainly removed the hyphen as part of his remodeling. The enlarged house and the shop were again separate buildings perhaps by the end of the century, although the 1798 tax record is ambiguous. Thus, Anne Catharine Green, in contrast to her husband and probably her son, chose literally to reconnect the domestic and work domains.

Muted Groups and Everyday Resistance

Moore (1988) suggests that some ideas of Edwin Ardener (1975a, 1975b) and James Scott (1985) may be useful in understanding women and gender relationships in male-dominated societies. Combining their ideas of muted groups and everyday resistance helps interpret Anne Catharine Green's choices and actions.

Ardener's notion of muted groups can apply to any subordinate group. Dominant groups generate and control the dominant modes of expression, through which subordinate groups must express themselves. An example of a dominant mode of expression is the mechanical model of science, mentioned above, which judges what is real and rational and what is absurd. Muted groups remain so because their models of reality and worldview cannot be expressed adequately through the modes and ideologies accepted by dominant groups. Mutedness is a result of the relations of dominance that inhibit the expression of alternative models.

Scott (1985) has studied protest and resistance embedded in all class relations and found everyday resistance pervasive: in "foot dragging, dissimulation, false compliance, pilfering, feigned ignorance, slander, arson, sabotage, and so forth" (Scott 1985:29). Peasant resistance is understood as a subordinate class of people "working the system . . . to their minimum disadvantage" (Hobsbaum quoted in Scott 1985:xv). The disadvantage is largely taken for granted because subordinate groups have little power with which to make any effective challenge to dominant groups. The "everyday forms of resistance" provide a way of approaching forms of protest embedded in gender relations (Moore 1988:181).

Muted groups that resist the dominant ideology must express themselves in ways they perceive to be effective but not dangerous. If muted, then groups may express themselves in alternative media, for example, through particular choices or uses of material culture, distinct rules of etiquette, or religion. Or they may refuse the dominant modes of expression by refusing to understand them. Mechal Sobel provides some telling illustrations. She notes that "members of the [Virginia] elite often found that their wives and children did not share their preoccupation with redeeming time" (Sobel 1987:65). William Byrd II accused his first wife, Lucy, "of not living up to 'proper' norms, of being negligent and disorganized, and of not 'improving' her time as he sought to improve his own" (Sobel 1987:65).

Members of another subordinate group in the English colonies, African Americans, were also resisting white, male ways. In Maryland in 1736 Edward Kimber observed that if "a new negro . . . must be broke . . . You would really be surpriz'd at their Perseverance; let an hundred men shew him how to hoe, or drive a Wheelbarrow, he'll still take the one by the Bottom, and the Other by the Wheel" (in Sobel 1987:47).

Sobel's work and its antecedents provide a useful analogy for a study of historic gender relationships. Eugene Genovese followed *The World the Slaveholders Made*

(1971) with *Roll, Jordan, Roll, the World the Slaves Made* (1974). The titles make the orientation of each work clear. In *The World They Made Together, Black and White Values in Eighteenth-Century Virginia*, Sobel argues that blacks and whites mutually created a distinctly new culture. Contributions by gender may be similarly assessed. Those made by men and women may be separated or they may be combined effectively to produce a holistic vision of history. Drawing a parallel between the historical archaeology of women and of African Americans serves both to imply wider issues of gender relationships and racial relationships and, within the context of those wider issues, to point out some shortfalls to avoid. One problem is false homogeneity. Another is mistaken analogy. The notion of "difference" is essential to addressing these problems.

In feminist thought, "difference" originally implied the difference between men and women and their experiences. Variability within women's experience quickly became apparent, particularly within anthropology. Race, ethnicity, nationality, and class all contribute to the variability (see, for example, Meese and Parker 1989). This now self-evident difference within gender (or difference within race) was initially not apparent because of our own gender ideology, which made women a peripheral and nonreducible category. Feminist historians have noted the polarization of the "universal" man and the "particular" woman. For example, Joan Scott (1989) documents the white male archetypical actor as the universal signifier. Women, and nonwhites, are marginalized and trivialized as particular instances peripheral to the experience of "everyman," who is worthy of history (his-story). Difference is both denied and recognized in such history—denied by refusing a different history and recognized by marginalizing other experience as irrelevant to the mainstream (Scott 1989:98). The universal man crept into expectations about universal woman (and others). Spector and Whelan (1989) stress that the deconstruction of the ideal of universal man and particular woman is essential to creating appropriate concepts for gender in archaeology.

The notion of difference allows false analogies to be exposed. Within the category of "women," difference allows class, race, and other categorizations to enter into the analysis. It is essential to understand that one woman's set of expensive china may indicate something about her economic status in relation to other women, but nothing about her status as a woman in relation to men of any class. It must be clear that an interpretation of gender relations relies as well on understanding something of group relations.

Muted groups have little choice but to express themselves through dominant groups' ideology and modes of expression or risk ostracism, condemnation, or belittlement by embracing their own. They have had little chance to be understood except through dominant modes of expression. Analyzing subordinate groups by means of mistaken analogies to dominant groups leads to the kind of analysis that Leone and Potter find "oddly apolitical" (1988:307–312). Discussing African American archaeology, they point out that some scholars can write about slaves' "quality of life" on the basis of the initial cost and presumed status of their material culture without considering past and present political implications. As archaeologists we need to understand social, economic, legal, political, and religious structures before we can understand anything about the material conditions of slavery or plantation life. "Quality of life" cannot be divorced from social constructs and judged on an entire context. The "cost" of products used by slaves is not the same cost as the "cost" of objects used by free people. The analogy of using one to understand the other is mistaken. Observing the "same" objects in very different cultural contexts should signal an anomaly rather than an analogy.

Archaeologists do not often set out to do an "archaeology of men" or of "whites." It is tacitly understood that social reality defies such simplistic and encompassing conceptualization. The same understanding must be applied to an archaeology of women, African Americans, and other groups so that such categories may be deconstructed and treated as nontrivial and nontoken. We currently may have an "archaeology of men," but that is due to the interpretive constructs we apply rather than to the material we excavate. Feminist archaeology is not about finding women's things or men's things documented in the ground but about exploring complicated gender relationships and gender ideology to understand how categories and therefore material culture are constructed, imagined, and represented (see, for example, Conkey 1991).

Discussion

The pieces known of Anne Catharine Green's life and of her times serve as one vantage point from which to view a feminist historical archaeology. That archaeology is constructed by examining the gender ideology and gender roles with which she lived and her visibility as a member of a muted group. Anne Catharine Green is not "everywoman." Nor is she to be marginalized as one particular, idiosyncratic case.

I presume that Anne Catharine Green was aware of the etiquette and the tools of etiquette expected of her gender and her class. The proliferation of manuals that sought to teach women their "natural" roles and attributes is an indication that gender roles and ideology were changing and were challenged. The dominant viewpoint in such behavioral guides is a male viewpoint. Guidebooks were not only aimed at women, they also functioned to separate classes. The new etiquette, which was developed and was adopted over a few centuries in Europe and its colonies, was inextricably intertwined with the developing cultures of capitalism. Gender ideology, which polarized men and women and separates women's domestic work from men's public work, was embedded in developing capitalism and its emergent two-tier economy. The development of the culture of capitalism and its attendant gender ideology was aided by religious cosmology and scientific epistemology, that is, by the prevailing attitudes toward understanding both the supernatural and the natural world.

The domestic role of women is clear in the life of Anne Catharine Green: she was a mother and a wife and she directed a household. The domestic sphere was not entirely separate from the nondomestic. Her supporting role in her husband's social endeavors was both domestic and public. She was also an artisan, supplying both the government and individuals. Her public role as a newspaper editor and publisher would have been important even in times that were not as politically volatile as the revolutionary era in the colonies. Those roles, however, were not necessarily acknowledged. They were something other than what a woman would do as a woman. The obituary written by Frederick Green makes this point. Anne Catharine is emphasized as relict of the printer to the province, not as a printer in her own right. She is an example to her sex because of her roles as wife and mother. Her "atypical" roles were made less visible by her contemporaries because they did not fit the emerging model of women's roles.

Because muted groups operate within a society that gives them little means of expression, it is difficult to discover their muted voices. For the most part, Anne Catharine Green followed the dominant mode of expression in her printing by continuing the newspaper's trend of standardization and segmentation. She did, however, revive an element of layout design in her embellishment of the initial letter, and she freely varied it for a year before standardizing the design. In the organization of her household after the death of her husband, Anne Catharine Green rearranged material to reflect her roles and perhaps a set of values rejected by the emerging dominant ideology. She physically reconnected domestic space and craft space. Craft and domestic items were not completely separated and the timepiece was removed from the print shop itself. Domestic labor was not separated from craft labor and task orientation was not replaced by a labor based on commodified time.

Such data add to a growing literature on the uses and organization of space by women and men (Ardener 1981; Moore 1986; Conkey 1991; Hastorf 1991; Tringham 1991).[4] The "social maps" (Ardener 1981) that begin to emerge allow archaeologists to see the varying coping strategies of men and women. Such possible expressions of different organization imply different values and worldviews. Kelly-Gadol's (1987) classic question, "Did women have a Renaissance?" emphasizes that women's historical experience, and the characterization of that experience, may be different from men's. The periods and developments deserving historical aggrandizement from a male point of view may not be those that would be important from a female point of view. A different history does not suggest a subordinate history, as separate spheres of responsibility do not necessitate one's subordination. A different history does not suggest a history that lagged behind or resisted "progress." A different history is not separate except insofar as it is separated artificially thorough historiography.

Gender and gender relationships are culturally constructed. Material culture provides a stage and a medium for expressing and learning cultural constructions. The possibilities for a feminist historical archaeology rely on recognizing and understanding the material culture and other expressions of muted groups within a dominant ideology. The archaeology of other muted groups such as African Americans is useful for creating appropriate concepts and for avoiding concepts and analogies that do not work. False homogeneity and misleading analogies to conditions of the dominant group need to be replaced by a recognition of "difference" and appropriate analogies based on complete cultural context.

Acknowledgments

The archaeological work at the Green house in Annapolis (18AP29) was carried out through the Archaeology in Annapolis project, sponsored by the University of Maryland and Historic Annapolis Foundation. I thank Paul Shackel and Paul Mullins for comments made on earlier drafts of this chapter, even if I did not always follow their good advice. Thanks also to Lois Carr for her encouragement in raising the question of gender differences using the probate data, in spite of the problems. Thanks to Alison Wylie, Mark Leone, Ed Heite and others for their interest in this work. And special thanks to the current owners of the property, R. R. and M. D. Brown, for generous permission to excavate on their property, and to M. D. Brown for sharing her research on the Green family.

Notes

1. M. D. Brown (1989), citing Randall (1984), comments that such early birth was not uncommon for the times and is likely to have been a result of planning, as proving one's fertility was important in the underpopulated colonies.

2. Between the writing of this chapter and its publication, at least three major publications on gender and archaeology have been published (Claassen 1992; Seifert 1991; Walde and Willows 1991).

3. Although there is potential for discussing public and private ceramics and their gender associations and meanings (Yentsch 1991), the vessels that may be attributed to either Anne Catharine Green or Jonas Green are too few to permit an analysis of changing gender roles.

4. Hastorf (1991) calls to attention the gender-related organization of space in modern Andean households. She cites Sikkink's (1988) work, which describes a different use of space between households with both male and female adults and those with only a female head of household. The interpretation that fewer constraints are placed on a woman who has no male counterpart in the household is certainly applicable to the case of Anne Catharine Green.

References Cited

Anderson, Bonnie S., and Judith P. Zinsser
1988 *A History of Their Own; Women in Europe from Prehistory to the Present*. Vol. 2. Harper and Row, New York.

Anne Arundel County
1767 Probate Inventories at the Maryland Hall of Records, Annapolis. Vol. 94, fol. 161; Box 74, folder 31.
1775 Probate Inventories at the Maryland Hall of Records, Annapolis. Vol. 119, fol. 344.

Ardener, Edwin
1975a Belief and the Problem of Women. In *Perceiving Women*, edited by S. Ardener, pp. 1–17. Dent, London.
1975b Belief and the Problem of Women Revisited. In *Perceiving Women*, edited by S. Ardener, pp. 19–27. Dent, London.

Ardener, Shirley (editor)
1981 *Women and Space, Ground Rules and Social Maps*. St. Martin's Press, New York.

Best, Michael R. (editor)
1986 *The English Housewife*, Gervase Markham (1568?–1637). McGill– Queen's University Press, Kingston and Montreal. Originally published 1615.

Breslaw, Elaine G. (editor)
1988 *Records of the Tuesday Club of Annapolis 1745–56*. University of Illinois Press, Urbana.

Brown, M. D.
1989 A Descriptive History of a House and Its Family. Unpublished manuscript.

Browne, Alice
1987 *The Eighteenth-Century Feminist Mind*. Harvester Press, Brighton, Sussex.

Carr, Lois Green, and Lorena S. Walsh
1980 Inventories and the Analysis of Wealth and Consumption Patterns in St. Mary's County, Maryland 1658–1777. *Historical Methods* 13:2:81–104.

Claasen, Cheryl (editor)
1992 *Exploring Gender through Archaeology, Selected Papers from the 1991 Boone Conference*. Monographs in World Archaeology, No. 11. Prehistory Press, Madison, Wisc.

Conkey, Margaret
1991 Contexts of Action, Contexts for Power: Material Culture and Gender in the Magdelenian. In *Engendering Archaeology, Women and Prehistory*, edited by J. M. Gero and M. W.Conkey, pp. 57–92. Basil Blackwell, Oxford.

Conkey, Margaret, and Joan Gero
1988 Towards Building a Feminist Archaeology. Paper presented at 53rd annual meetings, Society for American Archaeology, Phoenix, Ariz.

Conkey, Margaret, and Janet Spector
1984 Archaeology and the Study of Gender. *Advances in Archaeological Method and Theory* 7:1–38.

Deetz, James
1977 *In Small Things Forgotten*. Doubleday, New York.
1983 Scientific Humanism and Humanistic Science: A Plea for Paradigmatic Pluralism in Historical Archaeology. *Geoscience and Man* 23:27–34.

Demeter, Richard L.
1979 *Primers, Presses and Composing Sticks. Women Printers of the Colonial Period*. Exposition Press, Hicksville, N.Y.

Fox-Genovese, Elizabeth
1987 Women and the Enlightenment. In *Becoming Visible, Women in European History*, 2d ed., edited by R. Bridenthal, C. Koonz, and S. Stuard, pp. 252–277. Houghton Mifflin, Boston.

Genovese, Eugene D.
1971 *The World the Slaveholders Made*. Vintage Books, New York.
1974 *Roll, Jordan, Roll: the World the Slaves Made*. Pantheon Press, New York.

Gero, Joan M., and Margaret W. Conkey (editors)
1991 *Engendering Archaeology, Women and Prehistory*. Basil Blackwell, Oxford.

Glassie, Henry
1987 Vernacular Architecture and Society. In *Mirror and Metaphor, Material and Social Constructions of Reality*, edited by D. Ingersoll and G. Bronitsky, pp. 229–246. University Press of America, Lanham, Md.

Hare, R. R.
1963 Electri Vitrifrico Visits the Tuesday Club. *Maryland Historical Magazine* 58:1:62.

Hastorf, Christine A.
1991 Gender, Space and Food in Prehistory. In *Engendering Archaeology, Women and Prehistory*, edited by J. M. Gero and M. W. Conkey, pp. 132–159. Basil Blackwell, Oxford.

Keller, Evelyn Fox
1985 *Reflections on Gender and Science*. Yale University Press, New Haven, Conn.

Kelly-Gadol, Joan
1987 Did Women Have a Renaissance? In *Becoming Visible, Women in European History*, 2d ed., edited by R. Bridenthal, C. Koonz, and S. Stuard, pp. 175–201. Houghton Mifflin, Boston.

Labaree, L. W., R. L. Ketchum, H. C. Boatfield, and H. H. Fineman (editors)
1964 *The Autobiography of Benjamin Franklin*. Yale University Press, New Haven, Conn.

Land, Aubrey
1981 *Colonial Maryland, A History*. KTO Press, Millwood, N.Y.

Leone, Mark P.
1988 The Georgian Order as the Order of Merchant Capitalism in Annapolis, Maryland. In *The Recovery of Meaning: Historical Archaeology in the Eastern United States*, edited by M. P. Leone and P. B. Potter, Jr., pp. 235–261. Smithsonian Institution Press, Washington, D.C.

Leone, Mark P. and Parker B. Potter, Jr.
1988 Introduction: Issues in Historical Archaeology. In *The Recovery of Meaning: Historical Archaeology in the Eastern United States*, edited by M. P. Leone and P. B. Potter, Jr., pp. 1–22. Smithsonian Institution Press, Washington, D.C.

Little, Barbara J.
1987 *Ideology and Media: Historical Archaeology of Printing in 18th-Century Annapolis, Maryland*. Ph. D. dissertation, State University of New York at Buffalo, Department of Anthropology. University Microfilms, Ann Arbor.
1988 Craft and culture change in the 18th-century Chesapeake. In *The Recovery of Meaning: Historical Archaeology in the Eastern United States*, edited by M. P. Leone and P. B. Potter, Jr., pp. 263–292. Smithsonian Institution Press, Washington, D.C.

Little, Barbara J., and Paul A. Shackel
1989 Scales of Historical Anthropology: An Archaeology of Colonial Anglo-America. *Antiquity* 63:240:495–509.

Meese, Elizabeth, and Alice Parker
1989 "Grins . . . without the Cat": Introductory Remarks on "The Difference Within." In *The Difference Within: Feminism and Critical Theory*, edited by E. Meese and A. Parker, pp. 1–12. John Benjamin, Amsterdam/ Philadelphia.

Moore, Henrietta L.
1986 *Space, Text and Gender: An Anthropological Study of the Marakwet of Kenya*. Cambridge University Press, Cambridge.
1988 *Feminism and Anthropology*. University of Minnesota Press, Minneapolis.

Morgen, Sandra
1989a Gender and Anthropology: Introductory Essay. In *Gender and Anthropology, Critical Reviews for Research and Teaching*, edited by S. Morgen, pp. 1–20. American Anthropological Association, Washington, D.C.
1989b (editor) *Gender and anthropology, critical reviews for research and teaching*, pp. 1–20. American Anthropological Association, Washington, D.C.

Randall, Katharine
1984 Those Early Firstborns of Eighteenth Century America: Moral Lapses or Planned Parenthood? *New York Genealogical and Biographical Record* April:79–87.

Russo, Jean
1983 The Structure of the Anne Arundel County Economy. In Annapolis and Anne Arundel County, Maryland: A Study of Urban Development in a Tobacco Economy 1649–1776, edited by L. Walsh. NEH Report RS-20199– 1955.

Salmon, Marylynn
1986 *Women and the Law of Property in Early America*. University of North Carolina Press, Chapel Hill.

Scott, James C.
1985 *Weapons of the Weak, The Everyday Forms of Peasant Resistance*. Yale University Press, New Haven, Conn.

Scott, Joan W.
1989 History and Difference. In *Learning about Women; Gender,Politics, and Power*, edited by J. K. Conway, S. C.

Bourque, and J. W. Scott, pp. 93–118. University of Michigan Press, Ann Arbor.
Seifert, Donna J. (editor)
1991 Gender in Historical Archaeology. *Historical Archaeology* 25(4).
Shackel, Paul A.
1993 *Personal Discipline and Material Culture: An Archaeology of Annapolis, Maryland*, 1695–1870. University of Tennessee Press, Knoxville, Tenn.
Sikkink, Lynn
1988 Traditional Crop-Processing in Central Andean Households: An Ethnoarchaeological Approach. In *Multidisciplinary Studies in Andean Anthropology*, edited by V. J. Vizthum, pp. 65–87. Michigan Discussions in Anthropology No. 8. Ann Arbor.
Sobel, Mechal
1987 *The World They Made Together, Black and White Values in Eighteenth-Century Virginia*. Princeton University Press, Princeton, N.J.
Spector, Janet D., and Mary K. Whelan
1989 Incorporating Gender into Archaeology Courses. In *Gender and Anthropology, Critical Reviews for Research and Teaching*, edited by S. Morgen, pp. 65–94. American Anthropological Association, Washington, D.C.
Spruill, Julia Cherry
1972 *Women's Life and Work in the Southern Colonies*. W. W. Norton, New York. Originally published 1938.
Thomas, Isaiah
1970 *The History of Printing in America*. Weathervane Books, New York. Originally published 1810.
Thompson, E. P.
1967 Time, Work-Discipline, and Industrial Capitalism. *Past and Present* 38:56–97.
Tringham, Ruth E.
1991 Households with Faces: the Challenge of Gender in Prehistoric Architectural Remains. In *Engendering Archaeology, Women and Prehistory*, edited by J. M. Gero and M. W. Conkey, pp. 93–131. Basil Blackwell, Oxford.
Walde, Dale, and Noreen D. Willows (editors)
1991 *The Archaeology of Gender. Proceedings of the 22nd Annual Chacmool Conference*. Department of Archaeology, University of Calgary, Calgary, Alberta.
Weedon, Chris
1987 *Feminist Practice and Poststructuralist Theory*. Basil Blackwell, Oxford.
Yentsch, Anne
1991 The Symbolic Divisions of Pottery: Sex-related Attributes of English and Anglo-American Household Pots. In *The Archaeology of Inequality*, edited by R. H. McGuire and R. Paynter. Basil Blackwell, Oxford.

Appendix: Probate Inventories for Jonas Green and Anne Catharine Green

Jonas Green d. 1767

(Anne Arundel County; 1767 vol. 94, p. 161; Box 74, folder 31)

An Inventory of the Goods and Chattels belonging to the Estate of Jonas Green Deceased, appraised by us in Current Money being first duly Qualified for that Purpose Vizt

Sundry wearing apparrel	11. 5
1 Sword & Belt & 1 hangger & Belt	3. 2. 6
1 Silver Watch	3. 5. 0
1 large Walnut Oval Table	1.10. 0
1 Square Table	1. 0. 0
2 small Oval Tables	.10.
1 old Desk	1.15
1 Cherry tree Tea Table	1
1/2 doz. Black Walnut chairs	2. 8
1 arm'd Cherry Tree Ditto	.15.
2 Looking Glasses	3
6 old Maps, 3 Pictures & a Coat of Arms	.10.
1 small pine writing Desk & 1 Reading Frame	. 9.
2 old Tea Chests & Canisters	.15.
1 Set of China wanting 2 ps.	1.10
6 China Bowls	1.12
11 China Patty Pans	.12. 6
9 White China Cups & saucers	.10.
some old china & 1 teapot	.15.
1/2 doz Chocolate cups & saucers	.10.
2 small painted canisters & 4 glas Tumblers	4. 6
5 Decanters	. 8.
17 jelly glasses, 6 small glasses, 1 bucket glass, funnel glass candlestick	.19.
1 Glass tube, 1 hand glass, 1 magnifying glass (broke)	
3 Burning glasses	.10.
51oz 13d of old silver @ 6/6	16.15. 9
1 pr. gold sleeve Buttons	1. 5
5 Dollars, 2 English half crown, 1 P Portugal Silver	
15 Pens [?]	2.12. 8
1 Book Gold Leaf 2 Memorandum Books	3. 6
A Parcel of Books	9.10
1 Snuff Box, tin tobacco Box old knife & 2 ps Nipp	1. 6
1 wood candle screen & stand	3. 6
1 old Backgammon Table, Dice & Spooncase	12. 6
2 1/2 doz. stone & Delph Plates, 3 Dishes & 2 Tea Pots	.16.

A parcel of stone tea ware unsorted & 1 Lamp	5. 6
1 small Marble Mortar & Pistil	.10.
1 pr. Brass Scales & Weights & 1 pr. money Scales	1. 7. 6
2 pr Spoon Molds	.15.
a large tin canister	. 4.
3 1/2 [?] lb. Bohea Tea	.17. 6
1/4 lb Hyson Do & Canister	. 5.
14 lb coffee	.14.
4 lb [?] Chocolate	. 6.
1 Corner Cupboard	1.15.
19 dozn of bottles @ 2/9	2.12. 3
3 old Clothes Brushes, Hat Brush, hearth Brushes & chase ship [?]	. 5. 6
3 knife Boxes & a parcel of old knives & forks	. 8.
1 old Chest of Drawers & Black Dressing Glass	1. 5.
1 old close Stool chair & 2 pans	.15.
1 old case with 9 Bottles	. 2. 6
1 Bed Bedstead & Furniture	3. 5.
1 Ditto & Ditto	3. 5.
1 Bed press, Bedstead pr sheets & 2 old Bolsters	3.10
1 Bed, old Bedstead & Furniture	2.
1 Bed, Bedstead & Furniture	3.
1 small old Ditto & Do	1.10
1 childs Bed & Bolster	.12.
2 very old servants Beds & old Bedstead & some Furniture	.15.
1 suit of motheaten green curtains	1.
1 Rug & Gold Blankets	2.
6 old sheets	.15.
3 large Table Cloths & small Ditto	1. 6. 6
14 napkins & towels	.16.
6 old oznabrig towels & 5 ditto knife cloths	. 4.
1 old counterpain	.10.
3 cases with Bottles	3. 5
2 old pan Irons, 2 old chairs & a small pr tongs	7. 6
1 small Looking Glass & a gilt frame	2. 6
1 pine Desk	8
a small parcel of tools unsorted	6
a parcel of stone juggs & Butter Pots	1. 6. 0
1 meat sack [?] and weights	2.15. 0
3 old coffee Pots & 2 chafing Dishes	.15.
2 gridirons, 2 flesh forks & 2 or 3 skewers	. 8. 6
1 old warming Pan & 1 stew Pan	. 4.
2 old iron tea kettles & 2 old copper Do	.15.
3 spits, 1 Griddle & 1 trivit	. 9.
1 pr Bellows, old	. 2. 6
1 tin oven, apple Roaster, 9 tin Patty pans & 1 Bed Pan	.10.

1 pr. Hand Irons & 2 pr Tongs	2.
1 old Coffee Mill, Salt Box & 2 Rolling Pins	.11.
a Bell mettal Pestle & Mortar, broke	. 2. 6
15 pewter Candle Molds & stand	.12. 6
5 flat Irons & 1 Bread Toaster	.13.
1 old gratter, Candle Box, tin Pepper Box & 2 pr snuffers	. 1.
3 glass Salts & 1 glass Lanthon [?]	. 8. 6
1 old frying Pan & 3 pr. stilliards	.16.
6 Brass Candlesicks & stand for snuffers, old	.10.
6 old chairs, 1 arm'd Do, a stool & Clothes Horse	.12. 6
3 old Kitchen Tables	. 7. 6
1 pr Hand Irons Shovel & Tongs	1. 5.
3 pot Racks, Brass Skimmer & 1 cleaver	.19. 6
1 old safe & 1 Ditto for Meat	. 5.
1 old screen	. 7. 6
1 Bell mettal skillet	.16.
133 lb old hard mettal Pewter @ 1/3	8. 6. 3
123 of old common Do @ 9	4.12. 3
2 Iron Fenders & 2 tin Ditto	.14.
5 pr pott hooks & 2 old stills	1.13. 6
168 lb potmetal @3	2. 2. 0
a Mohogany Tea Board & 1 broken hand Board	.10.
1 old Copper kettle wt 48lb	2.
1 small old Brass Ditto	. 6.
145 Ells of oznabrigs @1	7. 5
12 yd blue linnen	.12
1 pattern of cloth for a suit & trimmings	7. 8
1 old chest, 1 old table & 2 chairs	.10.
1 small Looking glass	. 8.
1 small square table & 2 clothes chests	.17.
2 clothes Baskets	. 1.
1 old close stool & Pan	. 6.
a parcel of old wooken ware & some Pickle Bottles	.10.
1 very old Riding Chair & some Harness	1.10.
3 old Saddles & 2 Bridles	3.
1 little Hand Cart & 1 old wheel Barrow	. 7.
1 grind stone & 1 garden spade	.10. 6
2 pr small cast handirons, 1 shovel & 2 pr tongs & tin plate	.12. 6
1 Electrical wheel & some apparatus	.10.
5 old tables & 2 chairs	1. 5.
a small parcel of allum	. 1.
2000 feet of very indiff plank @4/6	4.10
7500 Cypress Shingles @ 14	5. 5.
500 Clapboards	2.
6 lb Bees wax	. 6.
2 soap jars	.15.
1 gallon Pot, broke, tin funnel & small Bason	. 7. 6
37/2 lb loaf sugar @10	1.11. 3

3/2 doub refine ditto	. 4.
27 gallons Rum @3	4. 1
197 lb bacon @ 4	3. 5. 8
10¾ of dry'd beef	. 2. 6
124 lb Hogs Lard @ 4	2. 1. 4
1 bag of Split pease 11 [?] Bushels Indian Pease	.19. 6
2 1/2 [?] Bushels of Beans & 4 Bushels of Corn	.16. 6
4 tin Boxes & a small Case of Pickle Bottles	.12.
a parcel of old Iron	. 8.
4 chamber pots	. 3. 6
1 large old Coffee Mill, out of Repair	. 3.
1 Remnant of silk	.15.
1 small Mare	2.
1 large chest	.10.
2 wine casks, 27-½ of lead	.13. 2
1 pr small Lottery wheels	1.
9½ Reams of Paper @ 15/	7. 2. 6
42 Reams of Gazette Paper @ 7-	14.14
30 Reams of Pot Paper @ 5/6	8. 5
a parcel of outside 2 wires of Paper, old votes [?] etc.	2.10.
a small Eight Day Clock	1.10.
2 old Printing Presses and a quantity of Printing materials, consisting of types calculated to be the Value of	90.14. 5
a parcel of old Binding materials	5. 3.
1 pr Bench vice, nippers & oyl stone	.10.
1 servant, Collin Malcolm, almost 2 years to serve	6.
1 ditto, Alexander Gordon, 5 years	12.
1 woman servant Margaret OBryans 5yrs 9mo Do	6.10.
16 lb Soap, 7 lb cotton in the seeds	.11.
3 Bottles, Turlington & some papers of jamess' Powders	.12. 6
2 Axes	. 8. 6
parcel old casks, lumber, etc.	1.12. 0
4 candle sconces & a Parcel of Jacket Buttons	0. 7. 6
	376.10. 6

[the under signing and oaths are ommitted here.]
Given under our Hand this 13th Day of July 1767

Rich Mackubin
Na Hammond

Kindred:

Wm Green
Rebecca Clapham
Oct 1st 1767 . . .

to wit came Anne Catharine Green, administrator of all and singular the Goods and Chattels of Jonas Green late of Anne Arundel County . . .

Anne Catharine Green d. 1775

(Anne Arundel County 1775 vol. 119, p. 344)

An Inventory of the goods and chattels belonging to the Estate of Anne Catharine Green, dec'd, appraised by us in current money being first duly qualified this 13 June 1775.

Sundry of the dec'd wearing apparrel	10. 0. 0
An old large oval table	1. 5
1 small square & 1 small Oval Table	0.15
12 Walnut Chairs leather bottoms	9. 0. 0
1 Armed Cherry tree Chair	0.15. 0
1 Large easy chair with Castors	1.10. 0
A Mahogany Cabinet	4. 0. 0
1 Old Desk	1. 5. 0
1 Large Looking Glass	2. 0. 0
A small 8-day clock	1. 0. 0
A Silver watch	3.
A Round tea table & 2 teaboards	1.
4 Pictures	0. 2. 0
A pr of hack irons, shovel, & tongs	1.
A hanger & a small sword	2. 5
An old desk & table	0.10
½ doz. chairs	3.12.
1 Bed, Bedstead, furniture, & a pr old curtains	7.10
1 Bed, Bedstead & furniture	3.
1 Bed, Bedstead & furniture	6.10. 0
1 small Bed, Bedstead & furniture	6. 0. 0
3 sheets, a blanket, & a rug	1.15. 0
1 looking glass, old & broke	0. 8. 0
1 Close stool Chair	0.10. 0
A small table, dressing glass & 2 old chairs	1.15. 0
237 lb single refined sugar @10	9.17. 6
157 lb brown sugar @4	2.12. 4
1 Marble pestle & Mortar	0.15. 0
11 Case Bottles	0. 7. 4
3 Old Chests, 2 old tables, & an old stand	1. 5. 0
An old meat Jack & 2 spits	1.10. 0
141 lb old pewter @[?]	7. 1
165 lb Hogslard @ 4	4. 8. 4
A pr. of hand irons, a shovel & 2 pr. tongs	2. 0. 0
2 old frying pans	0. 7. 6
2 old iton tea kettles & a copper do	1.
1 Bell Metal Skillet	0.12. 0
A flesh fork, ladle, skimmer, chafing dish, Grid iron, & 3 pr. pothooks	0.10. 0
A Coffee pott & 2 old candlesticks	0.10. 0
2 Flat Irons	0. 5.
1 Double Clothes horse	0.10. 0
209 lb pot metal @3	2.12. 3
7 old tubs & a Bread tray	0.10. 0

2 Stone pipkins	0. 4. 0
A dripping pan & knife box	0. 8. 0
A pr. of steelyards	0.15. 0
A large copper kettle	2.
A cross cut saw, wood saw, & 9 candle molds	0.16. 0
2 Pot Racks	0.12. 0
An old still	0.10. 0
A small parcel of plank & scantling [?]	2. 8. 0
An old brass kettle	0. 4. 0
1 pr. Lottery Wheels	1.
A bed pan	0. 8.
An old stew pan	0. 4.
An old leaden cooler	0. 6.
A parcel of tubs	0. 8.
A Cupboard Bedstead	2. 8. 0
An old bookstand	0. 1. 4
11 Reams Large Coarse paper	11. 0. 0
4 Reams Blue Paper	1.16.
A parcel of brown paper	0. 2. 0
A parcel of Laws & Votes & proceedings	4.
An old case & some bookbinders Utensils	0.16.
A pr. of old irondogs	0. 6.
Some volumes of the Gazette	2. 0. 0
A parcel of Blanks, Considerations, & part of the Treatise on Hemp	10. 8.
9 Tablecloths & 6 Napkins	9.
A Book, tea chest, and some paper	0. 4. 0
4 Papers Pins & Combs	0. 4. 6
1 Large tin cannister & 2 small do	0. 4. 0
1 pr scales & weights	0. 6. 0
A parcel Stoneware	0.16. 0
A parcel of delph, China, glass & stoneware	3.10. 0
An old carpet, rug, blanket, & 2 old beds	1.10. 0
2 old beds, bedstead, 3 old blankets, & a rug	1.10. 0
A Bookbinders press etc.	0.16. 0
50½ oz. silver @ 6/6	16. 8. 3
An Electrical Machine	0. 6. 0
2 Chamberpots	0. 2. 0
A parcel of books	1.
260 lb Bacon @ 4	3.18. 4
1 Pr. Spoon Molds	0. 6. 0
An old Cow	1.14. 0
12 Oil flasks 3 full	0. 6.
2 Stone Juggs, some old casks, Bags [?] etc	0. 9. 6
An old still	0. 6.
6 meat tubs, 2 large JARRS & a parcel of lumber	1.14. 0
A pr. Leather bucket & a Bag	1.
Robert Cowley, a servant, 3 yrs to serve	12. 0. 0
Wm. Richardson do do	12. 0. 0
John Eltham do 2 yrs to serve	10. 0. 0
James Ratcliff do do	10.
Thomas Sanon do do	10.
About 360 wt. English letter ¾ worn @ 3d	4.10.

About 390 small pica do @ 3d	4.17. 6
About 400 Long primer ½ worn @ 6d	10.
About 200 Burgeois do @ 7d	5.16. 8
About 600 do good for little	3.
About 300 different sorts a great deal worn @ 3d	3.17. 0
1 Press & furniture	10.
1 Very old do	2.
5 Friskets	1.
3 pr Tympans, 1 old	1.
4 pr. Pints, some broke	0. 1.
4 pr old Ball Stocks	0. 4.
9 pr. Iron Chases	1.12.
12 Composing Sticks	1.
20 Gallies & some slices	1. 4
14 letter boards	0. 8.
2 pr. old shears, 1 paste brush, tin fender, Board stand, pr. bellows, & a parcel of quoins & Reglet, 7 old frames	0.16. 0
2 Imposing Stones on Frames	1. 5. 0
a pr Leather Buskets & Bag	1.
Some old books, Brass Rule, & ½ doz. old knives & forks—a parcel of lumber in different places	0.14. 0
A parcel Quart bottles	0. 6. 0
	304. 1.10

Appraisers: Nath. Hammond, John Duckett
Kindred: John & Rebecca Clapham
Creditors: Charles Wallace, Joshua Frazier

July 13, 1775 Came Frederick Green, Administrator

XIII
CHAPTER

Antietam Furnace
A Frontier Ironworks in the Great Valley of Maryland

SUSAN E. WINTER

IN THE OPENING decades of the eighteenth century, influential and wealthy British and colonial merchants in the Chesapeake Bay region began searching for new avenues of investment outside the lucrative, but volatile, tobacco trade (Heite 1983; Skaggs 1984:282–283). A number of these entrepreneurs ventured into the uncharted course of iron manufacturing. Indeed, in 1728 Virginia governor William Byrd observed, "Many here are gone mine-mad, which proceeds from a passion to grow rich very suddenly" (Heite 1970:78).

The enthusiasm of these "mine-mad" merchants was not misplaced. Ports along the Chesapeake Bay and its navigable tributaries provided ample opportunity to ship iron to Britain, which had been importing iron from Baltic countries owing to a scarcity at home of wood for charcoal, the primary fuel for smelting ore. In addition, the hundreds of tobacco ships traveling to Britain required ballast, which created opportunities for transporting iron to the mother country at lower prices than would have prevailed if the vessels carried iron as their only cargo (Heite 1983:139; Skaggs 1984:284–285).

DEVELOPMENT OF THE CHESAPEAKE REGION IRON INDUSTRY

Establishing an ironworks required a tremendous capital investment for the physical plant, the huge tracts of land containing wood and ore reserves, and the relatively large, skilled work force (Heite 1983:139). To minimize risk, English and colonial merchants and planters formed formal partnerships (Paskoff 1983:4). In Virginia, Governor Alexander Spotswood, along with English investors, erected several furnaces along the Rappahannock-Rapidan river drainages around 1720 (figure 13.1). Two important firms that became involved in ironworks in the early 1720s were the Bristol Iron Company and the Principio Company. The Bristol Iron Company constructed several ironworks in Virginia, including Bristol Furnace along the Rappahannock River and Neabsco Furnace and Occoquan Forge along tributaries of the Potomac. The Principio Company constructed Accocceek Furnace on a tributary of the Rappahannock and the long-lived Principio Furnace at the head of Chesapeake Bay in Maryland (Heite 1983:145–146; Skaggs 1984:287–288). All of these ironworks sat on or near navigable streams.

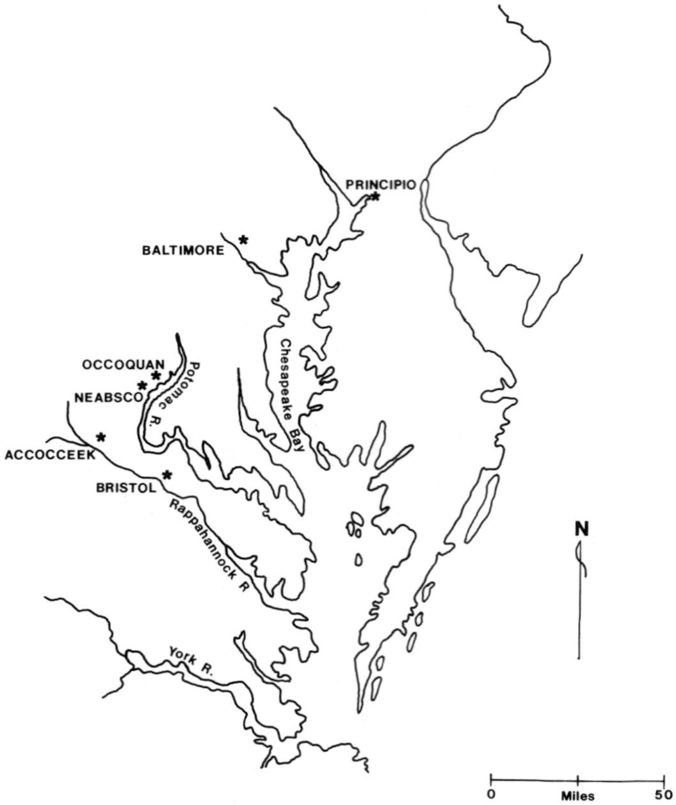

FIGURE 13.1. *Eighteenth-century iron furnaces established around the Chesapeake Bay region (adapted from Heite 1984:135).*

Five wealthy Marylanders, including several members of the influential Carroll family, created the Baltimore Company in 1731. This company, centered in Baltimore, soon became the largest ironmaking enterprise in the Chesapeake region, and along with the Principio Company dominated the export trade by the mid-eighteenth century. It is noteworthy that, with the exception of the Baltimore Company, most of the investment capital and managerial expertise for the early Chesapeake ironmaking enterprises originated in England (Skaggs 1984:287).

The Bristol Iron Company, Principio Company, Baltimore Company, and others all focused their energies on supplying English markets, rather than those in their own backyard. Paul F. Paskoff (1983:1), in a study devoted principally to the development of ironmaking in neighboring Pennsylvania, concluded that during the first half of the eighteenth century "Maryland, along with much of the South, lacked the population centers and the smaller but nonetheless vibrant hinterland settlements which could have absorbed the iron produced in [that] colony."

THE IRON INDUSTRY TURNS INWARD

After 1750, the high cost of entering the English markets against established giants such as the Baltimore and Principio companies encouraged new ironmaking firms to turn inward toward local markets (Skaggs 1984:9). Following the resolution of the border dispute between Maryland and Pennsylvania and the conclusion of the French and Indian Wars, settlements in the Great Valley of Maryland and Virginia multiplied. New markets opened for those willing to accept the risk and high probability of failure (Crapster 1985:1). In addition, large tracts of woodland became available in these newly open areas, furnishing a necessary component to all successful ironmaking establishments in their never-ending need for charcoal to fuel the smelting and forging operations (see Frye 1987 for a discussion of charcoal manufacturing).

One speculative ironmaking venture along the new frontier, and the first ironworks in western Maryland, was Antietam Furnace, established on the east edge of the Antietam (or Great) Valley of Maryland in 1761 (figure 13.2). Extensive archaeological excavations conducted at the main blast furnace of this complex provide a rare glimpse into the initial years of a developing frontier industry. This exceptionally well-preserved ironworks operated for only a short period (15 to 20 years) and was deliberately dismantled and covered over shortly after operations ceased, with the result that the site has been sealed from all disturbances for 200 years (Frye 1984). The unusually intact archaeological deposits, coupled with the short span of operation, make the Antietam Furnace site a "time capsule" of ironmaking technology and development during the latter half of the eighteenth century.

The remainder of this chapter documents the historical and technological development of Antietam Furnace, as well as the objects produced there, and shows how this early ironworks represents a tentative response to a new and challenging frontier environment and market. In addition, the apparent success of this ironworks and its successor, Mt. Aetna Furnace, is examined within the volatile political and economic climate of the American Revolution.

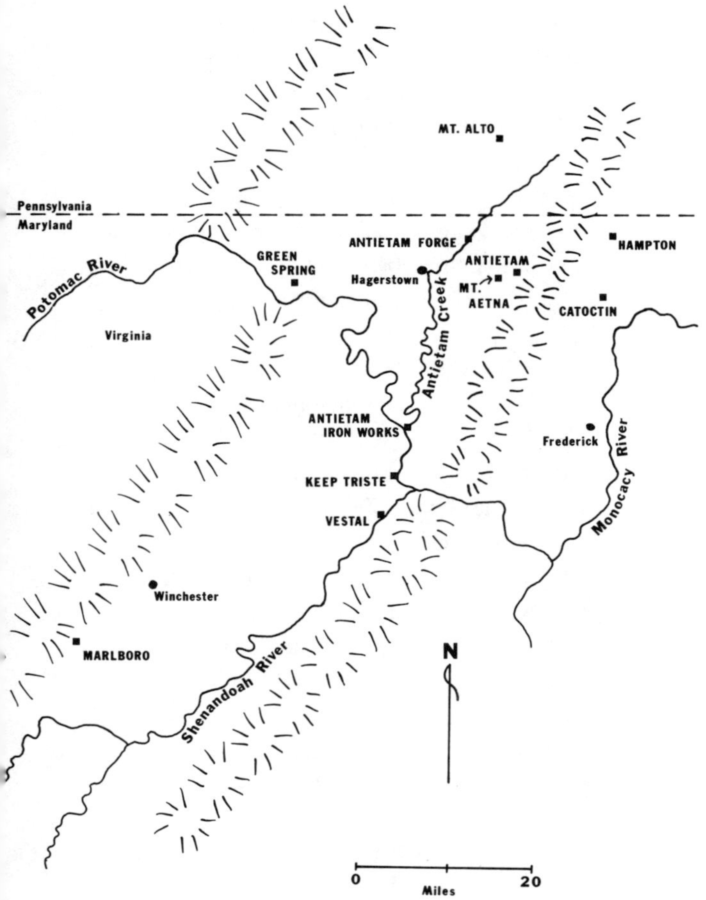

FIGURE 13.2. *Eighteenth- and early nineteenth-century iron furnaces established in the Great Valley of Maryland and the lower Shenandoah Valley of Virginia.*

Historical Background of Antietam Furnace

The site of Antietam Furnace lies at the west base of South Mountain, which today separates Frederick County on its east side from Washington County on its west side; the latter was carved from Frederick County in 1776. South Mountain also forms the east edge of a wide, fertile limestone valley, variously described as the Antietam, Great, or Lower Cumberland Valley. This valley was the focus of early settlement in present-day Washington County, and provided a well-traveled passage to the neighboring Shenandoah Valley in Virginia.

Early Settlement of Western Maryland

Settlement in western Maryland did not officially begin until 1732, when Lord Baltimore opened Maryland's backcountry through proclamation. Several factors stalled the initial development of this region, however, including border disputes, the fear of Indians, misconceptions about the land's fertility, and the speculative holding of large tracts of land (Porter 1975:329). A study of the earliest grants in Washington County has revealed that speculators from eastern Maryland held title to most of the surveyed land (Reed 1988:86). Around 1739, however, the colonial powers began awarding smaller land grants, primarily to German farmers arriving from Pennsylvania:

> As a result of this land speculation, the major thrust of settlement did not occur until the second half of the eighteenth century, and when it did happen, it was not by people moving west from tidewater Maryland, but rather by settlers from Pennsylvania, most of whom were Germans. (Reed 1988:86)

After the early settlers arrived, towns began appearing. Frederick, established in 1745, was the first town laid out in western Maryland. The backcountry developed by leaps and bounds, particularly east of South Mountain, and within five short years Frederick became the largest town in Maryland, with a population of 1,000 (that of Annapolis, for example, was 800) (Porter 1975:345–346). Hagerstown and Sharpsburg, located in present-day Washington County, were established in 1763 (Reed 1988:105).

Construction of Antietam Furnace

William James, a member of a long line of ironmasters, constructed Antietam Furnace in 1761 against the west base of South Mountain. Two of his partners were Baltimore merchants William Buchanan and Barnabas Hughes, and the third was an unidentified individual with the initials AD (Frye 1984:151). William Buchanan and the unknown AD apparently did not assume an active role in managing the new ironworks and dropped out of the partnership by 1765. In that year Barnabas Hughes—together with his three sons Daniel, Samuel, and John—expanded his general interest in the furnace operation by purchasing 2,500 acres along South Mountain from James (Maryland State Archives 1765b:245).

Although William James sold most of his land in western Maryland to the Hughes family, he retained part interest in the ironworks. An inventory of the Antietam

Furnace estate, recorded in May 1766 following Barnabas Hughes's death, lists "the goods and chattles [*sic*] of Barnabas Hughes late of Baltimore County deceased in cluding [*sic*] Wm. James undivided 1/3 appraised in current money" (Maryland State Archives 1766:159–164). Hughes's two-thirds interest was bequeathed to his sons as tenants in common, although John apparently remained a silent partner and was not involved directly with future transactions concerning Antietam Furnace (Maryland State Archives 1765a:47).

Daniel and Samuel Hughes's ironworking investments increased substantially with the acquisition of 4,550 acres from James Kennedy in 1766, for included in this transaction was a refining forge along Antietam Creek and a one-fifth interest in Hampton Furnace situated north of Frederick, near Emmitsburg, Maryland (figure 13.2; Frederick County Land Records 1766:870). The short-lived Hampton Furnace was constructed ca. 1765, and may never have been put in blast (Crapster 1985:5).

The Hughes brothers purchased Antietam Forge to complement their operations at Antietam Furnace. Pig iron produced at the furnace was converted at the forge into wrought iron, a more saleable item. A petition submitted to the Frederick County Circuit Court by Daniel and Samuel Hughes in August 1768 confirmed this supposition. In this document the brothers assert that

> they Labour under great inconvenience for want of direct roads from their forge on Antieatam to their coaling [charcoaling] ground and furnace the want of which lays it in the power of any ill disposed person living between to twin them round and Obstruct their Business when they please. Your petitioners therefore hope your worships will grant them a direct road from their forge aforesaid to their coaling ground belonging to the same and from their said forge to their furnace known by the name of Antieatam. (Frederick County Judgment Records 1768:326)

The petition was approved and the road laid out over the next year.

Between 1767 and 1771, Daniel and Samuel Hughes purchased more than 5,000 acres around Antietam Furnace, pointing to a significant expansion in their ironmaking operations (Frye 1984:18). These transactions included one with William James in 1769. James, identified by this time as a resident of Bedford County, Virginia, sold to the Hughes brothers 661 acres adjoining the furnace (Frederick County Land Records 1769:207). This was the last recorded reference to James, who must have conveyed his interest in Antietam Furnace to Daniel and Samuel prior to that date. Thus, on the eve of the American Revolution, the Hughes brothers owned Antietam Furnace, Antietam Forge, and at least 12,373 acres. To manage this growing and apparently successful enterprise, Daniel Hughes had moved from Baltimore to Antietam Forge sometime before 1770, and Samuel had established a residence at Antietam Furnace as well (Frye 1984:17–19).

Establishment of Surrounding Ironworks

Other ironworking establishments soon followed Antietam Furnace into the Great Valley of Maryland. Along the Virginia bank of the Potomac River, just above its confluence with the Shenandoah River, Scottish merchant John Semple (a partner in Occoquan Forge) purchased several hundred acres and erected Keep Triste Furnace in 1763–1764 (figure 13.2). Semple also acquired large tracts of land in Maryland and began constructing Frederick Forge at the mouth of Antietam Creek to complement the furnace operation at Keep Triste. In 1764, he conveyed the unfinished forge to a partnership of four men—Scottish merchants David Ross and Richard Henderson, local landowner Joseph Chapline, and Samuel Beall. While Keep Triste struggled as a result of Semple's mismanagement and was out of blast by the American Revolution, Frederick Forge prospered, and with the addition of a furnace around 1769, became the successful Antietam Iron Works (Thompson 1976:22–23; Skaggs 1984:289–295). As a side note, the owners of Frederick Forge were forced to purchase 175 tons of pig iron from Daniel and Samuel Hughes in 1767 when Semple could not, or would not, deliver the material from Keep Triste (Skaggs 1984:300).

By 1768, Thomas Johnson and Lancelot Jacques had purchased approximately 10,000 acres in the mountains along the west edge of Antietam Valley and erected Green Spring Furnace near Fort Frederick. This furnace remained in blast until around 1800 (Thompson 1976:67, 75). Thomas Johnson, governor of Maryland during the American Revolution, also constructed Catoctin Furnace around 1774 in partnership with his brothers. This successful ironworks, located north of Frederick, Maryland, operated throughout the remainder of the eighteenth century and most of the nineteenth century (Thompson 1976:63).

Three early ironworks were established in the upper Shenandoah Valley. William Vestal reputedly constructed a small establishment along the Shenandoah River around 1742 (figure 13.2), Lewis Stephens erected the Marlboro Ironworks on Cedar Creek below Winchester ca. 1756 (these works were purchased by Isaac Zane in 1768), and John Miller established the Mossy Creek Ironworks above Staunton in Augusta County around 1768. Although Miller concentrated on local markets, Zane imported considerable quantities of iron to the port towns of Falmouth and Alexandria during the 1760s and 1770s for export to Britain (Mitchell 1977:204).

Strangely, a short distance to the north, neighboring Franklin County, Pennsylvania, apparently did not have an iron furnace until 1783 (Wiestling 1922:15). No modern studies have been conducted in this area, however, which might expand upon research conducted earlier this century.

The American Revolution and Mt. Aetna Furnace

Antietam Furnace was thus one of the first ironmaking establishments constructed west of the Blue Ridge, and certainly the earliest in western Maryland. It also appears to have been successful, for it survived the rocky 1760s and early 1770s. At the outbreak of the American Revolution, Daniel and Samuel Hughes sought and received contracts from Maryland and the Continental Congress in Philadelphia to cast cannon, which ensured their continued prosperity and led to a sizable expansion of their operation (Thompson 1976:41; Frye 1984:19).

Initially, the manufacture of cannon ran into some problems. In February 1776, the cannon undergoing proof exploded, killing the man sent to inspect them (Maryland Historical Society 1892:122). Within a few months, the faulty casting was corrected, and cannon production continued unabated until the end of the Revolution. At some point during the opening months of the war, Daniel and Samuel Hughes constructed a new furnace, known as Mt. Aetna, for manufacturing the cannon (Scharf 1882:978; Frye 1984:22–23).

The Hughes brothers profited greatly from their involvement in the Revolution. In a 1783 tax assessment, Daniel and Samuel are listed jointly as the wealthiest property owners in Washington County (Frye 1984:23). The tax assessment listed Daniel and Samuel Hughes as owning a "forge"—most certainly referring to Mt. Aetna Furnace—in common, and Daniel as possessing two forges, the first being the old Antietam Forge. The second, Great Rock Forge, sat on Antietam Creek near the Pennsylvania border (figure 13.2) and most likely was constructed in 1781–1782 (Thompson 1976:51; Frye 1984:23). Since the earlier Antietam Furnace did not appear in the 1783 tax assessment, it apparently had ceased production by this time. Even so, by the end of the Revolution, the Hughes family possessed what probably was the largest ironmaking complex in western Maryland.

At the same time that Daniel and Samuel Hughes directed their ironworking enterprise, they participated actively in local government. The two were among the organizers of Washington County, formed in 1776 from Frederick County, and Daniel was appointed to the first body of the Levy Court (County Commissioners). Samuel served on the first Washington County delegation to the Maryland House of Delegates, sat as a Justice of the County Court in 1777, and was appointed a state senator upon the death of Charles Carroll in 1781 (Scharf 1882:987–991). Samuel also served as a member of the Washington County Committee of Safety during the Revolution, and both brothers served in the state militia (Thompson 1976:41). Daniel and Samuel Hughes clearly were influential and powerful men in western Maryland, with an extensive interest and involvement in local politics.

Following the American Revolution, Samuel conveyed half his interest in Mt. Aetna Furnace to his brother, and purchased an interest in the Principio Furnace near Baltimore. Confiscated as Royalist property during the Revolution, Principio was acquired by Hughes in partnership with others (Washington County Land Records 1781:529; Thompson 1976:50). From this time Samuel appears to have involved himself very little with Mt. Aetna, and in 1805 sold his remaining interest in the furnace to Daniel (Washington County Land Records 1805:471).

In 1807, Daniel and Samuel Hughes branched into ironmaking in Pennsylvania, with the construction of a furnace at Mt. Alto in neighboring Franklin County (figure 13.2). According to tradition, the pig iron produced at this works was transported to Williamsport, Maryland, and conveyed down the Potomac River in flat boats. Cast objects such as stoves, hollowware, and flat irons traveled by wagon to Baltimore (Wiestling 1922:18).

Upon Daniel Hughes's death in 1818, his three sons inherited Mt. Aetna Furnace, Great Rock Forge, and Mt. Alto Furnace (Washington County Land Records 1818:749; 1819:127), while his daughters received

Antietam Forge (Washington County Probate Records 1818:56–63). Daniel's sons apparently were not astute businessmen, and their ensuing financial difficulties forced them to close Mt. Aetna Furnace around 1820. Antietam and Great Rock forges remained open for at least another decade, receiving their pig iron from Mt. Alto Furnace a short distance across the Pennsylvania border (Frye 1984:27). In the long term, the Hughes family had maintained a strong hold on local ironmaking for almost seventy years—a significant accomplishment in such a volatile industry.

EIGHTEENTH-CENTURY BLAST FURNACE TECHNOLOGY

Several ingredients were essential for iron production in eighteenth-century America: iron ore, wood for charcoal to fuel the smelting process, a flux (generally limestone) to draw impurities from the ore to form the waste product slag, and waterpower. Most furnaces were located in relatively isolated areas close to these necessary resources. As a result of this isolation, "iron plantations" tended toward self-sufficiency, producing their own food and housing their own workers, which during this period often consisted largely of indentured servants and slaves in the mid-Atlantic and south (Kelley and Angel 1983; Dew 1974).

Eighteenth-century blast furnaces were substantial, stone-built structures shaped like truncated pyramids (figure 13.3). They typically measured 25 to 35 feet in height and 25 feet square at their base (Bining 1979:65–66; Heite 1983:167). The stone stack enclosed two chambers—the bosh and the hearth. The bosh received the ore, limestone, and charcoal through an opening in its top. The rectangular hearth, or crucible, formed a repository for the molten iron and slag after it had been processed in the bosh. Both chambers were lined with sandstone, which was less likely to melt and crack than other native stone (Overman 1854:453). One side of the hearth contained a small opening for the tuyere, defined as the nozzle or pipe that brought the forced air from the bellows to the furnace. These leather bellows, which measured 20 to 25 feet in length and several feet wide, were powered by huge waterwheels. These wheels often were set in the ground within stone-lined wheelpits to ensure sufficient water fall (Bining 1979:70–71).

Furnaces generally were constructed against the side of a hill to facilitate charging, or loading, of the furnace stack. A wooden bridge extended from the hillside to the top of the open stack. The ore, limestone, and charcoal were carried over the bridge and dropped into the furnace. A level area on the hillslope behind the bridge contained storage buildings for these materials. At the base of the furnace stack sat the casting house. Inside this structure, molten iron was tapped from the furnace twice a day into a long sand trench, referred to as the sow, and its side trenches, known as pigs. In addition, some iron was poured into molds to form stoves, hollowware, and other cast objects. These molds were prepared either in containers known as flasks, or pressed directly into the sand floor of the casting house (Thompson 1976:9; Heite 1983:174).

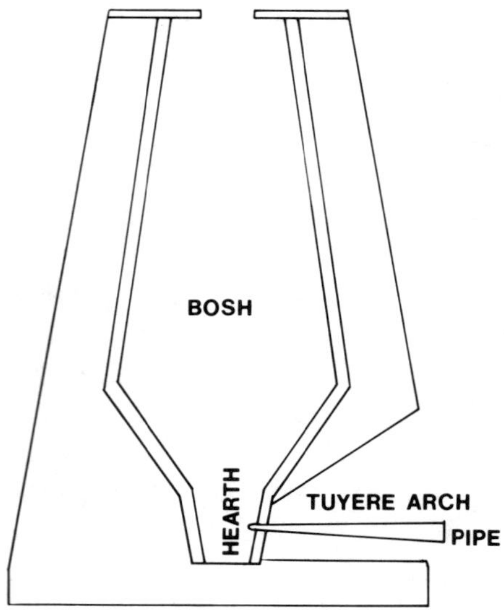

FIGURE 13.3. *Cross section of a blast furnace stack (adapted from Frye 1984:35).*

The furnace remained in blast for months at a time, discharging molten iron regularly on its twice-daily schedule. Eventually the furnace lining burned out and forced the furnace to shut down. A new interior was built, and the cycle begun anew.

ARCHAEOLOGICAL INVESTIGATIONS AT ANTIETAM FURNACE

In 1976, heavy earthmoving equipment partly exposed the front base of a long-forgotten furnace stack during expansion of the Mt. Aetna Volunteer Fire Department (Clark 1981). Archaeological fieldwork subsequently was conducted at the site of Antietam Furnace (in 1982 and 1983) under the auspices of the Maryland Historical Trust. Excavations concentrated on exposing the furnace stack, wheelpit, and bellows location (figure 13.4); remains of the casting house apparently had been destroyed during construction of the original fire hall and its addition (see Frye 1984 for a complete site report).

A thick layer of rubble directly underlay the present topsoil and sealed the site. The condition of this stone—much of it had been heated and some was coated with slag—suggested it originated from the stone furnace stack. Artifacts associated with this layer dated to the third quarter of the eighteenth century and consisted principally of discarded cast iron objects and some machinery, tools, and nails.

The base of the stone furnace stack lay underneath the rubble in the north half of the site. This stack measured 12 feet square at its excavated base and was oriented toward the cardinal directions, the crucible opening almost due west. The outer walls of the furnace were indifferently constructed of dressed limestone mortared with yellowish brown clay. The hearth interior measured 1.6 feet wide by 3.2 feet deep and consisted of cut sandstone coated with a thick layer of smooth, glossy black slag. The remains of a tuyere, or bellows archway, formed part of the south elevation of the furnace stack. A small tuyere opening cut through the south wall of the crucible.

Along the south half of the site sat the exceptionally

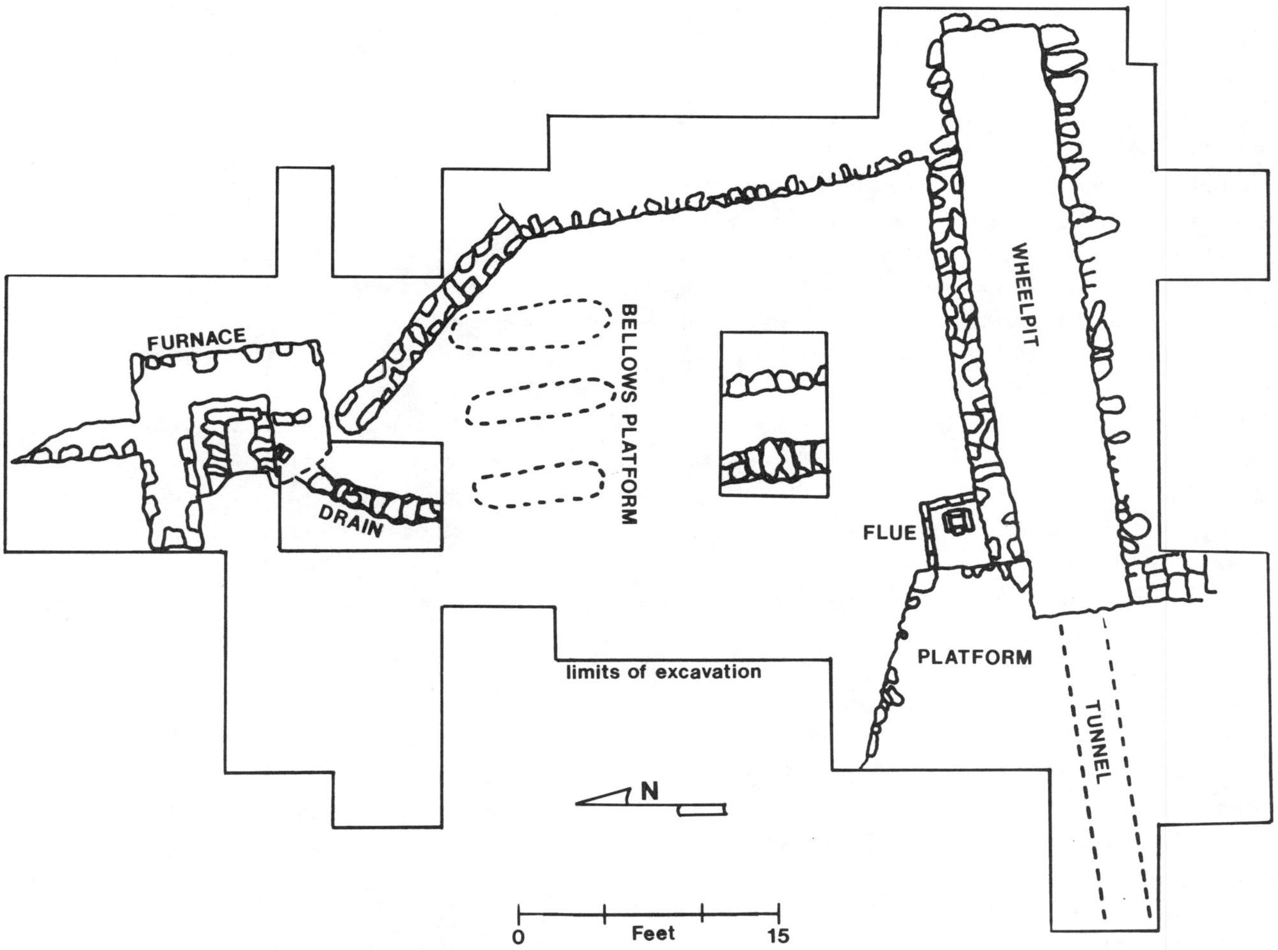

F I G U R E 13.4. *Plan of Antietam Furnace Site (adapted from Frye 1984:52).*

well-built and well-preserved wheelpit interior, which measured 33.5 feet long by 6.5 feet wide. Constructed on all four sides of dressed, dry-laid limestone, the pit extended at least 9.5 feet deep (the base was not exposed). A triangular-shaped tunnel entrance for wastewater cut through the west wall of the wheelpit about 4.5 feet below the present wall top. The tunnel interior consisted of a corbeled stone wall that extended in a west-southwest direction. A stone staircase constructed into the west end of the south wheelpit wall permitted access to this tunnel opening. Stone rubble and thick deposits of fine-grained ore, discarded as too small to use as fuel, filled the wheelpit.

Remains of a low-lying stone platform extended from the northwest corner of the wheelpit (bulldozing had destroyed the west half). Hard-packed rubble and clay created a relatively flat surface, probably for a structure. On the east side of the platform, against the north wall of the wheelpit, sat a small brick and stone feature measuring 4.5 by 3.25 feet. The stone formed a small, square-sided flue lined with glossy slag. A hole identified as a tuyere opening for bellows cut into the east side of this flue. Remnants of two short brick walls connected the stone flue to the north wheelpit wall and the platform.

With its bellows opening and slag-lined interior, the brick and stone feature apparently functioned as a flue for an ironworking process, possibly forming the base of a small forge chimney. If this were the case, the hard-packed stone and clay platform situated along the northwest corner of the wheelpit would have provided a suitable hearth base. Blacksmith's tools listed in the 1766 inventory of Antietam Furnace signify the presence of a blacksmith at the furnace complex (Baltimore County Inventory Records 1766:159–164). The possibility also exists that this feature represented an early, crude refining forge to produce malleable bar iron.

Archaeological investigations in the space between the furnace stack and wheelpit revealed the compacted, relatively level eighteenth-century working floor surface of the furnace complex. This surface was littered with small amounts of domestic debris, including about a half-dozen ceramic plates (creamware and slip-decorated redware) and mugs (redware), some glass bottles, and cut bones (principally cattle, with some pig and sheep). This small domestic assemblage probably represents items discarded on the furnace site after its abandonment, perhaps by residents of the nearby workers' village.

Three parallel trenches spaced approximately five feet apart cut through this floor along its north edge. These trenches extended about ten feet north-south, measured two to three feet in width, and were anchored at each end by postholes. The configuration and dimensions of the trenches and postholes suggested the remains of horizontal and vertical beams forming the base of the platform supporting the bellows mechanism.

Two additional features lay completely buried beneath the compact eighteenth-century floor level. The first consisted of a stone-capped drain which extended south from the base of the furnace stack toward the wheelpit. It is likely that the drain cut through the north wall of the pit and emptied into it. Such drains removed groundwater or runoff before it could penetrate the stack and cause an explosion (Overman 1854:154). The second feature, a sandstone wall, cut north-south through the center of the site. Only a small section of this wall was exposed; however, it appeared to continue south toward the center of the wheelpit. If it extended northward, the sandstone wall bisected the bellows support as well. The wall tentatively is interpreted as a support for the shaft leading from the waterwheel to the bellows.

Artifacts

In comparison with other archaeologically excavated ironmaking sites in the mid-Atlantic region, a large number of artifacts were recovered from the investigations at Antietam Furnace (Heite 1970;74; Orr and Orr 1975; Parrington and Schenck 1982). This high recovery rate may have been due to the fact that the complex was dismantled and covered shortly after it ceased operating, and thus had not been substantially scavenged or altered. Roughly 12 percent of the approximately 2,500 artifacts represent items cast at Antietam Furnace. Discussion focuses on what these artifacts reveal about the development of Antietam Furnace and the possible markets associated with it.

Furnace products were manufactured in the casting house, which provided the focus of activity at the blast furnace. Here the molten iron moved through trenches cut into a sand floor and then hardened into pigs; or, the iron was ladled into molds to form a variety of cast products. Although remains of the casting shed at Antietam have been destroyed, its primary products—pig iron, stoves, and hollowware—are amply represented in the archaeological record.

Pig Iron

Because smelted iron ore contains a high percentage of carbon, it has a relatively low melting point, which allows it to be molded into many forms. This same carbon, however, makes cast iron brittle and unworkable under a hammer. Before iron can be worked by a blacksmith, therefore, it must be refined into wrought iron, which is malleable and contains very little carbon. Pig iron (or ingots), cast directly from the blast furnace, formed an intermediary stage in the creation of wrought iron from cast iron. Once cooled, the long lengths of pig iron were broken into smaller pieces and sent to the refining forge. At the forge the pigs were melted in a finery hearth, a process that removed much of the carbon through oxidation. Following additional remelting and reworking, the end product became a wrought iron bar.

Of the 58 pig iron fragments recovered at Antietam Furnace, most were cut or broken at both ends. Half lay within rubble-fill layers covering the furnace site. Although metallurgical analysis has not been conducted on these fragments, surface examination of the pigs revealed that most of them had flaws, such as substantial accretions of slag and other impurities. Most likely the pigs represented rejects that had been broken up, perhaps for remelting.

Pig iron sometimes was marked with the name of the furnace at which it was produced or the year in which it was cast (Heite 1970:94; Parrington and Schenck 1982: 19). Two marked pigs were recovered at Antietam Furnace—one dated 1762 (figure 13.5) and the other containing the raised letter "M," which probably represented part of the word "Antietam."

Stove Plates

Five-plate and six-plate stoves were used almost exclusively by settlers of German descent. These stoves were produced principally in Pennsylvania, the Great Valley of Maryland, and the Shenandoah Valley of Virginia, where German settlement was concentrated (Mercer 1961). Antietam Furnace manufactured both stove types.

As the name suggests, five-plate stoves consisted of five heavy iron plates—one each for the top, bottom, front, right side, and left side. The box-like stove projected into a room, generally the parlor, through an opening in a wall. The back usually opened into a large fireplace in the kitchen. The stove plates were produced by open sand casting in a manner similar to pig iron. A wooden pattern pressed into the sand formed an impression of the desired plate, and molten iron was poured into it and allowed to cool. A copy of the pattern design formed on one side of the plate; the reverse side was rough and uneven (Groft 1981:19).

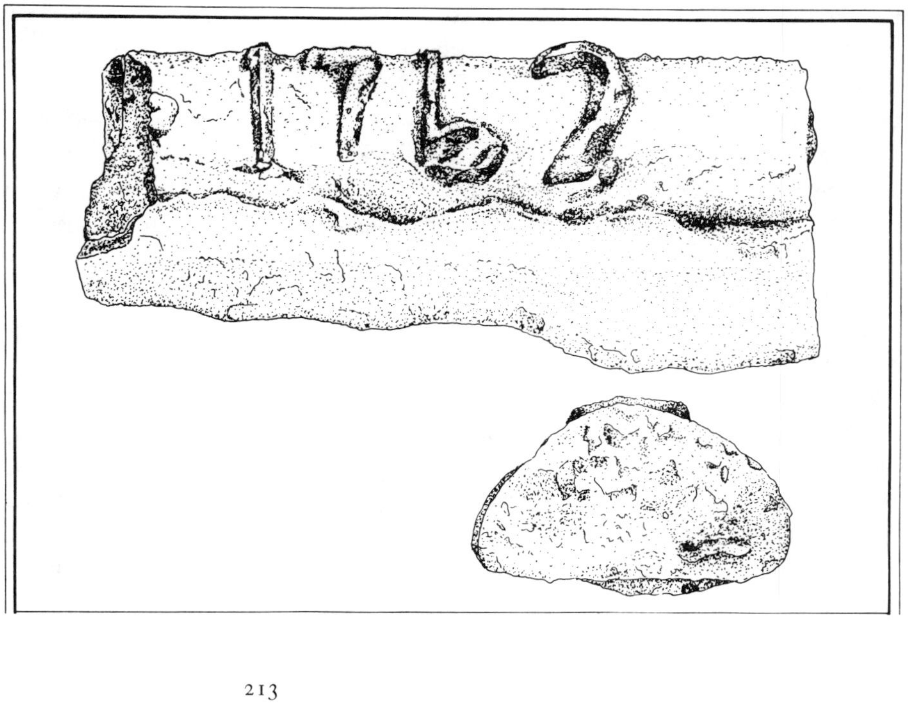

FIGURE 13.5. *Pig iron fragment dated 1762. (Courtesy of the Maryland Historical Trust, an agency of the Maryland Department of Housing & Community Development)*

Before 1750, the heavily decorated front and side plates displayed pictorial (primarily biblical) representations. After that date, a stylized floral pattern superseded these biblically inspired pictures. The central panel of the identical left and right side plates enclosed an inscription, generally an admonition from the Bible written in German. Sometimes these inscriptions continued from the side plate onto the front plate. By 1768, this central panel occasionally advertised the name of the furnace (Mercer 1961:44). Initials sometimes were set in the panel, their order indicating the relative importance of the ironmasters (Mercer 1961:72).

At Antietam Furnace, a total of 8 complete stove plates and 39 stove plate fragments were discovered. Bulldozing around the furnace base in 1976 uncovered almost half of these plates, including the 8 complete ones. As with the pig iron, the stove plate fragments with known provenience were found primarily within the fill layers overlying the furnace site.

A German-language inscription filled the central band of all eight plates, although it was totally legible on only two. It read "Dancket dem herrn dem" on one plate (figure 13.6), and "Dancket dem herrn den" on the other. Apparently the mold carver for the first plate made a mistake, for the second was the correct version and translated into a portion of the first verse of Psalm 106—"Give thanks unto the Lord for . . ." (Mercer 1961:218–219).

The verse was completed on the front plate, represented in the artifact collection by only a few small fragments but illustrated in Mercer (1961:plate 208). The inscription on the Mercer front plate reads "Er ist Freundlich," which translates to "He is good." The medallion of that plate contains the date 1762, which matches that on the pig iron fragment discussed above.

In addition to the biblical inscription, the plates share the same set of initials in their lower panels—WJ, WB, BH, and AD (figure 13.6). These initials represent the early owners William James, William Buchanan, Barnabas Hughes, and the unidentified AD and thus predate 1766. In fact, using design evolution in the floral-decorated stove plates, Mercer (1961:70–71) dates these plates to 1760–1763.

The free-standing, six-plate stove superseded the five-plate stove in the latter half of the 1760s (Mercer 1961:47–48). Six-plate as well as five-plate stoves were cast at Antietam Furnace. A fragment identical to a plate illustrated in Mercer was uncovered during construction activities around the fire hall (figure 13.7). The inscription on the plate in Mercer (1961:plate 227A) reads "D:S HUGHES FORNACE 1771." Apparently advertising that featured the names of the furnace owners rather than biblical inscriptions had become commonplace on six-plate stoves (Mercer 1961:82).

FIGURE 13.6. *Side plate from five-plate stove. (Courtesy of the Maryland Historical Trust, an agency of the Maryland Department of Housing & Community Development)*

The mid-1770s witnessed the development of the ten-plate stove, which contained an internal oven for baking (Mercer 1961:85–86). Archaeological investigations discovered no evidence of ten-plate stove manufacture at Antietam Furnace, although both ten-plate and Franklin stoves were produced at the later Mt. Aetna Furnace (Bast n.d.).

Hollowware

Hollowware, which referred to cast iron cooking implements such as pots, kettles, and skillets, was a major product at most eighteenth-century ironworks. Molten iron was ladled directly from the furnace crucible into wooden, sand-packed flask molds to form the various hollowware implements. When the iron had cooled, the flasks

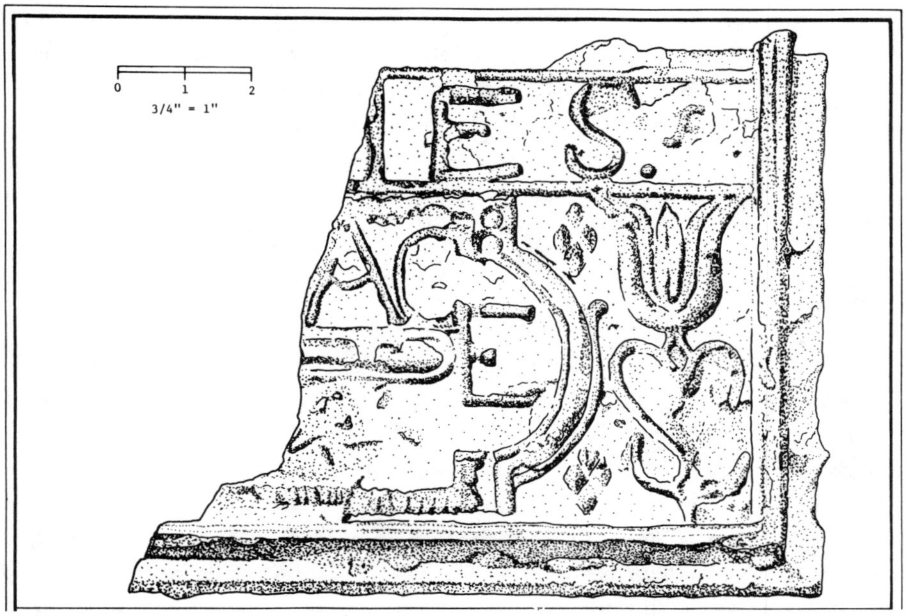

FIGURE 13.7. *Front plate fragment from six-plate stove. (Courtesy of the Maryland Historical Trust, an agency of the Maryland Department of Housing & Community Development)*

were removed and excess iron knocked off the casting (Frye 1984:100–102).

A total of 191 hollowware fragments and one large, complete pot were uncovered at the furnace site. Slightly more than half of the fragments lay in fill deposits covering the site. Investigations uncovered the cast iron pot in the one remaining small section of the casting floor. Stylistically, the numerous cast iron legs and handles all date to the mid-eighteenth century (Frye 1984:105).

Discussion

The historical background of Antietam Furnace, its physical configuration as uncovered through archaeological excavations, and the artifacts discovered during this investigation each reveal different facets of Antietam Furnace as an early, frontier ironworks.

The first owners of Antietam Furnace were not local investors, but rather merchants from Baltimore who did not move from that port city and who viewed the ironworks as a speculative venture and a supplement to their primary commercial enterprises. Their initiative was not misplaced, for old Frederick County was the fastest-growing area of Maryland in the early 1760s and shortly thereafter became the most populous county in the state (Thompson 1976:30). Under the merchants' long-distance tutelage, Antietam Furnace developed into a small, relatively self-sufficient community containing a store, residences, and a work force that included eight slaves and seven indentured servants (Baltimore County Inventory Records 1766:159–164).

The second-generation owners, Daniel and Samuel Hughes, apparently viewed the furnace operation not as just one of several business ventures, but concentrated most of their energy and capital on it. Following the death of their father Barnabas in late 1765, the two brothers quickly expanded their interests in the Great Valley by acquiring a refining forge along Antietam Creek and additional acreage. In 1769, the Hughes brothers purchased William James's remaining one-third interest in the furnace and continued acquiring more land. In addition, both Daniel and Samuel established their primary residences in the valley, Daniel at Antietam Forge and Samuel at the furnace. The two brothers became heavily involved in local politics, working hard to establish Washington County in 1776 and better transportation links with port cities to the east (Skaggs 1984:295).

In diameter, the furnace at Antietam measured only one-quarter the size of a typical eighteenth-century stack. The archaeological investigations uncovered no trace of an earlier, larger stack, so it must be presumed the furnace never measured any larger than 12 feet square. The small stack size suggests an early, tentative venture into a newly settled territory, where initial demand for furnace products would have been low, transportation networks poorly developed, and the expertise for furnace construction and operation in scarce supply. In fact, the skilled indentured and slave workers at Antietam Furnace were brought in from the outside. The small size and output of the furnace thus suggest an emphasis on local, easily saturated markets rather than commercial markets in the port cities to the east.

The large, well-constructed stone wheelpit with its corbeled-arch tunnel contrasted greatly with the small, crudely constructed furnace. Perhaps initial plans called for a larger stack, which was never constructed. The need for waterpower, which may have been in relatively short supply at this site, possibly required the construction of a deep, sturdy pit to hold the large wheel, which measured perhaps 20–25 feet in diameter.

The waterpower requirements of an apparent forge situated adjacent to the wheelpit, as indicated by the disturbed remnants of a stone and clay platform and the base of a small brick and stone flue, may also help explain the substantial size and construction of the wheelpit. This forge functioned either as a blacksmith shop or a small, crude refinery for producing wrought iron. The 1766 inventory of Barnabas Hughes's estate documented 608 pounds of bar iron at Antietam Furnace, as well as a substantial number of blacksmith tools (Baltimore County Inventory Records 1766:159–164). Whatever the function of the platform and flue, they, too, suggest production was restricted to the local market.

Cast iron products manufactured at Antietam Furnace, particularly stove plates, pointed to an emphasis on local markets as well. Five-plate stoves were produced for the many German settlers who entered Antietam Valley from Pennsylvania. A dated plate depicted in *The Bible in Iron* (Mercer 1961:plate 208) confirmed that the furnace was casting these plates in 1762, within a year of its construction. The 1766 inventory listed three sets of stove patterns at Antietam Furnace, which reinforce the importance of stove manufacturing to the furnace operation (Baltimore County Inventory Records 1766:159–164).

Not surprisingly, a pig iron fragment dated 1762 revealed this product was manufactured at Antietam at an early date. The question, however, is where the pig iron from this period was refined, for pig iron formed only an intermediary step toward the production of wrought iron. The probable forge uncovered adjacent to wheelpit remains a possibility, as Daniel and Samuel Hughes did not purchase Antietam Forge until 1766. The date at which the Antietam Forge itself began operating remains unclear, however, and pig iron possibly was transported there prior to the Hughes's ownership. Frederick Forge at the mouth of Antietam Creek, the only other one within traveling distance, did not begin operating until after 1762, although it did process 175 tons of iron from Antietam Furnace in 1767.

Since Daniel and Samuel Hughes evidently were able to transport pig iron overland to Frederick Forge, and thus to the Potomac River, they conceivably could have shipped iron down the Potomac to Georgetown or Alexandria, as well. At this date, however, the river remained unimproved and they would have had to undertake expensive portages around its numerous rapids. A proposal for improving river transportation outlined by John Semple, the owner of Keep Triste, reflected the difficulties early manufacturers experienced in conveying their products to relatively distant, but more lucrative and extensive markets (Thompson 1976:28–29).

The American Revolution forever altered the scope of the Hughes's ironmaking operations. Contracts received for casting cannon necessitated a total overhaul of their physical plant. In fact, in July 1776 the Provincial Convention of Maryland set aside £2,000 "for the encouragement of Daniel and Samuel Hughes to prosecute their cannon-foundry with spirit and diligence" (Scharf 1882:978). About that time a second furnace, known as Mt. Aetna, was constructed about 1 mile from the older and now obsolete Antietam Furnace.

No evidence has been found for the casting of cannon at Antietam Furnace. The stack was too small, and no deep casting pits were noted. At the site of Mt. Aetna Furnace, a number of flawed and rejected cannon have been discovered, whereas none have been uncovered around the earlier furnace. Artifactual evidence points toward the dismantling of Antietam Furnace before the end of the war, perhaps so that the bellows, waterwheel, and other equipment could be reused at Mt. Aetna. By 1783, Antietam Furnace had completely disappeared.

Conclusion

Archaeological investigations at Antietam Furnace yielded significant information unavailable in the historical record. First, this work proved that more than one furnace had existed at Mt. Aetna. Before this, memory of the early furnace survived only through local folklore. Second, excavations revealed a small, rather crudely constructed and experimental blast furnace complex. This complex, together with the remains of the items produced there, provide a picture of an early frontier operation erected by entrepreneurs eager to exploit the wooded mountain ranges and iron ore deposits of western Maryland, as well as local markets arising from extensive settlements after 1760. And third, archaeologists discovered a purposefully dismantled and sealed furnace complex, with a striking lack of post-1780 artifacts. This, together with the fact that no evidence of cannon production was uncovered at the site, strongly suggests it was abandoned after Mt. Aetna Furnace was constructed nearby, shortly after the beginning of the American Revolution.

The American Revolution substantially altered the overall complexion of the ironmaking industry in the Chesapeake region. Several large establishments that catered to foreign markets, such as the Principio and Baltimore companies, were destroyed through the confiscation of Loyalist property (Heite 1983:150,153). The Hughes family, however, apparently profited greatly from their contracts with the Continental Congress and continued to expand after the hostilities ended. Although Paskoff (1983:71), in his study of the Pennsylvania iron industry, contends that the Revolution "did less to stimulate the [iron] industry than it did to disrupt and retard its growth," this may not hold true for western Maryland and the Shenandoah Valley.

In conclusion, Antietam Furnace was one component of a far-flung enterprise that included Antietam Forge, the workers' village across the road from the stack, and a series of charcoal hearths, ore pits, and roads used to transport raw materials to the blast furnace. Like Antietam Furnace itself, these sites remain undisturbed and if studied as a whole would provide additional insight into the technological and social development of a frontier ironworks of the colonial period.

Acknowledgments

Funding for the archeological investigations at Antietam Furnace was provided by the Bowman Trust of Washington County and the Washington County Board of Commissioners. Wayne Clark, Richard Hughes, and Beth Cole of the Maryland Historical Trust, and Neal Trubowitz of Frostburg State College, provided administrative oversight and greatly assisted with the editing and publication of the original site report. Helpful comments for this essay were provided by Dennis Frye, Paul Shackel, and Barbara Little.

References Cited

Bast, Douglas
n.d. Manuscript Collection. Boonsboro Historical Museum, Boonsboro, Md.

Bining, Arthur Cecil
1979 *Pennsylvania Iron Manufacture in the Eighteenth Century*. Pennsylvania Historical and Museum Commission, Harrisburg.

Clark, Wayne E.
1981 Preliminary Survey of the Mt. Aetna Blast Furnace Site. Notes on file, Maryland Historical Trust, Annapolis, Md.

Crapster, Basil L.
1985 Hampton Furnace in Colonial Frederick County. *Maryland Historical Magazine* 80(1):1–8.

Dew, Charles B.
1974 David Ross and the Oxford Iron Works: A Study of Industrial Slavery in the Early Nineteenth-Century South. *William and Mary Quarterly* 31(2):189–224.

Frederick County Land Records
1766 Deed Book K:870.
1769 Deed Book M:207.

Frederick County Judgment Records
1768 Book P:326.

Frye, Susan Winter
1984 *Archeological Excavations at the Antietam Iron Furnace Complex (18WA288), Washington County, Maryland.* Maryland Historical Trust Manuscript Series No. 37. Annapolis, Md.
1987 Charcoal-Making in the Blue Ridge: A View from Maryland Heights. In *Uplands Archeology in the East: A Third Symposium*, edited by Michael Barber, pp. 2–14. U.S. Department of Agriculture, Forest Service, Southern Region, Cultural Resources Report 87-1.

Groft, Tammis Kane
1981 *Cast with Style: Nineteenth Century Cast-Iron Stoves from the Albany Area*. Albany Institute of History and Art, Albany, N.Y.

Heite, Edward F.
1970 Excavation of the Fredericksville Furnace Site. *Quarterly Bulletin, Archeological Society of Virginia* 25(2):259–296.
1983 The Pioneer Phase of the Chesapeake Iron Industry: Naturalization of a Technology. *Quarterly Bulletin, Archeological Society of Virginia* 38(3):133–181.

Kelley, Jennifer Olsen, and J. Lawrence Angel
1983 The Workers of Catoctin Furnace. *Maryland Archeology* 19(1):2–17.
Maryland Historical Society
1892 *Archives of Maryland* 11:122. Maryland Historical Society, Baltimore.
Maryland State Archives
1765a Baltimore County Probate Records 33:47.
1765b Maryland Land Patent Records BC&GS 27:245.
1766 Baltimore County Inventory Records 89:159–164.
Mercer, Henry C.
1961 *The Bible in Iron*. Bucks County Historical Society, Doylestown, Pa.
Mitchell, Robert D.
1977 *Commercialism and Frontier: Perspectives on the Early Shenandoah Valley*. University Press of Virginia, Charlottesville.
Orr, Kenneth G., and Ronald G. Orr
1975 *Field Report on the Archaeological Situation at the Catoctin Furnace Stack 2 Casting Shed Site, Frederick County, Maryland*. Division of Archeology, Maryland Geological Survey, Baltimore, Md.
Overman, Frederick
1854 *The Manufacture of Iron in All Its Various Branches*. Henry C. Baird, Philadelphia.
Parrington, Michael, and Helen Schenck
1982 *A Report on the Excavation of an Ancillary Area (Site 18FR320) of the Historic Ironworking Complex at Catoctin Furnace, Frederick County, Maryland*. Maryland Historical Trust, Annapolis, Md.
Paskoff, Paul F.
1983 *Industrial Evolution: Organization, Structure, and Growth of the Pennsylvania Iron Industry, 1750–1860*. Johns Hopkins University Press, Baltimore, Md.
Porter, Frank W. III
1975 From Backcountry to Country: The Delayed Settlement of Western Maryland. *Maryland Historical Magazine* 70(4):349–369.
Reed, Paula Stoner
1988 *Building with Stone in the Cumberland Valley: A Study of Regional Environmental, Technical, and Cultural Factors in Stone Construction*. Unpublished Ph.D. dissertation, Department of American Studies, George Washington University, Washington, D.C.
Scharf, J. Thomas
1882 *History of Western Maryland*. Louis H. Everts, Philadelphia.
Skaggs, David Curtis
1984 John Semple and the Development of the Potomac Valley, 1750–1773. *Virginia Magazine of History and Biography* 92(3):282–308.
Thompson, Michael D.
1976 *The Iron Industry in Western Maryland*. West Virginia University, Morgantown.
Washington County Land Records
1781 Deed Book B:529.
1805 Deed Book R:471.
1818 Deed Book Y:749.
1819 Deed Book DD:127.
Washington County Probate Records
1818 Will Book C:56–63.
Wiestling, Edward B.
1922 The Old Iron Works of the Cumberland Valley. *Kittochtinny Historical Society Papers* 10:7–21.

XIV
CHAPTER

The Archaeology of Ideology
Archaeological Work in Annapolis since 1981

MARK P. LEONE

"ARCHAEOLOGY IN Annapolis" began in 1981 with a two-part research design. The design actually evolved over a period of two years, but the key assumptions were part of the project from the beginning, at least as I envisioned it. The first part of the design was concerned with the archaeology of ideology, that is, the material supports for and manifestations of the taken-for-granteds that mask or facilitate unequal relations between groups of people. It was not the archaeology of wealth or wealth holding, but rather the archaeology of ideas, behaviors, practices, and disguises that enabled some people to acquire and hold large amounts of wealth while others did not. These questions concentrated on class relations, particularly on how they were maintained generation after generation in Maryland's capital city without eruptions of violence.

The second assumption behind the research design was that the archaeological work should be directed at exploring the roots of modern ideologies operating in Annapolis today. This was and remains a novel assumption for an archaeological research design and has been a difficult one to sustain, both because it is conceptually complex and also unpopular. This second assumption can be divided into several parts. To begin with, I have assumed that there is doubt about whether the purpose of archaeology is to explore the tie between past and present, since it usually fails in this purpose at both the scholarly and popular levels. In addition, I assumed that archaeology, in the context of historic preservation, may become part of the gentrification that often accompanies preservation activities. Given these assumptions, I thought that if archaeology explored the origin of the givens or taken-for-granteds that are used to sustain unequal relations today, and if archaeologists present their findings and themselves to the public directly, then absorption by the hierarchies who gentrify might be avoided. If such procedures were feasible, then the tie between the past and present could provide a credible purpose for archaeology since it would be concerned with the origins of contemporary ideology. This second part of our research design has been discussed elsewhere (see, for example, Leone 1983; Leone et al. 1987) and is not the topic of this essay. Rather, this chapter focuses on the archaeology and material culture of ideology and uses the known trend toward unequal distribution of wealth in Annapolis as evidence for the background cause of the existence of ideology and as the vehicle for changes within ideology. Because the logic of the tie between material remains and ideology has frequently been articulated, this chapter concentrates on a summary, by chronologically organized periods, of the archaeological manifestations of ideology.

I organize the data into five phases. They are by and

large the same phases that historians (Russo 1983) have used for 20 years to organize the history of the development of wealth in the city. Cross-cutting these will be two other categories: (1) artifacts and architectural remains and (2) landscapes.

1680–1700

Annapolis began as a small town around 1650 and became the colonial capital in 1694 when Sir Francis Nicholson, second royal governor, redesigned it in order to remove the capital from Saint Mary's City in strongly Catholic southern Maryland. The earliest probate inventories that survive in Annapolis date from later in this period and show few wealthy people and a fairly even distribution of wealth when compared to the net wealth described in the inventories of later periods. Before Annapolis became the capital, some of the wealthiest people lived in southern Maryland, and at this time there was little land speculation in the future capital. The wealth-producing institutions, which consisted of profitable enterprises or powerful arms of government, were not located there. But that changed after 1694.

The period before the city became the capital offers no archaeological record that can be analyzed quantifiably in a reliable way. The earliest archaeological data in Annapolis are from the 1680s and were uncovered at the Main Street site. Tin-glazed earthenware, sgraffito, and North Devon earthenware were found in an undisturbed context about 200 feet from the Maryland State House (Shackel 1986). The shards were found in association with a fieldstone house foundation aligned to Main Street, which in turn was laid out by Nicholson in 1694. The house had a small garden which was discovered when excavators exposed the shovel divot marks created during its cultivation. The house was not earthfast (which was then the traditional type of construction in the Chesapeake region), and it may have been one of the first houses built during the era when the city became the capital. The house's facade directly abutted the city's principal street and was not set back from direct access. The house stood 80 or 90 years, until the 1770s, when Thomas Hyde, who was on his way to becoming a wealthy merchant, built a five-bay, two-and-a-half-story Georgian-style town house on the location. The earlier house produced few artifacts, and there are too little data to know whether this family's behavior was affected by the habits of wealth coming into use in the city. In other words, using logic borrowed from Deetz (1977), there are too few ceramics and faunal remains to know whether dining patterns represent individual place settings and meals organized by portion and course. The question of the family's relation to wealth is of interest because, on the one hand, their location was close to the center of power and thus of some value after 1695, whereas on the other, their dishes and other artifacts show little indication of practices like the disciplining of the self or the notion of individualism and personal liberty that Deetz (1977), Foucault (1979), and I argue leads to the creation and maintenance of hierarchies based on wealth and power.

The more important and richest collection of seventeenth-century material comes from the Saint Mary's site (Kryder-Reid 1988). This site was the property of the Carroll family from 1701 until 1832, when it was deeded to the Roman Catholic Redemptorist Community, which still owns it. Four generations of Carrolls lived there, beginning with Charles Carroll the Settler, who came to the colony of Maryland as attorney general in 1693 and who bought his Annapolis property soon after the city became the capital. The third Carroll owner was Charles Carroll of Carrollton, who signed the Declaration of Independence and who in the 1770s created the large Georgian-style house and two-acre falling garden that is still present. The Carroll property has at least 600 feet of waterfront (Roulette and Williams 1987), which in the seventeenth century, before it became Carroll property, included part of the city's wharf, shipbuilding, and commercial area.

In 1987 archaeologists began an excavation on this land in their search for Proctor's Tavern, a seventeenth-century beachfront structure, possibly standing on what became the Carroll waterfront. Proctor's Tavern had been used as a temporary meeting place for the Maryland legislature from 1694 until the permanent state house was finished in 1700. While digging near the point where the present East Port bridge lands in the City of Annapolis, we recovered a small but varied collection of unmixed, late seventeenth-century ceramics, pipe stems, and bricks. The remains were found 6 to 7 feet below present ground level and 2 feet below water level. The labor and money required for a large-scale wet-site excavation, even of an untouched and historically significant seventeenth-century site, were beyond our capabilities and resources. Since it was not likely that the present owners would disturb the site, we felt no emergency existed that would justify expensive salvage efforts.

The areas of most important activity in late seventeenth-century Annapolis—the state house and waterfront—are the two in which we have found undisturbed, seventeenth-century material. Even though we have excavated more than two dozen other sites, including three that oral history places in the seventeenth-century, nothing else from that time has been found. Sites that might have dated earlier than 1700 include the Sands House (Shackel, personal communication), Calvert House (Yentsch 1986, 1990) and the Jonas Green House (Little 1984, 1988). No archaeological material from any of these sites dates from the period 1650 to 1680, the era before the city became the capital, probably because the remains from this period were destroyed during the rebuilding and expansion of Annapolis in its "Golden Age," from 1760 to 1780.

Thus, we can conclude that nothing archaeological that we know of dates to before 1680, although some undisturbed deposits date from 1680 to 1700. Since the baroque street plan was actually in place and functional by 1700 or earlier, the landscape was being built and used by 1700. And since that landscape was designed and built by royal authority, it was extended over the local population to absorb them into the hierarchy. Aside from the landscape of hierarchy, no other large collection of artifacts appears to be logically associated with this era.

1700–1720: Artifacts and Architecture

Social differences, unequal wealth, and secure claims to hierarchy were established in Annapolis by 1720. The city residents used Nicholson's plan to divide, lay out, and sell property and public space, and the city began to take on the shape—physically and socially—that it would have through the Revolution (Baker 1983). What had begun as a relatively egalitarian, but small city was now transformed by a series of economic processes that we can see through both the probate inventories and archaeological data.

Through archaeology, Paul Shackel (chapter 6) has shown one facet of the rise of hierarchy in the Sands House. According to oral history, the Sands House is the oldest surviving house in the city, built in the late seventeenth century. The house is still in its original location and has an irregular wing, which gives it an unbalanced appearance. Excavation was conducted on the house for three months in 1987. Parts of the site, including one wing and the backyard, were tested, and the underside of the rest of the house was examined carefully.

This archaeological work revealed that the original house was an earthfast building. An outline of postholes and postmolds was found beneath the standing walls of the wing. The upper parts of the posts were still intact as the vertical timbers framing the house. But around 1720 the frame was placed on a dry-laid fieldstone foundation. Then in the nineteenth century the building was raised onto brick piers, which still hold it up.

Around 1720, this house, unstable because its timbers needed periodic replacement because of rot, was made much more stable. Shackel argues that this change reflects a transition in the family's social relations, from extensive dependence on social bonds—because of the amount of labor required for the periodic replacements of the earthfast members, among other activities—to less dependence on the community once more permanent building materials became available. These materials may have allowed the family to redefine its social obligations and to place its resources in areas other than reciprocity with neighbors, who had to be equals because of the need for reciprocity.

Around 1720 or a little before, Shiplap House, constructed in 1713, also became more permanent. Shiplap is a wooden house with elements of seventeenth-century styling and elements of eighteenth-century symmetry. By 1720, its two fireplace ends were rebuilt in brick. This transition has long been attributed to a new city ordinance intended to prevent fires in wooden chimneys by mandating they be replaced with brick structures. But the change may also reflect the change in social ties, as Shackel argues for the Sands House. The cycle of reciprocal labor obligations that was generated by house fires and architectural decay was interrupted when the houses became less replaceable and people were suddenly free to initiate new and sometimes less egalitarian relations. According to Shackel, the self-sufficiency reflected in such architectural modification coincided with the substantial differentiation of wealth in the city by 1720, as shown in its inventories. In other words, egalitarian relations were replaced with hierarchical relations enforced through the legal building codes.

1700–1720: Landscape

The landscape of Annapolis, which consists of its street plan (formulated in 1694) and its building lots, was brought into being between 1700 and 1720 and is still largely intact. The 1694 street plan was only gradually turned into reality as streets were laid out and property boundaries surveyed. For example, State Circle, which was then called Public Circle, may not have been laid out until 1706 (Tony Lindauer, personal communication). Nicholson designed a plan that was regular and that employed circles and radiating streets (Baker 1983). Much of it was not built at once. The plan was not haphazard, although all of its idiosyncracies cannot yet be explained, and, in addition, it was designed to incorporate preexisting spaces and buildings into it. The landscape of Annapolis is in fact the product of a sophisticated and consciously baroque plan based on the principles of solid geometry employed in urban planning since Salviati and Palladio (Bacon 1968:93–148), on the one hand, and, on the other, the product of a gradual and episodic execution that matched, in varying degrees, the intended plan (Leone et al. 1989).

In the Nicholson plan, as it was drawn out on a map by Stoddart in 1718, all the streets entering both circles have parallel sides. Today, at least two of the streets that enter Church Circle and seven of the eight entries into State Circle have either diverging or converging sides (Read 1990). Since Stoddart's is the earliest written record of the plan and demonstrates a clear-cut use of plane geometry, we could conclude that nonparallel street sides were a later addition or a later accident derived from careless surveying. But our topographic surveying shows that Nicholson's intent in working from baroque principles of design was to use diverging lines of sight (as they would have been formed by the street lines and facades along the streets entering the two circles) to make distant objects, the Anglican Church and the state house, appear to be closer than they actually were, and to use converging lines to make close objects appear more distant than they actually were. Thus, it is possible that it is Stoddart's drawing that misrepresents reality and not the nonparallel sides of some present city streets. This is especially likely since no other streets in the core of the city have nonparallel sides. In other words, only those streets leading into the circles, which enclose the two centers of power, have converging or diverging sides; all the rest, which lead to views or places of less authority, are not controlled so as to effect an optical illusion.

Deeds show some gardens in Annapolis by 1720 (Shackel 1986). We do not know whether these were kitchen or ornamental gardens. It is unlikely that any of the gardens built early in the eighteenth century would have been similar to the huge falling ornamental gardens of the 1760s to 1780s (Leone 1984, 1987). Nonetheless, Nicholson clearly saw the city as one whole landscape. And it was gradually filled in according to that one design. Not everyone must have understood or agreed to the uniformity that was being imposed, but everyone was affected by the ground plan, for it attempted to create a single, hierarchical political entity.

1720–1760: Artifacts and Architecture

It was in the middle decades of the eighteenth century that Annapolis firmly established its hierarchical organization. This is when distinct classes appeared, renting increased dramatically, interest and wages emerged in the economy, and the difference between wealth and power—some with one, some with the other—began to be noticed and commented on. This is when Annapolis, but probably not its surrounding countryside, adopted eating habits, personal dress and cleanliness, and ways of keeping time associated with early modern life (Leone 1988).

Two trends in particular in the 1750s helped shape the era. First, practices and types of behavior that disciplined people in the world of profit making entered daily life. Inventories of the 1720s show that the wealthiest segments of the population were beginning to buy sets of tablewares. Forks, knives, dishes, napkins, chairs, and matched items like these show up in people's houses (Leone and Shackel 1987). They imply, as Shackel and I have argued (Leone 1988; Shackel 1987), an accompanying discipline, or etiquette, that users learned and that produced orderliness and uniformity by making people appear to be predictable (Foucault 1979). People internalized the rules of etiquette as they used these items in the dining room, kitchen, toilet, and elsewhere at home, and they turned themselves into punctual, orderly, segmentable beings, ideal for the marketplace and workplace. This is the ideology of individualism.

Early in the eighteenth century only a few people purchased the implements of this internalizing discipline. But many of these matched items appear archaeologically in the 1750s and became widespread by the 1780s and probably indicate the regular opportunity for breakage and loss, and thus disposal in trash that became the archaeological record. The sets of dining items created a world of apparent equality, with each individual having an equal place and array of personal items (Deetz 1977). Isaac (1982) has argued that equality, which was then called individualism, was considered a natural phenomenon, and we see that by 1750 the conceptual world of egalitarianism had appeared and was well established as an ideal in Annapolis; its purpose was to hide the new hierarchy.

The second major change to occur in the 1750s was a resistance to the new hierarchical distribution of wealth. There appeared an understanding and a critique of the new hierarchical structure, a structure that assigned some people a fixed, inferior place in Annapolis society using the new social practices. The Tuesday Club (Breslaw 1975) met in Annapolis between 1745 and 1757, and its records show conflict between the men of moderate and upwardly mobile means, but of considerable talent, on the one hand, and the uppermost class, on the other. The club members satirized and parodied the British ruling elite and mocked the governor and the whole—by then—unwelcome British colonial administrative apparatus. This included Parliament, the crown, and the whole royal system. The club's members also understood they were not a part of the local gentry, which was the very wealthy planter, slaveowning, landholding elite.

The Tuesday Club members wrote odes, composed music, performed these in public, and recorded them in two large surviving volumes (Breslaw 1988; Micklus 1990), which were also illustrated by at least 60 cartoons showing their activities. The book manuscripts, including the cartoons, constitute a corpus of material culture that shows a group of some wealth, but little power, which pushed for inclusion in the upper class by enforcing on themselves uniform modes of talking, debating, writing, and performing music. They enforced all these through performance in front of the wider public. With these practices, they showed they were as worthy as the elite and simultaneously attempted to claim leadership of the lower groups of their own society. The club members knew they had little power and attempted to claim, through the disciplines of language and song, to be the models of behavior for society as a whole. Using speech and music in an intensely musical society, the club attempted to set the rule for sound-making Annapolis. Society then, was one in which everyone from slaves to masters valued instrumental music, the government conducted its business in large part through debate, and the languages of African slaves were to be suppressed in order for their independence to be destroyed.

Annapolis showed its class structure in two new ways by 1720–1760. The first ideology, that of a naturally derived hierarchy based on a graduated order in nature, was in place as soon as the town became the capital and wealth became substantially differentiated. Then a second ideology appeared and was well-developed by the 1750s. This is the ideology called individualism and is one new event. Then, out of this ideology and in reaction to the idea of a natural hierarchy, came a second new event: satire and parody, or resistance, to the older ideology of inevitable hierarchy. These are two different but complementary events. I have argued that use of matched ceramics and the material culture of what Foucault (1979) calls the technologies of the self, constitute the training ground for individualism, which was the ideological mask for unequal wealth holding. This meant that instead of advertising hierarchy, it was disguised or misrepresented. Second, those not included in the upper circles objected to unequal wealth.

Protest against such exclusion and statements opposing hierarchy can be found in Annapolis at least by the late 1740s, according to the data collected to date. This is what the *Minutes* and *History of the Tuesday Club* represent to us in an argument about ideology. The argument is that because ideology is a misrepresentation of who has power and how and why wealth is disproportionately held, it can be identified readily by the exploited. The critique of ideology includes the idea that it is believed by those whom it protects but is seen as untrue and as unconvincing by those whom it exploits. The members of the Tuesday Club confirm both of these tendencies in their written records. Club members launched an 11-year parody on power, customs, and class. They recognized the fallacy of the notion that power is held naturally by those who currently have it. But they did not see it as a class matter; they saw it as arbitrarily excluding them, but not also as excluding everybody else. They then turned right around, never having actually pierced the ideology behind unequal power, and used it actively; that is, they recapitulated it, by placing themselves within it, and attempted to make themselves the masters of everyone else, especially those below them.

My work using Althusser's (1971) concept of ideology has been criticized by Hodder (1986), McGuire (1988), and most recently by Beaudry et al. (1991) and Cook (1989). They ask, where is the protest and resistance, how does anyone believe a misrepresentation for long, and are there other ideologies that complete? These are legitimate questions, and work with the Tuesday Club volumes, including the club's material items and cartoons, has begun to address them (Leone et al. 1992).

1760–1785: Artifacts and Architecture

During the American Revolution, the government changed, the flag changed, and the buildings changed, but the structure of wealth holding did not change (Leone and Shackel 1987, 1990). The hierarchical pattern that had emerged by 1720 and was partly rationalized by 1750, continued intact up to and beyond the Revolution, with 5 percent of the population continuing to hold 85 percent of the wealth held at death or measured in probate inventories. Now, however, the 5 percent that held the wealth also held the power. The British and their loyalists left, but a hierarchically organized society remained.

Jonas Green, the famous printer of the *Maryland Gazette*, died in 1767, and his printing business was carried on by his wife, Anne Catharine Green, and then by other family members. Excavation of his shop from 1983 to 1986 yielded nearly 10,000 pieces of printers' type, used to print the *Maryland Gazette* (Little 1984, 1986a, 1986b, 1986c, 1987a, 1987b, 1987c). Excavation and analysis of the type showed that the shop was never mechanized. Two inventories also showed that the shop had at least two presses in operation most of the time. Even though the format of the newspaper changed dramatically between 1747 and 1765, no new machinery or more complex organization of type was used. The newspaper became modern-looking at this time, with more columns, horizontal subdivisions, and quotation marks appearing only at the beginning and end of quoted passages, uniform capitalization of opening words and proper names, and the current usage of the short "s."

The distribution of the type can be tied to the ideology of individualism by logic developed from Foucault. By the 1750s, the *Maryland Gazette* had taken on a modern look; that is, the spacing and text were organized in a way that appears familiar to us today. Insofar as the type fonts can be dated, fonts of spaces—pieces of metal used to create space between words, paragraphs, and columns—came into use later in the shop's history. The increased use of spaces was the technical change that allowed for the visual and thus the conceptual separation of all the spatial elements in the newspaper and thus of those that conveyed meaning as well.

An archaeological effort concerned with ideology must focus on the way categories of reality, the givens in other words, acted to separate social life; how divisions were made. Individuals could be individuals in the first place because they were thought to be defined from within and on personally achieved merit. Words, letters, and meanings that were visual and that were thought to depend on the individual's training for recognition, could take on characteristics that would make them appear to carry their own meaning. Meaning did not inhere in them but depended on a reader recognizing the markers on and around the word. Thus, the proliferation of spaces has the same symbolic function as the means by which people, as individuals, were separated from each by their self-and social definition and by dishes, chairs, room divisions, toothbrushes, and the compartmentalizing technologies of all kinds.

Mass production and mass consumption enhanced these technologies of the self. The things that were made and used allowed people to learn and to carry out the disciplines that created individuals. Cheap, mold-made, look-alike dishes gradually became widely available, widely used, and widely broken in the late 1760s and early 1770s. English dishes were bought, used, and copied. With them came the rationale for the egalitarian treatment of the individual (Leone et al. 1987). To carry the argument a step further, such practice was an internalized discipline that extended to the workplace, where it produced the disciplined, reliable worker. By the 1760s–1780s in Annapolis, this worker-consumer, or modern person, was being widely produced and was widely producing. Creamware is found at Jonas Green's house, at Reynold's Tavern, 183 Green Street, which was a blacksmith's house and workyard, and at the Victualling Warehouse, where the owner or renter lived with his family in quarters in the warehouse. These businesses and families were from the middle class, did not become wealthy, gave up business at their home sites by about 1800, and still remained middle class. We see creamware appear on at least 10 archaeological sites of varying wealth groups, including the rich, as at the Hammond-Harwood (Dent 1985) and Thomas Hyde houses (Shackel 1986); the middle class at the Jonas Green house, Reynold's Tavern, 183 Green Street, and at the State House Inn site (Hopkins 1985); and among the not-so-rich, for example, at the Victualling Warehouse (Crosby 1984). I argue that that pattern of individual use was extensive by the Revolutionary era. That pattern acted recursively to build belief in the ideology that individual liberty and love of it was the highest right and natural aspiration of all men, meaning all male adult property owners on the revolutionary side. It is in this context that creamware and other mold-made wares were important because their users were the same middle-class people who supported the Revolution, even though it did not change their place in the hierarchy. Isaac argues that this is the ideology that linked the rich and the middle class, and even some of the laboring class, into a political unit whose joint effort cast out the British and ensconced the native gentry in their place. Thus, archaeologically recovered ceramics show no change with the Revolution, only a long, gradual, deepening of a process that had begun by 1720 and was affecting most city dwellers by 1780.

1760–1785: Landscape

Much of Annapolis was rebuilt in the 1760s and 1770s. The state house and State Circle were rebuilt and redesigned (Read 1990). The Greens expanded their house as did Charles Carroll of Carrolton and the Calvert family. James Brice built his large mansion over an earlier, turn-of-the century structure. While the city's archaeological record is intact, there is very little material from the era 1650 to 1750 because the 1760s and 1770s, Annapolis's golden age, saw a great deal of rebuilding. The new houses were often big, symmetrical, expensive, and highly decorated, the culmination of the style begun in the 1720s.

This style involved ornamental gardens, at least a dozen of which were built between 1765 and 1790, attached to the large, new houses (Leone 1984, 1987; Paca-Steele 1987; Roulette and Williams 1987; Ernstein 1989; Kryder-Reid 1989). These gardens were built on slopes, using the main proportions of their houses as base measures. The base measures were then combined to create volumes that controlled perspective by using foreshortening or, in reverse, lengthening, so as to manipulate the appearance of the object being viewed. Optical illusions were the desired result, and the gardens served the owners' wish to study, demonstrate, and control the laws of nature. Such efforts demonstrated place in the social hierarchy and thus a presumed natural right to govern, since society was a natural phenomenon also governed by natural laws. Two gardens in Annapolis have been mapped topographically, one was excavated extensively, and there are data on several others. These data suggest that gardens demonstrate the ideology of natural hierarchy. The era was one of a struggle with Britain over rights to appeal laws, rights to local manufacture, rights protecting investments, and rights to legal controls. In the short run, Britain won, and the local gentry spent its money on decorative arts, architecture, and ornamental gardens, all of which proclaimed the right to govern through knowledge of natural law: Power that did not yet exist.

The impact of such arguments made through material culture can be understood through the many gardens maintained by ordinary people like William Ferris, a silversmith/innkeeper of ordinary middle-class means (Sarudy 1988). Many people like Ferris (Popernack 1989) knew what gardening required in terms of labor, skill, knowledge, design and layout. Thus, people who owned and maintained a garden knew how to read the message of a large, rare falling garden. The message was that class or status was a natural position and those who knew nature well enough to copy and control it deserved to rule. Whether such middle-class people accepted what they copied is still an unresearched question, but the emulation does bring us a step closer to seeing that it is likely that a dominant naturalizing ideology was likely to have been believed.

Annapolis was filled with gardens, probably like the one at Main Street that dated to the 1720s. William Farris made a symmetrical and sophisticated flower garden right off Church Circle in the 1760s and 1770s (Sarudy 1988). He must have understood math, horticulture, hydraulics, and the physics of light and temperature in order to have sustained such a garden. Thus, he knew the ideology behind the landscapes at the homes of the wealthy and even imitated them. He may have commented on the ideology from his position as an ordinary craftsman, and if he did, he would have been acting like the members of the Tuesday Club, intimating that he would like to be included in the higher levels of wealth and hoped-for power. With this kind of data on the acceptance of hierarchy we can begin to see that the dominant ideologies, both of natural hierarchy and of individuality, had an effect on the groups in the middle.

1780–1820

Annapolis is widely thought to have reached the peak of its fame and importance during the postrevolutionary period, and then to have entered a long eclipse, which lasted throughout the nineteenth century, indeed, possibly until the 1950s. By the early nineteenth century, Baltimore had become Maryland's premiere center. By 1800 it had 8,000 people, whereas Annapolis had less than 2,000. Around 1820, wealthy Annapolis resident Charles Carroll of Carrollton moved to Baltimore permanently, having invested there in shipyards, in iron mines, then in the first U.S. railroad. He and others helped turn Baltimore into a true industrial city. This never occurred in Annapolis, which was not invaded by the industrial revolution, as we have come to view it stereotypically. Class distinctions remained, but mass production did not become established on a large scale.

The city remained a local port, even though it offered a route into the new capital at Washington. There is enough archaeological information to see that some businesses moved to specialized locations, whereas others left or died out (Crosby 1984). Small family producers disappeared, and so did the craftspeople who produced for the gentry. There were no more great houses built after 1790. Furthermore, Annapolis was no longer the transfer point of merchant's wealth, but we do not know whether its economy stopped being provincial from the point of view of London, only to become provincial from the point of view of Baltimore and cities like it.

To summarize, eighteenth-century Annapolis was a port town that became a capital city for a province and then, around 1790, became a little port again, even though it remained a state capital. All the while, it experienced the culture associated with land speculation, slave trading, and mercantile credit management. It was also a city whose architecture and landscape advertised the authority of a distant power that collected and exported substantial wealth. I have argued that these material remains, the architecture and landscape, are those of an ideology of natural hierarchy. The wealth came from elsewhere (that is, from the plantations), and from within the city itself, through slave trading, shipping, and rents. The businesses that served the royal government, the proprietary government, and the gentry disappeared with the older ideologies, or found new products and clienteles later. These businesses and the homes of their owners, workers, and customers show the material remains of the techniques associated with the concept of individualism.

In the era from 1695 to 1790, Annapolis was shaped by two circumstances, in particular. First, it was a colonial outpost with an essentially extractive economy, often called a provincial economy. As a result, capitalism appeared there but was subordinated to international interests, which meant that there was little reinvestment in the city. And second, it was a profit-making center for about 2,000 residents, but they were not allowed to invest the capital needed to invigorate businesses because of British mercantile restrictions. When the colonial government collapsed and local capital was freed, the early capitalist practices of Annapolis, which had been divorced in good part from investment, turned their attention to Baltimore, or appeared there independently. Some stayed locally to produce the small market economy that characterized Annapolis and many of the other small cities and towns around the Chesapeake Bay through the nineteenth century and well into the twentieth.

I would like to close this essay by explaining why it is productive for archaeologists to consider ideology in their analyses. First, the ideology of individualism and its accompanying techniques are at the core of the current American identity, and any exploration of their origins, of their incomplete expression, or of the time before the ideology existed helps to show the arbitrariness of the ideology itself. Ideology is not naturally there, nor is it eternal. Many people who come to Annapolis and who visit our excavations and exhibits and who fill out a questionnaire say they are surprised to learn to what extent "things stay the same" or that "things progress." Both impressions reveal people trapped inside an ideology and thus unable to pierce the notion that life is now as it always has been or that progress is inevitable. These conclusions show that our attempt at raising consciousness has failed in these cases. But they also show the durability of the ideologies we deal with. Thus, it is important to try to be aware of ideology.

Second, the standard interpretations emerging from other fields that deal with the same materials that are of concern to archaeology are very different. Professionals within the decorative arts stress connoisseurship, high-style craftsmanship, and aesthetic judgments and thus rank items on the basis of taste, quality, maker, chronology, and cost. Historians, in contrast, tend to see such materials as expressions of wealth and as reflections of people, institutions, and forces that are better studied through documents. Preservationists, as a third group, tend to see these materials as accurate ways of gaining access to the most desirable and beneficial aspects of the past.

As a consequence of these legitimate assumptions, historians of the decorative arts do not normally deal with vernacular items, the huge mass of archaeologically recorded materials, anonymous goods, or consumption or function. Some historians ignore material culture, fail to see its active side, do not see archaeology as being complementary to their epistemology, and have no conception of landscape. Preservationists have an essentialist view of the relationship between past and present, wherein these are mediated by authenticity, which is commonly called taste. This is in contrast to the positivist, Marxist, psychoanalyst and postmodernist, all of whom see a gap between past and present that can only be filled with assumptions that problematize the link. Thus, our common data are the springboard for profoundly different views, which allow us to claim an alternative opinion.

References Cited

Althusser, Louis
1971 Ideology and Ideological State Apparatuses. In *Lenin and Philosophy*, translated by Ben Brewster, pp. 127–186. Monthly Review Press, New York.

Bacon, Edmond N.
1968 *Design of Cities*. Viking Press, New York.

Baker, Nancy
1983 Annapolis, Maryland, 1695–1730. In Annapolis and Anne Arundel Country, Maryland: A Study of Urban Development in Tobacco Economy: 1649–1776. Lorena S. Walsh, ed. NEH Grant Number RS 20199-81-1955. On file at Historic Annapolis Foundation, Annapolis, Md.

Beaudry, Mary C., Lauren J. Cook, and Stephen A Mrozowski
1991 Artifacts and Active Voices: Material Culture as Social Discourse. In *The Archaeology of Inequality*, edited by Randall McGuire and Robert Paynter, pp. 150–191. Blackwell, Oxford.

Breslaw, Elaine G.
1975 Wit, Whimsy, and Politics: The Uses of Satire by the Tuesday Club of Annapolis, 1744–1756. *William and Mary Quarterly*, 3d ser. 32:2:295–306.
1988 (editor) *Records of the Tuesday Club of Annapolis, 1745–1756*. University of Illinois Press, Urbana.

Cook, Lauren J.
1989 Tobacco-Related Material and the Construction of Working-Class Culture. In *Interdisciplinary Investigations of the Boott Mills Lowel, Massachusetts*, vol. 3, edited by Mary C. Beaudry and Stephen A. Mrozowski. Culture Resources Management Study No. 21. Division of Cultural Resources, North Atlantic Office, National Park Service, Boston.

Crosby, Constance
1984 A Preliminary Site Report for the Victualing Warehouse, Annapolis, Md. On file at Historic Annapolis Foundation, Annapolis, Md.

Deetz, James
1977 *In Small Things Forgotten*. Anchor Books, Garden City, New York.

Dent, Richard J.
1983 Interim Report on Reynolds Tavern Excavation. On file at Historic Annapolis Foundation, Annapolis, Md.
1985 Archaeological Excavations at the Hammond-Harwood House, Annapolis, Md. Report on file at Historic Annapolis Foundation, Annapolis, Md.

Ernstein, Julie H.
1989 The Status of Landscape in Historical Archaeology and Some Comments toward a Deconstruction of Landscape. Paper presented at the Society for Historical Archaeology meetings, Baltimore, Md.

Foucault, Michel
1979 *Discipline and Punish*. Vintage Books, New York.

Hodder, Ian
1986 *Reading the Past: Approaches to Interpretation in Archaeology*. Cambridge University Press, Cambridge, U.K.

Hopkins, Joseph W., III
1985 State House Inn Preliminary Report. On file at Historic Annapolis Foundation, Annapolis, Md.

Isaac, Rhys
1982 *The Transformation of Virginia, 1740–1790*. University of North Carolina Press, Chapel Hill.

Kryder-Reid, Elizabeth
1988 Preliminary Report: St. Mary's Site, 18AP45. 1987 Excavation Season. Report on file at Historic Annapolis Foundation, Annapolis, Md.
1989 Political Landscapes and Landscape Politics: Contextual Archaeology and Myth at the Charles Carroll House, Annapolis, Maryland. Paper presented at the Council for Northeast Historical Archaeology annual meetings, October 15, 1989, Morristown, N.J.

Leone, Mark P.
1983 Method as Message. *Museum News* 62:1:35–41.
1984 Interpreting Ideology in Historical Archaeology: Using the Rules of Perspective in the William Paca Garden in Annapolis, Maryland. In *Ideology, Power and Prehistory*, edited by C. Tilley and D. Miller, pp. 25–35. Cambridge University Press, Cambridge, U.K.
1987 Rule by Ostentation: The Relationship between Space and Sight in Eighteenth-Century Landscape Architecture in the Chesapeake Region of Maryland. In *Method and Theory for Activity Area Research—An Ethnoarchaeological Approach*, edited by Susan Kent, pp. 604–633. Columbia University Press, New York.
1988 The Georgian Order as the Order of Merchant Capitalism. In *The Recovery of Meaning: Historical Archaeology in the Eastern United States*, edited by Mark P. Leone and Parker B. Potter, Jr., pp. 235–261. Smithsonian Institution Press, Washington, D.C.

Leone, Mark P., and Paul A. Shackel

1987 Forks, Clocks and Power. In *Mirror and Metaphor: Material and Social Construction of Reality*, edited by Daniel Ingersoll and Gordon Bronitsky, pp. 45–61. University Press of America, Lanham, Md.

1990 The Georgian Order in Annapolis, Maryland. In New Perspectives of Maryland Archaeology, edited by R. J. Dent and B. J. Little. *Maryland Archaeology.* 26(1,2):69–84.

Leone, Mark P., Parker B. Potter, Jr., and Paul A. Shackel

1987 Toward a Critical Archaeology. *Current Anthropology* 28:3:283–302.

Leone, Mark P., Julie H. Ernstein, Elizabeth Kryder-Reid, and Paul A. Shackel

1989 Power Gardens of Annapolis. *Archaeology* 42:2:34–39, 74–75.

Leone, Mark P., Elizabeth Kryder-Reid, and Janice Bailey-Goldschmidt

1992 The Rationalization of Sound in Mid-18th-Century Annapolis, Maryland. In *The Art and Mystery of Historical Archaeology*, edited by Anne E. Yentsch and Mary C. Beaudry, pp. 229–245. CRC Press, Boca Raton.

Little, Barbara J.

1984 AP29, Jonas Green Print Shop: Printers Type from the 1983 Excavation. On file at Historic Annapolis Foundation, Annapolis, Md.

1986a The Green Family Print Shop in Annapolis, Maryland. Paper presented at the Eastern States Archaeological Federation meetings in Wilmington, Delaware, October 1986. On file at Historic Annapolis Foundation, Annapolis, Md.

1986b Consuming Ideology: Printing and Printers in the Eighteenth-Century Chesapeake. Paper presented at the Society for American Archaeology meetings in New Orleans, LA, April 1986. On file at Historic Annapolis Foundation, Annapolis, Md.

1986c Changing Business and Domestic Structures of the Green Family of Printers in Annapolis, Maryland. Paper presented at the Northeast Anthropological Association meetings in Buffalo, N.Y., March 1986. On file at Historic Annapolis Foundation, Annapolis, Md.

1987a The Authorities of Media: Print Culture and Material Culture in the Colony and State of Maryland. Paper presented at the Society for American Archaeology meetings, Toronto, Canada, May 1987. On file at Historic Annapolis Foundation, Annapolis, Md.

1987b The Archaeology and History of Printing in Preindustrial Annapolis, Maryland. Paper presented at the Society for Historical Archaeology meetings, Savannah, GA, January 1987. On file at Historic Annapolis Foundation, Annapolis, Md.

1987c *Ideology and Media: Historical Archaeology of Printing in 18th-Century Annapolis, Md.* Ph.D. dissertation, State University of New York at Buffalo, University Microfilms, Ann Arbor.

1988 Craft and Culture Change in Eighteenth-Century Chesapeake. In *The Recovery of Meaning: Historical Archaeology in the Eastern United States*, edited by Mark P. Leone and Parker B. Potter, Jr., pp. 263–292. Smithsonian Institution Press, Washington, D.C.

McGuire, Randall

1988 Dialogues with the Dead, Ideology and the Cemetery. In *The Recovery of Meaning: Historical Archaeology in the Eastern United States*, edited by Mark P. Leone and Parker B. Potter, Jr., pp. 435–480. Smithsonian Institution Press, Washington, D.C.

Micklus, Robert (editor)

1990 *The History of the Ancient and Honorable Tuesday Club*, by Alexander Hamilton. University of North Carolina Press, Chapel Hill.

Paca-Steele, Barbara, with St. Clair Wright

1987 The Mathematics of an Eighteenth-Century Wilderness Garden. *Journal of Garden History* 6:4:299–320.

Popernack, Paul

1989 An Examination of 18th Century Land Records in Annapolis Maryland. On file, Department of Anthropology, University of Maryland, College Park.

Read, Esther Doyle

1990 Archaeological Investigations around State Circle in Annapolis, Maryland. On file at Historic Annapolis Foundation, Annapolis, Md.

Roulette, Billy Ray, and Eileen Williams

1987 A Topographical Survey Map of the Charles Carroll of Carrollton Garden. On file at Historic Annapolis Foundation, Annapolis, Md.

Russo, Jean

1983 The Structure of the Anne Arundel County Economy. In Annapolis and Anne Arundel County, Maryland: A Study of Urban Development in a Tobacco Economy, 1649–1776, edited by Lorena S. Walsh. NEH Grant No. RS 20199-81-1955. On file, Historic Annapolis Foundation, Annapolis, Maryland.

Serudy, Barbara W.

1988 *The Gardens and Grounds of an Eighteenth-Century Chesapeake Craftsman.* Master's thesis, University of Maryland, College Park.

Shackel, Paul A.

1986 Archaeological Testing at the 193 Main Street Site, 18AP44, Annapolis, Maryland. On file at Historic Annapolis Foundation, Annapolis, Md.

1987 *A Historical Archaeology of Personal Discipline.* Ph.D. dissertation, State University of New York at Buffalo, University Microfilms, Ann Arbor.

Shackel, Paul A., and Laura J. Galke, with a contribution by Stephen P. Austin

1988 Excavations in St. Anne's Churchyard, 18AP43, Church Circle, Annapolis, Md. On file at Historic Annapolis Foundation, Annapolis, Md.

Yentsch, Anne E.

1986 Preliminary Analysis of Features from Period 1

Associated with Postholes Buildings at the Calvert Site, Annapolis, Md. Calvert Interim Report No. 1. On file at Historic Annapolis Foundation, Annapolis, Md.

1990 The Calvert Orangery in Annapolis, Maryland: A Horticultural Symbol of Power and Prestige in an Early 18th-Century Community. In *Earth Patterns: Essays in Landscape Archaeology*, edited by William M. Kelso and Rachel Most, pp. 169–187. University of Virginia Press, Charlottesville.

XV
CHAPTER

Current Archaeological Perspectives on the Growth and Development of Williamsburg

MARLEY R. BROWN III AND PATRICIA SAMFORD

WILLIAMSBURG, THE capital of the colony of Virginia for more than three-quarters of a century, is one of the most studied of North America's colonial towns. From its modest beginnings as a cross-roads amid dispersed tobacco plantations, a place known in the seventeenth century as Middle Plantation, Williamsburg developed into a thriving eighteenth-century community. Much of the architectural skeleton of that community has been restored or reconstructed since 1928. Today, the former colonial capital of Virginia functions as a museum of living history where visitors can learn about both the important political events that took place there on the eve of the American Revolution and about daily life in the colonial period. One of the current goals of the Colonial Williamsburg Foundation, the museum organization that interprets Williamsburg's historic area to the public, is to teach early American history by portraying the evolution of American society in the seventeenth and eighteenth centuries (CWF 1985). This interpretive effort is deeply rooted in extensive documentary, archaeological, and architectural research, the most comprehensive of its kind ever undertaken in the Chesapeake, or anywhere else in the United States, for that matter.

Throughout its 60-year history, research at Colonial Williamsburg has been guided by the main goals of the foundation, which are "to restore, recreate, preserve, and interpret . . . eighteenth-century Williamsburg" (CWF 1989). Just as historians and architects were initially employed by the foundation to study the history of individual houses, the techniques of archaeology, or, more properly, excavation, were at first "a tool of the architectural restorer," used to track the footprints of individual buildings (Noël Hume 1983:72). Over the years, the scope of archaeological fieldwork at Williamsburg has been greatly expanded to encompass the interests of curators, social historians, archaeologists, and most recently, anthropologists. Questions asked by foundation archaeologists now reach far beyond the basic "what-where-when?" queries that motivated the digs of the late 1920s and 1930s and the more ambitious cross-trenching effort that followed World War II. No longer are archaeologists content only with measured drawings of brick footings or the retrieval of architecturally related artifacts such as hinges and door plates. These finds remain an essential core of evidence for current building reconstruction, just as they were for the early restoration efforts. So, too, do the domestic artifacts that have been systematically recovered from Williamsburg sites since the late 1950s, when Ivor Noël Hume introduced methods of stratigraphic excavation, and perfected the art of site-specific interpretation. In the past, these objects, numbering in the millions from Williamsburg sites, have been used to flesh out the furnishing plans of exhibit buildings, and to clarify the history of European ceramics and glass. Together with an increasingly diversified set of companion physical evidence from the ground, they are now being applied to the scholarly investigations of today's social historians and anthropologists, who are examining questions concerning the society and culture of the Chesapeake from the time of settlement through the early nineteenth century.

A Museum Framework for Archaeological Research

The current archaeological program at Colonial Williamsburg is guided by the museum's overall research and interpretive theme, recently articulated in an educational master plan titled *Teaching History at Colonial Williamsburg*. The theme is "Becoming Americans"—which refers to the transformation of the European and African cultures brought to the Virginia colony (CWF 1985). Each group of immigrants, whether arriving by choice or against their will, brought their own cultural traditions to the Chesapeake. Once there, they faced novel and often harsh conditions in the New World. The ways in which these groups adapted, both to their new environment and, more significantly, to one another, formed the roots of a new culture that began to take shape toward the end of the seventeenth century. From the interaction of European and African immigrants and the contact with the indigenous Native American population there emerged a regional American culture distinctively different from that of the homeland and other parts of the British colonial world (Mitchell 1983; Carr et al. 1988; Greene 1988). The Colonial Williamsburg Foundation seeks to better understand the character of this transformation by rigorously examining cultural elements that persisted in the Chesapeake and the changes from the Old to the New World as these were manifested in the lives and artifacts of Chesapeake town residents.

Inherent in this overarching educational theme is a commitment to "everyone's" history. The careers of wealthy white men who shaped public policy have hardly been forgotten, but the stories of men and women who heretofore had largely gone unnoticed in Williamsburg's exhibit buildings are now being told. The life experiences of common laborers, African American slaves and women, along with other long-neglected segments of the population, are being actively researched and interpreted. This effort has been greatly facilitated by the compilation of biographies of more than 2,000 late seventeenth- and eighteenth-century York County residents gathered from a wide range of primary historical sources, including deeds, probate records, and newspapers (Rowe 1988). Colonial Williamsburg historians have used the biographical files, together with information contained in more specialized data bases assembled from probate inventories and other materials, to examine a number of aspects of Williamsburg's demographic, economic, and social structure in relation to other rural and urban areas of the Chesapeake (Hellier 1987, 1989; Kelly 1988; Rowe 1988; Walsh 1989). These historical studies have contributed to a more general understanding of the role of towns within the Chesapeake, the emergence of a consumer society in the region, and the nature of the economic and social hierarchy in rural and urban areas.

During the past decade, the Department of Archaeological Research has joined in the investigation of these subjects, finding substantial common ground with colleagues in social and architectural history in the interrelated subjects of Williamsburg's physical growth and the material life of its inhabitants and of those living in nearby rural areas. In their pursuit of these goals, researchers have shifted away from what was the basic approach to archaeology at Williamsburg sites for more than twenty years. In part because of the implicit or explicit assumption that some level of on-site building reconstruction would take place, archaeological fieldwork within the historic area placed an intellectual premium on the accurate identification and dating of architectural features, artifacts, and the actions that produced them. This emphasis produced notable improvements in the field methods of historical archaeologists, especially the introduction of open-area stratigraphic excavation, and valuable refinements in the history of imported ceramics, glass, and other artifacts that now make it possible to date assemblages from colonial-period sites with some precision (Noël Hume 1968; 1969a).

Rather than abandon this approach to Williamsburg's archaeological record, the Department of Archaeological Research has expanded open-area excavation and embraced single-layer or single-context planning, combining these newer tools of stratigraphic interpretation with recently developed microcomputer techniques in order to enhance the "biographical" approach to Williamsburg sites (Derry and Brown 1987; M. Brown 1986; Harris

1989; Brown and Muraca, 1993). Contemporary stratigraphic units are now painstakingly reconstructed and correlated with the property ownership and occupation sequences of sites, blocks, and neighborhoods within Williamsburg that have been drawn together from historical sources (M. Brown 1985; G. Brown 1986c; Samford 1990). Archaeological evidence is linked with the data in the master biographical files created from historical records by reconstituting historical households and placing them in time and space. Not only is the household an especially appropriate analytical unit for bringing together historical and archaeological information, but it has shown potential for shedding light on a broad range of archaeological questions (Henretta 1978; Beaudry 1984; Mrozowski 1984; Kertzer 1985; Beaudry and Mrozowski 1989)

Williamsburg presents a unique opportunity for this type of research because of the ambitious scale at which historical households have been reconstructed and because of the care that has gone into placing them on the ground and tying them down to specific archaeological assemblages. No settlement in colonial America has produced archaeological data of the quality and quantity that now exist for Williamsburg—data that can be directly correlated in most cases with individual households whose members have at least some biographical material on file. This archaeological and historical record also makes it possible to raise the sights of comparative inquiry to encompass statistical patterning in the occurrence of household-related archaeological data within the town as a whole, and from the perspective of the Chesapeake, as well as other areas of the British colonial world (Brown 1990, 1991a, 1991b). Such a comparison, which is concerned with adding archaeology's fair share to reconstructing the material lives of *all* of the town's residents and drawing out any important differences that may have existed between town and country-dwellers, also benefits from a series of historical studies of eighteenth-century consumer activity relevant to the kind of domestic artifacts commonly found in the ground (Martin chapter 11, 1989; Miller 1991; Miller et al. 1992).

The remainder of this chapter will examine recent archaeological projects and explain how they have contributed to Colonial Williamsburg's overall research goals pertaining to the town's physical growth and the lives of previously underappreciated or poorly documented residents. The studies of physical growth have taken full advantage of recent innovations in the recovery and interpretation of environmental data from historic sites, and the studies of residents make use of both the unusually large collection of artifact assemblages recovered from Williamsburg during nearly 65 years of excavation and the innovative mass biography undertaken by the foundation's historians in the past decade.

The Physical Growth of Williamsburg

Part of Colonial Williamsburg's aim from the very beginning of the restoration was to recreate the physical landscape of the colonial past. In fact, Rev. W. A. R. Goodwin's and John D. Rockefeller's fascination with Williamsburg stemmed largely from the realization that in Williamsburg lay the opportunity to restore an entire town and its surroundings, thus giving its visitors a sense of complete immersion in the eighteenth century. Perhaps they, as James Deetz (1990:1) so eloquently expressed 60 years later, realized that the landscape was the "connective tissue that gives houses and communities their proper context." Much as today, the eighteenth-century landscape was a planned entity, a "mix of natural and man-made form" (Stilgoe 1982) reflecting the cultural views of the persons who created it. When Francis Nicholson drafted the town plan for Williamsburg in 1699, he imposed a rectilinear grid over the ridge between the James and York Rivers that the town now occupies. A series of late eighteenth- and early nineteenth-century maps document the town plan, detailing many of its contemporary buildings and natural surroundings, such as ravines, waterways, orchards, fields, and gardens. One map in particular (figure 15.1), created by an unknown French draftsman around 1782, was used in the 1930s and 1940s in conjunction with archaeological trenching to restore the town as it appeared on the eve of the American Revolution.

Archaeologists have long been interested in the reconstruction of past landscapes. Colonial Williamsburg's archaeologists have been no exception—their early efforts focused on unearthing and reconstructing eighteenth-century buildings and gardens. By 1934, six short years after the restoration began, 150 colonial buildings had been restored or reconstructed, and more than 400 more recent structures removed or destroyed. The resultant picture of the past was a landscape skewed in favor of upper-middle-class and gentry homes, quaint shops, box-

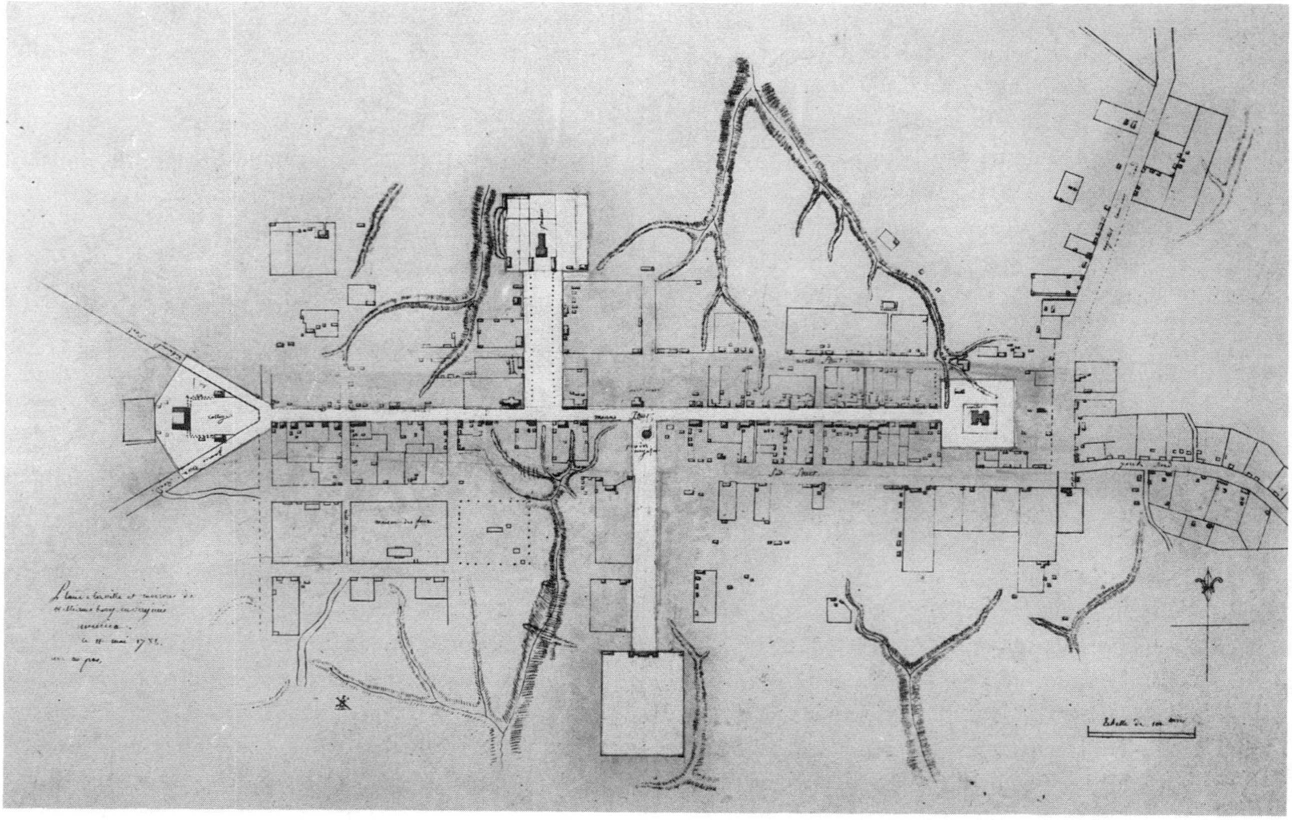

FIGURE 15.1. *Plan of the town of Williamsburg, prepared during the revolutionary war by an unknown French soldier as a barracks map. (Courtesy of Special Collections, Earl Gregg Swem Library, College of William and Mary)*

wood gardens, and grazing livestock. This vision of the past as a better, simpler time may have served a purpose in the Depression era of the 1930s, but was in reality a sterile, inaccurate image. Today, efforts have been made to view the physical landscape more objectively through the relatively unbiased eye of archaeology.

For example, the 1930s notion of the prevalence of formal garden spaces within colonial environments was apparently greatly exaggerated (Hosmer 1985; Brown and Samford 1990). Kitchen or utilitarian gardens seem to have been much more the norm, with the formal ornamental plantings prescribed by eighteenth-century garden manuals appearing much less frequently. For example, excavations on the site of Shields Tavern, a mid-eighteenth-century eating establishment, revealed four planting beds in the rear yard. Analysis of these beds and associated walkways and fencelines led to the reconstruction of a large kitchen garden behind the restored tavern, a garden that would have provided food for the tavern's kitchen. This type of working garden fit well with the commercial nature of the property.

In contrast, the gardens on the homelots of eighteenth-century statesman Sir John Randolph, of his son John, and of Judge Joseph Prentis would have been large formal gardens. Each man was an influential member of the Williamsburg gentry, and each was intensively interested in gardening. Recent research in Annapolis, Maryland (Yentsch 1984; Leone 1990), and at Governor Alexander Spotswood's Enchanted Castle in Orange County, Virginia (Sanford 1990), has shown that formal gardens, with their geometrically aligned beds and falling terraces, were perceived as a means of controlling the natural environment. These "demonstrations of the rules of nature observed and duplicated" (Leone 1988) were vivid social statements about the power of the gentry and were an expression of the "controlled rationalization of space"

(Leone 1984:25) that befit the Enlightenment. Such a control of space was expected for the urban plantations of the Randolphs and the Prentises.

However, the excavated planting beds and trenches on all three properties indicated the presence of only kitchen or utilitarian gardens, although the design and physical character of Sir John Randolph's garden suggested more than a passing knowledge of English gardening manuals. This urban plantation had four large planting beds at the northern end of the property, arranged with alleys between them. The various paving materials (wine-bottle glass, oyster shell, and bone) lining the different beds suggests that Sir John was experimenting with drainage materials. Seed analysis indicates that the planting bed was turned over to asparagus rather than ornamental plantings of boxwood or flowers.

Experimental kitchen gardening was also evident at Tazewell Hall, home of John Randolph, and at the Prentis site. Randolph, the attributed author of *A Treatise on Gardening* (1826), and Prentis, who wrote an unpublished garden calendar and garden book (Webb-Prentis Papers), were well-known gardening experts in the Virginia colony. These works must have been based on years of experimentation with gardening, and the excavation results show this to be the case at both sites. But nowhere on any of these properties was there evidence of the design elements so common in contemporary descriptions of eighteenth-century formal gardens.

In addition to determining the nature of garden design in Williamsburg, research has made environmental reconstruction possible. Recent advances in the areas of palynology (Bryant and Holloway 1983; Reinhard 1989), seed identification (Mrozowski 1987), and phytolith analysis (Rovner 1983, 1990) have enabled researchers to identify the flora actually growing in eighteenth-century Williamsburg and its gardens. Until recently, they had to rely on botanical material recovered from several colonial-period wells (Noël Hume 1969b, 1969c), but the information now available from pollen, seeds, and phytolith analysis expands the sample from the limited resources of anaerobic environments to trash pits, privy fills, and other similar sealed features (Brown 1990).

Gardens were only one small part of the larger picture that formed the eighteenth-century landscape of Williamsburg. This picture also included the natural environment of the town and its hinterlands. Because the colonists and their slaves interacted with and manipulated the physical world around them, another question of concern to archaeology is whether this changed through time and across cultural boundaries.

Virginia's Department of Archaeological Research currently employs a computerized geographic mapping program to assist in the accurate reconstruction of the built and natural environment. Developed by Dominic Powlesland of the Heslerton Parish Project in England, GEOBASE 4D facilitates the three-dimensional recovery of data from excavations. Excavated artifacts are piece-plotted with an electronic distance measurer (EDM) to determine artifact scatters, depositional patterns, and yard use. This relatively new program has been used on a few sites at Colonial Williamsburg. At the James Anderson site, for example, GEOBASE 4D was used during the recent excavation of a late eighteenth-century forge building. Point proveniencing of the horizontal and vertical location of each artifact from the building's earthen floor provided information on how space was used within the building (figure 15.2). Artifact plotting outside the building aided in differentiating work and storage areas in the forge yard.

GEOBASE 4D can also be used to discern past topographic levels and features and thus to reconstruct the

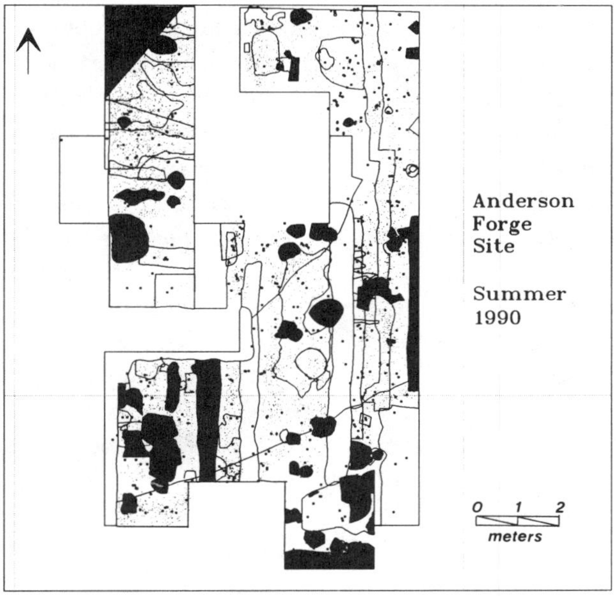

FIGURE 15.2. *Geobase map showing the location of all forge-related debris from the earthen floor of the James Anderson shop.*

town's natural environment during different periods of the past. When combined with large-scale utility projects across the town, GEOBASE can be used to map nonextant landforms, such as ravines, roadways, stream beds, old boundary lines, and street grades. Williamsburg, which is situated on a ridge between the James and York Rivers, was once heavily intersected by ravines. Eighteenth-century descriptions of the town document this rugged terrain; with GEOBASE it is possible to plot the perimeters of these landforms, link similar soil strata across the town, and "build" a topographically correct representation of Williamsburg during different time periods.

Another important facet of archaeological research at Colonial Williamsburg has been to document the growth and development of Williamsburg and its surrounding environs throughout the eighteenth century. Williamsburg has been a vital community, responding to meet the changing needs and functions of its inhabitants through time and across space. Colonial Williamsburg archaeologists, historians, and architectural historians have joined forces to study the colonial town in 10-year increments in an attempt to define the interrelationships between settlement patterns and the physical, social, and economic development of the community. One question being addressed in this project is how Williamsburg changed from a small seventeenth-century locus of dispersed farmsteads (Grim 1977) to the planned baroque community designed by Governor Francis Nicholson. Town development is being tracked through the building clause enacted to promote growth within the new town, existing maps of Williamsburg at various periods, and excellent documentation from the archaeological and architectural records. Growth is being charted in terms of actual property development, lot subdivision, and the development of peripheral areas. Work has also expanded to include the two ports or landings on the north and south sides of town, which were important centers for commerce and trade in the seventeenth and eighteenth centuries (Hudgins 1977; G. Brown 1986a, 1986b; Edwards 1986), and the various plantations, quarters, and industries located along the peripheries (Muraca 1991; Steen 1991).

Block 29 as a Case Study

Detailed analyses of archaeological, architectural, and historical data have been completed for several blocks within the town (G. Brown 1986c; Samford 1990). One block in particular, that bordering Palace Green and Market Square, two of the town's important social and political centers in the eighteenth century, has provided excellent historical, architectural, and archaeological information. The assumptions tested in this area concerned the changing functional roles of the town and their archaeological, historical, and architectural manifestations.

The first lots on Block 29 were purchased in 1713, thirteen years after the first lot sales were recorded in the town. In keeping with the building clause enacted during the early years of the town's development, structures were built on lots within two years of property purchase. During the first half of the eighteenth century, Block 29 showed a mixed commercial and residential character, with a gunsmith shop, theater, ordinary, bowling green, and apothecary shop coexisting with the residential buildings. The mixed character of the block, characteristic of colonial-period urban areas (Sjoberg 1960; Boulton 1987) can perhaps be explained by the wide range of functions Williamsburg served during the first half of the century as Virginia's leading urban center (O'Mara 1983:222). Although most service-related establishments, such as taverns and stores, were clustered at the eastern end of town, near the Capitol, such establishments overflowed into other parts of town, including Palace Green. The economic status of the residents was also mixed; the first three resident property owners were a middling artisan, an ordinary keeper or theater owner teetering on the edge of insolvency, and a wealthy merchant and physician.

With the completion of the grandly ornate governor's palace, and its subsequent mid-eighteenth-century upgrade, and with the gap between economic classes widening, the character of Block 29 slowly began to change. By the middle of the eighteenth century, the block had lost its industrial character, and the only commercial enterprise remaining was George Gilmer's apothecary shop. At the same time, the residents on the block became more consistently affluent—Thomas Everard, the mayor of Williamsburg and clerk of York County, now resided adjacent to the governor's palace, and his neighbors included Dr. Peter Hay and lawyers John Randolph and John Tazewell. Across Palace Green lived the lawyer and burgess George Wythe, and the treasurer and leader of the House of Burgesses Robert Carter. This homogenization of Block 29 into an upper-class residential area can be traced to the declining economic and social importance of Williamsburg during the third quarter of the eighteenth century (Smart 1986:26). The growth of new urban centers to the north and west, such as Fredericksburg and Richmond, reduced the need for consumer goods and services in Williamsburg. In addition, the labor of skilled slaves made many of the larger plantations in the Colony virtually self-sufficient; any goods not produced on the plantation could be ordered directly from England. Although on the wane socially and economically, Williamsburg, as the capital of the Virginia Colony, did remain politically important until 1780, when the capital was moved to Richmond. This status is reflected in the affluent nature of the neighborhood and the political ties of its residents.

Archaeological, architectural, and historical data reflect the changing character of the block and the upward mobility of its residents. While lots on the eastern end of town near the Capitol underwent subdivision typical of the increased demand for space, property size on Block 29 remained stable. Each resident owned 1½ to 2 acres—enough space for a house, a complement of outbuildings, and a spacious garden. In some respects, these properties were like the large "urban plantations" that had developed along Williamsburg's outskirts earlier in the eighteenth century. This emphasis on large lots for the affluent residents of Block 29 was not accidental; research using the 1798 tax list indicates that lot size was a significantly more important factor in determining property value or worth (and hence, economic status) than house size or detailing (Soltow 1989:65).

These residents were prospering materially as well: excavated artifacts indicate that both Gilmer and Everard consistently upgraded their ceramic table- and teawares while in residence (Samford 1990), moving from white salt-glazed stonewares to blue and white hand-painted Chinese porcelain, and eventually to overglaze decorated Chinese porcelain, the most expensive ceramic available at this time. Additional expenditures are also documented. Everard purchased livery for two of his young male slaves (Norton Papers); this action can only be interpreted as a public display of his wealth and power as the mayor of Williamsburg and the clerk of York County. Both Everard and Gilmer undertook renovations on their properties, as indicated by the construction debris in Everard's household garbage and a letter from Gilmer in 1752 to his merchant in England, which detailed the interior renovation of his house. In the letter, Gilmer comments:

> Mrs. Gilmer is perfectly satisfied with your conduct about her China. . . . I have just finished a closet for her to put it in as agreed on before you left us. I am wainscoting my dining room, which with a handsome marble chimney piece &c with glass over it, will make it a tolerable room for an Apothecary. (Brock Notebook)

But while the residents of Block 29 were prospering, a move was afoot that would bring about drastic changes for Williamsburg. The town had served as the capital of the Virginia colony for almost a century, between 1699 and 1780, but during the midst of the Revolutionary War, then-governor Thomas Jefferson decided to move the capital upriver to Richmond. With the departure of the government, gone too was the influx of planters who came to town for Public Times and various sessions of court and the General Assembly. Numerous tavernkeepers and businessmen, finding it no longer possible to support themselves on declining business, followed the government up to Richmond. The governor's palace, once the most opulent building in the colony, served a brief stint as a military hospital before being burned to the ground in 1781. Other public buildings shared similar fates, with the Capitol being used as a grammar school and court at the end of the eighteenth century (Reps 1972:190) and the powder magazine seeing service in the nineteenth century as a Baptist meetinghouse, a dancing school, and a livery stable.

This general transition was visible on Block 29 in several ways. The archaeological evidence indicated the focal point of the block had begun moving away from Palace Green. A new courthouse, constructed in 1770 on the open grassy field of Market Square along Duke of Gloucester Street, created a new locus of power and visual interest. In 1788, wealthy lawyer St. George Tucker purchased property on Block 29 containing an early eighteenth-century house. This house fronted on Palace Green, at that time a vista terminating on the former site of the governor's palace. One of Tucker's first actions as the new owner was to move the house to the southern end of the property, realigning it to face the new Courthouse and Market Square. The formerly prestigious frontage along Palace Street was downgraded to the location of the Tucker outbuildings; the voluminous personal papers of the Tucker family combined with archaeological research indicate a stable, bathhouse, and laundry were situated in the area. The Tucker move was not the only instance of this realignment behavior; on an adjacent block, the Peyton Randolph House was also rearranged to face Market Square. Although Block 29 remained principally residential, the character of the block's residents after the Revolutionary War returned to its early eighteenth-century mix of economic levels. St. George Tucker, the wealthy lawyer whose descendants still occupy the Tucker house, contrasts sharply with the late eighteenth-century owners of the Brush-Everard property. In the 10 years following the Revolution, four different middle-class families occupied this house.

Archaeological, documentary, and architectural information shows that changes in Block 29 throughout the eighteenth century reflected social, political, and economic changes that were taking place throughout Williamsburg. When the town was in the midst of its social, economic, and political heyday in the 1730s, Block 29 displayed a mixed residential-commercial character. As mentioned earlier, Williamsburg was the leading urban center of Virginia during the 1730s and performed a wide range of services. It continued to play this role into the 1750s but then began to be eclipsed by other service centers along the upper reaches of the James and Rappahannock rivers. Although its economic and social functions were becoming less important, Williamsburg, as the capital of the Virginia colony through 1780, did remain a center of political power. As the need for consumer services decreased, the commercial establishments disappeared from the block, and it was transformed into a gentry neighborhood. This status was maintained during the years preceding the Revolutionary War, as Williamsburg played a key role in the political events foreshadowing the British–American conflict.

After the removal of the capital, the types of residents on Block 29 changed. Persons connected with the government followed Jefferson to Richmond and Block 29 was inhabited by people connected with the College of William and Mary or the mental hospital. The block and the town remained much like this until the early twentieth century, when W. A. R. Goodwin and John D. Rockefeller set in motion the restoration of Williamsburg.

Standards and Styles of Living

Recent studies of eighteenth-century York County probate inventories provide profiles of households at various wealth levels throughout the century (Carson and Walsh 1981; Walsh 1983; Carr and Walsh 1991). When the information from these studies is compared with specific information on households gained from documentary and archaeological research, it is possible to determine and interpret patterns of behavior relating to the economic, political, and social forces at work in Williamsburg.

To carry out this comparison it has been necessary to reexamine some of Williamsburg's colonial citizens in light of new archaeological evidence. For years, the Colonial Williamsburg Foundation had portrayed John Brush, an early eighteenth-century Williamsburg gunsmith, as a middling artisan. The house he constructed on Palace Green around 1718 was a fairly modest one-and-a-half story frame structure (it measured 20 by 44 feet) built to meet the minimum standards required by the Williamsburg Building Act of 1705. The inventory of his estate, taken upon his death in 1727, portrayed a man of modest means; the £90 valuation of his combined household and his shop goods placed him squarely in the middle ranks of York County society. Yet, recent excavations on the John Brush property, combined with new architectural information, have brought about a reevaluation of John Brush and his position in Williamsburg and Chesapeake society.

During the fall of 1988, the Department of Archaeological Research excavated a privy constructed by John Brush that was filled with his household and shop debris during the 1720s (figure 15.3). The quality of the ceramics and table glass plus other dietary information recovered from the privy suggests that Brush enjoyed a much higher standard of living than his typical peers. Although some of Brush's furniture was described as "old" in the 1727 inventory, archaeology showed that he was able to set his table with finely painted English delft teawares and some vessels of Chinese porcelain (figure 15.4). These ceramics, plus the listing of a tea table in the estate inventory, indicate Brush had participated in the formal proceedings of the tea ceremony. In the third decade of the eighteenth century, only 33 percent of all York County inventoried estates valued at £226 to £490 listed tea or teawares (Carr and Walsh 1991). Because of the prohibitive cost of tea and its accoutrements, only the very wealthy had access to them. Brush, with his entire estate valued at only £90 at his death, certainly did not fit into this economic category. In fact, during that time period, no inventoried urban York County estates valued at £50 to £94 contained listings of tea or teaware.

Perhaps more surprising than the teawares was the dis-

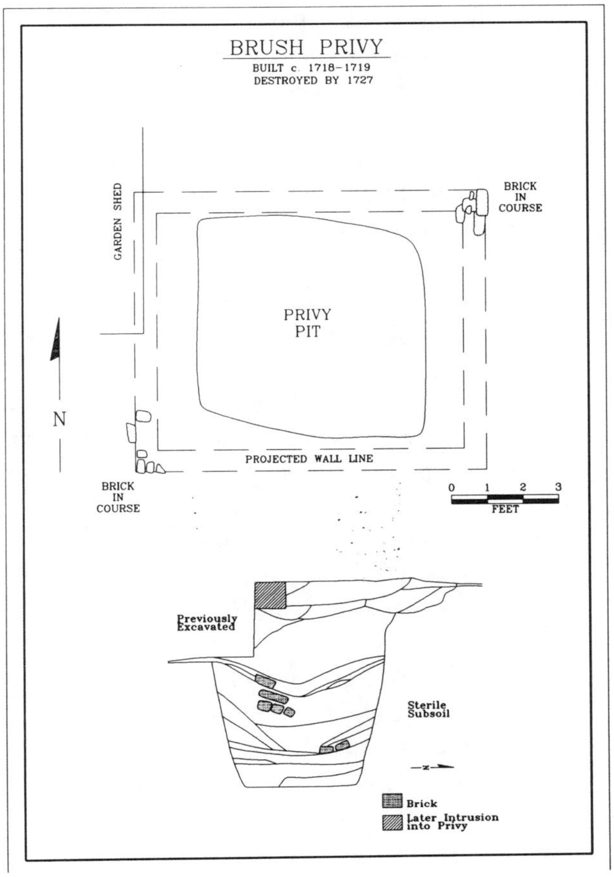

FIGURE 15.3. *Plan and profile of the John Brush privy. (Drawing by Kim Wagner)*

covery of Chinese porcelain tea- and tablewares in the privy and other Brush deposits on the site. The high cost of porcelain in the early eighteenth century guaranteed its place as a symbol of wealth and status. For this reason, porcelain was commonly found only in households of the upper class until the second quarter of the eighteenth century (Noël Hume 1969a:257) and was generally not available to the middle and lower classes in local stores until the 1740s (Martin 1988).

Although the faunal assemblage recovered from the privy contained the fairly typical complement of mainly cow and pig bone, the dietary pollen and seed samples (Reinhard 1989; Mrozowski 1991) suggested a varied diet for Brush and his household. This diet was flavored with spices and supplemented with fruits and vegetables such as potatoes and broccoli. Broccoli, which required specialized growing conditions, was one of the exotic vegetables favored by the elite (Stiverson and Butler 1977:34). The presence of spices (French parsley, sage, and thyme) was also highly unusual for the time. Some spices were used by the more wealthy families in the early eighteenth century, but like tea, they were uncommon among the middling classes (Carr and Walsh 1991).

These unexpected archaeological discoveries led to a reassessment of the documentary evidence, which revealed various other decorative and luxury items, such as a silver watch, a looking glass, and prints. In the 1730s, middling families were just beginning to acquire amenities,

FIGURE 15.4. *Delft teawares recovered from a 1717–1727 context in the John Brush privy. (Photograph by Tamera Mams)*

such as teawares, clocks, mirrors, and prints, which had been previously restricted to the gentry (Walsh 1983: 111). These items did not become standard possessions of urban artisans and laborers until later in the century, and thus owning them during the first quarter of the century set Brush apart from other artisans of the time.

If Brush's possessions suggest a higher standard of living than expected, then what about his house, restored to its eighteenth-century appearance on Palace Green? The house, as originally constructed by Brush around 1719, was a modest one, containing two rooms, a hall and a chamber, separated by a central passage. They were used for formal entertaining and family living, respectively. This central-passage floor plan had begun making its appearance in the Virginia colony during the first quarter of the eighteenth century (Wenger 1986). Since the house, as originally constructed, contained no dormer windows that would bring light into the second floor, it is believed that this second floor was used for little more than storage. Although it was formerly thought that Brush lived in this two-room house throughout his tenure on the lot, the results of recent dendrochronology tests on the structural timbers show that Brush added at least one and possibly two wings to his house within a few years of its construction (Heikkenen 1984). The addition of these wings had previously been attributed to a later eighteenth-century owner, Mayor Thomas Everard. With evidence from tree-ring dating, it was possible to obtain a more accurate assessment of the floor plan. The unusual placement of the hearths at the center back of the original structure suggests that the two wings were conceived as an integral part of the house before it was constructed. Although Brush may have only been able to construct a two-room house (whether to satisfy the city building code within the specified time allotted, or because of a lack of funds), he had obviously planned to build a house with almost double the square footage.

Recent research has suggested that many early eighteenth-century homes were built modestly and that multifunctional space was common (Upton 1979; Walsh 1983; Wenger 1989). It was only later in the century that the specialized use of rooms for dining or entertaining began to appear. Brush's estate inventory lists a minimum of furniture, but the clustering of items such as a clock, a desk, a looking glass, a tea table, and chest of drawers suggests that these items were placed together in one room. The nature of these items, plus their valuation of £12—the total value of Brush's estate was only £90—suggests that these were grouped in the more public room of his house. Perhaps here is evidence that the emphasis of Brush's buying power was being placed on public display areas and activities, such as the ritual of tea taking, as evidenced by the delft and porcelain teawares. This clustering in one room of items of high social display suggests that Brush had adopted the new concepts about segregation of space. His amenities make him an aberration for his time period and wealth category; it was not until several decades later that the middle class would push to have luxury items.

Although a gunsmith of middling wealth, Brush was leading a life-style beyond that documented for other artisans of the time in several respects. How can one explain Brush in light of his peers? Turning to the documents implies that perhaps his behavior can be attributed to the patronage of Governor Spotswood. Records suggest that Brush was brought over from England by Governor Spotswood to be the armorer to the Virginia colony. The placement of Brush's house adjacent to the governor's palace might suggest a benefactor relationship between the governor and Brush. About 50 years later, a similar relationship between Governor Botetourt and his former blacksmith, John Draper helps explain the relatively ostentatious possessions found at Draper's home (Brown et al. 1990).

The John Brush assemblage provides just one example of how a multidisciplinary approach integrating archaeological, documentary, and architectural information can provoke questions about behavior. More than 30 years of stratified archaeological excavation at Colonial Williamsburg has produced a number of tightly dated assemblages that can be subjected to this same type of analysis.

African American Lifeways

In addition to clarifying the history of documented citizens, archaeological research is providing new insight into the lifeways of groups that receive little mention in the historical record. At Carter's Grove, a colonial plantation owned by Colonial Williamsburg, archaeological excavations revealed the site of the plantation's late eighteenth-century farm quarter. Remains of three slave houses, delineated by patterns of root cellars and fencelines, have been reconstructed (figure 15.5) and represent one of the greatest interpretive challenges that the foundation has faced.

FIGURE 15.5. *Reconstructed slave quarters at Carter's Grove Plantation. (Courtesy of the Colonial Williamsburg Foundation)*

The reconstruction and furnishings of these cabins is the result of a joint effort of foundation archaeologists, historians, architectural historians, and curators. By combining archaeological evidence recovered throughout the Virginia and Maryland tidewater with extant descriptions of slave quarters and architectural information from the few surviving eighteenth- and early nineteenth-century slave houses, they were able to establish the general kinds of housing available to this social group. The reconstructed slave dwellings speak eloquently of the conditions in which most blacks, and indeed many Anglo-Americans, lived in the colonial Chesapeake. Such reconstructions make it possible to address the questions of master–slave relationships, African and English acculturation, and the development of slave communities by the mid-eighteenth century.

The search continues for traces of slave housing and material culture within the town of Williamsburg. In 1988, excavation revealed the remains of a mid-nineteenth-century slave house constructed specifically for the Tucker family mammy, Polly Valentine. Personal papers of the Tucker family provided information on this highly valued slave. The 15-by-25-foot house they built for Valentine and her husband Jim mirror the specifications for ideal slave housing detailed in contemporary Southern agricultural journals. Polly Valentine's house, her personal possessions as reflected through archaeology, and the family papers all document the paternalistic attitude of her master (Edwards 1990).

Conclusion

This brief survey of various facets of archaeological research at Colonial Williamsburg illustrates the contribution that excavation has been making to our understanding of Williamsburg's changing physical landscape, a subject being investigated by other urban historical archaeologists as well. Archaeological research has played a prominent role in defining the scope and character of landscape alterations, at various levels, from the individual houselot to the town as a whole. At least a partial picture of how Williamsburg emerged from the settlement, known as Middle Plantation, has been constructed. The real extent of topographic features depicted on period maps has now been traced, as have the manner and timing of their alteration.

On another level, archaeology is providing further insight into Williamsburg's physical growth by developing new tools for recording and analyzing spatial information about the town. As a result, more is now known about trends in the development and economic use of Williamsburg properties, and about the basic spatial patterns of individual houselots. As the computerized techniques for recording and modeling spatial evidence from both archaeological and documentary research become better refined and the results are further combined with the growing body of information on various ecofact categories such as pollen, phytoliths, oyster shells, and parasite remains, it will be possible to reconstruct Williamsburg's microenvironments with greater accuracy, particularly as they relate to health, sanitation practices, plant communities, and land-use patterns. More significantly, these studies can shed light on the environmental history of this one urban space within the broader context of the Chesapeake, by challenging or refining current conceptions of diet and nutrition, disease, and agricultural practices, to name but a few important topics.

Studies of the artifact assemblages recently recovered from tightly dated features such as John Brush's privy, together with a reanalysis of material recovered from earlier excavations within Williamsburg, will provide the basis for a detailed, yet comprehensive, view of the changing material life-styles of a broad cross-section of Williamsburg residents and those of surrounding rural counties during the course of the eighteenth century. This is a long-term project that will involve many Colonial Williamsburg researchers and will focus not only on archaeological remains, but also on evidence preserved in surviving buildings and in documentary sources.

Archaeology offers the unparalleled opportunity to study the actual things that people acquired, used, valued, and ultimately discarded. When such materials are retrieved from appropriate contexts using fine-grained techniques, they can be ascribed to persons and places and thus be used to trace an earlier society's physical imprint on the landscape. No other discipline can match that claim.

Yet the work of the archaeologist is necessarily slow and deliberate, and not all of the ground's surprises are auspicious ones. Many archaeologists want to say something profound, or at least provocative, about the colonial Chesapeake now. But they have been doing so in recent years with very little actual archaeological evidence to back them up. Historical archaeology's potential for contributing to such topics as landscape and environmental reconstruction is only just being recognized; the sample of sites will have to be greatly enlarged before archaeology can provide credible testimony concerning the material lives of most residents of the early Chesapeake. Historical archaeology stands to play a major role in documenting how people actually lived during this period, but even after a decade of concerted work, building on a respected tradition of nearly 30 years of previous archaeology, the real effort seems to be only just beginning at Colonial Williamsburg.

Acknowledgments

We would like to thank all those who assisted in the production of this chapter. Gregory J. Brown, Ann Smart Martin, and David Muraca, all of Colonial Williamsburg's Department of Archaeological Research, read and commented on earlier drafts of this essay, and it has benefited from their thoughtful insights and suggestions. Tamera Mams of the Department of Archaeological Research and Suzanne Brown and Cathy Grosfils of Colonial Williamsburg's Audiovisual Library helped with the photographs. Kim Wagner, also of the Department of Archaeological Research, prepared the privy map.

References Cited

Beaudry, Mary C.

1984 Archaeology and the Historical Household. *Man in the Northeast* 28(1):27–38.

Beaudry, Mary C., and Stephen Mrozowski (editors)

1989 *Interdisciplinary Investigations of the Boott Mills Lowell, Massachusetts*. Cultural Resource Management Study No. 21. Report prepared for the National Park Service by the Center for Archaeological Studies, Boston.

Boulton, Alexander O.
1987 The Transformation of Middle Plantation: Williamsburg before 1700. Ms. on file, Department of Archaeological Research, Colonial Williamsburg Foundation, Williamsburg, Va.

Brock Notebook
Manuscript volume in the Collection of the Virginia Historical Society, Richmond, Va.

Brown, Gregory J.
1986a Archaeological Investigations at the College Landing National Historic Site. Ms. on file, Department of Archaeological Research, Colonial Williamsburg Foundation, Williamsburg, Va.
1986b Phase I and II Archaeological Investigations of the Port Anne Development, Williamsburg, Virginia. Ms. on file, Department of Archaeological Research, Colonial Williamsburg Foundation, Williamsburg, Va.
1986c Block 9 in the Eighteenth Century: The Social and Architectural Context of the Shields Tavern Property. Ms. on file, Department of Archaeological Research, Colonial Williamsburg Foundation, Williamsburg, Va.

Brown, Gregory, Thomas Higgins III, David Muraca, S. Kathleen Pepper, and Roni H. Polk
1990 Archaeological Investigations of the Shields Tavern Site, Williamsburg, Virginia. Ms. on file, Department of Archaeological Research, Colonial Williamsburg Foundation, Williamsburg. Va.

Brown, Gregory, and David Muraca
1993 Phasing Stratigraphic Sequences at Colonial Williamsburg. In *Practices of Archaeological Stratigraphy*, edited by Marley R. Brown III and Edward Harris. Academic Press, New York. In press.

Brown, Marley R. III
1985 A Geographic Approach to Tidewater Urbanization. Paper presented at the annual meeting of the Pioneer America Society, Edenton.
1986 The Problem of Establishing Household Assemblages in Urban Archaeology: Some Examples from Eighteenth-Century Williamsburg. Paper presented in Symposium on the Historical Archaeology of the Household at the 53rd Annual meeting of the Eastern States Archaeological Federation, Wilmington, Del.
1990 Digging the Urban Places of Colonial America: The Perspective of Environmental Archaeology. Paper presented at the 4th Annual Colonial Williamsburg History Forum, Williamsburg, Va.
1991a New Ground Level Views of Eighteenth-Century America. Paper presented at the Colonial Williamsburg Antique Forum, Williamsburg, Va.
1991b The Comparative Archaeology of English Colonial Capitals: The Example of Williamsburg, Virginia, and St. George's, Bermuda. Paper presented at the Society for Historical Archaeology annual meeting, Richmond, Va.

Brown, Marley R. III, and Patricia Samford
1990 Recent Evidence of Eighteenth-Century Gardening in Williamsburg, Virginia. In *Earth Patterns; Essays in Landscape Archaeology*, edited by William Kelso and Rachel Most, pp. 103–121. University Press of Virginia, Charlottesville.

Bryant, Vaughn M. Jr., and Richard Holloway
1983 The Role of Palynology in Archaeology. In *Advances in Archaeological Method and Theory Volume 6*, edited by Michael Schiffer, pp. 191–224. Academic Press, New York.

Carr, Lois G., and Lorena Walsh
1991 Changing Lifestyles and Consumer Behavior in the Colonial Chesapeake. In *Of Consuming Interests: A Style of Life in the 18th Century*, edited by Ronald Hoffman and Cary Carson, in press.

Carr, Lois Green, Philip D. Morgan, and Jean B. Russo
1988 *Colonial Chesapeake Society*. Institute for Early American History and Culture, Chapel Hill.

Carson, Cary, and Lorena Walsh
1981 The Material Life of the Early American Housewife. Paper presented at the Conference of Women in Early America, Williamsburg, Va. CWF (Colonial Williamsburg Foundation)
1985 *Teaching History at Colonial Williamsburg*. Colonial Williamsburg Foundation, Williamsburg. Va.
1989 Colonial Williamsburg Seven-Year Objectives: 1989–1995. Ms. on file, Department of Archaeological Research, Colonial Williamsburg Foundation, Williamsburg, Va.

Deetz, James
1990 Prologue; Landscapes as Cultural Statements. In *Earth Patterns; Essays in Landscape Archaeology*, edited by William Kelso and Rachel Most, pp. 1–4. University Press of Virginia, Charlottesville.

Derry, Linda, and Marley R. Brown III
1987 Excavations at Colonial Williamsburg Thirty Years Ago: An Archaeological Analysis of Cross Trenching behind the Peyton Randolph Site. *American Archaeology* 6(1): 10–19.

Edwards, Andrew
1986 Archaeological Investigations at 44WB49, An Early 17th-Century Domestic Site in Williamsburg. Ms. on file, Department of Archaeological Research, Colonial Williamsburg Foundation, Williamsburg, Va.

Edwards, Ywone D.
1990 *Master–Slave Relations: A Williamsburg Perspective*. Unpublished Master's thesis, Department of Anthropology, College of William and Mary, Williamsburg, Va.

Frenchman's
1781 Plan de la ville et environs de Williamsburg en Virginie, 1782. Original map in Special Collections, Earl Gregg Swem Library, College of William and Mary, Williamsburg, Va.

Greene, Jack P.

1988 *Pursuits of Happiness; The Social Development of Early Modern British Colonies and the Formation of American Culture*. University of North Carolina Press, Chapel Hill.

Grim, Ronald

1977 *The Absence of Towns in Seventeenth Century Virginia: The Emergence of Service Centers in York County*. Ph.D. dissertation, University of Maryland. University Microfilms, Ann Arbor.

Harris, Edward

1989 *Principles of Archaeological Stratigraphy*. Academic Press, New York.

Heikkenen, Herman J.

1984 The Years of Construction for Eight Historical Structures in Colonial Williamsburg, Virginia, as Derived by the Key-Year Dendrochronology Technique. American Institute of Dendrochronology. Ms. on file, Department of Archaeological Research, Colonial Williamsburg Foundation, Williamsburg, Va.

Hellier, Cathleene

1987 Williamsburg at Mid-Century: A Population Profile. *Colonial Williamsburg Interpreter*. 8(5):1–2.

1989 National Endowment for the Humanities Final Report. Draft ms. on file, Department of Archaeological Research, Colonial Williamsburg Foundation, Williamsburg, Va.

Henretta, James A.

1978 Families and Farms: Mentalite in Pre-Industrial American. *William and Mary Quarterly*. 3d ser., 35(1):3–32.

Hosmer, Charles

1985 The Colonial Revival in the Public Eye: Williamsburg and Early Garden Restoration. In *The Colonial Revival in America*, edited by A. Axelrod, pp 52–70. W. W. Norton, New York.

Hudgins, Carter

1977 Historical Archaeology and Salvage Archaeological Excavations at College Landing: An Interim Report. Ms. on file, Virginia Department of Historic Resources, Richmond, Va.

Kelly, Kevin

1988 Some Demographic Characteristics of 18th-Century York County, Virginia. Ms. on file, Department of Archaeological Research, Colonial Williamsburg Foundation, Williamsburg, Va.

Kertzer, David

1985 Future Directions in Historical Household Studies: *Journal of Family History* 10:98–107.

Leone, Mark

1984 Interpreting Ideology in Historical Archaeology: Using the Rules of Perspective in the William Paca Garden, Annapolis, Maryland. In *Ideology, Power and Prehistory*, edited by Daniel Miller and Christopher Tilley, pp. 25–35. Cambridge University Press, Cambridge.

1988 The Georgian Order as the Order of Merchant Capitalism in Annapolis, Maryland. In *The Recovery of Meaning: Historical Archaeology in the Eastern United States*, edited by Mark Leone and Parker B. Potter, Jr., pp. 235–261. Smithsonian Institution Press, Washington.

Martin, Ann Smart

1988 "To Supply the Real and Imaginary Necessities": The Retail Trade in Table and Teawares, Virginia and Maryland, c. 1750–1810. Report submitted to the National Endowment for the Humanities. Manuscript on file, Department of Archaeological Research, Colonial Williamsburg Foundation, Williamsburg, Va.

1989 The Role of Pewter as Missing Artifact: Consumer Attitudes toward Tablewares in Late Eighteenth-Century Virginia. *Historical Archaeology* 23(2).

Miller, George

1991 A Revised Set of CC Index Values for Classification and Economic Scaling of English Ceramics from 1787 to 1880. *Historical Archaeology*. 25:1–25.

Miller, George, Ann Smart Martin, and Nancy Dickinson

1992 Changing Consumption Patterns: English Ceramics and the American Market from 1770 to 1840. In *Everyday Life in the Early Republic: 1780 to 1828*, edited by Catherine E. Hutchins. W. W. Norton, New York, in press.

Mitchell, Robert D.

1983 American Origins and Regional Institutions: The Seventeenth-Century Chesapeake. *Annals of the Association of American Geographers*. 73:404–420.

Mrozowski, Stephen A.

1984 Prospects and Perspectives on an Archaeology of the Household. *Man in the Northeast* 27:31–49.

1987 Exploring New England's Evolving Urban Landscape. In *Living in Cities: Current Research in Urban Archaeology*, edited by Edward Staski, pp. 1–9. Special Publications Series No. 5, Society for Historical Archaeology.

1991 A Preliminary Report of the Archaeobotanical Analysis of Context 29G—The Brush-Everard Site, Williamsburg, Virginia. Ms. on file, Department of Archaeological Research, Colonial Williamsburg Foundation, Williamsburg, Va.

Muraca, David

1991 Survey and Testing at Bruton Heights. Ms. on file, Department of Archaeological Research, Colonial Williamsburg Foundation, Williamsburg, Va.

Nöel Hume, Ivor

1983 *Historical Archaeology*. Alfred Knopf, New York. Originally published 1968.

1969a *A Guide to Artifacts of Colonial America*. Alfred A. Knopf, New York.

1969b Archaeology and Wetherburn's Tavern. Colonial Williamsburg Archaeological Series No. 3. Colonial Williamsburg Foundation, Williamsburg, Va.

1969c The Wells of Williamsburg; Colonial Time Capsules. Colonial Williamsburg Archaeological Series No. 4. Colonial Williamsburg Foundation, Williamsburg, Va.

Norton Papers

John Norton and Sons Papers. Manuscripts on file at the Colonial Williamsburg Foundation Library, Williamsburg, Va.

O'Mara, James

1983 *An Historical Geography of Urban System Development: Tidewater Virginia in the Eighteenth Century*. Geographical Monographs, No. 13. Atkinson College, Downsview, Ontario.

Randolph, John Jr.

1826 *A Treatise on Gardening by a Citizen of Virginia*. Edited by M. F. Warner. Reprinted from *The American Gardener of John Gardiner and David Hepburn*. 3d ed. Appeals Press, Richmond, 1924.

Reinhard, Karl

1989 Analysis of Latrine Soils from the Brush-Everard Site, Colonial Williamsburg, Virginia. Ms. on file, Department of Archaeological Research, Colonial Williamsburg Foundation, Williamsburg, Va.

Reps, John

1972 *Tidewater Towns; City Planning in Colonial Virginia and Maryland*. University Press of Virginia, Charlottesville.

Rovner, Irwin

1983 Plant Opal Phytolith Analysis: Major Advances in Archaeobotanical Research. In *Advances in Archaeological Method and Theory*, edited by Michael B. Schiffer, pp. 225–266. Academic Press, New York.

1990 Fine-Tuning Floral History with Plant Opal Phytolith Analysis. In *Earth Patterns; Essays in Landscape Archaeology*, edited by William Kelso and Rachel Most, pp. 297–308. University of Virginia Press, Charlottesville.

Rowe, Linda

1988 Peopling the Power Structure in Yorktown and Williamsburg 1691– 1780. Ms. on file, Department of Archaeological Research, Colonial Williamsburg Foundation, Williamsburg, Va.

Samford, Patricia

1990 *"Near the Governor's" : Patterns of Development of Three Properties along Williamsburg's Palace and Nicholson Streets in the Eighteenth Century*. Unpublished Master's thesis, Department of Anthropology, College of William and Mary, Williamsburg, Va.

Sanford, Douglas

1990 The Gardens at Germanna, Virginia. In *Earth Patterns; Essays in Landscape Archaeology*, edited by William Kelso and Rachel Most, pp. 43–57. University of Virginia Press, Charlottesville.

Sjoberg, Gideon

1960 *The Preindustrial City; Past and Present*. The Free Press, New York.

Smart, Ann Morgan

1986 *The Urban/Rural Dichotomy of Status Consumption: Tidewater, Virginia, 1815*. Unpublished Master's thesis, American Studies Department, College of William and Mary, Williamsburg, Va.

Soltow, Lee

1989 *Distribution of Wealth and Income in the United States in 1798*. University of Pittsburgh Press, Pittsburgh.

Steen, Carl

1991 Archaeology at Bassett Hall Woods. Ms. on file, Department of Archaeological Research, Colonial Williamsburg Foundation, Williamsburg, Va.

Stilgoe, John R.

1982 *Common Landscape in America 1580–1845*. Yale University Press, New Haven, Conn.

Stiverson, Gregory A., and Patrick H. Butler (editors)

1977 Virginia in 1732: The Travel Journal of William Hugh Grove. *Virginia Magazine of History and Biography* 85(1):18–44.

Upton, Dell

1979 *Early Vernacular Architecture in Southeast Virginia*. Unpublished Ph.D dissertation, Brown University, Providence.

Walsh, Lorena

1983 Urban Amenities and Rural Sufficiency: Living Standards and Consumer Behavior in the Colonial Chesapeake, 1643–1777. *Journal of Economic History* 42(1):109–117.

1989 Analysis of Inventoried York County Urban and Rural Decedents. Ms. on file, Department of Archaeological Research, Colonial Williamsburg Foundation, Williamsburg, Va.

Webb-Prentis Papers

Joseph Prentis' "Account Book and Garden Book". Manuscripts Department, University of Virginia Library, Charlottesville.

Wenger, Mark R.

1986 The Central Passage in Virginia: Evolution of an Eighteenth Century Living Space. In *Perspectives in Vernacular Architecture, II*, edited by Camille Wells, pp. 137–149. University of Missouri Press, Columbia.

1989 The Dining Room in Early Virginia. In *Perspectives in Vernacular Architecture, Volume III*, edited by Thomas Carter and Bernard L. Herman, pp. 149–159. University of Missouri Press, Columbia.

Yentsch, Anne E.

1984 Contrary to Nature: The Calvert Orangery as a Symbol of Power for a Patrician Household in Annapolis, Maryland. Paper presented at the 45th Conference on Early American History "The Colonial Experience: Eighteenth Century Maryland," 13 September 1984, Baltimore.

IV
PART

Nineteenth-Century Life

HISTORICAL archaeology of nineteenth-century sites is gaining momentum with the increasing attention being devoted to both industrialization and urban and regional issues of this period. Nineteenth-century studies have dealt with the cycles of capitalism (Paynter 1988), working-class life and modernization (Beaudry and Mrozowski 1989; Shackel 1991), landscape development (Ostrogorsky 1987), health conditions (Mrozowski et al. 1989), diet (chapter 10; Henry 1987), neighborhoods and settlement systems (Wall 1987), ethnicity and assimilation (see, for example, Schuyler 1980; Praetzellis et al. 1987; Little 1988; Staski 1990), and the role of the marketplace (Riordon and Hampton Adams 1985). Interest in nineteenth-century archaeology has also been stimulated by the hope of gaining new insight into our immediate past from a study of its material conditions.

Archaeologists have been particularly interested in the development of the ideologies underlying the modernization of industrial conditions. Sanitary conditions, for example, received the attention of the nineteenth-century industrialist when it became clear that an unhealthy work force meant decreasing productivity. Some industrial towns, like Lowell, Massachusetts, strongly supported the sanitary movements of the nineteenth and early twentieth centuries (Mrozowski et al. 1989), but others, like Harpers Ferry, West Virginia, neglected the new ideas about health and progress, with the result that health conditions remained relatively poor in these areas well into the twentieth century (Shackel 1993; see especially Ford 1993).

New ideologies concerning factory discipline also emerged and were sometimes resisted (see Smith 1977; Paynter 1989). This new work ethic emphasized strict time management as opposed to the old craft ethos. Some of the new ideas were not confined to the workplace, but crept into domestic life as well, where a new material culture was introducing profound changes. Many forces came into play during the industrialization of America—from the increasing standardization of the diet and increasing reliance on patent medicines in lieu of home remedies to the growing diversity of consumer goods.

The new work and domestic behaviors were sometimes resisted through new social movements such as the utopian-inspired organizations and millennialist religions. The effect of industrialization on everyday life and on social relations can be seen in the archaeological record. Research in Annapolis, Maryland, for example, suggests that African Americans, whose consumption patterns are often interpreted as being the result of poverty, opted for goods that reinforced their own cultural identity and ideological needs, rather than subscribe to the dominant culture (Leone et al. 1993).

In response to the problems that industrialization bred, nineteenth-century Americans created an ideology that acclaimed the moral and physical superiority of rural life. Paradoxically, many industrial towns established in the early nineteenth century were celebrated for their pastoral-like landscaping. Julia King's (see chapter 18) example of a nineteenth-century plantation in southern Maryland demonstrates how the industrial culture engulfed an antebellum family. Rather than adapt to a wage-labor system, as others in northern Maryland were doing, especially in Baltimore, the plantation owners clung to slave labor and used symbols of past generations to justify their everyday social relations.

Keith Barr, Pamela Cressey, and Barbara Magid (chapter 16) explain the repercussions of this attitude on the sugar industry in Alexandria, Virginia, where slave labor was used to perform many of the tasks in the refineries. Charles Cheek and Donna Seifert (chapter 17) point out some of the effects industrial society had on everyday social relations,especially gender relations, ethnicity, class, and neighborhood boundaries.

The Essays

In chapter 16, Keith Barr, Pamela Cressy, and Barbara Magid discuss the relationships between international, national, and local phenomena that affected the growth of the sugar industry. Sugar became a profitable venture early in the New World, first in the Caribbean. By 1700 the value of sugar was twice that of tobacco, and by the eve of the American Revolution there were 18 refineries in the New World. In 1800 Alexandria, Virginia had two refineries, which were owned by white middle-class families. Slaves provided most of the labor, but by the 1820s these industries began to fail and by the 1830s the industry had collapsed in Alexandria. Barr et al. explain that after the British outlawed slavery in the West Indies in 1832, the international trade shifted from sugar to coffee grown in South America. Alexandria did not have a large enough market for this new product, nor did it keep stride with the industries in Baltimore. The strong Quaker movement in Alexandria to free slaves may have contributed to the collapse of the sugar industry, since slave labor accounted for most of the work force.

From their work at the local factories, the authors provide a typology for individual earthenware sugar molds excavated in Alexandria. Spectrographic analyses indicate that the molds were probably locally made. The fact that archaeologists found no technologically advanced copper and iron molds suggests Alexandria experienced an industrial lag, which may have contributed to the eventual decline of its sugar industry. The locally made molds also indicate an international industry was relying on locally based manufacturing and the support of the local economy. Between 1830 and 1870 many of the smaller refineries in the nation closed down in the wake of large-scale industrialization, which Alexandria evaded; as a result, New York became the international leader of sugar refining.

Working with sites later in the century, Charles Cheek and Donna Seifert (chapter 17) examine a working-class neighborhood in Washington D.C. They diachronically compare the archaeological records from a brothel and a working-class household. The area examined, once known as Hookers Division and now called Federal Triangle, is close to the White House. In the 1890s it changed from a mixed residential-commercial area to a red-light district. By 1900 nearly all of the dwellings were brothels. In 1914 Congress outlawed prostitution in the District and in the 1920s purchased the land for development.

Cheek and Seifert divide their sample into early and late households, and working-class and prostitute households. They note a relatively higher frequency of ceramics in working- class households owing to the central place of meals in families' social reproduction. A surprisingly high percentage of toys, clothing, and tobacco pipes were found in the prostitutes' households; their presence may be explained in part by the higher available disposable income there. The authors find that white working-class neighborhoods in other areas have similar assemblages to the working-class neighborhood in Hooker's Division. African American neighborhoods show consumption patterns different from both the white working-class neighborhood and the prostitute's household.

Julia King (chapter 18) turns the discussion to rural areas. She describes the layout of the nineteenth-century Susquehanna farm owned by the Carroll family in southern Maryland, an area primarily involved in the tobacco industry. The landscape of Susquehanna farm not only reflected social divisions, but also shaped social interaction. King uses maps to show that the plantation was carefully planned in order to keep interaction between slaves to a minimum. Roads and fences served as barriers and probably inhibited or at least reduced social interaction between enslaved and free individuals. In this way landscape was manipulated to maintain social boundaries.

King analyzes the ideological use of cultural features by a particular family to create a long-standing claim to the past. Located about 10 feet from the main plantation house were the ruins of an older family mansion. This feature, in close proximity to the planter's dwelling, was a visible and integral part of the landscape until the cellar was filled in about 1870. Oral history claims that the Carrolls always intended to rebuild the old mansion. Even though they had 50 to 60 slaves to carry out the labor, little was done to "beautify" or alter the landscape by removing the ruins. The ruins seem to have served as a symbol of an earlier landscape, thereby providing a claim to precedent in the face of social and economic inequalities embedded in the plantation system.

As the essays in this section point out, broad cultural changes took place in American society in the nineteenth century. The new culture of capitalism and its accompanying standardized behavior were created and reinforced by the spread of mass-produced goods throughout the country. But this culture was far from homogeneous, despite the innovation of new transportation technologies, such as the railroad and canals. Regionalism and rural and urban differences were not erased. Not all people subscribed to the wage-labor system demanded by the culture of capitalism; some industrialists used slave labor for manufacturing (chapter 16). Others who continued to use slaves in their plantation economy called on the ideological mechanism of historical precedent to justify this practice (chapter 18). Industrialization obviously had a tremendous impact on everyday social relations and influenced class, gender roles, and ethnicity (chapter 17). The legacy of the nineteenth century is still very much with us.

References Cited

Beaudry, Mary C., and Stephen A. Mrozowski

1989 *Interdisciplinary Investigations of the Boott Mills, Lowell, Massachusetts. Volume III:The Boarding House System as a Way of Life.* Cultural Resources Management Series No. 21. National Park Service, North Atlantic Regional Office, Boston.

Ford, Benjamin

1993 Health and Sanitation in Nineteenth-Century Harpers Ferry. In *Interdisciplinary Investigations of Domestic Life in Government Block B: Perspectives on Harpers Ferry's Armory and Commercial District*, edited by Paul A. Shackel, pp. 12.1–12.38. Occasional Report No. 6. Regional Archeology Program. National Park Service, National Capital Region, Washington, D.C.

Henry, Susan

1987 A Chicken in Every Pot: The Urban Subsistence Pattern in Turn-of- the-Century Phoenix, Arizona. In *Living in Cities: Current Research in Urban Archaeology*, edited by Edward Staski, pp. 19–28. Special Publication Series No. 5. Society for Historical Archaeology.

Leone, Mark P., Barbara J. Little, Mark S. Warner, Parker B. Potter, Jr., Paul A. Shackel, George C. Logan, Paul R. Mullins, and Julie A. Ernstein

1993 An Archaeology of African Americans in Annapolis, Maryland: Who Asks the Questions? Who Listens to the Answers? In *I Too Am an American: Studies in African-American Archaeology*, edited by Theresa Singleton. University Press of Virginia, Charlottesville, in press.

Little, Barbara J.

1988 Echoes and Forecasts: Group Tensions in Historical Archaeology. *International Journal of Group Tensions* 18(4): 243–257.

Mrozowski, S. A., E. L. Bell, M. C. Beaudry, D. B. Landon, and G. K. Kelso

1989 Living on the Boott: Health and Well-Being in a Boarding House Population. *World Archaeology* 21(2):298–319.

Ostrogorsky, Michael

1987 Economic Organization and Landscape: Physical and Social Terrain Alteration in Seattle. In *Living in Cities: Current Research in Urban Archaeology*, edited by Edward Staski, pp. 10–18. Special Publication Series No. 5. Society for Historical Archaeology.

Paynter, Robert

1988 Steps to an Archaeology of Capitalism: Material Change and Class Analysis. In *The Recovery of Meaning: Historical Archaeology in the Eastern United States*, edited by Mark P. Leone and Parker B. Potter, pp. 407–433. Smithsonian Institution Press, Washington.

1989 The Archaeology of Equality and Inequality. *Annual Review of Anthropology* 18:369–99.

Praetzellis, Adrian, Mary Praetzellis, and Marley Brown III

1987 Artifacts as Symbols of Identity: An Example from Sacramento's Gold Rush Era Chinese Community. In *Living in Cities: Current Research in Urban Archaeology*, edited by Edward Staski, pp. 28–47. Special Publication Series, no. 5. Society for Historical Archaeology.

Riordon, Timothy, and William Hampton Adams

1985 Commodity Flows and National Market Access. *Historical Archaeology* 19(2):5–18.

Schuyler, Robert (editor)
1980 *Archaeological Perspectives on Ethnicity in America*. Baywood, Farmingdale, N.Y.
Shackel, Paul A. (editor)
1993 *Interdisciplinary Investigations of Domestic Life in Government Block B: Perspectives on Harpers Ferry's Armory and Commercial District*. Occasional Report No. 6. Regional Archeology Program. National Park Service, National Capital Region, Washington, D.C.
Smith, Merritt Roe
1977 *Harpers Ferry Armory and the New Technology*. Cornell University Press, Ithaca, N.Y.
Staski, Edward
1990 Studies of Ethnicity in North American Historical Archaeology. *North American Archaeologist* 11(2): 121–145.
Wall, Diana diZerega
1987 Settlement System Analysis in Historical Archaeology: An Example from New York City. In *Living in Cities: Current Research in Urban Archaeology*, edited by Edward Staski, pp. 65–74. Special Publication Series No. 5. Society for Historical Archaeology.

Suggested Readings from the Contributors

Borchert, James
1980 *Alley Life in Washington: Family, Community, Religion, and Folklife in the City, 1850–1970*. University of Illinois Press, Urbana.
Clemens, Paul
1980 *The Atlantic Economy and Colonial Maryland's Eastern Shore: From Tobacco to Grain*. Cornell University Press, Ithaca, N.Y.
Deetz, James
1982 Households: A Structural Key to Archaeological Explanation. In *Archaeology of the Households: Building a Prehistory of Domestic Life*, edited by R. L. Wilk and W. R. Rathje. *American Behavioral Scientist* 25:717–724.
King, Julia
1989 Archaeological Investigations at Susquehanna: A 19th-Century Farm Complex aboard Patuxent Naval Air Station, St. Mary's County. Jefferson Patterson Park and Museum, St. Leonard, Maryland.
Mintz, Sidney W.
1986 *Sweetness and Power, the Place of Sugar in Modern History*. Penguin Books, New York.
Rosen, Ruth
1982 *The Lost Sisterhood: Prostitution in America, 1900–1918*. Johns Hopkins University Press, Baltimore, Md.
Saint George, Robert Blair (editor)
1988 *Material Life in America, 1600–1860*. Northeastern University Press, Boston.
Sharrer, G. Terry
1977 Commerce and Industry. In *Alexandria: A Towne in Transition, 1800–1900*. Alexandria Bicentennial Corporation and Alexandria Historical Society, Alexandria, Va.
Smith, Merritt Roe
1977 *Harpers Ferry Armory and the New Technology*. Cornell University Press, Ithaca, N.Y.
Stilgoe, John R.
1982 *Common Landscapes of America, 1580 to 1845*. Yale University Press, New Haven, Conn.
Symanski, Richard
1981 *The Immoral Landscape: Female Prostitution in Western Societies*. Butterworths, Toronto.

XVI
CHAPTER

How Sweet It Was
Alexandria's Sugar Trade and Refining Business

KEITH L. BARR, PAMELA J. CRESSEY, AND BARBARA H. MAGID

SIDNEY MINTZ (1986) in his ground-breaking study of one food's use and influence in human history, *Sweetness and Power*, explored various aspects of sugar—its supply, production, labor, and consumption, as well as its influence on power relationships, demography, trade, slavery, health, and diet.

Our intent is to explore the relationships between sugar refining and supply, technology, owners, and laborers to gain insight into the changing economic role and power of one city in the first quarter of the nineteenth-century. Whereas Mintz considered sugar primarily in the European and Caribbean arenas, we look at America, the Chesapeake, and Alexandria, Virginia. Although the rise and demise of the sugar-refining business in Alexandria alone did not dictate the loss of its trading power, this experience illustrates how the town shifted from being a national leader of exports of wheat, tobacco, and sugar in an international arena to a provider of slaves, coal, and fish for domestic markets. Why sugar refining started in Alexandria did not continue, as it did in nearby Baltimore, Maryland, cannot be explained without considering both the larger sphere of power and trade in which the town functioned and the smaller sphere of the city's environment and leadership decisions.

An opportunity to study Alexandria's sugar industry arose in 1987, when proposed construction on a city parking lot led to archaeological excavations of the Alfred Street Sugar House (44AX96; figure 16.1). This business was one of two Alexandria refineries operating in the early years of the nineteenth-century. It was mentioned in the first economic history of the city, but little was known about Alexandria's refineries or their production of sugar. Alexandria Archaeology conducted excavations on this site in 1987 through 1989 and 1992. Parts of the Sugar House foundations were uncovered along with many, but very fragmentary, deposits of artifacts relating to the sugar-refining process. Foundations of homes that were both contemporary and subsequent to the refinery were also found and include the cellar of refiner Daniel Mclain's home. The refinery structure itself was partly obscured by two late nineteenth-century houses with full basements, but small outbuildings and wooden vats connected with the refinery were uncovered.

Another excavation in 1989, at a property one block from the Sugar House (900 King Street, 44AX113) revealed a cellar hole filled with sugar-refining pottery. This was once a grocery store associated with William Moore, the first owner of the Alfred Street Sugar House. Pottery from another Alexandrian sugar refinery—operated by Jacob Hoffman—was found in excavations at Alexandria's Lloyd House Library (44AX34) in 1990. The library building was once Hoffman's home and adjoined

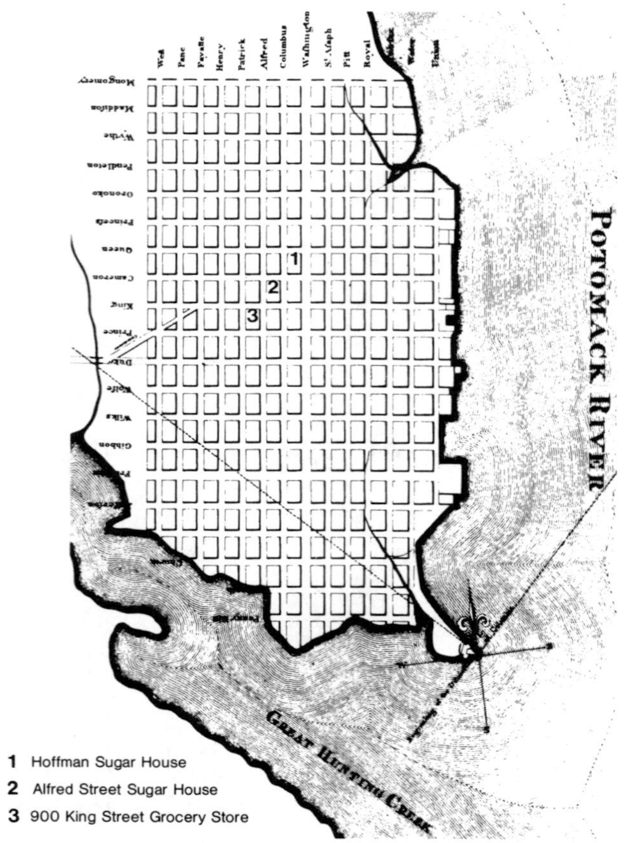

Figure 16.1. *Nineteenth-century Alexandria showing locations of three archaeological sites associated with sugar refining. (City of Alexandria, Va.)*

the refinery on Washington Street, just two blocks away from the Alfred Street Sugar House. These three investigations led to the study of Alexandria's sugar industry in the larger context of regional trade and manufacture.

Sugar in the World, the Region, and the City

The Spanish and Portuguese introduced sugar to the Atlantic islands, western Africa, and eventually to the New World. Columbus took sugarcane to Santo Domingo on his second voyage in 1493 (McCusker 1970:30–31). Despite the Spanish lead in the New World, Portuguese Brazil was the major sugar producer in the sixteenth century. As time passed, the Spanish and Portuguese concentrated on the quest for precious metals and left the production of marketable commodities to the northern European powers.

Although tobacco was one of the first New World products to build up a substantial European market, it was soon overtaken by sugar. The value of sugar reaching England and Wales in 1700 was double that of tobacco (Mintz 1986:35–37). Until this time sugar was a product enjoyed by a privileged few and utilized chiefly as a medicine or a spice, or sculpted in decorative displays as a sign of wealth. By the mid-eighteenth century the dramatic increase in British sugar production allowed even the poorer classes to enjoy sugar with their tea (Mintz 1986:45).

Refined sugar is far more valuable than raw sugar (muscovado). Theoretically, then, muscovado should have been the perfect mercantilist commodity. According to mercantilist doctrine of the period, raw materials were shipped from the colony in vessels from the mother country so that all processing could be done in the homeland. The colonies would then be dependent on the mother country for the upgraded, processed product. Yet, the British sugar-refining industry had strong competition from the colonies in the West Indies and America. Sugar refining in Barbados began as early as 1654, only a few years after it was first cultivated there. Illicit refineries quickly spread to Jamaica, Nevis, and other British Caribbean possessions (McCusker 1970:47–48).

The first sugar refineries in North America appeared in New England in the early eighteenth century (Hugill 1978:136). Sugar refining most likely arrived in the Chesapeake region when Charles Garts(z) and Company opened a refinery in Baltimore near the county wharf at the foot of Calvert Street. On March 14, 1784, the firm advertised in the Maryland *Journal* that it was making single- and double-refined sugars, as well as lump sugar, for which it had imported workmen from London (Scharf 1881:418).

In Washington D.C., Thomas Law, a colorful English-born entrepreneur, financed the establishment of the city's first sugar refinery at the end of the eighteenth century. The brother of an English peer, Law immigrated to the area in 1785 and became a large-scale real estate speculator. He attached himself to the local gentry by marrying the granddaughter of Martha Washington (Green 1962:19). Law was an antislavery man, and his sugar-refining business was part of a scheme to eliminate human bondage in the West Indies. Having spent some time in India, Law planned to import sugar raised by free but cheap Indian labor and thereby force emancipation on the West Indian planters by driving them out of the market (Townsend 1902:230–231).

Law hired James Piercy to operate the refinery at the foot of New Jersey Avenue. He advertised in the *Alexandria Gazette* in the spring of 1798 (May 22, 1798):

> The subscriber hereby gives notice, that at his new Sugar House in the City of Washington, on the Eastern Branch of the river Potomac; he will in a few days have ready for delivery a large quantity of
>
> Loaf and Lump Sugars,
>
> which he will sell wholesale at the Baltimore prices, for cash, indorsed notes, or flour delivered at the refinery, which is advantageously situated for that purpose.
>
> He has likewise ready for sale,
> Brown Muscovado Sugar
> and Molasses. . . .

Piercy probably expected his enterprise to become a major sugar refinery. The building was eight stories high, 47 by 46 feet, with a wing of five stories (Clark 1904:131). Piercy's mortgage, dated April 25, 1797, documented 500,000 bricks furnished by Daniel Carroll, the first brickmaker in the District of Columbia (Clark 1938:26). This building loomed over the landscape for decades; but the business failed within only three years.

Although Law's sugar enterprise failed, a number of changes in the international scene at the turn of the nineteenth century ultimately created an opportunity for new entrepreneurial pursuits. With the onset of the French Revolution and the subsequent wars between France and Britain, maritime commerce during the 1790s became steadily more dangerous. From 1800 to 1805, the belligerent European powers considered U.S. vessels neutral carriers. As in any wartime period, seaborne commerce had its dangers, but the unprecedented profits to be made outweighed them. One obstacle to American traders was the British law prohibiting neutrals in times of war from engaging in trade that mercantilist laws would have considered illegal in times of peace. Thus, if an American ship carried sugar from the Spanish colony of Cuba directly to Spain, the British claimed the right to capture it because such traffic was confined to Spanish ships during peacetime (Bauer 1988:62). American ship captains got around this law by the subterfuge of the "broken voyage" (Morison 1923:184). Ships stopping in the United States and passing through American customs, then immediately reexporting the Cuban sugar, technically made two separate voyages, each of which was legal under prewar Spanish law. This rationale satisfied the British admiralty court for a time (Bauer 1988:62).

During this period many merchants in the Chesapeake area took advantage of the dramatic increase in the reexport trade. Between 1803 and 1806 reexports from the United States jumped from $13 million to $60 million (Garraty and McCaughey 1987:206). Despite an embargo on foreign trade between December 1807 and March 1809, these were boom times.

The Rise and Demise of Sugar Refining in Alexandria

The first Alexandria sugar house was established on the 100 block of North Alfred Street. By April 22, 1803, John Leypold and Andrew Brunner "of Baltimore" had purchased a large property west of Christ Episcopal Church with a "pleasantly situated house in good order" and several vacant lots (Alexandria Deed Book 1802:D: 503–505; 1807:O:522). The following year, the city tax assessor recorded William Moore the owner of this half-acre (or one-quarter of the city block), which included a sugar house and a dwelling house.

The Early Refining Years

The *Alexandria Advertiser* printed the first notice of sugar production in the fall of 1804: "Sugar House—The subscribers have on hand at their Sugar House in Alexandria Loaf and Lump sugars and molasses, their own manufacturing, which they sell at the Philadelphia and Baltimore prices" (Brunner and Moore October 29).

In the tax records for the first few years of operation, Brunner—a business associate of John Leypold, who was Moore's relative by marriage—appears as co-owner of the sugar house. A Mutual Assurance Society declaration dated December 13, 1805, documents that the five-story sugar house sat 82 feet south of Moore's dwelling on North Alfred Street. Moore probably lived in the two-story frame residence shown on the declaration while operating the sugar refinery. In 1807, Andrew Brunner deeded the entire property to Moore for $9,000 (Alexandria Deed Book 1807:O:522 and 531). Moore began to expand his holdings and by 1811 had acquired about 1 acre, or half of the northern part of the block. These acquisitions were not without a degree of speculation and risk.

In 1808, Moore mortgaged the entire Alfred Street Sugar House property, including "all moulds, boilers, coppers, and implements made use of in the sugar refinery . . . together with the full benefit of a policy of Insurances to the amount of $3500 on the said sugar refinery and to the amount of $5000 on sugar and moulds contained in the said sugar refinery" (Alexandria Deed Book 1807:O:483). Hugh Smith, a prominent merchant, held this mortgage to secure a debt to another local merchant, Thomas Irwin. The following month, Moore sold a portion of his southernmost property on Alfred Street to Smith (Alexandria Deed Book 1808:Q:363).

About the same time as Moore set up his establishment west of Christ Church, a second sugar refinery started in Alexandria. Between 1802 and 1810 Jacob Hoffman, former mayor of the city, amassed several parcels encompassing nearly 1 acre. Located on the block north of Christ Church, the Hoffman sugar house was diagonally opposite the Moore refinery (figures 16.2, 16.3). Hoffman, a local merchant of imported fabrics from India, Germany, and Britain, probably built the refinery after 1802. He finally purchased the adjoining residence in 1810. Both house and refinery faced Washington Street, which had been designed only a decade before as one of the two widest roads in town. Eventually the street would become occupied by elite homes, professional offices, and cultural establishments. But in this period, the sugar refinery sat across from Joseph Harper's ropewalk on the 200 block of North Washington Street.

THE SUGAR HOUSE COMPOUND. The Hoffman estate included the brick refinery, a fine brick dwelling, garden, icehouse, smokehouse and a large two-story brick warehouse (Sharrer 1977:22). Like Moore, Hoffman lived on the lot adjacent to his sugar house, separated only by a garden. Tax records referred to both sugar houses as being five to six stories high. By 1825, the Hoffman refinery was "connected by a brick wall and shed with a large two story brick warehouse and smoke house" (*Alexandria Gazette*, May 14, 1825). A later tenant, Benjamin Hallowell, depicted this complex in an illustration (fig-

FIGURE 16.2. *Jacob Hoffman's Sugar House during its later use as a school in the second quarter of the nineteenth century, as illustrated by Benjamin Hallowell (Wedderburn 1907:35).*

FIGURE 16.3. *Jacob Hoffman's Sugar Refinery and tobacco warehouse. (Milton Grigg Collection, Alexandria Library, Lloyd House, Alexandria, Va.)*

ure 16.3; Wedderburn 1907:35). The smaller building was used as a "tobacco factory" and warehouse for cigars, cigar boxes, and tobacco (Alexandria Deed Book 1807:O:19).

The Moore and Hoffman refineries and adjoining homes were situated within a half block of Christ Church, near the very center of town—at King and Washington Streets. These manufacturing-residential compounds—with their sugar houses, slaves, white bourgeoisie families, large homes, and lovely gardens—were part of an urban landscape distinguished by its heterogeneity. The home at the Alfred Street refinery was described during a later period (1815–1822) by the owner's granddaughter as "surrounded by flower gardens in which my grandmother took much pride and pleasure." In fact, the family could "merely step from their garden into the [Christ] Church premises" through a turnstile (Wimsatt 1926:9).

SUGAR PRODUCTION AND SLAVE LABOR. By the time of the 1810 Federal Census of Manufactures, the two Alexandria sugar refineries were highly productive. The output from these two establishments alone placed the District of Columbia (of which Alexandria occupied the southwestern portion) third among the states in the nation for the volume of refined sugar produced. In 1810 Hoffman and Moore together produced 800,000 pounds of sugar and outpaced the entire state of Maryland, which produced about 756,000 pounds. Although they both produced less than one-third the refined sugar of the larger states of New York and Pennsylvania, for Alexandria's population of only 7,227, which was about one-tenth the size of Philadelphia or New York City, this production level was a major accomplishment.

The Moore and Hoffman refineries both relied on slave labor. Although the historic documents are typically devoid of data about slaves or their role in production, several primary sources permit some insight into the labor situation. In the 1810 census, Moore's household included 6 slaves, and Jacob Hoffman's included 13 (United States Census 1810). Ten years later, each refinery recorded that 7 slaves (5 men and 2 boys) supplied all their labor needs (U.S. Census of Manufactures 1820). This is the largest number of workers in any refinery in Maryland and Massachusetts. Only one refinery in Philadelphia (with 8 or 9 men) and two in New York City (with 13 men) had larger numbers of laborers.

Although some refiners did not completely fill out the 1820 census, and several forms are illegible or damaged, the federal survey of 24 refineries in five states does provide data against which to compare Alexandria's refineries. The fewest number of workers in the 24 refineries was 5, and the highest number was 13. The two Alexandria refineries were the only ones to use slave labor.

TRANSITION AT THE ALFRED STREET SUGAR HOUSE. Between 1811 and 1815, William Moore engaged in an array of speculative activities. He bought both rents and subdivisions in the northern outskirts of the city, as recorded in more than 50 deeds for this period. One of his last transactions brought him back in association with Thomas Irwin in the purchase of the City Hotel in January 1815 (Alexandria Deed Book 1815:Z:174). Yet, just three months later, he sold the entire sugar house property to Daniel McLean for $19,500 (Alexandria Deed Book 1815:AA:306). In May, Moore mortgaged his half of the City Hotel and other properties for debts to Irwin (Alexandria Deed Book 1815: Z:130). He left Alexandria and returned to Baltimore in the summer of 1815, perhaps because he had overextended himself (Revis 1990:5).

Moore repeated somewhat the same transactions in Baltimore. He purchased a sugar factory in 1816 on South Street near Pratt. He continued to buy lots, but fell prey to financial problems and mortgaged the properties to John McKim, Jr. By the 1820s Moore lived in Ann Arundel County, Maryland. His properties in Alexandria continued to be mortgaged to handle debts during this period, even after his death around 1830 (Revis 1990:5–7).

The Later Refining Years, 1815–1828

On 8 March 1815, exactly two months after Andrew Jackson's victory at New Orleans, the final battle of the War of 1812, Daniel McLean purchased Moore's sugar house (Alexandria Deed Book 1815:AA:306). McLean may well have been optimistic; postwar economic trends would have justified high hopes. Banks were investing in local manufacturing endeavors, and Alexandria's commerce had increased since mud banks blocked the Potomac River access to long-time rival Georgetown. In 1817 the city council invested in major community improvements, extending streets, providing street lighting, and building a new market house (Sharrer 1977:22).

McLean and his fellow townsmen could not have known that in that same year the prices for agricultural products would begin a dramatic decline. A barrel of flour dropped in price by nearly three-quarters in only four years. In the ensuing years the deed books filled with the bankruptcies, sales, and mortgages of prominent citizens (Sharrer 1977:23).

McLean and his partner Clement Weston kept the Alfred Street refinery operating, although the level of production may have decreased (Revis 1990:7). Their partnership continued until 1820, after which McLean continued the operation alone until his death on February 8, 1823.

In the 1820 Census of Manufactures, Hoffman and McLean recorded almost identical statistics: 500 boxes of (Havana) sugar valued at $20,000 consumed annually; 7 male slaves "employed"; 1 pan, cooler, cistern, and 5,000 moulds and pots; and $35,000 of capital invested, including the establishment. Hoffman also included $3,000 for contingent expenses and a sad comment on Alexandria on the eve of the 1830s: "For some time the demand has regularly declined owing to the general decline of trade" (U.S. Census of Manufacturers 1820).

His view was echoed in the 11 questionnaires filled out by other Alexandria manufacturers in 1820. Ezra Kinsey reported that his tannery had "sales less than usual stock increasing and the number of hands must be reduced." The Smoot and Brandt tannery's stock had increased and sales were "very dull." Two bake houses and the Entwistle brewery also remarked on diminishing demand, and a "dull and languishing condition."

This situation was not unique to Alexandria. One New York refiner commented in a similar vein on his questionnaire:

> The home consumption of Refined Sugar, has decreased so much in New York Since the peace, as to lesson the number of Refiners one half; this diminution of demand for this article may be attributed in the first place to the universal stagnation of business during the last five or six years and the consequent inability of people at large to indulge themselves in the use of an article that may be dispensed with. The most serious difficulty which the Refiner of Sugar in this country has had to encounter, was the want of encouragement on the part of the Government to place them on a footing with the Refiners of other Countries in foreign markets. (U.S. Census of Manufactures 1820)

During this difficult period, Jacob Hoffman served the town a second time as mayor, from 1818 until 1821. But financial difficulties hit him as well. He tried diversifying in 1823 by establishing a smokehouse for bacon (*Alexandria Gazette*, December 23, 1823). Eventually in 1824, the Hoffman family sold the sugar refinery, slaves, and residence because of their debts, and the site was no longer used for refining.

After Daniel McLean's death, his son Samuel continued to run the Alfred Street refinery for two years. But in 1825 neighbor John Hoffman was operating the Alfred Street Sugar House, just a year after his father had sold the Washington Street sugar refinery. The junior Hoffman managed to carry on the Alfred Street business for only three more years. There is no evidence that the Alfred Street refinery continued in operation after 1828. The last time that the property's association with sugar manufacturing was noted occurred in an 1836 tax assessor's reference: "old sugar house and lot . . . vacant."

The dwelling continued to be occupied by respected families, often widows. Hugh C. Smith purchased the refinery portion of the property and renovated it as his home in 1841. Archaeological evidence in excavations adjoining the Smith house indicates that some, or all, of the original refinery was dismantled during this renovation.

Alexandria's Economic Decline

As the 1830s wore on, Alexandria's economic fortunes continued to plummet. Commercial activities relied increasingly on only two products for domestic markets: fish and slaves (Sharrer 1977:23). Although steam power helped establish some new manufacturing operations, the city continued to be a commercial town rather than a large-scale manufacturing center.

A number of factors contributed to Alexandria's economic decline. Unlike Baltimore and its other rivals, it was not close to power sources, such as swift running water or fossil fuels. Alexandria had also had its share of difficulties with the British in 1814, plagues, falling prices, bankruptcies, and a major fire in 1827. Yet, other towns had had similar problems. As Sharrer writes, "What fundamentally stunted Alexandria's economic growth after the mid-1820s was the success Baltimore and Richmond achieved in drawing off the trade of Northern Virginia and the Shenandoah Valley" (1977:23).

Alexandrians did not try to use new technology to become the economic leader in the region. Baltimore's attitude was different: "Despite the hazards, enterprise was the watchword" (Olson 1980:24). Concerned that Baltimore would lose out to the competing spheres of Philadelphia and Georgetown, its citizens took a bold step. In 1827, the Baltimore and Ohio Railroad was incorporated (Olson 1980:71). By 1842, the B&O reached the Cumberland coal region. Major railroad improvements continued to be funded in Baltimore.

Other factors also contributed to Alexandria's lack of development, some of which were closely linked to the production of sugar. The town's economy was dependent on slave labor, as was the world sugar trade in general. Alexandria's sugar refineries relied solely on this source of labor. But the supply of slave labor and of raw materials was beginning to dwindle. The British had outlawed slavery in the West Indies in 1833, and this dramatically altered and decreased sugar production (Sharrer 1977:19; Mintz 1986:68). Trade shifted away from the West Indies and toward South America, particularly to Brazil, whose major export was coffee. However, Alexandria did not have a large market for this product; thus, it was passed by for northern ports. At the same time, sugar beet production, which was also based on slave labor, expanded in the American South. Thus, as Alexandria's source of sugar gradually disappeared, the lower South's local supplies increased.

Meanwhile, the rising percentage of free people in Alexandria's African American population altered the way the city did business. Through the first two decades of the nineteenth century, Quaker and other organized groups, as well as individuals, had worked to free slaves (Cressey and Shephard 1987:13). Alexandria's free population increased from 9 percent of African Americans in 1790 to 60 percent in 1840 (Cressey et al. 1984). But just as the number of free people was increasing, four new slave markets opened their doors during these decades.

Alexandria was caught between two different American sugar industries: one based on specialized labor in the northern cities and using imported sugar sources, the other centered on the southern sugar beet extractive refineries served by slave labor.

Sugar Refining Technology

The sugar industry underwent a number of technological changes in the early nineteenth century, and numerous treatises written in the 1830s and 1840s described both the old and the new methods in detail. The use of artifacts found in the excavation of the Sugar House can be ascertained through these writings.

The Sugar House Building and Equipment

An 1805 Mutual Assurance Society map described the Alfred Street Sugar House as "5 stories high covered with slate." Sugar houses were typically five or six stories high, to accommodate thousands of loaves of drying sugar. The usual layout placed the fill house on the ground floor, with a warehouse above. Workers boiled, filtered, and poured the sugar into molds in the fill house. They lifted the molds by a pulley system to the drying chamber in the upper floors (Porter 1843:207). A large stove, which measured 8 to 14 square feet and occupied one corner of the typical refinery, heated the drying chamber, or oven. The temperature on each floor could be regulated separately through iron doors on the chimneys. A surviving illustration of the Alexandria refinery operated by Jacob Hoffman showed the typical tall, narrow building (figures 16.2 and 16.3).

The 1820 Census of Manufacturers listed one copper pan, one cooler, and a cistern on the ground floor fill house of the Alfred Street refinery. The census also mentioned 5,000 cone-shaped earthenware sugar molds and 5,000 earthenware pots, or syrup jars. Other furnishings typically included a large vat for lime water and another for soaking the clay molds, a clay cistern for working the clay used in the claying process, and a scum cistern to hold the impurities for further refining. Commonly used tools included colanders, ladles, scummers, wooden sticks for working the clay, and baskets and blankets for filtering the scum (Porter 1843:208).

The Refining Process

The Alfred Street Sugar House and other refineries of the day used a lengthy refining process in which the sugar was boiled and filtered to remove impurities, was then cooled and crystallized, and placed in molds to drain and recrystallize. The first step in the refining process was to add lime water to the raw sugar during the boiling to help remove the molasses so that the sugar could crystallize (Porter 1843:205). A New York refinery described by Benjamin Silliman (1833:80) kept the lime water in a wooden cistern outside the building and conducted it through pipes to the copper pan. The unrefined sugar was added to the pans, mixed with an amount of lime water, which varied according to the quality of sugar being refined, and boiled.

A likely source of lime used at the Alfred Street refinery was coral and shell, possibly brought up as ballast from the Caribbean and ground up and burned at the site. More than 2,800 pieces of coral and shell were found at the Sugar House site, some amidst a carbonate-rich sandy sediment. The tropical-subtropical formanifera species *Archaias angulatus* and *Rotorbinella rosea* were identified by Dr. C. Wylie Poag, micropaleontologist with the U.S. Geological Survey, Woods Hole. According to Poag (personal communication 1988), these species of foraminifera are found no farther north than the Bahamas and are common along the north coast of Cuba, which was a source of sugar refined at the site. While the coral may have served another purpose at the site, its use in producing lime water for sugar refining was confirmed by a modern-day sugar refiner in the Philippines (Kuersteiner-Beck, personal communication 1988).

Fresh bullock's blood, egg white, or charcoal may then have been added to the pan as a clarifying agent (Porter 1843:213). Vegetable charcoal was introduced as a substitute clarifying agent in 1805, followed in 1811 by animal charcoal, which produced a clearer sugar (Evans 1848:146).

In the old method, as described by Silliman in 1833, the pan was heated to just below the boiling point for several hours, so that the blood, egg whites, and sediments rose to the surface as a scum several inches thick. The scum was removed with a long-handled perforated copper skimmer until a white milky-looking froth appeared.

The liquor (liquid sugar) was then transferred from the cooler to a copper cistern, open at the top. This cistern was topped with a woolen blanket in an oblong basket. A copper dipper was used to transfer the liquor into a wooden trough; the liquor then ran through the trough to the cistern, where it was filtered through the blanket. The sand and other substances caught in the blanket were discarded.

The pan was then washed and a portion of the liquor returned to it for evaporation. The liquor was boiled and stirred for 12 to 30 minutes until the foreman determined that it had reached the exact degree of viscosity. The fire in the furnace beneath the pan was dampened, but not extinguished, by throwing fresh coal and then water upon the flame.

The liquor was transferred from the cistern to a circular copper basin called a cooler. In the granulation process the liquor was stirred as it was poured so that it would not form a crust and was then agitated vigorously with the stirring oars until it began to crystallize. A second, third, and fourth portion of liquor, combined with that of previously refined sugar, was then evaporated in the boiler. It was at this stage that the granulated, or crystallized, sugar was transferred from the coolers to the molds to undergo the claying process (Silliman 1833:84–85).

In the claying process additional molasses was removed from the sugar, and thus a lower grade of sugar could be refined into one of a whiter, finer quality. The sugar was placed in a cone-shaped mold and topped with a wet clay slip. The water from the clay slowly percolated through the sugar, washing the syrup through and leaving a cap of dried clay on top (Knight 1841:167). The syrup dripped down through a hole in the pointed end of the mold, and into a pot, or syrup jar (figure 16.4). This procedure allowed the water to gradually percolate as it separated from

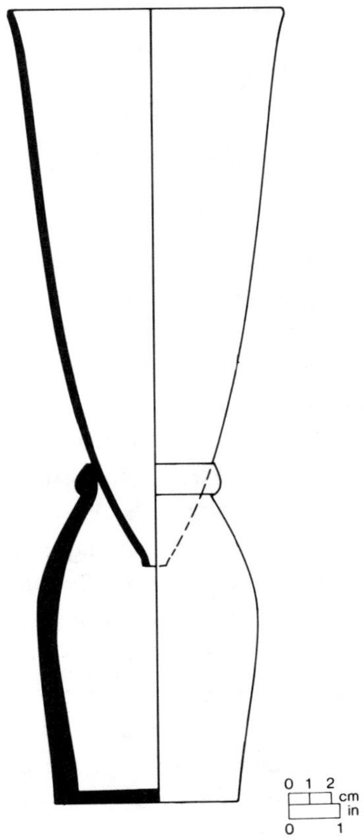

FIGURE 16.4. *Sugar mold inserted in a syrup jar, as positioned during the claying process. (City of Alexandria, Va.)*

the clay, since simply pouring water on top would have dissolved the sugar (Reed 1866:91–92). By the 1840s a faster process, called liquoring, had been developed, and it used a damp refined sugar in place of the clay (Scoffern 1849:135).

At the Sugar House site, excavators discovered lumps of white clay and many mold shards with a thin coating of clay adhering to the interior. The clay used in the refining process had to be white, clean, and free of stones, rust, and organic matter, so as not to discolor the sugar. American refineries used clay from such diverse sources as Federal Hill near Baltimore, the Delaware River drainage, Cow Bay on Long Island, Gay Head on Martha's Vineyard, and Holland (Silliman 1833:92).

Before claying, the molds were inserted in syrup jars on the upper floors of the refinery and were allowed to drain for 24 hours, during which time the sugar hardened. After the drainings were emptied from the syrup jars, the wet clay was poured over the mold and allowed to dry for at least five days. Finer grades of sugar would be clayed three times, and would sit for several more days in the molds.

A small portion of syrup usually remained at the narrow end of the lump and caused discoloration extending 3 to 5 inches. While this could be further refined, the tip was usually cut off and returned to the clarifier, and the end of the sugar was then shaped using a "nosing tool."

The finished loaves were removed from the mold, wrapped in blue paper, and placed on shelves to dry for several more days (Silliman 1833:96).

Sugar refining was substantially improved with the invention of the vacuum pan, or blow-up cistern, in 1813. The steam engine and vacuum pan were used in conjunction with bone charcoal to clear the color and eliminated the need for bull's blood or egg whites. The vacuum pan was widely used in European refineries and on the West Indies sugar plantations, but it was not introduced into the United States until 1831, when it was first used at the Louisiana Refining Company of New Orleans (Deer 1950:561). This was a few years after the demise of the Alfred Street Sugar House, ca. 1828. Benjamin Silliman (1833:69) described the transition to the new process: "All the refineries except three, are established on what is called the old method, by which is understood the method of evaporating in open pans. Indeed, very few have abandoned clarification by blood, and the use of clay. The three exceptions to the old system, are . . . in New York, Philadelphia and New Orleans: (Silliman 1833:69). Because of the War of 1812 and the ensuing economic depression, there was a delay in introducing the vacuum pan in American refineries. It was not until an economic revival was spurred by tariffs in 1824 and 1828 that the refineries had the margin of profit to experiment with the new methods.

Thus, when Anthony McLean (n.d.) recorded in a family history that "machinery coming into use obliged him [his father Daniel McLean, who purchased the refinery in 1815] to discontinue the old mode of refining," he is probably not referring to the vacuum pan because it was not yet introduced in this country. Anthony McLean gives no time frame or further explanation, so he may either have been referring to other improvements that his father made, or to the end of refining altogether around 1828.

A more common improvement seen in the United States prior to 1833 was the bascule pan, used instead of fixed copper boilers. This French invention consisted of a copper-lined wooden box that swung on chains, which allowed it to be raised, lowered, and tipped for pouring (Silliman 1833:100). Other inventions included various filters and the Baume aerometer, or saccharometer, which measured the density of fluid during heating.

Sugar refineries produced various grades of sugar. The best quality of sugar was the double-refined loaf or "family" sugar, followed by single loaves (once refined), "lump in three qualities," "piece," and "bastard," or brown sugar. The Alfred Street Sugar House's "500 boxes of Havannah Sugar," valued at $20,000 in the 1820 Census of Manufactures, most likely referred to partly refined Havana White sugar, which was further refined by McLean into the finest grade of loaf sugar. Nothing was wasted at the refinery—by-products were sold to distilleries for rum and vinegar. The Alfred Street refinery was also known to have produced candy (*Alexandria Gazette*, March 2, 1805), which was crystallized on string like the rock candy available today (Silliman 1833:101).

Artifacts of Alexandria's Sugar Refining Process

Excavations in Alexandria yielded a number of the artifacts associated with sugar refining, primarily sugar molds and syrup jars.

The Sugar Molds

Although 10,794 fragments of earthenware sugar molds were recovered at the Alfred Street Sugar House site (Magid 1987), these represent only 75 to 200 individual molds, and thus account for less than 4 percent of the 5,000 molds and pots reported at the sugar house in 1820 (U.S. Census of Manufactures).

Most of the sugar molds found in Alexandria are of a hard, sandy-tempered unglazed red earthenware (figure 16.5a). The porous unglazed ware enabled moisture to evaporate from the drying sugar, and the cone shape enabled the syrup to filter evenly from the sugar and to drip out through the narrow opening at the base. The molds had to be made of a hard material so that they would not break when they were tapped to release the loaves of sugar (Silliman 1833:93). The interior surface of the mold also needed to be very smooth so that the loaf would easily be released, and they had to be of a standard size to ensure that loaves were of a standard weight. The potter used a wooden or hollow cast-iron core mold or matrix to produce the sugar molds to these specifications (Regaldo-Saint Blancard 1986:161).

The technique, similar to that used for making ceramic drain pipes, involved turning the clay around the matrix, which was affixed to the potter's wheel. Horizontal lines on the interior of the Alexandria molds are evidence of the use of a fixed matrix, rather than one that turned with the wheel. The molds were manufactured in two stages. First they were turned around the mold, rim up, and then removed from the matrix and allowed to partially dry. Later they were returned to the wheel rim down, and the tip was formed (Regaldo-Saint Blancard 1986:161–165).

Molds came in various sizes according to the grade of sugar produced. At least four sizes were produced in Connecticut (Silliman 1833:93) and six in France (Regaldo-Saint Blancard 1986:153). The Alfred Street molds have five sizes of rim diameters, ranging from 6 to 14 inches. Although different size matrices were obviously used to produce molds of different sizes, it is not possible to determine the capacity of the molds without knowing the length, and this has not been determined for the Alexandria molds. However, the 12 and 14 inch diameters are most likely the bastard, or largest size molds used for brown sugar, while the smaller sizes would have been used for the finer loaf or lump.

Benjamin Silliman reported that the molds and pots were formerly all imported, from England, Holland,

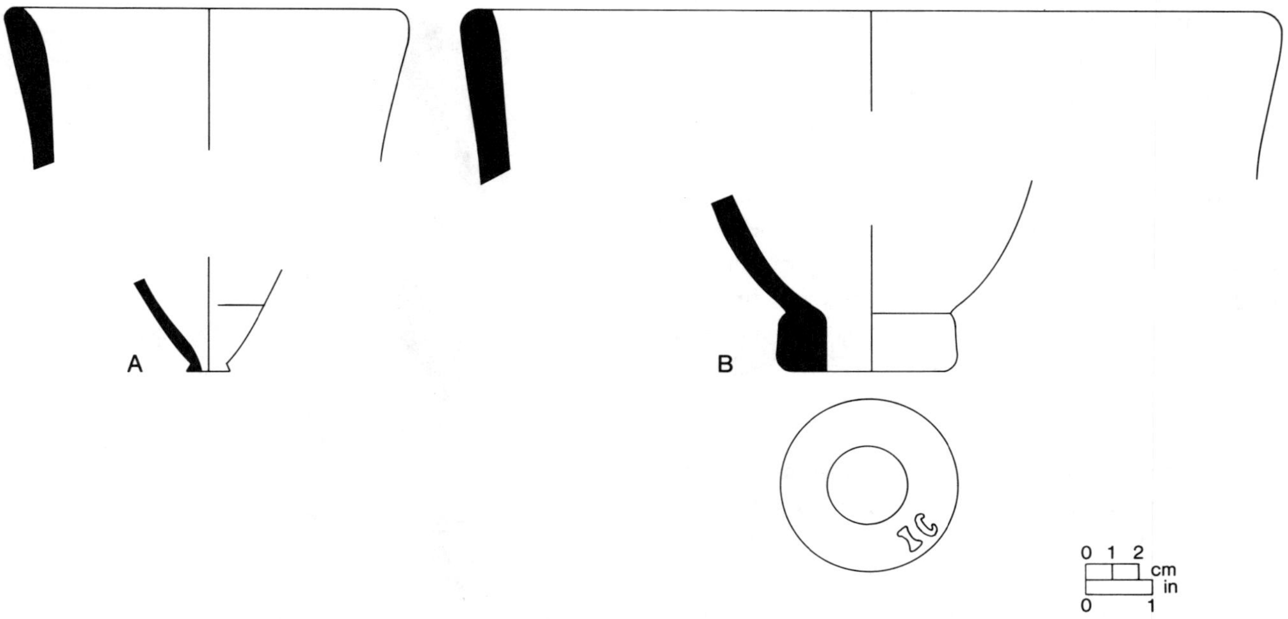

FIGURE 16.5. *Two types of sugar molds from the Alfred Street Sugar House: a. Rim and tip of sugar mold of hard, sand-tempered, dark red clay. The tip is perforated from the interior, with a small protuberance around the narrow opening. A line appears near the tip, from the template used to shape the end of the cone. These molds were probably made in Alexandria. b. Rim and tip of sugar mold of marbled clay, imported from France. The protruding tip has been turned and smoothed with a tool. (City of Alexandria, Va.)*

and France. The English wares were "smoother, firmer and stronger than the American, but (were) much more expensive" (Silliman 1833:93). In the early nineteenth century molds and pots were made in Norwalk, Connecticut, on Long Island, and in New Jersey. The Long Island and New Jersey clays were mixed with sand to make them firm enough to withstand the refining process.

The molds found in Alexandria were first thought to be imported, because they are much sandier and harder than any of the pottery known to have been produced in Alexandria. However, spectrographic analysis of a fragment of this pottery (Stenger 1988:1–4) showed it was similar in composition to shards from the six Alexandria pottery sites. Although this analysis covered only one shard of this ware, we cannot rule out the possibility that the molds were in fact manufactured locally, and that the sand temper was added, as in Long Island and New Jersey.

A second type of sugar mold found at the site was identified from 76 shards,which appear to represent just one or two molds. The material is a whitish-orange marbled clay, with a pale orange surface. These large molds have a flat, linear-profile rim, and spiral lines on the interior indicate that a turning matrix was used in their production. The most distinguishing feature is the protruding tip, which has been turned and smoothed with a tool . The tip measured 2 3/4 inches across, with a 1-inch opening, as compared to the 1/4-inch opening of the other molds. The flat face of the tip bears the stamped initials of the potter, "IC" or "IG." An identical mold is illustrated as "Sadirac Type 1E" by Regaldo-Saint Blancard (1986) in "Les Ceramique de Raffinage du Sucre: Typologie, Technologie," and dated to the second half of the eighteenth century. The mold found in Alexandria with a 12-inch diameter would correspond to the "demy melis" or "demy-batardes" size, with a height of 24 to 30 inches. Regaldo-Saint Blancard states that larger sugar molds (more than 12 inches in diameter) had tips with large turned holes, while small perforated holes appeared in the smaller molds.

The Syrup Jars

The Sugar House site yielded 1,700 fragments of syrup jars, and 9,375 more were recovered from a partly excavated cellar one block from the refinery (900 King Street, 44AX113; figure 16.1). The syrup jars, or pots, are tall with rounded shoulders and heavy rounded rims to support the weight of the molds (figure 16.4). The rim form is unique to sugar-refining pottery and unlike any other jar forms manufactured in Alexandria. Because their capacity was not as crucial as that of the sugar molds, these jars were wheel-thrown rather than molded, using techniques standard to domestic pottery making of the period (Regaldo-Saint Blancard 1986:158). The pots were locally made, as evidenced by their appearance and by spectrographic analysis (Stenger 1988:1–4), and confirmed by the presence of potters' marks on 15 of the vessels.

The mark, "J MILLER," above "ALEX" for Alexandria, refers to the potter James Miller, who appears in Alexandria records in 1797, 1800, and 1805 on three different sites with various partners. Miller is also listed in the 1820 census for the District of Columbia, of which Alexandria was a part, as a stoneware potter (Pickens n.d.). No stamped "J MILLER" pottery had previously been found in Alexandria.

The jar rims are folded outward to form a rounded rim. Some rims are turned partly outward to form a 1/2-inch deep lip (62 percent) (figure 16.6a), and others are folded completely down to form a 1-inch deep lip (38%) (figure 16.6b). Three 5-inch jars have straight rims shaped with a tool (figure 16.6c). These were probably lidded jars that served a different function. The first two styles appear in varying sizes, from 2 to 5 inches in inner diameter, increasing in half-inch increments. Of the six rims from the Sugar House and 1,014 rims measured from the 900 King Street cellar, 85 percent measured between 3 and 4 inches in their interior diameter. The four marked rims each measure 3 inches and have fully turned rims.

The color of the paste varies from a light buff orange to a darker red, and the interior lead glaze from yellow to orange, olive, and brown. These variations were not intentional, but were due to firing conditions in the kiln (Brooks 1983:4). Similar jars were used in England in the seventeenth and eighteenth centuries. The glaze has been worn away at the rim of these jars because the molds were repeatedly inserted (Brooks 1983:4). Similar wear can be seen on the Alexandria jars.

Other Artifacts

A few other artifacts from the Sugar House excavation also relate to the production of sugar. Large quantities of anthracite coal and clinkers remained from the fuel used to fire the ovens and boil the sugar. Lumps of white clay were found from the claying process, and coral, and coral probably used in the production of lime water, was found along with waterworn potshards and an eighteenth-century Spanish silver coin. Large, thick, curved pieces of iron may have been part of the stove or of a pan or cistern. A poorly preserved 9-inch-long, flat copper object may be part of a clasp for a brace used on the copper boiler or pan (Silliman 1833:30).

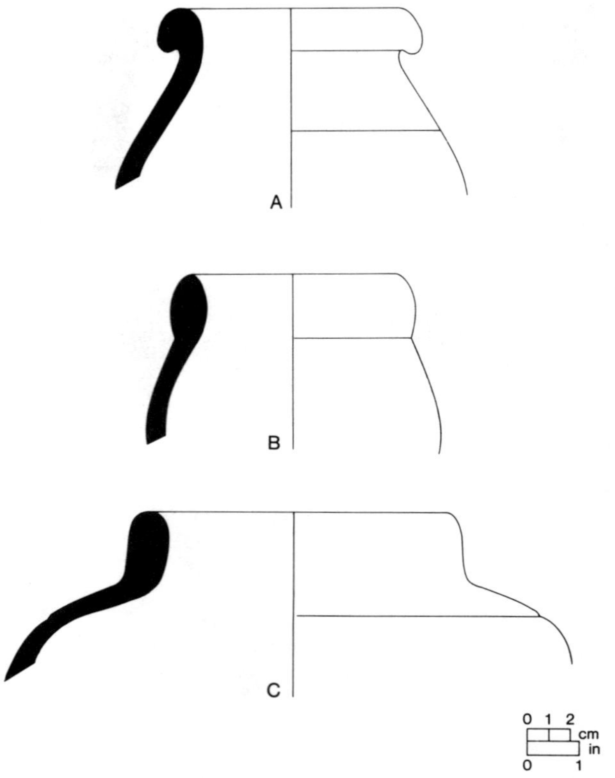

FIGURE 16.6. *Three types of syrup jars made in Alexandria: a. Partly turned rim, measuring 2 to 5 inches in diameter. b. Completely turned rim, measuring 2 to 5 inches in diameter. c. Straight rim, 5 inches in diameter. (City of Alexandria, Va.)*

Artifact Clues to the Refining Process

It is clear from the artifacts found that old refining methods continued to be used at the Sugar House. Claying was still used rather than the newer method of liquoring, which used refined sugar to cap the draining molds. Earthenware molds were used, rather than superior copper or iron ones, and the jars, and probably the molds, were locally made. There is also evidence of the use of lime water, which was generally omitted in the newer vacuum process. Traces of wood and nails from the wooden vats were found near the refinery's outbuildings. These may have held lime water or could have been used to soak the molds. Although many refiners were using animal charcoal by the time the Sugar House closed, no deposits of this were found on the site. The large copper equipment would have been disposed of at the time the refineries closed down, as it could be reused or melted down for profit.

Silliman wrote of an "impression which we find to be general, among the refiners who proceed upon the old plan, namely, that the new process by steam and the vacuum pans, if not ruinous, is, at best, so expensive, that its success, unless prosecuted upon a great scale, is very dubious" (1833:102). The Alfred Street Sugar House, with only one pan and 5,000 molds and pots, was operating on a moderate scale. This refinery used about 500 boxes of Havana sugar annually (U.S. Census of Manufactures, 1820) and produced less than one ton of refined sugar a day. The two-pan house of Seaman, Tobias & Co. in New York used 3,200 boxes of Havana White (of 475 pounds each) in one year (Silliman 1833:90), also with the old method. Only the larger refineries were able to afford the "apparatus upon the new plan, [which] is rather more than double of that upon the old" (Silliman 1833:119). Still, the new technology, which produced better-quality sugar in less time, was cost-effective after the initial investment. In 1833 only three houses had begun using the vacuum pan (Silliman 1833:69), but by 1841 "nearly all the principal sugar refiners now boil sugar in vacuo" (Knight 1841:164). Between the 1830s and 1870s many small houses closed while large refineries using vacuum pans refined up to 1,000 tons a day.

Conclusion

By 1840, the early industrialization experienced by other eastern ports had passed Alexandria by:

> As her star was descending others were ascending to take the place of the fallen brightness. . . . So fickle is fortune. Nor men nor cities can escape her innovations. But no city in the union perhaps has exhibited so sad a contrast as the one I am in . . . and the sight has been a melancholy one—especially to those who have seen Alexandria in her beauty and in her decay. (*Alexandria Gazette*, February 29, 1840)

The completion of the Alexandria Canal in the mid-1840s brought some increased prosperity to the town in the years prior to the Civil War. However, the railroad did not arrive in Alexandria until the 1850s, long after it had made a major contribution to Baltimore's growth. But even Baltimore, with the advantage of its major railroad connections, did not continue to control the region's sugar production for long. In the last years of the nineteenth century, sugar refining became a major monopoly, with outside interests purchasing and consolidating smaller operations. American Sugar Refining, a national trust based in New York, acquired the Baltimore Sugar Refining Company (Olson 1980:237). Despite technological innovations and the continuing activity in Baltimore's sugar trade in the twentieth century, the control of sugar was no longer in Baltimore's hands (Olson 1980:310). American Sugar Refining also acquired the three remaining Philadelphia refineries at the end of the century (Burt and Davies 1982:482).

The power within the eastern American sugar industry shifted from a shared and differentiated base of New York, Philadelphia, Baltimore, and Alexandria in 1810 to one fully dominated by New York at the turn of the twentieth century. Alexandria was the first to fall victim, but the others were eventually dominated by this one New York firm with worldwide ties. American sugar refining turned out to be a risky venture, as had Caribbean sugar growing. As Mintz states, "Sugar was never a sure thing" (Mintz 1986:45).

In Alexandria today, little evidence of the sugar industry remains above ground. The Hoffman residence and garden on Washington Street is home to a branch of the Alexandria Library specializing in history. Parts of the Alfred Street Sugar House may be attached to the townhouse remodeled or built by Hugh Smith in the early 1840s. A real estate firm now occupies this structure. Most of the Sugar House property is currently an asphalt parking lot owned by the City of Alexandria.

References Cited

Alexandria Deed Book
1802 Book D. Land Records Division, Alexandria Clerk of the Circuit Court.
1807 Book O. Land Records Division, Alexandria Clerk of the Circuit Court.
1808 Book Q. Land Records Division, Alexandria Clerk of the Circuit Court.

1815 Book Z. Land Records Division, Alexandria Clerk of the Circuit Court.

1815 Book AA. Land Records Division, Alexandria Clerk of the Circuit Court.

Alexandria Advertiser

1804 Sugar House. October 29.

Alexandria Gazette

1798 Advertisement by James Piercy, May 22.

1805 Advertisement for Alfred Street refinery, March 2.

1823 Bacon Smoking Establishment on Washington Street, 23 December.

1825 Valuable Property for Sale. . . . A Sugar Refinery, May 14.

1840 As Her Star Was Descending . . . , February 29.

Bauer, K. Jack

1988 *A Maritime History of the United States, The Role of America's Seas and Waterways*. University of South Carolina Press, Columbia.

Brooks, Catherine M.

1983 Aspects of the Sugar Refining Industry from the 16th to the 18th Century. *Post-Medieval Archaeology* 17:1–7.

Burt, Nathaniel, and Wallace E. Davies

1982 The Iron Age 1876–1905. In *Philadelphia: A 300-Year History*. W. W. Norton, New York.

Clark, Allen C.

1904 Why the City Went Westward. *Records of the Columbia Historical Society* 7:118–134.

1938 Daniel Carroll of Duddington. *Records of the Columbia Historical Society* 39:1–48.

Cressey, Pamela J., and Steven J. Shephard

1987 Geographical versus Social Scale in Alexandria: A Growing Perspective. Paper presented at the annual meeting of the Society for Historical Archaeology, Savannah, Ga.

Cressey, Pamela J., Barbara H. Magid, and Steven J. Shephard

1984 Urban Development in North America: Status, Distance, and Material Differences in Alexandria, Virginia. Report submitted to the National Endowment for the Humanities under Grant Ref: RS-1284-81. Alexandria Archaeology, Alexandria, Va.

Deer, Noel

1950 *History of Sugar*. Chapman and Hall, London.

Evans, W. J.

1848 *The Sugar Planter's Manual, Being a Treatise on the Art of Obtaining Sugar from the Sugar Cane*. Lea and Blanchard, Philadelphia.

Garraty, John A., and Robert A. McCaughey

1987 *The American Nation, A History of the United States to 1877*. Harper and Row, New York.

Green, Constance McLaughlin

1962 *Washington, A History of the Capital, 1800–1950*. Princeton University Press, Princeton, N.J.

Hugill, Anthony

1978 *Sugar and All That . . . A History of Tate & Lyle*. Gentry Books, London.

Knight, Charles

1841 A Day at the Sugar Refinery. *Penny Magazine of the Society of the Diffusion of Useful Knowledge*. Charles Knight, London.

Magid, Barbara H.

1987 The Sugar House Site, 44AX96: Interim Report, 1987 Field Season. Alexandria Archaeology, Alexandria, Va.

McCusker, John James

1970 *The Rum Trade and the Balance of Payments of the Thirteen Colonies, 1650–1775*. University Microfilms International, Ann Arbor.

McLean, Anthony

n.d. Family History. Lloyd House Library, Alexandria, Va.

Mintz, Sidney W.

1986 *Sweetness and Power, The Place of Sugar in Modern History*. Penguin Books, New York.

Morison, Samuel Eliot

1923 *The Maritime History of Massachusetts, 1783–1860*. William Heinemann, London.

Olson, Sherry H.

1980 *Baltimore, The Building of an American City*. Johns Hopkins University Press, Baltimore, Md.

Pickens, John K.

n.d. Collection of unpublished manuscripts on file at the Lloyd House Library, Alexandria, Va.

Porter, G. R.

1843 *The Nature and Properties of the Sugar Cane: With Practical Directions for the Improvement of Its Culture, and the Manufacture of Its Products*. Smith, Elder, London.

Regaldo-Saint Blancard, Pierre

1986 Les Ceramiques de Raffinage du Sucre: Typologie, Technologie. *Archaeologie du Midi Medieval* 4:151–168.

Reed, W.

1866 *The History of Sugar and Sugar Yielding Plants*. Longmans, Green, London.

Revis, Sara M.

1990 *The History of the North Alfred Street Sugar House*. Alexandria Archaeology, Alexandria, Va..

Scharf, J. Thomas

1881 *History of Baltimore City and County, Maryland*. Philadelphia. Reprinted 1971, Regional Publishing, Baltimore, Md.

Scoffern, John.

1849 *The Manufacture of Sugar at Home and in the Colonies*. Longmans, Brown, Green, and Longmans, London.

Sharrer, G. Terry

1977 Commerce and Industry. In *Alexandria: A Towne in Transition, 1800–1900*. Alexandria Bicentennial Corporation and Alexandria Historical Society, Alexandria. Va.

Silliman, Benjamin

1833 *Manual on the Cultivation of the Sugar Cane and the Fabrication and Refinement of Sugar*. Francis Preston Blair, Washington, D.C.

Stenger, Alison T.
1988 Spectrographic Analysis, Alexandria, Va., Department of Anthropology, Ceramics Analysis Laboratory, Portland State University, Oregon.
Townsend, George Alfred
1902 *Thomas Law, Washington's First Rich Man*, Records of the Columbia Historical Society, Washington, D.C. United States
1810 *Census of Manufactures for the District of Columbia.* Washington, D.C.
1820 *Census of Manufactures for the District of Columbia.* Washington D.C.
Wedderburn, Alex J.
1907 *Souvenir Virginia Tercentennial 1607–1907 Historic Alexandria Virginia, Illustrated.* n.p.
Wimsatt, Josephine Cleary
1926 *Recollections.* North China Star Press, Tientsin, China.

XVII
CHAPTER

Neighborhoods and Household Types in Nineteenth-Century Washington, D.C.
Fannie Hill and Mary McNamara in Hooker's Division

Charles D. Cheek and Donna J. Seifert

Hooker's Division was one of Washington, D.C.'s, most colorful neighborhoods. During the nineteenth century, as the federal district developed into a modern city, the working-class neighborhood south of Pennsylvania Avenue developed a distinctive character in response to the political, economic, and social history of the capital city (figure 17.1). The Civil War gave the neighborhood its name and early notoriety; the processes of capitalism and industrialization, in Washington, D.C., and throughout urban America, led to the differentiation and segregation of people, functions, and space. During the second half of the nineteenth century, industrial areas became separated from residential areas, and residential areas became segregated by class and ethnicity. The neighborhood known as Hooker's Division exhibited a distinct, definable character in terms of socioeconomic status, ethnicity, and household composition; this character is documented in the historical record and the archaeological record.

The artifact assemblages of Hooker's Division reflect the consumer behavior of Fannie Hill, madam of one of the neighborhood's brothels, and Mary McNamara, wife and mother of a neighborhood working-class family. Hooker's Division included two types of households—represented by neighborhood residents Fannie Hill and Mary McNamara—which manifested different patterns of consumption. The differences between the two types of archaeological assemblages are directly related to household composition and the differences in the work done by the women in each type of household. Mary McNamara was a working-class wife whose labor consisted of household tasks devoted to the social reproduction of the family. Although she may have engaged in income-producing labor, such as providing household services and meals for boarders in her household, the majority of her enterprise consisted of the production of goods and services for her family's consumption. Fannie Hill ran a brothel. Her labor was directed toward maintaining a household occupied by boarding prostitutes.

This study is based on the excavated collections from 10 house lots with stratified deposits on two blocks, squares 257 and 258 (figure 17.2). The two household types are defined in terms of distinctive artifact patterns. A comparison of these household types with households in other neighborhoods in Washington, D.C., reveals that the working-class household in Hooker's Division was similar to households in another white working-class neighborhood, and that both the prostitute and working-class

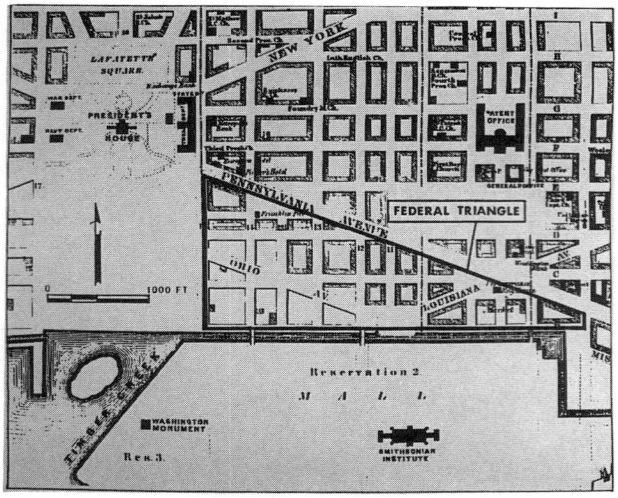

Figure 17.1. *Washington, D.C.'s, Federal Triangle (Keily 1850). Historic Hooker's Division is located in the west end of the modern Federal Triangle, the triangle formed by Pennsylvania Avenue, Constitution Avenue, and Fifteenth Street. The White House and the U.S. Treasury are a few blocks to the northwest, the Capitol is to the southeast, and the Smithsonian Mall is across Constitution Avenue (which replaced the abandoned Washington Canal) to the south. As in the nineteenth century, downtown Washington, D.C., is north of Pennsylvania Avenue.*

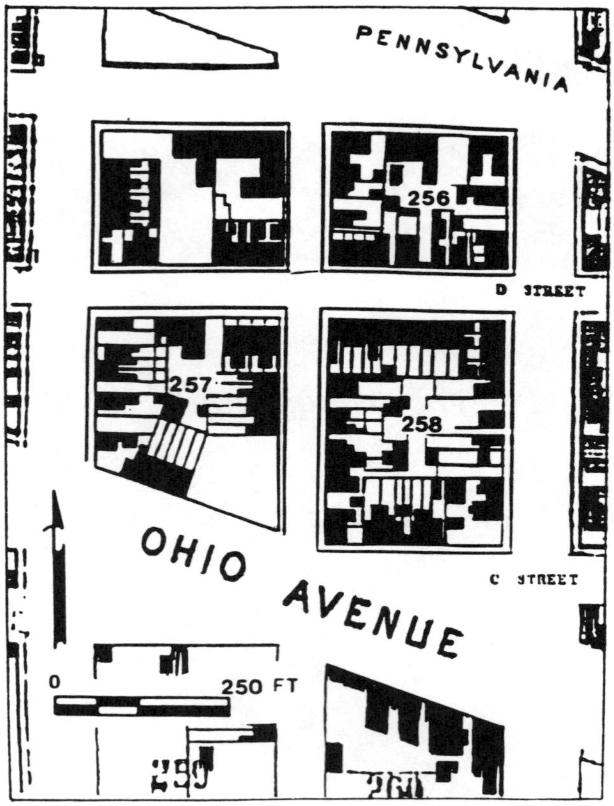

Figure 17.2. *Location of Squares 257 and 258 in Hooker's Division (Boschke 1857).*

households were distinguishable from households of black working-class neighborhoods.

Neighborhoods, Household Types, and Households

This chapter examines archaeological deposits on two levels of analysis: (1) household types within one neighborhood, Hooker's Division; and (2) household types across three nineteenth-century Washington, D.C., neighborhoods. Two other levels of analysis are considered but are not the subject of analysis: (3) archaeological household deposits linked to individual census households and (4) neighborhoods considered as a whole rather than as a set of household types.

Historical archaeologists have recently become interested in the neighborhood as a subject of study in its own right and as an analytical unit in archaeology (Cressey 1983; Rothschild 1987, 1990; Cheek and McCarthy 1990). Most studies of consumer behavior, however, focus on the household as the primary unit of analysis and use individual archaeological household deposits linked to individual census households (Deetz 1982; Beaudry 1984; Mrozowski 1984; LeeDecker et al. 1987; Spencer-Wood 1987). However, analysis based on the individual household presents both practical and theoretical problems (see Beaudry 1984; Mrozowski 1984; Brown 1987; Cheek and McCarthy 1990), which are best examined from the viewpoint of the neighborhood or household type. The central problem, especially in urban areas, is the correlation of the archaeological household with the historic household: the archaeological household (the artifact assemblage from a house lot) is not the direct material equivalent of the household defined by documents (Selby et al. 1984).

The historic household, a domestic residential group that inhabits a common dwelling and appears as a discrete group in the documents (Henry 1987:360 citing Laslett 1972:86), is usually considered a family group. However, the household may include unrelated boarders or servants. Furthermore, the unit of procurement and consumption and social reproduction is often wider than the kin-based residential group (Smith et al. 1984:8; Wong 1984:61). For example, historical and ethnographic data indicate that working-class African Americans participate in domestic networks composed of collateral and lineal kin that extend beyond the household; in fact, the household expands, contracts, and changes composition in response to the economic security of adults in the domestic network (Stack 1974a, 1974b; Borchert 1980). Even if such extensive domestic networks were limited to working-class blacks, consumption patterns of the domestic network affect the archaeological household through the recycling of goods (Schiffer et al. 1981). Thus, the artifact assemblage of the house lot may contain objects acquired by nonresident network members and lack objects acquired by household residents who contribute through exchange or gift to another household.

The correlation of historic and archaeological households is further complicated by site formation processes, the limitations in the documentary record, and the mobility of urban residents. Precise correlation of a documented family or household with an archaeological assemblage is rare. Because archaeological data are usually deposited continuously, it is difficult to identify discrete deposits that can be correlated with separate, documented households. Furthermore, historical research indicates that working-class urban residents were generally tenants and frequently moved in and out of cities (Hershberg 1978:18 citing Thernstrom and Knights 1970:264) and in and out of neighborhoods within a city (Blumin 1972:37). Even when an archaeological deposit and historical household can be correlated, data from a single stable household is not an accurate reflection of the norm, the transient working-class household.

Besides these practical problems, the central theoretical issue is whether any individual historical household is representative of a particular group (Henry 1989:18). This issue is important since archaeological samples are usually limited to a few houselots for any specific project.

Neighborhood analysis and household-type analysis address the problem of using a single archaeological sample as representative of a group. Neighborhood analysis aggregates archaeological households in areas segregated by function, historically known as neighborhoods. Each archaeological household in the aggregate is considered a sample of a neighborhood's historical households. Household-type analysis aggregates households according to household composition, economic status, ethnicity, or other variables that are thought to affect consumer behavior. Each archaeological household is considered part of a group characterized by certain socioeconomic characteristics. When aggregated, these archaeological deposits are considered representative of the group.

Urban historians, historical sociologists, and historical geographers in general agree that the modern neighborhood developed in response to the processes of industrialization and capitalism (La Gory and Pipkin 1981). These processes led to the differentiation and segregation of people, functions, and space. Discrete areas became restricted to industrial or residential function, for example, and residential areas became segregated by class and ethnicity. By the mid- to late nineteenth century, the modern segregated residential neighborhood had evolved.

Economic, sociocultural, and institutional forces affect the development and character of a neighborhood. Residents select their neighborhood on the basis of several economic and social factors, such as housing costs, life-style, and the desire to live among people of similar habits. This is true for working-class, middle-class, and elite households. Institutional forces are also important, particularly in limiting the choices of certain groups, such as blacks and immigrants (La Gory and Pipkin 1981:190–191). As a result of the economic, sociocultural, and institutional forces in the industrial city, modern neighborhoods are characterized by population homogeneity. The neighborhood also reflects consumer choice, because residents choose a neighborhood as they choose a house; neighborhood selection is limited by several factors, and choice is directed by the composition, economic status, and ethnicity of the household. Residents are, therefore, consumers of a neighborhood, which, like tableware or an automobile, reflects the values of the consumer. Furthermore, a neighborhood attracts particular kinds of consumers who buy certain kinds of goods. Therefore, a sample of households from a neighborhood represents the commonalities of the component households.

Household types can be characterized by the same variables as neighborhoods: household composition, socioeconomic status, and ethnicity. While the unit of procurement and consumption and social reproduction is often wider than the kin-based residential group, households are composed of people who share a common residence and pool resources to perform certain tasks. Thus, their consumer behavior is closely tied to their position in the socioeconomic structure of the society (Anderson 1988:157). Similar household types tend to cluster spatially in urban neighborhoods.

Studies of modern America by social scientists and archaeologists demonstrate that households with similar life-styles consume similar products (Rathje and McCarthy 1977; Weiss 1988) and live in discrete clusters (Shevky and Bell 1955; Timms 1971; Davies 1984) because they consume the same kind of living space or neighborhoods. Furthermore, modern studies of consumer behavior indicate that neighborhoods characterized by demographic variables are stable for decades: people move in and out of neighborhoods, but the life-style of the neighborhood remains the same (Tryon and Bailey 1970; Weiss 1988:14). If similar processes functioned in the past, material culture should differ from neighborhood to neighborhood (Cheek and McCarthy 1990). Therefore, it is appropriate to aggregate archaeological deposits, including those that cannot be assigned to a specific historical household, into household types and into neighborhoods. When archaeological deposits from a series of neighborhood houselots are aggregated into one assemblage, this assemblage represents the composite behavior of the neighborhood's households. The archaeological analytical unit then matches the historical analytical unit. The same is true for archaeological deposits aggregated on the basis of household type. Such an aggregated assemblage is a sample of the type and is more likely to represent the behavior of the people in this type of household than is one household linked to census documents.

Historical Context of Hooker's Division

The history of the neighborhood that came to be known as Hooker's Division begins with the establishment of the federal district in 1791. The location was hardly desirable; in fact, the land south of Pennsylvania Avenue from Fifteenth Street west to the Capitol was described as "a boggy morass covered with scrubby bushes and brambles, through which a path was cut" (Busey 1898:226). Tiber Creek separated the area from the parcel selected for the Smithsonian Mall. Improvement of the land began in the early nineteenth century. An 1801 enumeration of houses in the city for the Commissioners of the District of Columbia lists two houses in square 258 (Padover 1946:248). Tiber Creek was channelized in 1815; the new Washington Canal connected the Potomac with the Anacostia River (Green 1962:1:72). Although the canal was hailed as a boon to transportation, it soon silted up and transported neither barges nor the sewage it received.

During the early years of the nineteenth century, Washington, D.C., failed to compete with Alexandria and Georgetown for control of the local inland trade, which was then sent down the Potomac to Chesapeake Bay and on to other ports. The federal district became a city of politics and politicians, a city of seasonally fluctuating populations, and a city where services rather than trade or industry dominated the economy.

Although this picture of the city as a town of politicians with a service economy is accurate, it obscures the city inhabited by businessmen, white-collar workers, and skilled and unskilled workers who participated in the economic life of the nation and made homes and careers in the capital. The population of the city doubled between 1850 and 1860, when it reached approximately 60,000; by the end of the Civil War, the city had swollen to 130,000. By 1900, the population had more than doubled and doubled again before 1940 (Green 1962:1:183, 208; 2:89). Thus, from the beginning of the Civil War, there was a significant population living and working in the city. In many ways, Washington, D.C., was similar to urban areas in other parts of the country. Although the economy of Washington, D.C., was less dependent on trade and industry, the volume of business in the city rose slowly until the 1850s, when the value of manufactures doubled. Construction of federal buildings provided additional jobs throughout the nineteenth century and into the twentieth, as well. After the Civil War, manufactures increased nearly seven times by 1890, although most products were consumed by the expanding city rather than exported (Nolen 1976). Throughout the nineteenth century, Washington, D.C., experienced the problems that came with expanding urban populations, including vandalism, robbery, assault, and prostitution (Green 1962:1:215), problems that were magnified by the rapid population increase during the Civil War (Green 1962:1:251).

At midcentury, most of the squares between Pennsylvania Avenue and the canal had been developed (Keily 1850). The area was becoming one of the city's worst neighborhoods, known as a place of drinking, gambling, thieving, brawling, and prostitution, particularly around Fourteenth Street and Ohio Avenue (Townsend 1873:457; Press 1984:53). Despite this reputation, the 1860 census and city directories from 1858, 1860, and 1861 indicate that the project area was a working-class neighborhood.

The neighborhood reached a peak in notoriety during the Civil War. There was a marked influx of prostitutes, and thousands of off-duty soldiers in Washington, D.C., frequented the theaters, saloons, and brothels. In addition to the madams, prostitutes and their soldier clients, pickpockets, and resident laborers in the neighborhood, fugitive slaves seeking sanctuary in the federal district squatted in the area between Ohio Avenue and the Washington Canal (figure 17.1; Press 1984:58–60).

The neighborhood became known as Hooker's Division during the Civil War years. According to several histories of Washington, D.C., Major General Joseph Hooker (commander of the Union's Army of the Potomac in 1863) concentrated the city's prostitutes in the neighborhood south of Pennsylvania Avenue (see Brown 1930:373; Green 1962:I:251; Press 1984:56; Leech 1986:264; "Within Sight of the White House" [1895]). The provost marshal's 1864–1865 survey of bawdy houses reported more than 30 brothels on 11th, 12th, 13th, C, D, and E streets and more than 20 brothels at addresses on the "Island," the area south and west of the Washington Canal. An additional 20 brothels were scattered around the rest of the city (Provost Marshal 1865). Although Hooker's initiative appears to be undocumented, several local news items published in Washington's *Evening Star* (August 29, 1864:3) during the war refer to the neighborhood as Hooker's Division. It was said that during their off-duty hours, this was the place to find the men of General Hooker's Division (James O. Hall, personal communication 1989). Although the use of the term "hooker" for prostitute appears to predate the establishment of the division (Press 1984:56), the *double entendre* of Hooker's Division probably contributed to popularizing the term's usage.

After the war, the neighborhood retained its name. According to the 1870 census, several prostitutes lived in the area along with skilled and unskilled workers and their families. Laborers living in the neighborhood could walk to work in the city center, and the entertainments of the saloons and brothels were convenient to the downtown theater district and tolerated in a working-class neighborhood (see Ellis 1869:458). Several ethnic groups were represented in the neighborhood, including immigrants from northern Europe, England, and Ireland as well as native-born black and white residents.

The latter part of the nineteenth century witnessed several changes in the neighborhood, all probably related to its marginal location between Pennsylvania Avenue and the old Washington Canal. The first was the increase in industrial and commercial establishments in and adjacent to Hooker's Division. After the Civil War, the Somerville Brass Foundry and William Walter's Carriage Works were established (Boyd's City Directories 1868, 1870). By the early twentieth century, the division included a cornice works and lumber yard (Sanborn Map Company 1903). During the neighborhood's last years, an ornamental plaster works, cabinet works, plumbing and heating supply shops, a printer, and Potomac Electric Power Company contributed to the commercial and industrial character of the area (Sanborn Map Company 1928).

The second change was the marked increase in the number of black residents by 1870. The change in composition of the neighborhood (from 10 percent black in 1860 to 39 percent in 1870) probably reflects the influx of freed slaves who came to the neighborhood during and after the war.

The third change was the shift from a mixed residential-commercial-industrial neighborhood to a red-light district. Hooker's Division, like red-light districts in other urban centers, was in a working-class neighborhood close to the city's central business district (Symanski 1981:193; Shumsky 1986:665). In the 1890s, the number of prostitutes increased significantly, and by 1900 nearly all dwellings in the neighborhood were brothels. At the turn of the century, both Ohio Avenue and C Street experienced a small building boom. Wooden houses built in the mid-nineteenth century were replaced by two- and three-story brick Victorian townhouses. Several of these houses are identified on historic maps as brothels. It seems likely that houses were built as brothels when the concentration of prostitutes increased in the neighborhood. However, the documentary record does not reveal the intent of the builders or owners. Census records list these addresses as boardinghouses, each kept by a middle-aged woman and occupied by young female boarders for whom no occupation is given.

The District of Columbia's new office building, in the northeast end of the division, opened in 1908 (Press 1984:68), but the brothels remained. At the turn of the century there was increasing interest in revitalizing the city. Particular attention was devoted to the Smithsonian Mall; rehabilitation of the area between the Mall and

Pennsylvania Avenue called for replacing the existing neighborhood with government buildings (Press 1984: 64–65).

Since the 1890s, the division had received attention from reformers decrying the unlicensed sale of alcohol as well as prostitution only a few blocks from the White House ("Within Sight of the White House" [1895]). In February 1914, Congress passed an abatement act, banning houses of prostitution in the District of Columbia (Commissioners of the District of Columbia 1914:359–361; Press 1984:68; see also U.S. Senate 1913).

The brothels closed and the women left. Some undoubtedly went to other sections of the city where they could practice undetected (Press 1984:69). Some of the neighborhood's townhouses were occupied by a new wave of European immigrants, many with Italian names; many houses were apparently vacant. Commercial and industrial activity increased in the neighborhood after the passage of the abatement act, and there was some commercial construction. Until the late 1920s, the division continued to be a mixed residential-commercial-industrial neighborhood.

In 1918, the Public Building Commission recommended that the federal government purchase the remaining land within the triangle between Fifteenth Street, Pennsylvania Avenue, and North B Street (Constitution Avenue); in the late 1920s, Congress authorized the purchase of the entire triangle (Press 1984:69). By the early 1930s, the remaining buildings were razed (Cheek and Glendening 1988:12). Construction plans, however, were postponed because of the Great Depression. Although most of the Federal Triangle was developed after World War II, the Great Plaza, planned for the area from D Street to Ohio Avenue between Fourteenth and Thirteenth streets remained a parking lot (GSA 1981:24). The Federal Triangle Development Act, passed by Congress in 1987, revived plans to complete the development of the Federal Triangle.

The Archaeology of Hooker's Division

Hooker's Division included two types of households: houses occupied by working-class families and boarders and houses occupied by prostitutes. The neighborhood was also mixed ethnically: both blacks and whites were represented in working-class households and prostitute households.

Ten backyards of houselots and one cellar were chosen for excavation on the basis of historical research and testing. Few archaeological sites in Washington, D.C., have wells or privies into which trash was deposited. However, the backyards of houselots received considerable amounts of household debris, including food remains and artifacts, as well as ash and cinders, which were often the main component of the rear yard deposits. Because of rebuilding episodes, lot landscaping, or the introduction of water and sewer pipes, many of the deposits can be divided into chronologically separate deposits. Building permits documented construction that could be correlated with archaeological strata. These construction strata separated occupational deposits that could be associated with particular household types or even with individual documented households.

The dates of the chronologically separate archaeological deposits from the eight houselots that could be classified as working-class or prostitute households fall into two time periods: an early period, from 1860 to 1890; and a later period, from 1890 to 1920. These dates are based on datable archaeological deposits from the site, not on historically documented periods, although historic documents were used to associate census or directory households with archaeological deposits. There were four early deposits with two working-class and two prostitute households and five late households with two working-class and three prostitute households.

Analysis of the Data

The artifact pattern analysis, developed by Stanley (South 1977), consists of classifying artifact types by functional *groups* and *classes*. The artifact groups are kitchen, clothing, personal, tobacco, furniture, activities, architecture, and arms groups. All but the latter two are included in this analysis (tables 17.1 and 17.2). Each group is further subdivided into *classes* composed of specific artifact *types*. For example, the kitchen group includes such classes as ceramics, tumblers, glass tableware, and bottles, and the personal group includes the classes of coins, keys, and jewelry. The functions associated with the groups are self-explanatory, with the exception of the activities group. This group includes artifacts associated

TABLE 17.1. *Frequency of Selected Artifact Groups by Household Type and Time Period for Hooker's Division*

Time Period	Artifact Group[a]	Working Class Number	Working Class Percent	Prostitute Number	Prostitute Percent
Late					
1890–1920	Assemblage total (all groups)	7,699	100.00	10,727	100.00
	Kitchen ceramics[b]	2,823	23.68	1,273	11.87
	Clothing	34	0.44	240	2.24
	Tobacco	32	0.42	136	1.27
	Activities	303	3.94	1,354	12.61
	Personal	35	0.45	125	1.17
	Furniture	8	0.10	26	0.24
Early					
1870–1890	Assemblage total (all groups)	2,536	100.00	2,275	100.00
	Kitchen ceramics	963	37.97	477	20.97
	Clothing	10	0.39	21	0.92
	Tobacco	24	0.95	51	2.24
	Activities	136	5.36	128	5.63
	Personal	14	0.55	10	0.44
	Furniture	—	—	—	—

[a]South (1977).
[b]Only the ceramic class of the kitchen group is used here.

TABLE 17.2. *Frequency of Selected Artifact Groups by Neighborhood and Household Type*

	Working Class								Prostitute	
	Black				White				White & Black	
	Howard Road[b] 1870–1930		Quander Place[c] 1890–1940		N Street[c] 1880–1920		Hooker's Div. 1890–1920		Hooker's Div. 1890–1920	
Artifact Group[a]	Number	Percent	Number	Percent	Number	Percent	Number	Percent	Number	Percent
Assemblage total (all groups)	73,679	100.00	10,944	100.00	6,119	100.00	7,699	100.00	10,727	100.00
Kitchen ceramics[d]	6,838	9.28	711	6.50	1,293	21.10	1,823	23.68	1,273	11.87
Clothing	695	0.94	68	0.62	20	0.33	34	0.44	240	2.24
Tobacco	4	0.005	7	0.06	10	0.16	32	0.42	136	1.27
Activities	5,319	7.22	613	5.60	250	4.10	303	3.94	1,354	12.61
Personal	169	0.23	29	0.26	9	0.15	35	0.45	125	1.17
Furniture	5	0.007	9	0.08	3	0.05	8	0.10	26	0.24

[a]South (1977).
[b]Louis Berger & Associates (1985).
[c]Cheek et al. (1983).
[d]Only the ceramic class of the kitchen group is used here.

primarily with male activities, such as construction hardware, farm tools, and fishing gear, as well as miscellaneous artifacts such as toys.

The original purpose of South's procedure was to identify patterns in the percentages of the groups and classes. The identified patterns were to be an intermediate step that would stimulate and facilitate the investigation of the links between the patterns and the cultural and historical processes that caused assemblage differences and similarities (South 1988:27). South's method is used here to facilitate comparison among the households represented in the neighborhood. In addition, this method can be used to compare Hooker's Division households and other Washington, D.C., sites.

Because historical data indicated that there were two types of households in the neighborhood, variation in artifact pattern was expected. Distinct consumption patterns appeared when the archaeological households were grouped into four types: early and late working-class households and early and late prostitute households. Both blacks and whites lived in this neighborhood. However, the houselot deposits assigned to working-class households most likely represent white households. Three of the four houselots used in the analysis come from addresses for which there are no documented black residents. Furthermore, they come from Ohio Avenue, which always had a lower frequency of blacks than did 13 ½ Street. The fourth houselot, which is on 13 ½ Street, had black residents in an alley dwelling. However, the assemblage included in the analysis comes from deposits made after the alley dwelling had been torn down. The houselot deposits assigned to prostitute households may have included a black prostitute household in each period. However, a sample size of one is not sufficient for separate analysis.

Kitchen ceramics were thought to be particularly sensitive to household composition, since household composition in this neighborhood is clearly related to household members' occupations and household function. The working-class households were primarily composed of kin groups, that is, families with one or more wage-earners working outside the home. Some included boarders who also were employed outside the home. One such family household, occupying 1359 Ohio Avenue in 1880, was Pat and Mary McNamara and their eight children and as many as six boarders (U.S. Census Office 1880). Pat McNamara was a grocery clerk, and his two teenaged sons worked outside the home as a huckster and a telegraph messenger. Most households included family members at home, like the McNamara's youngest children, who probably were not involved in remunerative labor. Mary McNamara and her older daughter, Annie, probably contributed to the family's income by providing meals and household services for boarders. Food preparation and consumption was a primary function of the household. Whether or not household members ate together, most probably ate some meals at home each day.

The prostitute households, however, are composed of unrelated women living in a house that is also the place of employment. Fannie Hill lived at 314 13 ½ Street. She was listed as the proprietor of a *bagnio* (brothel) which also sold liquor without a District of Columbia license ("Within Sight of the White House" [1895]). Next door, at another *bagnio*, at 312 13 ½ Street, Ella Buchanan ran a "boardinghouse" with two unrelated young adult women for whom no occupation is listed (U.S. Census Office 1900). While the residents of a brothel probably ate in the house, and may have eaten together, the purpose of living together was not social support or even economic necessity, but a function of their employment. Other nonkin households (such as boardinghouses) might present data that would clarify the relation of kitchen ceramic frequencies to household composition, but no such household was included in the archaeological sample.

The percentages of kitchen ceramics in the archaeological deposits are related to occupation date and household composition: the percentages of kitchen ceramics decrease from the early to the late periods for both household types (table 17.1), but working-class households have higher percentages of kitchen ceramics in both periods. The decrease in ceramics in both household types is related to an increase in purchases of other consumer goods in general rather than to the increase in glass products alone, as has been suggested elsewhere (Garrow 1982:185–186; LeeDecker et al. 1987:250–251).

Two forces may account for the lower percentages of kitchen ceramics in the households of prostitutes in both time periods: household composition and the relative importance of meals to the purpose of the household. Providing food for its residents was not a primary purpose of the prostitute households. In working-class households, however, food and meals were central to one of the purposes of the family: social reproduction. The material culture of the archaeological household apparently reflects this difference in household purpose.

In addition to kitchen ceramics, other artifacts appear to be sensitive to household composition and occupation date. In fact, clothing and tobacco artifact percentages are consistently higher in prostitute households than in working-class households, whereas kitchen ceramics are consistently lower (table 17.1). Although there is no strong relationship between personal and furniture artifacts (such as drawer pulls and upholstery tacks) and kitchen ceramics, the percentages of these artifacts can also be understood by considering household composition and occupation date.

Household composition is significant in explaining percentage of clothing artifacts. In the early period, prostitute households had a higher percentage of clothing artifacts than the working-class households. In the late period, clothing percentages are higher in both types of households, although percentages are still highest in the prostitute households. Historical sources indicate that prostitutes had higher incomes than other working-class women, and prostitutes spent money to dress in style (Rosen 1982:106–107; Peiss 1986:66; Seifert 1991). The higher percentage of clothing artifacts, particularly buttons and other fasteners, may reflect an emphasis on stylish clothing as a mark of the profession.

The percentages of tobacco pipes are also higher in prostitute households from the early period. During the late period, percentages are lower for both types of households, but still higher for prostitute than working-class households. The artifacts from prostitute households probably represent tobacco pipes used and discarded by nonresident clients. Although women smoked by this time (Cook 1989:224), cigarettes were probably the preferred form of tobacco consumption. Brothel residents may have smoked some of the pipes recovered from these deposits, however. Even if clients did not smoke more than the general population, a larger number of smokers would visit the prostitute household per week than a working-class household, accounting for more pipes in prostitute than working-class households. The lower percentages in the late period may reflect the increasing popularity of cigarette smoking.

Although there is a slight decline over time in the percentage of the activities group in the working-class households, the percentage of this group increases and is higher in the prostitute households of the late period. The most noticeable addition in the later prostitute households is the higher percentage of toys, suggesting that one brothel, at least, included resident children.

Census records for Hooker's Division document a low incidence of children living in brothels. The high frequency of the toys is unexpected and may be related to a relatively high disposable income in prostitute households. The high frequency of flowerpots and lamp chimneys in the activities group in prostitute households may also reflect income used to decorate the brothels.

Prostitute households of the late period have higher frequencies of personal and furniture artifacts; both may reflect luxuries in prostitute households. Neither working-class nor prostitute households, however, have any furniture artifacts in the early period. This increased percentage of furniture in late-period households may represent the increasing variety of household furnishings available to, and purchased by, consumers in the late nineteenth and early twentieth centuries. Other artifact groups were examined, such as kitchen glass and architecture artifacts, but frequencies did not covary with kitchen ceramics, and no patterns were recognized.

Summary of Data Analysis

Differences in the percentage of kitchen ceramics are consistently related to household composition and date of occupation in the Hooker's Division neighborhood: early households differ from late households, and working-class households differ from prostitute households. Early working-class households have higher percentages of kitchen ceramics than contemporaneous prostitute households. Although the percentages are lower for both household types in the late period, late working-class household percentages are still higher than prostitute household percentages. Other artifact groups covary inversely with kitchen ceramics, including clothing and tobacco groups; activities, furniture, and personal artifacts are also higher in the late prostitute households.

In understanding the artifact percentages of the prostitute households, both the function and income of the household are important considerations. The lower percentages of kitchen ceramics and higher percentages of individual consumer goods in prostitute households reflect consumption patterns in which a smaller proportion of income is spent on goods related to social reproduction (represented by ceramic tableware), and a larger proportion of the income is spent on consumer goods for the individual and the residence. Individual consumer goods include clothing and personal items and tobacco pipes. Consumer goods related to the residence (which functioned as the workplace as well) include household furnishings such as lamp chimneys and flowerpots from the activity artifact group, as well as furniture.

These distinctive prostitute and working-class households have been defined by analyzing data from a working-class neighborhood with a few brothels, which changed at the end of the nineteenth century to a neighborhood composed primarily of brothels. The two household types in the neighborhood have been separated on the basis of archaeological and historical evidence. If neighborhoods attract people of similar consumption patterns resulting from similarities in socioeconomic status, family cycle, or ethnicity, then other neighborhoods in Washington, D.C., should also exhibit distinctive artifact patterns reflecting household type and consumption patterns.

Comparative Washington, D.C., Neighborhoods

Comparable data are available from two other Washington, D.C., neighborhoods. These sites were not studied specifically as neighborhoods; however, each includes data from several neighboring houselots within a block and household types could be identified from the data. Black working-class residents occupied the houselots excavated in the Howard Road Historic District during the period from 1870 to 1930 (Louis Berger & Associates, Inc. 1985, 1986). Working-class blacks also occupied the dwellings on Quander Place from 1890 to 1940, while working-class whites occupied the dwellings on the street face of the block, N Street, S.W., from 1880 to 1920 (figure 17.3; Cheek et al. 1983).

The comparable Howard Road and Quander Place–N Street data are from the late period represented in Hooker's Division (1890–1920). A comparison of these data with the late households from Hooker's Division indicated that the percentages of kitchen ceramics are related to both occupation date and ethnic composition of the household. The percentages of kitchen ceramics from the N Street samples are similar to those from the working-class households in Hooker's Division (table 17.2).

Other artifact percentages are comparable to the percentages from the working-class households in Hooker's Division. In the working-class households of both N Street and Hooker's Division, the percentages of cloth-

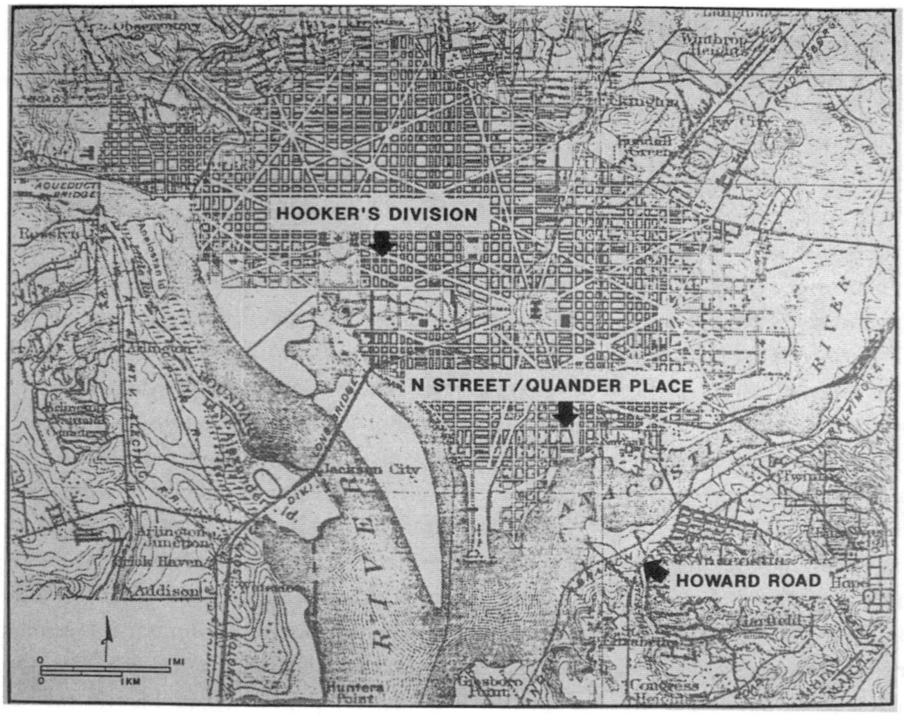

Figure 17.3. *Three Washington, D.C., neighborhoods (USGS 1898).*

ing, tobacco, personal, activities, and furniture artifact percentages are lower while kitchen ceramic percentages are higher than in prostitute households.

Percentages from the Howard Road and Quander Place households, however, are different from the working-class households in Hooker's Division and N Street: kitchen ceramics are lower, tobacco pipes are very low, clothing and activities are higher, and furniture is about the same. The data from black working-class households from Howard Road and Quander Place indicate that ethnicity is related to artifact pattern for this time period. The prostitute households in Hooker's Division are also distinct from the black working-class households. All the artifact categories from the prostitute households, including kitchen ceramics, are higher than the comparable categories from Quander Place and Howard Road.

Discussion

Archaeological and sociological research has demonstrated that distinctive combinations of three variables—socioeconomic status, ethnicity, and household composition—characterize neighborhoods and define household types. These three variables affect the consumption patterns of the households in the neighborhoods. This chapter used aggregate data on household type and neighborhood levels to examine the effect of these variables on consumer behavior.

Historical research determined that Hooker's Division was an integrated working-class neighborhood that underwent a major transformation between 1890 and 1900 from family households to a red-light district. Although the neighborhood was occupied by many prostitutes during the Civil War, the high prostitute population appears to have been restricted to the war years. Census data from 1860, 1870, and 1880 indicate that the neighborhood was occupied by primarily black and white working-class families with a few boarders, some of whom were prostitutes. After the transformation to a red-light district, the neighborhood was primarily composed of brothels inhabited by female boarders and madams, although some family households remained. The four types of historic households in Hooker's Division were white working class, black working class, white prostitute, and black prostitute. Each of these was present in both the early and late periods. However, no black working-class household deposits could be isolated for this analysis; only one black prostitute household from each period was identified, but a sample of one household was considered insufficient for reliable comparison.

Data from the houselots were grouped by household type and time period. Different patterns of consumption notable in the aggregate data were due to differences in household composition and function in Hooker's Division. The working-class household is composed of family members who live together because they are kin. The prostitute household is composed of unrelated women who live where they work. Mary McNamara kept house for her family; the goods and services she provided for boarders contributed to family income. Fannie Hill ran a brothel. Her labor in the household was remunerative work, contributing to the services provided by the household members.

Neighborhoods are composed of similar households. By grouping similar households in different neighborhoods, similarities and differences in household type across neighborhoods were defined. The pattern for white working-class households was identified in both Hooker's Division and at N Street. The black working-class households from Quander Place and Howard Road were similar to each other and different from both white working-class and prostitute households.

Three results of this analysis are noteworthy. First, the aggregation of data, either by household type or neighborhood, is useful for studying consumer behavior patterns in urban settings. Second, household composition is an essential variable in explaining the consumption patterns of households. Control of this variable is critical to understanding the archaeology of consumption. Third, evidence of differentiation between white and black working-class households in urban settings can be identified in the archaeological record. This suggestion was originally derived from the analysis of four houselots on Quander Place and N Street (Cheek and Friedlander 1990). Data from a larger number of comparative samples suggest that, besides the differences in foodways identified at Quander Place and N Street, there are differences in overall consumption patterns. Archaeologists should continue to explore ethnic differences between working-class blacks and whites.

Household type and neighborhood are useful, reliable analytical units for the archaeological study of consumer behavior. Aggregate data from several similar households within a neighborhood moderate the problems related to site formation processes, population mobility, and the representativeness of the single household. Aggregate data of household type and neighborhood should also prove useful in comparing consumer behavior among neighborhoods of different socioeconomic status.

ACKNOWLEDGMENTS

The success of a large project is the success of the project team. This project owes much to the individual efforts of our colleagues on the team. Patrick O'Bannon directed the historical research; he was assisted by Glenn Ceponis and Jo Balicki, who also prepared historic maps. Billy Ray Roulette, Jr., project archeologist, supervised the data recovery excavations and contributed to the interpretation of the site's stratigraphy. Dana Heck processed the artifacts, and Ann Martin and Patricia Joy prepared the tables.

Many others contributed to the success of the project by guiding us to sources and sharing their ideas. Roxanne Deane, Kathryn Ray, Mary Terness, and Matthew Gilmore, staff members of the Washingtoniana Division, Martin Luther King, Jr., Library in Washington, D.C., assisted us in the historical research. James O. Hall's knowledge of Civil War Washington, D.C., clarified how the division got its name. Nancy Kassner's interest and research leads directed us to several useful sources. James Gibb shared with us his observations on the gender biases and limitations of artifact pattern analysis.

The Hooker's Division data used in this chapter are from the 1988 and 1989 archaeological investigations at the site of the International Cultural and Trade Center/Federal Office Building in Federal Triangle (Cheek et al. 1991). The investigations were undertaken in accordance with the National Historic Preservation Act of 1966. The project was sponsored by the Pennsylvania Avenue Development Corporation and conducted by John Milner Associates, Inc. in cooperation with TAMS Consultants, Inc., and in consultation with the District of Columbia Historic Preservation Office and the Advisory Council on Historic Preservation.

REFERENCES CITED

Andersen, Margaret L.
1988 *Thinking about Women: Sociological Perspectives on Sex and Gender*. 2d ed. Macmillan, New York.

Beaudry, Mary
1984 Archeology and the Historical Household. *Man in the Northeast* 28:27–38.

Blumin, Stuart M.
1972 Residential Mobility within the Nineteenth Century City. In *The Peoples of Philadelphia: A History of Ethnic Groups and Lower-Class Life, 1790–1940*, edited by Allen F. Davis and Mark H. Haller, pp. 37–52. Temple University Press, Philadelphia.

Borchert, James
1980 *Alley Life in Washington: Family, Community, Religion, and Folklife in the City, 1850–1970*. University of Illinois Press, Urbana.

Boschke, A.
1857 *Map of Washington City, District of Columbia, Seat of the Federal Government*. A. Boschke, C.E. Map on file, National Archives and Records Administration, Alexandria, Virginia. Boyd's City Directories
1868 *Washington, D.C.* Boyd's City Directories. On file, Washingtoniana Room, Martin Luther King, Jr., Branch, District of Columbia Public Library, Washington, D.C.
1870 *Washington, D.C.* Boyd's City Directories. On file, Washingtoniana Room, Martin Luther King, Jr., Branch, District of Columbia Public Library, Washington, D.C.

Brown, George Rothwell
1930 *Washington: A Not Too Serious History*. Norman Publishing, Baltimore, Md.

Brown, Marley, III
1987 *"Among Weighty Friends": The Archeology and Social History of the Jacob Mott Family, Portsmouth, Rhode Island, 1640–1800*. Unpublished Ph.D. Dissertation, Department of Anthropology, Brown University.

Busey, Samuel C.
1898 *Pictures of the City of Washington in the East*. William Ballantyne and Sons, Washington, D.C.

Cheek, Charles D., and Amy Friedlander
1990 Pottery and Pig's Feet: Space, Ethnicity, and Class in a Working Class Neighborhood, Washington, D.C. 1880–1940. *Historical Archaeology* 24(1):34–60.

Cheek, Charles D., Amy Friedlander, Cheryl A. Holt, Charles H. LeeDecker, and Theresa E. Ossim
1983 Archeological Investigations at the National Photographic Interpretation Center Addition, Washington, D.C. Navy Yard Annex. Soil Systems, Inc., Alexandria, VA. Submitted to Leo A. Daly, Architects, Washington, D.C.

Cheek, Charles D., Donna J. Eifert, Patrick W. O'Bannon, Cheryl A. Holt, B. R. Roulette, Jr., Joseph Boalicki, Glenn G. Cepanis, Dana B. Heck
1991 Phase II and Phase II Archaeological Investigations at the Site of the Proposed International Cultural and Trade Center/ Federal Office Building Complex, Federal Triangle, Washington, D.C. John Milner Associates, Inc., Alexandria, VA. submitted to Pennsylvania Avenue Development Corporation.

Cheek, Charles D., and Cecile G. Glendening
1988 Phase I Archeological Investigations of the Site of the Proposed International Cultural and Trade Center/Federal Office Building Complex, Federal Triangle, Washington, D.C. John Milner Associates, Inc., Alexandria, VA. Submitted to TAMS Consultants, Inc., Washington, D.C.

Cheek, Charles D., and John H. McCarthy
1990 Neighborhood Analysis in Urban Archaeology. Paper presented at the Society for Historical Archaeology, Tucson, Ariz.

Commissioners of the District of Columbia
1914 *Acts of Congress Affecting the District of Columbia.* Commissioners of the District of Columbia, Washington, D.C.

Cook, Lauren J.
1989 Descriptive Analysis of Tobacco-Related Material from Boott Mill Boardinghouses. In *The Boarding House System as a Way of Life*, edited by Mary C. Beaudry and Stephen A. Mrozowski, pp. 187–208. Interdisciplinary Investigations of the Boott Mills, Lowell, Massachusetts, vol. 3. Cultural Resources Management Studies No. 21. Division of Cultural Resources, North Atlantic Regional Office, National Park Service, U.S. Department of the Interior, Boston.

Cressey, Pamela J.
1983 Sharing the Ivory Tower. In *Approaches to Preserving a City's Past*, pp. 3–20. Alexandria Urban Archaeology Program, City of Alexandria, Va.

Davies, Wayne K. D.
1984 *Factorial Ecology*. Grower Publishing Company, Limited, Hants, England.

Deetz, James
1982 Households: A Structural Key to Archaeological Explanation. In *Archaeology of the Households: Building a Prehistory of Domestic Life*, edited by R. L. Wilk and W. R. Rathje. *American Behavioral Scientist* 25:717–724.

Ellis, John B.
1869 *The Sights and Secrets of the National Capital: A Work Descriptive of Washington City in All Its Various Phases*. U.S. Publishing, New York.

Garrow, Patrick H. (editor)
1982 Archeological Investigations at the Washington, D.C. Civic Center Site. Soil Systems, Inc., Marrietta, Ga. Submitted to the Department of Housing and Community Development, Government of the District of Columbia, Washington, D.C.

General Services Administration (GSA)
1981 *Federal Triangle Master Plan, Historic Report.* Washington, D.C.

Green, Constance McLaughlin
1962 *Washington: A History of the Capital, 1800–1950*. 2 vols. Princeton University Press, Princeton, N.J.

Henry, Susan L.
1987 Factors Influencing Consumer Behavior in Turn-of-the-Century Phoenix, Arizona. In *Consumer Choice in Historical Archaeology*, edited by Suzanne M. Spencer-Wood, pp. 359–382. Plenum Press, New York.
1989 Consumers, Commodities, and Choices: a General Model of Consumer Behavior. Paper presented at the Annual Meeting of the Society for Historical Archaeology, Baltimore, Md.

Hershberg, Theodore
1978 The New Urban History: Toward an Interdisciplinary History of the City. *Journal of Urban History* 5(1):3–40.

Keily, James
1850 *Map of the City of Washington, D.C.* Lloyd van Derveer, Camden, New Jersey. Washingtoniana Room, Martin Luther King, Jr. Branch, District of Columbia Public Library.

Laslett, Peter
1972 Introduction: The History of the Family. In *Household and Family in Past Time*, edited by Peter Laslett and Richard Wall, pp. 1–89. Cambridge University Press, New York.

La Gory, Mark, and John Pipkin
1981 *Urban Social Space*. Wadsworth Publishing Company, Belmont, Calif.

Leech, Margaret
1986 *Reveille in Washington*. Carroll & Graf, New York.

LeeDecker, Charles H., Terry H. Klein, Cheryl A. Holt, and Amy Friedlander
1987 Nineteenth-century Households and Consumer Behavior in Wilmington, Delaware. In *Consumer Choice in Historical Archaeology*, edited by Suzanne M. Spencer-Wood, pp. 233–260. Plenum Press, New York.

Louis Berger & Associates, Inc.
1985 Technical Appendices. Archaeological, Architectural, and Historical Investigations at the Howard Road District, Washington, D.C., vol. 2. The Cultural Resources Group, Louis Berger & Associates, Inc., East Orange, N.J. Submitted to Washington Metropolitan Area Transit Authority, Washington, D.C. and Wallace Roberts & Todd, Philadelphia.
1986 Final Report. Archaeological, Architectural, and Historical Investigations at the Howard Road District, Washington, D.C., vol. 1. The Cultural Resources Group, Louis Berger & Associates, Inc., East Orange, N.J. Submitted to Washington Metropolitan Area Transit Authority, Washington, D.C. and Wallace Roberts & Todd, Philadelphia.

Mrozowski, S.
1984 Prospects and Perspectives for an Archeology of the Household. *Man in the Northeast* 28:27–38.

Nolen, John, Jr.
1976 Some Aspects of Washington's Nineteenth Century Economic Development. *Records of the Columbia Historical Society of Washington, D.C. 1973–1974*:524–531.

Padover, Saul K., editor
1946 *Thomas Jefferson and the National Capital: 1783–1818*. U.S. Government Printing Office, Washington, D.C.

Peiss, Kathy
1986 *Cheap Amusements: Working Women and Leisure in Turn-of-the-Century New York*. Temple University Press, Philadelphia.
Press, Donald E.
1984 South of the Avenue: From Murder Bay to the Federal Triangle. *Records of the Columbia Historical Society of Washington, D.C.* 51:51–70. University Press of Virginia, Charlottesville.
Provost Marshal
1865 List of Bawdy Houses in Washington, D.C. Provost Marshall's Department of Washington, 22d Army Corps, 1864–1865. Vol. 289, RG 393. National Archives and Records Administration, Washington, D.C.
Rathje, William L., and Michael McCarthy
1977 Regularity and Variability in Contemporary Garbage. In *Research Strategies in Historical Archaeology*, edited by Stanley South, pp. 261–286. Academic Press, New York.
Rosen, Ruth
1982 *The Lost Sisterhood: Prostitution in America, 1900–1918*. Johns Hopkins University Press, Baltimore, Md.
Rothschild, Nan A.
1987 On the Existence of Neighborhoods in Eighteenth-Century New York: Maps, Markets, and Churches. In *Living in Cities: Current Research in Urban Archaeology*, edited by Edward Staski, pp. 29–37. Special Publication Series No. 5. Society for Historical Archaeology.
1990 *New York City Neighborhoods: The 18th Century*. Academic Press, San Diego, Calif.
Sanborn Map Company
1903 *Fire Insurance Map of Washington, D.C.* Sanborn Map Company, New York. Map on file, Geography and Map Division, Library of Congress, Washington, D.C.
1928 *Fire Insurance Map of Washington, D.C.* Sanborn Map Company, New York. Map on file, Geography and Map Division, Library of Congress, Washington, D.C.
Schiffer, Michael B., Theodore E. Downing, and Michael McCarthy
1981 Waste Not Want Not: An Ethnoarchaeological Study of Reuse in Tucson, Arizona. In *Modern Material Culture: The Archaeology of Us*, edited by R. A. Gould and M. B. Schiffer, pp. 67–86. Academic Press, New York.
Seifert, Donna J.
1991 Within Sight of the White House: The Archaeology of Working Women. *Historical Archaeology* 25(4):82–108.
Selby, William M., Michael J. O'Brien, and Lynn M. Snyder
1984 The Frontier Household. In *Grassland, Forest and Historical Settlement: An Analysis of Dynamics in Northeast Missouri*, edited by Michael J. O'Brien, pp. 266–316. University of Nebraska Press, Lincoln.
Shevky, E., and William Bell
1955 *Social Area Analysis: Theory, Illustrative Applications and Computation Procedures*. Stanford University Press, Stanford, Calif.
Shumsky, Neil Larry
1986 Tacit Acceptance: Respectable Americans and Segregated Prostitution, 1870–1910. *Journal of Social History* 19:665–679.
Smith, Joan, Immanuel Wallerstein, and Hans-Deiter Evers (editors)
1984 *Households and the World-Economy. Explorations in the World-Economy: Publications of the Fernand Braudel Center*. Vol. 3. Sage Publications, Beverly Hills, Calif.
South, Stanley
1977 *Method and Theory in Historical Archeology*. Academic Press, New York.
1988 Whither Pattern? *Historical Archaeology* 22(1):25–28.
Spencer-Wood, Suzanne M.
1987 *Consumer Choice in Historical Archaeology*. Plenum Press, New York.
Stack, Carol B.
1974a *All Our Kin: Strategies for Survival in a Black Community*. Harper and Row, New York.
1974b Sex Roles and Survival Strategies in an Urban Black Community. In *Woman, Culture, and Society*, edited by Michelle Zimbalist Rosaldo and Louise Lamphere, pp. 113–128. Stanford University Press, Stanford, Calif.
Symanski, Richard
1981 *The Immoral Landscape: Female Prostitution in Western Societies*. Butterworths, Toronto, Ontario.
Thernstrom, Stephen, and Peter Knights
1970 Men in Motion: Some Speculations about Urban Population Mobility in Nineteenth Century America. *Journal of Interdisciplinary History* 1:7–36.
Timms, D. W. G.
1971 *The Urban Mosaic*. Cambridge University Press, New York.
Townsend, Geo. Alfred
1873 *Washington, Outside and Inside: A Picture and Narrative of the Origins, Growth, Excellences, Abuses, Beauties, and Personages of Our Governing City*. J. Betts, Hartford, Conn.
Tryon, Robert C., and Daniel E. Bailey
1970 *Cluster Analysis*. McGraw-Hill, New York.
U.S. Census Office
1860 Manuscript Population Census of the United States, 1860. Microfilm copy on file, National Archives and Records Administration, Washington, D.C.
1870 Manuscript Population Census of the United States, 1870. Microfilm copy on file, National Archives and Records Administration, Washington, D.C.
1880 Manuscript Population Census of the United States, 1880. Microfilm copy on file, National Archives and Records Administration, Washington, D.C.
1900 Manuscript Population Census of the United States, 1900. Microfilm copy on file, National Archives and Records Administration, Washington, D.C.
U.S. Geological Survey (USGS)
1898 Washington and Vicinity, Maryland-District of

Columbia-Virginia. USGS, Washington, D.C. Map on file, Geography and Map Division, Library of Congress, Washington, D.C.

U.S. Senate

1913 *Abatement of Houses of Ill Fame: Hearings before a Subcommittee of the Committee of the District of Columbia, United States Senate 62nd Congress, Third Session on S. 5861.* U.S. Government Printing Office, Washington, D.C.

Weiss, Michael J.

1988 *The Clustering of America.* Harper & Row, New York.

Within Sight of the White House

[1895] Unidentified newspaper clipping on file, Geography and Map Division, Library of Congress, Washington, D.C.

Wong, Claudia

1984 The Limits of Using the Household as a Unit of Analysis. In *Households and the World-Economy*, edited by J. Smith, I. Wallerstein, and H. Evers, pp. 56–63. Sage Publications, Beverly Hills, Calif.

XVIII
CHAPTER

Rural Landscape in the Mid-Nineteenth-Century Chesapeake

JULIA A. KING

ALTHOUGH FEWER and fewer members of the U.S. population are engaged directly in agricultural production, many Americans romanticize rural life and seek to perpetuate it. In many areas, the preservation of a community's rural character has become an important political issue (see, for example, Fedelchak and Wood 1988; St. Mary's County Government 1989). To the archaeologist, rural character is more than barns, fields, and farmhouses; it is a complex web of people interacting with one another and with the natural environment. However, barns, fields, and farmhouses, as well as other elements of the cultural landscape, reflect these interactions and the social relationships that exist in rural society. The material settings of these rural communities also shape social behavior, and they can provide valuable insight into the structure of contemporary and past rural life.

This chapter examines rural social relations in the mid-nineteenth century Chesapeake through the landscape and land-use patterns at the Susquehanna farm in southern Maryland. One of the largest and most productive farms in nineteenth-century southern Maryland, Susquehanna was home to the wealthy Carroll family, as many as 65 slaves, and possibly an overseer or tenant family on the eve of the Civil War. The structure of social relations at Susquehanna mirrored the structure of social relations found in southern Maryland at this time. At the top of the social hierarchy was a small elite upper class that controlled land, politics, and a good deal of the labor. In contrast, most free families struggled to make ends meet from year to year. At the bottom of the hierarchy was more than half of the population: slaves with few economic and legal rights.

The landscape of the Susquehanna farm in the mid-nineteenth century not only reflected these social divisions; it shaped the social interactions among these groups. The elite upper class of the region used the landscape to emphasize its access to and control of the two most important resources in the tobacco economy: land and labor. At the same time, access to the world of this oligarchic upper class was very limited, both economically and physically, in the landscape of the rural community.

This study challenges contemporary Americans to examine the popular ideology behind the preservation of community rural character through land-use planning and zoning. Deeply rooted in the American historical experience, this ideology celebrates the moral and physical superiority of the rural life: rural society, its adherents say, is egalitarian, democratic, and self-sufficient (see Rohrer and Douglas 1969; Stilgoe 1982:137–138, 262–264). In reality, however, rural life was rarely, if ever, any of these things. Rather, rural societies were usually organized along rigid social divisions based on wealth, ethnicity, gender, and legal status.

If social relationships are a reflection of the cultural manipulation of the landscape, this association must be considered in any assessment of the implications of landscape preservation efforts. This chapter challenges citizens, planners, preservationists, and politicians to preserve rural landscapes without reinforcing social structures based on the inferiority of certain members. This is especially important in the rural South, where social relations for more than four centuries have been defined in the context of the plantation economy.

THE PLANTATION ECONOMY IN NINETEENTH-CENTURY SOUTHERN MARYLAND

From the earliest years of colonization and arguably into the late nineteenth century, a plantation economy dominated the Chesapeake. Throughout the colonial period, this economy was based on the production of a single cash crop: tobacco. By the mid-eighteenth century, several areas, such as the Eastern Shore and the western part of Virginia's Northern Neck, had shifted to grain agriculture (Gouger 1976; Clemens 1980); in other areas, wheat farming was adopted in conjunction with tobacco cultivation, but tobacco remained the predominant crop. This was especially true in southern Maryland, which produced most of the state's tobacco in the middle decades of the nineteenth century.

Southern Maryland, a large peninsula of land located on the state's western shore (figure 18.1), includes all of St. Mary's, Charles, and Calvert counties and the southern parts of Anne Arundel and Prince George's counties. The Chesapeake Bay and the Potomac River form southern Maryland's eastern and southern and southwestern boundaries, and a number of smaller rivers and tributaries traverse the region. The topography ranges from flat lowlands to steep uplands, and the soils vary in the quality and quantity of tobacco they can yield (see Gibson 1978).

Tobacco, corn, and, to a lesser extent, wheat were the primary crops produced on southern Maryland farms in the early to mid-nineteenth century (see Marks 1979:81). Tobacco required large amounts of land and labor, but once harvested and cured, the leaf was exported to nonlocal markets for further processing. Corn was grown for home and for farm use. Wheat had been adopted by many farmers in this region by the late eighteenth century.

Little economic diversification or urban development existed in this region, and access to important economic resources—land and labor—remained concentrated in the hands of a small number of elite farmers and their families (Marks 1979). These families also controlled politics as a rural oligarchy (Ridgway 1979). The majority of the free population owned small tracts of land or, more likely, no land, and, after ca. 1820, many began experiencing serious downward economic and social mobility. More than half of the total population consisted of enslaved black men, women, and children, and these individuals are virtually invisible in the documentary record.

In the first half of the nineteenth century, the tobacco economy of southern Maryland was hit by a number of problems. Land and labor costs were too high to justify investment, and a series of economic depressions wiped out many farmers. Many landless families simply left the region, and new families did not arrive to take their place (Van Ness 1982:321). Consequently, Southern Marylanders found themselves increasingly isolated—socially, economically, and politically—from the rest of the state. The system would not collapse, however, as long as the families that controlled the land also controlled politics. For this small number of elite families, limited economic success was possible.

LANDSCAPE IN NINETEENTH-CENTURY SOUTHERN MARYLAND: DOCUMENTARY EVIDENCE

Visitors to southern Maryland in the early to mid-nineteenth century saw the economic and political isolation of the region reflected in the impoverished landscape. One traveler remarked:

> Nothing can present to the . . . eye a more dreary and miserable aspect, than the condition of most parts of the lower counties on the western shore of Maryland. . . . Dreary and uncultivated wastes, a barren and exhausted soil, half-clothed negroes, lean and hungry stock, a puny race of horses, a scarcity of provender, houses falling to decay, and fences windshaken and delapidating. (Anonymous 1819)

The cause of this misfortune, continued the visitor, was "the cultivation of tobacco as a sole and entire crop."

In 1844, John Skinner, writing in the *American Farmer*, commented on the "plantations of the middle and

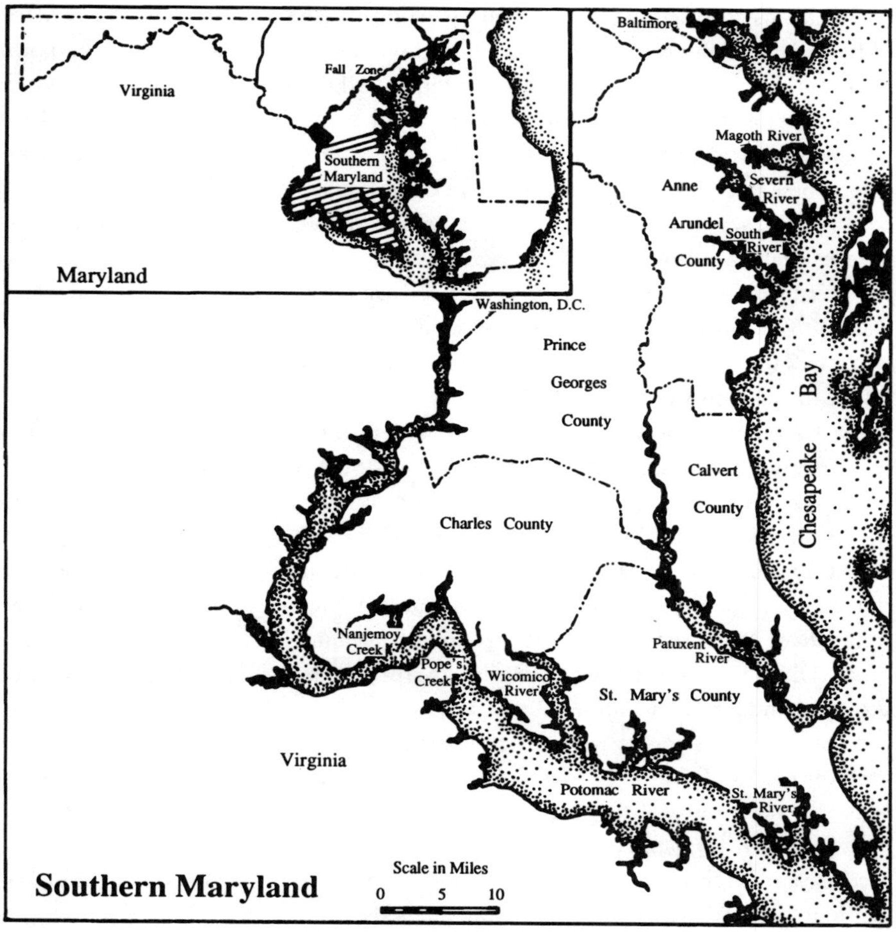

FIGURE 18.1. *The Southern Maryland region (from Garrow and Wheaton 1986).*

Southern states." "In too many instances," wrote Skinner, "houses [are] dark and dingy—windows broken—palings broken down—gardens demolished and lawns large enough for a New England plantation, rooted up by hogs, or grown up in weeds" ([Skinner] 1844). Other visitors were concerned about the system of shifting fields used in tobacco cultivation in both Maryland and Virginia: "In 1819 . . . this [field] was planted in corn. Just in my eye, are two tenements, deserted. The plantation will soon be covered with pine, which seems to delight in relieving desolation" (Anonymous 1844).

Frances Trollope's criticism was perhaps most biting. In a description of her visit to the home of a land-owning farmer and his family in southern Maryland, Mrs. Trollope commented: "The farm . . . consisted of about 300 acres of indifferent land, but all cleared. The house was built of wood, and looked as if the three slaves [of the farm] might have overturned it. . . . Near this mansion was a 'shanty,' a black hole, without any window, which served as kitchen and all other offices, and also as the lodging of the blacks" (Smalley 1949:241).

Southern Marylanders, in contrast, left few written descriptions of their perceptions of the landscape or remarks in defense of their life-styles (and landscapes). Thus, to examine emic views of the situation, it is necessary to consult the Annual Valuations of the Orphan's Court. In an effort to protect the estates left to orphaned children, these records describe in great detail the heirs' farms, their condition, and their management. Dwellings, outbuildings, farm buildings, gardens, orchards, and fields are often described in impressive detail. The records are clearly biased toward landowners, although tenant farms are also sometimes mentioned as part of some holdings. Eighty-nine valuations taken in St. Mary's County between 1840 and 1860 provide insight into the local perception of the landscape at midcentury.

The farms recorded in the valuations generally consist of fields planted in tobacco, wheat, or corn; domestic and farm buildings; gardens; orchards; and fencing. These farms contained an average of six wooden buildings, although one-third of the farms had four or fewer buildings. These structures would include a dwelling, kitchen, corn house, meat house, at least one barn, and a quarter. Dairies, stables, granaries, and carriage houses appeared in fewer than one-quarter of the valuations and are associated with wealthy households. The lack of specialized structures for crafts and cottage industries indicates that few of these farms were diversified or self-sufficient. All of the dwellings described in the valuations were of frame or, sometimes, log construction, and fully one-third of these were described as "in bad repair." Nearly every household had a frame kitchen; one-half of these were in poor condition. Only one brick building was noted, and this dwelling was described as "decayed" and unoccupied; it may have been used as a barn at this point. One landowning family occupied a one-room log dwelling with a dirt floor and a wooden chimney.

Farm buildings appear to be in slightly better shape. Only one-fifth of the meat houses required repair, and fewer than one-third of the corn houses were in bad repair. Orchards are found in more than one-half of the valuations, and slightly more than one-third of these were considered "old." Nearly half of the valuations also listed a garden, and most of these were in good shape. Fencing, on the other hand, was generally in much need of repair.

The Orphan's Court appraisers suggest that possibly one-third of landowners' farms in St. Mary's were generally in poor condition. Since tenant families could have afforded little investment in upkeep, an even larger proportion of the dwellings and farm buildings of these farmers was probably also in poor condition. According to Bayly Marks (1979:47), "times were hard [in St. Mary's County between the Civil war and World War II] and, while few could afford to maintain their buildings, neither could they afford to tear them down." This trend may have been under way for many households in the decades prior to the Civil War.

How were these dwellings, fields, and farm buildings organized to express and to guide relationships among the people who lived on these farms? For most families, the home farm and neighboring farms "encompassed their entire world," and long-distance trips away from the farm were rare (Marks 1979:46). Yet, the people who shared the home farm were not a homogeneous group. Rather, all of these individuals were guided by separate sets of rules. Archaeological and cartographic data are the spatial manifestations of these cultural rules and their relationship in the landscape. The information they provide can shed light on how landscape was manipulated to maintain social boundaries in an economic system that benefited only a few members of an oligarchic class.

Susquehanna

The Susquehanna farm provides a good opportunity to examine social relationships in mid-nineteenth-century southern Maryland and their manifestations in landscape and land-use patterns. In the mid-nineteenth century, Susquehanna was occupied by a well-to-do planter, his family, possibly a tenant and/or overseer family, and 41 slaves. Susquehanna is typical of the farms owned and managed by the elite families of this region. Members of these families controlled access to the large amounts of land and labor necessary to succeed in the tobacco economy. These families also had capital to invest in the production of other crops, especially wheat.

Fortunately, a comparatively rich documentary record concerning the farm survives, including a number of valuable cartographic materials depicting the Susquehanna landscape. The entire parcel that makes up the farm remains intact following its acquisition by the U.S. Navy in 1942. Further, federal preservation regulations and the fortuitous preservation of the principal structure at the Henry Ford Museum and Greenfield Village (in Dearborn, Michigan) have made it possible to generate an extensive historical and archaeological data base.

The Susquehanna farm was located on the west bank of the Patuxent River near its confluence with the Chesapeake Bay in St. Mary's County, Maryland (figure 18.2). English colonists had patented and settled Susquehanna by the mid-seventeenth century, and the land was continuously occupied by the same family from the late seventeenth century until 1894 (Walsh 1981). Beginning in 1894, the farm passed through a number of absentee owners until 1942, when the Navy acquired Susquehanna and nearby farms and established the Patuxent River Naval Air Test Center and Naval Air Station there. At that time, Susquehanna house, mistakenly identified as a seventeenth-century building, was moved to the Henry Ford Museum

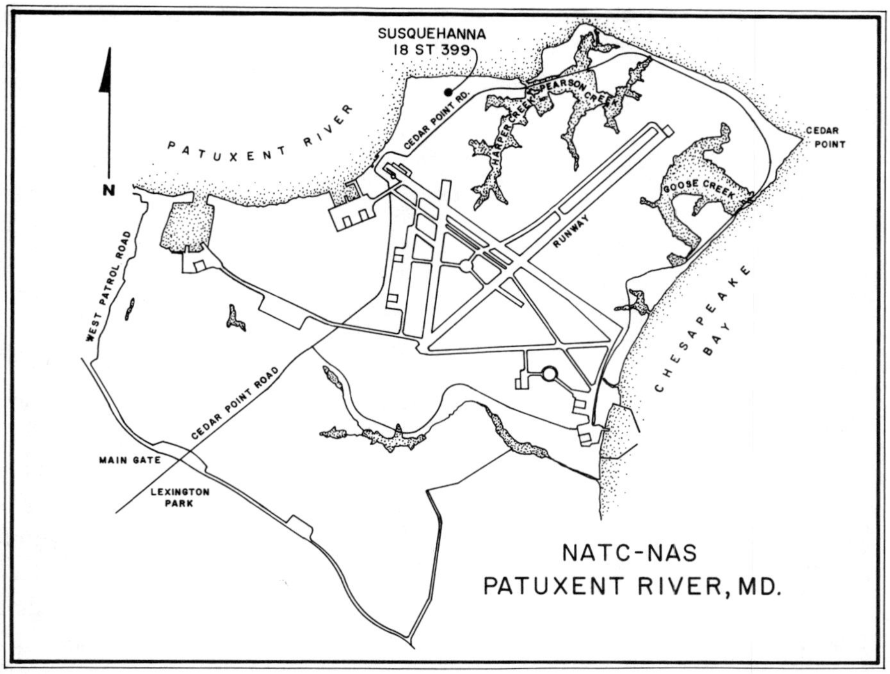

FIGURE 18.2. *Location of the Susquehanna site aboard Patuxent River Naval Air Station, St. Mary's County, Maryland (from King 1989).*

and is now one of the Greenfield Village exhibits at the museum.

In the nineteenth century, Susquehanna was a part of the farm community of Cedar Point. At least 11 farms have been identified for this period at Cedar Point, ranging in size from 15 to 750 acres, with a median size of approximately 300 acres. Susquehanna contained approximately 700 acres and was one of the largest farmholdings at Cedar Point and in St. Mary's County (U.S. Agricultural Census 1850). The soils found at Susquehanna and throughout most of the Cedar Point area are of the Matapeake-Mattapex-Sassafras association and tend to be very silty and well-drained. They are among the best agricultural soils in the county (Gibson 1978:9). Susquehanna's large acreage, fertile soils, and access to the Patuxent made it an especially valuable holding in rural St. Mary's county.

When Henry J. Carroll acquired a portion of the farm shortly before 1842, probably inheriting it from his father, his was the fifth generation of his family to have lived at Susquehanna. The agricultural census records that Carroll grew corn and wheat in 1850 and tobacco, corn, and wheat in 1860. He also produced some oats and hay, probably for farm consumption, and raised comparatively large numbers of horses, cattle, oxen, sheep, and pigs. The nineteenth century was a period of experimentation for farmers, who derived many of their ideas from such contemporary journals as the Baltimore-based *American Farmer*. Although there is no documentary evidence that Carroll used these publications, or their ideas and innovations, the agricultural censuses provide indirect evidence for careful farm management. The production of corn, wheat, and oats increased sharply at Susquehanna between 1850 and 1860 (figure 18.3), and an additional 20,000 pounds of tobacco were produced in 1860. Yet, Carroll had not improved any additional land at Susquehanna (U.S. Agricultural Census 1850, 1860). Although such increases are probably due to a number of factors, including a growing labor force and annual weather conditions, Carroll was no doubt paying close attention to issues of enclosure, soil fertility, and other farm management topics.

More than 70 persons occupied the home farm on the eve of the Civil War. In 1840, Carroll, a Catholic, had married Lucretia Leeds Briscoe, an Episcopalian and the daughter of a wealthy county planter (Fresco 1982:50). Lucretia died during the birth of their son, and Carroll remarried Elizabeth Ann Pyle, from neighboring Charles County, in 1845 (Fresco 1982:50). By 1850, the household consisted of Carroll, Elizabeth, their three children,

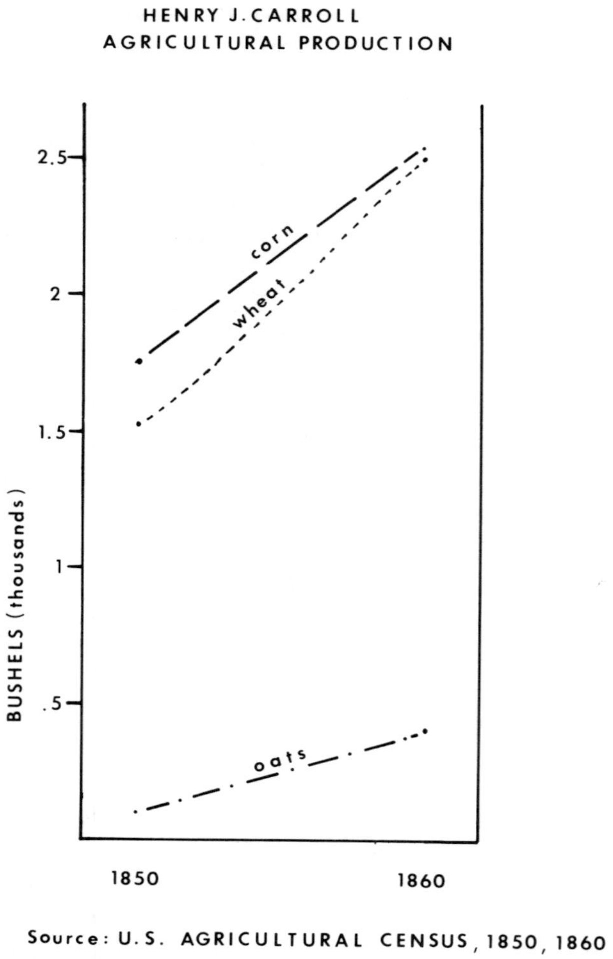

FIGURE 18.3. *Agricultural production at Susquehanna, 1850 and 1860 (not including tobacco) (from U.S. Agricultural Census 1850, 1860).*

and Carroll's son by his first wife (U.S. Population Census 1850a). In 1860, two more children were present. A school teacher, Elizabeth McCarty, also lived with the family (U.S. Population Census 1860a). Aside from the documented occupations of McCarty and Henry Carroll, little else is known about the specific activities of the Carroll household and how these activities were organized.

The majority of the documented population at Susquehanna consisted of slave men, women, and children. Forty-one slaves were reported at Susquehanna in 1850 and 65 slaves were present in 1860 (U.S. Population Census 1850b, 1860b). The large number of slaves present in both 1850 and 1860 made the farm one of the largest slave communities in St. Mary's County. Most of these persons were probably organized in families, but the slave schedules of the population census do not allow any reconstruction of slave families or households. The slave schedules do report, however, that these individuals were housed in cabins. These slaves were probably also organized by quarters on the home farm; that is, certain slaves were assigned to certain parcels of acreage at Susquehanna. This type of farm organization had been in use since the seventeenth century. By the nineteenth century, these quarters would be farmed either by slaves assigned to them or by free tenant families.

At least one and probably more overseers and their families may have also lived at Susquehanna. Unfortunately, surviving documents do not provide enough evidence to determine who these families were. The organization of the population census, for example, makes it difficult to assign families without land to certain farms, and the census does not record the status of these landless families as tenants or overseers. Historians have estimated that, at the most, a single supervisor could have managed no more than 10 laborers efficiently (Lois Green Carr, personal communication 1990). Although as many as one-half of the Susquehanna slaves were probably not considered prime laborers, at least two to three supervisors would nonetheless have been necessary to manage the agricultural operations. Much more research is required, however, before definitive statements can be made about any free families at Susquehanna other than the Carrolls.

The 700-acre Susquehanna farm provided the main setting for the lives of the Carroll family, their slaves, and probably an overseer or other tenant farmer. Nearly all of the members of this farm were engaged in agricultural production or its support, ultimately enhancing the wealth and prestige of Henry J. Carroll and his household. How was the space at Susquehanna farm organized to reinforce economic and social relations among those who lived there? How did Carroll maintain control of both the free and unfree populations that lived at or visited Susquehanna? How did these populations adjust to this control?

The Susquehanna Landscape at Midcentury

Both archaeological and cartographic data were used to examine landscape and land-use patterns at mid-nineteenth-century Susquehanna.

Data Collection

A Phase I archaeological survey of the Patuxent River Naval Air Station facility identified four nineteenth-century sites on what was formerly the Susquehanna farm (Pogue 1983). Subsequently, a more intensive pedestrian survey of the farm itself was undertaken in 1986 and 1987 and revealed that cultural elements associated with Susquehanna were still visible in the landscape (Stone 1986; King 1989).

In 1987 and 1988, archaeological investigations were conducted at the site of Carroll's dwelling to search for data on the composition and organization of the domestic yard. Field methodology consisted of a systematic shovel-test survey with limited additional testing. One hundred sixty shovel-test units were excavated at intervals of 10 feet in an area measuring 100-by-160 feet. This shovel-test strategy provided a wealth of spatial data while disturbing only 1 percent of the archaeological record. Twenty 5-by-5-foot excavation units were opened to examine subsurface features detected by the shovel-test survey (see King 1989).

Limited testing was also undertaken at a domestic site approximately 500 feet east of the Carroll dwelling and probably that of a slave cabin associated with the Susquehanna occupation. Although no structural features were identified, a late eighteenth- to nineteenth-century artifact assemblage was collected (King 1990). Descriptions of the form, style, and evolution of the Susquehanna dwelling now located at the Henry Ford Museum were also compiled (Cutler 1955; Ridout 1989).

An especially valuable source of data for this study was a set of topographic maps of the lower Patuxent prepared by the U.S. Coast and Geodetic Survey (1873) during the late 1840s and 1850s. These maps included dwellings, larger barns, fence lines, woodlots, roads, and a number of other cultural and natural features. They have been found to be fairly accurate for both nearby Sotterley plantation (Stone 1987) and Susquehanna (King 1989), and it is reasonable to assume that the maps are accurate for other farms as well. Certain cultural features, such as roads, rarely change their course, and the roads depicted on the maps are, almost without exception, in precisely the same locations as shown on modern maps.

Farm Landscape

One of the most important variables in landscape and land-use analysis is the legal property boundary of the home farm. Boundaries are "designed to isolate and protect objects or people within them" and "[to] stabilize social relationships" (Jackson 1984:13–15). Legal boundaries separate a farm and its residents from neighboring farms, placing arbitrary restraints on the potential for social interaction. The legal boundaries of Susquehanna and neighboring farms in the mid-nineteenth century have been reconstructed using historic maps and land deeds (figure 18.4). These boundaries were given visibility in the landscape through the use of both cultural and natural features (figure 18.5). The Patuxent River and Harper Creek, with their steep banks, defined most of the property boundaries at Susquehanna. A fenceline thickly bordered by trees separated Carroll's farm from neighboring Mattapany on the southwest. The public road to Cedar Point was located near the property's southeastern boundary.

The 1848 U.S. Coast and Geodetic Survey map indicates that Susquehanna consisted predominantly of level agricultural fields (see figure 18.5). According to the agricultural census, 530 acres, nearly three-quarters of the farm, were improved and presumably under cultivation or in other agricultural use. The remaining 180 acres contained marsh and woodlands located along the edges of the farm. These areas of unimproved land further defined the boundaries of Susquehanna. The marshland would have provided grazing for livestock, and the woodland provided building and fencing materials and fuel. This cocoon of natural boundaries formed by waterways, marsh, and woodland contained the agricultural fields, which appear to have been divided into five sections.

Henry Carroll's Susquehanna house was in a fairly central position among these level fields and about 1,000 feet inland from the Patuxent. Susquehanna house was readily visible to travelers in the busy Patuxent—so visible, in fact, that surveyors of the Patuxent included it as an important landmark for river traffic. Access to the house was from an avenue nearly 2 miles long which ran centrally through the farm. This completely straight avenue originated at the "Public Road" to Cedar Point, which crossed the southern portion of Carroll's land. A dirt path or road leading from the Patuxent at the northwestern edge of the property intersected the avenue slightly more than 1 mile from Carroll's dwelling. There was probably a landing and possibly a wharf at this location. Whether visitors to Susquehanna arrived by river or by the public road, however, they all moved along the principal avenue. The road thus symbolized movement and contact with the commu-

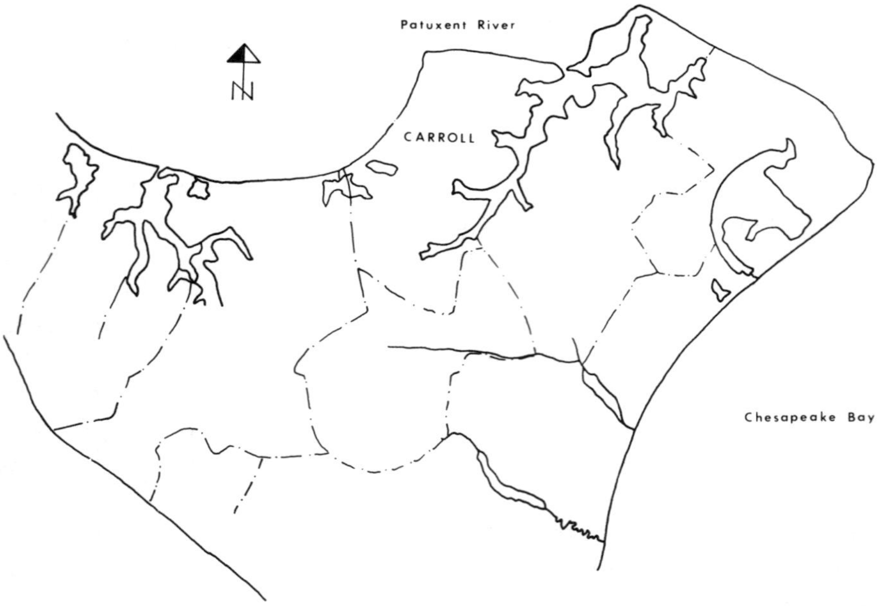

Figure 18.4. *Reconstructed legal property boundaries, Cedar Point area.*

nity and the world outside Susquehanna. The drive depicted in the 1848 map appears to be lined by trees, possibly cedar (figure 18.6). These trees would have emphasized the location of the principal road from most points on the farm. The road passed one building, probably a dwelling, enclosed by a rectangular fence. This dwelling may have been the home of an overseer and his family. This site was not located during the Phase I archaeological survey, probably because the survey was limited to a few cultivated strips in this vicinity (Pogue 1983:56).

The house and house yard were enclosed within an un-

Figure 18.5. *1848 U.S. Coast and Geodetic Survey map showing Susquehanna or Carroll farm.*

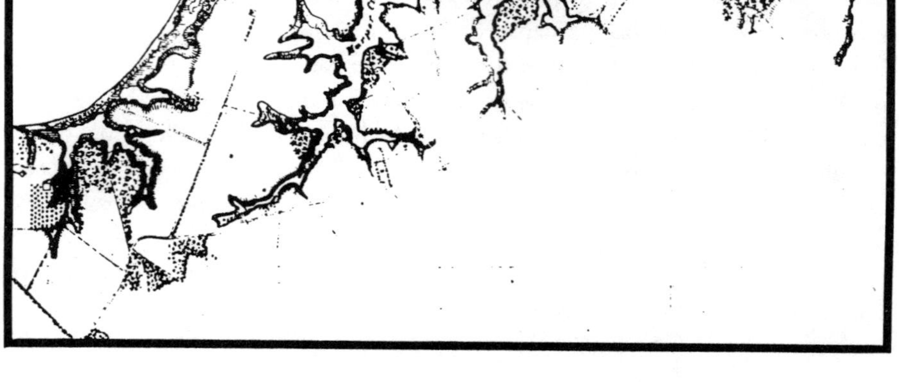

usual, elliptical-shaped fence (figure 18.6). Careful inspection of the 1848 map suggests that this fence, like the avenue, was also lined with trees. Unfortunately, the limited subsurface exposure provided by the shovel-test survey and subsequent testing did not reveal features that can be positively identified as this fenceline at this time. The overall accuracy of the 1848 map, however, suggests the elliptical fence probably did exist and formed yet another boundary between Carroll and his family and the rest of the farm population at Susquehanna.

Once inside the enclosed yard surrounding the house, a visitor to Susquehanna would have seen a number of buildings and other yard features. Foremost among these was Carroll's dwelling (figure 18.7). Susquehanna house is narrow and unusually long, with dimensions of 16-by-60-feet. Architectural and photographic evidence suggests that the house was originally constructed to be 60 feet long (Ridout 1989:102; Stone, personal communication 1989). Although rooms follow traditional Chesapeake functions and proportions, the basic organization of the house is unusual. Dendrochronology suggests the house was constructed in 1819, but this date may not be reliable owing to the numerous modifications it underwent following its move to Dearborn (Heikkenen 1989). Further, the historical evidence indicates that possession of the farm in the second and third decades of the nineteenth century was in a state of flux. The house may have been built as late as the 1840s. Porches on both facades probably date to the original construction (Ridout 1989:101).

The house follows a center-passage plan with a kitchen appended at one end, providing 960 square feet of interior living space on the ground floor (figure 18.8). The three ground-floor rooms are each heated by a fireplace; three small chambers in the loft are unheated. Like most dwellings in St. Mary's County, Susquehanna was a frame structure and one-and-a-half stories high. Documentary and archaeological research indicate that Susquehanna was one of the largest dwellings in St. Mary's County in the mid-nineteenth century. The house was well built and probably in very good condition when Henry J. Carroll acquired it in the early 1840s.

At least two outbuildings have been identified in the east house yard, including a dairy and an unidentified service structure (figure 18.9). The dairy, which was also moved to the Henry Ford Museum, measures 10 by 10 feet and has a pyramidal roof. Dairies were not common in nineteenth-century Southern Maryland, and most

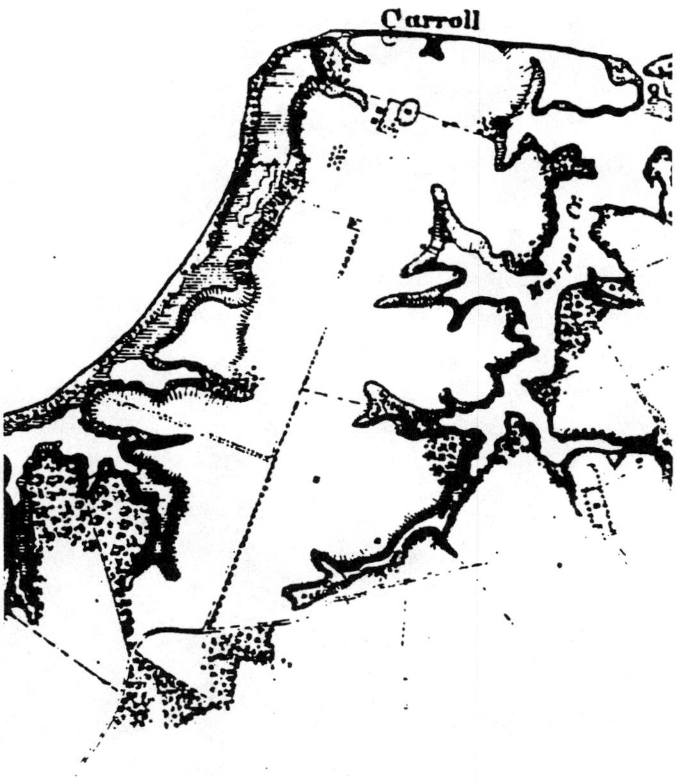

FIGURE 18.6. *Enlargement of 1848 U.S. Coast and Geodetic Survey map. Note what appear to be trees shown along avenue and elliptical fence.*

were owned by wealthier families. The second outbuilding was located through concentrations of wrought and cut nails, oyster shell, animal bone, and early to mid-nineteenth-century artifacts. Expanded testing in that area revealed two structural postholes and molds. No brick fragments or chimney foundation were found, however. Analysis based on current evidence suggests an unheated post- or block-supported frame or log building with associated domestic refuse. Identification is particularly difficult because the size of the building is unknown at this time. This structure may have been a quarter or, less likely, a kitchen with a wooden chimney.

The U.S. Coast and Geodetic Survey map of 1848 depicts an agricultural yard on the west side of the main dwelling yard and within a larger agricultural field (figure 18.5). An above-ground survey conducted in this vicinity in 1987 located the foundations of two and possibly three barns and a windmill, but these features date to the early twentieth century. According to the 1848 map, the

FIGURE 18.7. *The Susquehanna house as it appeared in 1941. (Photograph courtesy of the Henry Ford Museum and Greenfield Village, Dearborn, Michigan)*

mid-nineteenth-century agricultural yard consisted of a fenced enclosure abutting the elliptical fence of the house yard (figure 18.5). What appears to be an orchard is depicted in this enclosure; the Carroll family garden was probably placed here as well. The larger enclosed field contains two barns and a larger orchard.

Five buildings depicted on the 1848 map may have been slave cabins. One of these structures is shown along a fenceline leading from Susquehanna house to Harper Creek. The Phase I survey of the Patuxent River facility revealed a domestic site in this location dating to the late eighteenth and nineteenth centuries (Pogue 1983:71–73). Limited testing in this area revealed no architectural features, but the plowzone-derived ceramic collection suggested important variations between this site and the ceramics from Carroll's dwelling site. Although fewer transfer-printed and more undecorated refined earthenwares were recovered from this site, as expected, both assemblages contained identical distributions of Chinese porcelain (King 1990).

The remaining four structures shown on the map, which are believed to have been slave dwellings, are located along the bluffs of Harper Creek. Archaeological survey did not produce evidence of these three buildings, but two sites not shown were located (figure 18.10). Site 18St392 is located near Harper Creek and was identified on the basis of a scatter of Chinese porcelain, white salt-glazed stoneware, gray salt-glazed stoneware, and undecorated pearlware and whiteware (Pogue 1983:71–72). The second site (18St471) was identified on the basis of a scatter of handmade brick eroding out of the bank of Harper Creek. Limited testing exposed a brick wall 10

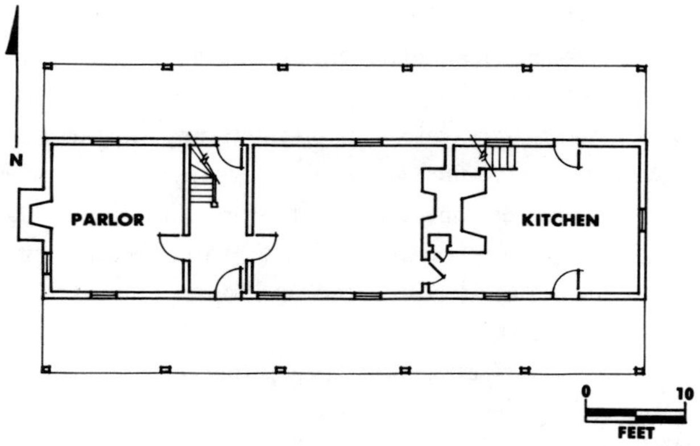

F I G U R E 18.8. *Plan of Susquehanna house (from King 1989).*

feet long overlaying an oyster shell midden, all at beach level (Pogue 1983:71, 81–82).

The structures along Harper Creek shown on the 1848 map and the archaeological sites probably represent domestic sites occupied by the large numbers of slaves at Susquehanna. No conclusions are fully warranted, however, until these sites are examined further, but it should be pointed out that these are the only nineteenth-century domestic sites, other than Carroll's dwelling, that have been located within the former boundaries of Susquehanna farm.

THE SUSQUEHANNA RUIN

The most interesting and unexpected element of the Susquehanna landscape was not a building, at least not one from the mid-nineteenth century. Shovel-test units excavated on the west side of the house yard revealed large concentrations of brick, mortar, and window glass, but virtually no other artifact types. Seven 5-by-5-foot test units were subsequently excavated to examine the source of these concentrations. This testing revealed sections of a brick footing and a filled cellar, located fewer than 10 feet

F I G U R E 18.9. *Susquehanna yard organization, mid-nineteenth century, based on results of archaeological investigation (from King 1989).*

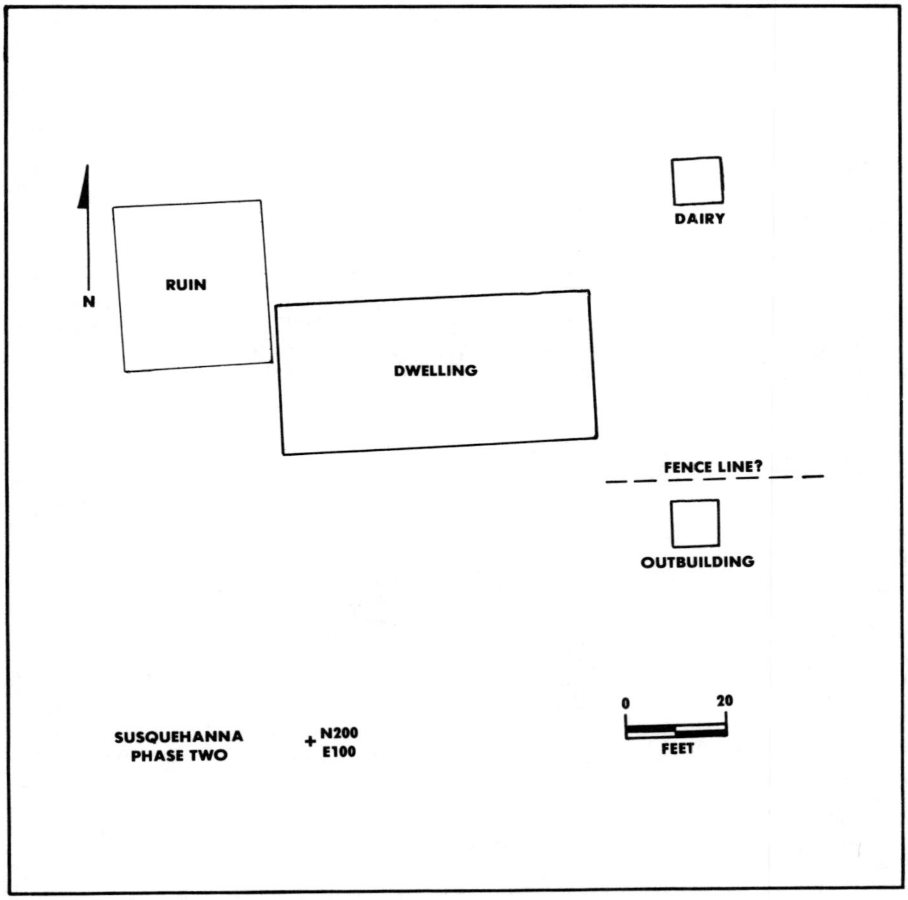

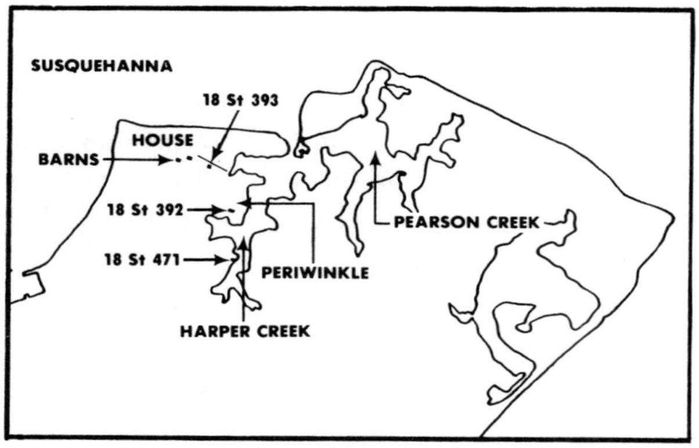

FIGURE 18.10. *Location of known archaeological sites at Susquehanna farm (from King 1989).*

from Susquehanna house (figure 18.11). The dimensions of the footing itself suggest a large building measuring approximately 25 to 30 feet by 30 to 35 feet.

A large number of eighteenth-century artifacts were also recovered, indicating occupation in this area prior to the construction of the surviving Susquehanna dwelling. The 1798 Federal Direct Tax Assessment describes a dwelling at Susquehanna farm as "one story of wood, in bad repair" measuring 28 by 32 feet. The estimated size of the structure revealed during the testing fits these dimensions; the footing's size suggests it supported no more than a one or one-and-a-half story building. The eighteenth-century artifacts and the architectural evidence suggest this feature is the dwelling mentioned in the 1798 tax assessment.

Documentary evidence indicates that the occupants of the dwelling described in that assessment, Henry Carroll's grandparents, left Susquehanna in 1813. It is not clear who then moved into the dwelling, which, 15 years earlier, had been described as being "in bad repair." The fact that no buildings are shown in this location on an 1824 U.S. Army Engineers map suggests that the surviving Susquehanna dwelling had not yet been built and that the earlier dwelling was no longer standing.

A small portion of the cellar fill was excavated in an effort to determine when this building was abandoned. Surprisingly, the datable materials found in the fill indicated that the cellar was not filled until the 1870s, and

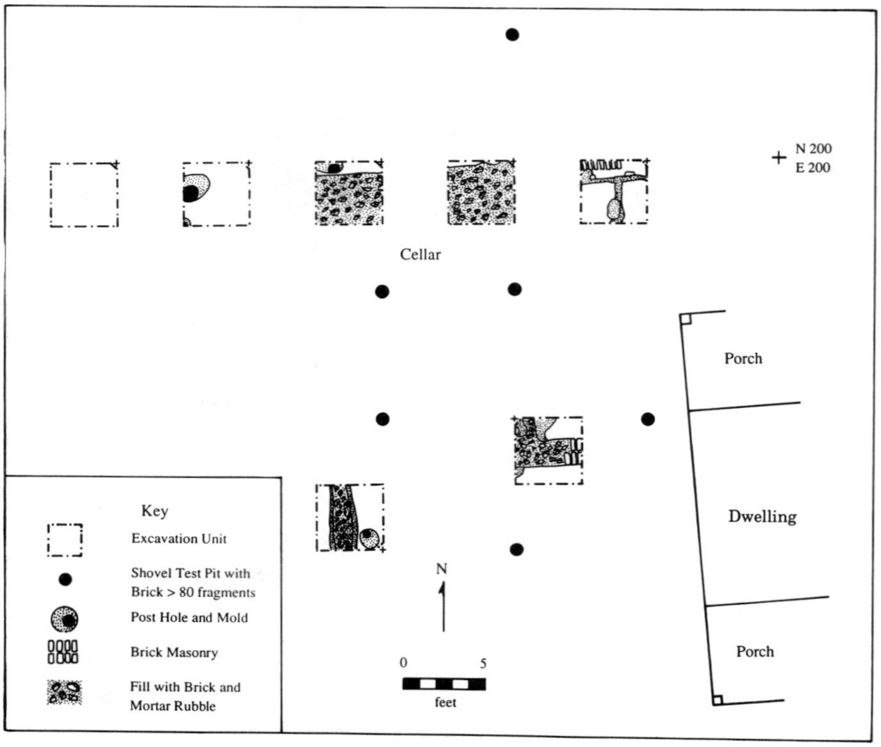

FIGURE 18.11. *Brick foundations and cellar located west of Susquehanna house.*

possibly later. A thick-walled, round-bottom ginger ale bottle dating to the last quarter of the nineteenth century, two wire nails, and 13 fragments of clear bottle glass strongly suggest the cellar was filled in the late nineteenth century. The dwelling ruin appears to have been open and thus visible at least into the late nineteenth century.

Fortunately, one piece of historical evidence survives that strongly supports the archaeological interpretation. Mrs. Fanny Combs Gough, a native of St. Mary's County, used to visit Susquehanna during the late nineteenth century and in 1947 she was interviewed about those visits (Gough 1947). She recalled that the site of this earlier dwelling was "nearby . . . where bricks and other signs of ruin were still to be seen" (Gough 1947:120). According to Mrs. Gough, this earlier structure "had been destroyed by fire [and] it was the purpose of the Carrolls . . . to rebuild what had been the mansion."

When combined, the historical, archaeological, and architectural evidence indicates that a visible structural ruin existed less than 10 feet from the Susquehanna house occupied by Henry J. Carroll and his family. The archaeological evidence recovered in the vicinity of the earlier dwelling offers no evidence of its destruction by fire. Further, Mrs. Gough's statement about the Carrolls' intent to rebuild "the mansion" may be more family lore than reality. The house transported to Dearborn was actually slightly larger than the earlier structure. If there had been a desire to reconstruct the earlier dwelling, Michael B. Carroll (the most likely builder) would certainly have been in a position to have done so. Finally, there is no evidence in the west wall of the surviving dwelling to suggest a connection between the new dwelling and the older one.

Although a structural ruin is not generally considered a typical yard feature, the ruin of the earlier Susquehanna dwelling was an integral component of the yardscape throughout the nineteenth century. With more than 40 slaves in 1850 and 65 slaves in 1860, Carroll surely had the labor necessary to remove and bury the ruin. When Carroll's family left Susquehanna in the 1890s, the ruin was immediately cleared and converted into an agricultural field by tenant farmers. Some of the footings may have been robbed at this time and the brick reused in the farm building foundations. Both the archaeological evidence and the documented recollections of Mrs. Gough provide convincing evidence that Henry Carroll consciously maintained a brick ruin adjacent to his impressive dwelling as part of the house yard.

Discussion

During the 20 years preceding the Civil War, Henry J. Carroll was one of the wealthiest farmers in St. Mary's County. His farm was one of the largest in the county, with rich agricultural soils and access to the Patuxent River. He owned one of the largest slave labor forces in St. Mary's, and this force expanded up until the Civil War. These two important resources—land and labor—and the ability to acquire more labor, had come to Henry Carroll through a line of inheritance that began 150 years earlier in the late seventeenth century. As a result, Carroll was one of a few successful farmers in an otherwise deteriorating economy.

For all Carroll's wealth, he left very little in the way of clues to his life. If any correspondence or other writings by the man survive, they have not been discovered. His involvement in local politics includes several minor appointments. An investment he made in the revival of the mills at nearby Clifton Factory is only briefly mentioned in the surviving documents. His family, slaves, and overseers are even less apparent in the documentary record. The U.S. population census provides the bulk of the limited information on Carroll's family and the slaves who lived and worked at Susquehanna.

Nonetheless, the combination of historical and archaeological research has revealed an important perspective of an elite-class nineteenth-century farmstead in St. Mary's County. Like most of his neighbors, poor and wealthy, Carroll used his land to raise tobacco, corn, and wheat. He grew other crops as well, probably for farm use, and raised relatively large numbers of livestock. Although only about one-quarter of the farm consisted of woodlands, these were carefully managed and preserved for their timber, fencing, and firewood. There is little evidence of erosion in this area between 1848 and the early twentieth century, which suggests Carroll paid close attention to farm management by preserving his rich topsoils as well. Carroll did this with his expanding slave labor force, which in 1860 was nearly eight times the size of Carroll's family.

By the early nineteenth century, Southern Maryland was the most economically depressed region in the State. Despite a failing economy stressed by a number of severe economic depressions, the area's free inhabitants clung tenaciously to the cultivation of tobacco and to the institution of slavery. By the second quarter of the nineteenth century, Southern Maryland was politically isolated as well. Farmers like Henry Carroll almost certainly read the Baltimore-based *American Farmer* and were aware of the frequent attacks on the southern Maryland economy and life-style. These men would have had extensive interaction with the commercial ports of Baltimore and, to a lesser extent, Alexandria. The increasing political and economic isolation of the southern Maryland region was almost certainly apparent to these farmers, and yet little evidence survives to suggest they made any effort to change this way of life.

At least two worlds, or communities, coexisted at Susquehanna. The first was the domestic sphere of Henry Carroll and his family, identified with Susquehanna house. With a well-defined avenue approach and an impressive dwelling, Henry Carroll signaled to the outside world and to other farm residents that this was the center of power and operations at Susquehanna. The unusual elliptical fence also set Carroll apart from both the outside world and from other farm residents. Susquehanna house and its occupants were at once highly visible and remote to both visitors and residents. Close to this domestic compound was the agricultural yard consisting of at least two barns, an orchard, and probably the household garden. Foodstuffs for household consumption by the Carrolls—including garden and orchard produce, dairy products, eggs, and meat—were produced here. Carroll probably also stored most of his farm machinery in this area, where he could have kept a watchful eye over its maintenance and storage.

In contrast, the slaves at Susquehanna lived in a world much less visible to the Carroll family and their visitors and, in many respects, to each other. Archaeological and cartographic evidence suggests that these families lived in isolated cabins scattered along the bluffs of Harper Creek, adjacent to the agricultural fields and accessible only by footpaths. It was not uncommon in colonial Chesapeake to place slaves near the fields in which they worked (Upton 1990:73). Although such a settlement pattern was an efficient way to organize labor over a large tract of land, it also isolated the members of the slave community. The houses shown on the 1848 map and the identified nineteenth-century domestic sites are situated 1,500 to 5,900 feet apart. Put another way, most of these dwellings were at least 1/4 mile apart, and one cabin is well over a mile from the majority of them. Although these distances are certainly manageable on foot, a slave's daily schedule may not have left much time for visiting other cabins, except on Sundays and holidays. Workdays would have been consumed by laboring for the farm and then domestic chores for the support of the slave household. The fields, creeks, and wooded edges along the bluffs of the creek, however, were probably the domain of the Susquehanna slaves and possibly the site of social interaction between slave households on holidays (see Upton 1990:74).

Although the details of the social interaction between the Carrolls, their overseer(s), and their slaves are as yet unclear, some general observations can be made. The distances between the domestic sites at Susquehanna suggest that interaction between households on a daily basis was limited to encounters in work spaces. In this arena, social relationships were guided by the traditional hierarchy of plantations: owners, overseers, and slaves. Slave households almost certainly interacted more extensively on holidays, but farm labor left little time for extended visits between scattered households. Interaction outside the work space between slaves and owners and overseers was probably limited. Although most of the slaves lived east of the avenue approach into the farm, Carroll and probably an overseer lived on the other side of it. Roads are considered symbols of movement, even a "potential menace" (Jackson 1984:15), and the Susquehanna drive could conceivably have been one of the "barriers or pitfalls" Upton (1990:74) suggests are evident in slaves' perceptions of the landscape. Although slaves had control over their quarters, they had no access to elaborate homelots across an important highway that, with their elaborate fencing, must have seemed fortified. Slaves may have attempted to enter the farmer's world, however, by mimicking social customs, such as the taking of tea; this would explain the presence of Chinese porcelain at the quarter site.

The ruin uncovered in the Susquehanna house yard deserves special mention in this analysis of rural landscape. Ruins of many kinds have existed in the historic American landscape, but their functions and meaning have generally not received much attention in landscape studies. Ruins, whether they are abandoned houses or charred foundations, serve as symbols of an earlier landscape, and these features are a constant reminder that the contemporary landscape is not unchanging. Notable ruins in the Chesapeake landscape can be traced to the colonial period. In the 1720s, Robert "King" Carter of Corotoman completed the construction of an imposing brick mansion incorporating classical architectural form. This "mansion" symbolized the economic success of Robert Carter and his efforts to distinguish himself in the eighteenth-century Virginia landscape. The distinction was short-lived; Carter's new home burned down in 1729. Carter spent the last three years of his life in an older and more modest dwelling adjacent to the charred ruin of his grand dwelling (Hudgins 1990:61–64). Perhaps Carter was too old to be concerned with either clearing or rebuilding the mansion. Nevertheless, Carter's diary suggests he was concerned with the look of the yardscape and in 1729 a ruin became part of that yard (Hudgins 1990:68).

Abandoned and ruined dwellings are occasionally mentioned in the Valuations of the Orphan's Court for St. Mary's County, and many of these structures had been converted to use for farm storage. Dilapidated structures, in particular, were simply left to decay, apparently not worth the cost of demolition. However, other documentary evidence uncovered in St. Mary's County suggests that certain architectural ruins may have been symbolic reminders of past events. A second "ruin"—that of the third Lord Baltimore's home at nearby Mattapany (abandoned ca. 1700)—was visible in the landscape in 1873 when surveyor George B. Dent recorded its location and provided an elaborate title for it (figure 18.12; Dent 1873). Other evidence of ruins is provided by documents pertaining to the dedication of the classroom building at the newly established St. Mary's Female Seminary. The seminary, located in the former capital at St. Mary's City, was established by the Maryland legislature in part to commemorate the bicentennial of the founding of Maryland. Emily Regina Thomas recorded her recollections of that dedication in her journal, noting that the ruins of Maryland's first state house lay less than 200 feet from the dedication ceremony. To those attending the dedication, the state house ruins represented the new and experimental ideas of Lord Baltimore's colony. St. Mary's City at that time was—and still is—popularly regarded as the birthplace of religious freedom in this country. Principles only recently articulated in the American experiment of the late nineteenth century had been tried nearly two centuries earlier in St. Mary's County.

The ruin at Susquehanna may have been such a "monument." According to J. B. Jackson (1980), monuments are "supposed to remind us of something important" and can range from a public facility to a "fragment of a ruined wall." Jackson cites a "proliferation of monuments" in the United States during the first half of the nineteenth century. These monuments (including ruined walls) are often public objects, but their purposes could have been appropriated by private individuals. At Susquehanna, an abstract cultural concept of inheritance placed one of the most valuable farms in Carroll's possession; the ruin—home to earlier generations of Carrolls—demonstrated that this spot had been the center of operations for more than 100 years, and it symbolized Carroll's right to this land.

Henry J. Carroll's family had played an important role

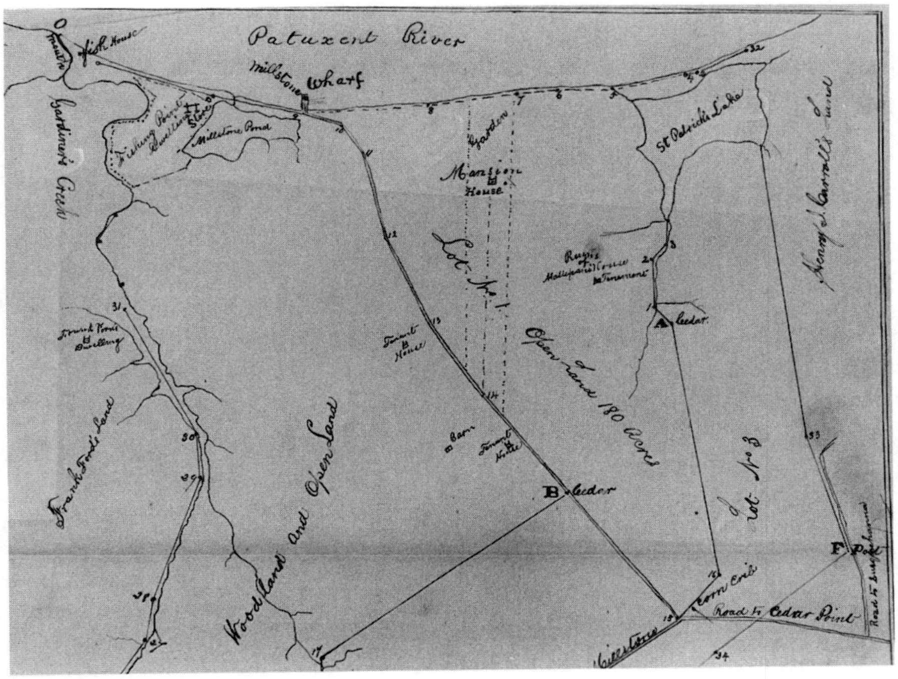

FIGURE 18.12. *Map showing the ruins of Lord Baltimore's dwelling at neighboring Mattapany. (Photograph courtesy of the St. Mary's County Historical Society and the St. Mary's County Courthouse)*

in the colonial period of Maryland history. He was descended from the Rousbys, who had acquired Susquehanna sometime in the second half of the seventeenth century. The Rousbys were a wealthy and politically influential family throughout the colonial period. The ruin at Susquehanna was associated with a dwelling constructed by Carroll's grandfather, Captain Henry Carroll, who had married into the Rousby family in the 1760s. Captain Carroll was a wealthy planter-merchant as well as the cousin of Charles Carroll of Carrollton. He had been a member of the General Committee for St. Mary's County, formed in late 1774 to enforce the resolutions of the Second Continental Congress (Hammett 1977:65–66). The younger Henry Carroll never knew his grandfather—he died in 1775—but he certainly knew of him. The ruin of this earlier dwelling may have provided a visible link to an important past associated with the events of the colonial and the revolutionary periods. On the one hand, southern Maryland was in a minority position, isolated economically, politically, and socially from the rest of the State; on the other, that same region had an important role in the founding of that state.

Historians and anthropologists have suggested that spatial arrangements and relationships among plantation dwellings reflect the degree of control exercised by one class over another (see Isaac 1982; Orser 1988; Upton 1990). At Susquehanna, the center of power was strongly evident through the use of roads, architecture, fencelines, and a garden ruin. The roads, architecture, and fencelines signaled both to the outside world and the home farm community the location of power at Susquehanna through the tremendous visibility of a place that was, in fact, really rather remote. In contrast, the dwellings for the bulk of the residents at the farm—the slaves—are scattered and, to some extent, isolated from one another. The lack of visibility and the apparent decentralization of the slave dwellings rendered the largest class element at Susquehanna virtually invisible to mainstream free society.

Acknowledgments

Funding for the Susquehanna project was provided by the Henry Ford Museum and Greenfield Museum and the Jefferson Patterson Park and Museum. The Patuxent River Naval Air Station provided laboratory and storage space for the project, as well as considerable logistical support. Both the Jefferson Patterson Park and Museum and the Maryland Historical Trust provided crucial administrative support for the research undertaken at Susquehanna. Statistical analyses and SYMAPS were completed on the VAX/VMS facility at St. Mary's College of Maryland.

I am also grateful to the following individuals for their assistance with this project: Karen Bescherer Metheny, Lois Green Carr, Peter Cousins, Julie Ernstein, Capt. Stuart J. Fitrell (Ret-USN), Regina Combs Hammett, Silas D. Hurry, Barbara Little, Patricia J. McGuire, Henry Prebys, Kyle Rambo, Orlando Ridout V, Paul Shackel, Lorena Walsh, and Carmen Weber.

References Cited

Anonymous
1819 A View of the Agricultural Condition of the Lower Counties of Maryland. *American Farmer* 1:98–99.
1844 *American Farmer* 6:250.

Clemens, Paul
1980 *The Atlantic Economy and Colonial Maryland's Eastern Shore: From Tobacco to Grain*. Cornell University Press, Ithaca, N.Y.

Cutler, Edward J., et al.
1955 Cutler Interview, Susquehanna House. On file, Henry Ford Museum. Dearborn, Mich.

Dent, George B.
1873 Survey Book of George B. Dent: Book B, 1872–1873. Ms. on file, St. Mary's County Historical Society, Leonardtown, Md.

Fedelchak, Marilyn, and Byrd Wood
1988 *Protecting America's Historic Countryside*. National Trust for Historic Preservation, Washington, D.C.

Fresco, Margaret K.
1982 *Marriages and Deaths, St. Mary's County, Maryland, 1634–1900*. Ridge, Md.

Garrow, Patrick H., and Thomas R. Wheaton, Jr.
1986 Final Report: Oxon Hill Manor Archaeological Site Mitigation Project, I-95/MD 210/I-295. Prepared for the Maryland Department of Transportation, State Highway Administration.

Gibson, Joseph W.
1978 *Soil Survey of St. Mary's County, Maryland*. U.S. Department of Agriculture, Soil Conservation Service, Washington, D.C.

Gouger, James B.
1976 *Agricultural Change in the Northern Neck of Virginia, 1700–1860: An Historical Geography*. Unpublished Ph.D. dissertation, University of Florida, Gainesville.

Gough, Fanny Combs
1947 Susquehanna, A Maryland House in Michigan. *Maryland Historical Magazine*: 115–123.

Hammett, Regina C.

1977 *History of St. Mary's County, Maryland*. Ridge, Md.

Heikkenen, Herman J.

1988 Report on the Dendrochronology of Susquehanna. On file, Henry Ford Museum, Dearborn, Mich.

Hudgins, Carter

1990 Robert "King" Carter and the Landscape of Tidewater Virginia in the Eighteenth Century. In *Earth Patterns: Essays in Landscape Archaeology*, edited by William M. Kelso and Rachel Most, pp. 59–70. University Press of Virginia, Charlottesville.

Isaac, Rhys

1982 *The Transformation of Virginia*. University of North Carolina Press, Chapel Hill.

Jackson, J. B.

1980 *The Necessity for Ruins and Other Topics*. University of Massachusetts Press, Amherst.

1984 *Discovering the Vernacular Landscape*. Yale University Press, New Haven, Conn.

King, Julia A.

1989 Archaeological Investigations at Susquehanna: A 19th Century Farm Complex aboard Patuxent River Naval Air Station, St. Mary's County, Maryland. Jefferson Patterson Park and Museum, St. Leonard, Md.

1990 A Comparison of Ceramic Assemblages from a Planter and a Slave Site in Early 19th Century Maryland. Paper presented at the Jamestown Conference on Archaeology, Association for the Preservation of Virginia Antiquities, Popes Creek, Va.

Marks, Bayly E.

1979 *Economy and Society in a Staple Plantation, St. Mary's County, Maryland*. Unpublished Ph.D. dissertation, University of Maryland, College Park.

Orser, Charles E.

1988 Toward a Theory of Power for Historical Archaeology: Plantations and Space. In *The Recovery of Meaning: Historical Archaeology in the Eastern United States*, edited by Mark P. Leone and Parker B. Potter, Jr., pp. 313–343. Smithsonian Institution Press, Washington, D.C.

Pogue, Dennis J.

1983 *Patuxent River Naval Air Station Cultural Resources Survey*. Vol. 1: *History and Archaeology*. Public Works Department, Naval Air Station, Patuxent River, Md.

Ridgway, Whitman H.

1979 *Community Leadership in Maryland, 1790–1840*. University of North Carolina Press, Chapel Hill.

Ridout, Orlando V

1989 Notes on the Architecture of Susquehanna. In Archaeological Investigations at Susquehanna, edited by Julia A. King, pp. 101–107. Jefferson Patterson Park and Museum, St. Leonard, Md.

Rohrer, Wayne C., and Louis H. Douglas

1969 *The Agrarian Transition in America*. Bobbs-Merrill, New York.

St. Mary's County Government

1989 Comprehensive Land Use Plan. On file, Office of Planning and Zoning, St. Mary's County, Leonardtown, Md. [Skinner, John S.]

1844 Letter. *American Farmer* 6(10):75.

Smalley, Donald (editor)

1949 *Domestic Manners of the Americans*, by Frances Trollope. Edited with a History of Mrs. Trollope's Adventures in America. Alfred A. Knopf, New York.

Stilgoe, John R.

1982 *Common Landscape of America, 1580 to 1845*. Yale University Press, New Haven, Conn.

Stone, Garry W.

1986 Susquehanna: Report on Site Reconnaissance of 24 November 1986. Ms. on file, Jefferson Patterson Park and Museum, St. Leonard, Md.

1987 Letter to Peter Cousins, January 13, 1987. On file, Jefferson Patterson Park and Museum, St. Leonard, Md.

U.S. Agricultural Census

1850 *Schedules for St. Mary's County*. Microfilm, Maryland State Archives, Annapolis.

1860 *Schedules for St. Mary's County*. Microfilm, Maryland State Archives, Annapolis.

U.S. Coast and Geodetic Survey

1873 Mouth of the Patuxent River. Traced from an 1848 copy. On file, National Oceanographic and Atmospheric Administration, Beltsville, Md.

U.S. Population Census

1850a Schedule for Free Persons, St. Mary's County. Microfilm, Maryland State Archives, Annapolis.

1850b Slave Schedules for St. Mary's County. Microfilm, Maryland State Archives, Annapolis.

1860a Schedule for Free Persons, St. Mary's County. Microfilm, Maryland State Archives, Annapolis.

1860b Slave Schedules for St. Mary's County. Microfilm, Maryland State Archives, Annapolis.

Upton, Dell

1990 Imagining the Early Virginia Landscape. In *Earth Patterns: Essays in Landscape Archaeology*, edited by William M. Kelso and Rachel Most, pp. 71–86. University Press of Virginia, Charlottesville.

Van Ness, James S.

1982 Economic Development, Social and Cultural Change: 1800–1850. In *Maryland: A History*, edited by Richard Walsh and William Fox, pp. 156–238. Hall of Records Commission, Department of General Services, Annapolis, Md.

Walsh, Lorena

1981 Documentary Research on Susquehanna Point Property, St. Mary's County, Maryland. Ms. on file, Jefferson Patterson Park and Museum, St. Leonard, Md.